Only a few centuries ago, the English language consisted of a collection of dialects spoken mainly by monolinguals and only within the shores of a small island. Now the English language includes such typologically distinct varieties as pidgins and creoles, 'new' Englishes, and a range of differing standard and nonstandard varieties that are spoken on a regular basis in many different countries throughout the world. English is also, of course, the main language used for communication at an international level. The use of English in such a diverse range of social contexts around the world provides us with a unique opportunity to analyse and document the linguistic variation and change that is occurring within a single language, on a far greater scale – as far as we know – than has ever happened in the world's linguistic history before.

This volume is intended to give a comprehensive account of our current knowledge of variation in the use of the English language around the world. Overview papers, written by specialist authors, survey the social context in which English is spoken in those parts of the world where it is widely used. Case study papers then provide representative examples of the empirical research that has been carried out into the English that is spoken in the area covered by the overview. The volume therefore contributes both to our understanding of the English language worldwide and to a more general understanding of language as it is used in its social context. It assesses the extent of our current knowledge of variation in the English language and points to gaps in our understanding which future research might set out to remedy.

D1120902

English around the world

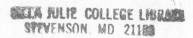
English around the world

Sociolinguistic perspectives

Edited by
JENNY CHESHIRE
Professor of Modern English Linguistics,
Universities of Fribourg and Neuchâtel

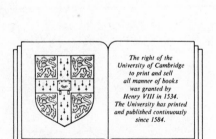

The right of the
University of Cambridge
to print and sell
all manner of books
was granted by
Henry VIII in 1534.
The University has printed
and published continuously
since 1584.

Cambridge University Press
Cambridge
New York   Port Chester
Melbourne   Sydney

Published by the Press Syndicate of the University of Cambridge
The Pitt Building, Trumpington Street, Cambridge CB2 1RP
40 West 20th Street, New York, NY 10011, USA
10 Stamford Road, Oakleigh, Melbourne 3166, Australia

First published 1991

Printed in Great Britain at the University Press, Cambridge

British Library cataloguing in publication data
English around the world: sociolinguistic perspectives.
1. English language. Usage. Social aspects
I. Cheshire, Jenny
428

Library of Congress cataloguing in publication data
English around the world: sociolinguistic perspectives/edited by
Jenny Cheshire.
    p. cm.
ISBN 0 521 33080 7
1. English language – Dialects. 2. English language – Variation.
3. English language – Social aspects. 4. English language – Foreign
countries. 5. Sociolinguistics. I. Cheshire Jenny, 1946–
PE1700.E49 1991
420 – dc20 89-78085 CIP

ISBN 0 521 33080 7 hardback
     0 521 39565 8 paperback

CC

72/24

Contents

Figures

Contributors

MOHAMED M. H. ABDULAZIZ
Department of Linguistics and
African Languages, University of
Nairobi, Kenya

DONN BAYARD
Anthropology Department,
University of Otago, New Zealand

ALLAN BELL
Department of Linguistics,
Victoria University of Wellington,
New Zealand

RICHARD A. BENTON
Maori Research Unit, New
Zealand Council for Educational
Research, New Zealand

EYAMBA G. BOKAMBA
Department of Linguistics,
University of Illinois, USA

DAVID BRADLEY
Division of Linguistics, LaTrobe
University, Australia

J. K. CHAMBERS
Department of Linguistics,
University of Toronto, Canada

JENNY CHESHIRE
University of Fribourg and
University of Neuchâtel,
Switzerland

J. KEITH CHICK
Department of General Linguistics
and Communication, University of
Natal, South Africa

MAURICE M. CHISHIMBA
Department of English, University
of Botswana, Botswana

SANDRA CLARKE
Department of Linguistics,
Memorial University of
Newfoundland, Canada

HUBERT DEVONISH
Department of Linguistics and Use
of English, University of the West
Indies, Jamaica

EDINA EISIKOVITS
Department of Linguistics, Monash
University, Australia

GENEVIEVE ESCURE
Department of English, University
of Minnesota, USA

xiii

JOHN H. ESLING
Department of Linguistics,
University of Victoria, Canada

NICHOLAS FARACLAS
Department of English and
Literature, University of Papua
New Guinea, Papua New Guinea

MARKKU FILPPULA
Department of English, University
of Joensuu, Finland

ANDREW B. GONZALEZ
De La Salle University, Philippines

GREGORY R. GUY
Department of Linguistics,
Stanford University, USA

JOHN HARRIS
Department of Phonetics and
Linguistics, University College
London, UK

JANET HOLMES
Department of Linguistics,
Victoria University of Wellington,
New Zealand

MUNZALI JIBRIL
Faculty of Arts and Islamic Studies,
Bayero University, Nigeria

JEFFREY L. KALLEN
School of Remedial Linguistics,
Trinity College Dublin, Ireland

THIRU KANDIAH
Department of English Language
and Literature, National University
of Singapore, Singapore

MUSIMBI R. A. KANYORO
The Lutheran World Federation,
Geneva, Switzerland

FARHAT KHAN
Youth Training, Barking and
Dagenham Education Authority,
Essex, UK

KOENRAAD KUIPER
Department of English Language
and Literature, University of
Canterbury, New Zealand

PETER H. LOWENBERG
Department of Linguistics,
Georgetown University, USA

RAJEND MESTHRIE
Department of Linguistics,
University of Cape Town, South
Africa

JAMES MILROY
16, The High Gate, Newcastle
upon Tyne, UK

PETER MÜHLHÄUSLER
Linacre College, University of
Oxford, UK

†JOHN PLATT
Department of Linguistics, Monash
University, Australia

JOHN R. RICKFORD
Department of Linguistics,
Stanford University, USA

SUZANNE ROMAINE
Merton College, Oxford

ANJU SAHGAL
Indira Gandhi National Open
University, India

CHARLENE J. SATO
Department of English as a Second
Language, University of Hawaii at
Manoa, USA

JOSEF J. SCHMIED
Universität Bayreuth, Germany

ALICE K. SIACHITEMA
Department of Literature and
Language, University of Zambia,
Zambia

JEFFREY SIEGEL
Department of Linguistics,
University of New England,
Australia

JOHN V. SINGLER
Department of Linguistics, New
York University, USA

KAMAL K. SRIDHAR
Department of Linguistics, State
University of New York at Stony
Brook, USA

MARGARET S. STEFFENSEN
Department of English, Illinois
State University, USA

MARY W. J. TAY
Department of English Language
and Literature, National University
of Singapore, Singapore

DONALD WINFORD
Department of Linguistics, Ohio
State University, USA

HOWARD B. WOODS
English Programme Development
Division, Public Service
Commission of Canada, Canada

Acknowledgements

Many people have helped in the preparation of this volume, far too many for all of them to be acknowledged by name. My first thanks, however, must be to all the contributors who sent in their papers within reasonable hailing distance of the deadline and who have been consistently courteous and cooperative during the lengthy production of the volume. It has been a pleasure to work with scholars of the English language from all over the world.

I would also like to warmly acknowledge the help of Richard Bailey, Braj Kachru, Loreto Todd and Peter Trudgill, who formed an advisory committee and provided extremely useful information on the research that has been carried out in the different parts of the world on which they have expert knowledge. Special thanks are due to Peter Trudgill, not only for encouragement and good advice during the planning stages of the volume but also for some very helpful comments on my own contributions.

I am very grateful to the authors of the overview papers in the volume, who made invaluable suggestions concerning the case study papers for the region of the world on which they were reporting.

Penny Carter of Cambridge University Press also deserves thanks for her encouragement and foresight during the earliest planning stages. The volume would not have taken the form that it has without her conception of the contribution that sociolinguistics can make to the study of English around the world. I would also like to thank Judith Ayling and Con Coroneos for their help during the final stages of preparation of the volume.

Finally, it is sad to have to report that John Platt died while this volume was in press. It was a special privilege to work with him and I am glad to have been able to include a paper in the volume that is representative of the lasting contribution that he made to our knowledge of English around the world.

Introduction: Sociolinguistics and English around the world

JENNY CHESHIRE

Only a few centuries ago, the English language consisted of a collection of dialects spoken mainly by monolinguals and only within the shores of a small island. Now it includes such typologically distinct varieties as pidgins and creoles, 'new' Englishes, and a range of differing standard and non-standard varieties that are spoken on a regular basis in more than 60 different countries around the world (Crystal 1985). English is also, of course, the main language used for communication at an international level.

Such diversity of form and function within what is nevertheless still thought of as a single language offers a unique opportunity to analyse and document the linguistic variation and change that is occurring on a far greater scale – as far as we know – than has ever happened in the world's linguistic history. It also allows us to investigate the relationship between language and the community in which it is used from a broader perspective than is usual. Academic disciplines tend to fragment into separate specialist fields: dialectology, bilingualism, pidgin and creole studies, and sociolinguistics, for example, are often treated as if they are relatively self-contained areas of study. All four of these fields, however, share the problems of describing and explaining linguistic variation, though the nature of the variation may differ; and all four fields investigate essentially the same social and educational issues arising from community attitudes that assign high prestige to some languages, or varieties of a language, and low prestige to others (see also Rickford 1988). Focusing on world Englishes in their social contexts, then, makes it easier to see what these disciplines have in common.

This introductory chapter does not attempt to summarise the contents of the volume. The papers speak for themselves, illustrating the range of variation that exists within the English language today and the diverse social contexts in which English is used. Instead, this chapter draws attention to the specific contribution that empirical research into English

1

around the world can make to our understanding of language in its social context and, conversely, to some of the reasons why a sociolinguistic perspective is important for the study of English around the world.

English around the world and sociolinguistics

Analysing sociolinguistic variation in the English that is used around the world poses an enormous challenge to sociolinguistics. One reason for this is that many fundamental concepts that have long been taken for granted within sociolinguistics become problematic when they are viewed from a multilingual perspective, rather than from the monolingual perspective in which they were originally developed. An example is the concept of the speech community. Early sociolinguistic surveys showed that social and stylistic variation could be incorporated into a single model of 'orderly heterogeneity' (Labov 1972), where all socioeconomic classes followed the usage of the higher socioeconomic classes in their more careful speech styles. Figure 1.1 (see chapter 1, page 18) illustrates this pattern of variation for the (th) variable in New York City. Such sociolinguistic patterning, together with tests of speakers' subjective evaluations of linguistic variants, led Labov to define the speech community as a group of speakers sharing a common set of evaluative norms (Labov 1966; see further Labov 1989). Romaine (1982) has already drawn attention to some of the problems that arise when applying this definition to (mainly) monolingual situations; the problems become still greater, however, when we investigate Creole communities (see Winford 1988) or the multilingual urban centres in 'developing' societies. As Guy (1988: 46) points out, in some cities of the 'third world' a majority of the population may have been born elsewhere, and many people may not even speak the official language or the standard dialect, so that they can hardly be said to form a speech community in the same way that New York City can.

There are other sociolinguistic concepts which are often taken as self-evident but which we are forced to question when analysing English as it is used around the world. 'Mother tongue' is not necessarily a useful or a meaningful concept in cities such as Lusaka, where population movement, language loss, language shift, and language attitudes may all affect the language that speakers consider to be their first language (see Siachitema, this volume). Furthermore, the distinction that has been drawn conventionally between the 'native speaker' and the 'non-native speaker' is becoming blurred and increasingly difficult to operationalise. At one time it may have been possible to make a distinction on the grounds that a non-native speaker of English had learnt the language through formal instruction, rather than acquired it as a mother tongue; but in many multilingual countries the functional range of English is changing rapidly, so that English is now used in informal domains as well as in more formal, official domains. This means that although English may still be learnt at school, it may also be acquired through informal use in everyday life (see further Kandiah, this volume). Similarly, some pidgin and creole varieties of English are easily identifiable as native speaker varieties (this is so for the varieties reported in the Caribbean and Pacific sections of this volume), but others may be second language varieties, learnt at school (Liberian English is an example; see Singler, this volume). Some pidgins are not termed 'English' and although English may have played an important role in their linguistic development it is not clear if they are perceived within the community as 'English': one such pidgin is represented in this volume (Faraclas' paper on Nigerian Pidgin). Other typological classifications of varieties of English as they are used around the world can also pose problems: it has been pointed out, for example, that the criteria used to identify ESL, EFL and other varieties of English that were once thought to be relatively discrete (such as the five types of English distinguished by Moag 1982) cannot do justice to the multiplicity of situations in which English is used (Görlach 1988: 181). All these problems of classification and description, then, challenge the early assumptions that were made in sociolinguistics, and force us to reflect on their validity. The discipline stands to benefit greatly from being forced to reassess its terminology and its conceptual frameworks in this way.

A second challenge that the analysis of English around the world offers to sociolinguistics concerns the methodology that is used in research. Many of the most widely used frameworks of analysis were developed during investigations into language use in Western industrial societies and have been shaped by underlying theoretical assumptions that were not always made explicit (see, for discussion, Milroy 1987). For example, the early Labovian framework of analysis linked the stylistic continuum to a functionalist model of social class, without explicitly acknowledging its dependence on this model. This meant that research results were interpreted as if they had resulted from a neutral, objective analysis rather than from an analysis tied to a theory-dependent model of class. For instance, the recurrent pattern of social and stylistic variation illustrated in figure 1.1 (chapter 1 below) was explained in terms of the prestige of the variants preferred by the higher socioeconomic classes; the persistence and spread of other, low-status, variants was then, correspondingly, accounted for by the notion of covert prestige (see, for example, Labov 1966; and, for further discussion, Milroy, this volume). As Milroy (1987: 99) points out, this type of interpretation can be illuminating, but the failure to acknowledge the dependence of Labov's view of sociolinguistic variation on a specific model of social class has meant that interpretations in terms of prestige have until recently been taken for granted. There has been very little consideration of alternative models of social class in sociolinguistics, and little meaningful debate on how linguistic variability can best be related to social structure. Shifting the focus of inquiry to non-Western societies, which are organised differently, forces us to give proper consideration to these questions (see, for example, the papers by Chishimba, Jibril, Rickford and Winford, this volume).

Similarly, analysing patterns of sex differentiation in English around the world puts into proper perspective the 'typical' finding that female speakers use a higher proportion of standard forms. Clearly, the finding is dependent on gender roles rather than simply on biological sex so that, at the very least, the interaction of speaker sex with other social variables must be analysed if we are to obtain a clear understanding of the inter-relationship between linguistic variation and social factors (see the papers by Escure and Clarke, this volume). Khan's paper in this volume demonstrates that in at least one English-speaking community, in India, the familiar pattern is reversed; Eisikovits' paper, on the other hand, shows far greater differentiation between the speech of male and female speakers in Sydney than has been documented for English-speaking societies before. Extending the analysis of sex differentiation in English to a wider range of societies, then, forces us to recognise that patterns of variation differ from community to community and that a simplistic approach to the analysis of sex differentiation in language use can give a very misleading impression of the nature and the function of linguistic variation.

An additional, important, perspective on language and gender is given by Kuijper's and Mühlhäusler's papers in this volume which, using qualitative approaches, demonstrate the cultural salience of gender divisions in two very different English-speaking communities. Sociolinguistics has tended to operate with preconceived ideas about the relative importance of different social parameters, and these ideas may have prevented us from understanding some crucial aspects of sociolinguistic variation. For example, it has been suggested that a preoccupation with the category of social class has led researchers to ask the wrong question about gender differentiation in language, by asking why women approximate to the norms of the class above them rather than, perhaps, approaching class differentiation in terms of gender differences (Milroy 1988: 581). Milroy refers to Coates' (1986) regraphing of data from several surveys carried out in the UK and the USA, which shows that the sex of speakers accounts for patterns of variation at least as well as, and sometimes better than, the social class to which they are assigned by the researcher. We are beginning to recognise, then, the importance of assessing the relative cultural salience of different social categories in the community whose speech is being investigated. A qualitative approach is one way in which this can be done; again, extending the scope of inquiry to a range of very different social settings forces us to look beyond those social categories that our own culture has conditioned us to believe are important, and helps us to formulate the kinds of questions that can lead to a fuller understanding of linguistic variation.

The studies of creole varieties and second language varieties of English in this volume are important in this respect, since they add new social parameters to those that have been commonly used in research into 'native speaker' varieties. These social parameters include residence in urban or rural communities, type of neighbourhood, age at which English is acquired, degree of Westernisation, and other languages spoken (including the problematic 'mother tongue'). The most important social factor in many communities is education, which interacts with other speaker variables such as gender, social status and neighbourhood (see further Sridhar 1985: 46). All these speaker variables pose problems of measurement which need to be resolved; and their diversity reminds us not only of the way in which language intimately reflects the social organisation of the community in which it is used but also, again, of the need to begin an analysis with an open mind about which social parameters should be taken into account. They point to the need to determine empirically the social salience of different speaker variables, perhaps by carrying out an ethnographic analysis before beginning the linguistic investigation, perhaps by experimental investigation, and ideally by the researchers being local residents themselves.

Several papers in this volume analyse statistical regularities in the linguistic constraints that govern variation. This approach to the analysis of variation in English around the world can lead to progress in our understanding of the physical and cognitive basis to the constraints. For example, Khan's paper in this volume finds that consonant cluster simplification in a variety of Indian English is subject to the same phonological constraints as it is in US varieties of English, thus confirming their presumed origins in articulatory processes. The papers by Singler and Platt in this volume are interesting in that they identify some linguistic constraints on morphological and syntactic variation, about which we still know relatively little. Many of these constraints may be language-specific, or variety-specific, but evidence is accumulating which suggests that speakers find certain syntactic environments more salient cognitively and perceptually than other environments, and that these environments may condition variation in many – perhaps all – languages. Platt's finding (this volume) that semantic similarity between a premodifier and a noun affects plural marking on nouns, and Faraclas' finding (also in this volume) that additional semantic distinctions in pronoun forms are established first in focused positions in the clause, each have parallels in analyses of variation in other varieties of English (see, for example, Stein, in press). A pressing research question is to investigate the universality of linguistic constraints such as these. This would necessarily involve analyses of a wide range of different languages, but at this early stage of enquiry a focus on a single language in a diverse range of social settings can help to establish comparisons and to suggest the kind of constraints on variation that are worth investigating on a wider scale.

Finally, there are many important aspects of language use which cannot be handled easily within the variationist framework; again, considering a single language in a range of diverse situations brings us face to face with these aspects and draws attention to the need for an eclectic approach to sociolinguistic research. Some of the papers in this volume illustrate the insights that can be achieved using qualitative methods (see, for example, the papers by Mühlhäusler, Kuijper, and Chick). Several contributors call for new perspectives and new models (see, for example, the papers by Kandiah, and by Tay; see also Kachru, 1985: 30); they also call for collaborative research between specialists in language and specialists in literature, and for an eclectic combination of analytical techniques and different theoretical models (see also Edwards 1988; Sridhar 1985). These needs have been articulated by others, some working in monolingual situations (for example, Cheshire 1987; Coupland 1988), and others working on languages other than English (for example, Van de Craen 1987). Once more, at this early stage in the development of sociolinguistics, a focus on analysing a single language in the very different social settings in which it is used may help to decide which of our existing models and methods can best be used in conjunction with each other, as well as the kinds of new models that can most usefully be developed.

Sociolinguistics and English around the world

A great deal of interest has been generated in the English language as a result of its spread around the world and its use as an international language. At least two academic journals are uniquely concerned with English around the world (Benjamins' *English World-wide* and Pergamon's *World Englishes*); there is also a popular magazine, *English Today*, published by Cambridge University Press. It is important that amid this understandable interest and enthusiasm we do not overlook the more undesirable consequences of the development of English as a world language. From a linguistic point of view, for example, the spread of English has all too often been associated with the death, or virtual death, of the indigenous languages in those countries to which it has been transplanted. England itself is a prime example. From a social and political point of view, the spread of English around the world was largely the result of exploitation and colonisation, and in many multilingual countries English is still the language of an exclusive social élite. In countries where English has been well established for many centuries (notably, though by no means only, Great Britain and the USA) there are difficult educational problems stemming from the coexistence of a standardised variety of

English and a range of associated local dialects, and the complex attitudes that are held towards these standard and non-standard varieties (see, for discussion of the UK situation, Cheshire and Trudgill 1989). Similar problems are now being seen on a world scale, albeit posed in a slightly different form (see the papers by Quirk and Kachru in Quirk and Widdowson 1985, and the discussion therein; see also Kachru 1986a, 1986b and 1986c). Finally, the immense amount of variation that exists in English around the world presents difficulties of codification and standardisation, as well as problems in the choice of a teaching model, none of which can be neglected in the English-language teaching context.

These, then, are some of the applied issues to which a sociolinguistic perspective on World Englishes can contribute. It can do so in several ways. First, it can contribute to English-language teaching issues by ensuring that descriptions of world varieties of English have a sounder empirical base than is the case at present. Current descriptions, whether of a non-standard dialect, a 'new' variety or even of a hypothetical international standard variety, are all too often given as lists of assorted departures from southern British standard English or from American standard English, with no attempt at determining the extent to which the local linguistic features function as part of an autonomous system (see further Sridhar 1985). In the absence of systematic empirical research, descriptions of different varieties of World English have often been based either on the writer's personal observations or on the recorded speech of a single person, so that there is no way of seeing how the linguistic features that are said to be characteristic of a given variety of English are governed by social and situational factors. It is impossible, from such descriptions, to distinguish reliably between features that are performance errors and features that are recurrent, 'legitimate' features of a local variety.

Where the variety that is being described is a second language variety of English, initially acquired mainly through formal instruction, a sociolinguistic analysis can help to answer the question of where learners' errors stop and where legitimate features of a local variety of English begin (see Hancock and Angogo 1984: 306). Learner, or performance varieties, may sometimes be nativised to the extent that they have some characteristic features reflecting the culture in which they are used (see Tay, this volume); but one of the principal differences between the variation that exists in learner varieties of English and the variation that exists in more stable varieties of the language is that stable varieties exhibit patterns of sociolinguistic variation which reflect the social organisation of the society in which they are used. These patterns do not come into existence until the variety is used as part of everyday social interaction between members of that society. It is interesting to note, in this context, that many of the features that English teachers in Kenya are instructed to see as interference phenomena (see Kanyoro, this volume) appear to function as markers of national and ethnic identity amongst educated Kenyan speakers of English (Schmied, this volume); they should therefore, it seems, be considered as characteristic of the local variety of English rather than as errors.

A sociolinguistic perspective is also important for identifying social attitudes both to the use of English relative to other languages in the community's verbal repertoire, and to the use of different varieties of English within that community. Several of the papers in this volume point to the need to take these attitudes into account in practical issues concerned with language planning, language teaching and language in public life generally (see, for example, the papers by Sato and Devonish). The question of language norms is an extremely sensitive issue in any society; in many of the countries represented in this volume the issues are particularly complex. Sometimes the complexity has arisen from a colonial legacy of a set of external reference norms, which now coexists with local norms (see, for example, the papers by Clarke, Woods and Guy in this volume). Several papers in this volume indicate that a change in local attitudes and norms is in progress (for example, Sahgal, this volume). The communities represented here often differ greatly from each other, yet the social, educational and political reactions to linguistic variation are essentially the same in them all, and there is the same danger of allowing prejudice and ill-informed views to cloud the issues. If they are to be discussed in a less impassioned and a more constructive and informed way than has often been the case in the past, it is vital that reliable information is available on the socially and linguistically patterned nature of variation within the different countries where English is spoken, as well as on the corresponding set of language attitudes and language norms, and on the function that local varieties may fulfill as markers of national identity or of other aspects of a person's social identity.

A sociolinguistic perspective on English around the world is crucially important in attempting to unravel some of this linguistic complexity. The papers in this volume provide a great deal of information on some of these important topics, but we still have a long way to go before we will be ready to meet the practical challenges of English-language teaching in a world context, or to decide whether it is really necessary to attempt to engineer the use of a planned variety of international English. As always, more empirical research is needed in order that these, and other pressing issues, can be properly addressed. One of the aims of this volume, therefore, is to stimulate further empirical research into English in its social contexts around the world. A further aim is to assess the extent of our current knowledge, in order to show where there are gaps which future research might set out to remedy. Above all, however, the volume aims to represent the rich diversity in the form and function of English as it is used around the world today.

Organisation of the volume

In order to ensure comprehensive and systematic coverage, the contents of the volume have been divided into eleven geographical areas. For each of these areas, a specialist author with extensive experience of living and working in that part of the world was invited to write an overview paper which would survey the more important sociolinguistic research that had been carried out in that area and which would point to the research that is still needed. The overview authors were also asked to cover a short list of specified topics in order to give some background information about the use of English in that area of the world and to enable clear comparisons to be drawn between the different regions. Academics are independent creatures, however, and the specialist authors did not always follow their instructions to the letter – and perhaps the volume is all the better as a result. The overview papers for each of the eleven areas are followed by case studies, often chosen with the help of the specialist author or of the advisory committee for the volume. These case studies provide representative examples of the sociolinguistic research that has been carried out in that part of the English-speaking world.

There have, inevitably, been problems, not the least of which lay in the definition of the geographical areas. Dividing the world into a small number of separate areas defies logic, and many criticisms will doubtless be made of the decisions that were eventually reached. To forestall some of the more obvious objections, it should perhaps be explained that at an early stage in the planning of the volume it was decided to exclude the UK and the USA, as far as possible, on the grounds that the research that has been carried out there has been very widely disseminated. It seemed more important to give space to other areas of the world from which the research findings are less well known or have been less readily accessible. These two countries, however, could hardly be excluded completely from a collection of papers that aimed to represent 'World' English; furthermore, the research that has been carried out in the UK and the USA has often been very influential in shaping research carried out elsewhere in the world, and it should therefore be represented in some way. The decision was therefore made to include a single overview paper on sociolinguistic aspects of English in the UK and the USA, but to exclude case study papers for these countries (although there is a case study from Northern Ireland in the section of the volume that is concerned with Ireland and the section on 'The Pacific' includes a case study paper from Hawaii, one of the states of the USA).

It was also decided, at an early stage in the planning of the volume, to treat New Zealand separately from Australia, in an attempt to break away from the tradition of treating these two countries as a single linguistic area. Given their different histories and their different social, political and cultural situations, it was considered important to clearly stress their sociolinguistic distinctiveness in this volume. Inevitably, however, this decision restricted the space that was available for other countries, so that some countries now have to sit uneasily with others that have been assigned to the same geographical area. Hong Kong, for example, is included here as part of South-East Asia. Some geographical areas have a more sociolinguistically complex makeup than others; many, such as the Caribbean and the area that I have named the 'Pacific', are so complex that they each merit a separate volume in their own right. There can, of course, be no perfect way of dividing the English-speaking world into separate areas; the divisions that have been made here are best seen as simply providing a reasonably coherent organisational framework for the volume.

Other aspects of organisation and categorisation have posed problems. The intention was to exclude countries such as Japan or the Netherlands, where English is used mainly as a foreign language rather than as a language of everyday communication within the country. It is not always possible, however, to establish a clearcut division between those countries where English is a foreign language and those countries where it is a second language, since the status of English in the language policies of a country can – and does – change. In Tanzania and Malaysia, for example, English is no longer an official language, though it was until relatively recently. Case studies for these two countries have in fact been included in the volume. As mentioned earlier, the division between native and non-native varieties of English, or between first and second language varieties, is also difficult to establish. The distinctions that are drawn between different varieties of English and the terminology that is used by different writers are currently inconsistent, and they are changing rapidly. Terminology is understandably a sensitive issue, as some of the contributors to the volume make clear. For these reasons, I have not attempted to change the terms that the contributors have chosen to use. Instead, I have tried to ensure that although their terminology sometimes differs, the distinctions that the contributors wish to draw are clear from the contexts in which the terms are used. I have also done my best to refrain from imposing my own variety of English on the contributions to the volume.

Many of the case studies describe research that has been carried out within a quantitative, variationist framework of analysis, reflecting the worldwide influence of this approach. Not all the case studies are of this type, however. There are some sociolinguistic questions for which a quantitative analysis is not the most appropriate approach; and there are other methodologies that are equally valuable. However, although the case studies differ in their approaches and, sometimes, in their aims, they all have one thing in common: all are empirical analyses of English which are firmly based on sociolinguistic research that has been carried out in the community in which the language is used. They therefore contribute both to our understanding of the English language as it is used around the world and to a more general understanding of language as it is used in its social context.

REFERENCES

Cheshire, J. 1987. Syntactic variation, the linguistic variable and sociolinguistic theory. *Linguistics* 25: 257–82

Cheshire, J. and Trudgill, P. 1989. Dialect and education in the UK. In Cheshire, J., Edwards, V., Münstermann, H., and Weltens, B. (eds), *Dialect and Education: Some European Perspectives*. Clevedon: Multilingual Matters, pp. 94–109.

Coates, J. 1986. *Women, Men and Language*. Harlow: Longman.

Coupland, N. 1988. *Dialect in Use*. Cardiff: University of Wales Press.

Crystal, David 1985. How many millions? The statistics of English today. *English Today* 1: 7–11

Edwards, W. F. 1988. Morphosyntactic acculturation at the rural/urban interface in Guyana. Paper presented to the 6th Society for Creole Studies Meeting, Jamaica.

Görlach, M. 1988. *Varietas delectat*: Forms and functions of English around the world. In Nixon, G, and Honey, J. (eds.) 1988, *An Historic Tongue: Studies in English Linguistics in Memory of Barbara Strang*. London: Routledge, pp. 167–208.

Guy, G. 1988. Language and social class. In Newmeyer, F. J. (ed.), *Linguistics: The Cambridge Survey. Volume 4: Language: The Socio-Cultural Context*. Cambridge: Cambridge University Press, pp. 37–63.

Hancock, I. F. and Angogo, R. 1984. English in East Africa. In Bailey, R. W. and Görlach, M. (eds.), *English as a World Language*. Cambridge: Cambridge University Press, pp. 306–23.

Kachru, B. B. 1985. Standards, codification and linguistic realism: the English language in the outer circle. In Quirk, R. and Widdowson, H. G. (eds.), *English in the World: Teaching and Learning the Language and Literatures*. Cambridge: Cambridge University Press in association with the British Council, pp. 11–30.

Kachru, B. B. 1986a. Native and non-native norms. In Kachru, B. B., *The Alchemy of English*. Oxford: Pergamon, pp. 100–14.

1986b. New Englishes and old models. In Kachru, B. B., *The Alchemy of English*. Oxford: Pergamon, pp. 115–23

1986c. Regional norms. In Kachru, B. B., *The Alchemy of English*. Oxford: Pergamon, pp. 87–99.

Labov, W. 1966. *The Social Stratification of English in New York City*. Washington DC: Center for Applied Linguistics.

1972. *Sociolinguistic Patterns*. Philadelphia: University of Pennsylvania Press.

1989. The exact description of a speech community: Short *a* in Philadelphia. In Fasold, R.W., and Schiffrin, D. (eds.), *Language Change and Variation*. Amsterdam: John Benjamins, pp. 1–57.

Milroy, L. 1987. *Observing and Analysing Natural Language: A Critical Account of Sociolinguistic Method*. Oxford: Blackwell.

1988. Review of Horvath, B., *Variation in Australian English: The Sociolects of Sydney. Language in Society* 17: 577–81.

Moag, R. F. 1982. On English as a foreign, second, native and basal language. In Pride, J. (ed.), *New Englishes*. Rowley MA: Newbury House, pp. 11–50.

Quirk, R. 1985. The English language in a global context. In Quirk, R. and Widdowson, H. G. (eds.), *English in the World: Teaching and Learning the Language and Literatures*. Cambridge: Cambridge University Press in association with the British Council, pp. 1–6.

Rickford, J. R. 1988. Connections between sociolinguistics and pidgin-creole studies. In Rickford, J. (ed.), *Sociolinguistics and Pidgin-Creole Studies.* (*International Journal of the Sociology of Language* 71 (3)), pp. 51–7.

Romaine, S. 1982. What is a speech community? In Romaine, S. (ed.), *Sociolinguistic Variation in Speech Communities*. London: Arnold, pp. 13–24.

Sankoff, D. 1988. Sociolinguistics and syntactic variation. In Newmeyer, F. J. (ed.), *Linguistics: The Cambridge Survey. Volume 4: Language: The Socio-Cultural Context*. Cambridge: Cambridge University Press, pp. 140–61.

Sridhar, K. K. 1985. Sociolinguistic theory and non-native varieties of English. *Lingua* 68: 39–58.

Stein, D. In press. *Natural Factors and Syntactic Change* Berlin: de Gruyter.

Van de Craen, P. 1987. Networks, language variation and the relevance of sociolinguistics. In Blanc, M. and Hamers, J. (eds.), *Theoretical and Methodological issues in the Study of Languages/Dialects in Contact at Macro- and Micro-Levels of Analysis*. Quebec: International Centre for research on Bilingualism.

Winford, D. 1988. The Creole continuum and the notion of the community as the locus of change. In Rickford, J. (ed.) *Sociolinguistics and Pidgin-Creole Studies.* (*International Journal of the Sociology of Language* 71 (3)), pp. 91–105.

1

The UK and the USA

JENNY CHESHIRE

Introduction

More research has been carried out on the English that is spoken in the UK and, particularly, in the USA, than anywhere else in the world. It is impossible to survey this vast array of research within a single chapter, and I shall make no attempt to do so.

Nevertheless, as mentioned in the Introduction, a volume whose subject matter is English around the world can hardly exclude the two countries where English has been institutionalised longer than anywhere else, and whose standard varieties have, until very recently, held an unchallenged position as reference models for the teaching of English throughout the world. This chapter, therefore, briefly discusses some sociolinguistic aspects of English as it is used in the UK and the USA, keeping broadly to the format that the authors of the overview papers were asked to use, in order to make comparisons possible between different areas of the world.

Whilst admittedly very different, the UK and the USA share some important characteristics. Perhaps the most important of these is that both countries are overwhelmingly monolinguistic in their official orientation, even though throughout their history they have always been multilingual. A further similarity is that the standard varieties of English in the USA and in southern Britain each have well codified norms, enshrined in their different national dictionaries and grammars; and within each country the existence of a standard variety has given rise to similar sets of attitudes towards the uncodified non-standard varieties (which are spoken by the majority of the population) and has resulted in a similar set of social and educational problems. The phonetic, phonological, lexical and syntactic differences between the two national varieties have long been recognised and described (though discourse structure and discourse strategies have yet to be researched) – see, for example, Mencken 1936; Trudgill and

Hannah 1987 – and lexical and syntactic differences are usually considered
to be relatively minor (Greenbaum 1988: 38). This means that there is no
need to treat the UK and the USA separately in this volume in order to
stress their linguistic distinctiveness, as is currently the case, for example,
for Australia and New Zealand.

Status of English

Neither the UK nor the USA has ever had a legally sanctioned official or
national language[1]. It has been suggested that this reflects a cultural and
philosophical view of the freedom of the individual in language choice and
language use, as in other forms of social behaviour, which makes legislation unpalatable. This may also account for the absence of a British
institution with an equivalent role to the Académie Française (see Heath
and Mandabach 1978; Greenbaum, 1988: 35). Heath and Mandabach
further suggest that legislation in England has been unnecessary because
of the strength of social sanctions on those individuals who exercise their
choice in ways that differ from those of the powerful established groups in
society. Wales is a special case: the Acts of Union in 1536 and 1542
demanded that Wales be ruled in English (see Leith 1983: 179; Bellin
1984: 450), but the Welsh Language Act of 1967 has now given equal
validity to the Welsh language in Wales. In England and Scotland the
absence of overt linguistic legislation has not prevented the English
language from encroaching on the indigenous languages of Britain, so that
it has now become the language used by the majority of the population
in virtually all areas of public life (for details of the use of Gaelic in
Scotland see MacKinnon 1984; for Northern Ireland see Harris, this
volume). Many other languages are spoken in the British Isles, mainly in
private domains (see, for details, Trudgill 1984; Linguistic Minorities
Project 1985); but there has been relatively little research to date which
has focused on language contact between English and other languages.
An exception is Romaine and Chana's work on the language of Panjabi–
English bilingual speakers in Birmingham: Romaine (1983) documents
the spread of English into the private domains of schoolchildren; Chana
and Romaine (1984) investigate attitudes towards Panjabi–English code-
switching; and Romaine (1986) analyses the code-mixed compound verb
in Panjabi–English bilingual discourse, as in the example *Mə apni
language learn kərni*, 'I want to learn my own language' (from Romaine
1989: 129). Romaine (1989) contains further discussion and analysis of
Panjabi–English bilingual discourse. There have been a number of studies
carried out by social psychologists, which investigate the ethnolinguistic
vitality of minority groups; these studies focus on language as both a
determinant and a reflection of ethnolinguistic vitality (see, for example,
Sachdev, Bourhis, D'Eye and Phang 1990). British Black English has been

analysed by Sutcliffe 1982, 1984; Sebba 1984; and Edwards 1986, 1989a, 1989b.

When English was transported to the USA it continued its encroachment on other languages, now on the other side of the Atlantic. The tradition of having no specified official or national language was also continued. Neither the Declaration of Independence nor the American Constitution specified an official language for the USA, although the documents were written in English (Marshall 1986: 8). This was a planned political strategy, recognising the need to attract new immigrants who might speak other languages, and perpetuating the philosophy of individual choice (and trusting that this would eventually result in a single language being used throughout the country). The strategy subsequently changed, however; by 1923 there were 34 states with statutes denying school instruction in languages other than English, and the Nationality Act of 1940 required an alien seeking citizenship to speak English (see Heath 1976, 1977; Marshall 1986). In 1985 a constitutional amendment was put before Congress, urging that English should be the official language of the USA and that Congress should have the power to enforce this legislation. Several federal states, influenced by the English Language Amendment, have now passed their own versions of the Amendment. The Amendment has been criticised and challenged by many professional societies concerned with language (see, for discussion, Fishman 1986); the implications for teachers of English are discussed by Judd (1987), who stresses the relationship between language teaching and political ideology. This relationship, of course, is extremely pertinent to the role of English as a world language (see, for discussion, Phillipson 1988).

There has been a great deal of research in the USA on the role of English in the linguistic repertoires of bilingual speakers and on the effects of language contact on the English spoken by bilinguals. The language with the largest number of speakers in the USA, other than English, is Spanish (Ferguson and Heath 1981: 216) and, despite Toon's view that scant attention has been paid to Hispanic American varieties of English (Toon 1984: 219), several studies have been carried out into Spanish–English bilingualism (see, for example, Wolfram 1973, Teschner, Bills and Craddock 1975; Ornstein-Galicia 1983; Penfield and Ornstein-Galicia 1985; Ornstein-Galicia, Green and Bixler-Marquez 1988). There has also been research on contact between English and Italian (for example, Biondi 1975, Di Pietro 1976; see Correa-Zoli 1981 for some further details), and on English and several other languages in the USA (see, for some illustrative discussion, Ferguson and Heath 1981). Haugen (1969) analyses contact between Norwegian and English in the USA.

There have been many studies of Black English Vernacular, too numerous to detail (but see, for example, Wolfram 1969; Labov 1972a; and many of the papers in Montgomery and Bailey 1986). A current interest is the extent to which black and white varieties of English may – or may not – be diverging (see, for example, Bailey 1987; Bailey and Maynor 1987; Labov 1987; Wolfram 1987).

Regional variation

There is a long tradition of regional dialect study in Britain. The best known and most comprehensive dialect research was the *Survey of English Dialects* (Orton *et al.* 1962–71), which was followed by the *Linguistic Atlas of Scotland* (Mather and Speitel 1975, 1977) and the Tape-Recorded Survey of Hiberno-English (see Harris, this volume). Some aspects of regional variation and its relation to social variation are described in Hughes and Trudgill 1987; regional accents are described in Wells (1982). Far less is known about regional variation in morphology and syntax than about phonetic and phonological variation; for an overview of research into British dialect grammar up until 1983 see Edwards, Trudgill and Weltens 1984; for some descriptions of regional syntax see Milroy and Milroy 1989.

It is generally agreed that, in the UK, traditional rural dialects of the kind described in the *Survey of English Dialects* are declining, but that the pattern of population movement since World War II is giving rise to new urban dialects (see Milroy 1984). Lass (1987) sees Britain as becoming increasingly characterised by distinctive broad regional types, with focal points in the large conurbations that form the regional population centres, such as Edinburgh and the Lothian region, Clydeside, Tyneside, Leeds-Bradford, Birmingham-Wolverhampton, Merseyside, or London. Though intuitively appealing, this has yet to be empirically validated. A preliminary investigation of dialect levelling in urban centres in Britain is reported in Cheshire, Edwards and Whittle (1989); this suggests that certain features of non-standard syntax are now used in virtually all the major urban centres of Britain. These features include demonstrative *them*, as in *look at them big spiders*; relative *what*, as in *the film what was on last night was good*; and the participle form *sat*, as in *she was sat over there looking at her car*.

There is a similar tradition of rural dialectology in the USA, stemming from the foundation of the American Dialect Society in 1889. *The Linguistic Atlas of New England* (Kurath *et al.* 1939–43) was followed by atlases for the Atlantic coast from New Brunswick to Georgia (Kurath 1949; Atwood 1953; Kurath and McDavid 1961). Cassidy (1984:196) expects the entire USA (and English-speaking Canada) to be mapped by the end of the century. As in the UK, sociolinguistic research tends to focus more on urban dialect forms than on rural forms, reflecting the present-day distribution of the population (Preston 1986:13). Sociolinguistic surveys carried out in various parts of the USA as well as in Britain have confirmed that the use of regionally characteristic dialect features is generally correlated with the socioeconomic status of speakers; in other words, that regional variation is inseparable from social variation (see, for illustrative examples for the USA, Labov, 1966; Wolfram and Christian 1976; Feagin 1979; and, for the UK, Trudgill 1974; Petyt 1985; Macaulay 1977).

Sociolinguistic variation

Labov's early research in New York City (Labov 1966) provided the impetus for a large number of quantitative investigations into linguistic variation and change – not only in English, of course, but in an increasing number of other languages. The results have, for the most part, been very widely reported and discussed. The standard textbooks give brief accounts of some of the better known studies (see, for example, Chambers and Trudgill 1980; Hudson 1980; Trudgill 1983a; Wardhaugh 1986); accounts of the early methodology and of Labov's own early research findings are given in Labov (1966, 1972a, 1972b). The papers in Trudgill (1978), Romaine (1982), Labov (1982), Sankoff (1986) and Fasold and Schiffrin (1989) illustrate some of the refinements and adaptations to the methodology that have been made by scholars working on English, and other languages, in the UK and the USA as well as in some other countries.

It is impossible to summarise the patterns of sociolinguistic variation that have emerged from such a large body of research; in any case, the findings are now so complex and disparate that it would be unrealistic and counterproductive even to attempt a summary. It will perhaps be useful, however, to briefly restate some of the better known approaches, so that readers can appreciate the extent to which some of the contributions to this volume have been influenced by the quantitative, Labovian framework. It may also be useful to briefly mention some of the more important criticisms of the framework that have been made since about 1980, and to consider some alternative approaches to sociolinguistic analysis.

'Status-based' approaches

Early investigations carried out within the Labovian framework used sampling methods to select speakers from a hierarchy of socioeconomic classes, on the basis of indicators such as income, education and housing. Interviews were conducted in such a way that they could elicit different styles of speech, which were considered as ranging along a continuum from very careful speech to relatively spontaneous speech. The frequency of occurrence of a number of carefully defined linguistic variables was then analysed for each group of speakers in each stylistic context.

A typical pattern of social and stylistic variation that emerged from

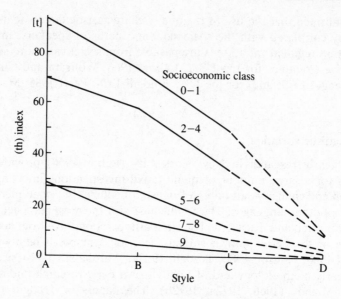

Figure 1.1   Social and stylistic variation in the use of (th) in New York City (from Labov 1972b: 113). A: casual speech; B: careful speech; C: reading style; D: word lists. Socioeconomic class scale: 0—1, lower class; 2—4, working class; 5—6, 7—8, lower middle class; 9, upper class.

early studies using this methodology is shown in figure 1.1. In New York the vernacular pronunciation of English *th* in words such as *three* or *thing* is [t]. As figure 1.1 shows, members of the lower working class in New York City use the vernacular [t] variant more frequently than speakers from other socioeconomic classes; in fact, the frequency of use of the vernacular form reflects the social 'ranking' of the classes on the socioeconomic hierarchy. As speech style becomes progressively more careful, all speakers use a lower proportion of the vernacular variant, so that in their more careful styles they approximate more closely to the usage of the higher status socioeconomic group.

The finding that linguistic variation is not free, as had previously been supposed, but is systematically constrained by the social and stylistic context in which language occurs, was of major importance, and has been replicated in sociolinguistic surveys carried out in other cities in the USA (see, for example, Shuy, Wolfram and Riley 1967; Wolfram 1969; Wolfram and Christian 1976; Feagin 1979) and in the UK (Trudgill 1974; Macaulay, 1977; Petyt 1985). The neat relationship between social and stylistic variation that was found in the early surveys has not been replicated in all communities, however; this is the case, for example, in some divergent dialect communities such as that investigated by Johnston (1983) in Edinburgh; see further Milroy, this volume.

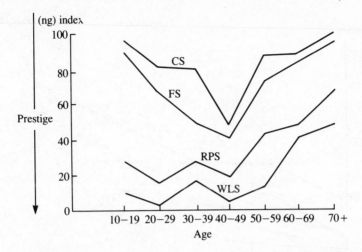

Figure 1.2 Norwich (ng) by age and style (after Chambers and Trudgill 1980: 91).
CS = casual style; FS = formal style; RPS = reading passage style;
WLS = word list style.

A further recurrent, well known and contentious finding that emerged from early sociolinguistic surveys was that, other things being equal, female speakers tended to use a higher proportion of variants that were identified as the 'prestige' forms (see Introduction, this volume; Milroy, this volume). Regular patterns of age differentiation also emerged, with variables that were not involved in linguistic change showing a curvilinear pattern of social and stylistic variation (see Cheshire 1987a for discussion). Figure 1.2 illustrates this pattern of age differentiation, for the (ng) variable in Norwich.

Variables that enter into irregular patterns of social or stylistic variation were commonly considered to be involved in linguistic change; this is the case, for example, for the (r) variable – the pronunciation of postvocalic (r) in words such as *card* – in New York City (Labov 1966). As figure 1.3 shows, speakers from the lower middle class (classes 6–8) used a higher percentage of postvocalic /r/ than speakers from the class above them (see Labov 1972b: 122–42, for discussion).

'Solidarity-based' approaches

A second influential approach to the quantitative analysis of sociolinguistic variation has focused on the social relationships that speakers enter into with others. This approach is not necessarily incompatible with a status-based approach (see Milroy 1980: 201); Romaine (1982: 8), for example, sees the two approaches as focusing on the place of the individual speaker at different

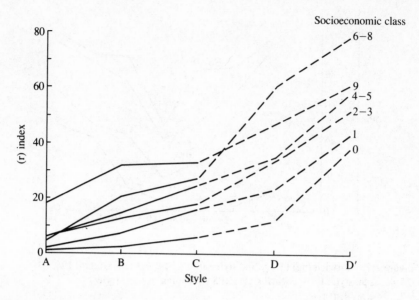

Figure 1.3   Class stratification of (r) (from Labov 1972b: 125). A: casual speech; B: careful speech; C: reading style; D: word lists. Socioeconomic class scale: 0−1, lower class; 2−4, working class; 5−6, 7−8, lower middle class; 9, upper class.

levels of abstraction in linguistic analysis, within the following hierarchy: individual, network, social group, speech community, language. An example of an investigation at the network level of analysis is reported by Labov (1972c), who analysed the relationship between the peergroup status of black adolescent and pre-adolescent speakers, and the frequency with which they used certain features of Vernacular Black English (one such feature is the deletion of *is* as a realisation of the copula BE, in phrases of the kind *he fast in everything he do* − see Labov 1972d: 67). Cheshire (1982) found that the use of non-standard verb forms characteristic of the English spoken in Reading, England, was related to the degree to which male adolescents participated in the local vernacular culture (a delinquent youth culture). Milroy's well-known analysis of the English spoken in Belfast (Milroy 1980, 1987a) applied the notion of social network (see Boissevain 1974) to the analysis of linguistic variation in three Belfast communities. A network strength scale was constructed using five indicators which reflected the relative multiplexity and density of a speaker's personal social network (specifically, the extent to which kin, work and friendship ties were contracted within a territorially based neighbourhood). Edwards (1986), investigating language in a British Black community, analysed the relationship between social network and the use of Patois, using a network strength scale with indicators based on patterns of work, friendship and leisure within the community. The Patois variants included phonological features (for example, /o/ in words such as *fun* or *run*) and morphological and syntactic features (for example, the pronoun forms in *me feel happy, im put it away, dem like di baby*; and the negative construction in phrases such as *di boy no want it*); see Edwards 1986: 80). Speakers with higher social network scores were found to use Patois more frequently.

Social network analysis has provided insights into the mechanisms of linguistic change, showing how dense and multiplex networks act as norm-enforcing mechanisms, hindering linguistic change; and how, conversely, weak network ties can lead to linguistic innovation. The spread of /a/ backing (in words such as *bad*) from a Protestant east Belfast community to a Catholic west Belfast community can be explained in this way, as can the spread of recent changes in the use and social evaluation of the (*pull*) variable (see Milroy and Milroy 1985; J. Milroy, this volume).

Criticisms

Now that a large amount of research has been carried out within the Labovian framework, it is possible to reflect on the accumulated findings and on the interpretations that have been offered, to evaluate the methodology and to assess its theoretical implications. In fact, almost every aspect of the analytical frameworks mentioned above has now been criticised. For example, attention has been drawn to problems in the sampling methods used in sociolinguistic surveys (Romaine 1980a), to the theoretical inadequacy of the original Labovian model of style (Traugott and Romaine 1985; Wolfson 1976; and, especially, Bell 1984); to the unacknowledged dependence of the Labovian status-based approach on a functionalist model of social class (Milroy 1987b; Guy 1988; Rickford 1986); and to a 'male-as-norm' bias in the analysis and explanation of sex differences in language behaviour (see Cameron and Coates 1985, 1989). Coupland (1988: 5) comments on the subjectivity that is involved in the construction of a socioeconomic class index, where individual indicators are selected and weighted, at the expense of others; Cameron and Coates (1985, 1989) make a similar point with reference to the indicators that are chosen to enable social network structure to be measured. There has been a long debate, still unresolved, on the question of whether the linguistic variable should be extended from the analysis of phonological variation, for which it was originally used, to the analysis of variation in syntax and in discourse (see Labov 1978; Lavandera 1978, 1988; Romaine 1980b; Dines 1980; Weiner and Labov 1983; Winford 1984; Cheshire 1987b; Sankoff 1988). A comprehensive, critical review of the Labovian framework of analysis is given in Milroy (1987b; a shorter review is given by Walters (1988).

As Milroy (1987b) points out, critical appraisal should be welcomed as a sign that the discipline of sociolinguistics has matured. Some of the controversies, however, have had some unfortunate consequences. For example, although the difficulties of applying the linguistic variable to the analysis of syntax has not prevented some researchers from analysing syntactic variation within a quantitative framework (see, for example, Cheshire 1982; Weiner and Labov 1983), it does seem to have stopped any real progress being achieved in this area of enquiry. It is still the case that there are more quantitative analyses of phonetic and phonological variation in English than there are of syntactic variation; and much of the quantitative research that is currently being carried out into syntactic variation in English (for example, Biber 1986; Du Bois 1987; Chafe 1980) cannot really be considered to be sociolinguistic in its orientation, since it pays little attention to the social context in which language is used (see further Macaulay 1988: 158). A great deal of research that aims to analyse the syntactic and discourse structure of face-to-face conversation does not use quantitative methods (or, if it does, it makes only subsidiary use of them) and, again, focuses more on the linguistic organisation of discourse than on the social context (see, for example, Stubbs 1986; Coates 1987, 1989; Schiffrin 1987; Cameron, McAlinden and O'Leary 1989; Cheshire 1989).

There are, in addition, some important aspects of sociolinguistic analysis which have so far received very little critical attention. In particular, sociolinguistic research has paid relatively little attention to the 'socio-' part of sociolinguistics. One reason for this is that the emphasis in research is frequently on linguistic systems, aiming to analyse the place of variability in the structure of linguistic systems, and the mechanisms of linguistic change (see, for example, Labov 1982; Trudgill 1983b: 2–3). Faced with the necessity of observing and organising linguistic data that have been recorded in a social context, and with a potentially infinite number of non-linguistic variables to take into account (see, for discussion of many of these, Preston 1986), researchers have tended to categorise speakers in terms of the demographic variables that are typically used in human geography and other social sciences, such as socioeconomic class or status, sex, age and ethnic group (termed by Preston (1986: 15) 'the big four of modern sociolinguistics'). As Milroy (1987b: 97) points out, it is difficult to see how an investigation could proceed without some recourse to such large-scale categories in the initial stages.

Even when the research focus is primarily on the linguistic system, however, it is clearly important to recognise the theoretical status of the social categories that are used to categorise the data. Sometimes the categories appear to represent simply the shared intuitions of researchers about the sources of variation in society (see, for discussion, Smith, Giles and Hewstone 1980: 285; Smith 1984: 11), or to be merely the social dimensions for which data are most easily available or most easily observable. A person's social class in the UK, for example, is readily

classifiable in accordance with the Registrar-General's published classification of occupations; and the researcher's own assessment of a person's
apparent age group and sex is used in studies based on rapid and
anonymous observation (see, for example, Labov 1972e; Labov 1981;
Rimmer 1982).

Bell (1984) argues convincingly that speakers' evaluations of social
differentiation in language determine the extent of their style shifting
(stylistic variation, in other words, is the mirror image of social variation);
if we accept this view of linguistic behaviour, it becomes essential to
determine what speakers themselves see as the important parameters of
social variation, rather than to unthinkingly analyse the linguistic data in
terms of the more conventional parameters that researchers may assume
to be important (see Rickford, this volume, for an example of an analysis
of age differences and social class differences in terms of the distinctions
that are relevant to community members). The taxonomy mentioned
earlier (Preston 1986) assumes that the categories of age, socioeconomic
class and ethnicity will be connected to 'community labels'; it must be
said, however, that in practice researchers in both the UK and the USA
have paid very little attention to the social divisions that are seen as
important within the community whose linguistic behaviour is being
analysed.

Eckert's work on white adolescent social structure and the spread of a
vowel change (see Eckert 1988) is an example of the insights that can be
gained from analysing linguistic data in terms of the social categories that
speakers themselves perceive to be relevant. Eckert analysed patterns of
change in the backing and lowering of the (uh) variable in the Detroit
area. Three years of participant-observation in high schools in the suburbs
of Detroit revealed that the adolescent participants tended to polarise into
groups, referring to themselves and known by their peers as, respectively,
'Jocks' and 'Burnouts'. These categories were culturally salient to all the
adolescents who took part in the study, including those who did not
consider themselves as belonging to either of the groups (these speakers
usually referred to themselves as 'In-Betweens', describing themselves
with reference to the characteristics of the two polarised groups). The
social category to which individual speakers felt they belonged was
associated with different network structures and with a different orientation to the urban area of Detroit; all these factors, in turn, had a significant
effect on the realisation of (uh). Although the social class of the adolescents (here, the social class of their parents) was related to their
affiliation to either the Jocks or the Burnouts, it was the group affiliation
that predicted linguistic variation in the use of (uh), rather than social
class. In other words, the social category that best predicted linguistic
variation was the category that the adolescents themselves perceived as
important, rather than the category which might otherwise have been

imposed on them by the researcher; and it was by approaching the data in terms of this categorisation that Eckert was able 'to find the intervening variables between broad demographic categories and the daily realities of social and linguistic life' (1988: 206).

Qualitative approaches to sociolinguistic analysis

Eckert's work, for all its originality, still has as its aim the understanding of linguistic change and the place of linguistic variation in the language system. It has been argued that work carried out within the Labovian framework is 'sociolinguistics proper' (Trudgill 1978: 11), and the space that has been given in this chapter to this approach to sociolinguistic research reflects the dominance that it has had since the 1960s in work on English in its social context, in both the UK and the USA. It is, however, by no means the only approach to sociolinguistic research that has been developed, and a necessarily brief mention should be made of two of the more influential qualitative approaches to the analysis of language in its social context.

One of these is 'interpretative sociolinguistics' (see Gumperz 1982a, 1982b). The aim here is to analyse the interactive processes underlying face-to-face interaction. Quantitative sociolinguistics is of very limited use for this purpose, with its reliance on grouping individuals into predetermined social categories. Interactional sociolinguists generally prefer to see social categories as 'symbolic entities' which individuals can manipulate in everyday conversation in order to achieve their communicative goals – though an important proviso, of course, is that an individual's ability to perform this manipulation is subject to social constraints imposed by history and economic forces (1982a: 26).

The focus in interpretative sociolinguistics is on selected instances of natural conversation (although role playing has sometimes been used to generate conversation). The participants' interpretations of the interaction are often elicited after the event, together with interpretations from 'judges' who view the interaction. The aim of the analyst is to deduce the inferences and social assumptions that speakers must have made in order to have acted as they did, and to determine empirically the contribution that specific linguistic features have made to the interpretation process. A good example of the insights to be gained from this approach is Chick's paper (this volume). Inferences are more unstable and therefore less subject to agreement than ideas about, for example, speech norms, but it nevertheless seems reasonable to suppose that speakers from similar social backgrounds share similar social knowledge and that this leads them to draw similar inferences. Gumperz therefore argues that certain linguistic features act as 'contextualisation cues', which lead participants to foreground certain aspects of their background knowledge and to underplay others (see also Goffman 1974; Eco 1984).

Clearly, the aims of interpretative sociolinguistics are different from those of quantitative sociolinguistics, and research carried out within the interpretative framework leads to an understanding of different aspects of language in its social context.

Where the participants in a conversation are from different cultural backgrounds, research results have sometimes been presented in terms of 'miscommunication' between participants in a conversation who, it is said, have interpreted contextualisation cues differently (see, for example, Gumperz and Cook-Gumperz 1982; Jupp, Roberts and Cook-Gumperz 1982, on ethnic differences; see also Maltz and Borker 1982 for an interpretation of sex differences in this way). This view, however, has been criticised as being culture-bound, failing to take account of the effect of institutionalised power structures on the interpretation of minority speakers' utterances (Singh and Martohardjono 1985; Singh, Lele and Martohardjono 1988).

A second approach that should be mentioned is Brown and Levinson's model of politeness (Brown and Levinson 1987), which is influenced by Goffman's theory of face (Goffman 1967). The aim, again, is to explain language behaviour in terms of the processes governing human interaction. Brown and Levinson argue for a shift in emphasis away from the analysis of linguistic indicators of social origin and identity (as in the quantitative Labovian approach) towards a focus on patterns of verbal interaction as the expression of social relationships, and for a shift away from the usage of linguistic forms to an emphasis on the relation between form and complex inference (1987: 2, 49). Like Gumperz, Brown and Levinson see language use as a reflection of communicative strategies and speaker intent, urging that 'sociolinguistics should be applied pragmatics' (1987: 281); unlike Gumperz' approach, however, their model does not provide a methodology for conducting research, but instead provides a theoretical framework which has been mainly used for *post hoc* interpretations of the results of an increasingly wide range of linguistic analyses (see, for example, Kuiper's paper, this volume). These analyses extend beyond what has traditionally been considered to come under the umbrella of 'sociolinguistics', to include empirical investigations of second language learning, child language acquisition, discourse and conversation analysis, and even some aspects of theoretical syntax (see, for discussion, Brown and Levinson 1987: 28–47; 257). The model has also been used to reinterpret the results of some quantitative research into variation in English (see, for example, Deuchar 1987).

The generality of the model thus allows a very wide range of language behaviour to be considered within the same conceptual framework. Despite this achievement, however, it has been pointed out that the model, like the others mentioned in this chapter, suffers from being determinist and overly simplistic (Coupland, Grainger and Coupland 1988), and that it assumes too much rational choice, propositional clarity and clear turn-taking than in fact exists in conversational discourse (Hymes 1986). We still have some way to go, it seems, before achieving a coherent and integrated account of language in its social context.

Most writers who see this as a viable research aim assume that interdisciplinary collaboration is needed to account for the complexity of language as we use it in daily life (see Van de Craen 1985; Cheshire 1987b; Coupland 1988); and it is not surprising, perhaps, that recent advances in understanding linguistic variation and change have come from interdisciplinary work – for example, by combining ethnographic and sociolinguistic analysis (Milroy and Milroy 1985; Eckert 1988), or by interpreting sociolinguistic research findings within the social psychological theory of speech accommodation (Bell, 1984; Trudgill 1986). Coupland (1980, 1984, 1988) was perhaps the first to combine sociolinguistic and social psychological methodologies, analysing phonological variation in Cardiff English (including the realisation of word initial /h/, word final -ng, intervocalic /t/ and final consonant clusters) from the point of view of speech accommodation and social identity marking processes. His recent work on language and the elderly aims to develop psychosociolinguistics (Coupland, Coupland, Giles and Henwood 1988: 35).

Attitudes

There has been a great deal of research into attitudes to linguistic variation in English, both in the USA and the UK. A comprehensive overview of this research, up to about 1980, is given in Edwards (1982). Briefly, several British studies of accent evaluation have shown that judges will assess accents according to stereotyped reactions which reflect differentiated views along a number of dimensions. Typically these dimensions are considered to fall into three groups, reflecting competence, personal integrity and social attractiveness (see Lambert 1967). In England, Wales and Scotland, RP generally has connotations of competence and status, whilst regional accents have connotations of integrity and attractiveness, though judges' reactions are affected by factors such as the formality of the context (Bourhis, Giles and Tajfel 1973; Creber and Giles 1983) and by the perceived socioeconomic status of the speaker (Abrams and Hogg 1987).

Similar patterns of evaluation have been found in US studies investigating attitudes towards 'Network' English, Black English and a number of regional American accents (Fraser 1973; Irwin 1977; Zahn and Hopper 1985), and towards standard English and Spanish-accented English (Ryan and Carranza 1975; Arthur, Farrar and Bradford 1974). 'Degree' of accent has been found to affect evaluation, with 'broader' non-standard accents generally being evaluated less favourably (Ryan, Carranza and Moffie 1977; Brennan and Brennan 1981; Ryan and Carranza 1977). In an attempt to standardise the methods used in research and to make the results of different studies more directly comparable, Zahn and Hopper (1985) offer the SEI (Speech Evaluation Instrument); this identifies three factor groups, labelled 'superiority', 'attractiveness' and 'dynamism'.

Most of the studies mentioned above use the matched guise technique (introduced by Lambert, Hodgson, Gardner and Fillenbaum 1960) to investigate language attitudes (or, more precisely, attitudes to speakers – see Edwards 1982). Although this method is very widely used, as many of the overview papers in this volume testify, it has been criticised on several counts, mainly for its alleged artificiality (Agheyisi and Fishman 1970; Robinson 1972; see, for discussion, Edwards 1982). Edwards (1982: 31) points to the need for a greater awareness of the distinction between attitude and belief, as a way of discovering why judges' evaluations take the forms they do; and to the need to relate experimental findings to observations in natural settings (Edwards 1982: 32). Again, then, interdisciplinary cooperation seems to be the best way of progressing towards a fuller understanding not only of linguistic variation, but also of the relationship between linguistic variation and language attitudes.

NOTE

1. At the time of writing the English Language Amendment (see page 15) is still before the US Congress.

REFERENCES

Abrams, D. And Hogg, M. A. 1987. Language attitudes, frames of reference, and social identity: a Scottish dimension. *Journal of Language and Social Psychology* 6: 201–13.

Agheyisi, R. and Fishman, J. A. 1970. Language attitude studies: a brief survey of methodological approaches. *Anthropological Linguistics* 12: 131–57.

Arthur, B., Farrar, D. and Bradford, G. 1974. Evaluation reactions of college students to dialect differences in the English of Mexican-Americans. *Language and Speech* 17: 255–70.

Attwood, E. B. 1953. *A Survey of Verb Forms in the Eastern United States*. Ann Arbor: University of Michigan Press.

Bailey, G. 1987. Are black and white vernaculars diverging? *American Speech* 62 (1): 32–40.

Bailey, G. and Maynor, N. 1987. Decreolisation? *Language in Society* 16: 449–73.

Bell, A. 1984. Language style as audience design. *Language in Society* 13:145–202.

Bellin, W. 1984. Welsh and English in Wales. In Trudgill, P. (ed) (1984), pp. 449–79.

Biber, D. 1986. Spoken and written textual dimensions in English. *Language* 62: 384–414.

Biondi, L. 1975. *The Italian-American Child: His Sociolinguistic Acculturation*. Washington, D.C: Georgetown University Press.

Boissevain, J. 1974. *Friends of Friends: Networks, Manipulators and Coalitions*. Oxford: Blackwell.

Bourhis, R. Y. Giles, H. and Tajfel, H. 1973. Language as a determinant of ethnic identity. *European Journal of Social Psychology* 3: 447–60.

Brennan, E. M. and Brennan, J. S. 1981. Measurements of accent and attitude toward Mexican-American speech. *Journal of Psycholinguistic Research* 10: 487–501.

Brown, P. and Levinson, S. 1987. *Politeness: Some Univerals in Language Usage*. Cambridge: Cambridge University Press.

Cameron, D. and Coates, J. 1985. Some problems in the sociolinguistic explanation of sex differences. *Language and Communication* 5: 143–51. Revised version in Coates, J. and Cameron, D. (eds.) 1989, pp. 13–26.

Cameron, D., McAlinden, F. and O'Leary, K. 1989. Lakoff in context: the social and linguistic functions of tag questions. In Coates, J. and Cameron, D. (eds.) 1989, pp. 74–93.

Cassidy, F. G. 1984. Geographical variation of English in the United States. In Bailey, R. W. and Görlach, M. (eds.), *English as a World Language*. Cambridge: Cambridge University Press, pp. 177–209.

Chafe, W. (ed.). 1980. *The Pear Stories: Cognitive, Cultural and Linguistic Aspects of Narrative Production*. Norwood, NJ:Ablex.

Chambers, J. and Trudgill, P. 1980. *Dialectology*. Cambridge: Cambridge University Press.

Chana, U. and Romaine, S. 1984. Evaluative reactions to Panjabi-English code-switching. *Journal of Multilingual and Multicultural Development* 5: 447–53.

Cheshire, J. 1982. *Variation in an English Dialect: A Sociolinguistic Study*. Cambridge: Cambridge University Press.

1987a. Age and generation-specific use of language. In Ammon, U., Dittmar, N. and Mattheier, K. (eds.) (1987), *Sociolinguistics: An International Handbook of the Science of Language and Society*. Volume 1. Berlin: de Gruyter, 760–7.

1987b. Syntactic variation, the linguistic variable and sociolinguistic theory. *Linguistics* 25: 257–82.

1989. Addressee-oriented features in spoken discourse. *York Papers in Linguistics* 13: 49–63.

Cheshire, J., Edwards, V. and Whittle, P. 1989. Urban British Dialect Grammar: the question of dialect levelling. *English World-Wide* 10: 185–225.

Coates, J. 1987. Epistemic modality and spoken discourse. *Transactions of the Philological Society* pp. 110–31.

1989. Gossip revisited: gossip in all-female groups. In Coates, J. and Cameron, D. (eds.) (1989), pp. 94–122.

Coates, J. and Cameron, D. (eds.). 1989. *Women in their Speech Communities: New Perspectives on Language and Sex*. Harlow: Longman.

Correa-Zoli, A. 1981. The language of Italian Americans. In Ferguson, C. A., and Heath, S. B. (eds.) 1981, pp. 239–56.

Coupland, N. 1980. Style-shifting in a Cardiff work-setting. *Language in Society* 9: 1–12.

1984. Accommodation at work: some phonological data and their implications. *International Journal of the Sociology of Language* 46: 49–70.

1988. *Dialect in Use: Sociolinguistic Variation in Cardiff English*. Cardiff: University of Wales Press.

Coupland, N., Coupland, J., Giles, H. and Henwood, K. 1988. Accommodating the elderly: invoking and extending a theory. *Language in Society* 17: 1–42.

Coupland, N., Grainger, K. and Coupland, J. 1988. Politeness in context: intergenerational issues. *Language in Society* 17: 253–62.

Creber, C. and Giles, H. 1983. Social context and language attitudes: the role of formality-informality of the setting. *Language Sciences* 5: 155–62.

Dawe, A. 1970. The two sociologies. In Thompson, K. and Turnstall, J. (eds.), *Sociological Perspectives*. Harmondsworth: Penguin.

Deuchar, M. 1987. Sociolinguistics. In Lyons, J., Coates, R., Deuchar, M. and Gazdar, G. (eds.), *New Horizons in Linguistics 2*. Harmondsworth: Penguin, pp. 311–35.

Dines, E. 1980. Variation in discourse – and stuff like that. *Language in Society* 9: 13–31.

Di Pietro, R. 1976. *Language as a Marker of Italian Ethnicity*. Rome: Studi di Emigrazione.

Du Bois, J. W. 1987. The discourse basis of ergativity. *Language* 63: 805–55.

Eastman, C. M. 1985. Establishing social identity through language use. *Journal of Language and Social Psychology* 4: 1–20.

Eckert, P. 1988. Adolescent social structure and the spread of linguistic change. *Language in Society* 17: 183–208.

Eco, U. 1984. *Semiotics and the Philosophy of Language*. London: Macmillan.

Edwards, J. 1982. Language attitudes and their implications among English speakers. In Ryan, E. B. and Giles, H. (eds.), *Attitudes towards Language Variation*. London: Arnold, pp. 20–33.

Edwards, V. K. 1986. *Language in a Black Community*. Clevedon: Multilingual Matters.

1989a. The speech of British Black women in Dudley, West Midlands. In Coates, J. and Cameron, D. (eds.) 1989, pp. 33–50.

1989b. Patois and the politics of protest: Black English in British classrooms. In Garcia, O. and Otheguy, R. (eds.), *English across Cultures, Cultures across English*. Berlin: de Gruyter.

Edwards, V. Trudgill, P. and Weltens, B. 1984. *The Grammar of English Dialect: A Survey of Research*. London: Economic and Social Research Council.

Fasold, R. W. 1986. Linguistic analyses of the three kinds. In Sankoff, D. (ed.) (1986), pp. 361–6.

Fasold, R. W. and Schiffrin, D. (eds.). 1989. *Language Change and Variation*. Amsterdam: Benjamins.

Feagin, Crawford. 1979. *Variation and Change in Alabama English: A Sociolinguistic Study of the White Community*. Washington DC: Georgetown University Press.

Ferguson, C. A., and Heath, S. B. (eds.). 1981. *Language in the USA*. Cambridge: Cambridge University Press.

Fishman, J. F. (ed.). 1986. *The Question of an Official Language: Language rights and the English Language Amendment*. (*International Journal of the Sociology of Language* 60).

Fraser, B. 1973. Some 'unexpected' reactions to various American-English dialects. In Shuy, R. W. and Fasold, R. (eds.), *Language Attitudes: Current Trends and Prospects*. Washington DC: Georgetown University Press, pp. 28–35.

Giles, H. (ed.). 1984. *The Dynamics of Speech Accommodation*. (*International Journal of the Sociology of Language* 46).

Giles, H., Mulac, A. Bradac, J. J. and Johnson, P. 1986. Speech accommodation theory: the next decade and beyond. In McLaughlin, M. (ed.), *Communication Yearbook 10*. Beverly Hills: Sage, pp. 13–48.

Goffman, E. 1967. *Interaction Ritual: Essays in Face to Face Behaviour*. New York: Anchor Books.

1974. *Frame Analysis*. New York: Harper and Row.

Greenbaum, S. 1988. *Good English and the Grammarian*. Harlow: Longman.

Gumperz, J. J. 1982a. *Discourse Strategies*. Cambridge: Cambridge University Press.

(ed.). 1982b. *Language and Social Identity*. Cambridge: Cambridge University Press.

Gumperz, J. J. and Cook-Gumperz, J. 1982. Interethnic communication in committee negotiations. In Gumperz, J. J. (ed.) 1982b, pp. 145–62.

Guy, G. 1988. Language and social class. In Newmeyer, F. J. (ed.), pp. 37–63.

Haugen, E. 1969. *The Norwegian Language in America: A Study in Bilingual Behaviour*. Cambridge: Cambridge University Press.

Heath, S. B. 1976. A national language academy? Debate in the new nation. *International Journal of the Sociology of Language* 11: 9–43.

1977. Language and politics in the U.S. In Saville-Troike, M. (ed.), *Linguistics and Anthropology*. Washington DC: Georgetown University Press.

Heath, S. B. and Mandabach, F. 1978. Language status decisions and the law in the U.S. Washington DC: National Institute of Education. Reprinted in Cobarrubias, J. and Fishman, J. A. (eds.), 1983. *Progress in Language Planning: International Perspectives*. The Hague: Mouton, pp. 87–105.

Hudson, R. A. 1980. *Sociolinguistics*. Cambridge: Cambridge University Press.

Hughes, G. A. and Trudgill, P. 1987. *English Accents and Dialects: An Introduction to Social and Regional Varieties of English*. London: Edward Arnold. 2nd edition.

Hymes, D. 1986. Discourse: scope without depth. *International Journal of the Sociology of Language* 57: 49–89.

Irwin, R. 1977. Judgements of vocal quality, speech fluency, and confidence of southern black and white speakers. *Language and Speech* 20: 261–66.

Johnston, P. 1983. Irregular style variation patterns in Edinburgh speech. *Scottish Language* 2: 1–19.

Judd, E. 1987. The English Language Amendment: A case study on language and politics. *TESOL Quarterly* 21 (1): 113–35.

Jupp, T. C., Roberts, C., and Cook-Gumperz, J. 1982. Language and disadvantage: the hidden process. In Gumperz, J. J. (ed.) 1982b, pp. 232–56.

Kurath, H. 1949. *A Word Geography of the Eastern United States*. Ann Arbor: University of Michigan Press.

Kurath, H., Hanley, M. L., Bloch, B., Lowman, G. S. and Hansen, M.L. 1939–1943. *Linguistic Atlas of New England*. 3 vols. in 6 parts. Providence: Brown University Press.

Kurath, H., and McDavid, R. I. 1961. *The Pronunciation of English in the Atlantic States*. Ann Arbor: University of Michigan Press.

Labov, W. 1966. *The Social Stratification of English in New York City*. Washington DC: Center for Applied Linguistics.

1972a. *Language in the Inner City: Studies in the Black English Vernacular*. Philadelphia: University of Pennsylvania Press.

1972b. *Sociolinguistic Patterns*. Philadelphia: University of Pennsylvania Press.

1972c. The linguistic consequences of being a lame. In Labov 1972a, pp. 255–92.

1972d. Contraction, deletion and inherent variability of the English copula. In Labov 1972a, pp. 65–129.

1972e. The social stratification of (r) in New York City department stores. In Labov 1972b, pp. 43–69.

1978. Where does the linguistic variable stop? A reply to Beatriz Lavandera. *Working Papers in Sociolinguistics* 44. Austin, Texas: Southwest Educational Development Laboratory.

1981. Field methods used by the project on linguistic change and variation. *Working Papers in Sociolinguistics* 81. Austin, Texas: Southwest Educational Development Laboratory.

(ed.) 1982. *Locating Language in Time and Space*. New York: Academic Press.

1987. Are black and white vernaculars diverging? *American Speech* 62 (1): 5–12.

1989. The exact description of a speech community: Short *a* in Philadelphia. In Fasold, R. W. and Schiffrin, D. (eds.) 1989, pp. 1–57.

Lambert, W. E. 1967. A social psychology of bilingualism. *Journal of Social Issues* 23: 91–109.

Lambert, W. E., Hodgson, R., Gardner, R. C. and Fillenbaum, S. 1960. Evaluational reactions to spoken languages. *Journal of Abnormal and Social Psychology* 60: 44–51.

Lass, R. (1987). *The Shape of English*. London: Dent.

Lavandera, B. 1978. Where does the sociolinguistic variable stop? *Language in Society* 7: 171–83.

1988. The study of language in its socio-cultural context. In Newmeyer, F. J. (ed.), pp. 1–13.

Leith, D. 1983. *A Social History of English*. London: Routledge.

Linguistic Minorities Project. 1985. *The Other Languages of England*. London: Routledge.

Macaulay, R. K. S. 1977. *Language, Social Class and Education; A Glasgow Study*. Edinburgh: University of Edinburgh Press.

1988. What happened to sociolinguistics? *English Worldwide* 9:153–69.

MacKinnon, K. 1984. Scottish Gaelic and English in the Highlands. In Trudgill, P. (ed.), pp. 499–516.

Maltz, D. N. and Borker, R. A. 1982. A cultural approach to male–female miscommunication. In Gumperz (ed.) 1982b, pp. 196–216.

Marshall, D. F. 1986. The question of an official language: language rights and the English Language Amendment. *International Journal of the Sociology of Language* 60: 7–75.

Mather, J. Y. and Speitel, H. H. 1975. *The Linguistic Atlas of Scotland. Volume 1.* London: Croom Helm.

1977. *The Linguistic Atlas of Scotland. Volume 2.* London: Croom Helm.

Mencken, H. L. 1936. *The American Language.* New York: Knopf. 4th edition.

Milroy, L. 1980. *Language and Social Networks.* Oxford: Blackwell.

1984. Urban dialects in the British Isles. In Trudgill, P. (ed.), pp. 199–218.

1987a. *Language and Social Networks.* Oxford: Blackwell. 2nd edition.

1987b. *Observing and Analysing Natural Language: A Critical Account of Sociolinguistic Method.* Oxford: Blackwell.

1988. Review of Horvath, B. *Variation in Australian English: The Sociolects of English. Language in Society* 17: 577–81.

Milroy, L. and Milroy, J. 1985. Linguistic change, social network and speaker innovation. *Journal of Linguistics* 21: 339–84.

(eds.). 1989. *Regional Variation in British English Syntax.* London: Economic and Social Research Council.

Montgomery, M. B. and Bailey, G. 1986. *Language Variety in the South.* Alabama: University of Alabama Press.

Newmeyer, F. J. (ed.) 1988. *Linguistics: The Cambridge Survey. Volume IV: The Socio-Cultural Context.* Cambridge: Cambridge University Press.

Nordberg, B. 1987. Aims of research and methodology. In Ammon, U., Dittmar, N. and Mattheier, K. (eds.), *Sociolinguistics: An International Handbook of the Science of Language and Society.* Berlin: De Gruyter.

Ornstein-Galicia, J. L. (ed.) 1983. *Form and function in Chicano English.* Rowley MA: Newbury House.

Ornstein-Galicia, J. L., Green, G. K., Bixler-Marquez, D. J. (eds.). 1988. *Research Issues and Problems in United States Spanish.* (Rio Grande Series in Language and Linguistics no. 2). Brownsville TX: Pan American University.

Orton, H. *et al.* 1962–71. *Survey of English Dialects.* 4 vols., each in 3 parts. Leeds: E. J. Arnold.

Orton, H., Sanderson, S. and Widdowson, J. (eds.). 1978. *The Linguistic Atlas of England.* London: Croom Helm.

Penfield, J. and Ornstein-Galicia, J. L. 1985. *Chicano English: An Ethnic Contact Dialect.* Amsterdam: Benjamins.

Petyt, K. M. 1985. *Dialect and Accent in Industrial West Yorkshire.* Amsterdam: Benjamins.

Phillipson, R. 1988. Linguicism: structures and ideologies in linguistic imperialism. In Skuttnab-Kangas, T. and Cummins, J. (eds.), *Minority Education: From Shame to Struggle.* Clevedon: Multilingual Matters, pp. 341–58.

Preston, D. 1986. Fifty-some odd categories of language variation. *International Journal of the Sociology of Language* 57: 9–47.

Rickford, J. 1986. The need for new approaches to social class analysis in sociolinguistics. *Language and Communication* 6: 215–21.

Rimmer, S. 1982. On variability in Birmingham speech. *MALS Journal* 7: 1–16.

Robinson, W. P. 1972. *Language and Social Behaviour*. Harmondsworth: Penguin.

Romaine, S. 1980a. A critical overview of the methodology of urban British sociolinguistics. *English World-wide* 1: 163–98.

1980b. On the problem of syntactic variation: a reply to Beatriz Lavandera and William Labov. *Working Papers in Sociolinguistics* 82. Austin TX: Southwest Educational Development Laboratory.

(ed.). 1982. *Sociolinguistic Variation in Speech Communities*. London: Arnold.

1983. Collecting and interpreting self-reported data on the language of linguistic minorities by means of 'language diaries'. *MALS Journal* 8: 3–30.

1986. The syntax and semantics of the code-mixed compound verb in Panjabi-English bilingual discourse. In Tannen, D. and Alatis, J. E. (eds.), *Languages and Linguistics: The Interdependence of Theory, Data and Application*. Washington DC: Georgetown University Press.

1989. *Bilingualism*. Oxford: Blackwell.

Ryan, E. B. and Carranza, M. 1975. Evaluative reactions of adolescents toward speakers of standard English and Mexican American accented English. *Journal of Personality and Social Psychology* 31: 855–63.

1977. Ingroup and outgroup reactions toward Mexican American language varieties. In Giles, H. (ed.), *Language, Ethnicity and Intergroup Relations*. London: Academic Press. pp. 59–82.

Ryan, E. B., Carranza, M. and Moffie, R. W. 1977. Mexican American reactions to accented English. In Berry, J. W. and Lonner, W. J. (eds.), *Applied Cross-cultural Psychology*. Amsterdam: Swets and Zeitlinger B.V., pp. 174–8.

Sachdev, I., Bourhis, R. Y., D'Eye, J. and Phang, S. 1990. Cantonese-Chinese vitality in London (UK). *Journal of Asian Pacific Communication*. 1(1): 209–27.

Sankoff, D. (ed.). 1986. *Diversity and Diachrony*. Amsterdam: Benjamins.

1988. Sociolinguistics and syntactic variation. In Newmeyer, F. J. (ed.), pp. 140–61.

Schiffrin, D. 1987. *Discourse Markers*. Cambridge: Cambridge University Press.

Sebba, M. 1984. Language change amongst Afro-Caribbeans in London. *Amsterdam Creole Studies* 7: 1–11.

Shuy, R. W., Wolfram, W. and Riley, W. K. 1967. *A Study of Social Dialects in Detroit*. Report on Project No. 6–1347. Washington DC: Office of Education.

Shuy, R. W., Baratz, J. C., and Wolfram, W. A. 1969. *Sociolinguistic Factors in Speech Identification*. NIMHR Project MH-15048-01. Washington DC: Center for Applied Linguistics.

Singh, R., and Martohardjono, G. 1985. Review of Gumperz, J., *Discourse Strategies*. *Journal of Multilingual and Multicultural Development* 6: 193–9.

Singh, R., Lele, J. and Martohardjono, G. 1988. Communication in a multilingual society: some missed opportunities. *Language in Society* 17: 43–60.

Smith, P. 1984. *Language and the Sexes*. Oxford: Blackwell.

Smith, P., Giles, H. and Hewstone, M. 1980. Sociolinguistics: A Social Psychological Perspective. In St Clair, R. N. and Giles, H. (eds.), *The Social and Psychological Contexts of Language*. Hillsdale NJ: Lawrence Erlbaum, pp. 283–98.

Stubbs, M. 1986. 'A matter of prolonged fieldwork': notes towards a modal grammar of English. *Applied Linguistics* 17: 1–25.

Sutcliffe, D. 1982. *British Black English*. Oxford: Blackwell.

1984. British Black English and West Indian Creoles. In Trudgill (ed.), pp. 219–37.

Teschner, R. V., Bills, G. D. and Craddock, J. R. (eds.). 1975. *Spanish and English of United States Hispanos: A Critical, Annotated Linguistic Bibliography*. Arlington VA: Center for Applied Linguistics.

Toon, T. E. 1984. Variation in contemporary American English. In Bailey, R. W. and Görlach. M. (eds.), *English as a World Language*. Cambridge: Cambridge University Press, pp. 210–50.

Traugott, E. K. and Romaine, S. 1985. Some questions for the definition of 'style' in sociohistorical linguistics. In Romaine, S. and Traugott, E. K. (eds.), *Papers from the Workshop on Sociohistorical Linguistics. Folia Linguistica Historica* 6: 7–39.

Trudgill, P. 1974. *The Social Differentiation of English in Norwich*. Cambridge: Cambridge University Press.

(ed.) 1978. *Sociolinguistic Patterns in British English*. London: Arnold.

1983a. *Sociolinguistics*. Harmondsworth: Penguin. 2nd edition.

1983b *On Dialect: Social and Geographical Perspectives*. Oxford: Blackwell.

(ed.). 1984. *Language in the British Isles*. Cambridge: Cambridge University Press.

1986. *Dialects in Contact*. Oxford: Blackwell.

Trudgill, Peter and Hannah, Jean. 1987. *International English: A Guide to Varieties of Standard English*. London: Arnold. 2nd edition.

Van de Craen, P. 1985. Networks, language variation and the relevance of sociolinguistics. In Blanc, M. and Hamers, J. (eds.), *Theoretical and Methodological Issues in the Study of Languages/Dialects in Contact at Macro and Micro-Levels of Analysis*. Quebec: International Centre for Research on Bilingualism, pp. 76–96.

Walters, K. 1988. Dialectology. In Newmeyer, F. J. (ed.), pp. 119–39.

Wardhaugh, R. 1986. *An Introduction to Sociolinguistics*. Oxford: Blackwell.

Weiner, E. J. and Labov, W. 1983. Constraints on the agentless passive. *Journal of Linguistics* 19: 29–58.

Wells, J. 1982. *Accents of English. Vol. 2. The British Isles*. Cambridge: Cambridge University Press.

Winford, D. 1984. The linguistic variation and syntactic variation in Creole continua. *Lingua* 62: 267–88.

Wolfson, N. 1976. Speech events and natural speech: some implications for sociolinguistic methodology. *Language in Society* 5: 189–209.

Wolfram, W. 1969. *A Sociolinguistic Description of Detroit Negro Speech*. Washington DC: Center for Applied Linguistics.

1973. *Sociolinguistic Aspects of Assimilation: Puerto-Rican English in New York City*. Washington, DC: Center for Applied Linguistics.

1987. Are black and white vernaculars diverging? *American Speech* 62 (1): 40–8.

Wolfram, Walt and Christian, Donna. 1976. *Appalachian Speech*. Washington DC: Center for Applied Linguistics.

Zahn, C. J. and Hopper, R. 1985. Measuring language attitudes: the speech evaluation instrument. *Journal of Language and Social Psychology* 4: 113–23.

Ireland

2

Ireland

JOHN HARRIS

Historical and political background

Since 1921, Ireland has been divided into two political entities: the independent 26-county Republic of Ireland (earlier the Irish Free State, capital city Dublin) and the six-county statelet of Northern Ireland (capital Belfast) which is currently part of the United Kingdom. Although the latter is frequently referred to as Ulster, it excludes three of the counties which comprise the historical province bearing that name.

The long-standing dispute over the political status of the Six Counties reflects the divided loyalties of its population. Broadly speaking, the nationalist community (largely Roman Catholic) desires a united independent Ireland, while the unionist community (largely Protestant and descended from Scottish and English settlers who arrived in the seventeenth century) professes allegiance to the British crown. The present ascendency of the unionist cause stems from the fact that the boundaries of the Six Counties were originally drawn in such a way as to ensure a Protestant majority. The current ratio of Protestants to Catholics in Northern Ireland is roughly two to one.

The English language first established a foot-hold in Ireland with the Anglo-Norman invasions of the twelfth century. For several centuries after this date, it made little headway against the Irish Gaelic of the indigenous population. In fact the influence of English waned to such an extent that by 1600 it was more or less restricted to a small enclave on the east coast. Relic dialects of this form of English survived into the nineteenth century (see Ó Muirithe 1977a). (For overviews of the history of English in Ireland, see Hogan 1927; Barry 1982.)

It was the plantation schemes of the seventeenth century, under which thousands of English and Scottish settlers arrived in Ireland, that laid the foundations for the steady advance of English towards the position of majority language which it has today. By 1800, English was the first language of about half of the population, with Irish becoming increasingly associated with poverty and disadvantage (see de Fréine 1977). During the nineteenth century, various factors contributed to the continuing rapid decline of Irish: the introduction of universal English-language education, the adoption of English by both the nationalist movement and the Roman Catholic church, and famine and large-scale emigration which hit the Irish-speaking areas hardest. Today the *Gaeltacht* (Irish-speaking district) is restricted to a few areas on the west coast. Current estimates put the number of native Irish speakers at around two per cent of the total population (Ó Huallacháin 1970).

The status of English

Irish

A series of language-planning initiatives undertaken by the government of the 26 Counties has failed to arrest let alone reverse the decline in the use of Irish as a first language. Nevertheless, Irish enjoys a special status in this part of Ireland. Article 8 of the constitution of the Republic declares that 'the Irish language as the national language is the first official language', while 'the English language is recognised as a second official language' (*Bunreacht na hÉireann*, 6). The teaching of Irish as a compulsory school subject at secondary level has ensured that the majority of the population has at least some competence in the language, however restricted (see Ó Huallacháin 1970). There is a flourishing literature in Irish. It is used in a range of official functions, including broadcasting and government publications. Nominal qualifications in the language are required for entrance to many government services. In most of these domains, however, Irish is usually employed side-by-side with English, and in many instances the use of Irish has no more than a ceremonial function. (Convenient summaries and discussions of the successess and failures of the Irish language planning case are provided by Macnamara 1971 and Edwards 1984.)

    As regards the position of Irish in the Six Counties, the language has up until now never enjoyed official status. However, it is taught in the independent Catholic schools which provide education for the majority of the nationalist population. And at the time of writing, there are indications that sustained pressure from within the nationalist community will result in Irish receiving some kind of official recognition in the near future.

Standard and vernacular varieties of English

In spite of not being officially recognised as the national language in the Republic, English is the medium of everyday communication for the vast majority of the population of Ireland. The functional link between institutionalised forms of English and the spoken vernacular varieties which have developed in Ireland has remained unbroken since the seventeenth century. The result is that there exists no fully independent Irish English vernacular. Instead we have the familiar pattern of a continuum of varieties ranging from least to most standard-like.

Besides *Irish English*, other terms employed in the academic literature to refer to vernacular varieties of English spoken in Ireland include *Anglo-Irish* and *Hiberno-English*. The former, which was favoured in earlier writing (e.g. van Hamel 1912), has largely fallen out of use (although see Henry 1977 who reserves the label for varieties that have been heavily influenced by the Irish substrate). The term *Hiberno-English* has recently gained some currency (Bliss 1972; Sullivan 1980; Filppula, this volume; Kallen, this volume). Convenient structural outlines of Irish English are provided by Bliss (1984) and Harris (1984a).

Standard English is employed in Ireland in the full range of public domains associated with its use in countries such as Britain and the United States. The written model is more or less indistinguishable from that of standard British English. As might be expected, there are a few items of vocabulary, generally borrowed from Irish, which refer to local customs and institutions (e.g. *taoiseach* 'prime minister', *dáil* 'parliament'), but these are hardly sufficient to warrant speaking of an autonomous local written standard. When used in formal institutional contexts (such as news broadcasts, religious sermons and lectures), spoken English tends to follow the norms of the written standard in matters of grammar and lexis.

There is a long tradition of representing Irish English speech in fiction and drama, stretching back at least to the beginning of the seventeenth century (Bliss 1979). In fact the portrayal of vernacular speech in the works of such writers as Synge, Yeats, Joyce, O'Casey and Behan has provided material for much of the research into Irish English (e.g. van Hamel 1912; Sullivan 1980).

The question of whether it is possible to identify locally established standard norms for the pronunciation of English in Ireland has not been investigated in great depth. One point is clear: there is no such thing as a set of codified norms defining a standard Irish English accent. Although external models, such as British 'Received Pronunciation', may influence the way in which some speakers standardise their phonology, total assimilation to such norms is extremely rare, even in the most formal of settings. Several authors assume the existence of informally-defined local standards of pronunciation, based on Dublin in the 26 Counties (e.g. Masterson *et al.* 1983) and on Belfast in the Six Counties (e.g. Douglas-Cowie 1984). However, being unsupported by empirical research, these claims remain largely conjectural.

The only researcher who has attempted to address the issue of informal standard norms of Irish English pronunciation in any systematic way is

J. Milroy (1982, and this volume). His quantitative results indicate that it would be misguided to assume the direction of accent standardisation in Irish English to be determined by a unitary external target such as RP. Using sociolinguistic data collected in Belfast, he argues that the main structural effect of standardisation in northern Irish English is a reduction of allophony. In some cases, the direction of this process is at variance with external prestige norms, with the result that some lower-status pronunciations actually sound more like RP than do higher-status ones.

Regional variation

Most of the work on regional variation in Irish English has been carried out within the framework of traditional dialectology. Some charting of lexical variables has been undertaken (e.g. Henry 1964), but most attention has been devoted to the description of phonological variation. Filppula (1986a, this volume) is exceptional in providing quantitative analyses of a number of regionally differentiated syntactic variables. The preliminary report on regional variation provided by Henry (1958) has been followed up by the large-scale Tape-Recorded Survey of Hiberno-English Speech or TRSHES (Barry 1981a). As with the major dialect surveys of Europe and North America, the target population of this questionnaire-based project is largely rural. However, the TRSHES has included speakers from three age-levels in each of its targeted localities. Preliminary examination of age-differentiated variables has enabled the researchers to uncover apparent-time information on the shifting of isoglosses across geographical space (e.g. Tilling 1981; Adams 1981).

Initial results reported by the TRSHES researchers confirm earlier impressionistic accounts of a major dialect boundary between northern and southern Irish English (Barry 1981b). A bundle of phonological isoglosses occurs along a line which, very roughly speaking, coincides with the boundary of the historical province of Ulster.

Little is known about the regional distribution of linguistic differences within southern Irish English. Claims by Adams (1977: 56) and Bliss (1972: 36; see Filppula, this volume) that southern varieties constitute a relatively homogeneous group have not been checked and do not appear to be borne out by the reports of lay observers. The latter readily identify pronunciation variables which differentiate the vernaculars of major southern population centres such as Dublin and Cork. The main linguistic input which distinguishes northern from southern Irish English is Lowland Scots, reflecting the high level of Scottish settlement in Ulster in the seventeenth century. Within the northern region itself, it is still possible to isolate areas where the linguistic impact of Scots has been more marked than elsewhere. The boundaries of the 'core' Ulster Scots (or 'Scotch-Irish') dialect areas have been researched by Gregg (1972, 1985).

The Irish substratum

Research on the linguistic structure of Irish English vernacular has traditionally proceeded on the assumption that its markedly non-standard characteristics can be directly attributed to substratal transfer from Irish (e.g. van Hamel 1912; Hogan 1927; Hughes 1966; Bliss 1972; Adams 1980; Sullivan 1980; Hickey 1986). Much of the evidence cited in this work is anecdotal and, with a few exceptions (e.g. Henry 1957), is treated rather unsystematically. More recently, however, the substratum case has come under closer scrutiny. Much more theoretically and methodologically rigorous analyses, which generally speaking support the substratum position, have been provided by Filppula (1986a, b) and Kallen (1986a, b). Although the question has not yet been investigated thoroughly, the impression is that the incidence of substratal features is both regionally and socially stratified, with the greatest degree of Irish infuence being manifested in rural low-status speech. Some attempt has been made to relate discussion of the origins of Irish English to the more general debate about the role of substrata and linguistic universals in the development of vernaculars which have evolved in conditions of language contact and shift (e.g. Guilfoyle 1983, 1986; Harris 1987a).

It has long been acknowledged that Irish English has preserved a number of linguistic features which were once current in vernacular Early Modern English but which have since disappeared from general use (e.g. Hume 1878). More recent research indicates that this factor has played a more prominent role in shaping modern Irish English than has generally been appreciated. It has been argued that many of the non-standard characteristics of Irish English which were previously attributed to the exclusive influence of Irish are more likely to represent archaic English forms (e.g. Harris 1984b, 1987b). In some cases, it seems necessary to view particular features as reflecting a convergence of substratal and earlier superstratal inputs.

For various historical reasons, issues surrounding the evolution of Irish English have a direct bearing on debates about the origins of particular linguistic features in New World Englishes. The periods during which English became firmly established in Ireland and the New World overlap to a large extent; and there was a considerable Irish presence in most parts of the New World (including the Caribbean – see Le Page and Tabouret-Keller 1985; Williams 1986) during the early years of English-speaking settlement. In some areas of North America where Irish settlement was at its densest, the influence of Irish English on the development of local vernaculars is unmistakable, e.g. Newfoundland (Clarke 1986, and this volume) and the Ottawa Valley (Pringle and Padolsky 1981).

More controversial is the claim that certain features of New World Black Englishes can ultimately be traced to an Irish English source (e.g.

Bailey 1982). The most likely explanation for the undoubted structural similarities that exist between these varieties appears to involve a convergence of inputs, among which borrowing is only one. Rickford (1986) claims that some of the Irish-like features of decreolised Black Englishes represent relexifications, perhaps influenced by Irish English models, of creole forms which derive directly from the West African substrate. Harris (1986) argues that, while the functions of such features may have substratal origins, the selection of particular morphs to encode them was dictated by the existence of parallel forms in certain regional dialects of British English.

Sociolinguistic variation

A number of studies have presented impressionistic accounts of sociolinguistic variation in Irish English (see, for example, Bertz's 1975 description of phonological variables in Dublin). However, the purpose of this section is to review research which takes an explicitly quantitative approach to the analysis of linguistic variability.

Douglas-Cowie (1978) investigated the use of a number of phonological and lexical variables in the rural community of Articlave, County Derry. Each variable consists of a local Ulster Scots variant and a more standardised variant. She demonstrates how the occurrence of particular variants is sensitive to a range of social and social-psychological factors, including the regional background of those present at the interview, the topic of conversation, and the declared social ambition of the subject. Generally speaking, more standardised variants were favoured by the presence of an English fieldworker, by conversational topics dealing with education and occupation, and by speakers with a high degree of social ambition. Douglas-Cowie describes her results in terms of bidialectalism and code-switching. However, it is clear from her discussion that we are not dealing here with switching between structurally discrete varieties, such as occurs in classic diglossic situations. Rather, we have a pattern of style shifting involving quantitative differences in the use of individual sociolinguistic variables.

The sociolinguistic situation in the northern city of Belfast has been the focus of two major research projects directed by James and Lesley Milroy. The results of this work are presented in two reports (J. and L. Milroy 1977; J. Milroy et al. 1983) and discussed in a number of publications, including J. Milroy (1981), Harris (1985), L. Milroy (1987a, 1987b) and J. Milroy (forthcoming). The first project, Speech Community and Language Variety in Belfast, centred on three inner-city areas of Belfast with a main quota sample of 48 speakers (four speakers being drawn from each of twelve cells defined by area, sex and two age groups). As described by L. Milroy (1987a), the social network method of contacting speakers was employed rather than the random-sampling procedures followed in some other sociolinguistic projects. That is, speakers were selected on the basis of their participation in sets of interlocking relationships centred around territoriality, kinship, social contact and the work place. An important aspect of the method was that the fieldworker was accepted within the communities as a second-order contact ('friend of a friend'), which permitted the extensive use of participation-observation techniques. In this way, maximal access was gained to spontaneous vernacular speech and the social settings in which it is normally used.

Using essentially Labovian methods of quantification, the researchers were able to measure the stratification of phonological variables according to such familiar extralinguistic factors as age, sex and area (J. and L. Milroy 1978). However, the most influential aspect of the research carried out as part of the first project related to an attempt to explain sociolinguistic differences between speakers in terms of social network structure (L. Milroy 1987a; L. Milroy and Margrain 1980). The basic hypothesis here is that the more deeply embedded an individual is within a given local community, as gauged by the number and nature of ties contracted with other members of the community, the more likely he or she is to be subject to local cultural, including linguistic, norms. To test this hypothesis, Milroy devised a five-point network scale for measuring the strength of an individual's ties to the local community. The hypothesis was largely confirmed. She was able to demonstrate significant correlations between individuals' scores for a range of phonological variables and their network scores. All else being equal, higher network scores predicted a higher incidence of local vernacular variants.

The second project, *Sociolinguistic Variation and Linguistic Change in Belfast*, extended the methods employed in the first to two outer-city areas and also incorporated a random-sample survey of the whole city as well as a smaller community study based in the town of Lurgan (for details of the latter, see Pitts 1985, 1986). Studies arising out of this later research have focused on the analysis of linguistic change in progress. J. and L. Milroy (1985) apply the social network model to the issue of how linguistic innovations diffuse through social space (see also L. Milroy 1987a (ch. 7) and J. Milroy, this volume). Harris (1985) examines the factors which influence the direction of change in urban communities when linguistic norms deriving from different hinterland dialects are in competition.

The bulk of the Belfast research was concerned with phonological variation. A number of smaller quantitative studies of Irish English have focused on syntactic variables. Most of these have been concerned with linguistic and pragmatic constraints on variation and contain little in the way of information on the social and stylistic factors that are potentially involved. Some of the results of Filppula's (1986a) study of one urban (Dublin) and two rural communities (Wicklow and Kerry/Clare) are summarised in his contribution to this volume. Kallen's work (1986a, this volume) provides the only other quantitative analysis of linguistic variation in Dublin. Several publications deal with a range of syntactic variables in Belfast (Policansky 1982; Harris 1984b; Finlay and McTear 1986).

Language attitudes

A striking fact about the sociolinguistic status of the Irish language in Ireland is that, although it is no longer the medium of everyday communication for the vast majority of the population, it is nevertheless viewed by many as the embodiment of Irish nationalism. Survey data cited by Macnamara (1971) and Brudner and White (1979) confirm that, in spite of low fluency rates, attitudes towards Irish among the population of the Republic are overwhelmingly positive. Thus, although Irish no longer plays a major communicative role in Irish life (despite its official status in the Republic), it none the less fulfils an important symbolic function. In Fasold's words, the language can be said to play a *nationalist* but not a *nationist* role (1984: 282).

Against this background, it might be expected that reactions towards English would be correspondingly negative. Indeed, English has been viewed by some nationalists as symbolising British colonial oppression (e.g. Pearse 1976). However, as the relatively rapid shift to English bears witness, the perceived value of the language as a means of gaining access to improved economic conditions both within Ireland and overseas has clearly been sufficient to override such sentiments.

Attitudes towards different accents of Irish English have been investigated in a number of subjective reaction tests. These conform to the by now familiar design in which judges are presented with speech samples and asked to rate subjects on a series of semantic-differential scales relating to various personality and background attributes (such as intelligence, integrity, enthusiasm, sense of humour and likely school achievement). The studies have focused on stereotypical reactions to various accents differentiated by class (Edwards 1977a, 1979a, 1979b; Masterson *et al.* 1983) and/or region (Milroy and McClenaghan 1977; Edwards 1977b; Masterson *et al.* 1983; Killian 1986). The results of these investigations coincide to a large extent with those of similar studies conducted elsewhere in the world. As might be expected, more standardised accents were generally rated higher on dimensions of overt prestige, while local vernacular accents received more favourable ratings on dimensions of solidarity. Thus, while methods which involve directly eliciting opinions about language in Ireland indicate that a high degree of symbolic prestige attaches to Irish, indirect methods have disclosed a range of attitudes towards English which reflect its position as the main language of communication in the country.

Future research

We conclude this overview by referring to two areas in the study of Irish English which deserve closer attention from researchers than they have received up to now: Irish–English bilingualism, and the identification of overt and covert prestige norms governing language use.

Systematic investigation of the linguistic behaviour of Irish–English bilingual speakers might be expected to make significant contributions to our knowledge in at least two areas. Firstly, it would seem to be an obvious research site for testing assumptions about the influence of Irish on the development of Irish English. Secondly, it would be likely to shed light on the linguistic and social processes involved in the selective use of Irish and English in the *Gaeltacht* areas. In a less narrow perspective, research of this nature might be expected to provide input to the wider debate about the role of substrata versus linguistic universals in the genesis of contact vernaculars and to contribute towards the elaboration of a general theory of code-switching and code-mixing. In fact, it is surprising how little empirical research with either of these goals has been carried out. (Ní Ghallchóir 1981 is exceptional in this respect.)

Our knowledge of the way in which institutionalised and vernacular linguistic norms determine patterns of linguistic variation and change in Irish English is still somewhat sketchy. The Milroys' social network studies have already begun to yield promising results which further our understanding of why, in the face of standardising pressures, local non-standard linguistic norms should remain so resilient. However, we are still very much in the dark when it comes to identifying the processes which underlie the establishment of overt prestige models in both parts of Ireland.

It would be oversimplying things to equate overt prestige in Irish English with external standard (e.g. British) models and covert prestige with local nonstandard norms. Not only would this overlook the potential existence of locally-based overt prestige models; but it would also ignore the possibility that change in Irish English is subject to externally-based covert influences. It has been noted by various researchers that large-scale Irish migration has had a long-term effect on the linguistic development of some British urban vernaculars, such as that of Liverpool (e.g. Knowles 1978). Current patterns of migration raise the possibility that the linguistic influence might also work in the opposite direction. During the post-war years, thousands of Irish immigrants in British cities have retained a strong connection with Ireland through frequent visits home and, in many cases, through eventual permanent resettlement. It is likely that such people represent potentially important conduits of linguistic change in Irish English. In particular, it is worth considering the possibility that they are responsible for the importation of covert prestige norms associated with British urban vernaculars. This would provide an explanation for why

Dublin English, for example, appears to be increasingly acquiring a number of linguistic characteristics which are typical of British urban speech but which are not found in the city's hinterland dialects. (These include: glottalling of /t/ in syllable codas, diphthongisation of the nuclei in the DAY and GO word-classes, and velarisation of /l/.) The issue warrants further investigation.

When considering the issue of sociolinguistic norms in the context of the Six Counties, the question arises as to whether it is at all possible to speak of a unified speech community (as, for instance, Douglas-Cowie 1984 implies). There is reason to suspect that political affiliation in the North helps define overt and covert prestige norms for language use; the local wisdom is that 'Catholics speak differently from Protestants'. In Belfast, this phenomenon appears to reflect the fact that the two communities migrated, broadly speaking, from different hinterland dialect areas (J. Milroy 1981). In some geographically peripheral areas of Northern Ireland, however, it is difficult to avoid the conclusion that unionists and nationalists simply do not share the same set of prestige linguistic norms (see Todd 1984). Moreover, Hickey's (1986) claim that 'in neither of the two states in Ireland is it considered desirable to emulate the phonological norm of the other' (1986: 2) is debatable, at least as it applies to the Six Counties. The impression that strikes anyone who is familiar with the sociolinguistic situation in the North is that, for some nationalists, linguistic targets dictating the direction of standardisation appear to be defined at least in part by southern norms.

It should be obvious from the tentative nature of these remarks regarding the identification of overt and covert norms in Irish English that the conclusions are based on no more than anecdotal evidence. Future empirical research into this area is to be welcomed not only for the light it may shed on the complexities of the sociolinguistic situation in Ireland but also for the contribution it may be expected to make to a general understanding of the role played by sociopolitical factors in shaping the course of linguistic change.

REFERENCES

Adams, G. B. 1977. The dialects of Ulster. In Ó Muirithe (ed.) 1977b, pp. 56–70.
    1980. Common features in Ulster Irish and Ulster English. In R. Thelwell (ed.),
        Linguistic Studies in Honour of Paul Christophersen. Coleraine, Co. Derry:
        New University of Ulster, pp. 85–103.
    1981. The voiceless velar fricative in northern Hiberno-English. In Barry (ed.)
        1981c, pp. 106–17.
Bailey, C.-J. N. 1982. Irish English and Caribbean Black English: another joinder.
    American Speech 57: 237–9.

Barry, M. V. 1981a. The methodology of the tape-recorded survey of Hiberno-English Speech. In Barry (ed.), 1981c, pp. 18–46.

1981b. The southern boundaries of northern Hiberno-English speech. In Barry (ed.), 1981c, pp. 52–95.

(ed.). 1981c. *Aspects of English Dialects in Ireland*. Belfast: Institute of Irish Studies, Queen's University Belfast.

1982. The English language in Ireland. In Bailey, R. W. and Görlach, M. (eds.), *English as a World Language*. Ann Arbor: University of Michigan Press, pp. 84–133.

Bertz, S. 1975. *Der Dubliner Stadtdialekt I: Phonologie*. Published PhD thesis. Freiburg i. Br: Albert-Ludwigs-Universität.

Bliss, A. J. 1972. Languages in contact: some problems of Hiberno-English. *Proceedings of the Royal Irish Academy* 72: 63–82.

1979. *Spoken English in Ireland 1600–1740*. Dublin: Dolmen.

1984. English in the south of Ireland. In Trudgill (ed.) 1984, pp. 135–51.

Brudner, L. and White, D. 1979. Language attitudes: behavior and intervening variables. In Mackey, W. and Ornstein, J. (eds.), *Sociolinguistic Studies in Language Contact: Methods and Cases*. The Hague: Mouton, pp. 51–98.

Bunreacht na hÉireann. 1937. Dublin: Government Publications Office.

Clarke, S. 1986. Sociolinguistic patterning in a New World dialect of Hiberno-English: the speech of St John's, Newfoundland. In Harris *et al.* (eds.), 1986, pp. 67–82.

de Fréine, S. 1977. The dominance of the English language in the nineteenth century. In Ó Muirithe (ed.) 1977b, pp. 71–87.

Douglas-Cowie, E. 1978. Linguistic code-switching in a northern Irish village: social interaction and social ambition. In Trudgill (ed.) 1978, pp. 37–51.

1984. The sociolinguistic situation in Northern Ireland. In Trudgill (ed.) 1984, pp. 517–32.

Edwards, J. 1977a. The speech of disadvantaged Dublin children. *Language Problems and Language Planning* 1: 65–72.

1977b. Students' reactions to Irish regional accents. *Language and Speech* 20: 280–6.

1979a. Judgements and confidence in reactions to disadvantaged speech. In Giles H. and St Clair, R. (eds.), *Language and Social Psychology*. Oxford: Blackwell, pp. 22–44.

1979b. Social class differences in the identification of sex in children's speech. *Journal of Child Language* 6: 121–7.

1984. Irish and English in Ireland. In Trudgill (ed.) 1984, pp. 480–98.

Fasold, R. 1984. *The Sociolinguistics of Society*. Oxford: Blackwell.

Filppula, M. 1986a. *Some Aspects of Hiberno-English in a Functional Sentence Perspective*. University of Joensuu Publications in the Humanities 7. Joensuu: University of Joensuu.

1986b. The equative sentence in Hiberno-English: another area of interference from Irish? In Harris *et al.* (eds.) 1986, pp. 111–20.

Finlay, C. and McTear, M. 1986. Syntactic variation in the speech of Belfast schoolchildren. In Harris *et al.* (eds.) 1986, pp. 175–86.

Gregg, R. J. 1972. The Scotch-Irish dialect boundaries in Ulster. In Wakelin,

M. F. (ed.), *Patterns in the Folk Speech of the British Isles*. London: Athlone, pp. 109–39.

1985. *The Scotch-Irish Dialect Boundaries in the Province of Ulster*. Ottawa: Canadian Federation for the Humanities.

Guilfoyle, E. 1983. Habitual aspect in Hiberno-English. *McGill Working Papers in Linguistics* 1: 22–32.

1986. Hiberno-English: a parametric approach. In Harris *et al.* (eds.) 1986, pp. 121–32.

Harris, J. 1984a. English in the north of Ireland. In Trudgill (ed.) 1984, pp. 115–34.

1984b. Syntactic variation and dialect divergence. *Journal of Linguistics* 20: 303–27.

1985. *Phonological Variation and Change: Studies in Hiberno-English*. Cambridge: Cambridge University Press.

1986. Expanding the superstrate: habitual aspect markers in Atlantic Englishes. *English World-Wide* 7: 171–99.

1987a. Conservatism versus substratal transfer in Irish English. In Boretzky, N., Enninger, W. and Stolz, T. (eds.), *Bochum-Essener Beiträge zur Sprachwandelforschung* 4. Bochum: Brockmeyer, pp. 143–62.

1987b. On doing comparative reconstruction with genetically unrelated languages. In Ramat, A. G., Carruba, O. and Bernini, G. (eds.), *Papers from the 7th International Conference on Historical Linguistics*. Amsterdam: Benjamins, pp. 267–82.

Harris, J., Little, D. and Singleton, D. (eds.). 1986. *Perspectives on the English Language in Ireland: Proceedings of the First Symposium on Hiberno-English*. Dublin: CLCS, Trinity College Dublin.

Henry, P. L. 1957. *An Anglo-Irish Dialect of North Roscommon*. Dublin: University College Dublin.

1958. A linguistic survey of Ireland: preliminary report. *Lochlann* 1: 49–208. Supplement to *Norsk Tidsskrift for Sprogwidenskap* 5.

1964. Anglo-Irish word-charts. In Adams, G. B. (ed.), *Ulster Dialects: An Introductory Symposium*. Cultra, Co Down: Ulster Folk Museum, pp. 147–62.

1977. Anglo-Irish and its Irish background. In Ó Muirithe (ed.) 1977b, pp. 20–36.

Hickey, R. 1986. Possible phonological parallels between Irish and Irish English. *English World-Wide* 7: 1–21.

Hogan, J. J. 1927. *The English Language in Ireland*. Dublin: Educational Company of Ireland.

Hughes, J. P. 1966. The Irish language and the 'brogue': a study in substratum. *Word* 22: 257–75.

Hume, A. 1878. Remarks on the Irish dialect of the English language. *Transactions of the Historic Society of Lancashire and Cheshire* 3: 93–140.

Kallen, J. L. 1986a. Linguistic fundamentals for Hiberno-English syntax. PhD thesis. Dublin: Trinity College Dublin.

1986b. The co-occurrence of *do* and *be* in Hiberno-English. In Harris *et al.* (eds.) 1986, pp. 133–48.

Killian, P. A. 1986. English in Ireland: an attitudinal study. In Harris *et al.* (eds.) 1986, pp. 271–82.

Knowles, G. O. 1978. The nature of phonological variables in Scouse. In Trudgill (ed.) 1978, pp. 80–90.

Le Page, R. B. and Tabouret-Keller, A. 1985. *Acts of Identity: Creole-Based Approaches to Language and Ethnicity.* Cambridge: Cambridge University Press.

Macnamara, J. 1971. Successes and failures in the movement for the restoration of Irish. In Rubin, J. and Jernudd, B. (eds.), *Can Languages be Planned?* Honolulu: University Press of Hawaii, pp. 65–94.

Masterson, J., Mullins, E. and Mulvihill, A. 1983. Components of evaluative reactions to varieties of Irish accents. *Language and Speech* 26: 215–31.

Milroy, J. 1981. *Accents of English: Belfast.* Belfast: Blackstaff.

1982. Probing under the tip of the iceberg: phonological normalisation and the shape of speech communities. In Romaine, S. (ed.), *Sociolinguistic Variation in Speech Communities.* London: Arnold, pp. 35–48.

In press. *Society and Language Change.* Oxford: Blackwell.

Milroy, J. and Milroy, L. 1977. *Speech Community and Language Variety in Belfast.* Report to the Social Science Research Council. Grant no. HR 3771.

1978. Belfast: change and variation in an urban vernacular. In Trudgill (ed.) 1978, pp. 19–36.

1985. Linguistic change, social network and speaker innovation. *Journal of Linguistics* 21: 339–84.

Milroy, J., Milroy, L., Harris, J., Gunn, B., Pitts, A. and Policansky, L. 1983. *Sociolinguistic Variation and Linguistic Change in Belfast.* Report to the Social Science Research Council. Grant no. HR 5777.

Milroy, L. 1987a. *Language and Social Networks.* Oxford: Blackwell. 2nd edition.

1987b. *Observing and Analysing Natural Language: A Critical Account of Sociolinguistic Method.* Oxford: Blackwell.

Milroy, L. and McClenaghan, P. 1977. Stereotyped reactions to four educated accents in Ulster. *Belfast Working Papers in Language and Linguistics* 2 (4).

Milroy, L. and Margrain, S. 1980. Vernacular language loyalty and social network. *Language in Society* 9: 43–70.

Ní Ghallchóir, C. 1981. Aspects of bilingualism in northwest Donegal. In Barry (ed.) 1981c, pp. 142–70.

Ó Huallacháin, C. 1970. Bilingual education program in Ireland: recent experiences in home and adult support, teacher training, provision of instructional materials. *Georgetown University Round Table on Languages and Linguistics 1970.* Washington DC: Georgetown University Press, pp. 179–93.

Ó Muirithe, D. 1977a. The Anglo-Normans and their English dialect of southeast Wexford. In Ó Muirithe (ed.) 1977b, pp. 37–55.

(ed.) 1977b. *The English Language in Ireland.* Dublin: Mercier.

Pearse, P. H. 1976. *The Murder Machine and Other Essays.* Cork: Mercier.

Pitts, A. H. 1985. Urban influence on phonological variation in a northern Irish speech community. *English World-Wide* 6: 59–85.

1986. Differing prestige values for the (ky) variable in Lurgan. In Harris *et al.* (eds.) 1986, pp. 209–42.

Policansky, L. 1982. Grammatical variation in Belfast English. *Belfast Working Papers in Language and Linguistics* 6: 37–66.

Pringle, I. and Padolsky, E. 1981. The Irish heritage of the English of the Ottawa Valley. *English Studies in Canada* 7: 338–52.

Rickford, J. R. 1986. Social contact and linguistic diffusion: Hiberno-English and New World Black English. *Language* 62: 245–90.

Sullivan, J. P. 1980. The validity of literary dialect: evidence from the theatrical portrayal of Hiberno-English forms. *Language in Society* 9: 195–219.

Tilling, P. M. 1981. Age-group variation in the speech of Kinlough, Co Leitrim. In Barry (ed.) 1981c, pp. 96–105.

Todd, L. 1984. By their tongue divided: towards an analysis of speech communities in Northern Ireland. *English World-Wide* 5: 159–80.

Trudgill, P. (ed.) 1978. *Sociolinguistic Patterns in British English*. London: Arnold.

(ed.) 1984. *Language in the British Isles*. Cambridge: Cambridge University Press.

van Hamel, A. G. 1912. On Anglo-Irish syntax. *Englische Studien* 45: 272–92.

Williams, J. P. 1986. Hiberno-English and white West-Indian English: the historical link. In Harris *et al.* (eds) 1986, pp. 83–94.

3

Urban and rural varieties of Hiberno-English

MARKKU FILPPULA

Introduction

While there is a substantial body of literature on the general characteristics of Hiberno-English (HE), relatively little is known about grammatical variation within this variety of English, although the circumstances in which HE has evolved have varied in different parts of the country, depending mainly on the position and strength of the formerly dominant vernacular, Irish. Given the paucity of empirical research into spoken HE, descriptions of regional and social differences within HE have remained at a rather general level. For example Bliss (n.d.:5), setting aside the Scottish dialects of Ulster, simply makes a distinction between rural HE, urban HE and the speech of educated Irishmen (cf. Henry 1977: 20, for a somewhat different view). Of these, the rural varieties are said to display most clearly grammatical features which go back to the corresponding features of Irish, whereas the educated variety is closest to standard English. Urban speech is characterised as being somewhere in between: while it has been influenced by contact with Irish, it has also been open to standardising and, perhaps, other influences from outside the country, especially from Britain (for further discussion, see Bliss n.d.).

Despite these general differences, Bliss (n.d.: 4 f; 1972: 36) emphasises the relative *uniformity* of HE as a whole. This he explains by the special historical continuity of the conditions in which knowledge of English was transmitted among the originally Irish-speaking population: because of a lack of social intercourse between Irish-speakers and speakers of standard English, not to mention the lack of competent teachers, Irish people learnt their English from members of their own community, whose English was usually heavily influenced by Irish. This led to a cumulative process whereby in each generation the learner's English was a little more influenced by Irish than the model's, and the unbroken tradition of passing on English from model to learner in this way explains why Irish features

51

still persist even in the dialects of those areas in which Irish died out long ago (n.d.; 1972).

This paper examines how far the claimed uniformity of HE with regard to Irish influence extends and, more specifically, whether it applies to urban speech as well as the rural varieties.[1] The following discussion is based on the analysis of a corpus of spoken HE, which I collected for my doctoral dissertation (Filppula 1986).

Three linguistic features are discussed, the first of which is the so-called cleft construction or 'clefting'; for example:

(1)   It was the window that John broke.

Clefting is a device which is employed in discourse to give special thematic and focal prominence to a constituent placed in the 'hinge' position of the sentence (cf. Quirk *et al.* 1972: 951).

The second feature I refer to as 'topicalisation'. This is an operation which moves a constituent to the very beginning of its clause and assigns thematic and focal prominence to it in a way very similar to that of clefting. This is illustrated by (2), where *the window* is placed in the 'topic' position and thus made the point of focus:

(2)   The window John broke (not the door).

The third feature studied is a peculiarly HE construction, which involves the use of *and* to introduce a subordinate clause lacking a finite verb. The following example, taken from Harris (1984: 305), illustrates this construction which, following Harris, I call 'subordinating *and*':

(3)   He fell and him crossing the bridge (i.e. '. . . while he was crossing the
         bridge').

Instead of a present participle, the clause introduced by *and* may contain a past participle, an infinitive, an adjective or an adverbial phrase (further examples will be cited below).

As Harris (1984: 305) notes, subordinating *and* has a very idiomatic parallel in the Irish adverbial structure *agus* 'and' + subject pronoun + *ag* 'at' + verbal noun (cf. also Henry 1957: 206 and Bliss 1984: 147). The Irish rendering of (3) would be as follows (my source is again Harris 1984):

(4)   Thit sé agus é ag dul thar an droichead.
         'Fall + past he and he at go over the bridge'.

Thus, any influence on HE usage from this Irish pattern may be character-ised as being *direct*, as opposed to *selective* and *preservative*, which is the case when, given a choice between two or more equally acceptable structures of English, the one chosen or preferred by the HE speaker is that which corresponds closest to the structure of Irish (cf. Bliss, no date: 5; see also Weinreich 1974: 36 for examples of selective influence from other contact vernaculars). Both clefting and topicalisation fall into this latter category: they are perfectly acceptable and usable in English, but there are certain peculiarities of Irish which can be expected to have led to a particularly extensive exploitation of these constructions in HE, too.

First, Irish obeys a very rigid VSO word order, which makes it almost impossible to resort to word-order arrangements for purposes of emphasis, for instance. Secondly, since Irish – unlike English – does not use sentence stress for the expression of emphasis or contrast, it must have recourse to structural devices, principally the so-called copula construction. This is virtually the same operation as clefting in English, except that the clefted sentence starts with the verb-like copula *is*. Thirdly, since it is not stressed, the copula is often omitted in speech, and the sentence begins with the focused constituent. Thus the Irish copula construction is structurally and functionally not far from the English topicalised sentence, although it has its closest parallel in the English cleft sentence. Consequently, one can expect that the Irish tendency to shift the information focus to the beginning of the sentence by means of the copula construction is reflected in HE speech, particularly in the frequencies of use of such constructions as clefting and topicalisation, which work towards the same end. Let us now turn to the data from spoken HE to see how it supports this expectation.

The empirical set-up of the study

The three linguistic features – clefting, topicalisation and subordinating *and* – are examined on the basis of material from three varieties of HE, two of which are rural and one urban. The first of the rural varieties comprises the (south-) western dialects of Counties Kerry and Clare, which together represent the most recent direct contact with Irish. In these areas Irish still retains a certain presence and has been spoken within living memory. The other rural variety is that spoken in the mountain areas of County Wicklow, which is on the east coast, just south of Dublin. Irish died out from this area quite early: according to de Fréine (1977: 75), most of County Wicklow had become English-speaking by 1750. The urban variety of HE is that spoken in Dublin. As in Wicklow, the Irish language lost its position here towards the end of the 18th century (for statistical evidence, see Ó Cuív 1951: 21).

The speech material from these three varieties consists of openly recorded, fairly informal interviews with 23 informants: 10 from Kerry and Clare, 6 from Wicklow, and 7 from Dublin. The fieldwork was done by several people, including myself (see Filppula 1986: 273 ff, for further details). No questionnaires were used, nor were the informants told that the interviews might be used for purposes of linguistic analysis. The topics of the interviews ranged from local history and traditions to various aspects

Table 3.1. *Frequencies of clefting in the varieties investigated*

Variety	Size of corpus in words	Total of clefting	Total/1,000 words
Kerry and Clare	69,747	192	2.8
Wicklow	41,986	77	1.8
Dublin	42,173	54	1.3
ESE	40,247	28	0.7

of the personal lives and work of the informants. Measured by the numbers of words, the sizes of the corpora are as follows: Kerry and Clare 69,750, Wicklow 42,000 and Dublin 42,150 words. The total of 153,900 words amounts to a little over 19 hours of recorded speech.

The most important criteria in choosing informants included age, place of birth, length of residence in the area, level of education and social standing. All the informants were elderly, their ages varying from 50 to 95 years. They were all 'born and reared' in the area and had spent most of their lives there. None had more than the minimum education i.e. National School, and their social standing was about the same: all informants from the rural communities worked, or had worked, in the traditional occupation of farming (including sheep-rearing), while those from Dublin represented various working-class occupations, such as work on the docks and tramways, street-trading, modest clerical work and service in the British and Irish armies. The informants from Wicklow and Dublin generally had very little or no knowledge of Irish, whereas those from Kerry and Clare had at least some knowledge of it, although their first language was English.

In addition to the HE material, a corpus of spoken southern British English is used as a further basis for comparison. This corpus, which consists of openly and surreptitiously recorded interviews with ten people, may best be described as representing Educated Spoken English (henceforth ESE) i.e. the variety which comes closest to the spoken form of standard southern British (English) English. The size of the corpus is 40,250 words.[2]

Clefting

The frequencies of clefting in the varieties studied are given in table 3.1 above. To facilitate comparison between the varieties, the rightmost column provides the average frequencies of cleft sentences per variety per 1,000 words. Word-counting was chosen as the basis for quantitative comparisons because of the obvious difficulties involved in counting reliably the number of clauses or sentences in the corpora (for further justification and discussion of the various problems of delimitation of cleft sentences, see Filppula 1986: 113, 87–91).

The results show a clear continuum: the western rural variety, Kerry and Clare, is at the top with its average of 2.8 clefts per 1,000 words; the eastern rural dialect, Wicklow, is somewhat lower at 1.8, while the urban variety spoken in Dublin displays the lowest average frequency among the HE varieties, viz. 1.3 clefts per 1,000 words. On the other hand, Dublin speech distinguishes itself from southern British English (ESE), which is well behind with its average of only 0.7 clefts per 1,000 words.

These figures do not include individual scores or variation among them. In order to take into account the possible effect of individual differences among the speakers of each variety, the figures were put to an analysis of variance.[3] This confirmed that the differences among the HE varieties are significant at the 0.002 level. If ESE is included, the probability of all being at the same level is as low as 0.00.

The *linguistic* significance of these quantitative differences is further confirmed by several qualitative features of clefting. Thus Kerry and Clare speech, but not the other varieties, contains several instances of clefts with the universal quantifier *all* in the focus position, as in (5); for ease of interpretation, the examples from my corpus are given in their proper textual contexts (the cleft sentence is in italics; 'I' stands for the informant):

(5)   Topic of conversation: The informant's house
        I: He (i.e. the informant's father) made the house . . . narrow, and . . .
        he roofed and slated it . . . Probably it was thatched, because it was all
        . . . *it was all thatched houses was here one time*, you know.

The most likely source of the HE *all* in this type of context is Irish, where the universal quantifiers *uilig, go léir* and *ar fad* can readily occur in the focus of the copula construction.[4]

Although the western rural variety shows the clearest traces of the syntactic freedom so characteristic of the Irish cleft construction (cf. Stenson 1981: 99 ff), similar influences are also detectable in Wicklow speech. To mention just one example, a (part of a) periphrastic verb phrase cannot occur in the focus of clefts in British English, but this restriction is not obeyed in rural HE. The existence of the pattern in Wicklow speech is one indication of the uniformity of rural HE dialects (here 'a' represents the interviewer):

(6)   Topic of conversation: Farming in Wicklow
        a: Have many people left this area at all, or . . . or given up farming at
        all or . . .?
        I: Ah, very little's give up farming round this area.
        It's looking for more land a lot of them are.

Table 3.2. *Frequencies of topicalisation*

Variety	Size of corpus in words	Total of topicalisation	Total/1,000 words
Kerry and Clare	69,747	97	1.4
Wicklow	41,986	59	1.4
Dublin	42,173	36	0.9
ESE	40,247	18	0.4

Topicalisation

Table 3.2 gives the frequencies of topicalisation in each of the varieties.[5]

An immediate observation is that topicalisation is generally less frequent than clefting, in all the varieties. Moreover, the differences between the varieties are not so marked, although the two rural varieties seem to differ from the urban language of Dublin and, in particular, from British English. An analysis of variance showed the differences between ESE and the HE varieties to be significant, but not the differences between the three HE varieties, because of the large amount of individual variation.

Although the quantitative evidence remains inconclusive in the case of topicalisation, there are certain qualitative features which suggest some differences between the varieties. Consider the following two examples from the western dialects of Kerry and Clare:

(7)   Topic of conversation: Tom Leary, the Land League activist
        I: But Tom Leary was as strong as ever. And . . . *a pastime he used to have*. His father used to keep a bull . . .
(8)   Topic of conversation: The informant's family
        I: One son. He is workin' over there. *In some building he is workin' with the couple of weeks.*

What is special about these examples is the *function* of topicalisation: far from implying contrast with something in the preceding context, topicalisation serves to introduce a new discourse referent or provides further specification of a piece of information already conveyed. This function, coupled with fairly neutral stress on the fronted constituent and with the discoursal newness of the referent of the topicalised constituent, makes these examples sound very odd, at least to a speaker of standard English. Moreover, in my HE corpus this type was confined to the rural dialects. While they are most prominent in the west, very similar occurrences are encountered in the Wicklow material, as can be seen from (9):

Table 3.3. *Frequencies of subordinating* and

Variety	Size of corpus in words	Total of subord. *and*	Total/1,000 words
Kerry and Clare	69,747	22	0.32
Wicklow	41,986	13	0.31
Dublin	42,173	4	0.09
ESE	40,247	0	0.00

(9)   Topic of conversation: Driving the cattle to the fair
        I: Oh, you couldn't drive them one . . . Too much traffic. *Too much motors you'd be meetin'*. You couldn't drive them.

As in the case of clefting, the Irish tendency for the information focus to come first in the sentence suggests itself as the most plausible source for these peculiarly rural uses of topicalisation. However, it is also possible that HE topicalisations reflect patterns which were current in the Early Modern English period. In this period, which was crucial from the point of view of the formation of HE, constraints on word-order shifts were not so stringent as they are in present-day English, and, as Traugott (1972: 161) notes, emphasis, for instance, was quite readily expressed by simple word-order shifts. Given that the HE predilection for topicalisation can be explained both by language transfer from Irish and by historical considerations, the safest conclusion is that these two influences intermingle; the role of Irish has thus been preservative and reinforcing rather than direct (cf. Harris 1984 for a similar conclusion concerning the peculiarities of the HE tense and aspect system).

Subordinating *and*

With subordinating *and* we move on to a feature which is quite rare in HE speech, as can be seen from the figures given in table 3.3.

Despite the low frequencies, the general pattern is strikingly similar to those documented for clefting and, even more so, for topicalisation: the rural varieties use this construction to the same extent, whereas Dublin speech is again at a lower level with its average of only 0.09 instances per 1,000 words. No statistical test was applied to these figures, but it is of interest that subordinating *and* was recorded from eight of the ten speakers from Kerry and Clare and four of the six informants from Wicklow, but from only two of the seven Dubliners.

It is interesting that subordinating *and* also occurs in the urban variety. The following example from Dublin speech shows that, there too,

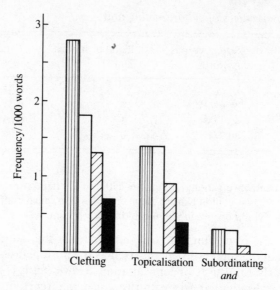

Figure 3.1   Frequencies of clefting, topicalisation and subordinating *and* in the varieties investigated. ⦀ = Kerry & Clare; ☐ = Wicklow; ▨ = Dublin; ■ = ESE.

it has the usual function of expressing a temporal relation between two clauses:

(10)   Topic of conversation: Historical characters
         I: Now, there is one man . . . I only thought of him there *and I cooking my dinner*.

While all four instances from Dublin speech contain a present participle, those examples from the rural varieties have a past participle, an adjective or even an adverbial phrase in the same position. The last two are exemplified by (11) from Kerry and Clare and (12) from Wicklow:

(11)   Topic of conversation: A local musician and the 'Fairy Reel'
         I: Father and mother was givin' him hell. 'Twas in harvest time *and the weather bad*.
(12)   Topic of conversation: A fox attacking hens
         I: I went over to see what it was, and here it was a fox, *and he with a hen*.

Summary

The frequencies of clefting, topicalisation and subordinating *and* are summarised above, in figure 3.1.

It can be seen that the most significant difference within HE is that between the rural dialects and the urban speech of Dublin. This difference emerges with respect to all three features, whether they represent selective or direct Irish influence. It is evident that although the urban variety of HE can be shown to preserve noticeable traces of Irish impact, it has moved further towards standard British (English) English patterns than the rural dialects. Reasons for this development are probably to be found in the closer contact that Dubliners have with the 'outside world'.

As for the rural varieties investigated here, the frequencies do not point to clear differences, except in the case of clefting. Although some of the most markedly Irish features are encountered in the west, Wicklow speech, too, preserves a perhaps surprising number of Irishisms in view of the fact that Irish has not been spoken there for well over 200 years. My results thus lend some support to the view that HE dialects are relatively uniform. The greater frequencies of clefting in Kerry and Clare speech are most probably due to the almost identical structure of the Irish and the English cleft constructions: because of this close resemblance the English cleft construction has been particularly susceptible to the selective and reinforcing influence from the Irish substratum, and this influence has been strongest in those areas where Irish has held out longest against the English language. Thus, grammatical variation within HE is better described in terms of *continua* rather than in terms of discrete varieties with clear-cut boundaries. As the foregoing discussion shows, these continua receive different values or profiles depending on the linguistic feature, the type of substratum influence, and regional and social considerations.

NOTES

1. In the preparation of this article I have been greatly helped by Jenny Cheshire and John Harris, whose comments on earlier drafts have suggested a need to see Hiberno-English in a wider sociolinguistic context. I hope that this paper goes some way towards doing this.
2. Half of the ESE corpus was collected by Mr J. A. Stotesbury, of the University of Joensuu, in England in 1979 and 1980, and the other half was drawn from the spoken English texts included in Svartvik and Quirk's *A Corpus of English Conversation* (for a detailed description, see Filppula 1986: 82 ff).
3. My thanks are due to Mr E. Korpelainen of the Department of Statistics, University of Joensuu, for his crucial help in the planning and computing of the analyses of variance.
4. The information about Irish has been confirmed by Mr Liam Mac Con Iomaire, a native speaker of Irish from Carraroe, County Galway.
5. Note that only fronted constituents which realise the main information focus of their clauses are included in the category of topicalisation (see Filppula 1986: 182 ff, for a fuller account of the delimitation problems).

REFERENCES

Bliss, A. J. (no date). The English language in Ireland. MS, University College, Dublin.

1972. The language of Synge. In Harmon, M. (ed.), *J. M. Synge Centenary Papers 1971*. Dublin: The Dolmen Press, 35–62.

1984. English in the south of Ireland. In Trudgill, P. (ed.), *Language in the British Isles*. Cambridge: Cambridge University Press, 135–51.

de Fréine, S. 1977. The dominance of the English language in the 19th century. In Ó Muirithe (ed.) 1977, 71–87.

Filppula, M. 1986. *Some Aspects of Hiberno-English in a Functional Sentence Perspective*. Joensuu, Finland: University of Joensuu Publications in the Humanities 7.

Harris, J. 1984. Syntactic variation and dialect divergence. *Journal of Linguistics* 20: 303–327.

Henry, P. L. 1957. *An Anglo-Irish Dialect of North Roscommon*. Dublin: University College, Dublin.

1977. Anglo-Irish and its Irish background. In Ó Muirithe, (ed.) 1977, 20–36.

Ó Cuív, B. 1951. *Irish Dialects and Irish-Speaking Districts*. Dublin: Dublin Institute for Advanced Studies.

Ó Muirithe, D. (ed.). 1977. *The English Language in Ireland*. Dublin: The Mercier . Press.

Quirk, R., Greenbaum, S., Leech, G. and Svartvik, J. 1972. *A Grammar of Contemporary English*. London: Longman.

Stenson, N. 1981. *Studies in Irish Syntax*. Tübingen: Gunter Narr Verlag.

Svartvik, J. and Quirk, R. (eds.). 1980. *A Corpus of English Conversation*. Lund: CWK Gleerup.

Traugott, E. C. 1972. *The History of English Syntax*. New York: Holt, Rinehart and Winston.

Weinreich, U. 1974. *Languages in Contact: Findings and Problems*. The Hague/ Paris: Mouton.

4

Sociolinguistic variation and methodology: *after* as a Dublin variable

JEFFREY L. KALLEN

Introduction

Perhaps because of the interest and controversy which has been associated with the link between the Irish language and Hiberno-English, purely synchronic studies in which the direct influence of Irish can be effectively discounted are very rare. Classic descriptive studies such as those of Henry (1957, 1958) concentrate on rural dialects, while structural analyses such as those of Bliss (1972), Henry (1960–61), and others have tended also to look at Hiberno-English only in comparison with Irish. Although some early writers (e.g., Hayden and Hartog 1909) have also given space to a consideration of the role of earlier English forms in the development of Hiberno-English, these writers too were concerned only with rural varieties in which both Irish influence and dialectal 'conservatism' might be strongest. Recent studies by Harris (1983, 1984) have examined aspects of Hiberno-English more rigorously, while still using a contrast between this variety and 'standard English' or Irish as a point of departure.

We examine here a well-known syntactic feature of Hiberno-English, the use of *after* as a perfective marker, whose origins, though still not well documented, may lie in the large-scale contact between English and Irish speakers in the seventeenth century (see Bliss 1979 and Kallen 1986). What is of concern, though, is the set of factors which governs the contemporary use of *after* in Dublin, a large urban centre in which the Irish language can effectively be ruled out as a direct influence on the modern use of English. Situating the study of *after* in Dublin has two major consequences: (1) it eliminates questions related to the structural relationship between Irish and English, except as a historical matter, and (2) it invites examination in terms of relevant sociolinguistic categories such as social class, age or context of use. Focusing on the use of *after* as it occurs in actual speech also has the consequence of re-defining this feature of Hiberno-English grammar, in that previous semantic accounts of it can be shown to be inadequate. Thus, sociolinguistic methodology may enrich the understanding of language as an abstract system by basing abstractions on actual usage rather than on intuitions or exemplars.

Nature of the variable

Definitions of *after* generally refer to notions of recency or completion: van Hamel (1912: 276) stated that *after* denotes that 'a thing has just happened a moment ago', while Goeke and Kornelius (1976: 5) argue that *after* refers to an action 'immediately preceding the time of speaking', and Harris (1984: 308) sees *after* as a 'hot news' perfect referring to 'a point that is separated from but temporally close to the present'. Hume (1878: 25), on the other hand, noted *after* as designating that 'the action [is] complete', while Henry (1957: 64) states that *after* signifies an 'action accomplished' or (1958: 177) that 'an action has just been concluded'.

Starting with a more neutral view of *after* simply as a perfect marker, however, we see that *after* covers the range of semantic functions for the perfect as described in languages generally. Kiefer (1982: 312–313) points out that 'achievement of the goal' is only one source of perfect usage, while Dahl (1985: 133) has joined the various often overlapping usages found for the perfect across languages under the notion that these forms all 'involve a point of reference . . . which is different from the "point of event"'. To illustrate the diversity of perfect markings shown by *after* in Dublin, consider the schema suggested by McCawley (1971: 263–8) listed below. Under each of McCawley's subcategories of the English perfect, I have given an example from the Dublin corpus which forms the basis of this study. Reference numbers after each example refer to a unique informant number given to each speaker contributing to the corpus, as well as an indication of the speaker's sex and age group.

I   *'Universal' perfect in which 'a state of affairs prevailed throughout some interval stretching from the past into the present'*

(1)   All the week is after being cold /7M45–65/
(2)   We're after bein livin there for the past 21 years /128M18–25/

II *'Existential' perfect denoting the 'existence of past events'*

(3)   Three times she's after changing it /53F26–45/
(4)   The traffic is after being fierce /144M25–45/

III *'Hot news' perfect based on relative recency and the presupposition that the 'addressee does not yet know the news'*

(5)   Leo! I'm just after sending a lady up that way /15F45–65/
(6)   Glenn's just after being on to me /121F18–25/

IV '*Stative*' *perfect indicating that '*the direct effect of a past event still continues*'

(7)   What you're after gettin in the budget is nothing /17F44–65/
(8)   He's after taking the child up the North /134F25–44/

Note that the linguistic or extra-linguistic context of the above examples makes their determination in McCawley's schema clear: (1) was uttered when speaker and interlocutor were agreed that the weather was cold at the moment of speaking, (2) was stated by someone still resident 'there,' (7) refers to the continuing effects of a budget with no tax or price reliefs, etc.

The above inventory shows that *after* cannot be seen as a marker of any single semantic distinction, but rather must be seen in distribution with other perfective markers such as *be* and *have*, illustrated below in '*extended present*' and '*be-*resultative*' examples (see also Harris 1984 and Kallen 1986):

(9)   The one you have for forty years /44F65–80/
(10)   Mr Q. is married for forty-five years /38F18–25/
(11)   Sadie is just gone asleep about two minutes ago /11F26–44/

Though a complete study of the perfect in Hiberno-English would need to examine these and other perfective markers, this study is concerned only with the use of *after*. Lexical, pragmatic, and contextual factors are examined for their respective influences on the distribution of this marker.

Analysis

This discussion is based on a corpus of 114 tokens of *after* obtained from 74 speakers in Dublin. The method used here is one of ethnographic participant observation, in which everyday language encountered by an observer living in the community is seen within a system of shared social relations and meanings. Data came from a variety of conversational genres: family interactions, conversations between friends and workmates, service encounters, public meetings, radio and television interviews, and non-artistic writing. In the majority of cases, I was an interlocutor in the conversation: in some cases, however, I noted overheard conversations and was also fortunate to receive further examples from Margaret Mannion, who was in a position to collect tokens from similar domains. Though surreptitious tape recording was occasionally used, the most common method of data collection involved the making of notes in a small diary or the taking of notes in shorthand. Slightly more than 10 per cent of the corpus comes from my own extended family, including children from 2 to 18 years of age. Some taped interviews were used, and while they yielded only one token, they did establish that a subsequent shift towards the use of *after* could be observed when the same speaker is observed more informally (one speaker, for example, used no *after* tokens in an hour-long interview, but subsequently used it once in a ten-minute chance encounter on the bus).

The advantage of this method is that it allows for tokens and relevant contextual information to be noted whenever and wherever possible, subject only to limitations of the observer's ability to make an accurate note at the time of speaking. Harris (1984) notes the relative rarity of *after* in the archives of the Tape-recorded Survey of Hiberno-English, finding (p. 317) only three examples in 15 hours of interview, as opposed to 119 other 'non-standard' perfect forms and 98 forms using *have*. Similarly, Greene (1979) has noted the rarity of the comparable structure in Irish language conversational and formal corpora, underlining his contention that the low functional yield of this category in Irish is mirrored in a peripheral role for *after* in Hiberno-English. As long as observations take place in environments where the use of *after* is pragmatically appropriate, however, *after* tokens may readily be obtained.

Although the corpus includes the utterances of speakers from all major social classes, a wide range of ages, and both sexes, no claim is made here that the balance of groups in the sample reflects that found in the population as a whole. The logical question which this study attempts to answer, then, is not 'How is the use of *after* distributed in the Dublin speech community,' but 'Where, when, and from whom could an observer looking for *after* expect to find it?'. This question is not far from a vital question of language acquisition: if we picture a child learning English in Dublin, we may reasonably ask from whom and in what domains is the child liable to hear *after* being used. Moreover, we may suggest that this child's language learning experience, while not identical to the linguist's field explorations, will be sensitive to the same constraints which shape our corpus (excluding errors of perception or measurement), rather than to the more abstract distributional constraints found in an abstract entity such as 'the whole society.' The following subsections, then, present the major linguistic and non-linguistic constraints which have shaped the corpus.

Verb types and speech acts

Though *after* co-occurs with a wide range of verbs (56 in the corpus), the distribution of these verbs is far from even. Four closely related verbs account for 35 tokens (31 per cent of the total), while over half of the sample (54 per cent) is accounted for by adding eight more verbs to this subset. Thus, note the following frequencies: *getting* (N=12), *being* (copula) (N=10), *being* (auxiliary/passive) (N=7), *taking* (N=6), *having, making, coming* (N=4 per verb), *falling, doing, asking, changing* (N=3 per verb), with 44 other verbs accounting for 52 tokens. Active verbs (transitive and intransitive) predominate over perceptive verbs, but the only absolute limitation which holds in the corpus is the non-appearance of truly stative predicates i.e., those in which there is no change in the entities denoted. This characteristic, however, is predicted by the remarks of Kiefer (1982) as a general feature of perfect aspect, a point which further underscores the broadly perfective nature of *after*. Examples (12) – (17) illustrate the major types:

(12)   I'm after *gettin* the wrong cigarettes /5M26–44/
(13)   She's after *gettin* very big /31F18–24/
(14)   I'm after *bein* on my knees /13F45–65/
(15)   I'm after *bein* away for three weeks /81F45–65/
(16)   That's where I'm after *bein looking* /23F45–65/
(17)   It was after *bein* spring *cleaned* /132F45–65/.

At the boundary between linguistic and non-linguistic constraints on *after* lies its function in speech acts. I have already shown that *after* can be found in any of the semantically-defined aspectual categories given by McCawley (1971) and others. Noting Dahl's (1985: 133) distinction between 'types of perfect' and 'types of *uses*' of the perfect, I would argue that the commonly cited categorisations of perfect aspect are components of *meaning*, but that categories of *use* must take account of (a) the relations among temporal reference points, and (b) the pragmatic intent or effect of the use of aspectual markers. Considering (a), temporal reference points may be defined to include the moment of speaking (S_t), the time of the event or state of affairs referred to in the utterance (E_t), and a reference point or points from which aspect is determined (R_t): see Kiefer (1982) and Dahl (1985) for discussion. The usage categories for *after* which appear below make use of three major types of temporal relationship: what I have termed 'immediate,' in which S_t is virtually simultaneous with the completion of the act referred to in the utterance, 'proximate,' in which significantly more time has elapsed between E_t and S_t, and 'non-proximate,' in which E_t is relatively distant from S_t.

While the relationship between the propositional versus the illocutionary significance of *after* (in the sense of Searle 1969) has yet to be fully explicated, the data below also suggest that *after* covers a distinct set of speech acts. Each usage category thus represents a different orientation with respect both to the temporal setting and to the speaker–hearer relationship: each category tries to 'do' something different with *after*.

The usage categories for *after* which appear in the corpus may be defined and exemplified as follows: ('durative' used here refers to a state of affairs which can be subdivided, while 'non-durative' refers to an act which is indivisible. The term 'giving out' is borrowed from general Hiberno-English usage.)

I *Giving out.* Immediate reference to a concluded action or event, with speaker expecting an apology or change of attitude/behaviour by listener.

(18)　　You're after breakin the gate! /147F6–11/

II *Announcement.* Immediate reference to a concluded non-durative action/event.

(19)　　I'm after spilling a drop of that in the saucer /9F26–44/

III *Report.* Proximate reference to a concluded action/event (non-durative) or state of affairs (durative).

(20)　　She's only after joining /125F18–25/ (Non-durative)
(21)　　They're just after bein used up /12M18–25/ (Durative)

IV *Comment.* Reference to a state of affairs which continues from a non-proximate past through the moment of speech; S_t occurs at the interruption rather than the completion of E_t, while shared knowledge of the state of affairs is presupposed.

(22)　　It's after gettin real long /134F25–44/

V *Narrative.* Narration of past event; typically using past tense (pluperfect).

(23)　　I was just after saying to Áine . . . /10F26–44/

VI *Non-factual.* Hypothetical/counterfactual, related uses.

(24)　　A student will be after accomplishing an academic task /126F18–25/

VII *Reported speech.* Quoted uses of types I–V, with embedding as appropriate.

(25)　　I wouldn't want you comin over and saying, 'Look, what're you after doin to it?' /122M26–44/

　　Table 4.1 shows the distribution of the corpus across these usage categories.

　　Two main points arise from considering the distributional characteristics of *after* discussed above. (1) Speakers may be sensitive to distinct pragmatic properties attached to *after*. Thus, for example, while *You're after breakin the gate* and *You've broken the gate* have the same propositional content, the unmistakable force of *after* in chastising within the speech community renders these two examples fundamentally distinct. (2) The favouring of 'actions,' 'immediacy,' and 'completion' referred to in traditional accounts of *after* is relative and not categorical: durative *reports*, for example, deal with states and not actions, while *announcements, reports, comments*, and *narratives* all differ significantly in their relationships

Table 4.1. *Frequency of usage categories for* after

Usage category	Tokens	Frequency (%)
Report		
non-durative	34	30
durative	21	18
Announcement	27	24
Narrative	11	10
Comment	7	6
Giving out	7	6
Reported speech	4	4
Non-factual	3	3

between E_t, the moment of speaking (S_t) and 'completion' of an action or state of affairs.

Age, conversational domain, and social class

It is generally recognised that characteristics of speakers such as age, sex, social class, social network and mobility may have an effect on socially marked linguistic phenomena. Because of the way in which data were collected for this study, not all logically occurring combinations of these variables could be observed: nevertheless, the spread of speakers which was observed is wide enough to obtain information which can be analysed to suggest significant patterns in the use of *after*. The general picture which emerges is that (1) *after* is not restricted to any single social group, nor is it used by any group in all environments where it may occur, and (2) the differential tendency to use *after* is determined not alone by semantics or the speech act, but by the social relations which characterise a conversation in which *after* is used. The corpus allows for the analysis of three variables with potential significance for constraining the use of *after*: age, type of conversation, and social class.

Age is often seen as significant not only in conditioning the use of sociolinguistic variables, but as a factor indicating language change in progress. Cheshire (1982) points out that age-related research has yielded contradictory results, in that different speech communities have shown different tendencies with regard to the status of different age groups in age stratification. Significant age-related patterns do not appear in the corpus under analysis here.

After in Dublin is acquired at an early age, with one example in the corpus coming from a two-year old child; *after* is also found among speakers from the 66–80 age group. The relative contribution of different age groups to the corpus appears to be a function of the observer's social network and the different sizes of the age groups themselves. Thus, while the largest number of tokens (41) comes from the 26–44 age group, with only 5 tokens from the 6–11-year-olds and 13 tokens coming from the 12–17 age group, the greater size of the first mentioned age range and the correspondingly larger number of speakers falling within it are clearly the factors determining its weighting. Since there was ample opportunity to observe adolescent and pre-adolescent speakers in contexts which could lead to the use of *after*, I would suggest that had these age groups been significantly disproportionate in their use of *after*, some indication in terms of mean tokens per speaker or a similar measure would have been observable in the corpus.

Not only is there no indication of age stratification in the use of *after*, there does not appear to be any sign of a semantic shift in progress. Greene (1979: 126) has stated that the perfect using *after* indicates 'that an action has just be[en] concluded' (cf. Henry 1958, quoted above), but has suggested that in Irish, at least, the comparable verbal category has been expanding beyond this domain of temporal reference. We saw earlier that *after* covers a wide range of temporal reference categories, while table 4.1 showed that relatively recent reference is favoured: if a change comparable to that described by Greene (1979) were in progress in Dublin, the correlation of age groups with the usage categories of table 4.1 would have shown a greater use of *comments* and *reports* (especially durative ones) among younger speakers, with older speakers favouring *announcements*. Both *comments* and durative *reports*, however, are well spread by age group: of the 19 durative *report* tokens, for example, the 26–44 and 45–65-year-old groups yielded 8 and 7 tokens respectively, with a further 3 such tokens coming from the 18–25-year-old group and one coming from 66–80-year-old speakers. Although the small numbers in some of these categories preclude a definitive statement, it would appear that if the use of *after* outside of *announcements* does reflect a historical shift, it is a shift which has already taken place in Dublin.

Social factors which may condition the use of *after* can be seen either as components of some wider social structure, or as characteristics of individual interactions. The first approach usually focuses on issues such as social class, exemplified particularly by work such as that of Labov (1966), while the second may focus on networks of face-to-face social interaction or on socially significant characteristics of interlocutors (see, for example, Milroy 1980 and Wolfson 1982, respectively). Insofar as the data of the corpus permit, the following discussion looks at issues raised by both approaches, suggesting a link between interlocutor relations and the use of *after*, cross-cutting with usage constraints related to social class.

Consider first the analysis by type of social interaction. Each token in the corpus has been categorised according to the nature of the interaction in which it occurred: the categories consist of '*friendly*' conversations

Table 4.2. *Conversational domains for* after

Conversational Domain	Tokens	Frequency (%)
Friendly (work)	26	23
Friendly (general)	22	19
Family	20	18
Shops	20	18
Public (strangers)	5	4
Interview	4	4
Writing	2	2
Public (neighbours)	2	2
Friendly (casual)	1	1
Public meetings	1	1
Unclassified	10	9

(defined by interpersonal relationships and the stylistic feature which Hymes (1971: 65–66) denotes as 'key' or 'tone') in settings such as employment, the neighbourhood, etc., *family* conversations, *'shop'* service encounters almost always occurring in small neighbourhood shops, *interviews, public meetings, writing,* and *public encounters* between strangers or socially distant neighbours. The relative frequencies of these domains for *after* are given in table 4.2.

It must be noted here that the frequency of tokens in each domain is not a function of the amount of time spent in the domain: because collection of tokens could take place at any time, the amount of time spent in all domains was considerable. As an extreme example, consider that hundreds of hours spent in public meetings of various degrees of formality have yielded only one token of *after*, while a brief time spent in the neighbourhood fruit and vegetable shop yielded tokens fairly quickly.

The significance of the *shop* category is not to be underestimated: the small shops where these examples were found are ones in which informal conversation and the interweaving of personal and business roles are common, and they may be contrasted with more impersonal service domains such as supermarkets or government offices. Note, too, that of the four *interview* tokens, none came from sociolinguistic interviews: two were from media interviews in which speakers described recent disasters (gas explosions in both cases), one was from an interview for a place in college, and the fourth was from a tape-recorded journalistic interview (see Kallen 1983 for an edited transcript). The figures in table 4.2 thus show clearly that 'friendly' domains are favoured for *after*, while formal ones are not.

Some discussion is in order on whether social class should be seen as a

variable to be correlated with the use of *after*. Although early studies by
Labov (see Labov 1972) showed promising results in analysing variation
and the possible dynamics of linguistic change within social class structures,
arguments such as those of DeCamp (1971), as well as Milroy's (1980)
social network model, and Wolfson's (1982) observations on the importance of the relative status of interlocutors rather than the background of
the speaker alone all suggest that simple correlations of socioeconomic
group and token frequency may be inadequate. (Arguments over social
class definition in terms of subcultural group vs. definition by external
factors such as income or occupational prestige are not new in sociology:
see Leach 1967, for example.) The problem is complicated in this study by
the possibility that social class models developed for large industrial
societies are not necessarily appropriate to Ireland, and that the sociolinguistic dynamics seen in studies such as Labov (1966) may therefore not
exist.

Nevertheless, it is also possible that social class in a relatively stratified
society such as that in Dublin (see Whelan and Whelan 1984 for cross-
cultural comparisons) may correlate roughly, at least, with either social
network or subcultural definitions of social organisation. The data in table
4.2 are taken from different social groups and include both intra- and
inter-class interactions; the following social class analysis is therefore
presented as a complementary analysis which, given the ethnographic
methodology used, should be taken as indicative rather than definitive.
What the analysis seeks to uncover is any pattern in the use of *after* that is
conditioned by the socioeconomic background of speakers, without preju-
dicing the possibility that further studies using other social categorisations
may also yield valid results.

The social classifications used here are adapted from the definitions of
Whelan and Whelan (1984), modified to include women and dependent
children. Six major classes based on occupational status are used: **Class I**
(Higher professional/managerial, proprieters), **Class II** *(Lower pro-
fessional/managerial)*, **Class III** *(Routine non-manual)*, **Class IV** *(Technical, supervisors of manual workers, petty bourgeoisie)*, **Class V** *(Skilled
manual)*, **Class VI** *(Semi-skilled/unskilled manual)*.

Class-based patterns appear to be largely subservient to the pattern
established in the hierarchy of interpersonal domains (see table 4.2). Class
I speakers, for example, used *after* only in *friendly* (work and general) and
family domains (11 tokens from 7 speakers), while Class II speakers used
after largely in these domains (17 tokens from 7 speakers), with the corpus
also showing three tokens from three further speakers in this class in the
writing, casual friend, and *public meeting* domains.

The 'shop' interaction, however, appears to be a linguistic watershed in
the use of *after*. While speakers from Class III also favoured the use of
friendly and *family* domains (9 tokens from 5 speakers), four speakers

from this group also accounted for four of the *shop* tokens. Likewise, speakers from Class VI showed a favouring of the friendly and family domains (22 tokens from 5 speakers), but significant use (7 tokens from 4 speakers) in shops. (Not enough speakers were found from Classes IV and V to permit analysis here.)

The limitations imposed by anonymous observation mean that only 40 of the 74 speakers contributing to the corpus could be positively ascribed to a social class: this limitation probably under-represents the size of the trend towards a wider distribution of domains for the use of *after* among speakers outside Classes I and II. Almost all the tokens taken from anonymous observation were heard in areas where members of Classes I and II are distinctly in the minority, such as inner-city shopping districts and public transportation in inner-city areas. To the extent that phonological clues could be taken as evidence of social class, very few of the unclassified tokens (i.e. used by speakers who could not definitively be assigned to a social class) appeared to come from speakers in Classes I and II. In this unclassified group, again the strongest weighting is towards the *friendly* and *family* domains (9 speakers yielding 9 tokens), but it is from this group as well that the *public* tokens are found (5 speakers giving 5 tokens) and from which 7 speakers contribute 7 further *shop* tokens. While there are clues to suggest that as many as three of the nine speakers in this 'unclassified' group who used *after* in the *friendly/family* domains could be from Class I or II, none of the speakers in the unclassified group who used *after* in the *public* or *shop* domains could be thought to be from Classes I or II on the basis of location, phonology, or any other observable indications.

The trend in terms of class analysis, then, is that while all social class groups use *after* and all favour the use of *after* in friendly or family interactions, the use of *after* outside such domains was rarely observed in speakers from Classes I and II. Note here that *shop* usages came from customers as well as shop assistants. Though all tokens from shop assistants would be ascribed to Class III by definition, with those from owners of small shops without employees ascribed to Class IV, customers using *after* could in principle have come from any social class. In describing *shop* encounters as a watershed, then, I suggest that it is in the shop that social distinctions are made manifest: while informal conversations using *after* may take place 'across the counter' among speakers from Classes III–VI, speakers from Classes I and II may restrict *after* more specifically to *family* and *friendly* domains, using it very rarely in service or public encounters.

Conclusion

After in Dublin may be seen as a realisation of perfect aspect, cutting across generally recognised varieties of the perfect, but favoured for use in contexts where the relationship between the time of the designated event/state of affairs and the time of speaking (mediated by a temporal reference point relevant to the use of the perfect in general) is fairly recent. Description of its semantic value, however, is inadequate to account for its use, which is governed by a combination of linguistic and non-linguistic factors.

Chief among the discourse factors conditioning *after* is the favouring of 'friendly' and family domains. While usage in formal meetings, writing, interviews, etc., is not ruled out, it is relatively rare. Also rare is the co-occurrence of *after* with past tense *be* (11 tokens or 10 per cent of the corpus), a single non-factual 'future' with *will be* plus *after*, and one co-occurrence with negation. Though Greene (1979) argued that this aspect category intrinsically excluded negation, (26) below, in which the speaker is commenting on the effect of a recent gas explosion on an old flat, should be noted as a counterexample:

(26)   It's not after makin it any better /146F–/.

Social class analysis suggests that all social classes follow the same general hierarchy of linguistic and non-linguistic constraints, but that some social groups appear to use *after* in domains where members of other groups use it more rarely. These results emphasise the importance of basing an understanding of *after* on a corpus which is large enough to show minor constructions and minor domains, and of refraining from the tendency to offer the categorical definitions given in more traditional accounts.

This study raises further questions for sociolinguistic methodology. Taking the infrequency of *after* tokens in interviews for granted, the results here show the necessity literally to be 'in the right place at the right time' to hear *after* being used. The favouring of *after* in *announcements, reports, giving out*, and *comments* (accounting for 96 tokens or 84 per cent of the corpus) suggests that the observer simply must be close to (or even in the middle of) the event/state of affairs in order to hear *after* being used. More precisely, the speaker must also choose to encode the account of events so as to reflect this proximity: it is entirely possible, and was commonly done by speakers who contributed to the corpus, to refer to proximate events using some other form of perfect or using the simple past. It is difficult to imagine an interview which could elicit examples of *giving out* except as reported speech, and the relative rarity of reported speech forms in the corpus suggests that speakers may not recount verbatim every *after* token which they hear.

The primacy of solidarity domains for the use of *after* also affects the methodology necessary to understand it. Had I not been in the position to observe professional class family and close friend interactions at close range, for example, I would have been led to the (erroneous) conclusion that *after* is not used in these class groups but is restricted to the Class III and Class VI groups from whom I more readily obtained tokens in anonymous, service, and other less solidary domains. The non-use of *after* in interviews by speakers who subsequently used it in chance encounters or family contexts suggests again that an interview would be an unlikely place to find *after*, and that a corpus based only on tokens collected in interviews would not reflect actual usage.

The method used here does lose something in terms of control of data. It has not been possible, for example, to compare the use of *after* with the frequency of other perfect markers in Hiberno-English. Furthermore, since an observer cannot predict that *after* is about to be used, surreptitious note-taking will almost never include the utterances preceding the *after* token: it can certainly be useful to work from transcripts rather than from isolated notes. Despite these losses, however, the ethnographic method can clarify previously existing questions about the use of *after* and suggest further detailed accounts of variation in speech communities. Even the phonological variants of Dublin *after* ([aftər] vs. [aṭər]) could be investigated along the lines used here. I suggest that such studies will come closer to describing the sociolinguistic reality facing real speakers than other, more idealised, methods.

REFERENCES

Bliss, A. J. 1972. Languages in contact. Some problems of Hiberno-English. *Proceedings of the Royal Irish Academy* 72, Section C: 63–82.

1979. *Spoken English in Ireland: 1600–1740*. Dublin: Dolmen Press.

Cheshire, J. 1982. *Variation in an English Dialect*. Cambridge: Cambridge University Press.

Dahl, Ö. 1985. *Tense and Aspect Systems*. Oxford: Basil Blackwell.

DeCamp, D. 1971. Implicational scales and sociolinguistic linearity. *Linguistics* 73: 30–43.

Goeke, D, and Kornelius, J. 1976. On measuring Irishisms. *Fu Jen Studies* 9: 45–60.

Greene, D. 1979. Perfects and perfectives in Modern Irish. *Ériu* 30: 122–141.

Harris, J. 1983. The Hiberno-English 'I've it eaten' construction: what is it and where does it come from? *Teanga* 3: 30–43.

1984. Syntactic variation and dialect divergence. *Journal of Linguistics* 20: 303–27.

Hayden, M. and Hartog, M. 1909. The Irish dialect of English: its origins and vocabulary. *The Fortnightly Review* New series 85: 777–85, 933–47.

Henry, P. L. 1957. *An Anglo-Irish Dialect of North Roscommon*. Dublin: Department of English, University College Dublin.

1958. A linguistic survey of Ireland: preliminary report. *Lochlann* 1: 49–208.

1960–61. The Irish substantival system and its reflexes in Anglo-Irish. *Zeitschrift für Celtische Philologie* 28: 19–50.

Hume, A. 1878. *Remarks on the Irish Dialect of the English language*. Liverpool.

Hymes, D. 1971. Sociolinguistics and the ethnography of speaking. In E. Ardener (ed.), *Social Antropology and Linguistics*. London: Tavistock, pp. 47–93.

Kallen, J. 1983. Politics is for everybody. *Gralton* No. 9, August/September: 14–16.

——— 1986. Linguistic fundamentals for Hiberno-English syntax. Unpublished PhD thesis, Trinity College Dublin.

Kiefer, F. 1982. The aspectual system of Hungarian. In Kiefer, F. (ed.), *Hungarian Linguistics*. Amsterdam: Benjamins.

Labov, W. 1966. Hypercorrection by the lower middle class as a factor in linguistic change. Reprinted in Labov 1972.

——— 1972. *Sociolinguistic Patterns*. Philadelphia: University of Pennsylvania Press.

Leach, E. 1967. Caste, class and slavery. Reprinted in Laumann, E., Siegel, P. and Hodge, R., (eds.) 1970, *The Logic of Social Hierarchies*. Chicago: Markham Publishing.

McCawley, J. 1971. Tense and time reference in English. Reprinted in J. McCawley (1976), *Grammar and Meaning: Papers on Syntactic and Semantic Topics*. London: Academic Press. Corrected edition.

Milroy, L. 1980. *Language and Social Networks*. Oxford: Basil Blackwell.

Searle, J. R. 1969. *Speech Acts*. Cambridge: Cambridge University Press.

van Hamel, A. 1912. On Anglo-Irish syntax. *Englische Studien* 45: 272–292.

Whelan, C. and Whelan, B. 1984. *Social Mobility in the Republic of Ireland: A Comparative Perspective*. Dublin: The Economic and Social Research Institute.

Wolfson, N. 1982. *CHP: The Conversational Historical Present in American English Narrative*. Dordrecht: Foris.

5

The Interpretation of Social Constraints on Variation in Belfast English

JAMES MILROY

Introduction

In linguistic terms, the city of Belfast (like many other areas in the British Isles) is what Johnston (1985) has called a 'divergent dialect' community. Not only is the city vernacular highly divergent from what we usually call 'standard English', but also the range of variation within the city is very wide. In such communities, many of the patterns observed are discontinuous, and these do not fit comfortably into unidirectional scales of variation corresponding with the socioeconomic class of the speakers (of the kind used by Labov, 1966, in New York City). For example, whereas in Belfast back-vowel realisations of /a/ (pronouncing, e.g., *man* as 'maun') are favoured at one level of the social hierarchy (and people are moving towards back /a/), a higher status level reverses the trend and favours fronting of /a/ (J. Milroy 1982). Thus, the socioeconomic class pattern revealed is not unilinear, but is a zig-zag pattern, incorporating a reversal of evaluation. Lower status speakers are moving away from front values of /a/ towards back values, whereas the middle to upper status groups are reverting again to front values.

There are other respects in which the variation revealed fails to conform with the predictions of the Labov model (1966, 1972). The zig-zag pattern, for example, is frequently replicated in the stylistic continuum. Speakers move towards the so-called 'careful' or 'prestige' variants in the 'careful' spoken styles only to return to the casual ('vernacular') variants in reading styles (which, according to Labov, are the most carefully monitored styles). In table 5.1, below, ten out of thirteen speakers show this zig-zag pattern for (a), and this is not unusual (see discussions by L. and J. Milroy 1977; L. Milroy 1987a). Similar patterns have more recently been located in quantity in Johnston's study of Edinburgh; he has found what he calls *humpback* and *saddle* patterns, but also complete *reversals* of the patterns predicted by the status model (Johnston 1985). The status model can

Table 5.1. *Linguistic variable scores in
three styles for thirteen Ballymacarrett
informants*

	(a) (index score)		
	SS	IS	WLS
Donald B	3.00	2.66	3.00
George K	4.15	3.40	4.62
Mary T	2.05	1.40	1.00
Elsie D	2.65	1.60	2.31
Millie B	2.80	1.85	2.69
Brenda M	2.80	2.15	2.69
James H	3.30	2.75	2.92
Terence D	2.90	3.35	3.15
Brian B	3.65	2.65	3.00
Stewart M	4.05	2.80	3.00
Alice W	2.55	2.20	2.69
Lena S	2.40	1.92	2.46
Rose L	1.35	1.55	1.50

SS   = Spontaneous style.
IS   = Interview style.
WLS = Word list style.

therefore be criticised on the grounds that it is not practical in these
circumstances; it does not succeed in helping us to interpret the variation
revealed in a community like Belfast. More generally, the failure of the
model to work in these circumstances raises broader questions about the
social motivation of linguistic change. The most obvious one is the role of
prestige in change.

In order to understand and explain the complex patterns that we have
found, we require a model of speech community significantly different
from the classic New York one; in particular, it seems that we cannot
readily accept prestige as a primary explanatory principle, as patterns do
not move consistently in the 'prestige' direction. What we have in fact
done is to develop a model based on the idea of language *maintenance*,
and have proposed that patterns of language variation are maintained in
communities by solidary social patterns. To the extent that social ties
between individuals are dense and multiplex, language patterns will tend
to be maintained. In this perspective, it follows quite logically that relative
weakening of ties will lead to the possibility of language change (Granovetter 1973, 1982; J. and L. Milroy 1985). It is in solidary communities that
shared values will be found and change impeded: only to the extent that

values are *not* shared will change be possible. The Belfast study therefore sought from its inception to find a way of explaining why highly divergent forms and varieties (which often seem to have low status) can be maintained through generations and even centuries.

It is worth commenting at this point that the underlying notion of prestige (and class mobility) has affected the interpretation of variation in other dimensions. This is particularly true of sex differentiation, which seems to be universal, and which is virtually always skewed in the same direction. Females are usually found to be 'moving upwards' in speech when it is measured against a social class continuum (see, however, Khan, this volume) and it is therefore suggested that since females usually have less access to power and influence than males do, they attempt to acquire status 'by proxy' through their use of language. But surely such an interpretation is slavishly dependent on the notion of prestige. Clearly, if it is men who actually acquire status, it is difficult to see why *their* language should not be considered status-ful, and why, for example, the wives of successful men do not simply imitate the language of their husbands. We have elsewhere (J. Milroy 1986; L. Milroy 1987b) discussed the possible role of sex differentiation independently of the prestige model. In this paper, I shall examine certain broader patterns of variation in Belfast, rejecting the notion of prestige as a primary explanatory principle, and using network as a model to assist in interpreting the patterns revealed by our analysis of the language.

Patterns in the inner city

The most striking characteristic of phonological variation in Belfast as a whole is the remarkable phonological complexity of inner-city speech as against that of the outer city. In the account that follows, we bear in mind two important points. The first is the principle enunciated by Weinreich, Labov and Herzog (1968) that variability in language is *functional*. People do not maintain variation in language for no reason at all: they use it for social purposes. The second principle arises from ethnographic work on small solidary communities (Cohen 1982: 8), which distinguishes between the 'voice to the outside world' and the 'much more complicated' voice of the community 'to its own members'. According to this view, in-group variation (in social affairs generally) is not only functional within communities, but also highly complicated and difficult for outsiders to access. We are interested in locating these complex patterns of linguistic variation, understanding the functional pressures that maintain them, and finally identifying the patterns of simplification that arise to the extent that in-group ties are weakened.

For our present purposes, there are two main senses in which the inner-city phonology can be said to be complicated: first, there is a much higher

Table 5.2. *Range of realisations for /a/ in inner-city Belfast*

ε	æ	a/ä	ɑ	ɔ
bag	back	back	grass	bad
bang	flash	bag	bad	man
		flash	man	can
		chap	pal	hand
		hat	hand	
		can't	can	
		ant		
		aunt		
		dance		

degree of 'low-level' allophonic variation in the inner-city than in outer areas, resulting in a wide range of variation and frequent overlap between phonemes (J. Milroy 1984); yet, this variation can be shown to be rule-governed; second, there is a high incidence of what I shall call *phonolexical alternation* in the inner city, which is much reduced in outer-city communities. We have shown in various studies that lexical alternants (of the *pull* type – see below) are highly salient in the community and encode values of greater and lesser solidarity. In what follows my main purposes are: (1) to demonstrate the patterns of simplication that can be traced by comparing our inner-city data with that of our city-wide random sample survey and our outer-city community studies, and (2) to consider how far a theory of strong and weak ties can account for maintenance of complex patterns and the development of simpler ones. My first example concerns allophonic complexity. I shall use here the data on short /a/, but similar conclusions hold true of other vowels (for greater detail, see for example, J. Milroy 1976, 1981; Harris 1985).

Table 5.2 is a simplified representation of the range of /a/, in terms of following consonantal environments. It is simplified in many ways; it ignores patterns of length, diphthongisation and rounding, and excludes post-velar environments, as in *cab, castle*. Yet it is still sufficiently detailed to make our main points.

The pattern displayed here incorporates variation, but the heterogeneity in the system is orderly: it can, in principle, be described in terms of variable rules. Similarly, it can be described phonologically in terms of a set of subscales, in which the potential for lowering and backing will vary in degree for different subsets.

We had much evidence during field-work that limits on permitted variation are maintained by community pressures: for example, when a young East Belfast informant applied a strategy of front-raising (similar to

RP) to the item *chap* (on a word-list), the mockery of his companions was deafening: a strategy of front-raising cannot be used in this social group.

To return to the main point about allophonic complexity: it is obvious, even from the simplified displays in table 5.2, that these complex patterns are not easily learnable for outsiders, even though they are regular. How, for example, could an outsider know that backing is not permitted in velar environments and fronting not possible in most others? Therefore, it seems that these patterns can only be maintained by insider knowledge depending on the extent to which speakers belong to relatively close-knit groups. To the extent that these close-knit social relations are weakened, it is predicted that these linguistic complexities will be reduced. I shall adduce evidence from the outer city, which suggests that this view is correct.

A second sense in which the inner-city language may be said to be complex is in the incidence of lexical items which have two alternative vowel pronunciations quite distinct phonetically from one another. There are several such sets, and most of them (such as the MEET/MEAT alternation) are highly salient in the inner city. They are discussed by J. Milroy (1980, 1981), J. Milroy and Harris (1980), and Harris (1985).

The set we have studied in most detail is the (pull) set, which alternate in vowel realisation between [ʌ] and [u]. The membership of this limited set is not predictable by environmental phonological rules; for example, whereas *shook*, *look* belong to it, *cook*, *book* do not. The items *wood*, *wool*, *hood* and probably *soot* used to belong to it, but do not now. Nevertheless, inner-city speakers know, in this alternating set (and others), precisely which items can alternate and which cannot. Again, it seems that the best explanation for the survival of this kind of insider knowledge in inner-city speakers is a theory of close ties, which function as norm-enforcement mechanisms.

Furthermore, as we might expect, these alternations are functional. The existence of these sets provides an important sociolinguistic resource for inner-city speakers, and survival of these alternants must surely depend on this. First, in a broad sense, the 'in-group' variant ([ʌ]) can be held to affirm group identity. More importantly, I think, the alternative choices can encode messages of social nearness or social distance – or, if you like, degrees of social distance. The in-group form encodes messages of intimacy and closeness, and, like the T pronoun, can actually be *required* amongst close friends in casual circumstances: its strong affective meanings, however, are not easily accessible to outsiders. The other alternant is the out-group form, and this of course is used in interactions with those who have relatively weak ties with *ego*, or in situational contexts in which social distance is present. Again, we have evidence from fieldwork about the functions of these alternants; one man of 27 commented that during his years away from Northern Ireland, he had stopped using what I have called the in-group alternants. The most obvious explanation for this is that during his years away from home, he would develop a large number of relatively weak ties; in such circumstances, the in-group alternant would cease to have any function for him and so could be abandoned. This functional explanation seems to me more satisfactory than, and logically prior to, one based on prestige, as this individual's activities away from home had not been upwardly mobile.

It is to be expected that within the wider social structure of a city, social distance between groups will develop. In such circumstances, the norm enforcement mechanisms that maintain the complex structure of inner-city phonology (and other patterns of language use) will be weakened, and simplification is likely. The findings of our random sample survey of the city and of the outer-city community studies appear to confirm this.

Linguistic patterns in the wider speech community

I have elsewhere shown (J. Milroy 1982) that the range of variation in (a) is greatly reduced in speakers outside the inner city. Table 5.3 below, which is from the random sample survey of speakers throughout the city, shows total convergence on a low front vowel for /a/, and table 5.4 demonstrates another interesting point. In it the two front-raised items (*castle*, *dabble*) appear to be randomly front-raised rather than governed by any systematic rule. The vernacular rules predict that *dabble* will be subject to backing – certainly not front-raising, and it is unlikely that this speaker is following the highly recessive rule for front-raising after velars in the item *castle* (this has been largely abandoned by younger low-status speakers). Table 5.5, based on the output of 60 speakers, shows that the reduction in range for this vowel throughout the city is clear and consistent (statistically, the pattern is very highly significant). Furthermore, it is sex-graded; females are more likely to simplify than males. Very similar patterns were revealed for other variables, and in these also females were consistently in the lead in moving away from the more complex traditional patterns. Thus, it may well be worth considering the possibility that sex differentiation in language contributes to simplification patterns and hence to the establishment of supra-local norms.

We now turn to the findings of the two outer-city community studies, which also show a pattern of reduction of allophony. The social characteristics of the speakers are of course very different from the inner city: they can be characterised as upper working to lower middle class, and the territorially-based network indicators that we used in the inner city (L. Milroy 1987a: 141–2) do not yield high scores. In these 'loose-tie' conditions, the prediction is that, owing to the weakening of norm-enforcement mechanisms and the reduction in the everyday functional value of the use of in-group forms, complexity of both kinds will be reduced. Additionally, it may be the case that realisations will be less

Table 5.3. /a/ *range for a middle class Belfast speaker: word-list style*
(random sample survey)

	ɛ	æ	a	ä	ɑ	ɔ
bag			+			
back			+			
cap			+			
map			+			
passage			+			
cab			+			
grass			+			
bad			+			
man			+			
castle			+			
dabble			+			
passing			+			

Index score of convergence on [a]: 0 (max. convergence)
Range score   0 (min. range)

Table 5.4. /a/ *range for a middle class Belfast speaker: word-list*
style(random sample survey)

	ɛ	æ	a	ä	ɑ	ɔ
bag			+			
back			+			
cap			+			
map			+			
passage			+			
cab			+			
grass			+			
bad			+			
man			+			
castle		+				
dabble		+				
passing			+			

Index score of convergence on [a]: 2
Range score: 1

subject to rule, and some apparently random variation (as in table 5.4)
may be encountered.

   Table 5.6 lists the following consonantal environments that we used in the
outer-city studies in the quantification of (a), (o) and (ɛ) (as in *cat, stop, bet*).

Table 5.5. *Range*

Average range scores (maximum 5):		
Lower group	(LWC-MWC):	2.83
Upper group	(UWC-MC):	1.97
No. of speakers with range of 1 or less:		
Lower group	1	(4 per cent).
Upper group	11	(31 per cent).
No. of males and females with range of 1 or less:		
Males	3	(10 per cent).
Females	9	(30 per cent).
No. of speakers with range of 3 or more:		
Lower group	16	(66.7 per cent).
Upper group	10	(27.7 per cent).

Table 5.6. *Consonantal environments used in the quantification of (a), (o) and (ɛ)*

T = voiceless stop (incl. affricate) or sonorant + voiceless obstruent
TS = environment described in T + a following syllable in same morpheme
D = voiceless fricative or any voiced consonant not immediately followed by a voiceless segment
DS = environment described in D + a following syllable in same morpheme.

Tables 5.7 and 5.8 demonstrate the narrowing of the range of realisations in the outer city; for (ɔ), the extreme left-hand column is empty, and for (ɛ), both the extreme left- and extreme right-hand columns are empty. In the inner city, however, not only is the full range exploited, but the left-hand columns (for environment T in the inner city), which are empty here, are in the order of 100 per cent (i.e. categorical) for virtually all the males (young and old) in the sample (for details see L. Milroy 1987a: 217–18). This compares with quantities close to zero in the outer city, for most speakers. Similarly, the range from low to high-mid (in the case of (ɛ) is reduced to a very narrow range in table 5.8. Thus, these findings support the findings of the random sample, in which, as we have seen, the range of realisations is reduced in higher status speakers. There is also some indication that the appearance of particular items in particular

Table 5.7. /ɔ/ *in Andersonstown*

ä	ɑ	ɒ	ɒ:	ɔ	ɔ:
	T got (2)		T shop		
	DS Polytech				
	T shop			DS probably	D job (3)
	T pot	DS concentrated			D of
		DS vodka			D God
				TS bottom	

Table 5.8. /ɛ/ *in Andersonstown*

ä	ɛ	ɛ:	ẹ	ẹ:	e:
	T set-up (2)		DS specials	D red	
	T lent		T went	D tell	
	T went (2)			D ten	
	DS specials (3)				
	DS remember				
	TS twenty				

columns is more likely to be random than in the inner city. Space does not permit a full discussion of this, but it is worth noting that this confirms our view that the situation is less focused than in the inner city.

Conclusions

The general picture that emerges from these patterns of variation is one in which simplification patterns and loss of regularity and consistency are made possible by the weakening of network strength and the development of patterns of weak ties. Complex patterns, which (as we have argued) are functional in close communities, are maintained by the norm-enforcement function of dense and multiplex networks. For those whose ties are uniplex and (relatively) open-ended, these patterns are no longer functional and it is for this reason, and not primarily because of speakers' desire for prestige, that they disappear.

These findings have revealed important patterns of change that are not readily captured in a quantitative paradigm that measures a unilinear scale of phonetic variation against a unilinear scale of socioeconomic class. If we argue, nevertheless, that prestige models can still account for the trend to simplification and uniformity that we have revealed, we then have to explain *why* simplification should carry prestige. The trend to uniformity (not always necessarily simplification) that is often found in so-called prestige accents (such as RP) would seem itself to be related to functional factors. As Jakobson perceived long ago, those varieties that have supra-local functions and which tend to develop in the direction of *koinés* display simpler systems than varieties that have purely local functions (for an excellent discussion of simplification and complexity in a range of language situations, see Andersen 1986). It may well be that, in varieties that have supra-local functions, a high degree of complexity (at any level) becomes dysfunctional.

In the social status dimension, of course, the network model is also explanatory, as different status levels in society are normally characterised by different degrees of network density and multiplexity. At the lowest and highest levels, network strength is normally high (as L. Milroy 1987a has pointed out): it is chiefly in the middle ranges of society that social and geographical mobility lead to the development of large numbers of relatively weak ties; individuals at these levels have more uniplex and diffuse ties. At these levels, the complex variation which encodes rich social meanings to insiders simply becomes progressively more and more redundant: it is no longer functional for these mobile people. The 'voice' of these people is directed more to 'the outside world' than to close-tie communities, whose 'voice' to their own members (as Cohen 1982: 8 points out) is indeed more complicated.

Finally, in the dimension of sex differentiation, our studies indicate that females lead in the development of supra-local norms (including those that involve systemic simplification). This perception, I would suggest, is closer to providing an explanation for sex differentiation in language than explanations based on prestige, and this is a matter that should be more fully investigated.

NOTE

I am grateful to all those colleagues who took part in the Belfast research, particularly John Harris, Rose Maclaran, Lesley Milroy and Zena Molyneux, for their contributions to that research; and to the UK Social Science Research Council for funding. My thanks also to Jenny Cheshire and John Harris for their helpful comments on this paper.

REFERENCES

Andersen, H. 1986. Center and periphery; adoption, diffusion and spread. Paper delivered to the International Historical Dialectology Conference. Poznan.
Coates, J. 1986. *Women, Men and Language*. London: Longman.
Cohen, A. (ed.). 1982. *Belonging*. Manchester: Manchester University Press.

Granovetter, M. 1973. The strength of weak ties. *American Journal of Sociology* 78: 1,360–80.

1982. The strength of weak ties: a network theory revisited. In Marsden, P. V. and Lin, N. (eds.), *Social Structure and Network Analysis*. London: Sage.

Harris, J. 1985. *Phonological Variation and Change*. Cambridge: Cambridge University Press.

Johnston P. 1985. Irregular style variation patterns in Edinburgh speech. *Scottish Language* 2: 1–19.

Labov, W. 1966. *The Social Stratification of English in New York City*. Washington DC: Center for Applied Linguistics.

1972. *Sociolinguistic Patterns*. Philadelpha: University of Pennsylvania Press.

Milroy, J. 1980. Lexical alternation and the history of English. In Traugott, E. *et al.* (eds.), *Papers from the 4th International Conference on Historical Linguistics*. Amsterdam: Benjamins.

1981. *Regional Accents of English: Belfast*. Belfast: Blackstaff.

1982. Probing under the tip of the iceberg phonological normalization and the shape of speech communities. In Romaine, S. (ed.). *Sociolinguistic Variation in Speech Communities*. London: Edward Arnold, pp. 35–47.

1984. Present-day evidence for historical changes. In Blake, N. F. and Jones, C. (eds.), *English Historical Linguistics: Studies in Development*. Sheffield: University of Sheffield, pp. 173–91.

1986. The methodology of urban language studies: the example of Belfast. In Harris J. *et al.* (eds.) *Perspectives on the English Language in Ireland*. Dublin: Trinity College Dublin.

Milroy, J. and Harris, J. 1980. When is a merger not a merger? The MEAT/ MATE problem in a present-day English vernacular. *English World-Wide* 1 (2): 199–210.

Milroy, J. and Milroy L. 1985. Linguistic change, social network and speaker innovation. *Journal of Linguistics*, 21: 339–84.

Milroy, L. 1987a *Language and Social Networks*. Oxford: Blackwell. 2nd edition.

1987b. *Observing and Analysing Natural Language*. Oxford: Blackwell.

Milroy, L. and Milroy, J. 1977. Speech and context in an urban setting. *Belfast Working Papers in Language and Linguistics* 2: 1–85.

Patterson, D. 1860. *The Provincialisms of Belfast*. Belfast: Mayne.

Weinreich, U., Labov, W. and Herzog, M. 1968. Empirical foundations for a theory of language change. In Lehmann, W. and Malkiel, Y. (eds.), *Directions for Historical Linguistics*. Austin, TX: University of Texas Press, pp. 95–188.

Canada

6

Canada

J. K. CHAMBERS

Introduction

Canada occupies a vast territory, embracing several regions distinguished from one another by climate, topography, network ties, orientation, and all the other factors that naturally accrue to geophysical spread. Sociocultural perspectives are further complicated by the existence within the Canadian boundaries of two long-standing national consciousnesses which simultaneously share Canadian nationality and maintain their own. Québec is the power base for the francophone minority, equal partners in Confederation since its inception in 1867. Newfoundland joined Confederation only in 1949 after centuries of colonial ties to Britain and self-government.

Linguistically, their presence affects Canadian English (hereafter CE) in interesting and very different ways. Québec's location interrupts the continuity of the English-language majority, splitting the Atlantic provinces from the central and western provinces, and it perpetuates bilingual buffer zones in the adjacent provinces of New Brunswick on the east and Ontario on the west. Newfoundland, though overwhelmingly anglophone, did not share mainland Canadian settlement history, and her political autonomy gave rise to an indigenous standard accent which is only now beginning to reflect the influence of mainland CE. Any generalisations that might be hazarded about CE must necessarily be qualified – implicitly or explicitly – by their presence.

Counterbalancing these sources of Canadian diversity are several other factors of crucial importance to Canadian national unity. Demographically, the population of 25,675,200 (as of October 1986) is often called 'sparse', and undoubtedly correctly so when one considers the thousands of square kilometres available for settlement, but in fact the great majority of Canadians are geographically concentrated. Most Canadians live within a belt two or three hundred kilometres wide parallel to the US–Canadian border: even that area is far from small, of course, because the national borders adjoin for more than 4,000 kilometres, but the concentration belies any 'mental map' of Canada as a country of isolated homesteads.

Socioeconomically, Canadians are not only highly urbanised but also overwhelmingly middle-class, to an extent that can scarcely be comprehended by outsiders, except perhaps by Americans and Australians. As in the New World societies of the United States and Australia, two apparently unrelated factors conspired to determine the relatively monochromatic class structure. On the one hand, Canada's earliest settlements had too few amenities to support an aristocracy, and settlers with aristocratic pretensions either returned to the Old Country or joined the commonality. On the other hand, the earliest political initiatives fostered geographical mobility as a means of uniting the enormous expanses that needed to be governed. The combination of social egalitarianism and freedom of movement led to occupational and social mobility on a scale unknown in the colonising nations.

Social trends in the first half of this century further increased the class homogenisation. Urbanisation shrank the agricultural class to less than 10 per cent of the population and occupational mobility keeps the unskilled labour group at less than 5 per cent (Camu, Weeks and Sametz 1971). More than 85 per cent of the population is thus middle-class, sharing to a greater or lesser degree their values, aspirations, living standards, and (outside of Québec and Newfoundland) speech standards.

Most of the linguistic research on CE has been carried out in the framework of traditional dialectology rather than sociolinguistic dialectology. Three overviews based on traditional materials already exist (Avis 1973; Chambers 1979b; Bailey 1982) and access to the dialect literature is facilitated by annotated bibliographies (Avis and Kinloch [1978]; Lougheed 1988). No purpose is served by recapitulating the traditional studies and generally I will not do so unless they have useful social implications or are the sole source of social inferences. More recent sociolinguistic studies will be supplemented by historical and sociological sources.

The Status of English

English and French are the official languages of Canada, and all regions are institutionally bilingual. According to 1981 census figures, 67.0 per cent of Canadians are monolingual English speakers, 16.6 per cent are monolingual French, 15.3 per cent are English-French bilinguals, and 1.2 per cent have a mother tongue neither English nor French. The concentration of the francophone population shows up dramatically when Québec is left out of the demolinguistic calculations: English is the mother tongue of 87.2 per cent of the rest of the population as compared to slightly more than 4 per cent French (Lachapelle and Henripin 1982: 20). Of the Canadians whose mother tongue is neither English nor French, almost all – perhaps 95 per cent – speak English, not French as their second language (Joy 1972: 57–63).

The growth of anglophone Canada took impetus from four significant waves of immigration, all of which have linguistic consequences.

The first, from 1776 to 1793, was the wholesale movement of American anti-revolutionaries from the United States, the populace known in Canadian history as 'United Empire Loyalists' (those who arrived by 1783, the end of the Revolution) and the 'Late Loyalists.' About 34–40,000 sought refuge in Nova Scotia, where they easily outnumbered the 20,000 inhabitants, many of whom were francophone, and about 7,500–12,000 went to Upper Canada (now Ontario) where they became the first significant settlers (Stewart 1985: 128). Most of them were from the states of Vermont, New York, New Jersey and Pennsylvania, and their American accents became the local standard in all the towns and villages they founded.

About four decades later, and peaking in 1851–61, waves of British settlers, especially Scots and Irish, arrived in Canada as part of a concerted effort by the British governors to counteract the growing sentiment for American republicanism in the country. Most came to Upper Canada. When they settled in established towns, as most did, their British accents disappeared after a generation or so, but when they themselves founded communities in unsettled areas of the Ottawa Valley, Peterborough County north of Lake Ontario and Elgin County on the north shore of Lake Erie in southwestern Ontario, the colonial lineage of their Scots and Irish accents remains to this day.

In 1901–11, another wave of British settlers, especially Scots, and many Germans, Dutch and Belgians arrived. For the most part, their descendants assimilated the standard Canadian accent, but those descendants today often identify Scotticisms with the speech of their grandparents' generation, ascribing its features to age rather than nationality. A few rural communities founded by Germans retain traces of their founders' accents, including Waterloo county in southern Ontario. Before this wave arrived, the vast territory west of Ontario, originally Rupert's Land, had been settled largely by Ontarians and partitioned into the provinces of Manitoba (1870), Saskatchewan (1885), Alberta (1885) and British Columbia (1886). Many of these immigrants of 1901–11 settled in the west, with the predictable linguistic results for their offspring. As a result, all of urban, middle-class Canada (again, except Québec and Newfoundland) speaks a remarkably homogeneous accent (Priestley 1951; Chambers and Hardwick 1986). Linguistic traces of German ancestry were still discernible in German-founded towns a generation ago (Graham 1957), but have now largely disappeared.

In 1951–61, immigrants from much more diverse homelands reached a peak in a wave that continues today. Thousands of Germans, Italians, Ukrainians, Greeks, Chinese, Portuguese, and other immigrants moved into Canada's urban areas, especially the major conurbations surrounding Toronto, Vancouver, Edmonton, Winnipeg and Montréal. In Ontario more than one person in six has a mother tongue other than English or French (Chambers 1979a). Many of the immigrants arrive as labourers. Their numbers are large enough and their residential communities often self-contained enough (Breton 1964) for the native CE of their offspring to show features not found in standard CE, and sometimes those features are retained by the next generation as well. If the features persist, they will be a source of variants in urban CE accents, but so far they appear to be transitional.

Autonomy of CE

Both Newfoundland English and inland CE appear to have established themselves as autonomous national varieties, but their autonomy now seems rather precarious. Evidence of increasing heteronomy comes from close studies of changes in progress in both varieties, and is by no means conclusive at this early stage. Evidence of established autonomy comes from the much more obvious indicators of 'codification' (Jolly 1983) and public awareness.

Among North American settlements, Newfoundland has an extraordinarily long, colourful and complex history (Story 1965, Clarke in this volume). The uniqueness of Newfoundland English in the North American context makes it a ready marker of national identity, and public awareness of its autonomy has been fostered by numerous archival and research projects based at Memorial University of Newfoundland in St John's. Its distinctiveness is codified in the *Dictionary of Newfoundland English* (Story *et al.*1982), a dialect dictionary exceptionally rich in citations from tapes as well as literary sources.

The autonomy of Newfoundland English is threatened by her joining the Canadian confederation in 1949. Newfoundland had close ties to Canada before confederation as a result of geography and trade, but the ties are now more intimate. Recent research by Clarke (1985, and this volume) shows age-grading for a number of linguistic variables, with the younger speakers adopting CE variants regardless of social class or other independent variables. Her results suggest an incipient shift in the direction of heteronomy in the post-confederation generation (see below).

CE itself may be undergoing a shift in the direction of heteronomy. By most criteria, CE's autonomy appears to be well-established, though relatively recent. The term 'Canadian English' first appeared in print in 1857, ten years before confederation (Geikie 1857). There is a general awareness among Canadians of their linguistic independence from British and US varieties. According to Pringle (1985b: 183–4), Canadians may even overstate the case for their linguistic uniqueness in order to 'assert the reality of a Canadian linguistic identity which, Canadians sometimes fear, is not as obvious or even as real as they would like it to be. This they do,' he says, 'by exaggerating the differences between Canadian and American English (which often entails disparaging American English), and by asserting that in at least some respects Canadian English is more like British English, and is therefore better.'

For whatever motive, the codification of CE proceeds on several fronts. Books on language proclaiming their Canadian content include dictionaries such as the CE dialect dictionary (Avis *et al.* 1967) and several desk and classroom dictionaries, usage guides (Secretary of State 1985), and textbooks at several levels (for example, Scargill and Penner 1966: Chambers 1975: McConnell 1979: O'Grady and Dobrovolsky 1987).

It is perhaps disquieting, then, to discover that the feature of CE that most readily distinguishes it from American English is undergoing a change that could conceivably erase the difference. The rule called 'Canadian raising' raises the onsets of diphthongs before voiceless consonants as in *house* and *wife* such that they contrast phonetically with low back onsets in *how, houses, why* and *wives* (Joos 1942: Chambers 1973). Recently, younger Canadians throughout the inland urban area tend to pronounce the back-gliding diphthong in words such as *house, houses, how* the same, with an onset that is low and front (see below for more details). The pronunciation is thus the same as in general American English. Faced with this linguistic similarity, I attempted to correlate the linguistic change with pro- and anti-American sentiments expressed by different age groups in Toronto (Chambers 1981). In some of its details the correlation is inconclusive but the results undoubtedly show that younger Canadians are more attuned and receptive to things American than their elders. This 'gross correlation' suggests that the linguistic change in progress may be a response to a shift from Canadian autonomy to North American heteronomy.

Regional variation

In Canada, the correlation between regions and dialects appears to present a unique geolinguistic pattern. Instead of the expected gradation of accents on a geographical continuum, Canada has a remarkably homogeneous urban middle-class standard accent from sea to sea except in Newfoundland and Québec, and enclaves of other accents and dialects in non-urban regions spread discontinuously across the country (Chambers 1985: Pringle 1985a).

The discontinuity of the regional accents and the diverse sources from which they sprang makes for a bewildering variety. Categorising them according to the ethnicity of the founders, as I do below, indicates gross similarities among them at the expense of the indigenous features that each has developed during their period of independent development on Canadian soil.

Because many of the enclaves were founded by Scots-Irish and Irish settlers, the regional accents often share certain features with Newfoundland speech in spite of the geographical discontinuity and complete absence of contact. One of them, Peterborough County, about 150 kilometres north-east of Toronto, remains unstudied linguistically and, sadly, may now be best suited for studying the progress of standardisation, but the features used by the most isolated speakers include final clear [1], retroflex post-vocalic [r], and centralized onsets for [əɪ] in all environments. None of these features is shared with standard CE spoken in the near-by city of Peterborough or in Toronto, but all are heard in Newfoundland (Paddock 1974). Among the inland enclaves of Scots-Irish and Irish origin, only the Ottawa Valley has been studied (see below). Others that need studying include Cape Breton Island in Nova Scotia, the Cornwall-Maxville district on the St Lawrence River near the Québec border, and eastern Elgin county in south-western Ontario.

Scots-based linguistic groups of a very different sort developed in the Prairie provinces as a result of intermarriage with native women in the eighteenth century. The Hudson's Bay Company favoured Scots and Orkneymen as their trappers and factors in Rupert's Land while the rival Northwest Company employed Québecois. The men of both groups married Cree and Ojibwa women, and their unions established in the territory a French creole (Douaud 1982) and an English creole. The best-known English creole is called Bungee, from Ojibwa *panki*, 'mixed' (Stobie 1967–68), spoken in the Red River district in Manitoba. Linguistic data are sparse but the following features are mentioned by Scott and Mulligan (1951): [s] and [ʃ] merge (making *shot* homophonous with *sot*), the only mid front vowel is lax (*paper* is homophonous with *pepper*), and the grammar blends lexicon and constructions from English and Algonquian. Scott cites the following sentence: *Bye me I kaykatch killed it two ducks with wan sot.* meaning 'Boy, I nearly killed two ducks with one shot'. Whether Bungee survives today is uncertain.

The best-known regional dialect founded by German settlers is that of Lunenburg, Nova Scotia. Emeneau (1935) described numerous lexical and surnaming regionalisms there as well as some phonological features. The principal phonetic feature was the lack of post-vocalic [r], attributable to New England influence rather than to German.[1] Emeneau's description was apparently recollected from what he remembered hearing as a youth, and was written and published long after he had left. By the time the next linguist arrived (Wilson 1958), the distinctive Lunenburg features were either gone or going. Wilson (1975: 44) concluded, 'The forces of history have tended to wear away the German element and preserve the Yankee features which are constantly reinforced by the surrounding [Nova Scotian] population.' Other German settlements across Canada are numerous but are unstudied linguistically, apart from the Saskatchewan settlements (Graham 1957).

Also unstudied, for the most part, are the rural dialects founded by Ukrainian, Dutch, French, Polish, and other immigrant groups which arrived after the Scots, Irish and Germans but which in many cases have now been in place for three or more generations. Europeans have not been the only source: rural communities in Canada have also been founded by Oklahoma blacks in northern Alberta (Emery 1971), Pennsylvania Dutch in the Niagara Peninsula in Ontario (Gleason 1977), Japanese in the Kootenays of British Columbia, and other groups. In the larger areas such as the Ottawa Valley the founders have intermingled with successive ethnic waves (Pringle and Padolsky 1983) and in the more populous areas such as the Niagara Peninsula they have been surrounded by conurbations. The linguistic results of all this ethnic diversity can only be guessed until they are studied.

Varieties of English as a second language

With two official languages and numerous third languages, Canada is as rich in varieties of English as a second language (ESL) as in first-language varieties. The points of French-English contact differ from the points of third language-English contact because the former are more or less stable bilingual situations and the latter are usually transitional. The ESL varieties are not as well studied in either case as are the other languages (Woods 1985).

The most stable bilingual areas are, of course, the bilingual belts on either side of the Québec border. Even here, stability is relative rather than absolute, as the 'width' of the band has fluctuated over the years. In the Acadian bilingual area of New Brunswick, the relative proportion of francophone school-age children dropped from 45 per cent in 1951 to 38 per cent in 1961, apparently as a result of emigrations from the province (Joy 1972: 80–2). On the Ontario side, in the counties adjoining Québec, the francophone population has steadily increased since confederation, showing a proportional growth from 21 per cent in 1871 to 29 per cent in 1961 (Joy 1972: 119).

Sociolinguists seem more attracted to fluctuation than to relative stability, and the existence for more than a century of French-coloured English in the bilingual belts is largely unstudied. However, impressive results are being achieved on the French spoken there and in the predominantly anglophone areas to the west, with methods that will readily adapt to the

English of the same regions. The key determinant of English variation, as of French, seems likely to be 'language-dominance,' for which Mougeon *et al.* (1980) developed a questionnaire and an index for their research in the francophone community in Welland, Ontario. Language dominance is itself determined by a complex set of social variables, including intermarriage (Mougeon 1977), media exposure, language-dominance of each parent, and so on, each of which must be weighted (Cichocki 1986: 140–65). Individual indices for French or English dominance have so far been demonstrated to correlate strongly with several linguistic variables including preposition use (Beniak and Mougeon 1984), auxiliary verbs and pronominals (Mougeon *et al.* 1982), and intonation (Cichocki 1986: 157–65). A similar index developed by Poplack (1984) in the Ottawa-Hull area correlates strongly with code-switching.[2] Similar results might be anticipated for sociolinguistic research on English in stable bilingual contexts.

In the bilingual situations where immigrant languages and English come together, the research again is sparse, and most of it has been directed at the immigrant languages rather than English. Chamak-Horbatsch (1987) illustrates the decline of Ukrainian by studying the language of mother–child interactions among second-and third-generation Torontonians. Probably the best studied immigrant language is *Italese*, the Italian interdialect used in Toronto, where the community is large (over 400,000) and the interdialect has been current for almost three generations. Italese has adapted and nativised hundreds of English lexical items (Clivio 1976: Danesi 1985).

Sociolinguistic variation

The Labovian enterprise, correlating linguistic variation with social variables, has made sharp impact upon CE studies, as elsewhere. Sociolinguistic studies in several regions hold out the promise of clarifying CE dialectology and bringing its data to bear on issues of language change and social function. In what follows, I can attempt no more than a broad survey of these projects, which are as varied in scale and purpose as the landscape they cover.

Variation in Regional Accents

St John's, Newfoundland   Clarke's first results (1984a, 1985, this volume) show age as the crucial independent variable in the speech of the Newfoundland capital. It is the only social factor that affects all 13 variables, and the most significant gap in age stratification consistently separates speakers 55 and over from the others. The explanation, Clarke notes (1984a: 151), lies in 'the much greater exposure of residents of the city to speech models of a standard North American variety over the past forty years, in particular since the confederation of Newfoundland with Canada in 1949.' She also notes that age is the crucial sociolinguistic variable in smaller Newfoundland communities (Reid 1981; Colbourne 1982; King 1983) as further support for her explanation.

Prince Edward Island   An interesting indication of the regional spread of a linguistic variant comes from Pratt's study (1982) of the variable [əɪ] in *time, light, sky*, and so forth, on Prince Edward Island (hereafter PEI). The variant [oɪ] or [ɔɪ] occurs throughout the Atlantic provinces, in the Ottawa Valley, and in other areas in which the Irish formed a significant part of the population. It does not occur in inland urban CE. On PEI, where about 25 per cent of the population is of Irish descent, Pratt shows that the variant no longer correlates with ethnicity. Several other social variables are more likely possibilities, although, as Pratt says, 'none of the samples were large enough to be compelling'. The variant appears to be more frequent among less well educated speakers, among older women, and among young people who intend to remain on PEI, but the clearest conclusion is that the variant appears to be relatively stable at about 30 per cent of all tokens for PEI speakers, regardless of age, gender, ethnicity, or the rest.

The Ottawa Valley   The Ottawa Valley survey promises to unearth a profusion of linguistic variants of diverse origins. The area is large and its population unstratified and spread thinly throughout the area. Pringle and Padolsky (1983: 338–40) outline the extraordinarily diverse settlement history and claim that the present inhabitants are speakers of nine (or more) accents or dialects: 'three Hiberno-English speech-types, no fewer than six other varieties of English – varieties which are often sharply distinguished from each other, especially in their phonology, but also in their morphology, their syntax, and their lexicon.' So far, none of these has been described. Instead, the published results illustrate several variants for (aɪ) and (au) for three men from the village of Navan (Pringle and Padolsky 1983: 334–9) and one 72-year-old farmer (Pringle, Dale and Padolsky 1984). The amount of variation and its apparent failure to correlate with independent variables have led the investigators to conclude that 'there is no linguistic baseline' in the Ottawa Valley (Pringle and Padolsky 1983: 339). This extraordinary result awaits more thorough documentation.

Montréal   Although Montréal English has long been acclaimed as different from the inland urban CE, the details of those differences are not clearly identified. Phonologically, we now have a preliminary indication of how Montréal English differs from other urban CE varieties. Hung (1987) replicated a Toronto survey (Chambers 1980) with a small sample of middle-class Montréalers in three age groups in order to determine their onsets for the variable (au), which is undergoing a change in other urban settings (see below). Her results show little comparability with the group results from other cities, and no evidence for the linguistic change in progress. Where adults elsewhere contrast with younger speakers by having back onsets, in Montréal all tend to have non-back onsets. The inconsistency of the variability in Montréal allows the possibility that a few of Hung's individual subjects might fit into samples from other cities as speakers of more-or-less standard CE with respect to variable (au), but 'perhaps the most reasonable interpretation of the results,' she says, 'is that Montréal never had as its standard the raised back vowel in words like /haus/' (Hung 1987:138), that is, Canadian raising. The inconsistencies among individual speakers in her sample probably reflect anglophone fragmentation in post-1940 Montréal (Lieberson 1965, 1970).

Variation in inland urban CE

Vancouver   The Survey of Vancouver English (SVEN), directed by R. J. Gregg, conducted interviews from 1976 to 1981 with 300 Vancouverites spread across the urban area. Its scope and methods are admirably ambitious (Gregg *et al.* 1981), and the archiving methods (Gregg *et al.*1984) make it an incomparable databank for CE. Archiving the data has necessarily preoccupied the research team's efforts in the first stages, but its eventual analysis will be enhanced by its deliberate comparability at some points with real-time data from Gregg's earlier research (1957a, 1957b), and at most points with synchronous data from Ottawa (Woods 1979), which Gregg calls 'a serendipitous spin-off from the early stages of our current Vancouver enterprise'. Several points of comparison between the Ottawa and SVEN surveys are outlined by De Wolf (1984) and Murdoch (1984).

So far, the most fully analysed results from SVEN deal with local lexical items (Gregg 1983) and grammatical usage (Gregg 1984). Gregg shows that the indigenous lexicon, including items such as *saltchuck* 'tidal flats' and *oolichan* 'a small fish', retain some currency but perhaps diminishingly so, because the words are less likely to be known by younger speakers and, when they are known to them, their knowledge is often passive. The usage section of the survey checked choices among speakers on several points of contention (*different from/than, between you and me/I* and others), and Gregg's results divide the sample by education (postsecondary or not) and further divide it by identifying the subset of teachers, with the expected results. Both studies indicate something of the social dimensions available in SVEN for analysis of other aspects of variation. The databank is also being analysed instrumentally for sociophonetic information at the acoustic laboratories of the University of Victoria (see Esling in this volume).

Ottawa Howard Woods' sociolinguistic study of urban Ottawa (1979), prepared as a doctoral thesis under the supervision of Professor Gregg, surveys 100 speakers in five contextual styles (minimal pairs, word list, picture responses, reading passage, 'free speech') with respect to 27 phonological features and 71 vocabulary and usage items. Woods' analysis is straightforward and methodical. For each item, he presents graphic representations showing style on the abscissa and group frequencies (as a percentage) on the ordinate. Speakers are grouped by social class indices in one graph and usually recombined by other social factors (urban–rural, over 40–under 40, male–female) in other graphs. In the completeness of the analysis, Woods' work is unrivalled in the literature on CE.

As important as it is in its own right, it also offers numerous points of departure for subsequent studies both in Ottawa and elsewhere in the inland urban CE region (as in Woods' article in this volume). His discussions and interpretations of the results are minimal, but productive lines of inquiry suggest themselves throughout.

Woods' results for the onsets of the 'Canadian diphthongs', which he calls (i) and (ou) (1979: 123–9, 131–7), show indices for all social classes high on the scale – 60 per cent or higher – with no style shifting and insignificant class stratification, indicating the relative stability of this feature. However, the reanalysis of (ou) by age and gender (1979: 128) indicates lower onset vowels for females under 40 than the other groups. This result is consistent with findings for this variable in Toronto, Vancouver and Victoria (see below), where there is a change in progress led by younger women. The lower index score for younger women in Ottawa presumably reflects the tendency noted among their counterparts in Toronto, and is stated as follows: 'The tendency not to raise the onset of the diphthong in front of a voiceless consonant is greater when the vowel is fronted than when it is [back]. Thus the females in each age group not only use fronted vowels more frequently . . . but they also fail to raise more frequently' (Chambers 1980: 25).

On this point, and potentially on dozens of others, Woods' Ottawa results provide useful inferences for sociolinguistic research on CE.

Comparative variability in urban middle-class CE As Woods (1979: 33) remarks, 'A uniform Canadian dialect covers a larger land mass than any other one dialect in the world.' The explanation for this uniformity, reviewed above, lies in the linguistic similarity of the founding populations of the inland region, from Ontario to British Columbia. In the course of time, one might expect that regionalisms will accumulate, ultimately diversifying Canadian urban accents.

At present, the best available evidence suggests that the tendency towards homogeneity remains a sociolinguistic force. A recent sound change, described first in Toronto (Chambers 1980, 1981, 1984) and then in Vancouver (Chambers and Hardwick 1986) and Victoria (Davison 1987), is progressing similarly in all these cities and presumably in Ottawa, as indicated above, and elsewhere as well. (On its non-occurrence in Montréal, see above, pp. 97–8). The surveys in Toronto, Vancouver and Victoria elicited the variable (au) in three contextual styles from middle-class speakers in three age groups (12, 22, 46+) of both genders. The onset vowel varies similarly in all locations: for older speakers, it is generally back ([ʌu] before voiceless consonants, [ɑu] elsewhere) but occasionally for them and much more frequently for younger speakers it is fronted ([ɐu], [ɛu], [au] or [æu] before voiceless, one of the latter two elsewhere). As mentioned above, there is a tendency in all cities for the fronted onsets to be unraised, suggesting that the present phonetic diversity may eventually be simplified by eliminating the non-low onsets, which would have the effect, incidentally, of eliminating the Canadian raising rule from CE phonology. This tendency is not yet well-defined, although it is more evident in Vancouver and Victoria than Toronto. In all three cities, the main aspects of the change, socially and linguistically, are the same: younger speakers are more advanced than older and females are ahead of males, and the 'elsewhere' environment promotes fronting more often than the voiceless one. The striking similarities of so recent a change across such distances may find their explanation in the increasing heteronomy of the middle class (see above).

Language attitudes

The methodology for empirical studies of attitudes toward dialects was developed by Wallace Lambert and his associates in Montréal (Lambert *et al.*1960). Their conclusions, showing that both anglophone and franco-phone listeners downgraded French-accented CE, sent shock waves through Canadian officialdom and perhaps added some impetus to the legislation supporting the status of French both in Québec and in the rest of Canada. Lambert's methodology has now been used in numerous studies around the world, with similar results about the stereotyping of non-standard accents. The time is probably ripe for a replication of the original studies in Montréal as a check on attitudinal changes after a quarter century. The methodology has not been often applied elsewhere in Canada, perhaps because urban CE is not sufficiently differentiated to make it useful. Clarke (1981) used it in Newfoundland and discovered that both urban and rural listeners downgraded regional accents in predictable ways. One of her results showed, unpredictably, that teachers were less critical than their students in their evaluations. Clarke later refined her analysis (1984b) in several important dimensions, showing that non-standard phonological features in the speech sample used as a stimulus weighed more heavily with the listeners than other linguistic features, and the particular accent of the listeners significantly affected their responses to the speech stimuli, as did several other social variables. She concludes that the failure by investigators to control these variables may 'unknowingly inject a bias into their work' (1984b: 28).

Generally, linguistic attitudes of CE speakers are part and parcel of their attitudes toward things British and things American (Pringle 1985b). Since mid-century, things American have greatly outweighed things British in the Canadian world-view, but Canadian attitudes toward the US are by no means simple or stable. Hultin (1967) shows that attitudes about American English have swung from grudging approval to mild contempt at irregular intervals. Such historical soundings necessarily rely on written reports rather than linguistic behaviour. A recent attempt to discern attitudes indirectly from responses in linguistic interviews (Chambers 1981) indicates that younger Canadians are much more receptive than their elders to American speech as well as American media and other cultural aspects. Warkentyne (1983) correlated attitudes of subjects toward Canada, Britain and the United States with their evaluations of taped speech samples from the three countries. Although his results were inconsistent, there was a tendency for subjects who expressed highly favourable attitudes toward Britain and Canada to downgrade the American speech samples.

Attitudinal studies may be scarce for a good reason. Compared to many nations, Canada appears to be relatively tolerant linguistically. To some extent, this tolerance no doubt determines governmental policies upholding linguistic diversity, and may, in turn, be fostered by those policies. In any event, no other nation has endorsed diversity so broadly. In 1977, a government document entitled *A National Understanding* proclaimed:

> It is precisely the rejection of uniformity, the refusal to accept a homogeneous view of themselves and their country, that constitutes the most authentic and widely shared experience of Canadians. The affirmation and preservation of differences, personal, social, local, regional, cultural, linguistic, has consumed the minds and hearts of Canadians all through their history. It is the Canadian response to the question of identity. Our unity – and it is a real and profound unity if we will only bring ourselves to see it – arises from the determination to preserve the identity of each of us. (Quoted by Wardhaugh 1983: 59.)

It is difficult to assess how, or whether, statements such as this one, by no means unfamiliar in Canadian politics, translate themselves into the linguistic attitudes of individual citizens. Canadians are certainly aware that their country differs from at least the United States in exactly this respect. As Pringle (1983) puts it, 'The linguistic aspect of the Canadian mosaic owes something to the fact that the pressure on newcomers to "adjust" has always been less forceful in Canada than in the United States.'

What it might mean in the most mundane sense is that Canadians, more than most other nationalities, place linguistic non-conformity low on their list of contentious issues. The linguistic patchwork of regional accents has never been the basis of internecine feuds, and the standard CE accent, the fabric on which all those patches are stitched, confers no special privileges on its speakers, as standard accents elsewhere appear to do.

Hard evidence for this is hard to come by, but anecdotal evidence is abundant. For instance, a current television commercial for dry cat food proclaims it the favourite of 'Canadian cat lovers,' and by way of proof offers a testimonial from a middle-class suburbanite speaking a modified London (England) accent. Our American cousins would surely be outraged by such a discrepancy between citizenship and accent, and our more distant relatives, we can guess, would howl in protest, but in Canada the commercial is enjoying a long, unnoticed run. Slightly harder evidence comes from an undergraduate essay by Evan Wayne of the University of Toronto, who set out to compare the use of four minor Toronto variants (*'kilometre/ki'lometre, exclamation mark/point, slept in/overslept, porridge/ oatmeal*) with their occurrence in the nearest large American city, Buffalo. Stationing himself at shopping malls in the two cities, he stopped hundreds of shoppers on their daily rounds. The Buffalo shoppers were unanimous: they all said the same thing, the 'American' word (second in each pair). His Toronto shoppers offered, as expected, one or the other of the variants, in varying degrees (68/32 per cent, 93/7 per cent, 69/31 per cent, 87/13 per cent, respectively). Yet all, of course, were speaking 'Canadian.' With this kind of tolerability abroad in the land, Canada should remain fertile soil for sociolinguists for years to come.

NOTES

I am grateful to Jenny Cheshire, Sandra Clarke, Howard Woods, and Malcah Yaeger-Dror for comments on and corrections of an earlier version.

1. Canada has few non-rhotic accents other than Lunenburg. Another exists in the area of Conception Bay, Newfoundland, including Trinity Bay (Reid 1981), Port de Grave and Bay Roberts (Seary *et al.* 1968), and perhaps in enclaves beyond these as well (Sandra Clarke personal communication). Another non-rhotic region is rumoured to exist in southernmost New Brunswick at the Maine (US) border, but it has apparently not been investigated.
2. Butler and King (1984) suggest several independent variables as possible

explanations of extremely high code-switching (13.2 per hour) in a Newfoundland bilingual community, but the variables would likely resolve coherently into
an index of language-dominance.

REFERENCES

Avis, Walter S. 1973. The English language in Canada. In Sebeok, Thomas A.
(ed.). *Current Trends in Linguistics 10: Linguistics in North America.* The
Hague: Mouton, pp. 40–74.
Avis, Walter S., Crate Charles, Drysdale Patrick, Leechman Douglas, and Scargill
M. H. 1967. *A Dictionary of Canadianisms on Historical Principles.* Toronto:
W. J. Gage Limited.
Avis, Walter S., and Kinloch, A. M. 1978. *Writings on Canadian English
1792–1975. An Annotated Bibliography.* Toronto: Fitzhenry & Whiteside.
Bailey, Richard W. 1982. The English language in Canada. In Bailey, Richard W.
and Görlach, Manfred, (eds.). *English as a World Language.* Ann Arbor:
University of Michigan Press, pp. 134–76.
Beniak, Edouard and Mougeon, Raymond, 1984. Possessive *à* and *de* in informal
Ontarian French; a long-standing case of linguistic variation. In Baldi, P,
(ed.), *Papers from the XII Linguistic Symposium on Romance Languages.*
Amsterdam: Benjamins.
Breton, Raymond. 1964. Institutional completeness of ethnic communities and the
personal relations of immigrants. *American Journal of Sociology* 70: 193–205.
Reprinted in Blishen, B. R., Jones, F. E., Naegele, K. D. and Porter, J.
(eds.), 1971. *Canadian Society: Sociological Perspectives.* Toronto: Macmillan
of Canada, pp. 51–68.
Butler, Gary R. and King, Ruth. 1984. Conversational strategies in a bilingual
context: code-switching in L'Anse-á-Canards, Newfoundland. In Barnstead,
J. Gesner, B. E., Gordon, W. T., and Holder, M. (eds). *Papers from the
Eighth Annual Meeting of the Atlantic Provinces Linguistic Association.*
Halifax: Dalhousie University, pp. 11–18.
Camu, Pierre, Weeks, E. P. and Sametz, Z. W. 1971. The People. In Blishen, B.
R., Jones, F. E., Naegele, K. D. and Porter J. (eds.). 1971. *Canadian Society:
Sociological Perspectives.* Toronto: Macmillan of Canada, pp. 21–50.
Chamak-Horbatsch, Roma. 1987. Language use in a Ukrainian home: a Toronto
sample. *International Journal of the Sociology of Language* 63: 99–118.
Chambers, J. K. 1973. Canadian raising. *Canadian Journal of Linguistics* 18:
113–35.
(ed.). 1975. *Canadian English: Origins and Structures.* Toronto: Methuen
Limited.
1979a. Introduction. In Chambers J. K. (ed). *The Languages of Canada.*
Montréal: Didier Ltée, pp. 1–11.
1979b. Canadian English. In Chambers, J. K. (ed). *The Languages of Canada.*
Montréal: Didier Ltée pp. 169–204.
1980. Linguistic variation and Chomsky's 'homogeneous speech community'. In
Kinloch, A. M. and House, A. B. (eds). *Papers from the Fourth Annual*

Meeting of the Atlantic Provinces Linguistic Association. Fredericton: University of New Brunswick, pp. 1–32.

1981. The Americanization of Canadian raising. In Miller, M. F., Masek, C. S. and Hendrick, R. A., (eds.). *Parasession on Language and Behavior*. Chicago: Chicago Linguistic Society, pp. 20–35.

1984. Group and individual participation in a sound-change in progress. In Warkentyne (ed.), 1984, pp. 119–36.

1985. Three kinds of standard in Canadian English. In Lougheed (ed.), 1985, pp. 1–15.

Chambers, J. K. and Hardwick, Margaret F. 1986. Comparative sociolinguistics of a sound change in Canadian English. *English World-Wide* 7: 123–46.

Cichocki, Wladyslaw. 1986. Linguistic applications of dual scaling in variation studies. Unpublished PhD thesis, University of Toronto.

Clarke, Sandra. 1981. Dialect stereotyping in rural Newfoundland. In Pratt, T. K. (ed.). *Proceedings from the Fifth Annual Meeting of the Atlantic Provinces Association*. Charlottetown: University of Prince Edward Island, pp. 39–57.

1984a. Sociolinguistic variation in a small urban context: the St John's survey. In Warkentyne (ed.). 1984, pp. 143–53.

1984b. Role of linguistic feature types in dialect stereotyping. In Barnstead, J., Gesner, B. E., Gordon, W. T. and Holder, M. (eds.). *Papers from the Eighth Annual Meeting of the Atlantic Provinces Linguistic Association*. Halifax: Dalhousie University, pp. 19–32.

1985. Sociolinguistic patterning in a New-World dialect of Hiberno-English: the speech of St. John's, Newfoundland. Paper presented at the First Symposium on Hiberno-English, Dublin.

Clivio, Gianrenzo. 1976. The assimilation of English loan-words in Italo-Canadian. In Reich, P. A. (ed.). *The Second LACUS Forum*. Columbia, South Carolina: Hornbeam Press, pp. 584–9.

Colbourne, B. Wade. 1982. A sociolinguistic study of Long Island, Notre Dame Bay, Newfoundland. Unpublished MA thesis. Memorial University of Newfoundland.

Danesi, Marcel. 1985. Loanwords and Phonological Assimilation. *Studia Phonetica* 20. Ville LaSalle. PQ: Didier.

Davison, John 1987. On saying /aw/ in Victoria. In Avery, P. (ed). *Toronto Working Papers in Linguistics* 7. Toronto: Linguistics Graduate Course Union, University of Toronto, pp. 109–22.

DeWolf, Gaelan. 1984. Methods in statistical analysis of compatible data from two major Canadian urban sociolinguistic surveys. In Warkentyne (ed.) 1984, pp. 191–6.

Douaud, Patrick C. 1982. All mixed: Canadian Métis sociolinguistic patterns. *Sociolinguistic Working Paper* No. 10, Austin, TX: Southwest Educational Development Laboratory.

Emeneau, M. B. 1935. The dialect of Lunenburg, Nova Scotia. *Language* 11: 140–7. Reprinted in Chambers (ed.), 1975, pp. 34–9.

Emery, George. 1971. Negro English in Amber Valley, Alberta. In Darnell, R. (ed.), *Linguistic Diversity in Canadian Society*. Edmonton: Linguistic Research, Inc., pp.45-59.

Geikie, Rev. A. Constable. 1857. Canadian English. *Canadian Journal of Science. Literature and History* 2: 344–55.

Gleason, H. A., Jr. 1977. Church distribution as evidence for settlement patterns – Germans in the Niagara Peninsula. Paper presented at the East Lakes Division. Association of American Geographers.

Graham, Robert Somerville. 1957. The transition from German to English in the German settlements of Saskatchewan. *The Journal of the Canadian Linguistic Association* 3: 9–13.

Gregg, R. J. 1957a. Notes on the pronunciation of Canadian English as spoken in Vancouver, British Columbia. *The Journal of the Canadian Linguistic Association* 3:20–6.

1957b. Neutralisation and fusion of vocalic phonemes in Canadian English (Vancouver). *The Journal of the Canadian Linguistic Association* 3: 78–83.

1983. Local lexical items in the sociodialectical survey of Vancouver English. *Canadian Journal of Linguistics* 28: 17–23.

1984. Grammatical usage. In Warkentyne (ed.). 1984, pp. 179–84.

Gregg, R. J., Murdoch, Margaret, Hasebe-Ludt, Erika and DeWolf, Gaelan. 1981. An urban dialect survey of the English spoken in Vancouver. In Warkentyne, H. J. (ed). *Papers from the Fourth International Conference on Methods in Dialectology*. Victoria: University of Victoria, pp. 41–65.

Gregg, R. J., Murdoch, Margaret, DeWolf, Gaelan and Hasebe-Ludt, Erika 1984. The Vancouver survey: analysis and measurement. In Warkentyne (ed.). 1984, pp. 179–200.

Hultin, Neil C. 1967. Canadian views of American English. *American Speech* 42: 243–60.

Hung, Henrietta 1987. Canadian raising à la Montréalaise. In Avery, P. (ed.). *Toronto Working Papers in Linguistics* 7. Toronto: Linguistics Graduate Course Union, University of Toronto, pp. 123–39.

Jolly, Grace 1983. La codification de l'anglais canadien. In *La Norme linguistique*. Québec, pp. 731–62.

Joos, Martin. 1942. A phonological dilemma in Canadian English. *Language* 18: 141–4. Reprinted in Chambers (ed.), 1975, pp. 79–82.

Joy, Richard J. 1972. *Languages in Conflict:The Canadian Experience*. Carleton Library 61. Toronto: McClelland & Stewart Limited.

King, Ruth. 1978. Le parler français de l'Anse-à-canards/Maisons d'hiver. Unpublished MA thesis. Memorial University of Newfoundland.

1983. Variation and change in Newfoundland French: a sociodialectal study of clitic pronouns. Unpublished PhD thesis. Memorial University of Newfoundland.

Lachapelle, Réjean, and Henripin, Jacques 1982. *The Demolinguistic Situation in Canada: Past Trends and Future Prospects*. Montréal: The Institute for Research on Public Policy.,

Lambert, W. C., Hodgson, R. C. Gardner, R. C. and Fillenbaum, S. 1960. Evaluational reactions to spoken language. *Journal of Abnormal and Social Psychology* 60: 44–51.

Lieberson, Stanley 1965. Bilingualism in Montreal: a demographic analysis. *American Journal of Sociology* 71: 10–25. Reprinted in Dil, A. S. (ed.) 1981

Language of Diversity and Language Contact. Stanford, CA: Stanford University Press pp. 131–57.

1970. Linguistic and ethnic segregation in Montreal. *International Days of Sociolinguistics.* Rome: Instituto Luigi Sturzo, pp. 69–81. Reprinted as above, pp. 218–48.

Lougheed, W. C. (ed.). 1985. *In Search of the Standard in Canadian English.* Strathy Language Unit Occasional Papers No. 1. Kingston, Ont: Queen's University.

1988. *Writings on Canadian English 1976–1987: A Selective, Annotated Bibliography.* Strathy Language Unit Occasional Papers No. 2. Kingston, Ont: Queen's University.

McConnell, R. E. 1979. *Our Own Voice: Canadian English and How It is Studied.* Toronto: Gage Educational Publishing.

Mougeon, Raymond 1977. French language replacement and mixed marriages: the case of the francophone minority in Welland, Ontario. *Anthropological Linguistics* 19: 368–77.

Mougeon, Raymond, Brent-Palmer, Cora. Bélanger, Monique. and Cichocki Wladyslaw 1980. *Le français parlé en situation minoritaire,* Vol. 1 Toronto: Ontario Ministry of Education.

Mougeon, Raymond, Beniak, Edouard and Bélanger, Monique. 1982. Morphologie et évolution des pronoms déterminatifs dans le français parlé à Welland. *Canadian Journal of Linguistics* 27: 1–22.

Murdoch, Margaret 1984. A proposal for standardization of computer coding systems in linguistic surveys. In Warkentyne (ed.) 1984, pp. 185–90.

O'Grady, William and Dobrovolsky, Michael. 1987. *Contemporary Linguistic Analysis:An Introduction.* Toronto: Copp. Clark Pitman.

Paddock, Harold J. 1974. Some variations in the phonology and grammar of Newfoundland English. Ms.

Poplack, Shana. 1984. Contrasting patterns of code-switching in two communities. In Warkentyne (ed.). 1984, pp. 363–85.

Pratt, T. K. 1982. 'I dwell in possibility': variable (ay) in Prince Edward Island. *Journal of the Atlantic Provinces Linguistic Association* 4: 27–35.

Priestley, F. E. L. 1951. Canadian English. In Partridge, E. and Clark, J. W. (eds.). *British and American English Since 1900.* London: Andrew Dakers. pp. 72–9.

Pringle, Ian. 1983. The concept of dialect and the study of Canadian English. *Queen's Quarterly* 90: 100–21. Reprinted in Allen, H. B. and Linn, M. D. (eds.). 1985, *Dialect and Language Variation.* New York: Academic Press, pp. 217–36.

1985a. The complexity of the concept of standard. In Lougheed (ed.) 1985, pp. 20–38.

1985b. Attitudes to Canadian English. In Greenbaum, Sidney (ed.). *The English Language Today.* Oxford: Pergamon Institute of English, pp. 183–205.

Pringle, Ian and Padolsky, Enoch. 1983. The linguistic survey of the Ottawa Valley. *American Speech* 58: 325–44.

Pringle, Ian, Dale, R. H. and Padolsky, Enoch. 1984. Procedures to solve a methodological problem in the Ottawa Valley. In Warkentyne (ed.) 1984, pp. 477–94.

Reid, Gerald 1981. The sociolinguistic patterns of the Bay de Verde speech community. Unpublished MPhil thesis, Memorial University of Newfoundland.

Scargill, M. H. and Penner, P. G. 1966. *Looking at Language: Essays in Introductory Linguistics.* Toronto: W. J. Gage Limited.

Scott, S. Osborne and Mulligan, D. A. 1951. The Red River dialect. *The Beaver* 282: 42–5. Part I, by Scott, reprinted in Chambers (ed.) 1975, pp. 61–63.

Seary, E. R., Story, G. M. and Kirwin, W. 1968. *The Avalon Peninsula of Newfoundland: an Ethno-Linguistic Study.* Bulletin 219, Anthropological Series 81. Ottawa: National Museum of Canada.

Secretary of State 1985. *The Canadian Style: A Guide to Writing and Editing.* Toronto: Dundurn Press.

Stewart, Walter. 1985. *True Blue: The Loyalist Legend.* Toronto: Collins.

Stobie, Margaret. 1967–68. Backgrounds of the dialect called Bungi. *Historical and Scientific Society of Manitoba – Transactions,* Series III. No. 24: 65–75.

Story, G. M. 1965. Newfoundland dialect: an historical view. *Canadian Geographical Journal* 70: 127–31. Reprinted in Chambers (ed.) 1975, pp. 19–24.

Story, G. M. Kirwin, W. J. and Widdowson, J. D. A. 1982. *The Dictionary of Newfoundland English.* Toronto: University of Toronto Press.

Wardhaugh, Ronald. 1983. *Language and Nationhood: The Canadian Experience.* Vancouver: New Star Books.

Warkentyne, H. J. 1983. Attitudes and language behaviour. *Canadian Journal of Linguistics* 28: 71–6.

(ed.). 1984. *Papers from the Fifth International Conference on Methods in Dialectology.* Victoria, British Columbia: University of Victoria.

Wilson, H. Rex. 1958. The dialect of Lunenburg County. Unpublished PhD thesis, University of Michigan.

1975. Lunenburg Dutch: fact and folklore. In Chambers (ed.) 1975, pp. 40–44.

Woods, Howard B. 1979. A socio-dialectal survey of the English spoken in Ottawa: a study of the sociological and stylistic variation in Canadian English. Unpublished PhD thesis, University of British Columbia.

1985. Variation in English as a second language in Canada. In Lougheed (ed.) 1985, pp. 139–51.

7

Phonological variation and recent language change in St John's English

SANDRA CLARKE

Introduction

Newfoundland English

The English spoken in Newfoundland has long been recognised as a distinct variety of North American English (see, for example, Bailey 1982: 163; Chambers, this volume). Unlike much of the rest of eastern Canada, Newfoundland received little if any settlement of United Empire Loyalists from the eastern United States in the post-revolutionary period. Rather, most present-day Newfoundlanders are the descendants of immigrants from two highly concentrated areas in the British Isles: southwest England (particularly the counties of Dorset, Devon, Somerset and Hampshire – see Handcock 1977) and southeast Ireland (especially the counties of Waterford, Wexford, Kilkenny, Tipperary and Cork – see Mannion 1977a). While the beginnings of permanent settlement in Newfoundland can be traced back to the early seventeenth century, the peak period of immigration to the island came two centuries later; Irish immigration was particularly high in the periods 1811–1816 and 1825–1833 (Mannion 1977a: 7).

Within Newfoundland, the Irish were to settle primarily on the Avalon peninsula, south of the present-day capital, St John's (see figure 7.1). Much of the remainder of the long coastline of the island was inhabited by those of West Country English stock. As a result of sparse overall settlement, as well as the lack of inland transportation links until well into the present century, many of the small fishing communities or outports that dotted the coast remained fairly isolated from the outside world; some remain so even today.

The relative geographical isolation of Newfoundland has had obvious linguistic repercussions. By comparison to much of mainland North America, Newfoundland constitutes a linguistic relic area. Thus, most communities outside the Avalon peninsula have preserved to this day, to

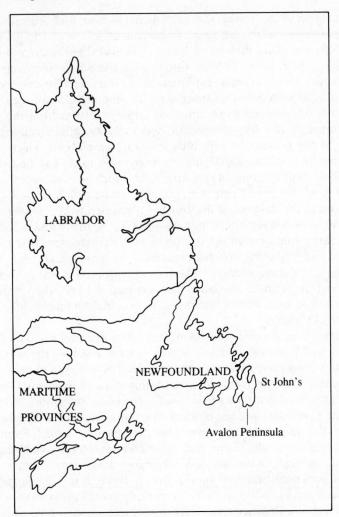

Figure 7.1   St John's

differing degrees, phonological, grammatical and lexical features characteristic of various West Country dialects.[1] The Irish communities of the
southern Avalon peninsula of Newfoundland have likewise preserved
many features of the speech of the homeland. Among the phonological
traits of southern Hiberno-English origin still found in Newfoundland are
'clear' or fronted variants of post-vocalic /l/, as in *pill* or *pull*; a slit fricative
pronunciation of post-vocalic, non-preconsonantal /t/ in words such as *bit*
or *pity* (cf. Wells 1982: 429–30); lowered and monophthongal variants of
the tense mid vowels /e/ and /o/, as in *made* or *go*; a rounded and retracted

pronunciation of the vowel /ʌ/ in such words as *strut*; and neutralisation of the oppositions /ɔɪ/ vs. /aɪ/ (e.g., *toy/tie*), and /or/ vs. /ɑr/ (e.g., *port* vs. *part*). Newfoundland dialects of Irish origin also share with local dialects which have their source in West Country English an alveolar stop variant as by far the most common realisation of the interdental fricatives /θ/ and /ð/, leading to such pronunciations as *tin* for *thin*, and *den* for *then*.

If much of Newfoundland remained largely isolated from the outside world through the late nineteenth and early twentieth centuries, the middle of the present century brought two major events which were to transform its political, social and economic structure. The first of these was World War II, one of the effects of which was to vastly increase contact with mainland North America. The strategic importance of Newfoundland in the defence of the North Atlantic led to the construction of both Canadian and American military bases on the island and in Labrador; the resulting employment opportunities hastened the developing urbanisation by contributing to the movement in population from smaller outports to the larger centres.[2] The second major event was of course the formal shift in political allegiance that occurred in 1949, when Newfoundland ceased to be a British dominion, to become the tenth and youngest province of Canada.

The increasing focus on mainland North America over the past 40 years has also had a major linguistic impact – most notably, the widespread diffusion within the province of the mainland North American standard. This has not stemmed from any great in-migration of mainland Canadians to the province, since Newfoundland's economic inferiority within the Canadian Confederation has ensured that out-migration of Newfoundlanders to the mainland far outweighs the reverse trend.[3] Even those Newfoundlanders who have had no direct interaction with mainland Canadians would, none the less, regularly come into contact with a General American standard speech variety through the dissemination of this speech model on the airwaves – especially via the nation-wide network of the Canadian Broadcasting Corporation, introduced to the province in 1949.

The speech of St John's

The largest city in the province, St John's, has a present-day population of approximately 162,000 in the metropolitan area; the 96,000 population of the city proper constitutes almost one-fifth of the entire Newfoundland and Labrador population of 568,000. The capital city lies on the northern periphery of the Irish-settled Avalon. Since through the nineteenth and early twentieth centuries St John's contained a somewhat higher proportion of residents of Irish than of English descent, the traditional standard accent of the city incorporates a number of features of Hiberno-English origin. The economic attraction which St John's would have held – particularly in the present century – for residents of small outports settled by the West Country English has proven to have some linguistic impact. Wessex initial /h/ deletion, for example, a non-standard feature which characterises the dialect spoken by many recent in-migrants, is highly stigmatised within the city as a sign of 'bayman' or outport speech.

The present-day linguistic situation in St John's suggests a speech community in a state of flux. Many older residents of the city exhibit obvious Irish phonological features that would clearly differentiate them from central Canadians of comparable age, while the speech patterns of certain teenage groups would be, to the untrained observer at least, virtually indistinguishable from those of teenagers in such major Canadian centres as Toronto or Vancouver. In short, the speech community of St John's offers an ideal laboratory in which to examine the sociolinguistic implementation of what appears to be a not inconsiderable amount of phonological change over the past 40 years. It is this which will be the focus of the following sections.

The St John's sociolinguistic study

The conclusions to be drawn in this paper are based on a sociolinguistic investigation of St John's (henceforth SJ) English, the data for which were collected in 1981–82. The study was conducted within a Labovian framework. It consisted of a series of approximately two-hour interviews designed to capture both casual or Free Conversation style (henceforth FC), as well as a range of formal reading styles, including the usual Minimal Pair List, Word List (WL), and connected Reading Passage (RP).[4] The study utilised a stratified random sample of 120 subjects representing four social variables: age, sex, socioeconomic status (SES), and religion.[5] This sample is represented in table 7.1.

Data collected in the SJ investigation were quantified as to relative frequency of use of individual linguistic features on the part of each of the 120 subjects.[6] In order to determine whether significant linguistic differences existed among the various social groups represented in the study, subject means were treated via the statistical test known as analysis of variance, using the ANOVA subroutine of the Statistical Package for the Social Sciences (SPSS). Results presented in this paper are based on a $4 \times 2 \times 5 \times 2$ Anova design (Age $\times$ Sex $\times$ SES $\times$ Religion).

In addition to presenting empirical evidence in support of the hypothesis that SJ speech is undergoing considerable phonological change in the direction of Canadian English (CE) heteronomy, this paper will also address the broader issue of the social implementation of phonological change in the SJ speech community. The literature dealing with sociolinguistic variation in urban centres in the western world has been remarkably

Table 7.1. *The 120-subject St John's sample*

By age group		By sex		By religion	
15–19	29	Male	64	Roman Catholic	62
20–34	32	Female	56	Protestant	58
35–54	32				
55 and over	27				

By socioeconomic index

Group 1	22	(SES score of 0–10) – 'Upper' class
Group 2	27	(SES score of 11–15) – 'Upper Middle' class
Group 3	31	(SES score of 16–20) – 'Middle' class
Group 4	28	(SES score of 21–25) – 'Lower Middle' class
Group 5	12	(SES score of 26–30) – 'Working' class

consistent in its findings. In spite of some evidence to the contrary (e.g., Feagin 1979, Nichols 1983), females have typically proven to use more standard linguistic features than do males of corresponding social status. In the SJ context, then, there is reason to hypothesise that females rather than males are in the vanguard when it comes to the adoption of CE variants. Socioeconomic stratificational patterns associated with the implementation of language change also tend to be fairly consistent. Labov (1981) suggests that, in the early and middle stages of linguistic change, socioeconomically intermediate groups are more advanced than are peripheral groups, whether upper or lower classes. It will be of interest to determine whether, in the SJ speech community, it is in fact the middle classes who are spearheading the drive towards the adoption of the CE norm.

Since the methodology used is not the most appropriate one for the investigation of grammatical features,[7] the SJ study has focused on some 20 phonological variables. In the following sections, a representative selection of these will be discussed.

Results

Language change in apparent time

Statistical analysis reveals that, of the four social variables examined in the SJ study, age is by far the most important. Indeed, for every one of the phonological variables examined, age is the only factor for which significant differences in language use are evident in the 120-subject sample, in at least one style. Thus the earlier-noted impression of fairly rapid phonological change in SJ speech is given empirical support by the present study.

As anticipated, the pattern of age stratification which emerges reflects a general tendency among younger generations of city residents to replace local pronunciations with variants which more closely resemble the CE norm. Without exception, all the local Irish features noted in the Introduction, above, are affected by this trend. Two of these features – the use of a clear variant of post-vocalic (1), and a monophthongal variant of (o) – are represented in figures 7.2 and 7.3 in terms of their relative frequency of use in three speech styles.[8] Both displays indicate a substantial usage difference between the members of the sample aged 55 and over and the two younger age groups – that is, between those who were adults or young adults by the beginning of World War II, on the one hand, and, on the other, city residents who are members of the post-war and post-Confederation generations. For both variables, the usage of the 35-54-year-old group constitutes a transition between older and younger group usage.

The role of gender and socioeconomic status in the implementation of phonological change

As suggested above, change within the SJ speech community in the direction of CE heteronomy may be expected to be more advanced among females than males, and among the middle classes rather than those classes occupying the extremities of the socioeconomic hierarchy. It follows, then, that the greatest amount of local (or, from the CE perspective, nonstandard) variant retention may be expected to be found not simply among older residents of the city, but also among SJ males, as well as among those lower on the socioeconomic scale.

Quantitative analysis proves this to be the case. What emerges is a fairly consistent pattern: local features characteristic of older age groups, and increasingly infrequent among the young, also typically display gender stratification, which is often accompanied by SES stratification. An outline of major trends follows.

Linguistic conservatism among older males The gender stratification exhibited by several features of SJ English that are age-stratified seems to have as its source the linguistic behaviour of the two older groups of males investigated in the sample, particularly males aged 55 and over. In brief, males who grew up in SJ prior to World War II seem to have been considerably less affected by the CE norm than have females who grew up in the same period.

While older males exhibit a high local variant retention rate with respect to many of the linguistic features examined in the SJ investigation, this

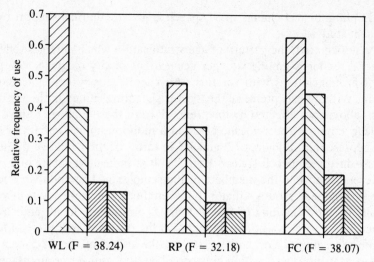

Figure 7.2   Clear (l) use by age group. ▨ = 55+; ▧ = 35−54; ▨ = 20−34; ▨ = 15−19. ($p < 0.001$, df = $\frac{3}{83}$).

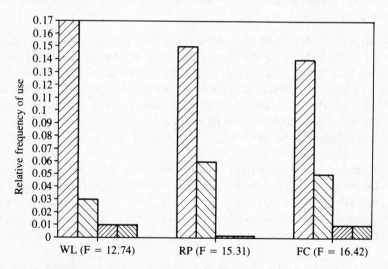

Figure 7.3   Monophthongal (o) by age group in 3 speech styles. ▨ = 55+; ▧ = 35−54; ▨ = 20−34; ▨ = 15−19. ($p < 0.001$, df = $\frac{3}{83}$).

appears most evident in the case of local non-standard vowel pronunciations – among them, monophthongal variants of tense mid (e) and (o),
retracted and rounded pronunciations of (ʌ), and unrounded variants of
the nucleus of the (ɔɪ) diphthong. An example is provided in figure 7.4,
which represents a monophthongal or steady pronunciation of the vowel

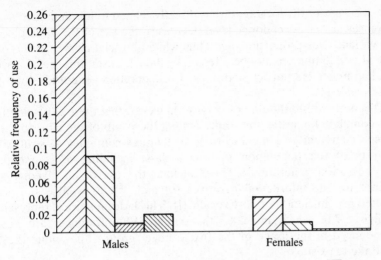

Figure 7.4 Monophthongal (o), age by sex in casual (FC) speech style 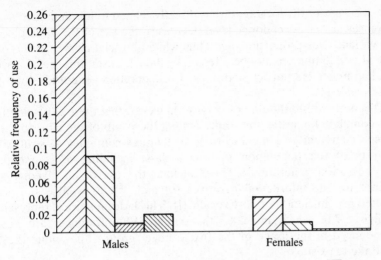 = 55+; = 35−54; = 20−34; = 15−19. ($p < 0.001$, F = 9.37, df = $\frac{3}{83}$).

(o), in terms of its casual speech style use by males and females in each of the four age groups. As the figure demonstrates, males aged 55 and over – followed by males in the 35 to 54 age group – are by far the greatest users of the monophthongal variant. Females of all age levels, on the other hand, make very little use of the local feature. Indeed, it seems to have fully disappeared among the two youngest female groups.

In short, there is considerable evidence from the SJ study to indicate that while males tend to favour local speech norms, females are quicker to embrace the external standard variety.[9] It is interesting that exactly the same tendency has been noted in at least one sociolinguistic study conducted in a small rural Newfoundland community (Colbourne 1982).

Markers of socioeconomic status The vowel features noted above play more of a role in the present-day SJ speech community as age and gender markers than as markers of SES. Nonetheless, they also display obvious links with social class.

The picture that emerges, however, is not that of a simple correlation between local non-standard variant usage and lower social classes. For most of these variables there are interactions between social class and age. An example is provided in Figure 7.5, which again represents the local monophthongal variant of (o) in casual speech style; here, relative frequencies of use are presented in terms of both subject age and socioeconomic level.[10] What is striking is that the monophthongal pronunciation occurs very rarely among members of the two younger age groups, no matter what their socioeconomic status. Among the two older groups, however, use of the local feature is directly related to age and SES: as age increases and socioeconomic level decreases, the use of the monophthongal variant rises proportionally. Thus while all social classes of the postwar SJ population seem to be affected by the CE norm, this speech variety has had much less impact among pre-Confederation generations of lower class speakers.

This observation should not suggest, however, that there exists anything like complete linguistic uniformity among the youth of the city. In the SJ speech community, a number of local features continues to stratify the entirety of the population by social class, including of course post-Confederation generations. These include the use of an alveolar stop variant for the interdental fricatives (θ) and (ð), as well as the clear, fronted pronunciation of post-vocalic (l). This latter feature is represented in figure 7.6, which indicates that while SES differences are not as pronounced in the usage of the two younger groups, they none the less continue to exist.

Incipient shifts in SJ speech The previous sections have shown that, in the SJ context, loyalty to the vernacular norm is most evident among older speakers, males, and lower social strata. While the obvious inference may be that the spread of the CE standard within the SJ speech community bears close links not only with age but also with gender and social class, such links require empirical confirmation. This can best be provided by examining what appear to be very recent linguistic innovations in SJ speech.

During the course of the investigation, several features of vowel pronunciation were noted which through their profile in apparent time suggest the recent incursion of the perceived mainland Canadian norm. One of these involves the pronunciation of the low front vowel (æ) in words such as *trap* or *back*. Newfoundlanders characteristically use a more raised variant of this vowel than do their central Canadian counterparts. Indeed, an [æ⊥]-like pronunciation that to central Canadian ears would appear raised and somewhat fronted characterises the two older age groups of the sample, particularly in formal speech styles.[11] Younger groups, however, use a greater proportion of a lowered and slightly retracted [æ⊤] or [æ⊢] pronunciation, one more closely approximating the CE variant (0.08 for the teenagers in casual speech style, as opposed to 0.04 for the other groups; $p = 0.10$).

The extent to which (æ) is lowered and retracted is not simply a function of age in SJ speech, however, but also has close links to SES level and gender. Figure 7.7 provides a Sex × SES breakdown of the mean usage of this variant in casual and formal speech styles. In all three styles, it is upper class females who make by far the greatest use of the CE-like pronunciation.

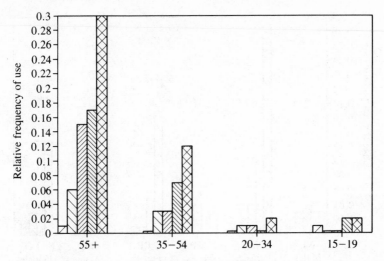

Figure 7.5   Monophthongal (o), age by SES in casual (FC) speech style. ▨ = SES1; ▨ = SES2; ▨ = SES3; ▨ = SES4; ▧ = SES5. ($p < 0.05$, F $= 2.06$, df $= \frac{12}{83}$).

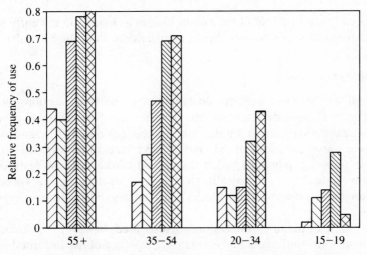

Figure 7.6   Clear (l) use, age by SES in casual (FC) speech style ▨ = SES1; ▨ = SES2; ▨ = SES3; ▨ = SES4; ▧ = SES5. (Not significant; $p = 0.11$).

Females of the upper classes play a similar role with respect to other incipient linguistic changes favouring the adoption of perceived mainland Canadian features, among them the centralisation of the mid and high back vowels, as well as the fronting of the nucleus of the (au) diphthong (concerning this latter change in CE, see Chambers, this volume). Thus

SANDRA CLARKE

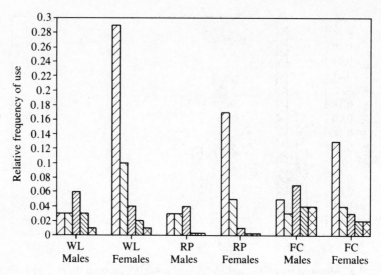

Figure 7.7   Lowered (æ) use, sex by SES in 3 speech styles. ⧄ = SES1;
⧅ = SES2; ⧄ = SES3; ⧅ = SES4; ⧈ = SES5.

the usually attested role of the middle classes as leaders in the early stages
of language change does not appear at all evident from the SJ study.

Stylistic stratification

Several of the local variants documented in previous sections do not
display much stylistic stratification. In other words, features like monophthongal pronunciation of the mid vowels (e) and (o), rounded and
retracted pronunciations of (ʌ), and clear variants of (l) have the stylistic
profile of social indicators rather than social markers. These features are
socially rather than stylistically stratified, characterising the speech of
certain social groups within the city, particularly older and working-class
males.

For some of the linguistic features investigated, however – including the
incipient shifts outlined above – relative frequency of use in formal versus
informal styles is particularly illuminating in clarifying the spread of
standard CE features within the SJ speech community. While the study
has confirmed the general impression of fairly rapid phonological change
in SJ English, stylistic profiles suggest that local features are not in fact
disappearing as rapidly as might be surmised. While a number of standard
CE features characterise the speech of younger rather than older generations of community residents, what is extremely interesting is that such
features differentiate age groups more extensively in formal than in casual
speech styles. For certain variables, in fact, the speech behaviour of

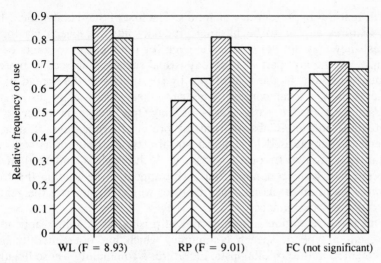

Figure 7.8   Interdental (ð) by age group in 3 speech styles. ⊿ = 55+;
⧄ = 35–54; ⧄ = 20–34; ⧄ = 15–19. ($p < 0.001$, df = $\frac{3}{83}$).

younger generations may not differ significantly from that of older
genertions in casual speech, but simply in formal style. An example is
provided in figure 7.8, which represents the use of a standard, interdental
fricative variant of (ð) in three speech styles, on the part of the four age
groups of the sample.

   In short, while CE features are obviously spreading among SJ youth,
they may not as yet be firmly entrenched as part of the casual speech
norm. Rather, younger groups have become fairly adept at code-switching,
incorporating CE features into their formal, more conscious, speech styles.
There is evidence that this pattern of stylistic diffusion of standard
linguistic variables is not unique to St John's; an analogous situation has
been documented in the rural Newfoundland context (Colbourne 1982).

Conclusion

This paper has shown that, as expected, the SJ speech community exhibits
a considerable amount of ongoing phonological change, in the general
direction of the CE speech model. In fact, the speech of post-Confederation generations differs significantly from that of pre-Confederation generations with respect to most of the phonological features traditionally
associated with SJ speech.

   In spite of the marked tendency to CE heteronomy, there is none the
less a substantial indication that SJ English will retain its distinct phonological identity for some time to come. There are two basic pieces of
evidence to justify this conclusion, both indicating restrictions on the use

of CE features in present-day St John's. The first of these is stylistic. Many CE features appear to be filtering gradually into SJ speech via formal styles; they may not yet constitute, even for the teenage speakers of the sample, an integral part of everyday casual speech. The second piece of evidence pertains to the role played by social class in the spread of CE features in the local context. The curvilinear social class distribution characteristic of the early stages of language change in other urban contexts is noticeably absent from the present investigation. Rather, SJ speech is characterised by a linear social class distribution as well as a linear age profile. In other words, it is the highest rather than the intermediate socioeconomic groups who appear to be leading the trend towards adoption of phonological features which characterise the general North American standard.

This last observation is perhaps not surprising, as St John's appears to represent a type of speech community which has not generally been documented in the sociolinguistic literature: a community whose linguistic standard is being defined in terms of an external norm. Given the socioeconomic inferiority traditionally experienced by Newfoundland/ Labrador, it is not surprising that the most upwardly mobile segment of its principal city would be the upper classes, or those who are most aware of the value of the standard CE speech variety. The SJ study clearly suggests that, in certain contexts, social classes other than intermediate ones may play a major role in phonological change. In light of the linguistic behaviour of the upper classes of St John's, it is obvious that hypotheses concerning the sociolinguistic implementation of language change must be considerably broadened.

NOTES

The St John's English investigation was supported by grants 410-81-0386 and 410-83-0351 from the Social Sciences and Humanities Research Council of Canada. I am also grateful to the Institute of Social and Economic Research of Memorial University for its financial support. Special thanks must be extended to John Porter, who was responsible for the phonetic transcription, as well as to Robert Hollett, Margot French, Winnifred Flynn, and Philip Hiscock, all of whom participated extensively in the project.
1. Phonological features include (variable) word-initial fricative voicing, as in the pronunciation of *fir* as *vir*/*var*; word-final consonant cluster simplification; non-standard initial /h/ patterning; steady or monophthongal variants of the tense mid vowels /e/ and /o/ in such words as *made* or *goat*; and a tendency to neutralise each of the following pairs of vocalic oppositions: /ɪ/ and /ɛ/ (e.g., *pin* vs. *pen*), /or/ and /ar/ (e.g., *port* vs. *part*), /er/ and /ir/ (e.g., *bear* vs. *beer*), /or/ and /ur/ (e.g., *pore* vs. *poor*).
2. It is estimated that during the war period, one-quarter of the Newfoundland

population came into direct contact with foreign military personnel, the number of which prior to the end of the war was equivalent to almost one tenth of Newfoundland's population of 322,000(MacLeod 1986).

3. 1901 census figures show that less than 2 per cent of the population was foreign-born; in 1945, that figure had declined to just over 1 per cent. According to the 1981 census, some 93 per cent of the Newfoundland population was actually born in the province.

4. This paper will provide results for a maximum of three stylistic levels: FC, WL and RP. As in several other sociolinguistic investigations – among them Woods (1979), Milroy (1980), and Davis (1983) – the Reading Passage proved a somewhat unreliable device for eliciting a stylistic level intermediate between FC and WL styles.

5. Religion was included since it constitutes one of the most reliable indicators in Newfoundland of Irish versus English ethnic background (cf. Handcock 1977: 24; Mannion 1977a: 7). The five SES groups used in the investigation were based on an SES index containing independent scores for each of the factors of occupation, income, father's occupation, education and housing. For further details, see Clarke (1985).

6. In each case, a decimal score or mean was obtained, representing the ratio of actual use of a given variant to total use of all variants of the linguistic variable of which it forms part. The total number of tokens of any variant reported on in this paper ranges, per style, from a minimum of approximately 1,000 to a high of approximately 10,000.

7. The fairly low frequencies of occurrence of grammatical variables yielded by interviews of this type have been noted by, among others, Cheshire (1982: 28).

8. The relatively flat stylistic profile exhibited by these variables indicates a lack of stylistic stratification. This will be touched on later in this paper.

9. None the less, older SJ females proved more linguistically conservative than older males in the case of several features associated not with CE, but with the standard British speech model, which commands considerable prestige in the Newfoundland context (see Clarke 1982). These features include retention of a voiceless non-flapped variant of intervocalic (t), and maintenance of +glide pronunciations in words like *new* or *tune*.

10. For an interpretation of the five socioeconomic groups (SES1-SES5) in terms of corresponding social class, see table 7.1.

11. Mean or average use of the fronted local variant of (æ) in WL style is 0.49 for the 55 and over group, 0.50 for the 35–54-year-olds, 0.36 for the 20–34 age group, and 0.30 for the teenagers ($p = 0.001$, $F = 5.97$, df = 3/83).

REFERENCES

Bailey, R. W. 1982. The English language in Canada. In Bailey and Görlach (eds.) 1982, pp. 134–76.

Bailey, R. W. and Görlach, M. (eds.). 1982. *English as a World Language*. Ann Arbor: University of Michigan Press.

Cheshire, J. 1982. *Variation in an English Dialect. A Sociolinguistic Study.* Cambridge: Cambridge University Press.

Clarke, S. 1982. Sampling attitudes to dialect varieties in St John's. In Paddock, (ed.) 1982, pp. 90–105.

   1985. Sociolinguistic variation in a small urban context: the St John's survey. In Warkentyne (ed.) 1985, pp. 143–53.

Colbourne, B. W. 1982. A Sociolinguistic Study of Long Island, Notre Dame Bay, Newfoundland. Unpublished MA, thesis, Memorial University of Newfoundland.

Davis, L. M. 1983. The elicitation of contextual styles in language: a reassessment. *Journal of English Linguistics* 16: 18–26.

Feagin, C. 1979. *Variation and Change in Alabama English.* Washington DC: Georgetown University Press.

Handcock, G. 1977. English migration to Newfoundland. In Mannion J. (ed.). 1977b, pp. 15-48.

Labov, W. 1981. What can be learned about change in progress from synchronic description? In Sankoff and Cedergren (eds.). 1981, pp. 177–99.

MacLeod, M. 1986. *Peace of the Continent, The Impact of Second World War Canadian and American Bases in Newfoundland.* St John's, Nfld: Harry Cuff Publications Ltd.

Mannion, J. J. 1977a. Introduction. In Mannion (1977b). 1–13.

   (ed.) 1977b. *The Peopling of Newfoundland. Essays in Historical Geography.* St John's, Nfld: Institute of Social and Economic Research, Memorial University.

Milroy, L. 1980. *Language and Social Networks.* Oxford: Basil Blackwell.

Nichols, P. 1983. Linguistic options and choices for black women in the rural south. In Thorne, Kramarae and Henley (eds.) 1983, pp. 54–68.

Paddock, H. (ed.) 1982. *Languages in Newfoundland and Labrador,* 2nd edn. St John's: Memorial University of Newfoundland.

Sankoff, D. and Cedergren, H. (eds.) 1981. *Variation Omnibus.* Edmonton, Alberta: Linguistic Research, Inc.

Thorne, B., Kramarae, C. and Henley, N. (eds.). 1983. *Language, Gender and Society.* Rowley MA: Newbury House.

Warkentyne, H. J. (ed.). 1985. *Papers from the 5th International Conference on Methods in Dialectology.* Victoria, British Columbia: University of Victoria.

Wells, J. C. 1982. *Accents of English.* Vol. 2. Cambridge: Cambridge University Press.

Woods, H. 1979. A Socio-dialectology Survey of the English Spoken in Ottawa: A Study of Sociological and Stylistic Variation in Canadian English. Unpublished PhD thesis, University of British Columbia.

8

Sociophonetic variation in Vancouver

JOHN H. ESLING

This study of Vancouver English using instrumental procedures suggests the following sociophonetic generalisations: (1) the speech of men and women differs systematically in the particular vowels that function as social indicators, (2) individual vowels differ systematically in quality between working class speech and middle class speech, (3) class-based differences in vowel quality are realised as superimposed secondary articulations representing prosodic shifts in vocalic phonology, (4) class-based differences in speech extend to consonant articulation as an acoustic result of choice of habitual voice setting, and (5) subtle shifts in voice setting, which affect the acoustic realisation of vowel and consonant articulations, function as salient social indicators and potential markers of style.

English in Vancouver is consistent with the general characteristics of heartland Canadian English as far as the urbanised and relatively uniform social structure of its anglophone residents is concerned (Chambers 1979: 190). There is considerable representation of other varieties of English as well as other languages including German, Cantonese, Punjabi and Vietnamese, to the extent that up to 40–50 per cent of students in many school districts do not speak English as a first language. Varieties of English from the British Isles are in strong evidence and play a large role in the way people in Vancouver think about speech and its prestige value. The status of English as a second language also holds a place in how people think about language, in social interaction and in political rhetoric. The dynamics of social interaction within a varied population implies that performance in spoken language varies according to context of situation, and that perceptions of people based on their speech depend on many more factors than just the relationship of their speech to a single standard model. These are all fruitful areas for sociolinguistic exploration. This case study, however, examines only the speech of Vancouverites born and raised in the greater urban area who are native speakers of Canadian English.

The instrumental investigation of variation within the community focuses on a single context in an interview setting. Data are excerpted from the records of the Survey of Vancouver English (Gregg *et al*. 1981, 1985), which includes extensive interviews with 240 subjects randomly selected from the Greater Vancouver Directory. Subjects in the survey are divided into three age groups: 16–35, 36–60, and over 60 at the time of selection (1979–81). In this study, only the youngest age group is examined, which includes 80 men and women born between 1946 and 1963.

Subjects in the original survey are divided into four socioeconomic status divisions according to indices developed using Murdoch's 1979 Index of Social Stratification based on subject's occupation, father's occupation, education, income, residential location and housing type (Gregg *et al*. 1981). Scores for occupations rely on Blishen and McRoberts' (1976) socioeconomic indexing scale. For the purposes of the present study, these groups are termed (1) MWC, middle working class, (2) UWC, upper working class, (3) LMC, lower middle class, (4) MMC, middle middle class. Individual subjects represent the extremes of the social scale, but this sampling probably best reflects a middle range of society. Original survey cells each contain ten speakers. Because of poor quality or local interference during recording, two speakers from each cell had to be excluded, leaving eight subjects in each cell with acceptable speech for acoustic measurements, 32 females and 32 males. Comparisons of vowels across the four socioeconomic status groups sample some 600 female and 600 male vowels.

The immediate objective of this study is to determine whether vowels of Vancouver English are articulated differently as a function of socioeconomic status, given comparable contexts of speaking and identical vowel tokens within those contexts. A theoretical objective is to identify phonetically the acoustic shifts between socioeconomic status groups in order to describe the function of long-term habitual voice settings as social indicators.

Social indicators in men's and women's speech

Normally, in comparing vowels as phonological variables in the socially stratified speech of a community, variants are counted to arrive at either an index for each social group collectively (Trudgill 1974) or a set of relative frequencies on an individual subject basis (Clarke 1985). In the present study, phonological items from identical text and linguistic environments in story-reading style are examined for each of the ten vowels of Canadian English (i.e. excluding diphthongs and /ər/), and compared acoustically to identify the pattern of phonetic variation separating the four social groups for both men's and women's speech.[1]

Results suggest that the speech of men and women differs systematically in the individual vowels which function as social indicators. All ten vowels are significantly differentiated across the four socioeconomic status (SES) divisions of the Survey of Vancouver English for female subjects in the 16–35 age range. Individual vowels of male subjects demonstrate less separation of the four SES groups than female subjects' vowels. Considering female subjects' vowels in each SES group collectively reveals a distinct pattern of acoustic shift in vowel quality. Male subjects' vowels taken collectively parallel this pattern, especially in the case of UWC and MMC groups, but to a less significant degree.

The difference in vowel quality separating SES groups is illustrated in figure 8.1 for female subjects on the articulatorily oriented formant chart. Each group's vowel system can be identified with a separate corner of the two-dimensional vowel space. Some vowel classes are particularly susceptible to this systematic shift, while other vowel classes change comparatively little from one SES group to another.[2] In general, MWC vowels have high F1, low F2 values, UWC vowels have low F1,F2 values, LMC vowels have low F1, high F2 values, and MMC vowels have high F1,F2 values. Individual vowels, however, differ in their degree of separation. For example, female speech and male speech both differentiate the central vowel /ʌ/ as a social indicator, but while female speakers differentiate /e/ /i/ and /o/, these vowels do not alter significantly for male speakers of different SES groups. Furthermore, while male speakers differ in their production of /ɑ/, this vowel is not a social indicator for female speakers.

The rank order of vowels which best indicate social status in female speech differs considerably from the order of vowels that function as social indicators in male speech.[3]

> Female rank order: /ʊ e ɛ ʌ i o æ u ɪ ɑ/
> Male rank order: /ɛ ɪ ʌ ɑ æ u ʊ e o i/

There seems no obvious principle for the rank order of significantly differentiated vowels for female speakers, other than that some mid, front to central vowels tend to be better differentiated than some back or open vowels. UWC and MMC groups are successfully differentiated by all ten vowels individually. Even for MWC and LMC groups, the most difficult to differentiate, all ten vowels except /ɒ/, /ɪ/, /æ/ and /ʌ/ separate these two groups. On the whole, clusters of individual vowel classes behave in the same way as all vowels taken collectively, for female speakers. A possible interpretation of the relationship between male SES groups is that /i/ acts as a pivotal vowel, virtually identical in all four groups, and that tense vowels /e/ and /o/ also remain more or less constant while the

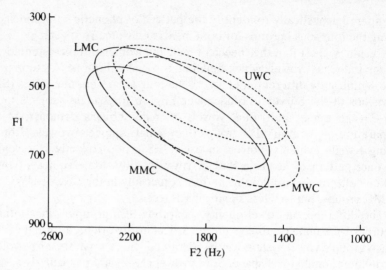

Figure 8.1   Generalised vowel quality shifts as SES indicators in Vancouver English:
female speech, 16–35 age group. MWC (– – –); UWC (-----); LMC (– –);
MMC (——).

majority of shifting to signal social status appears in half-open to open and
in front to central vowels: /ɪ ɛ ʌ æ ɑ/.

Systematic vowel quality shifts as SES indicators

The majority of individual vowels differ systematically in quality between
working class speech and middle class speech. The clearest class-based
distinction in vowel quality, for both males and females, occurs between
UWC pronunciation, characterised by lingual retraction and raising as in
velarisation, and MMC pronunciation, characterised by lingual fronting
and nasalisation. MWC vowel quality suggests lingual retraction and
lowering (laryngo-pharyngalisation) while LMC vowels are fronted and
raised (palatalised), although the separation of these two groups is less
obvious. These systematic shifts in vowel quality are more distinct in the
case of females (illustrated in fig. 8.1) than of males.

Articulatory identifications are based on the relationship between vowel
formant locations of SES groups and known values of model data.[4] In
general, individual vowel phoneme comparisons of UWC and MMC
speakers with velarised and nasalised models confirm rank orders of
susceptibility of phoneme classes to the shift from group to group. Vowels
at the top of the order as male social indicators are identified as velarised
for UWC speakers and nasal for MMC speakers, whereas vowels lower in
the order do not demonstrate these clear distinctions. In any case, larger

samples of individual vowels from additional speaking styles are needed to support articulatory associations.

These findings introduce some interesting and unexpected comparisons with the vowel systems of other varieties of English. For instance, collective vowel systems of a WC Vancouver accent and a sample of Houston English are both associated with a tongue-retracted, velarised setting. The southern US variety, represented by 14 black, male community college students, all natives of urban Houston recorded in reading style in 1984 (Esling and Dickson 1985: 159–60), is acoustically similar to WC Vancouver vowels but not to MC Vancouver vowels.[5] The auditorily predicted difference between the southern states accent and the Canadian accent, therefore, appears only in the case of MC Vancouver English and not WC Vancouver English. This method of cross-dialect comparison introduces the possibility of identifying globally similar acoustic patterns despite obvious phonological divergence in vocalic inventory.

Relating vowel systems to voice setting

The consistent pattern of vowel quality shifts in figure 8.1 indicates that more than just individual vowels are involved in the phonological distinction separating and identifying social status. The systematic acoustic patterns observed for a majority of vowels imply the long-term, habitual or 'quasi-permanent' presence of auditory features or qualities that represent the voice setting level of phonetic description (Abercrombie 1967). The labels to describe habitual articulatory configuration (Honikman 1964), or voice setting (Laver 1980), that most appropriately identify the four SES divisions of the Vancouver survey are: laryngo-pharyngalised voice (MWC), velarised voice (UWC), palatalised voice (LMC), and nasal voice (MMC).

It is the uniformity of the vowel shifts separating SES groups in Vancouver which suggests strongly that these patterns can be related to long-term superimposed background settings. The motivation for considering voice setting originates with Abercrombie (1967: 89–95) who describes accent as not only a product of segmental articulatory gestures but also of dynamic and voice quality properties. It is the concept of voice quality as a voluntary, acquired, continually present secondary articulation or setting that lends itself to examination as a long-term feature and potential sociolinguistic variable.

Voice setting can be predicted to interact with vowels and consonants of a phonology so as to alter their acoustic values systematically in a given direction. The distinct directions of shift favoured by the different SES groups in Vancouver illustrate acoustically the contrasting articulatory settings described by Honikman (1964) to characterise variation in accent across languages. Figure 8.1, therefore, is interpreted to mean that class-based differences in vowel quality are realised as superimposed secondary articulations representing prosodic shifts in vocalic phonology.

Long-term average spectral (LTAS) analysis adds support to the argument that socially differentiated speech patterns result from generalised shifts in the configuration of the articulators.[6] For each of the 64 Vancouver subjects, spectra computed over 45 seconds of continuous reading represent the average vocal tract response of all voiced speech in the utterance. This technique captures not only the magnitudes of a speaker's vowels over time, which are the longest-duration, highest-energy components, but also the effect of consonantal voicing. Approximately 275 vowels in all positions of stress and 200 voiced consonants are represented in each LTAS (with 200 voiceless consonants being excluded in the present technique).

The long-term accent characteristics of female SES groups in Vancouver corroborate vocalic analyses in separating female UWC speech from MMC speech, as well as from MWC speech. The dominant LTAS contrast for male SES groups is also between UWC speakers and MMC speakers, with LMC and MMC groups also differentiated significantly. Articulatory interpretations of the distribution of first spectral peaks (P1,P2) parallel results of vowel formant analyses based on F1,F2. The linguistic behaviour of WC and MC social groups is therefore distinguished not only by a shift in the acoustic properties of a majority of vowels, but also by a parallel shift in long-term features of accent. This implies a difference at the level of voice setting, particularly between UWC and MMC SES groups for both female and male speech.

Social variation in consonantal articulation

Instrumental analysis of the Survey of Vancouver English also indicates that consonant articulation varies systematically to mark class-based divisions in speech. In the same way that vowels shift according to SES group, consonants differ in acoustic properties as a result of the generalised voice settings that characterise those groups. The choice of a given setting, therefore, is equivalent to introducing a habitual secondary articulation as a prosodic register which affects not only vocalic sounds but also consonantal quality.

LTAS analysis provides evidence that socially differentiated speech registers extend beyond the level of individual vowel classes. Articulatorily controlled models contrasting 12 voice quality settings are compared with Vancouver survey group spectra, confirming a number of the associations evident in vowel formant analyses. The phonetic principles of this system of voice analysis are described in Laver (1968, 1974, 1980) and applied in Esling (1978, 1981).[7] As before, associations between tongue-retracted

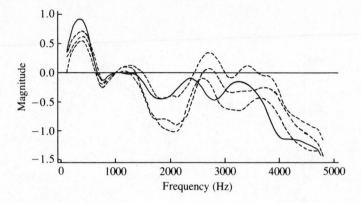

Figure 8.2 The male UWC group LTAS mean (——) parallels the LTAS characteristics of the velarised model (☰☰).

settings and the WC end of the SES scale and between nasal voice and the MC end of the scale are significant.

Velarisation and uvularisation characterise MWC and UWC groups, while palatalisation and nasal voice apply to the MMC group. Although these classifications do not identify degrees of fronting or backing as accurately as vowel formant mapping, they demonstrate that WC accents differ from MC accents in the influence of long-term setting on all voiced portions of speech. The LTAS displays in figure 8.2 compare the male UWC mean with controlled performances of three velarised model texts. The first two peaks of each spectrum (P1,P2) are analogous to the formant frequencies of a homorganic vowel to that setting, of a high back vowel, for example, in the case of velarised voice. Due to sample length, vowel reduction in varying positions of stress, and inclusion of voiced consonants, P1,P2 values are predictably lower in frequency than F1,F2 values of a corresponding vowel set.

The two-dimensional comparison of F1,F2 means and P1,P2 means in figure 8.3 represents graphically the directions of shift that characterise both the vowel systems and long-term speech of the four Vancouver SES groups. Only the relationship between LTAS of LMC and MWC groups is undifferentiated. Four corresponding model settings parallel SES group patterns of differentiation. While the added spectral information in long-term speech samples results in lower absolute frequencies, the relative orientation of models and SES groups is maintained. The most salient relationship between models and SES groups is the association of tongue-retracted settings (laryngo-pharyngalised and velarised voice) with WC accents and tongue-fronted (palatalised voice) and nasal settings with MC accents. Each SES group is distinguished by a single feature in the tongue height, front-back, or nasality dimension. Of methodological importance

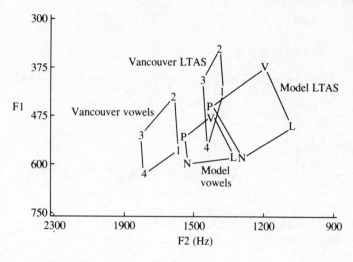

Figure 8.3   Combined male/female Vancouver survey SES groups are associated with four voice setting models. Vocalic and LTAS means: (1) MWC, (2) UWC, (3) LMC, (4) MMC; (L) laryngo-pharyngalised voice, (V) velarised voice, (P) palatalised voice, (N) nasal voice.

is that LTAS analysis appears as valid a measure of difference between groups as formant frequency information.

Conclusions

The results of this case study reveal that subtle shifts in voice setting, which affect the acoustic realisation of vowel and consonant articulations, function as salient social indicators. Vowels of Vancouver English, identical with respect to linguistic environment and spoken in a relatively formal story-reading context, contrast in quality to differentiate groups of young men and women according to socioeconomic status. This contrast governs a majority of vowel classes in each SES group, operating as a generalised acoustic shift. UWC and MMC groups realise the greatest contrast in vowel quality in both male and female speech, and all four SES divisions of the Survey of Vancouver English in the 16–35 age range contrast in direction of shift for female speakers. The contrast in voice setting can be thought of as the choice of a superimposed secondary articulation with its consequent effect on not only the vowels but also consonant articulations as they occur during speech. In this manner, the voice settings that have been identified for each SES group in Vancouver are also available to function as potential markers of style if members of one group were to adopt features of another group as a vehicle of accommodation. This possibility needs to be examined in further research.

The systematic single-feature shift in vowel quality that differentiates each class of speakers suggests that socially salient speech patterns are defined not only by selections of alternative phonological variants, but also by changes in voice setting. Phonetically, WC groups demonstrate acoustic characteristics of tongue retraction as a constant, background secondary articulation. MC speakers demonstrate tongue fronting or nasality as a habitual configuration or voice setting. Corresponding shifts in long-term speech characteristics, identified using long-term average spectral analysis which responds to differences in acoustic properties of voiced consonants as well as of vowels, support these conclusions.

Articulatorily, UWC Vancouver speakers' vowels and LTAS are associated with velarisation, while MMC speakers demonstrate lingual fronting and nasalisation. MWC vowels indicate more extreme, laryngo-pharyngalised retraction than their UWC counterparts as a habitual setting, while LMC vowels indicate palatalised fronting but little nasality. Not all vowels respond to a given background setting in the same way, so that those vowels that show greatest shift for female speakers are not the same vowels that show greatest shift across male groups. In other words, female speech differs from male speech in the particular vowels which are most susceptible as SES indicators. These associations can now be posited as tentative articulatory explanations of the voice setting component of accent in Vancouver English, and tested in further research procedures. The present results are a positive indication that sociophonetic variation in the speech of an urban community can be identified phonetically and differentiated socially at the long-term level of accent using both vowel formant analysis and LTAS analysis techniques.

NOTES

The cooperation and technical assistance of B. C. Dickson, J. Clayards, M. Doyle, M. Keating, and S. K. Wong are gratefully acknowledged. Appreciation is extended to R. J. Gregg, G. de Wolf and J. K. Chambers for their helpful comments and advice in the preparation of this report. This acoustic investigation of the Survey of Vancouver English was supported by grant No.410-85-0481 from the Social Sciences and Humanities Research Council of Canada.

1. Initial measurements of vowel formants are made using the ILS speech analysis system (Signal Technology 1983) on the PDP-11 minicomputer. Later corroboratory measurements are made with the Micro Speech Lab system developed in the Centre for Speech Technology Research at the University of Victoria on the IBM-PC microcomputer (Dickson 1985). Automatic ILS procedures compute first and second formant peaks (F1,F2) which are filed by group for statistical processing.
2. Principal component analysis and canonical discriminant analysis are used to

generate a between-class correlation matrix, giving a probability of relationship between sets of first and second formant (F1,F2) values. Using log-mean speaker normalisation, a scaling factor is applied to minimize the effects of individual speaker idiosyncrasies (Hindle 1978). A generalised squared distance measure computes percentages of F1,F2 coordinates located nearest each group centroid, classifying unknown test values into known reference groups.

3. To establish rank order, instances of significant separation of groups for the six-way pairings of the four groups for each vowel are summed at the $p < 0.001$, $p < 0.01$, and $p < 0.05$ significance levels, producing a count for each vowel where (6,6,6) is the highest possible score. At $p < 0.05$, 77 per cent of pairings of the ten vowels are socially distinct across female SES groups, and 62 per cent across male groups. The Spearman correlation coefficient relating male and female rank orders is negative (rho = -0.24), indicating that the two lists do not correlate, although there is a tendency for the orders to be negatively related.

4. The model-matching approach, assessed using generalised squared distance, compares phonetically controlled performances of contrasting voice settings on identical texts with survey group values (Esling and Dickson 1985: 163–66). Contingency tables indicate an association between UWC and MMC groups and the velarised and nasalised models, respectively: $\chi^2 = 30.53$ with 1 d.f., and $\chi^2 = 70.22$ with 3 d.f. including velarised, nasalised, laryngo-pharyngalised, and palatalised models ($p < 0.0001$).

5. MWC/UWC Vancouver vowels are associated statistically with the Houston sample vowels ($p < 0.82$; 68 per cent by generalised squared distance distribution). LMC/MMC Vancouver vowels are not significantly associated with the Houston data ($p < 0.003$; 32 per cent by squared distance), or with corresponding MWC/UWC Vancouver vowels ($p < 0.0001$).

6. Such long-term differences are attested in distinguishing the French and Flemish accents of bilingual Belgians (Harmegnies and Landercy 1985).

7. The settings include close rounding, close jaw, dentalisation, retroflexion, palatalisation, uvularisation, velarisation, laryngo-pharyngalisation, nasalisation, faucal constriction, raised larynx, and lowered larynx. Models reflect performances of three phonetic texts (90 seconds of speech). Euclidean (root-mean-squared) distance measures indicate high internal consistency of the models across texts. Statistical calculations compare male SES groups at regular intervals along the spectrum of each of the eight subjects in each group, and with the spectrum of each model.

REFERENCES

Abercrombie, D. 1967. *Elements of General Phonetics*. Edinburgh: Edinburgh University Press.

Blishen, B. R. 1967. A socio-economic index for occupations in Canada. *Canadian Review of Sociology and Anthropology* 4: 41–53.

Blishen, B. R. and McRoberts, H. A. 1976. A revised socioeconomic index for occupations in Canada. *Canadian Review of Sociology and Anthropology* 13: 71–9.

Chambers, J. K. 1979. Canadian English. In Chambers, J. K. (ed.), *The Languages of Canada*. Montréal: Didier, pp. 169–204.

Clarke, S. 1985. Sociolinguistic variation in a small urban context: The St John's survey. In Warkentyne (ed.) 1985, pp. 143–53.

Dickson, B. C. 1985. *User's Manual for Micro Speech Lab*. Victoria: Software Research Corporation.

Esling, J. H. 1978. The identification of features of voice quality in social groups. *Journal of the International Phonetic Association* 8: 18–23.

1981. Methods in voice quality research in dialect surveys. In Warkentyne (ed.) 1981, pp. 126–38.

Esling, J. H. and Dickson, B. C. 1985. Acoustical procedures for articulatory setting analysis in accent. In Warkentyne (ed.) 1985, pp. 155–70.

Gregg, R. J., Murdoch, M., Hasebe-Ludt, E. and de Wolf, G. 1981. An urban dialect survey of the English spoken in Vancouver. In Warkentyne (ed.) 1981, pp. 41–65.

Gregg, R. J., Murdoch, M., de Wolf, G. and Hasebe-Ludt, E. 1985. The Vancouver survey: Analysis and measurement. In Warkentyne (ed.) 1985, pp. 179–200.

Harmegnies, B. and Landercy, A. 1985. Language features in the long-term average spectrum. *Revue de Phonétique Appliquée* 73–74–75: 69–79.

Hindle, D. 1978. Approaches to vowel normalization in the study of natural speech. In Sankoff, D. (ed.), *Linguistic Variation: Models and Methods*. New York: Academic Press, pp. 161–71.

Honikman, B. 1964. Articulatory settings. In Abercrombie, D., *et al* (eds.), *In Honour of Daniel Jones. Papers contributed on the Occasion of his Eightieth Birthday, 12 September 1961*. London: Longman, pp. 73–84.

Laver, J. 1968. Voice quality and indexical information. *British Journal of Disorders of Communication* 3: 43–54.

1974. Labels for voices. *Journal of the International Phonetic Association* 4: 62–75.

1980. *The Phonetic Description of Voice Quality*. Cambridge: Cambridge University Press.

Signal Technology, Inc. 1983. *Interactive Laboratory System* V4.1. Goleta, California.

Trudgill, P. 1974. *The Social Differentiation of English in Norwich*. Cambridge: Cambridge University Press.

Warkentyne, H. J. (ed.). 1981. *Papers from the Fourth International Conference on Methods in Dialectology*. Victoria: University of Victoria.

Warkentyne, H. J. (ed.). 1985. *Papers from the Fifth International Conference on Methods in Dialectology*. Victoria: University of Victoria.

9

Social differentiation in Ottawa English

HOWARD B. WOODS

Introduction

Ottawa, the capital of Canada, is Canada's fourth largest city with a population of 819,263 inhabitants. It is bilingual, English (71 per cent) and French (29 per cent) and multicultural, situated on the bilingual belt which extends from Sudbury, Ontario to Moncton, New Brunswick. Ottawa and the area surrounding it, called the Ottawa Valley, was settled during the 1830s, 40s and 50s by Scots, Irish, English, Americans and French Canadians. Although there remains a great deal of interest in and popular writing about the 'Ottawa Valley Twang', a dialect derived from a mixture of the several Irish and Scots dialects, little of this 'Twang' can be found today as most of the surrounding area and all the city have assimilated to General English (Chambers 1975: 55–9).

Recently, the federal government has placed great importance on making its institutions bilingual. Although some 57,000 anglophone federal public employees have undergone extensive French language training and a much larger number of English-speaking school children attend total-immersion French elementary school instruction, the English in Ottawa remains representative of urban Canadian English. English in Ottawa, and in Canada generally, appears to be very little influenced by its contact with French, though research on this topic is sparse (see Chambers, this volume).

Canadian English is, however, strongly and increasingly influenced by American English in nearly all functions of communication; it is also strongly influenced by British English in governmental, administrative, academic, religious, and fine arts areas of communication. These two major influences and Canada's unique mixture of these sources are of major interest throughout the study of Ottawa English.

This case study of urban sociodialectology investigates the social differentiation and stylistic variation of English in Ottawa. The method used for

134

Table 9.1. *Number of speakers in each socioeconomic class*

Socioeconomic class	Number of speakers
Working class	14
Lower Middle class	26
Middle class	35
Upper Middle class	15
Lower Upper class	10

collecting, analysing, and presenting the data conforms in most respects to that established by Labov (1966) and Trudgill (1974). The study presents an analysis of a sample of Canadian English, as spoken by people whose mother tongue is English and who were born and raised in Ottawa. The analysis investigates whether and to what degree the participants vary their speech patterns according to the tasks that they were asked to perform; and whether variation in usage and style is correlated with age, gender and socioeconomic class. An hour-long interview was conducted with 100 participants using a set format to elicit five styles of speech (see Woods 1979 for details). In this case study I will report on six phonological variables and one discourse feature.

The covariation of the phonological variables with social and stylistic parameters.

The five contextual styles are shown as a linear continuum in figures 9.1–9.10, ranging from the most formal, Minimal Pairs (MP), through Word List (WL), Pictures (P)[1] and Reading (R) to Free Speech (FS), which is assumed to be the most informal style. In the figures that follow, the index scores for one variant of each phonological variable are displayed as percentages. These percentages represent the frequencies of that variant in all occurrences of the variable in the speech of all members of a given social group. The different social groups are represented by a number of symbols, as shown in the figures, and the lines on the graphs connect the scores obtained by each social group in each of the five contextual styles. The social classes represented in the figures are: Working Class (W), Lower Middle class (LM), Middle class (M), Upper Middle class (UM) and Lower Upper class (LU). Table 9.1 shows the number of speakers in each of the five socioeconomic classes; the number chosen to represent each class is roughly proportionate to the size of that class in Ottawa society (see Woods 1979 for details).

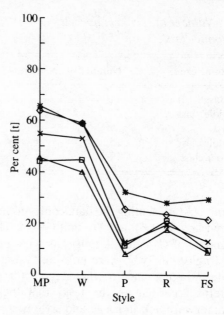

Figure 9.1   Percentage frequency of [t] by social class. □ = working; △ = lower middle; × = middle; ◇ = upper middle; ＊ = lower upper.

The variable (t)

This variable is the post-tonic /t/, pronounced [t] or [d], which is found between vowel sounds as in *city, Ottawa, out of* or between the liquids /l/ and /r/ and vowels, as in *shelter, belted, dirty, quarter*. In addition, this variable occurs frequently after most voiceless fricatives: after /f/ in *after, often, fifteen and fifty*; after /s/ in words such as *sister, sixteen, mister, twister, blister*; and after /ʃ/ in phrases such as *wished our, washed (h)is, finished it*. It occurred in 150 words and phrases in the corpus that was analysed. A similar pattern of variation also occurs after /n/, in words such as *carpenter, seventy, seventeen*; this is not included here, but is analysed separately in the following section.

Figure 9.1 shows the percentage frequency of the [t] variant for the five social classes in each of the five contextual styles. It can be seen that this variable is involved in a considerable amount of ordered social class differentiation, with an almost perfect linear sequencing of the classes in each of the five styles. Furthermore, a 20 per cent separation is maintained in each style between the frequency indices of the highest class (the Lower Upper class) and the two lowest classes (Working and Lower Middle).

There is also a considerable amount of stylistic variation within each group of speakers, with scores generally decreasing, for the two higher socioeconomic classes, as we progress from more formal speech styles to more informal styles. The remaining classes show irregular patterns of stylistic variation, with the percentage frequency of the [t] variant increasing in Reading style. It is also worth noting that the Lower Upper class (the highest socioeconomic class) also uses a higher proportion of the [t] variant in Free Speech style than in Reading style. The scores drop 45 per cent for some classes. Group frequences range between 67 and 7 per cent; a few individuals scored 100 per cent in Minimal Pairs style and 0 per cent in Free Speech style. Some members of the Working Class, however, showed almost no stylistic variation, with percentage frequencies below 15 in all styles.

Figure 9.2 shows the percentage frequency of the [t] variant analysed according to gender and age groups. We can see that female speakers over 40 years have the lowest frequency of /t/ voicing (i.e. the highest frequency of the [t] variant) throughout the entire range of styles, while young male speakers consistently have the highest frequency; this is a pattern which recurs frequently in our study.

There is no parallel study of North American usage of this variable and consequently no comparisons can be made with other varieties of North American English. However, it is interesting to note that *Webster's Third International Dictionary* transcribes words with post-tonic medial /t/, such as *city*, with [d] as first choice, suggesting that the voiced variant is the US norm.

The variable (ntV)

This variable occurs in 48 words in the corpus, including *plenty*, *centre*, *twenty* and *winter*. It has three possible realisations, namely [nt], [n], or [nd]. Figure 9.3 shows the percentage use of the [nt] variant by the four groups defined by age and gender. We can observe that female speakers use the [nt] variant more frequently than male speakers in all speech styles, and that age does not appear to be a significant factor affecting variation. There is considerable stylistic variation amongst all four groups of speakers.

The [n] variant was the most frequently uttered variant in Free Speech, while the [nd] variant occured infrequently in all styles for all groups of speakers.

The variable (-ing)

This variable is the morphological suffix which marks progressive aspect and the gerund. It also occurs as a nominalising suffix in words such as *building* and *clothing*, and occurs as the final portion of monomorphemic

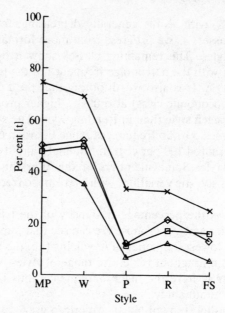

Figure 9.2   Percentage frequency of [t] analysed by gender and age.
□ = males 40 years of age and older; △ = males younger than 40 years of age.
× = females 40 years of age and older; ◇ = females younger than 40 years of age.

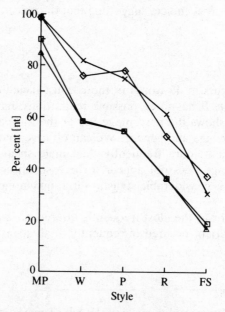

Figure 9.3   Percentage frequency of [nt] analysed by gender and age.
□ = males 40 years of age and older; △ = males younger than 40 years of age.
× = females 40 years of age and older; ◇ = females younger than 40 years of age.

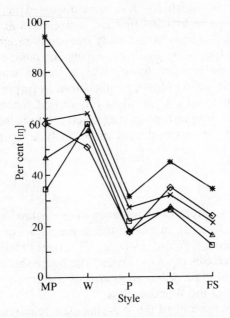

Figure 9.4   Percentage frequency of [ɪŋ] by social class. □ = working;
△ = lower middle; × = middle; ◇ = upper middle; ✳ = lower upper.

words such as *morning* and *evening* (but not in monosyllabic words such as *thing, sing* or *wing*). It does not normally carry stress and is pronounced in three different ways in the data, namely [ɪŋ], [in] and [ən].

Figure 9.4 shows the percentage frequency of the [ɪŋ] variant for the five social classes. The graph illustrates fairly consistent social differentiation according to class, although there are some unusual cross-over patterns. Group frequencies range from 94 per cent for the Lower Upper class to 34 per cent for the Working class in Minimal Pair style, with a separation of about 20 per cent maintained between these classes in all other speech styles. In Reading style the nominalising suffix in words such as *building*, and monomorphemic words such as *morning* and *evening*, have a 20 to 30 per cent higher frequency of [ɪŋ] than has the verbal suffix in words such as *making* or *sitting*.

Other studies of this variable (Labov 1966: 394–99; Trudgill 1974: 91–5) consider the pronunciation [n] as the only alternative to [ŋ], paying little or no attention to vowel quality. However, our study reveals – and preliminary investigations elsewhere in Canada substantiate – that neither [ən] nor [ɪŋ] are the most frequent realisation of the (-ing) variable, but that [in] is. The percentage frequencies for all speakers for the [in] variant are 72, 61 and 61 in Picture, Reading and Free Speech styles, respectively.

This pronunciation, which has not been discussed in the literature, is treated as usage to be avoided by CBC newscasters in Tilden and Rich (1978: 2). The participants in this study frequently pronounced as homophones words such as *being* and *bean*; *paying* and *pain*; *playing* and *plain*; and, especially, *beings* and *beans*, with a longer vowel in the word containing the *-ing* suffix. Most pronunciations as [in] in the data carried tertiary stress (or lower). Only when [in] carried secondary or primary stress, did some listeners react negatively; otherwise its occurrence passed unnoticed, or was evaluated as perfectly acceptable (see Woods 1979).

The variable (tj, dj, nj)

This variable is the presence or absence of the palatal glide [j] after [t], [d], or [n], and before [u], in words such as *tune, due,* or *new*.[2] Figure 9.5 presents the percentage frequency of the [j] variant of variable (tj, nj, nj), for all five social classes in all five styles. The figure shows that there is an ordered pattern of class differentiation (but not stylistic differentiation) for all classes except the Working class.

The linguistic behaviour of the Working class requires some comment. For a number of phonological items analysed in Woods (1979), the Working class and the Lower Upper and Upper Middle classes show similar patterns of variation. An explanation lies in the fact that Ottawa and the surrounding Ottawa Valley was settled in the 1830s, 1840s and 1850s by Scots and Irish, of mainly humble social standing. Many of the descendants of these settlers have now reached the Upper Middle and Lower Upper classes of Ottawa society, but a large number have remained in the Working class. The results found for this feature and for others described in Woods (1979), such as (ou), (a), (ar) and (or), all point to this common heritage. The remaining classes, the Lower Middle and Middle, are to a large extent made up of newcomers, many of whom follow more closely the patterns of General Canadian English.

Female speakers over the age of 40 have much higher frequency indices than the other gender and age groups, as figure 9.6 shows. The percentage frequency of [tj, dj, nj] remains fairly high in all five styles, with a mean percentage frequency (i.e. for all speakers) of about 50 per cent in Minimal Pairs style and about 30 per cent in Free Speech.

Most Ottawans perceive [tj, dj, nj] to be 'correct' and associate this pronunciation with British usage, assuming the [t,d,n] variant to be American and 'incorrect'. In spite of the fact that Canadian English is (geographically, at least) a variety of North American English, many Canadian speakers emulate certain southern British English forms as markers of independence from the American forms and of (assumed) superiority.

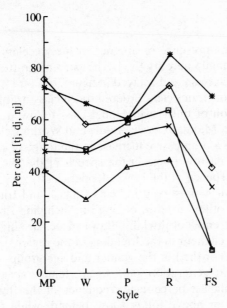

Figure 9.5 Percentage frequency of [tj, dj, nj] by social class. □ = working;
△ = lower middle; × = middle; ◇ = upper middle; ✻ = lower upper.

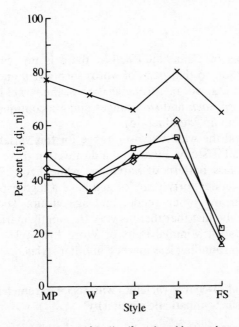

Figure 9.6 Percentage frequency of [tj, dj, nj] analysed by gender and age.
□ = males 40 years of age and older; △ = males younger than 40 years of age.
× = females 40 years of age and older; ◇ = females younger than 40 years of age.

The variable (hw)

This variable is the presence or absence of the voiceless labial glide [ʍ], represented informally here by [hw]. The percentage frequencies of [hw] for all five social classes are displayed in figure 9.7.

Figure 9.7 demonstrates clear ordered social class stratification, with the pattern of variation of the Lower Upper class followed, in sequence, by the Upper Middle, Middle, Lower Middle and Working classes. The figure also demonstrates a progressive increase in the range of stylistic variation, from a relatively narrow range in the speech of the Working class, to a wide range in the speech of the Lower Upper class.

The [hw] variant is preserved in Scots English and Irish English but is recessive in most other varieties of English, including English English. It may be that occurrences of [hw] in Ottawa speech are high because of the Scottish and Irish element in the founding of the region.

The distribution of [hw] in the gender and age groups, shown in figure 9.8, reveals a clear generation gap. Again, female speakers aged 40 or above have the highest percentage frequency of the [hw] variant. Male speakers aged 40 or above follow close behind, while the two younger gender and age groups have much lower percentage frequencies, in all styles.

The variable (ɒ)

In most varieties of Canadian English, there is no phonemic contrast between /ɒ/ and /ɑ/, so that pairs of words such as *cot* and *caught* are not distinguished. In Ottawa, the pronunciation of the vowel in words such as *cot, caught, soccer, sock* and *stop* ranges along a continuum from full lip rounding [ɒ], to no lip rounding, [ɑ].

Our data reveal the widest stylistic range for this variable than for any other analysed in the study. Figure 9.9 indicates that there is no systematic socioeconomic class pattern of variation, while figure 9.10 shows that female speakers under forty years of age have a higher frequency of use than speakers in any other gender and age group. The sharp stylistic gradients reflect the fact that there is very frequently marked lip rounding in isolated words (in Minimal Pairs or Word List style) and in stressed syllables, with lip rounding less marked in other styles.

The covariation of discourse variables with social parameters: 'social contracting' versus 'sympathetic circularity'

In a further attempt to find those linguistic items which vary in relation to the social characteristics of speakers, we decided to investigate the covariation of socioeconomic class with the prefixing of phrases of 'social

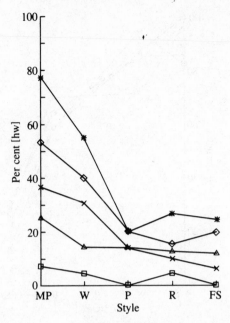

Figure 9.7 Percentage frequency of [hw] by social class. □ = working;
△ = lower middle; × = middle; ◇ = upper middle; * = lower upper.

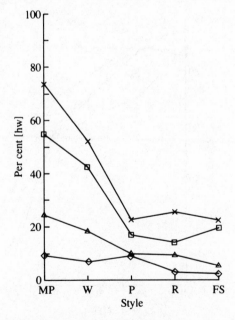

Figure 9.8 Percentage frequency of [hw] by gender and age.
□ = males 40 years of age and older; △ = males younger than 40 years of age;
◇ = females 40 years of age and older; * = females younger than 40 years of age.

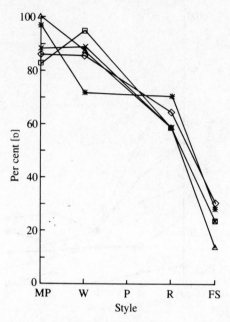

Figure 9.9   Percentage frequency of [ɒ] by social class.   □ = working;
△ = lower middle;   × = middle;   ◇ = upper middle;   ✳ = lower upper.

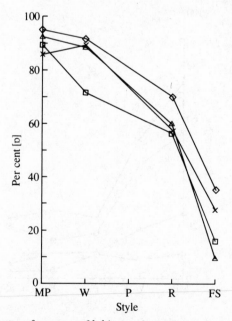

Figure 9.10   Percentage frequency of [ɒ] by gender and age.
□ = males 40 years of age and older;   △ = males younger than 40 years of age;
× = females 40 years of age and older;   ◇ = females younger than 40 years of age.

contracting' and the suffixing of tags of 'sympathetic circularity'.[3] Our inspiration for this part of the study came from Bernstein (1973), who postulated that, in England, the higher social classes preface much of what they are about to say with sequences of 'social contracting', such as *in my opinion* . . ., or *I believe* . . . . Bernstein assumed that these opening phrases make it clear that the speaker is offering his or her own view; the addressee is not necessarily expected to agree, and some disagreement and discussion are often expected. On the other hand, the lower socioeconomic classes are assumed to have a tendency to add signals of 'sympathetic circularity' to the end of an utterance (Bernstein 1973: 130–7). These signals, such as *you know, isn't that right, don't you think*, and, in Canadian English, the narrative and confirmative *eh*,[4] were thought to signal an assumed agreement between speaker and addressee on what had been said or to seek confirmation that the speaker is with like-minded addressees. In order to express disagreement the addressee would have to make an abrupt and unexpected interruption. Despite their obvious differences, both types of sequence have an equivalent function, that of establishing and maintaining social rapport. Discourse features such as these have now been analysed in more detail, with attention paid to the varied discourse functions that they can fulfil (see, for example, Holmes 1986, 1987; Schriffin, 1986; Coates 1987; Bell and Holmes, this volume); although our analysis did not attempt to distinguish different discourse functions for individual features, the results are nevertheless of interest, since they reveal the greatest amount of ordered socioeconomic stratification of all the features analysed in the Ottawa survey.

Opinion openers

During the interviews the following phrases occurred as signals that a personal opinion was to follow:

I think, I would think, I think generally, To my way of thinking, I'm more apt to think;
In my opinion, As far as I'm concerned, I'm inclined to think, I am biased;
I feel, I believe, I guess, I assume, I presume, I imagine, I suppose, I would say, I would probably say, I have the feeling;
It appears to me that, It looks to me like, It seems to me, To me, To me anyway, For me, To my mind, Myself I; I'm speaking generally, Generally speaking, Generally, I would think generally speaking, Basically, I find this with a great many things;
I don't know but, I don't think in terms like that but, I'm not sure but, I have absolutely no idea but, I would really be hard put to, I have no idea but, I don't feel, I don't know whether this is right or not, I'm not exactly sure;

Apparently from what I can tell, Presumably, Probably, Obviously, Ostensibly, Undoubtedly.

The frequency of occurrence of these phrases was analysed in the speech of each of the five socioeconomic classes. The results are shown in table 9.2.

Table 9.2 shows that the percentage of speakers in each socioeconomic class who use one or more opinion openers increases as we move up the social hierarchy. It also shows that there is clear socioeconomic class patterning in the frequency with which opinion openers occur in the corpus.

Sympathetic circularity

The phrases used by the participants in the study to signal 'sympathetic circularity' were few in number, but occurred very frequently. They were: *you know, eh, (isn't that) right* and *don't you think*; *eh* was frequently used where a tag question could have occurred. Again, the occurrence of these phrases was analysed in the speech of each of the five socioeconomic classes. The results are shown in table 9.3.

It can be seen from table 9.3 that the percentage of speakers who use signals of symapthetic circularity is high in all socioeconomic classes, with percentages ranging from 69 per cent to 80 per cent. It can also be seen that the mean number of occurrences per speaker is highest for the Working class and, with the exception of the Lower Middle class, progressively lower for classes higher in the social hierarchy (the Lower Middle class was generally more taciturn in responding to the open-ended questions during the interview). The number of signals used by members of the two upper classes was considerably lower than for the other socioeconomic classes.

In our data, then, the upper socioeconomic classes used more opinion opening gambits than the lower socioeconomic classes and, conversely, the lower socioeconomic classes used more signals of sympathetic circularity than the upper socioeconomic classes. This analysis needs considerable refinement in order to take account of the different functions that a given discourse feature may fulfil in the utterance in which it occurs; but these results are interesting and seem worth reporting.

Final remarks

Several of the patterns of variation found in this study differ from those that have been found in other sociolinguistic surveys. Firstly, all the phonological variables analysed here show a greater degree of stylistic variation than of social differentiation; this difference is most extreme for

Table 9.2. *Frequency of use of Opinion Openers by socioeconomic class*

Socioeconomic class (No. of speakers)	% of speakers who used opinion openers (No. of speakers per class)	Mean occurences (No. of occurrences per class)
WC (14)	43 (6)	0.79 (11)
LM (26)	42 (11)	2.20 (57)
M (35)	54 (19)	2.70 (94)
UM (15)	87 (13)	5.90 (89)
LU (10)	100 (10)	5.00 (81)
Total (100)	(59)	3.32 (332)

Table 9.3. *Frequency of use of phrases signalling Sympathetic Circularity*

Socioeconomic class (No. of speakers)	% of speakers who used signals of sympathetic circularity (No. of speakers per class)	Mean occurences (No. of occurrences per class)
WC (14)	74 (11)	9.43 (132)
LM (26)	73 (19)	4.23 (110)
M (35)	69 (24)	6.49 (227)
UM (15)	80 (12)	3.07 (45)
LU (10)	80 (8)	3.00 (30)
Total (100)	(74)	5.44 (544)

the (ɒ) variable (see figure 9.9). This is the reverse pattern to the one that has usually been found in urban sociolinguistic surveys, as Bell (1984) points out. Secondly, for the (-ing) and (hw) variables the upper class shows a considerably higher degree of style shifting than the lower classes (see figure 9.4 and figure 9.7); this is also an unusual pattern of sociolinguistic behaviour. Thirdly, there were some unusual patterns of stylistic variation for some variables, in the speech of some social classes: for example, the Lower Upper class (the highest socioeconomic class) voiced medial [t] more often in their Reading style than in their Free Speech style (see figure 9.1), and all classes used the [ɪŋ] and [tj, dj, nj] variants more frequently in Reading Style than in Free Speech (see figure 9.4 and figure 9.5). The clearest patterns of social differentiation were for the discourse features that were analysed.

These unusual patterns of sociolinguistic variation have yet to be explained. It is presumably relevant, however, that where there was a choice of variants for a given variable, the choice was frequently between a British form and a North American form. It seems that Canadians have two sets of linguistic norms; and Canadian English (or the variety of Canadian English spoken in Ottawa, at least) obtains a great deal of its uniqueness by exercising its choice between these British and American variants.

NOTES

1. Participants in the study were asked to identify objects shown to them in pictures and photographs in order to elicit short responses. It was assumed that 'reading' pronunciations and spelling pronunciations were avoided in this speech style.
2. In most varieties of Canadian English the palatal glide [j] is not normally heard in the word *suit* nor in the word *pursue*; /f/, /v/, /m/, /h/ and /k/ are usually followed by [ju] in words such as *few, view, music, hew* and *cue*.
3. We were motivated to undertake this type of analysis by several applied linguists who, at that time, were defining functional-communicative syllabuses for second language teaching; among the published works were Johnson and Morrow (1978); Munby (1978) and Widdowson (1979). For discussion of the need and use of this type of discourse analysis, see Woods (1985).
4. One of the most characteristic features of Canadian English is its wide use of the tag *eh* (see Bailey 1984: 161). The functional types of *eh* which we have distinguished are the following: agreement, confirmation, surprise, imperative, exclamation, interrogative, echo, narrative, pardon, friendly reprimand, gratitude, congratulation, pet talk and teacher talk. Only the narrative and confirmation users of *eh* are relevant for this analysis of markers of 'sympathetic circularity'.

REFERENCES

Bailey, R. W. 1984. The English language in Canada. In Bailey, R. W. and Görlach, M. (eds.), *English as a World Language*. Cambridge: Cambridge University Press, pp. 134–76.

Bell, A. 1984. Language style as audience design. *Language in Society* 13: 145–202.

Bernstein, B. 1973. *Class, Codes and Control, Volume 1: Theoretical Studies towards a Sociology of Language*. St Albans, Herts: Paladin.

Chambers, J. K. 1975. The Ottawa Valley 'twang'. In Chambers, J. K. (ed.), *Canadian English: Origins and Structures*. Toronto: Methuen, pp. 55–9.

Coates, J. 1987. Epistemic modality and spoken discourse. *Transactions of the Philological Society* 110–17.

Holmes, J. 1986. Functions of *you know* in women's and men's speech. *Language in Society* 15: 1–21.

1987. Hedging, fencing and other conversational gambits: an analysis of gender differences. In Pauwels, A. (ed.), *Women and Language in New Zealand Society*. Sydney: Australian Professional Publications, pp. 59–79.

Johnson, K. and Morrow, K. 1978. *Functional Materials and the Classroom Teacher*. Reading: Centre for Applied Language Studies, University of Reading, UK.

Labov, W. 1966. *The Social Stratification of English in New York City*. Washington, DC: Center for Applied Linguistics.

Munby, J. 1978. *Communicative Syllabus Design*. Cambridge: Cambridge University Press.

Schiffrin, D. 1986. *Discourse Markers*. Cambridge: Cambridge University Press.

Tilden, L. and Rich, G, (eds.). 1978. *You Don't Say*. Toronto: CBC.

Trudgill, P. 1974. *The Social Differentiation of English in Norwich*. Cambridge: Cambridge University Press.

Widdowson, H. 1979. *Explorations in Applied Linguistics*. Oxford: Oxford University Press.

Woods, H. 1979. A Socio-Dialectology Survey of the English Spoken in Ottawa: A Study of Sociological and Stylistic Variation in Canadian English. Unpublished PhD thesis, University of British Columbia.

1985. Variations in English as a second language in Canada. In Lougheed, W. (ed.), *In Search of the Standard in Canadian English*. Occasional Papers no. 1. Kingston, Ontario: Strathy Language Unit, Queen's University.

New Zealand

10

New Zealand

ALLAN BELL AND JANET HOLMES

English, Maori and minority languages

New Zealand is one of the world's most monolingual nations. English is the first language of 95 per cent of the 3.4 million population – and the only language of 90 per cent, most of whom are of British descent. English dominates all public domains – media, education, government, law – despite efforts to increase the use of the language of the indigenous Maori people (cf. Benton 1987).

Maori are the largest minority group, constituting about 12 per cent of the population. Maori (a Polynesian language) has gained increasing official recognition, although the change appears too late to reverse a century of neglect and opposition which has brought it to the edge of extinction as a language of everyday interaction.[1] Now less than 25 per cent of Maori people (and still fewer younger Maori) can speak their language fluently (Benton 1979a). Even in isolated rural areas it has virtually been replaced by English (Benton 1979b). Maori is therefore following the typical pattern of an indigenous tongue overwhelmed by an imperial language, and has reached a point from which few languages have recovered. Nevertheless, language revival efforts are underway, with bilingual schooling the most promising initiative (Hirsh 1987).[2] While Maori may eventually be lost as an everyday tongue, it may survive as the language of formal speech events in Maori culture.[3] Benton's survey in this volume presents more detail on the relationship of English and Maori.

New Zealand has been the target of migration from the South Pacific islands since the 1950s. About 3 per cent of the country's population are estimated to be Polynesians of Pacific Island descent, comprising Samoans, Cook Islanders, Niueans, Tongans and Tokelauans. Immigrant European groups are smaller still and include Dutch, Yugoslavs (mainly Dalmatians), Poles, Greeks, Hungarians, Italians and Scandinavians. There are also small Asian minorities, in particular Chinese (mainly Cantonese) and

153

Indians (mainly Gujerati). For most of these groups English has gradually displaced the mother tongue in all but the most domestic domains. In a familiar pattern (Fishman 1980) minority groups in New Zealand have suffered language loss often by the second generation and certainly by the third. Hirsh (1987) documents current language maintenance and revival efforts by a wide range of groups. Although the pattern of language shift to English has been widely noted (e.g. Young 1973; Kroef 1977; Stoffel 1982; Jakich 1987) detailed published studies of the process are lacking. Nor do we have a great deal of information about domains of use.

Research in this area has often focused on the English language skills of young children (e.g. Cheung 1971; Clay 1971; Wee 1974; Natusch 1978; Moynihan 1980). Jamieson (1976) undertook a comprehensive study of the language proficiency of all 102 five- and seven-year-old Tokelau children in New Zealand. Their English language skills were less developed than those of Pakeha children at the same ages,[4] but about 80 per cent also spoke Tokelauan at least 'moderately'. Watkins' (1976) study of children from the Samoan community in Auckland, New Zealand's largest city, observed that the desire for their children's advancement led some parents to speak English at home. Others spoke Samoan while their children responded in English. Watkins found her 20 young adolescent subjects could be divided into three groups – a few recent arrivals still learning English, two children monolingual in English, and the majority bilingual in varying degrees. In a multi-ethnic suburb of the capital city, Wellington, Jamieson (1980) found a wide variety of languages used alongside English. Groups varied in the degree of language maintenance. Greek families insisted on Greek in the home, whereas in Cook Island families mothers reported a decided shift to English. No group reported more than 50 per cent of its children maintaining the ethnic language in the face of English.

Other researchers report broadly similar findings, with the extent of non-English language maintenance influenced by community size, concentration and speech event. While 63 per cent of nine-year-olds in the vital Wellington Samoan community were described as fluent in Samoan (Fairbairn-Dunlop 1984), really fluent speakers of Cantonese were predominantly aged over 50 (Greif 1974). The few published studies conclude that while the first generation of immigrants usually maintain ethnic languages in the home and sometimes for community speech events, there is a substantial shift to English in other domains. Few children of migrants speak their parents' language even at home.

No systematic research has been undertaken on code switching or mixing between New Zealand English (NZE) and other languages. There is a little micro-level research into the influence of English on minority languages, often described as studies of 'interference' (e.g., Barham 1965; Benton 1966), and extensive discussion of the use of Maori vocabulary in

NZE (e.g. Turner 1966, 1970). A small study of Maori–English code switching revealed metaphorical switching to English according to topic changes (Smith 1978). Benton (1985, this volume) observes that where Maori structures used to be seen as affecting the English of Maori children, for the past 20 years the influence has been in the opposite direction.

Variation in New Zealand English

While there has been research into NZE lexicon and phonology for some time (e.g., Turner 1966; Bennett 1970; Hawkins 1973a, 1973b; Northcote-Bade 1976; Eagleson 1984; Bauer 1986), variation within NZE has been little researched, still less in a quantitative framework. The most substantial work to date in a Labovian mould is Bell (1977), which is concerned only secondarily with the NZE data base. Maclagan and Gordon have contributed significant findings on variation in NZE vowel systems (and on language attitudes), but Bayard (1987, this volume) is the pioneering quantitative research on the NZ speech community.

NZE has often been described as an adjunct to studies of Australian English, for example in Ramson's *English Transported* (1970) – a title appropriate to the convict origins of Australian English, but not to NZE. Linguists have typically treated variation in NZE in terms of the three-way division of accents into Cultivated, General and Broad, devised for Australian English (see Guy, this volume), making Mitchell and Delbridge (1965) one of the most frequently cited works in writings on NZE. But the validity of this division for NZE has not been established. Bayard (1987) finds evidence in broadcast speech for a continuum from Cultivated to Broad (see further Bayard, this volume); in Abell's (1980) language attitude work, subjects evaluated Broad above General on most parameters; and Durkin (1972) found the division between General and Broad was fluid and had to add a fourth category, 'Modified', to cater for speakers who had undergone speech training. She classified 50 per cent of her West Coast speakers as Broad, 25 per cent General, 19 per cent Educated, and 6 per cent Modified. Although Durkin quantifies the numbers of occurrences of each vowel variant, she collected no sociological data on her speakers.

Regional variation

While regional variation within NZE vocabulary has been noted (see, for example, Turner 1966), almost every description comments on its absence in phonology and syntax. The only regional difference universally acknowledged by both linguists and the public is the occurrence of postvocalic /r/ in Southland and part of Otago, attributed to the Scottish origin of early settlers. Even this had not been studied until Bayard (1990b) analysed /r/-pronouncing speakers from his quantitative study of

86 mainly southern speakers. Ten speakers had considerable Southland /r/, with the average age of 50 indicating that the feature is probably being lost.

Despite linguists' contention – admittedly assumed rather than demonstrated – that there is little regional variation, New Zealanders frequently insist they can identify accent differences from areas such as Northland, Auckland, Taranaki, Wellington, Christchurch, or the West Coast, a remote mining and forestry region. Durkin's major articulatory study of NZ vowels (1972) was prompted by others' perception of her West Coast accent. She reported that Coasters spoke with a more consistently 'broad' accent than those from the more status-conscious Canterbury region, and recognised that the finding suggested social class rather than regional variation. However, in an acoustic analysis comparing the speech of 30 men from a rural Northland town with Auckland city speech, Hall (1976) found Northland close vowels were more open, open vowels closer, and back vowels further forward than in Auckland. The evidence to date on regional variation remains inconclusive.

Social class

Linguists increasingly agree there are social class differences in NZ speech, but, until Bayard's work, findings were largely incidental, or small scale. Despite the acknowledged limits to the social, regional and stylistic range of his data, Bayard (1987, this volume) found a general increase in RP-like vowel variants with higher social classes.[5] The salient diphthongs /ei, ai, au, ou/, centralisation of /ɪ/, merger of the vowels in *ear* and *air*, and vowel variants before /l/ showed clear social stratification. Bayard's paper in this volume summarises his most significant findings.

The *ear/air* distinction is examined in some detail by Gordon and Maclagan (1985), who conclude the diphthongs are tending to merge on the more open variant /eə/.[6] Their sample recorded a short conversation, sentences, word lists and minimal pairs from 90 adolescents. No distinction was made by 24 per cent of their subjects, with 9 per cent merging on the closer variant /iə/, and 15 per cent on /eə/. The distinction was made by 13 per cent, and the remainder showed no clear trend. The researchers offer the 'highly tentative' conclusion that higher class females tended to use /eə/ and lower class males /iə/. A small but well-executed analysis by Morton and Williams (1977) examined the social stratification of five diphthongs /ei, ai, au, ou, oi/ in the speech of ten teenage boys from two neighbouring but socially divergent Auckland schools. The first four diphthongs, often considered diagnostic of NZE, all showed significant differences. In particular, the lower class boys started the /ai/ diphthong well back and open, compared with the upper class rather fronted first element. For /au/, the lower class vowel started forward and open, and the upper class much further back.

Ethnic group

Early research into Maori English was largely in the 'deficit' mould, prompted by concern over the educational performance of Maori children. Two later studies offer findings suggestive of distinctive morphology and phonology in Maori English. McCallum (1978) found vernacular forms in the English spoken by 5 per cent of children with professional Pakeha parents, 6 per cent of other Pakeha children, 11 per cent of urban Maori children, and 16 per cent of rural Maori-speaking children. In Hall's (1976) sample of 15 Maori and 15 Pakeha men, Maori speakers tended to have closer front vowels and opener back vowels, with most vowels a little further back than those of Pakeha men. The English vowels of L1 Maori speakers were further away from Pakeha English than the vowels of Maori speakers whose first language was English. Hall concludes that acquiring Maori as a first language accounts for these differences. However, other researchers (e.g., Barham 1965; Simon 1979) have found no differences between Maori and Pakeha children's speech. Benton's more detailed survey in this volume concludes that the widespread NZ belief in the existence of a stable, distinctive Maori dialect of English is not confirmed by his own or others' research to date.

The other principal ethnic dialects of English recognised by New Zealanders are spoken by Pacific Islanders. Watkins' (1976) study of Samoan adolescents in Auckland found a good deal of vernacular syntax and morphology, with double negatives, subject-verb inversion in indirect questions, and lack of number concord and tense marking. However, her analysis does not demonstrate the existence of a distinctively Samoan English.

Gender

The available evidence suggests that in New Zealand, as in Britain and the United States, women tend to use prestigious phonological variants more often than men do. Bayard (1987, this volume) found that women used more of the RP-like variants for /ai, ei, ou/, although Maclagan's (1982) acoustic study of NZ vowels found male and female vowel systems were very similar.

The principal studies on gender variation in NZE are comparisons by Holmes and others of conversational patterns in men's and women's speech.[7] The use of syntactic hedges such as tag questions, and pragmatic particles such as *you know*, *I think* and *sort of*, have been suggested as characteristic of tentativeness in women's language (Lakoff 1975). However, Meyerhoff (1986) found few gender differences in the use of noun phrase hedges or approximators in a picture description task.

Holmes (1984, 1985, 1986a, 1987) takes account of how such particles function in different contexts and of a speaker's role in an interaction. The number of occurrences of a form often did not differ between men and women, but the forms tended to serve different functions. An interesting example is the particle *I think*. In this case New Zealand men, in fact, used more instances of *I think* than women (the reverse of Lakoff's suggestions). Moreover, men used more instances of 'tentative' *I think*, while women used more tags as conversational facilitators. A number of small-scale student projects offer interesting if preliminary findings. Men tended to take more of the speaking time than females (Franken 1983; Sollitt-Morris and Brown 1985), but in a less formal situation women's picture descriptions averaged 100 words longer than men's (Meyerhoff 1986). Two apparently similar studies of interrupting and feedback behaviour provided opposing results. Stubbe (1978) reported little evidence that men interrupted women more often than women interrupted men. But Hyndman (1985) found men were responsible for 73 per cent of interruptions and women were interrupted three times as often as men. Generally NZ data mirror the finding elsewhere that women tend to encourage and support other participants.

In related research Holmes (1988) found NZ women, like Americans, give more (67 per cent) and receive more (74 per cent) compliments than men. Indeed there is some suggestion that while compliments function as solidarity-expressing strategies for women, men may experience them as 'face threatening acts' (Brown and Levinson 1978, 1987). This provides an intriguing mirror-image of Kuiper's analysis (this volume) of how insults, which would certainly be experienced as face-threatening by women, perform a solidarity-maintaining function for some males. Kuiper examines the contrasting verbal styles of two male sports groups, one of which affirms its members, while the other achieves commitment through verbal denigration.

Age grading and linguistic change

Researching the historical development of NZE, Gordon (1983a) concluded that a distinctive New Zealand accent was observable by about 1900. The pronunciation of final [i:] in *pretty*, of /ai/ with an open back first element, and the similarity of /a/ and /ʌ/ were noted in written records as early as 1887. By the early 1900s the distinctive diphthongs /ei, ai, au, ou/ and centralised /ɪ/ were noted.

Bayard (1987, this volume) found a general increase in prestigious, RP-like variants with increasing age. New Zealand retention of /ʍ/ is very low in people under 40, and Bayard predicts it will vanish within the next

30 years. The *ear/air* merger is clearly a historical change in progress. Gordon and Maclagan's data (1985) from teenage speakers were supplemented by interviews with a group of elderly people. The merger is not recent, since half the older speakers merged some distinctions on either diphthong, although less often than the adolescents. The pairs *cheer/chair* and *sheer/share* collapsed by the older speakers are those most frequently merged by the young sample. The evidence was strong that the change is taking place through lexical diffusion. Two minimal pairs merged on /iə/ – *really/rarely* and *kea/care*.[8] Five pairs merged on /eə/ – *beer/bear*, *ear/air*, *cheer/chair*, *spear/spare*, *shear/share*. Four other pairs remained distinct: *here/hair*, *fear/fare*, *fear/fair*, *tearful/careful*.

Bayard (1990b) notes that /t/ glottalisation in word-final position occurred in up to 30 per cent of contexts for younger speakers, but was rare in speakers aged over 30. He also found 'rare to frequent' use of postvalic /r/ among a subsample of younger NZ speakers, but considers it may be an 'ephemeral, age-graded phenomenon'. He attributes both changes to possible media influence.

Stylistic variation

The principal quantitative research on style shift in NZE is by Bell (1977, 1982a). With a sample of 35 hours of recorded radio news, Bell found consistent differences in the radio stations' language styles which could be explained only in terms of the social stratification of the stations' audiences. The linguistic variables included auxiliary and negative contractions, consonant cluster reduction and intervocalic /t/ voicing. Particularly striking were the cases where individual newsreaders consistently shifted style when broadcasting on different radio stations. Bell (1984b) expands these and other findings into the Audience Design hypothesis that style differences in face-to-face interaction can largely be correlated to differences in a speaker's audience.

Bell (1982b, 1985) examines the effect of opposing linguistic norms on language in NZ media. For some variables, media speech seems to be moving away from a traditional BBC-oriented norm of quasi-RP towards an American-based norm. Bell (1990) analyses accents in NZ television advertisements, 40 per cent of which use non-native accents (mostly RP, Cockney and American). Of particular interest is the New Zealand prestige accent used by only a handful of media professionals, which mixes NZE, RP and phonetically intermediate vowel variants.

Discourse types and registers

The most significant sociolinguistic research accomplished to date in New Zealand uses local data but does not focus on its distinctive New Zealand character. Often concentrating on a particular discourse type or register, a great deal of this work is based on the premise of its likely generalisability to other Englishes. Into this category falls much of the research by Lane on courtroom language, by Holmes and her associates on compliments and gender differences in conversation, by Bell on style and media language, by Kuiper and associates on different types of discourse, and by Pride on ESL varieties in other countries and on cross-cultural communication difficulties. Some of the research makes explicit comparisons with, or even concentrates on, data from other countries (Pride 1982, 1985; Kuiper and Tillis 1985; Holmes 1987; Bell 1988).

Kuiper and Haggo (1984) and Kuiper and Austin (1990) develop important theoretical insights on oral formulae through analysis of two characteristically New Zealand forms of discourse: the livestock auction and the horse-racing commentary. The analyses are ethnographically as well as linguistically illuminating, examining the prosodic techniques and formulaic lexicon and syntax by which these speech professionals perform their tasks. In another area where linguistic formulae abound, Holmes (1988, in press) shows that compliments in New Zealand are as formulaic as in America. Compliments are most frequently used between equals (79 per cent of the compliments in the data base), and appearance is the most common topic. New Zealanders overwhelmingly prefer to accept compliments than to reject or evade them: 61 per cent of responses in the data base were acceptances, 29 per cent were evasions, and 10 per cent were rejections.

The language used in district court trials in Auckland has been recorded and analysed by Lane (1985) to identify sources of miscommunication between Pakeha legal personnel and Polynesian witnesses for whom English is a second language. Courtroom communication problems are often located in 'question cycles', where a question is re-stated several times and augmented with requests for confirmation or clarification. Long question cycles were much more frequent in cross-examination of non-native speakers, often leading to their being evaluated as unreliable, inconsistent or evasive. In research on language in another social institution, Bell examines the function of media language as a standard within a speech community (1983), and the use of personal descriptions in news language (1985). A syntactic analysis of news editing (Bell 1984a) showed how editors manipulate variable rules to re-style copy to suit particular media house styles, often with semantic repercussions which introduce errors into news copy.

Language attitudes

Denigration of NZE in comparison with RP has a long local history and is still commonly expressed in media correspondence columns. Gordon (1983a, 1983b) surveyed historical comments on NZE in the reports of school inspectors between 1880 and 1930. From 1912 onwards, references to 'impure vowels' and 'colonial twang' increased, with specific criticism of /ɪ/ and the diphthongs.

Research broadly confirms that RP is still regarded as the prestige variety. Huygens and Vaughan (1983) asked 120 Pakeha psychology students in Auckland to identify the accents and evaluate the social and personal characteristics of recorded speakers. The speakers represented four ethnic groups – British, Maori, Dutch and Pakeha – with three social statuses distinguished for the Pakeha group. Upper-status Pakehas and British English speakers were rated most favourably on the social scales.

Other studies have found RP to be rated more highly than upper-status Pakeha speech. For example, Abell (1980) found RP was rated markedly higher than 'Cultivated' NZE on social prestige parameters such as education, income and ambition. Her study recorded and classified four speakers – RP, Cultivated, General and Broad – whose accents were evaluated by 14-year-old subjects in Christchurch for social and personal characteristics. The Cultivated accent was rated well above other NZE accents on all parameters, although on two personal attractiveness indicators the other two accents came closer. The General and Broad accents were rated close together for all variables, with General usually below Broad. Bayard (1990a) also found that RP topped most scales, followed by North American, with Cultivated less highly rated. His sample of 86 university students in Dunedin identified the social class of speakers quite accurately, and registered a particular dislike of (in this case female) working class accents. Bayard found that 80 per cent of respondents identified RP, but 16 per cent classed it as New Zealand. He also discovered – like Huygens – that Cultivated NZE is often classified as British (by 48 per cent of his respondents), while lower class accents are mistaken for Australian (Huygens 1979). RP-speaking Britishers were sometimes labelled New Zealanders. 'About one-third of the subjects seemed to accept the speech of the distant "mother country" as belonging to New Zealand' (Huygens 1979: 57). The findings confirm that RP is regarded as a part of – the top of – the NZ speech continuum.

In contrast to findings in other countries, the most marked local accents tend to be ranked low for personal attractiveness as well as social prestige. Bayard (1990a) found that Broad, lower class NZ accents were rated lowest even for friendliness and sense of humour, and very low for intelligence, ambition and income. Abell (1980) concluded that NZE has some covert prestige, but the Cultivated accent rather than Broad is regarded as attractive in a person. By contrast Huygens and Vaughan (1983) found that lower class speakers were highly rated for warmth and easy-going nature.

These apparently contradictory findings may represent genuine regional differences. The more rural, conservative South Island (Bayard, Abell) values RP above Cultivated NZE on prestige scales, and Cultivated NZE above Broad for attractiveness. The more urbanised, progressive northern North Island (Huygens) values Cultivated NZE as highly as RP, and rates Broad well on attractiveness scales.

The studies also reflect popular stereotypes about the ethnic groups involved, with the Maori regarded as most warm but least intelligent and the British speakers as most self-confident (Huygens and Vaughan 1983). Maori and Pakeha accents were often indistinguishable, with only 25 per cent of respondents successfully identifying Maori speakers. Gould (1972) found Maori speakers were incorrectly classified as Pakeha by 55 per cent of subjects, while Pakehas were correctly classified by 87 per cent. It seems that some Maori people sound distinctive but most do not. The stereotype also seems to link Maori and Polynesian accents with low status. Bayard (1990a) found that one lower class subject's Broad accent was sometimes classed (wrongly) as Maori or Polynesian.

Conclusions

The strength of much New Zealand sociolinguistic research has been on data generalisable to other Englishes. New Zealanders have focused on and made significant contributions to issues of general linguistic and sociolinguistic interest. While not questioning the value of such work (to which much of our own research belongs), we feel there is a pressing case for paying more attention to what makes NZE distinctive rather than what it shares with other Englishes. One obvious feature for investigation is the intonational rise at the end of a declarative sentence. Researched in Australia by Guy *et al.* (1986) as the High Rise Terminal, the form functions identically in NZ speech. Although Guy *et al.* describe it as unique to Australia, NZ use considerably pre-dates its reported appearance there.

More information on patterns of language use, maintenance and shift among NZ minority group communities is needed. For some communities available data are pitifully small, out of date, or purely anecdotal. Patterns of code switching and mixing with minority languages offer a virtually unresearched field. Empirical work on distinctively New Zealand English has mostly been fragmented or small-scale. Even the larger projects have tended to be deficient in their sociological, methodological or linguistic approaches. Stratified samples and sociological information on speakers have on occasions been collected but not used to the full. The captive populations of school children, and to a lesser extent university students, have provided most of the samples. The bulk of the speech used to analyse pronunciation has consisted of reading aloud of word lists or, at best, a continuous passage. Ad lib speech has rarely been elicited, and a casual style only for studies of pragmatic features of conversation.

The lack of information should be corrected by a large-scale sociolinguistic survey of NZE which is currently in progress, drawing its data from a range of speakers, obtaining and using information on their social characteristics, and sampling a variety of styles including casual speech. We will then be much better placed to identify linguistic forms unique to or characteristic of NZE, and to establish and describe what regional, social, ethnic and stylistic variation exists within the New Zealand English speech community[9].

NOTES

1. Kennedy (1982) discusses the extent to which English is a second language in NZ, and Kaplan (1981) surveys the use of other languages. Benton (1981) reviews the place of Maori language in NZ society.
2. *Kohanga reo* or 'language nests' provide a Maori-speaking environment for pre-school children (see Benton, this volume).
3. See, for example, Salmond's (1974) description of the Maori ritual of encounter.
4. Pakehas are New Zealanders of European descent.
5. Analysis of NZ vowels (e.g., Maclagan 1982; Gordon and Deverson 1985; Bauer 1986) generally represents /e/ as very close, /æ/ half close, and /ɪ/ and /u/ as centralised. The salient diphthongs are /ei/ which closes from an open rather central first element [ʌɪ]; /ai/ starting open back and closing forwards [ɒɪ]; /au/ starting open front and centering [æə], and /ou/, closing from an open central first element [ʌə]. Hall's acoustic analysis (1976) found /i, ɪ, e/, and /a,ʌ/, tended to overlap in quality.
6. Gordon and Maclagan (1985) note that the distribution and nature of the merger has been simplified by Wells (1982) and by Fromkin *et al.* (1984), who assert the merger is on /iə/.
7. Meyerhoff (1987) provides a detailed review of gender and language research in NZ.
8. *Kea* (a mountain parrot) is normally pronounced [kiːə] by Pakehas, although the Maori pronunciation is [kea].
9. Since this paper was written in 1987, research on NZ English and its use has blossomed. A large proportion of a million-word Corpus of NZ English has been gathered. The first major research project to record and analyse everyday New Zealand speech has been completed. The pioneer collection of papers on NZE has been published (Bell and Holmes 1990). Papers presented at a conference on Language and Society, held at Victoria University in May 1990, demonstrated the rapid growth in research on NZE throught the country.

REFERENCES

Abell, M. 1980. A Study of Sociolinguistic Stereotyping by Fourth Form Students in Christchurch. Unpublished MA thesis, Christchurch: University of Canterbury.

Barham, I. H. 1965. *The English Vocabulary and Sentence Structure of Maori Children*. Wellington: New Zealand Council for Educational Research.

Bauer, L. 1986. Notes on New Zealand English phonetics and phonology. *English World-wide* 7: 225-58.

Bayard, D. 1987. Class and change in New Zealand English: a summary report. *Te Reo* 30: 3–36.

1990a. 'God help us if we all sound like this!': attitudes towards NZE and other English accents. In Bell, A. and Holmes, J. (eds.), *New Zealand Ways of Speaking English*. Clevedon: Multilingual Matters, pp. 67–96.

1990b. Minder, Mork, and Mindy? -T glottalisation and postvocalic -R in younger NZE speakers. In Bell, A. and Holmes, J. (eds.), *New Zealand Ways of Speaking English*. Clevedon: Multilingual Matters.

Bell, A. 1977. *The Language of Radio News in Auckland: A Sociolinguistic Study of Style, Audience and Subediting Variation*. Unpublished PhD thesis, Auckland: University of Auckland.

1982a. Radio: the style of news language. *Journal of Communication* 32: 150-64.

1982b. This isn't the BBC: colonialism in New Zealand English. *Applied Linguistics* 3: 246–58.

1983. Broadcast news as a language standard. *International Journal of the Sociology of Language* 40: 29–42.

1984a. Good copy – bad news: the syntax and semantics of news editing. In Trudgill, P., (ed.), *Applied Sociolinguistics*. London: Academic Press, pp. 73–116.

1984b. Language style as audience design. *Language in Society* 13: 145–204.

1985. One rule of news English: geographical, social and historical spread. *Te Reo* 28: 95–117.

1988. The British base and the American connection in New Zealand media English. *American Speech* 63: 326–44.

1990. Audience and referee design in New Zealand media language. In Bell, A. and Holmes, J. (eds.) *New Zealand Ways of Speaking English*. Clevedon: Multilingual Matters, pp. 165–94.

Bell, A. and Holmes, J. (eds.) 1990. *New Zealand Ways of Speaking English*. Clevedon: Multilingual Matters

Bennett, J. A. W. 1970. English as it is spoken in New Zealand. In Ramson (ed.), 1970, pp. 69–83. (Reprinted from *American Speech* 18, 1943.)

Benton, R. A. 1966. *Research into the English Language Difficulties of Maori School Children, 1963–64*. Wellington: Maori Education Foundation.

1979a. Who speaks Maori in New Zealand? *Set* 1, Item 6. Wellington: New Zealand Council for Educational Research.

1979b. *The Maori Language in the Nineteen-Seventies*. Wellington: New Zealand Council for Educational Research.

1981. *The Flight of the Amokura: Oceanic Languages and Formal Education in the Southern Pacific*. Wellington: New Zealand Council for Educational Research.

1985. Maori, English, and Maori English. In Pride (ed.) 1985, pp. 110–20.

1987. From the Treaty of Waitangi to the Waitangi tribunal. In Hirsh (ed.) 1987, pp. 63–73.

Brown, P. and Levinson, S. 1978. Universals in language usage: politeness phenomena. In Goody, E. N. (ed.), *Questions and Politeness: Strategies in Social Interaction*. Cambridge: Cambridge University Press, pp. 56–310.

1987. *Politeness: Some Universals in Language Usage*. Cambridge: Cambridge University Press.

Cheung, K. Y. 1971. The Effects of Bilingualism on School Learning Studied in a Group of Chinese Children in Christchurch. Unpublished MA dissertation, Christchurch, University of Canterbury.

Clay, M. M. 1971. The Polynesian language skills of Maori and Samoan school entrants. *International Journal of Psychology* 6: 135–45.

Durkin, M. E. 1972. A Study of the Pronunciation, Oral Grammar and Vocabulary of West Coast Schoolchildren. Unpublished MA dissertation. Christchurch, University of Canterbury.

Eagleson, R. D. 1984. English in Australia and New Zealand. In Bailey, R. W., and Görlach. M. (eds.), *English as a World Language*. Ann Arbor MI: University of Michigan Press, pp. 415–38.

Fairbairn-Dunlop, P. 1984. Factors associated with language maintenance: the Samoans in New Zealand. *New Zealand Journal of Educational Studies* 19: 99–113.

Fishman, J. 1980. Bilingualism and biculturalism as individual and as societal phenomena. *Journal of Multilingual and Multicultural Development* 1: 3–15.

Franken, M. 1983. Interviewers' strategies: how questions are modified. MS, Wellington, Victoria University.

Fromkin, V., Rodman, R., Collins, P. and Blair, D. 1984. *An Introduction to Language* (Australian edition). Sydney: Holt, Rinehart & Winston.

Gordon, E. 1983a. New Zealand English pronunciation: an investigation into some early written records. *Te Reo* 26: 29–42.

1983b. 'The flood of impure vocalisation' – a study of attitudes towards New Zealand speech. *The New Zealand Speech-Language Therapists' Journal* 38: 16–29.

Gordon, E. and Deverson, A. 1985. *New Zealand English: An Introduction to New Zealand Speech and Usage*. Auckland: Heinemann.

Gordon, E. and Maclagan, M. A. 1985. A study of the /iə/~/eə/ contrast in New Zealand English. *The New Zealand Speech-Language Therapists' Journal* 40: 16–26.

Gould, P. 1972. Assessment of status by accent: an aspect of sociolinguistic competence. MS, Wellington, Victoria University.

Greif, S. F. 1974. *The Overseas Chinese in New Zealand*. Singapore: Asia Pacific Press.

Guy, G., Horvath, B., Vonwiller, J., Daisley, E. and Rogers, I. 1986. An intonational change in progress in Australian English. *Language in Society* 15: 23–52.

Hall, M. 1976. An Acoustic Analysis of New Zealand Vowels. Unpublished MA thesis, Auckland, University of Auckland.

Hawkins, P. 1973a. A phonemic transcription system for New Zealand English. *Te Reo* 16: 15–21.

1973b. The sound-patterns of New Zealand English. In *Proceedings and Papers of the 15th Congress*. Sydney: Australasian Universities Language & Literature Association 13. 1–8.

Hirsh, W. (ed.) 1987. *Living Languages: Bilingualism and Community Languages in New Zealand Today*. Auckland: Heinemann.

Holmes, J. 1984. Hedging your bets and sitting on the fence: some evidence for hedges as support structures. *Te Reo* 27: 47–62.

1985. Sex differences and mis-communication: some data from New Zealand. In Pride (ed.) 1985, pp. 24–43.

1986a. Functions of *you know* in women's and men's speech. *Language in Society* 15: 1–22.

1986b. Compliments and compliment responses in New Zealand English. *Anthropological Linguistics* 28: 485–508.

1987. Hedging, fencing and other conversational gambits: an analysis of gender differences in New Zealand speech. In Pauwels, A. (ed.), *Women and Language in Australian and New Zealand Society*. Sydney: Australian Professional Publications, pp. 59–79.

1988. Paying compliments: a sex-preferential positive politeness strategy. *Journal of Pragmatics* 12: 445–65.

Huygens, I. 1979. Sociolinguistic Stereotyping in New Zealand. Unpublished MA thesis, Auckland, University of Auckland.

Huygens, I. and Vaughan, G. 1983. Language attitudes, ethnicity and social class in New Zealand. *Journal of Multilingual and Multicultural Development* 4: 207–23.

Hyndman, C. 1985. Gender and language difference: a small study of interrupting behaviour. MS, Wellington, Victoria University.

Jakich, M. 1987. The Yugoslav language in New Zealand. In Hirsh (ed.) 1987, pp. 117–24.

Jamieson, P. 1976. The Acquisition of English as a Second Language by Young Tokelauan Children living in New Zealand. Unpublished PhD thesis, Wellington, Victoria University.

1980. The pattern of urban language loss. *The Australian and New Zealand Journal of Sociology* 16: 102–9.

Kaplan, R. B. 1981. The language situation in New Zealand. *Linguistic Reporter* 23: 1–3.

Kennedy, G. D. 1982. Language teaching in New Zealand. In Kaplan, R. B. (ed.), *Annual Review of Applied Linguistics 1981*. Rowley MA: Newbury House, pp. 189–202.

Kroef, A. P. M. 1977. The Use of Language in a Three-Generational Group of Dutch Immigrants in New Zealand. Unpublished MA thesis, Auckland, University of Auckland.

Kuiper, K. and Austin, P. 1990. They're off and racing now: the speech of the New Zealand race caller. In Bell, A. and Holmes, J. (eds.) *New Zealand Ways of Speaking English*. Clevedon: Multilingual Matters, pp. 195–220.

Kuiper, K. and Haggo, D. 1984. Livestock auctions, oral poetry, and ordinary language. *Language in Society* 13: 205–34.

Kuiper, K. and Tillis, F. 1985. The chant of the tobacco auctioneer. *American Speech* 60: 141–49.

Lakoff, R. T. 1975. *Language and Woman's Place*. New York: Harper & Row.

Lane, C. 1985. Mis-communication in cross-examinations. In Pride (ed.) 1985, pp. 196–211.

McCallum, J. 1978. In search of a dialect: an exploratory study of the formal speech of some Maori and Pakeha children. *New Zealand Journal of Educational Studies* 13: 133–43.

Maclagan, M. A. 1982. An acoustic study of New Zealand vowels. *The New Zealand Speech Therapists' Journal* 37: 20–6.

Meyerhoff, M. 1986. 'The Kind of Women who put "-ish" behind Everything and "sort of" in front of it' – A Study of Sex Differences in New Zealand English. Unpublished MA thesis, Wellington, Victoria University.

    1987. Language and sex: research in New Zealand. In Pauwels, A. (ed.), *Women and Language in Australian and New Zealand Society*. Sydney: Australian Professional Publications, pp. 32–44.

Mitchell, A. G. and Delbridge, A. 1965. *The Speech of Australian Adolescents*. Sydney: Angus & Robertson.

Morton, R. and Williams, L. 1977. An investigation into the diphthongs of New Zealand English. MS, Auckland, University of Auckland.

Moynihan, I. 1980. A Comparative Study of the Language used by New Zealand Children of European and Samoan Descent aged 6 years 10 months to 8 years in a Conversation with an Adult. Unpublished PhD thesis, Palmerston North, Massey University.

Natusch, B. 1978. The Development of English and Japanese Phonology in a Bilingual Child 1 year 3 months to 1 year 8 months. Unpublished MA thesis, Palmerston North, Massey University.

Northcote-Bade, J. 1976. An introduction to New Zealand English. *Englisch* 4: 147–51.

Pride, J. B. (ed.) 1982. *New Englishes*. Rowley MA: Newbury House.

    (ed.) 1985. *Cross-Cultural Encounters: Communication and Mis-Communication*. Melbourne: River Seine Publications.

Ramson, W. S. (ed.) 1970. *English Transported: Essays on Australasian English*. Canberra: Australian National University Press.

Salmond, A. 1974. Rituals of encounter among the Maori: a sociolinguistic study of a scene. In Bauman, R. and Sherzer, J. (eds.), *Explorations in the Ethnography of Speaking*. London and New York: Cambridge University Press, pp. 192–212.

Simon, J. A. 1979. Maori English: does it exist amongst urban Maori children? MS, Auckland, University of Auckland.

Smith, L. 1978. Code-switching in a Maori university seminar. MS, Wellington, Victoria University.

Sollitt-Morris, L. and Brown, A. 1985. Do sex-based differences in language really exist? MS, Auckland, University of Auckland.

Stoffel, H.-P. 1982. Language maintenance and language shift of the Serbo-Croatian language in a New Zealand Dalmatian community. In Sussex, R. (ed.), *The Slavic Languages in Emigré Communities*. Carbondale, Illinois and Edmonton, Canada: Linguistic Research Inc., pp. 121–39.

Stubbe, M. 1978. Sex roles in conversation: a study of small group interaction. MS, Wellington, Victoria University.

Turner, G. W. 1966. *The English Language in Australia and New Zealand*. London: Longmans.

    1970. New Zealand English today. In Ramson (ed.) 1970, pp. 84–101.

Watkins, A. L. 1976. Samoan English: Some Linguistic Features of the Speech of Samoan Adolescents. Unpublished MA thesis, Auckland, University of Auckland.

Wee, M. L. 1974. A study of English Oral Skills of School Entrant Chinese in New Zealand. Unpublished MA thesis, Auckland, University of Auckland.

Wells, J. C. 1982. *Accents of English* Vol. 3. Cambridge: Cambridge University Press.

Young, M. L. 1973. The Auckland Chinese: A Community in Transition. Unpublished MA thesis. Auckland, University of Auckland.

11

Social constraints on the phonology of New Zealand English

DONN BAYARD

Background

Although speakers of northern hemisphere varieties of English perceive few, if any, differences between New Zealand English (NZE) and that of Australia (Wells 1982: 605; Trudgill and Hannah 1985: 18), New Zealanders have been aware of differences in their own speech for at least a century (Gordon 1983a, 1983b). All Kiwis share the stereotypes of the broad-accented cow cocky and the refined university professor.[1] However, the notion that accent varies according to socioeconomic 'class' distinctions stands in direct conflict with the cherished belief that New Zealand is a 'classless' society, at least in theory (Sinclair 1980: 316–17; Ausubel 1960: 27ff). The economic difficulties of the years after 1973 have weakened the myth, but its influence may have contributed to a lack of interest in sociolinguistic variation in NZE.

A second factor which impressed me as an American immigrant to New Zealand in 1970 was an apparent feeling of inferiority about the NZE accent (cf. Bayard 1990a) – a belief that it was little more than a colonial, non-standard variety of RP. When I began this study in 1984, very little quantitative research into NZE sociolinguistics had been done. The phonetic research which had been carried out relied on 'general NZE' speakers (Hawkins 1973a, 1973b; Maclagan 1982), only roughly defined along the lines of Mitchell and Delbridge's (1965) 'broad-general-culti-vated' trichotomy in Australia (see Guy, this volume).

I was interested not only in ascertaining if such a trichotomy was present in NZE, but also the degree of correlation with socioeconomic level, age, and sex. Obvious targets were 'class' variation in the values of the four 'stigmatised diphthongs' (ai) (au) (ei) (ou), but also variation in a series of mergers currently taking place: /ʍ/ and /w/; /eə/ and /iə/; /ʌʊl/ and /ɒl/ (and sometimes /ʌl/ as well); and /æ/ and /e/ before /-l/. I also investigated changes in pronunciation of some lexical items and replacement of others

169

Table 11.1. *NZE sample by age group and socioeconomic index*

Age group	Socioeconomic index											No.	%
	3	4	5	6	7	8	9	10	11	12	13		
6–11	–	4	1	4	11	–	–	–	–	–	–	20	14.2
12–19	5	2	3	1	2	–	1	–	2	3	–	19	13.5
20–29	1	3	5	3	2	6	8	4	7	5	1	45	31.9
30–39	–	–	1	3	4	2	3	–	4	1	–	18	12.8
40–49	–	1	2	4	2	–	1	1	2	–	2	15	10.6
50–59	–	3	–	2	–	1	1	–	–	–	–	7	5.0
60–69	–	1	1	–	2	–	2	3	–	–	1	10	7.1
70–74	–	2	–	–	3	–	1	1	–	–	–	7	5.0
No.	6	16	13	17	26	9	17	9	15	9	4	*141*	
%	4.3	11.3	9.2	12.1	18.4	6.4	12.1	6.4	10.6	6.4	2.8		*100*

under the rapidly increasing impact of American English on the New Zealand spoken media; results have been summarised elsewhere (Bayard 1989). This study will concentrate on the ten phonological variables which proved to be significantly associated with the rather simplistic definition of 'class' used here, and also with the age of NZE speakers; a few sex differences which emerged will be discussed briefly.

Scope and methods

Informants and sociological variables

Ideally the informants used should have been selected by a stratified random sampling technique such as those employed in the now classic studies of Labov (1966) and Trudgill (1974); however, as these authors admit, the difficulties in obtaining such a sample are many. Instead, the selection method used here was similar to the 'networking' procedure employed in Horvath's study of Sydney sociolects (1985): through selection of initial informants and informants' family, friends, and acquaintances, I attempted to obtain a fairly balanced sample in terms of age, sex, and socioeconomic level. As the number of values for age group and socioeconomic level I wished to employ were considerably larger than Horvath used (eight vs. two and eleven vs. three respectively), I was unable to attain the five-per-cell 'ideal' sample she employed; including sex, this would have entailed a sample of 880.

As table 11.1 shows, the final sample of 141 is not ideal; the 20–29 decade is over-represented and the three decades from 50 up are correspondingly under-represented. The socioeconomic spread is rather more even, save for the upper and lower extremes. A second important limitation on the sample is that it is strongly biased towards speakers from the southern half of the South Island (77 per cent from Dunedin city, Otago and Southland), and hence cannot be said to be fully representative of the country as a whole. However, an accent attitude study suggests that the average NZE speaker is unable to correctly distinguish regional variants of NZE, although these are popularly believed to exist (Bayard 1990a; see further Bell and Holmes, this volume). Enough of a sample of rural vs. urban speakers was present to allow inclusion of an urban – rural dichotomous variable in the analysis. Finally, the very important question of ethnic variation in NZE (as covered in Horvath's Sydney study) is not examined here, due to difficulties in obtaining a fully comparable sample of non-Pakeha informants in Dunedin (Pakehas are New Zealanders of European descent).[2] Despite these limitations, the results from this sample can certainly be taken as suggestive, if not definitive.

The socioeconomic index (SEI) employed here utilised not only occupation (based on Elley and Irving's 1972 classifications), but education (scaled from 1: primary school/Form V only, through 5: advanced degree[s]) and amount of private/boarding schooling). Overall SEI values were arrived at by summing these three scores, similar to the method used by Trudgill in his Norwich study (1974: 41). Predictably, occupation and private schooling showed a highly significant ($p < 0.001$) degree of rank-order correlation with education. The lower, middle, and upper middle socioeconomic 'classes' referred to below (Lower class = socioeconomic index groups 3–5; Middle class = socioeconomic index groups 6–11; Upper middle class = socioeconomic index groups 12–13) are those which produced the most clearcut breaks in several of the analyses, and are not to be interpreted as sociologically 'real'; 'class' in New Zealand is still probably best viewed as a continuum rather than as a number of discrete groups.

The speech sample and phonological variables

Informants were asked to read a 170-word passage at normal speed, and then 'slowly and carefully'; the passage was designed to include at least two occurrences each of Wells' 27 lexical sets (1982: 127–68). They were then asked to read a series of word lists to test for features of NZE discussed earlier by Hawkins (1973a, 1973b) and, since this research, more thoroughly described by Gordon and Deverson (1985) and, particularly, Bauer (1986). Speech samples for each informant were about four minutes long (considerably longer in the case of some younger informants).

Variables were auditorily scored on a 1–4 scale, with 4 representing 'conservative' RP values and 1 representing 'innovative'/'broad' values. As the text contained only two to ten tokens of each variable, I thought

Table 11.2. *Phonological variables, methods of scoring and percentage of sample having each value*

(hw): merger of initial /ʍ/ and /w/, as in *which/witch*

Scores	Percentage of total sample with score
1 = all [w]	66
2 = [ʍ] in word lists	9
3 = [ʍ] in word lists and slow reading	4
4 = all [ʍ]	21

Mean value: 1.81

(æ~e): merger of /æ/ and /e/ before /l/, as in *Ellen/Alan*

Scores	Percentage of total sample with score
1 = all items /æ/ or all items /e/	40
2 = some items slightly distinct	9
3 = all items distinct except *Ellen/Alan*	14
4 = all items distinguished (no merger)	34
	(3% missing)

Mean value: 2.44

(ʌ~ɒ~ou l): merger of /ʌ/, /ɒ/, /ou/ before /l/, as in *dull/doll/dole*

Scores	Percentage of total sample with score
1 = all merged as /ɒ/	4
2 = /ʌ/ in *dull*; /ɒu/ in both *doll* and *dole*	50
3 = all three distinct as /ʌ, ɒ, ɒu/	38
4 = all three distinct as /ʌ, ɒ, əu/	9
(as with some RP speakers)	

Mean value: 2.50

(l): final /l/ vocalisation ('dropping'), as in *hole*

Scores	Percentage of total sample with score
1 = /l/ always vocalised	4
2 = /l/ vocalised in reading texts, retained in word lists or, sometimes, vocalised in both	13
3 = /l/ reduced in reading texts or word lists	26
4 = /l/ fully retained	57

Mean value: 3.38

Table 11.2. *Continued*

(/iə~eə/): merger of /iə/ and /eə/, as in *fear/fair*

Scores	Percentage of total sample with score
1 = all unselfconsciously merged as [iə] or [eə]	40
2 = pauses, selfconsciously largely merged	11
3 = some pairs slightly distinguished	20
4 = all distinct, /iə/ versus /eə/	29

Mean value: 2.38

(ou): initial element in diphthong, as in *goat*

Scores	Percentage of total sample with score
1 = mid-low back [ɤʊ]	16
2 = mid-low back central [ʌʊ]	75
3 = mid-central [əʊ]	9
4 = mid-fronted [ɜʊ]	0

Mean value: 1.93

(ei): initial element in diphthong, as in *face*

Scores	Percentage of total sample with score
1 = low-mid central [ɐɪ]	2
2 = low-mid, slightly fronted [ɐ˖ɪ]	48
3 = mid-front, slightly backed [ɛ˗ɪ]	41
4 = mid-front [eɪ]	9

Mean value: 2.57

(au): initial element in diphthong, as in *mouth*

Scores	Percentage of total sample with score
1 = low-mid front [æʊ]	18
2 = intermediate [a˖ʊ]	55
3 = low front or central [aʊ] or [ɑ˖ʊ]	27
4 = low central-back [ɑʊ]	0

Mean value: 2.09

(ai): initial element in diphthong, as in *price*

Scores	Percentage of total sample with score
1 = low back [ɒɪ]	18
2 = low back [ɑɪ] or [ʌɪ]	69
3 = low back-central [ɑ˖ɪ]	9
4 = low central or central-front [aɪ]	4

Mean value: 1.99

Table 11.2. *Continued*

====

(i): diphthongisation of /i/, as in *speech*

Scores   Percentage of total sample with score
1 = marked diphthongisation as [əi]   6
2 = slight to marked diphthongisation, in range [əɹi] to [ɪi]   27
3 = slight diphthongisation as [ɪi]   57
4 = minimal or no diphthongisation; [i] usual   10

Mean value: 2.72

(linking /r/): as in *for it*
based on 5 possible occurrences in the reading passage

Scores   Percentage of total sample with score
1 = present in most or all cases, in both readings   42
2 = present in most or all cases in first reading; some
    omitted on second (slow) reading   35
3 = some present in first reading, none present in second
    (slow) reading   17
4 = none or only one present on both first and second
    readings   6

Mean value: 1.87   (1%) missing

(intrusive /r/)
based on two possible occurrences (*idea is, banana under*) in reading passage

Scores   Percentage of total sample with score
1 = present in both cases, in both readings   5
2 = present in both cases in first reading; one or both
    skipped on second (slow) reading   13
3 = one present in first reading, one or none on second   45
4 = none present in either reading   34

Mean value: 3.11   (3%) missing

====

that absolute quantification would give a false sense of precision; nor did I wish to convert each value on the 'innovative'–'conservative' scale into a variable in itself, based on an *a priori* 'broad'–'cultivated' classification (the approach adopted by Horvath 1985). Instead, a mean value was determined as the score for each speaker's use of each variable; in most cases little variation in values was noted for each speaker, and the procedure presented few difficulties, at least for a broad-spectrum study of this sort.

Of the 15 phonological variables investigated, 10 proved to have considerable social significance. The values used in scoring these are

Table 11.3. *Rank-order correlation coefficients for phonological variables with sociological variables*[1]

	SEI[2]	Age	Sex	URBR[3]	(ou)	(ei)	(au)	(ai)	(i)	(æ~e)	(ʌ~ɒ~ou)	(l)	(iə~eə)
Age	12												
Sex	−09	02											
	19	10	−06										
	02												
(ou)	35	01	18	06									
	00		03										
(ei)	22	05	19	−09	53								
	01		02		00								
(au)	37	03	14	01	61	57							
	00				00	00							
(ai)	24	15	22	02	48	49	62						
	00		01		00	00	00						
(i)	39	32	06	06	34	35	42	55					
	00	00			00	00	00	00					
(æ~e)	47	07	−14	18	28	21	19	14	29				
	00			04	00	01	02		00				
(ʌ~ɒ~ou)	24	24	−10	09	17	25	17	29	32	32			
	00	00			04	00	05	00	00	00			
(l)	34	33	02	19	22	14	18	22	34	27	29		
	00	00		02	01		03	01	00	00	00		
(iə~ea)	34	35	−12	15	17	24	14	20	41	48	29	31	
	00	00			05	00	02	00	00	00	00	00	
(hw)	03	58	07	−07	11	14	12	15	24	08	08	19	30
		00							01			03	00
	SEI[2]	Age	Sex	URBR[3]	(ou)	(ei)	(au)	(ai)	(i)	(æ~e)	(ʌ~ɒ~ou)	(l)	(iə~eə)

[1] decimal point omitted, two decimal places shown; significance [2-tailed t test] shown only when at 95% confidence level or above; see table 11.2 for abbreviations.
[2] SEI = Socioeconomic index
[3] URBR = Urban versus rural

presented in table 11.2. As presence or absence of linking and intrusive /r/ proved to have significant associations with the speaker's sex, they are included as well.

Data were analysed using SPSS[x] package programmes for rank-order correlation coefficients (Spearman's ϱ), partial correlation coefficients, factor (principal components) analysis, and discriminant analyses.

Results

The rank-order correlations given in table 11.3 make it apparent that significant associations are present between age and socioeconomic 'class' on the one hand and all ten of the phonological variables considered here. All of the latter are significantly associated with the socioeconomic index at $p \leq 0.01$ save (wh); (i), (ʌ~ɒ~ou), (l), and (iə~eə) are about equally associated with age, while (wh) is ascciated with age only. The correlations are of course not particularly high ones: in the range of what Fasold has called 'definite but small relationship' ($\pm$ 0.2–.4) or 'substantial relationship' ($\pm$ 0.4–.7; Fasold 1984: 104). This is, of course, to be expected when a number of different sociological variables are acting simultaneously on the phonological variables.

Partial correlation coefficients controlling for socioeconomic index predictably show a particularly strong association (+ 0.65) between /ʍ/ retention and greater age; (iə~eə) merger also appears to be more closely associated with youth than lower socioeconomic index. On the other hand, (æ~e) merger and (l) vocalisation are more positively correlated with lower socioeconomic index when age is controlled for, as are three of the four 'stigmatised diphthongs', (au), (ei), and (ou). (i) diphthongisation and (ʌ~ɒ~ou) merger are about equally correlated with lower socioeconomic index and youth. Some idea of the actual distribution of the values among the sample by age group and socioeconomic 'class' can be gained by examining the percentage figures presented in tables 11.4 and 11.5, and figures 11.1 and 11.2. Table 11.4 and figure 11.1 demonstrate that all of the ten phonological variables save (hw) show clear variation within the threefold arbitrary division of the socioeconomic spectrum employed here, with the 'lower class' using a higher proportion of the 'broad' variant and the 'upper middle class' using a higher proportion of the more 'conservative' variant (closer to RP).

The situation with those variables sensitive to age or to both age and class seems equally clear. Table 11.5 and figure 11.2 show that /ʍ/ is clearly on the point of vanishing as an effective contrast in NZE, as it has elsewhere. (iə~eə) merger and (ʌ~ɒ~ou) merger begin to predominate in the 30s to 50s decades, and both mergers may well become normal characteristics of NZE. (i) dipthongisation appears to be a more recent phenomenon (*if* we asume that these figures represent 'apparent time' – and there is evidence in my analyses of the pronunciation of items such as *lieutenant* and *schedule* that the concept is not quite as neat and tidy as it seemed to be 20 years ago; see Bayard 1987).

Space precludes detailed discussion of sex differentiation and urban – rural disinctions; however, table 11.6 summarises the results for those variables that were found to be differentiated for sex of speaker with a significance of < 0.05. Table 11.6 and figure 11.3 show, for those speakers who used a given variant of each variable, the percentage of speakers who were male and the percentage who were female. As has been found in numerous other studies, women showed a greater preference for the 'conservative' or more 'acceptable' variants (i.e., those given a value of 3 or 4);

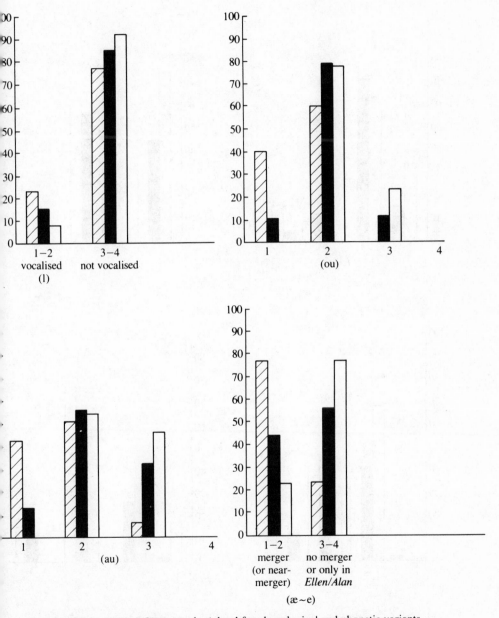

Figure 11.1 Percentage frequency by 'class' for phonological and phonetic variants.
▨ = 'lower'; ■ = 'middle'; ☐ = 'upper middle'; 1 = 'broad' variant;
4 = 'cultivated' variant.

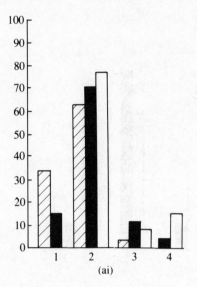

(ai)

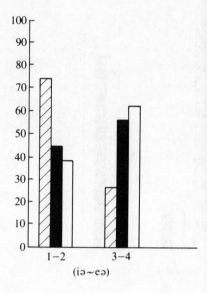

(iə~eə)

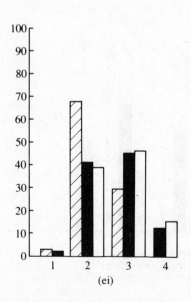

(ei)

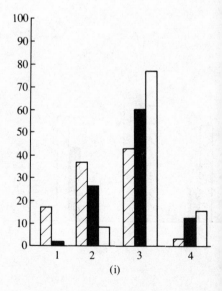

(i)

Figure 11.1 (continued)   Percentage frequency by 'class' for phonological and phonetic variants. ▨ = 'lower';   ■ = 'middle';   ☐ = 'upper middle'; 1 = 'broad' variant; 4 = 'cultivated' variant.

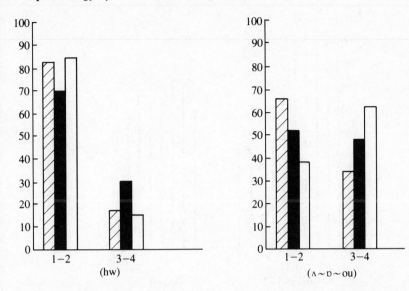

Figure 11.1 (continued) Percentage frequency by 'class' for phonological and phonetic variants. ▨ = 'lower'; ■ = 'middle'; ☐ = 'upper middle'; 1 = 'broad' variant; 4 = 'cultivated' variant.

Table 11.4. *Percentages by 'class' for phonological variants*

Variable	(au)				(ae~e)		(l)		(ou)				(ei)			
Value	*1*	*2*	*3*	*4*	*1–2*	*3–4*	*1–2*	*3–4*	*1*	*2*	*3*	*4*	*1*	*2*	*3*	*4*
Class:																
Lower	43	51	6	0	77	23	23	77	40	60	0	0	3	68	29	0
Middle	12	56	32	0	44	56	15	85	10	79	11	0	2	41	45	12
Upper middle	0	54	46	0	23	77	8	92	0	77	23	0	0	39	46	15

Variable	(i)				(ai)				(iə~eə)		(hw)		(ʌ~ɒ~ou)	
Value	*1*	*2*	*3*	*4*	*1*	*2*	*3*	*4*	*1–2*	*3–4*	*1–2*	*3–4*	*1–2*	*3–4*
Class:														
Lower	17	37	43	3	34	63	3	0	74	26	83	17	66	34
Middle	2	26	60	12	15	70	11	4	44	56	70	30	52	48
Upper middle	0	8	77	15	0	77	8	15	38	62	85	15	38	62

See table 11.2 for abbreviations and values.

only in the case of (æ~e) did female speakers show a greater tendency towards merger, and the correlation was not significant at the 0.05 level.

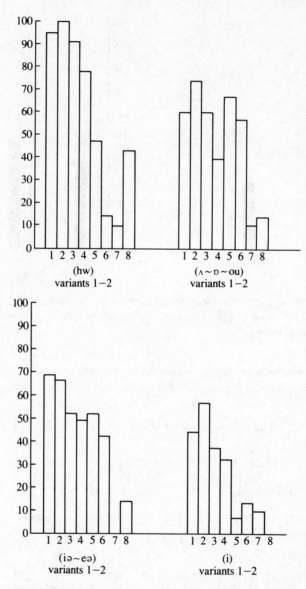

Figure 11.2 Percentage frequency by age group for variants of selected variables. Age groups: 1 = 6–11 years; 2 = 12–19 years; 3 = 20–29 years; 4 = 30–39 years; 5 = 40–49 years; 6 = 50–59 years; 7 = 60–69 years; 8 = 70+ years.

Significant contrasts between the urban–rural variable and phonological variables were limited to positive correlations between 'urban' and 'innovative' values of (æ~e) and (l), and this could well be due to the fact that the lower-socioeconomic index informants scored significantly lower on

Table 11.5. *Percentages by age group for selected phonological variables*

		Age Group							
		6–11 N=20	*12–19* N=19	*20–29* N=45	*30–39* N=18	*40–49* N=15	*50–59* N=7	*60–69* N=10	*70+* N=7
(hw)	1–2	95	100	91	78	47	14	10	43
(hw)	3–4	5	0	9	22	53	86	90	57
(ʌ~ɒ~ou)	1–2	60	74	60	39	67	57	10	14
(ʌ~ɒ~ou)	3–4	40	26	40	61	33	43	90	86
(iə~eə)	1–2	70	68	53	50	53	43	0	14
(iə~eə)	3–4	30	32	47	50	47	57	100	86
(i)	1–2	45	58	38	33	7	14	10	0
(i)	3–4	55	42	62	67	93	86	90	100

See table 11.2 for abbreviations and values.

Table 11.6. *Sex significant phonological variables, by per cent of sex using each value*

	(linking /r/)				(intrusive /r/)				(ai)				(ei)				(ou)			
	1	*2*	*3*	*4*	*1*	*2*	*3*	*4*	*1*	*2*	*3*	*4*	*1*	*2*	*3*	*4*	*1*	*2*	*3*	*4*
Male	57	41	29	25	86	42	51	31	69	41	42	17	100	49	47	8	61	45	23	0
Female	43	59	71	75	14	58	49	69	31	59	58	83	0	51	53	92	39	55	77	0

See table 11.2 for abbreviations and values.

the urban–rural variable (i.e., they were more 'urban') than those in socioeconomic index 8 and above.

Factor analyses of the phonological variables – both with and without sociological variables included – provided good corroboration of the overall pattern: a cluster containing (hw) only clearly associated with age alone; a second cluster containing the four 'stigmatised diphthongs' associated with socioeconomic index alone; and a third large cluster containing the remaining five variables, associated with both socioeconomic index and age. The two (r) variables, (linking /r/) and (intrusive /r/), formed a fourth cluster clearly associated with sex. However, it is important to point out that these three factors together accounted for only 24 per cent of the variance (socioeconomic index 14.9 per cent; age 5.2 per cent; sex 4.2 per cent).

Finally, we might ask how predictable the variables are as 'indicators' of

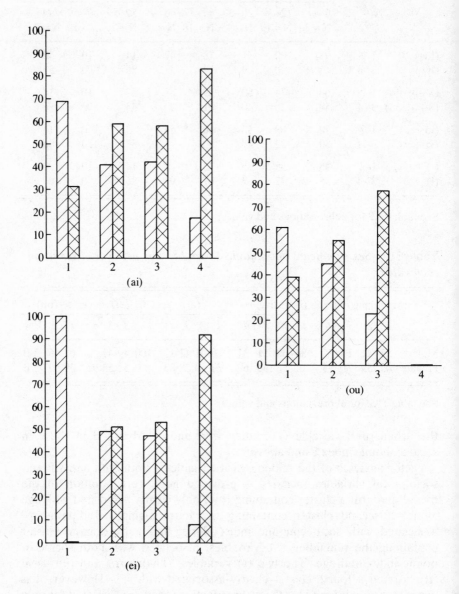

Figure 11.3   Percentage of male and female speakers using each variant of five variables. ▨ = male speakers; ▨ = female speakers; 1 = 'broad' variant; 4 = 'cultivated' variant.

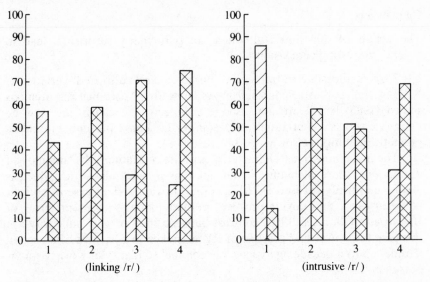

Figure 11.3 (continued)   Percentage of male and female speakers using each variant of five variables.   ⧄ = male speakers;   ⧆ = female speakers; 1 = 'broad' variant; 4 = 'cultivated' variant.

socioeconomic level. Several stepwise discriminant analyses were carried out to determine the degree to which this technique could predict class membership on the basis of the phonological variables alone. The analyses ranked these (in descending order) as (æ~e) (au) (ou) (iə~eə) (i) (ai) (ʌ~ɒ~ou) (ei) (l); (hw) had little or no discriminating power. A discriminant analysis including the nine significant variables, with the boundary between 'lower' and 'middle' class set at socioeconomic index 5/6, gave fairly clear-cut results: 'lower' and 'middle/upper middle' informants were classified correctly in 83.2 per cent of cases, and a three-way analysis with breaks at socioeconomic index 5/6 and 11/12 assigned 73.0 per cent correctly. I think most would agree that social stratification here is not as clearly marked as in the UK, and this is reflected in the overlaps present in the groups defined for the last two analyses: while the two-class analysis defined 95 per cent of the 'middle/upper middle' group correctly, 53 per cent of the 'lower class' were included as well. Similarly, while the 'lower class' group was assigned with 47 per cent correctness and the 'middle class' with 93 per cent in the three-class analysis, the 'upper middle' group was totally incorrect; all were placed in the 'middle' group.

    In short, while this study supports the presence of 'lower' and 'middle' socioeconomic classes in New Zealand, there is obviously considerable overlap. The 'upper middle' class arbitrarily defined here is supported only by the percentage figures given in table 11.4, and not by discriminant analyses.

Conclusions

The results of this study, although not particularly surprising, lead to several interesting conclusions.

1. It seems possible to talk about 'broad-general-cultivated' varieties of NZE as well as Australian English. As Horvath's Australian research has shown (1985), these are not discrete sociolects, but can in my view be better viewed as a continuum; at least in NZE.[3] I have presented tentative phonetic definitions elsewhere (Bayard 1990a).

2. The most 'notorious' characteristics of the continuum, the 'stigmatised diphthongs' (here including /i/ but not – as in Australia – /u/, which is almost uniformly realised as [ʉ] in NZE) provide a clear case of conflict between overt and covert prestige, perhaps better viewed in terms of Brown and Gilman's (1960) contrast between 'power' and 'solidarity': in this case the power and prestige of RP as spoken in what was often called 'Home' up to a decade ago versus the colonial solidarity of Kiwis vis-à-vis outsiders.[4]

3. New Zealand has been undergoing considerable social and economic change since the end of World War II, accelerating rapidly and profoundly after the twin shocks of oil price rises and Britain's entry into the EEC in 1973. This has been reflected in an increased nationalism (legal recognition of a distinct national anthem in 1977, and of a national flag only in 1981). It has also seen an apparent lessening of RP as a positive model, and substitution of 'general' NZE in many contexts, although TV newsreaders, after a period of rapid change from RP or near-RP in the early 1970s to something approximating 'cultivated' NZE, have lagged behind the trend (Bayard 1987, 1990a). If the discriminant analyses undertaken here are an even approximate indicator, there is a possibility that a real 'class'-based dichotomy – or at least a thin spot in the continuum – will emerge between the 'lower' and 'middle/upper middle' socioeconomic classes; such a development was predicted almost 30 years ago by Ausubel (1960: 229).[5] However, I cannot see the evolution of anything approaching the situation in the UK.

4. The relative weakening of RP and increased prestige of local models may well be helped by the impact of American English via the spoken media. This has been massive on the lexicon, idiom, and pronunciation of certain words (Bayard 1987, 1989), but the impact on NZE phonology has thus far been minimal aside from weakening the position of RP as an oft-heard prestige model. Indeed, the only possible candidate for incoming phonological influence on NZE at present is the apparently increasing frequency of final /-t/ glottalisation; if this does become a standard feature of NZE phonology it will of course be an importation from non-standard English English rather than General American (Bayard 1990b).

Finally, it is obvious that a very great amount of work remains to be done on NZE. Of particular importance is the investigation of 'ethnic' varieties (Maori and Pacific Island varieties in particular); and style and register variation in NZE. As a relatively isolated South Pacific speech community undergoing rapid social change, developing an increasingly independent political stance, and suffering a rather paradoxical increase in American influence, New Zealand has considerable potential as a sociolinguistic laboratory.

NOTES

1. Typified in the 1970s by John Clarke's archetypal Kiwi farmer Fred Dagg on the one hand and RP newsreaders on the other – what I have termed elsewhere the 'Dagg to Dougal' continuum (Bayard 1990a).
2. Unfortunately, Horvath's study reached me only in early 1987 – well after my research had been completed.
3. Horvath chooses to divide her 'periphery' and 'core' continua into discrete sociolects; I feel, however, that the apparently intuitive drawing of clusters she employs imposes a rather arbitrary subdivision (Horvath 1985: 74, 76).
4. Accent attitude surveys I have recently carried out suggest strongly that Australian and even General American accents are viewed positively in solidarity-related traits; RP and near-RP accents are not (Bayard 1990a). This same research also indicates a continuing feeling of inferiority about the NZE accent vis-à-vis RP and even General American.
5. I do not wish to imply support for all or even most of the conclusions in Ausubel's controversial work; as an ex-American I find many of them exaggerated or simply erroneous.

REFERENCES

Ausubel, David P. 1960. *The Fern and the Tiki: an American view of New Zealand National Character, Social Attitudes, and Race Relations.* New York: Holt, Rinehart & Winston.
Bauer, Laurie. 1986. Notes on New Zealand English phonetics and phonology. *English World-Wide* 7: 225–58.
Bayard, Donn. 1987. Class and change in New Zealand English: a summary report. *Teo Reo* 30: 3–36.
1989. 'Me say that? No way!': The social correlates of American lexical diffusion in New Zealand English. *Te Reo* 32: 17–60.
1990a. 'God help us if we all sound like this!' Attitudes to NZE and other English accents. In Bell, A. and Holmes, J. (eds.), *New Zealand Ways of Speaking English*. Clevedon: Multilingual Matters, pp. 67–96.
1990b. Minder, Mork, and Mindy? -T glottalisation and postvocalic -R in

younger NZE speakers. In Bell, A. and Holmes, J. (eds.), *New Zealand Ways of Speaking English*. Clevedon: Multilingual Matters, pp. 149–64.

Brown, Roger and Gilman, Albert. 1960. The pronouns of power and solidarity. In Sebeok, T. (ed.), *Style in Language*. Cambridge MA: Massachusetts Institute of Technology Press.

Elley, W. B. and Irving, J. C. 1972. A socio-economic index for New Zealand based on levels of education and income from the 1966 census. *New Zealand Journal of Educational Studies* 7(2): 153–67.

Fasold, Ralph. 1984. *The Sociolinguistics of Society*. Oxford: Blackwell.

Gordon, Elizabeth. 1983a. 'The flood of impure vocalisation' – a study of attitudes towards New Zealand speech. *New Zealand Speech-Language Therapists Journal* 38(1): 16–29.

1983b. New Zealand English pronunciation: an investigation into some early written records. *Te Reo* 26: 29–42.

Gordon, Elizabeth and Deverson, Tony. 1985. *New Zealand English: An Introduction to New Zealand Speech and Usage*. Auckland: Heinemann.

Hawkins, Peter. 1973a. The sound-patterns of New Zealand English. In *Proceedings and Papers of the 15th Congress*. Sydney: Australasian Universities Language and Literature Association 13. 1–8.

1973b. A phonemic transcription system for New Zealand English. *Te Reo* 16: 15–21.

Horvath, Barbara. 1985. *Variation in Australian English: The Sociolects of Sydney*. Cambridge: Cambridge University Press.

Labov, William. 1966. *The Social Stratification of English in New York City*. New York: Center for Applied Linguistics.

1972. *Sociolinguistic Patterns*. Oxford: Blackwell.

Maclagan, Margaret A. 1982. An acoustic study of New Zealand vowels. *New Zealand Speech Therapists' Journal* 37(1): 20–6.

Mitchell, A. G. and Delbridge, Arthur. 1965. *The Speech of Australian Adolescents: A Survey*. Sydney: Angus & Robertson.

Sinclair, Keith. 1980. *A History of New Zealand*. Revised and enlarged edition. Harmondsworth: Penguin.

Trudgill, Peter. 1974. *The Social Differentiation of English in Norwich*. Cambridge: Cambridge University Press.

Trudgill, Peter and Hannah, Jean. 1985. *International English: A Guide to Varieties of Standard English*. London: Edward Arnold.

Wells, J. C. 1982. *Accents of English*. 3 vols. Cambridge: Cambridge University Press.

12

Maori English: a New Zealand myth?

RICHARD A. BENTON

English and Maori in New Zealand

At the end of the 1970s it was estimated that there were about 70,000 fluent Maori speakers in New Zealand (Benton 1979a), less than 20 per cent of the total Maori population (385,000 in 1981), or about 3 per cent of the population of the country as a whole. Practically all of the Maori-speakers would have been bilingual, and the majority of them middle-aged or elderly. About half as many people again were thought to be passively bilingual (i.e., able to comprehend conversational Maori with little difficulty, but with limited speaking proficiency). A very much larger number of New Zealanders had some slight contact with the language – it had been included in the curriculum of many primary schools, for example, and had also obtained a foothold in radio broadcasting (although it did not feature regularly on television until the introduction of a five-minute daily news broadcast in Maori in 1986). However, for Maori and other New Zealanders alike, English has now long been the dominant language in most aspects of daily life.

The recent history of Maori and English in New Zealand has thus been characterised by a loss of functions by Maori on the one hand, and a corresponding expansion of functions (amounting often to an almost complete takeover) by English, on the other, within the former Maori speech community (cf. Metge 1964; Benton 1979a, 1979b, 1984a, 1986). These trends are illustrated in table 12.1, drawn from interviews conducted in 6,500 Maori households in cities, towns and rural areas throughout the North Island of New Zealand in the course of the sociolinguistic survey of Maori language use conducted by the New Zealand Council for Educational Research between 1973 and 1979 (Benton 1983).

By the 1970s, the only overwhelmingly Maori-language domain nationally was the *marae* in the strictest use of that term – the plaza in front of a meeting house where ceremonial speeches are made and rituals of encounter conducted – and then only during formal welcoming and speech-making; younger speakers, however, were tending to use English even there. Maori remained *relatively* strong in other circumstances in the *marae* environment, as well as in some religious practices, and was preferred in principle as a language for everyday conversation by many people who in practice spoke English most of the time. Homes where there were no young children were more likely to have Maori as a household language than those where children were present, indicating the generational differences in the conversational use of Maori (cf. Benton 1984a). A follow-up to the original survey in a few communities in 1986 (Benton 1987b) showed the pub to be analogous to the informal aspects of the *marae*: for older Maori-speakers, it was a place where Maori was preferred, and where younger speakers could be expected to use the language whenever possible.

English, however, now dominates in the home generally, and especially in interactions with (and between) children. The school has been an English-only domain until very recently, but education is the one domain in which Maori has made some inroads during the last decade; as well as the small number of (mainly) primary school classrooms where Maori is used as a medium of instruction, the language is widely taught as a subject in secondary schools, and is also increasingly used informally across the curriculum as part of a bicultural approach to schooling.

None the less, there has been a steady displacement of Maori by English throughout the twentieth century, which by the 1980s has reduced the number of Maori-speaking communities from hundreds to one or two. Maori has continued to be very important as a social bond between those who still speak it, and is an essential component of ceremonial aspects of Maori social life (cf. Salmond 1975; Metge 1976). However, it has become increasingly assumed that English is the lingua franca for most practical purposes, even within Maoridom. Assumptions concerning children have been particularly important; for at least a generation, most adults have come to assume that children either cannot speak Maori at all, or that their competence is limited to an ability to handle a few linguistic routines.

As with Gaelic in Scotland and Ireland (cf. Durkacz 1983), the replacement of Maori by English in New Zealand has been accomplished rapidly, with bilingualism leading not to diglossia (in the sense of stable bilingualism accompanied by language maintenance), but rather marking a brief interlude in the replacement of one language by the other. Vigorous attempts are now being made to reverse this process, through early-childhood Maori immersion programmes (the *kohanga reo* or 'language nests', 500 or more of which have been established since 1982), bilingual education, and intensive Maori language courses for adults. Maori has also very recently (July 1987) been accorded the status of an official

Table 12.1. *Use of English and Maori in various social contexts*

Domain/situation	Percentage* reporting use of		
	Maori	Both	English
Predominantly Maori domains			
Marae – formal			
Formal speechmaking (Elder)	94	5.6	0.4
Formal speechmaking (Informant)	73	10	17
Religion			
Prayers for sick (Northland)**	54	15	31
Opening prayers at meetings	50	26	24
Mixed and polarised domains			
Religion			
Prayers for sick (Overall)	46	15	41
Church services	42	35	23
Sermons	42	32	26
Grace at meals	41	13	46
Marae – social			
Chatting at a *hui* (meeting)	32	28	40
Home – no young children			
General language+	27	40	33
General language preference			
Prefer to speak . . .	42	28	30
Predominantly English domains			
Reading and writing			
Reading books and magazines	4	36	60
Reading preference	17	29	54
Writing preference	16	29	55
Workplace			
With workmates++	6	29	65
Neighbourhood			
With neighbours	11	25	64
Home			
Children to parents***	4	14	82
Parents to own children***	7	24	69
Adults to others' children	4	11	75
General language (children present)+++	4	42	54

* N = approx. 7,000, except where indicated; ** N = 740; *** N = 5,600; + N = 1,278; ++ N = 3,227; +++ N = 5,113

language, although its status under the new law is still inferior to English even for most bureaucratic purposes (cf. Benton 1987a).

The Maori language has not yet had the same degree of influence on English spoken by non-Maori New Zealanders that Hawaiian has had on colloquial English in Hawaii; nor, despite some portrayals of such speech in caricatures of Maori people in literature as late as the 1940s (cf. Pearson 1968) did an interlanguage evolve into a distinctive creole. Nevertheless, both New Zealand English and New Zealand Maori have influenced each other, although the extent and nature of these influences are not clear.

The most obvious influence of Maori on New Zealand English has been at the lexical level, with a large number of words for flora and fauna, some cultural concepts such as *mana* ('prestige', 'standing'), and a few expressions such as *taihoa* (anglicised to /taɪhou/) 'wait a bit'. In some regions where there has been long and intensive contact between the two speech communities, New Zealand English phonology may also have been influenced by Maori (cf. Hall 1976).

The effects of English on New Zealand Maori have been even less well studied. Most research into New Zealand Maori has concentrated on either cultivated or literary varieties. Even the formal or literary language has assimilated many English vocabulary items; the appendix to the most recent edition of Williams' dictionary lists about 600 such items, mostly nouns. What published evidence there is suggests that in less formal speech there is a much greater degree of English influence, extending to some aspects of syntax as well as unassimilated English loans in the Maori speech of children whose first language was Maori (Benton 1980, 1985a).

Maori English: Myths and theories

The existence of a distinctive Maori ethnic dialect or variety of English has long been assumed, both by creative writers (cf. Pearson 1968) and educators. One of the educationally-oriented investigations (the findings of which will be touched on again below) posited a Maori English comprising a set of subdialects, originating in the acquisition of English by earlier generations of Maori speakers and involving semantic, lexical and grammatical features 'transferred' from Maori and standardised in adult speech (Benton 1966: 79). Other commentators interested in the question of 'language problems' also took the existence of Maori English, in the sense of a stable dialect of New Zealand English, for granted.

Jack Richards, for example, stated that there were probably four dialects of English indigenous to New Zealand: Pakeha English 1, the prestige variety (presumably the closest to RP),[1] and Pakeha English 2, which differed mostly in pronunciation, together with Maori English 1, noted in popular folklore for the 'purity of its vowels', and Maori English 2, which differed from all three other varieties in aspects of grammar, vocabulary *and* pronunciation (Richards 1970: 131). He noted that 'most school teachers condemn [Maori English 2] and try to get their pupils to use either Maori English 1 or one of the Pakeha dialects'. Commenting on the linguistic aspects of Maori schooling, Byron Bender suggested that there were three major varieties of New Zealand English: Standard, Colloquial, and Maorified Colloquial (Bender 1971: 47). Many New Zealanders commanded all three varieties, but those who controlled only two could be at a disadvantage in some social situations, particularly if they were children in a classroom where the teacher regarded the Maorified variety as a problem to be eradicated.

Many commentators stressed the legitimacy of Maori English. One even pointed out that, based on what had been written about the non-standard features of Maori children's speech, the dialect could be regarded as superior to other New Zealand dialects, in that it was 'redundancy reduced', thus being a more efficient medium of communication, as well as serving as an instrument of social solidarity (George 1969: 37). Some official attitudes have not been so enthusiastic, however. A Department of Education handbook for primary school teachers claimed that

> The language used in many Maori homes is a dialect form of English, in which some of the non-standard usages are due to the influence of the Maori language . . . This distinctive element, which is easily recognized in the speech of many Maori children, can distract the teacher's attention from the basis of the dialect, which is a very restricted form of the English language. (Dept. of Education 1971: 21; cf. Benton 1975: 25–7)

The search for evidence

Two extensive collections of data on the English speech of Maori children (Barham 1965; Benton 1966), and another smaller-scale one (Anderson and Aitken 1965) were made in the 1960s. All these studies concentrated on the presence or incidence of deviations from what their authors considered to be New Zealand standard English, particularly in syntax and vocabulary, in children's speech, with the first two including non-Maori children as comparison groups.

The Barham study was confined to 6- and 8-year-olds, divided into three groups (selected by teachers): bilingual Maori, monolingual English-speaking Maori, and Pakeha children. Using Strickland's (1962) level 1 measure (based on sentence length) as his primary index of linguistic maturity, he found no significant differences between the Maori and Pakeha samples. He did find, however, that the Pakeha and monolingual English-speaking Maori children performed better on the verbal sections of an intelligence test and similar measures than the bilingual children, and that the vocabulary of Maori children was less wide-ranging than that of the Pakeha children.

The Benton study included children at all levels of the primary school system, and some from rural secondary schools. Again, Maori-speaking children were identified, in this case by the researcher. It was estimated that in the rural areas only 25 per cent of the children were monolingual English-speakers. Many teachers greatly underestimated the extent to which both passively and actively bilingual children could speak and understand Maori. In Auckland City, however, 65 per cent of the children were classed as monolingual in English. From information supplied by teachers and an analysis of recordings of children's speech, a lengthy catalogue of non-standard forms was produced, some of which could be accounted for in terms of influences from the Maori language on the acquisition of English in a bilingual environment, and others which were found in both Pakeha and Maori speech.

A reanalysis of the Barham data (Scott 1970), using a number of measures of linguistic complexity and maturity, found little difference between the speech of the supposedly monolingual English groups, but that the Maori-speaking children had made no growth in linguistic maturity between the ages of 6 and 8, and appeared to have more restricted vocabularies than the English speakers. He also found no 'errors' which were peculiar to either Maori group. He did however list a number of usages 'peculiar to children', without further analysis: lack of subject/verb concord, uninflected stem signalling past tense, and so on.

Other authors had also pointed out that the same non-standard forms occur in the English of both Maori and non-Maori children in New Zealand (cf. Reid 1966; Richards 1968; Durkin 1972). However, in planning a study designed specifically to test the hypothesis that Maori English exists as a distinctive dialect of New Zealand English, McCallum, following Labov et al. (1968), noted that these were just the kinds of structures which, when analysed for relative frequency of occurrence in the speech of different classes of people, might signal the presence of a non-standard dialect (McCallum 1973: 4).

The McCallum study (McCallum 1978) looked at the English speech of four groups of children – Pakeha children from high socioeconomic status families, monolingual English speaking Pakeha and Maori children from lower SES families, and Maori speaking children from a rural community. She did find some differences, particularly between the extremes ('Professional Pakeha' and Maori-speaking Maori), the most noticeable of which was the use by the Maori speakers of *went to* or *went and* plus stem to indicate simple past tense, as in:

> . . . and the butterfly went to pass, and they went to make a house . . .

(this structure was also noted as particularly prevalent in the speech of Maori children by Benton 1966: 28, 51). None the less, she felt compelled to conclude, after a careful examination of the data, that:

the similarities vastly outweigh the differences, for both Maori groups are in fact producing between 84 and 90 per cent standard verb forms. This is scarcely convincing evidence for the development of a separated potentially stable dialect. (McCalum 1978: 142)

Simon (1979), in a study of the speech of Maori children in Auckland, also found that many of the structures identified by Benton 1966 as more common among Maori children were still used by these city children, but nevertheless concluded that the evidence was not strong enough to establish the existence of a Maori English dialect.

The few studies dealing with phonological aspects of New Zealand English in relation to ethnicity have similarly failed to establish clear differences between Maori and other variants of New Zealand English. In her acoustic study of the characteristics of vowels in the speech of adult Maori and Pakeha New Zealanders in a Northland town, Hall (1976) set out to investigate the presence of regionalism in New Zealand speech, and to identify the differences (if any) in speech between Pakeha and Maori (bilingual and monolingual in English), and the influence of Maori on spoken English. She found some common characteristics (e.g., a 'telescoping of articulation') shared by her Northland informants and Aucklanders included in a separate study, when compared with RP norms, which could have arisen from a combination of isolation, the influence of the Maori language, and social factors such as the development of a New Zealand identity.

She was able to indentify some differences between the Maori speakers and the others (e.g., opening of back vowels and more articulatory movement with diphthongs) which seemed to reflect familiarity with two articulatory systems, and having acquired Maori before English. There were a few characteristics which differentiated the speech of all Maori informants from their Pakeha counterparts, most noticeably an even greater flexibility in the production of monophthongs (so that /i/, /ɪ/ and /e/ overlapped to a high degree, compared with /i/ and /e/ among the Pakeha), and a larger diphthong triangle, so that there were more distinctions between the vowels 'even among [iə, eə, eɪ] which are composed of the most overlapping phonemes'. These distinctive characteristics, however, were most marked among informants who had acquired Maori before English.

It is not surprising, therefore, that attitude and psycholinguistic studies (like those by Gould 1972; Huygens and Vaughan 1983; and Bayard 1990, discussed by Bell and Holmes in this volume) have found that Maori and Pakeha accents have been indistinguishable much of the time, and that Pakeha speakers with a 'broad' or 'working class' accent are often misindentified as Maori. Since there is a disproportionate number of Maori people in the lower socioeconomic categories, this again is unremarkable.[2]

Table 12.2. *School Certificate Pass Rates in Maori and English (third-year students only)*

	Year, and percentage of candidates passing				
	1981	1982	1983	1984	1985
English					
Maori candidates	29.0	29.3	40.2	40.5	37.5
Other candidates	57.7	57.2	60.5	60.5	61.0
Maori					
Maori candidates	40.0	41.4	46.0	57.3	60.4
Other candidates	46.5	46.6	41.5	64.0	56.1

Source: Department of Education 1982–6

There is also a possibility that the most significant differences between Maori and other variants of New Zealand English are those which are least accessible to direct observation: that is, that they lie in the areas of semantics and metaphor. This possibility has been discussed in Benton 1985a (cf. also Metge 1979). Maori children included in the trial group for the standardisation of a test of scholastic abilities had particular difficulty with items concerning certain common idioms, such as *to turn turtle, to have a close shave*, and *the coast is clear*, which led to these being excluded from the test (cf. Reid and Gilmore 1983: 26). Yet Maori speech (in English or Maori) is far from devoid of figurative language.

This kind of evidence suggests that there are differences at the semantic and especially the metaphorical levels which neither Maori nor Pakeha interlocutors may recognise: that is, that there are (with very minor exceptions) practically identical syntactic and phonological rules governing the English speech of Maori and Pakeha alike, a few semantic differences – mainly in terms denoting certain religious and cultural concepts – but that the figurative codes (cf. Steinmann 1973) may be very different.

This may help to explain some of the differences in performance of Maori and non-Maori students in the subjects English and Maori respectively in the national school certificate examination (taken in the third year of high school). As can be seen from table 12.2, there are large and consistent differences between the two groups of students in pass rates in English, whereas in Maori the differences are smaller, and do not consistently favour either group. One reason for this may be that no effort is made to control the figurative content of the English examination, where most of the candidates are assumed to be native speakers, whereas the Maori examination is prepared for second language learners, and therefore, ironically, is likely to be much more literal in style and content.

A tentative conclustion

Although the evidence for the existence of Maori English as a distinct and stable (or at least autonomous) variety of New Zealand English is at best tentative and ambiguous, it would be surprising if the largely English-speaking population comprising the identifiable and distinctive Maori subculture in New Zealand (cf. Fitzgerald 1977: 140–52) did not in some way manifest this identity and distinctiveness in the English speech of its members. In fact, this identity *is* manifested linguistically in Maori usage of English, perhaps semantically and figuratively (as suggested above), and certainly by the use of a number of devices reflected also in many passages in stories by contemporary Maori authors.

One such device is the systematic use of non-standard forms, which are not themselves confined to Maori New Zealanders; the effect is often heightened in writing by a contrasting standardisation of the equivalent form in the speech of Pakeha characters. Another is the representation of 'Maori' pronunciations of a number of common terms, making use, for example, of the /i, ɪ, e/ overlap noted in Hall's 1976 study – thus 'fellow' becomes *fulla* instead of *fella*. A third, almost universally employed, is the use of Maori words and phrases, especially in 'stream of consciousness' narrative involving memories of older Maori-speaking relatives. These importations from Maori may go beyond the range of Maori vocabulary with which most Pakeha New Zealanders would be familiar, or consist of relatively well known words (like *kai*, 'food') which, though well known, would seldom be used by Pakehas in normal conversation with each other. Pakeha insensitivity (or incompetence) in the pronunciation of proper nouns and other Maori words by using English rather than an approximation of Maori phonology may also be emphasised.

All these devices are illustrated in a short story published recently in a Maori bimonthly magazine. The alienation of the principal character is symbolised by the way in which the Pakeha actors mangle or stumble over his name:

> 'T'tuki Row-paata!' The voice and cop again. 'Ya here? Row-paata?'
> It broke Tuki's peace, the foreign sounds leaving him cold, like the room within which he sat.

> 'Yes, Mr Findlay,' he heard the judge say. 'You have talked to Mr Ro . . .' A slight hesitation, then: 'Ropata. Yes, Ropata, I take it?' (Anonymous 1986:62)

In the story, the Maori character habitually uses the form 'Yeah', where the counsel and judge are equally punctilious in using 'Yes'. Similarly, the 'Maori English' *fulla* makes its appearance:

'Wanna plead guilty,' Tuki replied. 'I hit that pakeha fulla', he said to the floor.

In the principal character's memories of conversations with his grandfather on the power of words, Maori words and phrases (emphasised and translated in the examples below, but not in the original) are used to give a Maori flavour to the narrative:

'The power of the word, *e moko* [grandson] . . .'.

His *koro* [grandad] paused, melancholy, remembering.

'. . . Your *tipuna* [ancestors], they hear them . . .' 'You shoot something into the sky, what happens? You watch, watch, watch. Ha! Goes out of sight. *Ne ra*? [Doesn't it?]'

At present, Maori English could perhaps most confidently be described as a variety (or set of varieties) of New Zealand English, varying according to the setting, and possibly also in some aspects according to the class-related variety of non-Maori English habitually spoken by each interlocutor. It would more commonly be encountered in settings in which most or all of the interlocutors were Maori, than where the majority were Pakeha. It certainly incorporates lexical items and phonological features derived directly (and often consciously) from the Maori language. It is possible that there are, as well, other features not unique to Maori English, but perhaps employed by Maori English speakers in ways different from those characterising the speech of other New Zealanders. It is also possible that there is an 'inaudible' form of Maori English, with a different 'figurative code' from that employed by other New Zealand English speakers, but syntactically and phonologically indistinguishable from 'normal' New Zealand speech.

There is obviously plenty of scope for research on the vocabulary, syntax, semantics and figurative structure of English spoken by New Zealanders who are members of the Maori community. However, such research is sensitive in nature in an atmosphere where 'non-standard' is still frequently interpreted as 'substandard,' where dialect is often a pejorative term, and where Maori people are increasingly suspicious and resentful of research which has the effect of exposing their social anatomy and physiology to the world at large, with little if any demonstrable benefit to them individually or as a people (cf. Stokes 1985). The mysteries of Maori English are thus likely to remain opaque to scholars for some considerable time to come.

NOTES

1. Pakehas are New Zealanders of European descent.
2. At the time of the 1981 Census, 75 per cent of the Maori population aged 15 and over had incomes below NZ$10,000 a year, compared with 66 per cent of the rest of the population in that age group. More significantly, perhaps, less than 5 per cent of Maori full-time workers were in positions classified as professional and technical or administrative and managerial, compared with more than 18 per cent of the non-Maori full time workforce (Department of Statistics 1982, 1983).

REFERENCES

Anderson, L. and Aitken, R. 1965. A study of the speech and idiom of Maori children in the Western Bay of Plenty. MS, Auckland, Auckland Teachers College.
Anonymous. 1986. Sticks and stones. *Tu Tangata* 32: 62–4.
Barham, I. H. 1965. *The English Vocabulary and Sentence Structure of Maori Children*. Wellington: New Zealand Council for Educational Research.
Bayard, D. 1990. 'God help us if we all sound like this!': attitudes to NZE and other English accents. In Bell, A. and Holmes, J. (eds.), *New Zealand Ways of Speaking English*. Clevedon: Multilingual Matters, pp. 67–96.
Bender, B. W. 1971. *Language Factors in Maori Education*. Wellington: New Zealand Council for Educational Research.
Benton, R. A. 1966. *Research into the English Language Difficulties of Maori School Children 1963–1964*. Wellington: Maori Education Foundation.
1975. Language and the Maori child. In McDonald, G. (ed.), *Children and Language*. Wellington: Association for the Study of Childhood.
1979a. *Who Speaks Maori in New Zealand?* Wellington, New Zealand Council for Educational Research.
1979b. *The Maori Language in the nineteen-seventies*. Wellington: Maori Unit, NZ Council for Educational Research.
1980. Changes in language use in a rural Maori community. *Journal of the Polynesian Society* 89: 455–78.
1983. *The NZCER Maori Language Survey: Notes on the Purposes and Methodology of the Sociolinguistic Survey of Language Use in Maori Households and Communities*. Wellington: Maori Unit, New Zealand Council for Educational Research.
1984a. Bilingual education and the survival of the Maori language. *Journal of the Polynesian Society* 93: 247–66
1984b. Smoothing the pillow of a dying language: official policy towards the Maori language in New Zealand since World War II. In Gonzalez, A. B. (ed.), *Language Planning, Implementation and Evaluation: Essays in Honor of Bonifacio P. Sibayan on his Sixty-Seventh Birthday*. Manila: Linguistic Society of the Philippines, pp. 24–39.
1985a. Maori, English, and Maori English. In Pride, J. B. (ed.), *Cross Cultural*

Encounters: Communication and Mis-Communication. Melbourne: River Seine Publications.

1985b. *Bilingual Education Programmes Evaluation: Final Report*. Wellington: New Zealand Council for Educational Research.

1986. Schools as agents for language revival in Ireland and New Zealand. In Spolsky, B. (ed.), *Language and Education in Multilingual Settings*. Clevedon: Multilingual Matters.

1987a. From the treaty of Waitangi to the Waitangi Tribunal. In Hirsh, W. (ed.), *Living Languages: Bilingualism and Community Languages in New Zealand*. Auckland: Heinemann.

1987b. *The Maori Language at School and in the Community: The Views of Parents in Eight Districts*. (Community Research Report No. 4). Wellington: Maori Unit, New Zealand Council for Educational Research.

Biggs, B. G. 1968. The Maori language past and present. In Schwimmer, E. (ed.), *The Maori People in the Nineteen-Sixties*. Auckland: Blackwood and Janet Paul, pp. 65–84.

Department of Education. 1971. *Maori Children and the Teacher*. Wellington: Government Printer.

1982–6. *School Certificate Examination Statistics 1981 . . . 1985*. Wellington: Department of Education.

Department of Statistics. 1982. *New Zealand Census of Population and Dwellings 1981, Volume 8A: Maori Population and Dwellings*. Wellington: Department of Statistics.

1983. *New Zealand Census of Population and Dwellings 1981, Volume 5: Incomes and Social Security Benefits*. Wellington: Department of Statistics.

Durkacz, V. E. 1983. *The Decline of the Celtic Languages*. Edinburgh: John Donald.

Durkin, M. E. 1972. A study of the pronunciation, oral grammar and vocabulary of West Coast schoolchildren. Unpublished MA thesis, University of Canterbury.

Fitzgerald, T. K. 1977. *Education and Identity: A Study of the New Zealand Maori Graduate*. Wellington: New Zealand Council for Educational Research.

George, H. V. 1969. Language and social equality. *Te Kaunihera Maori* Autumn Issue: 31–7.

Gould, P. 1972. Assessment of status by accent: an aspect of sociolinguistic competence. MS, Department of English, Victoria University of Wellington.

Hall, M. 1976. An acoustic analysis of New Zealand vowels. Unpublished MA thesis (English), University of Auckland.

Huygens, I. and G. Vaughan. 1983. Language attitudes, ethnicity and social class in New Zealand. *Journal of Multilingual and Multicultural Development* 4: 207–23.

Labov, W., Cohen, P., Robins, C. and Lewis, J. 1968. *A Study of the Non-Standard English of Negro and Puerto Rican Speakers in New York City*. Final Report, Cooperative Research Project 3288 (2 vols.). New York: Office of Education.

McCallum, J. 1973. Review and preview of research into Maori English. Working paper. Wellington: New Zealand Council for Educational Research.

1978. In search of a dialect: an exploratory study of the formal speech of some

Maori and Pakeha children. *New Zealand Journal of Educational Studies* 13: 133–43.

Metge, J. 1964. *A New Maori Migration: Rural and Urban Relations in Northern New Zealand.* London: The Athlone Press.

1976. *The Maoris of New Zealand: Rautahi.* London: Routledge & Kegan Paul.

1979. The translation of culture. Paper presented at the Symposium on Cross-cultural aspects of Cognition, 49th Congress of the Australian & New Zealand Association for the Advancement of Science, Auckland.

Mitcalfe, B. 1967. Survivals of Maori in English. *Education* 16 (8): 20–22.

Pearson, B. 1968. The Maori and literature 1938–65. In Schwimmer, E. (ed.), *The Maori People in the Nineteen-Sixties.* Auckland: Blackwood and Janet Paul, pp. 217–56.

Reid, C. T. 1966. Why call it a Maori difficulty? *National Education* 48: 74–5.

Reid, N. and Gilmore, A. 1983. Pupil performance on TOSCA: some additional information. *New Zealand Journal of Educational Studies.* 13: 133–43.

Richards, J. C. 1968. Language problems of Maori children. *Comment* 36: 23–32.

1970. The language factor in Maori schooling. In Ewing, J. and Shallcrass, J. (eds.), *Introduction to Maori Education.* Wellington: New Zealand Universities Press, pp. 122–32.

Salmond, A. 1975. *Hui: A Study of Maori Ceremonial Gatherings.* Wellington: A. H. & A. W. Reed.

Scott, D. I. 1970. Some structural analyses of the colloquial English of certain urban Maori and Pakeha children aged 6 and 8. Unpublished MA thesis, University of Auckland.

Simon, J. A. 1979. Maori English: does it exist among urban children? MS, Department of Anthropology, University of Auckland.

Steinmann, Martin, Jr. 1973. Figurative language and the two code hypothesis. In Fasold, R. W. and Shuy, R. (eds.), *Analyzing Variation in Language: Papers from the Second Colloquium on New Ways of Analyzing Variation.* Washington DC: Georgetown University Press, pp. 220–7.

Stokes, E. 1985. *Maori Research and Development: A Discussion Paper.* Wellington: National Research Advisory Council.

Strickland, R. G. 1962. The language of elementary school children: its relationship to the language of reading textbooks and the quality of reading of selected children. *Bulletin of the School of Education* (Indiana University) 38 (4).

13

Sporting formulae in New Zealand English: two models of male solidarity

KOENRAAD KUIPER

Introduction

This is a study of two ways in which adult males in New Zealand become members of groups. It is, in other words, a study in solidarity. The models which will be put forward both achieve the same ends: induction into a group through the acquisition of certain routines, specifically certain linguistic routines. These routines are most clearly seen in the acquisition and use of a set of routine formulae (Coulmas 1979, 1982) which exemplify the strategies the two groups use to make men members of their groups. The two strategies are quite different. In one group, formulae are used to save face; specifically, the face of players in a recreational volleyball squad. In the other group, sexual humiliation is used as a means of creating group solidarity through the loss of face the individuals who belong to the group suffer.

Preliminary remarks

If I use the New Zealand English formula *Gidday* with a wink and a characteristic quick southeast to northwest movement of the head, the conditions of use for such a greeting are relatively specific; it is an informal greeting to one with whom one is not intimate. It is not middle class but characteristically working class, and/or rural. It is often used when no response is expected.

While learning the linguistic aspects of such a formula can be regarded as a part of language acquisition, learning conditions of use is a function of acculturation:

> patterns of message construction, or 'ways of putting things', . . . are part
> of the very stuff that social relationships are made of (or, as some would

prefer, crucial parts of the expression of social relationships). (Brown and Levinson 1978: 60)

In previous work (Kuiper and Haggo 1984) it has been shown that being an auctioneer involves mastering a set of specialised formulae used only for auctioning and, for each formula, mastering its conditions of use. It is clear from the speech of auctioneers that the acquisition of these formulae is almost sufficient to make one who has acquired them a member of a group whose identity is a partial function of such knowledge. To generalise, vocabulary acquisition is a function of socialisation and the particular sub-vocabularies which one acquires as a native are no exception.

As a consequence, group membership can be identified by particular kinds of vocabulary acquisition. But it is possible to take a further step in the case of some groups. There are groups which do not need to share a common vocabulary to be a group. For example, sports teams share a common goal of playing a particular game together for a particular purpose which may, for example, be recreational or competitive. Yet many sports teams develop a common vocabulary which is only tangentially related to the game the team is playing. Some formulae will be common to all those playing the particular game, or playing that game in a particular place or for a particular club. Other formulae may be unique to a particular team. Such formulae can serve primarily to create group solidarity. How they do that is the question posed in the present study.

Face saving as a strategy for solidarity: recreational volleyball formulae

The group which provides the model for the first pattern meets twice a week for recreational volleyball. Its members are all male employees of a large organisation and they come from all over the organisation. Few of them meet each other regularly in the normal course of events; in fact, many members of the group meet only through their membership of the group which plays recreational volleyball.

When the group meets to play there are no set teams, since attendance fluctuates. The official rules of the game are regarded as a guideline only for what is done. There is a set of common law rules which includes a number of the official rules and the absence of others as well as additional conventions developed over the years. As a result, overly legalistic members of the group tend either to adapt or to leave in frustration. The game is played for a set period rather than to win and frequently players do not know or care what the score is.

As well as playing volleyball, members of the group frequently talk and shout to and at each other during play. This verbal interaction is partly oral-formulaic in that the group knows a number of formulae which are used on a regular basis in the game. The inventory of formulae is not large and it is not the only way that the members of the group address each other. It is, however, an interesting indication of the dynamics of the group.

The formulae used in recreational volleyball are related to particular episodes in the game as it is played.

Start of game formula:

1.   Our serve.

This is a formula very frequently used to start the game after the warm up.

Serving formulae:
There is a set of formulae used before a serve. Many of these are used only by particular individuals but they are recognised as belonging to the group.

2.   They drop quickly.
3.   Watch the spin on these.

These two formulae are spoken by the server and addressed to the receiving team to warn them of the quality of the coming serve.

4.   Once today.

This formula is addressed to the server by a member of the receiving team and is an invitation to the server to serve into the net or out of bounds.

Formulae used between the gaining of a point and the next serve being taken:

5.   It's like taking candy off a baby.

This formula is said by a member of the team which has just scored an easy point.

6.   Always a winner.

This formula is used by the winner of a point when that point has been won by the unorthodox method of punching the ball over the net and the opposing team having failed to return it. It is also used ironically when the same tactic results in the ball going under or into the net or out of bounds. In such a case it is almost always used by someone in the team opposing the user of the punch tactic.

7.   He's worth two to the opposition any day.

This formula is used with reference to one player only and is used by someone in the team opposing that in which this particular player plays. It is used when the particular player has made an error costing a point or a service turn.

8.   Two points for that one.

This formula is used by a player when someone in his team has scored a point which is regarded as having been done particularly well.

9.   The old one, two, three.

This formula is used by a member of a team which has scored a point as a result of touching the ball on its side of the net the normal three times.

10.   The old sucker shot.

This formula is used by a member of a team when that team has just scored a point through a ball being directed into the net at close range by a member of the opposing team.

11.   Justice!

This formula is used when a team considers, after winning a point, that the previous point won by the opposing team was unfairly won (for example, if it was won as a result of someone insisting that the rules of the game should be invoked.)

12.   Play the setups.

This formula is used by a member of a team when a player in that team who should know and be able to do better does not set the ball up for the other players in the team. Note that this is always a general exhortation and it is never said when a player is new to the group or relatively less able at volleyball.

13.   Where was the block on that one?

Used by a member of a team which has just lost a point to a particularly hard spike. Used ironically, since conventional blocking as used in actual volleyball is a rare occurence in recreational volleyball particularly when the spike looks to be a hard one.

Scoring formula:

14.   14–3.

This formula is used, usually by the serving team, after a point has been scored, when the score has not been kept track of, or merely as a jocular way of confusing the opposition. (The winning point in a match is usually fifteen. The formula thus indicates that the team which has just won a point is only one point away from winning the game.)

There are other formulae which might be similarly analysed for their role in discourse. However, what is interesting about the above cases is the question of why they are used at all. They are clearly a response to situations in the game, but they serve no function in the game as game. The rules of volleyball explicitly forbid excessive calling on the court. Their use therefore has to be explained on grounds other than their role in the game. Their role can be explained in terms of the theory of politeness developed by Brown and Levinson (1978, 1987) who suggest that politeness is a way of saving face: either saving the speaker's face or the hearer's face. Face 'is the public self image that everyone wants to claim for himself, consisting of two related aspects:

(a) negative face . . . the freedom of action and freedom from imposition
(b) positive face: the positive consistent self image or 'personality' (crucially including the desire that this self image be appreciated and approved of) claimed by interactants'. (Brown and Levinson 1978: 66)

Let us call a face-threatening act which threatens positive face 'humiliating' and one which threatens negative face 'coercive'. Politeness strategies thus mitigate humiliating or coercive acts.

In social volleyball there are ample opportunities for the loss of positive face, that is, for humiliation. The players are not terribly proficient and therefore there are frequent errors. Since it is a game where a score is kept (even if in a perfunctory way), an error may result in a loss of positive face for the team, namely in defeat. Furthermore, the players are drawn from the whole of the organisational hierarchy and thus someone higher in the hierarchy may lose face in the eyes of people lower down, whereas people lower down may have their position on the hierarchy reinforced if they make playing errors of which their organisational superiors are aware. However, the purpose of the game is recreational and therefore some way has to be found for there to be no loss of face. Most of the formulae outlined above have this function if their relationship to the discourse is reanalysed in terms of politeness strategies.

The serving formulae tell the receiver (and everyone else) that the serves to come (which everyone knows to be suitably innocuous) may for the purposes of politeness be perceived as particularly dangerous. Thus, if a receiver fails to deal adequately with the serve there is no loss of face in that for the receiver. If the receiver does not fail, so much the more credit. The formula *on the line* which is said in the face of the evidence says to the player who has just served the ball out, that as far as the members of the player's team are concerned the serve was good, without it making any practical difference. The point is always conceded. Thus, the player who has served out saves face through the politeness strategy which is inherent in the use of the formula. The formula *justice!* might be used on the next exchange to show the server again that the serve was good in the eyes of team members, without there being faulty perception of the actual facts.

The formula *14–3* which is used after winning a point tells everyone that the score is of so little relevance that there is no loss of face in losing the game. (It also functions as a morale booster for one's own team, of course.) Even the formula *He's worth two to the opposition any day* can be regarded as a politeness formula since, although it expresses an element of censure against a particular player, it does so in terms which suggest that the player is of worth even if it is to the opposition team which uses this formulae. The fact that the censure does not come from the members of the censured player's own team allows a measure of face saving. Thus most of these formulae receive a functional explanation as face-saving politeness formulae.

What effect does the use of these formulae have? Clearly it has the potential to create group solidarity. Just simply learning the formulae of a small group can have this result, but in the case of these formulae it is even more likely, since players who are members of the group know, when they know the group's formulae, that the group has and uses the resources of a set of politeness formulae which will allow any player, regardless of status, to save face in potentially face-threatening situations. This makes belonging to the group agreeable. It is clear that a group whose members use such politeness strategies as the dominant mode of verbal interaction can be termed civilised.

Face-threatening rituals of sexual humiliation as a strategy for solidarity: rugby football locker room formulae of address

The contrasting situation is based on the verbal interaction of members of a rugby team before and after a game or practice. The formulae here do not have specific links with episodes in the game. Instead they function in the banter that seems to pervade locker rooms. The examples which will be used here are modes of address, greetings and vocative formulae. The following are not the only modes of address, but they have been selected to illustrate a particular and dominant strategy:

15. . . . , cock.
16. Morning girls.
17. . . . , you fucking old woman.
18. . . . , you fucking ugly girl.
19. If I left it any longer, cunts, you'd say I was fucking around.
20. You're late, cunt.
21. . . . , you wanker.
22. . . . , you bastard.
23. . . . didn't catch the name; girl's blouse, was it?
24. . . . fuck-face.

25.   . . . get a fucking great dog right up you.
26.   . . . you great penis.
27.   Fuck off, wanker.

One dominant and characteristic function of these formulae is sexual humiliation; that is, these vocatives threaten the hearer's (and sometimes the speaker's) positive face in the sexual domain. This can be shown by an analysis of their ritual value. For example, a number of the formulae use as a form of address the word *wanker*. Literally the word *wanker* in New Zealand English denotes a male who masturbates. But it is also used as a general term of abuse among New Zealand males. Masturbation is popularly regarded as a sign of sexual inadequacy. Therefore a wanker is one who is sexually inadequate. *Cunt*, like *wanker*, is also a popular form of abuse among these males. It denigrates a man's masculinity by apparently suggesting that he is a part of the female sexual anatomy. The phrase *get a great dog right up you* again denigrates male sexuality by suggesting that the one addressed will be subjected to anal intercourse by a large dog. Even the forms of address *cock* and *you great penis* are demeaning, since they suggest that the man being addressed is no more than a sexual organ. Since, in New Zealand society, the public exhibition of a penis is illegal, equating a man with a penis is to say that he himself is a proscribed form of sexual exhibition and thus a sexual embarrassment. Forms of address which equate men with women and girls hint at effeminacy and thus, it can be argued, at sexual inadequacy and impotence.

But why sexually humiliate one's team mates in the intimate surroundings of the locker room? Clearly, if the locker room is a place where one's sexuality is called into question in an arbitrary fashion, then the team all know the formulae of sexual humiliation and every member of the team knows that he can both use these formulae and be the object of their use. This, then, is a factor creating solidarity partly because mutual knowledge of a restricted vocabulary is involved but also because that vocabulary is coercive. It ensures that everyone who knows this vocabulary, that is all the members of the team, can both in the privacy of the locker room and, potentially, outside it, damage any team member's face since, in New Zealand society, sexual humiliation is one of the most damaging actions social beings inflict on each other. Thus solidarity is created through fear of sexual humiliation: actual humiliation in private and potential humiliation in public. The way to avoid it is clear to team members; it is not to make mistakes, such as showing fear, in the game. This is, of course, always and only temporary since there are always further games.

We have here a clear case which runs counter to Brown and Levinson's assertion (1978: 65) that 'it will in general be to the mutual interest of two MPs (Model Persons) to maintain each other's face'. It may be that the men involved in the above strategy are not model persons. More likely they participate in a social group which does not value face within the group and instead uses potentially and actually face-threatening acts as a coercive strategy to maintain solidarity and discipline in a group which is involved in physically dangerous activity.[1] We can call this side of politeness phenomena 'the dark side'. The rituals of sexual humiliation thus promote solidarity by making all the men in a group which uses such rituals active and passive participants (perpetrators and bystanders) in a positive and negative face-threatening strategy. Far from such rituals being deviant, as Brown and Levinson suggest, they seem instead to be a different but equally significant human interactional strategy. That such rituals are threatening to positive face is clear. If others outside the group know that one is thought by one's male friends to be involved in bestial anal intercourse, one is unlikely to be thought well of. But such rituals are also coercive; that is, threatening to negative face. This is because their object is to make men conform to group requirements and thus they impede 'the freedom of action and freedom from imposition' (Brown and Levinson 1978: 66).

Note too that the solidarity ritual of sexual humiliation has a significant double bind consequence outside of the membership of the team, since it suggests that heterosexual activity cannot help in making one accepted as a man among men. This is because women or their sexual organs are seen in the rituals of sexual humiliation as contemptible, and thus hetero-sexual activity with them is portrayed as just as contemptible as with a dog – since *getting a great dog up you* and *cunt* are functionally equivalent as supposedly jocular terms of address. Rugby football itself thus becomes the only acceptable norm for sexual activity. Initially this seems absurd. It is not.

> The tone of men's house culture is sadistic, power oriented, and latently homosexual, frequently narcissistic in its energy and motives. (Millett 1977: 50).

Phillips (1984) supports this view by showing how the same ethos is to be found in New Zealand myths about the nature of New Zealand soldiers and rugby players round the turn of the twentieth century.

> It was claimed that rugby, like Cadets, provided moral discipline. The chairman of the Southern Rugby Club in 1904 argued that the success of the club team was in itself 'evidence of a clean life'. Cleanliness, of course, meant in particular sexual repression . . . (Phillips 1984: 99)

Thus, rugby and war become sublimated sexual activity and a man's partners in this activity are his mates. And they are partners, at least in part, because of their mutual knowledge of the destructive potential of the strategies of sexual humiliation.

208 KOENRAAD KUIPER

Conclusion

The analysis of the two sets of sporting formulae tells us a number of things. First, it supports the following suggestive comment:

> Idioms . . . set up shared frames for perception, culturally transmitted boundaries with which individuals tacitly recognise or ignore patterns of phenomena. (Herdt 1981: 197)

Second (and in conflict with some radical feminist ideology), it suggests that while some New Zealand men may not always be model persons in the terms of Brown and Levinson (1978), others are, at least some of the time. The two contrasting rituals of face-saving and face-threatening which these men use create two contrasting kinds of solidarity, the first of which I have termed civilised.

Third, it has shown that there is a dark side to politeness, a side where humiliation and coercion are the object of language use. It remains to be seen whether such dark-side strategies are solely the preserve of men.

NOTES

The research reported in this paper was supported by research grants from the New Zealand University Grants Committee and the University of Canterbury. An earlier and longer version of this paper was read at the 8th Commonwealth Conference in Laufen, West Germany. I am grateful to the following for helpful comments on earlier drafts of this paper: Paddy Austin, Robyn Carston, Gareth Cordery, Michele Dominy, Geoff Fougere, Colin Goodrich, Elizabeth Gordon, Janet Holmes, Rosemary and David Novitz.

1. I am not suggesting that this strategy is the only one which can be used in physically dangerous circumstances. It does, however, appear to be a common one among men.

REFERENCES

Brown, P. and Levinson, S. 1978. Universals in language usage: politeness phenomena. In Goody, E. (ed.), *Questions and Politeness: Strategies in Social Interaction*. Cambridge: Cambridge University Press. 1987. Revised and extended version published as *Politeness: Some Universals in Language Usage*. Cambridge: Cambridge University Press.

Coulmas, Florian. 1979. On the sociolinguistic relevance of routine formulae. *Journal of Pragmatics* 3: 239–66.

1982. *Conversational Routine*. The Hague: Mouton.

Herdt, Gilbert H. 1981. *Guardians of the Flutes*. NY: McGraw Hill.

Kuiper, Koenraad and Haggo, Douglas, C. 1984. Livestock auctions, oral poetry and ordinary language. *Language in Society* 13: 205–34.

Millett, Kate. 1977. *Sexual Politics*. London: Virago.

Phillips, J. O. C. 1984. Rugby, war and the mythology of the New Zealand male. *The New Zealand Journal of History*. 18: 83–103.

Australia

14

Australia

GREGORY R. GUY

Introduction

The English language is now completing 200 years of continuous usage in
Australia. In that time it has supplanted the original languages of the
continent, and recruited most descendants of non-English speaking immigrants, so that today it is the overwhelmingly dominant tongue throughout
Australia. Several features of the Australian situation yield a unique
insight on the development and diversification of English: its geographic
isolation, its social origins as a penal colony, and its recent wave of non-
English speaking immigrants. Australian English (AE) has experienced
language and dialect contact, but for most of the last two centuries
Australia may have had the highest proportion of monolingual English
speakers of any country in the world, aside from England itself. This
bicentennial survey will hopefully serve to illuminate the Australian branch
of 'English around the world' – in this case, about as far around the world
as it could go.

The status of English in Australia: the national language

The status of the English language in Australia is today, and has been
since British colonisation, that of THE national language. It overwhelmingly
dominates the linguistic landscape, both demographically and functionally.
This is not to say that Australia is a monolingual country; on the contrary,
a large number of languages are spoken within its borders. But the English
language dwarfs all others in terms of both number of speakers and the
social roles it is used for.

Demographically speaking, English is 'regularly used', according to the
1976 census, by 98.6 per cent of the population over the age of 5 (Clyne
1982: 6). Of these, over four-fifths speak English natively, with the balance
having greater or lesser ability as second language speakers. The teaching

213

of English as a second language is a small industry, with extensive government supported programmes such as the Adult Migrant Education Service providing initial ESL instruction to most newly arriving immigrants.

In terms of social domains of use, English is again paramount. For most of the population it is the first and only language, and hence is used in all domains and activities. It is the language of government, education, the courts, business, and public life generally. For most people it is also the language of the home, of child-rearing, and private social interaction. Even among non-native speakers there is a certain amount of shift to English in private domains.

The languages other than English (LOTEs) that are spoken in Australia include surviving languages of the aboriginal population and languages of non-English speaking immigrants. Both groups have tended toward linguistic decline and death in the face of assimilatory pressures from English.

The original languages of Australia, those such as Guugu Yimidhirr, Wirradhurri, and Pitjantjatjara, which had been spoken in Australia for 40,000 years, numbered about 200 when the First Fleet of anglophones arrived (Dixon 1980: 18). Today only a quarter of these survive as active languages of a community. The trend for these languages has been continuous decline since 1788, either through the extermination of their speakers by English weapons and diseases, or through the recruitment of their children into the English-speaking community. Aborigines today constitute only one per cent of the Australian population, and those who still speak an Aboriginal language natively are largely located in remote areas in the interior, primarily in the Northern Territory. Even there assimilation to English is still progressing, spread by contact with schools, jobs, and government agencies. In recent decades an admirable effort has been mounted by tribal organisations and institutions such as the School of Australian Languages to strengthen these speech communities, so they may resist linguistic assimilation. Nevertheless, language deaths will continue to occur among languages now spoken only by adults. Those languages that do survive will likely do so as the first language of a community which also speaks English.

The other principal non-users of English are recent migrants. Since World War II, non-English speaking migrants have come to Australia in huge numbers. Greeks, Italians, Lebanese, and Vietnamese have all come and formed substantial communities in major Australian cities. These communities are following a fairly typical course of linguistic assimilation, with some shift to English in the first generation, and mostly English dominance in second and later generations. Against this trend, however, many communities are engaged in language maintenance efforts, usually through special community schools emphasising fluency and literacy in the community language and knowledge of the community culture and homeland.

For the most part the use of LOTEs is confined to private, within-community interactions. But some LOTEs with substantial numbers of speakers are used publicly on a small scale. In areas with high residential concentrations of one linguistic group, there are often shops and other small businesses where the language can be used in commerce. Media services are available: there are multi-lingual radio and television channels, and newspapers and magazines are published in more than a score of LOTEs. Access and information in LOTEs are provided in many government agencies and public facilities through signs, brochures, and the provision of interpreters and translators. Significantly, the recently promulgated national language policy (Lo Bianco 1987) sets a national goal of having all Australians learn a second language. But for the present, English dominates public and private life.

Thus, the status of English in Australia is like that of English in the United States: commanding the linguistic landscape, the language of virtually all public life and most private life, but coexisting with a number of indigenous and immigrant LOTEs. English has taken root and flourished in Australia, developing into a distinctive and unique variety. In subsequent sections we will attempt to characterise this Australian variety of English, focusing on three issues: first, the autonomy of Australian English: the unique aspects of its nature and history; second, its apparent unity from the standpoint of dialect geography; and third, its great internal social diversity. These aspects of AE have long attracted the attention of linguistic observers, yielding a large literature to which we can only provide a modest introduction in the present format.

The autonomy of AE

That AE is now an autonomous variety, following its own evolutionary course, is perhaps clearer to the linguist than the layperson. As we will see in our discussion of language attitudes, there is a certain ambivalence among some Australians about AE, a suspicion that perhaps British English should really be the norm. The publication of an authoritative Australian reference work, the *Macquarie Dictionary* (Delbridge 1981), is helping to establish the independence of a standardised AE in the public mind. But, for the linguist, evidence of the autonomy of AE lies more in its unique history and its present-day sociolinguistic patterning. The former topic is discussed in this section, and the latter in subsequent sections.

The point of departure for understanding the history of AE is its origin as a 'colonial variety' characterised by an abrupt break in the historical continuity of the speech community (Trudgill 1986: 127). AE began when a new community was suddenly assembled in a new land from individuals of diverse social and linguistic backgrounds. Out of such sociolinguistic melting pots, distinctive new alloys emerged, such as the varieties of

English which are the subject matter of this volume. In understanding the development of such a dialect we will want to look at two principal influences: contact with other languages in the new locale, and the dialectal makeup (both social and geographic) of the founding population.

Language contact

The principal sources of language contact were the indigenous languages of the native inhabitants, and languages spoken by non-English immigrants. The former source of contact was rapidly eliminated by the early colonisers. Australian Aborigines were mostly displaced and linguistically destroyed wherever they were found occupying land coveted by the colonisers. Australia is like North America in this respect: indigenous languages now have very few speakers. This is very different from the rest of the erstwhile British Empire: in Africa and India indigenous languages thrive, and their speakers are a large majority.

The impact of Aboriginal languages on English has been small, limited principally to the lexicon. There are thousands of place-names of Aboriginal origin in Australian English: for example, *Wollongong*, *Murrumbidgee*, *Warrumbungle*. Other borrowed words include large numbers of terms for native flora and fauna – *kangaroo*, *koala*, *wallaby* – and features of aboriginal material and cultural life: *boomerang*, *woomera*, *corroborree*. Outside of the lexicon there is no evidence that the indigenous languages of the continent had any impact on the English of white Australians in any component of the grammar or the sound system.

It should be noted, however, that there has been clear Aboriginal language influence on a spectrum of language varieties used by Aboriginal speakers. There are the non-standard varieties sometimes called Aboriginal English (cf. Kaldor and Malcolm 1985). And there are several creole languages which arose from contact between English and Aboriginal languages (cf. Crowley and Rigsby 1979; Sandefur 1984; Sandefur and Harris 1986). Steffensen's article in the present volume discusses variation in the use of one of these creoles and its relation to cultural context. Other sociolinguistic studies bearing on English-Aboriginal contact include Shnukal (1985), Schmidt (1985), and Bavin and Shopen (1985).

The remaining potential sources of contact for AE were other immigrant languages. But for 150 years after the First Fleet dropped anchors at Botany Bay, the non-Aboriginal population of Australia was overwhelmingly English-speaking. As a penal colony for the first half-century, the founding population consisted mainly of transported English criminals and their English jailers. Non-British European immigrants were rare, and Asians virtually non-existent (aside from a brief spurt of Chinese immigration in the mid nineteenth century). Only since World War II have non-English speaking immigrants come in large numbers, and their impact on English has been minimal.

The one sizeable group of speakers of another European language in early Australia was the Irish. It is estimated that, around 1800, Gaelic was spoken by about half the population of Ireland, and Irish prisoners constituted over a quarter of all transportees to Australia (Hughes 1986: 190–5). So speakers of Irish Gaelic may have numbered above 10 per cent of the early population of New South Wales. But their linguistic effect was mitigated by several factors. Most Irish people knew English, at least as a second language. And since Irish prisoners were considered particularly prone to rebellion, a policy of dispersal and repression of the Irish evolved which would have prevented Gaelic speakers from forming much of a linguistic community (Hughes 1986:194). Some linguists trace certain features of modern Australian English to an Irish English input (Horvath 1985:39, Trudgill 1986:139–41), but direct impact from Gaelic was probably minor.

Thus, language contact has not been a major factor in the development of AE, perhaps even less influential than in British North America, where English was in contact from the earliest days with French, Dutch, German, and Spanish. Aside from lexical borrowing from Aboriginal languages, and a possible modest Irish influence, the sociolinguistic history of Australian English has been mainly one of an overwhelmingly monolingual anglophonic community.

Dialect contact

If language contact has made only a modest contribution to the distinctive character of AE, we are left with dialect contact in the founding population as the probable principal determinant. What varieties of English were originally transported to the Antipodes? Diversity was present from the first: most English dialects were represented among the early settlers and convicts. But many characteristic features of AE are derived from a small number of dialects whose speakers were numerically dominant in the early years of colonisation.

In broad terms this means the south of England – the most populous part of England and the site of its great metropolis. AE broadly conforms to linguistic characteristics of southeastern England in the late eighteenth century, such as *r*-lessness. Among the convicts, working class speakers from metropolitan areas predominated, especially speakers of Cockney – the dialect of working class London. Hence, many features of working class AE are reminiscent of Cockney, such as the chain-shift pattern in long vowels described later in this chapter (cf. Trudgill 1986: 135; Labov in press). But other dialects also must have had an impact, including Irish English, East Anglian varieties (Trudgill 1986: 136–7), and the dialects of the Midlands, an area then undergoing rapid industrialisation with concomitant social turmoil and increase in crime. And finally, the jargon of British sailors was represented in the early working class of Australia, due to their economic importance. The upper-class of early Australia, however, presented a different dialect picture. Officers, government officials, clergymen, and wealthy settlers tended to be educated people who probably lacked the marked regional traits of working class speakers, and converged on some ancestral version of what is now called RP.

Thus the founding population of Anglo-Australia spoke many varieties of English, although with an identifiable dialectal central tendency. But none of these people spoke 'Australian English': this was the invention of the 'Currency' – the first generations of Australian-born whites who had to process this diversity of dialect inputs into a coherent usage of their own. They probably knew nothing of the regional significance of English dialects, but socially significant differences were a vivid phenomenon in their lives.

In view of this social history, three conclusions can be drawn about the subsequent development of a nativised Australian variety of English. First, the emergent AE was not simply a transplanted equivalent of any single English dialect. Rather it was a new development, with some features traceable to some dialects of England, but with other entirely original developments. AE is not a graft but an alloy, like bronze or steel, with characteristics of its own that do not come from any single one of the elements that make it up. Second, social diversity was an original condition of the dialect, present from the beginning. Language, like all social institutions in early Australia, could hardly escape the profound divisions between convicts and jailers, the bound and the free. Finally, language change must have been a prominent feature of early AE. Dialect contact and sociolinguistic diversity are the engines that drive linguistic evolution, and for at least the first two or three generations, anglophone Australians certainly experienced plenty of both.

The unity of AE

Australia is often described as lacking geographic dialectal differentiation, which is surprising in view of its huge territorial extent. If true this would make it quite different from English-speaking North America, where several markedly different regional dialects are found. There are two issues to resolve here: how much uniformity is there, and how was it achieved?

The historical source of AE unity appears to lie in settlement history. Most early settlement in Australia disseminated from a single original point: Sydney. Places such as Hobart, Newcastle, and Brisbane were all established as penal outstations from Sydney, rather than by new fleets direct from England. The diversity in North America is due to multiple foci of settlement established at different times by different constituent populations, but Australian colonisation was a centralised, government-run operation. Also,

North America had relatively little population movement between settlements in the early days, while the isolation of Australia from the rest of the anglophone world promoted internal communication at the expense of communication with England, a situation which tended to minimise regionalisation. There were frequent intersettlement transfers of convicts and soldiers. A struggling young colony at Melbourne or Adelaide was more likely to find needed settlers, skills, tools, and trade in Sydney than on the other side of the globe in Liverpool or London. And throughout the nineteenth century internal migration was stimulated by a series of goldrushes.

But there remains the empirical question of how different the regions of Australia really are. It may be that dialectal unity has been overstated. Some of the best evidence on this matter comes from recent studies of vowel variation in AE. The work of Bradley (1980, 1989) reveals a number of phonetic and phonological differences, including monophthongisation of /uə/ and /iə/ (e.g. *tour, fear*) in Sydney (versus maintenance of the diphthong in Melbourne); extreme raising of the front lax vowels in Melbourne; less rounding of back vowels and diphthongs in Sydney. Bradley's article in the present volume discusses regional differences in the realisation of the /a/-/æ/ alternations in *dance, castle*, etc. Work by Oasa (1979) has revealed regional differences such as: a backing glide in the diphthongal realisations of /u:,ou/ in Sydney, versus a fronting direction of movement in the rest of Australia; a marked lowering and backing of vowels before /l/ in Adelaide. Taken in conjunction with well-known regional differences in the lexicon, we may conclude that AE is perhaps not quite so geographically homogeneous as has been supposed.

The diversity of AE

Many observers of Australian English have commented on its great social diversity. However a certain confusion has existed over whether it follows the same kinds of social patterning found in other English speaking countries, particularly as regards the questions of the social correlates of the variation, and the discreteness of continuity of the varieties.

The most influential work on these questions is that of Mitchell and Delbridge (1965a, 1965b). They describe AE in terms of three relatively discrete varieties, which they label 'Broad', 'General', and 'Cultivated'. The principal criterion for differentiating these varieties is vowel quality particularly the pronunciation of the six long vowels /i:, u:, eɪ, ou, aɪ, au/ (in *beat, boot, say, so, high, how*). These vowels have phonetic values relatively close to British English RP norms in 'Cultivated Australian', but show a systematic chain-shift in 'Broad Australian' whereby the first four of these (the non-low long vowels) are diphthongal with centralised and lowered nuclei, while the last two have respectively backed and fronted nuclei. This yields approximately the following set of pronunciations: [əɪ,əʊ,ʌɪ,ʌʊ,ɔɪ,æu]. The 'General Australian' pronunciations fall between these two extremes.

Mitchell and Delbridge's interpretation of their data has coloured much of the subsequent discussion of sociolinguistic variation in AE. Working in the dialectological tradition, they treat the vocalic variables in terms of discrete 'diaphones', and assemble these into sets which characterise the separate named 'varieties'. Individual speakers in their corpus are also treated categorically, in that they are assigned to one of the three varieties based on an overall assessment of their usage. However, they retreat from categoriality when they come to the question of the social distribution of the 'varieties', often seeming to deny that class, or sex, or education has any decisive effect on a speaker's linguistic comportment. For example, in one early article Mitchell states that the varieties of AE 'occur according to no clear principle of social or geographical division' (1951: 13). In a later work Delbridge asserts that 'Every Australian speaker can make his own linguistic choices from a number of available styles and variants . . .' (1977: 209).

The sociolinguistic tradition developed in Britain and North America in the last 25 years takes a different approach on all of these points. Works such as Labov 1966 and Trudgill 1974 do not define discrete categories for either particular linguistic variables or the overall spectrum of speech varieties; rather, both are seen as continuous. Individuals may occupy points on the continuum, but are not assigned to discrete named lects. And most importantly, the overall social distribution of variants is seen as highly structured and finely stratified, with strong correlations between particular variants and social dimensions such as class, sex, and age.

What is the explanation for these contrasts? Is Australian English really very different, in effect a classless society where one's tastes in language are as individual as one's favourite flavour of ice-cream? Or does the answer lie in differences in theory and method and points of emphasis between the two research traditions?

Recent analyses of AE, involving both new data and new interpretations of the sociolinguistic facts, suggest that the second answer is the correct one. In other words, AE does display the same kind of continuous variability and social stratification found elsewhere in the English-speaking world. Vowel pronunciations are of course as continuously variable in AE as in other human languages, and this is acoustically verified in work by Bernard, Bradley, Oasa, and others. The division of the community into the three named varieties is clearly a theoretical construct, and a relatively arbitrary one. Mitchell and Delbridge themselves acknowledge that a single speaker rarely is confined to all 'broad' or all 'general' variants, and this is confirmed by Horvath's quantitative studies (1985: 67–95). And finally, the variables in AE show clear correlations with the important social dimensions, especially class and sex, with higher-status and female speakers using more 'cultivated' forms, and lower-status and male speakers favoring 'broad' forms. Delbridge acknowledges this social patterning in his 1970 review article:

> Statistically, at least, one can say that the choice a person makes of a speech variety is affected by a complex set of factors . . . Girls tend towards Cultivated and General forms, boys towards General and Broad. Cultivated speech correlates significantly with the higher [status] occupations . . . (1970: 20).

This point has been confirmed quantitatively. Horvath (1985: 20) demonstrates that the class and sex correlations can be observed in Mitchell and Delbridge's own data: 'Broad' varieties are attributed to 41 per cent of speakers with lower working class occupations, and 51 per cent of all males, but to only 22 per cent of middle class speakers and 19 per cent of females. Further confirmation is found in Horvath's own data. Whereas Mitchell and Delbridge categorised each speaker as Broad, General, or Cultivated based on an overall impression of their pronunciation, Horvath conducted quantitative studies of each variable in the speech of each informant. The results are clear: on virtually every measure speakers with the highest-status occupations are skewed toward the higher-prestige end of the linguistic continuum, as are females.

Thus the overall picture in AE is compatible with the standard Western sociolinguistic situation that Weinreich, Labov and Herzog (1968: 100) call 'orderly heterogeneity': individuals vary in their proportion of use of the socially distinct linguistic variants (rather than in membership of discrete categories), and there are certain systematic relationships along social dimensions that probabilistically predict an individual's proportion of use (upper class speakers use more of the high-prestige variants than lower class speakers, women more than men, etc.). Mitchell and Delbridge's named varieties are essentially points on a continuum of sociolinguistic variation, rather than discrete 'dialects'. Their disclaimers about social systematicity quoted above were a matter of methodological focus. They were working in the framework of structuralist dialectology, and were unable to find clear socially demarcated boundaries for the varieties they identified. As Delbridge puts it: 'There emerged no geographical or cultural boundaries for diaphones' (1970: 20). Casting a categorical net in continuous waters, they came up empty. Working with the benefit of recent advances in sociolinguistic theory and method, we can now discern the 'clear social principles' that eluded Mitchell.

The available data concerning style-shifting, while limited, also tend to bring the Australian picture into agreement with sociolinguistic findings elsewhere. Both anecdotal observations and explicit studies have shown that speakers shift toward the 'cultivated' end of the spectrum in more formal contexts. For example, Bernard (1969: 68) has noted the difficulty of studying 'broad' speakers in the laboratory: finding themselves in a formal, unfamiliar context, such speakers would automatically shift towards their more careful varieties, and their 'broadness' would evaporate. And Eisikovits' work (1981) with adolescents reveals a tendency to avoid in more formal situations a range of non-standard features in syntax and lexicon.

While it is gratifying to the sociolinguistic theorist to find that Australia thus conforms to our general models, we should not at the same time lose track of what is unique in AE. One striking feature that sets it apart is that sex differentiation appears to be a great deal more prominent than has been found in the USA and Britain. We have mentioned above the strong association between male speakers and broadness in the Mitchell and Delbridge data. And in Horvath's sample, no men at all used the highest-prestige 'sociolect' (one which is devoid of all 'broad' vowels and has at least 70 per cent 'cultivated' vowel realisations.) Eisikovits' work (1981, this volume) adds a further complication: on certain non-standard variables connoting masculinity the boys actually increase their use in formal styles and as they get older, while the girls are decreasing. Other studies also support the point that men and women are strongly linguistically differentiated in Australia (e.g. Guy et al. 1986; Bryant 1980.) While it is usual in Western societies to find women tending toward prestige variants, one rarely finds differentiation to the AE extent. This may have been a further contributing factor to Mitchell and Delbridge's conclusions about class: since males at all class levels are appreciably 'broader' in their usage than their female counterparts, the class pattern is harder to discern.

Major studies

The previous discussion has made references to a number of sociolinguistic studies of AE. It may be useful to the reader to briefly survey the recent research that has used quantitative methodology. The most substantial body of work in the past decade has come from Horvath and her associates at Sydney University. Horvath's book (1985) is the most ambitious quantitative treatment of AE yet undertaken, drawing on an excellent corpus of sociolinguistic interviews which now includes over 200 speakers comprising a stratified sample of the Sydney speech community. The work examines a broad range of sociolinguistic variables, including the vowels previously discussed as well as six consonantal variables: (θ), initial (h), (-ing), medial (t), post-vocalic (r), and palatalisation of apical obstruents (t,d,s,z). She also undertakes a ground-breaking study of discourse variation, and addresses questions of historical development and change in progress. Her work on the internal sociolinguistic structure of the Sydney speech community is also discussed in Horvath and Sankoff 1987. Nesbitt 1984 analyses t, d deletion in Horvath's corpus.

The Sydney group have also conducted a series of studies of the use of 'question' intonation (high-rising terminal contours) in declarative clauses.

Contrary to the common English usage in which this creates a *de facto* yes/ no question, this 'Australian questioning intonation' (Bryant 1980) has an interactional meaning of approximately 'do you understand?' Guy *et al.* (1986) demonstrate that it is a relatively recent innovation in Australian English, and still spreading rapidly. Studies of this phenomenon by other researchers include McGregor (1978) and Allan (1984).

Eisikovits (1981, this volume) also focuses on Sydney, but the work was done separately from Horvath's group. This study addresses morphological and lexical variability among adolescents. Most of the non-standard forms reported are common throughout the English speaking world, but some of the sociolinguistic facts are unique, particularly the divergence of the sexes mentioned above.

Shnukal's studies (1978, 1982) of Cessnock, a mining town in New South Wales, contain careful quantitative work on phonological and syntactic variables. Of particular note is the (-ing) variable, which in addition to the common alternation [-ɪn/-ɪŋ] shows a realisation as [ɪŋk]. This is a non-standard feature widespread in Cessnock, but also found occasionally in other parts of Australia. Shopen (1978) looks at this feature in Canberra, and both Horvath and Eisikovits examine its occurrence in Sydney.

Code-switching and mixing

Despite the availability of many bilingual Aborigines and migrants, code-mixing and code-switching have not received much attention from scholars in Australia. One recent survey of these phenomena in Aboriginal communities is McConvell (1985), who describes code-switching as 'common throughout a wide area of Northern Australia' (p. 96). He even cites cases of trilingual code-switching involving Gurindji, Wanyjirra, and English. McConvell concludes that the same kinds of linguistic and social factors are at work in Aboriginal code-switching as are reported elsewhere, but emphasises that the principal usage is to convey social meanings. In migrant communities also switching and mixing occur. Some example texts appear in Bettoni (1985). Migrants switch between English and their community language to make a cultural or emotional point, to exclude outsiders (and children with limited competence), and to fill lexical gaps. These patterns may not be so conventionalised in the Australian cases as they apparently are among New York Puerto Ricans, for example, but they at least occur as individual initiatives. However, this remains an understudied area in Australian linguistics.

Language attitudes

Language attitudes in Australia are a topic much discussed but little researched. There is a certain ambivalence about the national variety: in comparison with British English, for example, AE is both derided as crude and admired as unaffected and earthy. There is, in many sections of the community, hostility to the non-native accents of migrants and Aborigines. A smattering of quantitative research is beginning to reveal the attitudes of Australians towards their own social variation. Berechree and Ball (1979) find that their subjects give distinctly more positive evaluations of 'cultivated' voices on several scales of competence and social attractiveness. However, a sex-differentiated norm is apparent: 'broad' female speakers are ranked significantly lower than 'broad' males. Interestingly a reversal of evaluation occurred on a scale of perceived confidence. Here 'cultivated' male speakers were heard as being very low in confidence. This suggests some 'covert prestige' associating 'broadness' with masculinity and self-confidence.

An attitude study by Guy and Vonwiller (1984) shows similar mixed responses to Australian questioning intonation: negative evaluations on scales of job-suitability and maturity, but positive reactions on scales of friendliness and solidarity. It would seem that there is still linguistic insecurity on the part of many Australians: a desire for a uniquely Australian identity in language mixed with lingering doubts about the suitability and 'goodness' of AE. This ambivalence may explain the apparent converging change that Horvath discerns in her data: a movement from both ends of the sociolectal continuum towards the middle 'General Australian' variety.

Conclusions

Australian English is an autonomous national variety, undergoing internal developments independent of the other major varieties of English around the world. It has acquired its unique national character primarily through dialect contact and levelling in the early years of settlement. Internally it shows a relative absence of geographic differentiation combined with a striking presence of social differentiation. Both features are traceable to aspects of its social history: high internal mobility combined with the 'tyranny of distance' from England yielded geographic homogeneity, while the social divisions between convicts and guards in the early period perpetuated sociolinguistic diversity. It is a national language in all senses, dwarfing in both public and private domains all the other languages spoken in Australia. An emerging tradition of quantitative sociolinguistic studies is beginning to demonstrate the insights that AE can offer us into the nature and continuing diversification of that multinational language once spoken only by the English.

REFERENCES

Allan, K. 1984. The component functions of the high-rise terminal contour in Australian declarative sentences. *Australian Journal of Linguistics* 4: 19–32.

Bavin, E. and Shopen, T. 1985. Warlpiri and English: languages in contact. In Clyne (ed.) 1985, pp. 81–94.

Berechree, P. and Ball, P. 1979. *A Study of Sex, Accent-Broadness, and Australian Sociolinguistic Identity*. MS, University of Tasmania.

Bernard, J. R. 1969. On the uniformity of spoken Australian English. *Orbis* 18: 62–73.

Bettoni, C. 1985. Italian language attrition: a Sydney case study. In Clyne (ed.) 1985, pp. 63–79.

Bradley, D. 1980. Regional differences in Australian English phonology. *University of Melbourne Working Papers in Linguistics* 6: 73–93.

1989. Regional dialects in Australian English phonology. In Collins, P. and Blair, D. (eds.) 1989, pp. 260–70.

Bryant, P. 1980. Australian Questioning Intonation: An Addition to Speakers' Response Seeking Repertoire. Unpublished BA honours thesis, Australian National University.

Clyne, M. 1982. *Multilingual Australia*. Melbourne River Seine Publications.

(ed.) 1985. *Australia, Meeting Place of Languages*. (*Pacific Linguistics* C-92) Canberra: Australian National University, RSPacS, Dept. of Linguistics, pp. 95–125.

Collins, P. and Blair, D. (eds) 1989. *Australian English: the Language of a New Society*. St. Lucia: University of Queensland Press.

Crowley, T. and Rigsby, B. 1979. Cape York Creole. In T. Shopen (ed.), *Languages and Their Status*. Cambridge MA: Winthrop, pp. 153–207.

Delbridge, A. 1970. The recent study of spoken Australian English. In W. S. Ramson (ed.), *English Transported*. Canberra: Australian National University Press, pp. 15–31.

1977. Australian English. In *The Australian Encyclopedia*. Sydney: Grolier Society.

(editor-in-chief) 1981. *The Macquarie Dictionary*. St Leonards, NSW: Macquarie Library.

Dixon, R. M. W. 1980. *The Languages of Australia*. Cambridge: Cambridge University Press.

Eisikovits, E. 1981. Inner-Sydney English: An Investigation of Grammatical Variation in Adolescent Speech. Unpublished PhD thesis, University of Sydney.

Guy, G. R. and Vonwiller, J. 1984. The meaning of an intonation in Australian English. *Australian Journal of Linguistics* 4: 1–17.

Guy, G. R., Horvath, B. M., Vonwiller, J., Daisley, E., and Rogers, I. 1986. An intonational change in progress in Australian English. *Language in Society* 15: 23–52.

Horvath, B. M. 1985. *Variation in Australian English*. Cambridge: Cambridge University Press.

Horvath, B. M. and Sankoff, D. 1987. Delimiting the Sydney speech community. *Language in Society* 16: 79–204.

Hughes, R. 1986. *The Fatal Shore: The Epic of Australia's Founding*. New York: Alfred A. Knopf.

Kaldor, S. and Malcolm, I. 1985. Aboriginal children's English educational implications. In Clyne (ed.) 1985, pp. 223–40.

Labov, W. 1966. *The Social Stratification of English in New York City*. Washington: Center for Applied Linguistics.

In press. The three dialects of English. In P. Eckert (ed.), *New Ways of Analyzing Sound Change*. New York: Academic Press.

Lo Bianco, J. 1987. *National Policy on Languages*. Canberra: Australian Government Publishing Service.

McConvell, P. 1985. Domains and code-switching among bilingual aborigines. In Clyne (ed.) 1985, pp. 95–125.

McGregor, R. L. 1978. High-Rising Tone in Non-Question Forms in Sydney Australian English. Unpublished MA thesis, Macquarie University, New South Wales.

Mitchell, A. G. 1951. Australian English. *Australian Quarterly*. 23: 9–17.

Mitchell, A. G. and Delbridge, A. 1965a. *The Pronunciation of English in Australia*. Sydney: Angus & Robertson. Revised edition.

1965b. *The Speech of Australian Adolescents*. Sydney: Angus & Robertson.

Nesbitt, C. 1984. The linguistic constraints on a variable process: /t,d/ deletion in Sydney speech. Unpublished BA Honours thesis, University of Sydney.

Oasa, H. 1979. Is regional dialectology possible in Australia? A quantitative study of systematic regional variations in the pronunciation of Australian university students. MS. Australian National University, Canberra.

1989. Phonology of current Adelaide English. In Collins, P. and Blair, D. (eds.) 1989, pp. 271–87.

Sandefur, J. 1984. A Language Coming of Age: Kriol of Northern Australia. Unpublished MA thesis, University of Western Australia.

Sandefur, J. and Harris, J. 1986. Variation in Australian Kriol. In Fishman, J. A. *et al.* (eds.) *The Fergusonian Impact. Vol. 2: Sociolinguistics and the Sociology of Language*. Berlin: de Gruyter, pp. 179–90.

Schmidt, A. 1985. Speech variation and social networks in dying Dyirbal. In Clyne (ed.) 1985, pp. 127–50.

Shnukal, A. 1978. A Sociolinguistic Study of Australian English: Phonological and Syntactic Variation in Cessnock, NSW. Unpublished PhD thesis, Georgetown University.

1982. You're getting somethink for nothing: two phonological variables of Australian English. *Australian Journal of Linguistics* 2: 197–212.

1985. Multilingualism in the eastern Torres Strait islands. In Clyne (ed.) 1985, pp. 265–79.

Shopen, T. 1978. Research on the variable (ING) in Canberra. *Talanya* 5: 42–52.

Trudgill. P. 1974. *The Social Differentiation of English in Norwich*. Cambridge: Cambridge University Press.

1986. *Dialects in Contact*. Oxford: Basil Blackwell.

Weinreich, U., Labov, W. and Herzog, M. 1968. Empirical foundations for a theory of language change. In Lehmann, W. and Malkiel, Y. (eds.) *Directions for Historical Linguistics*. Austin TX: University of Texas Press, 95–188.

15

/æ/ and /a:/ in Australian English

DAVID BRADLEY

Various previous studies have claimed that there are no regional differences within Australian English phonology. The main recent proponent of this view has been Bernard (1969: 62, 1981); see also Hammarström (1980: 42) and Turner (1966). Others, such as Mitchell and Delbridge (1965a, 1965b), while finding a different form of /ou/ in Adelaide, have generally agreed. Conversely, in an ongoing study (Bradley and Bradley 1991) quite a number of regional phonological differences have been identified, one of which, the lexical diffusion involving /a:/ and /æ/ in words such as *castle* or *dance*, is a popular regional stereotype and also shows social and stylistic differences. It may also reveal something about the process of lexical diffusion and the phonetic characteristics of the corresponding vowels in southeastern British English at an earlier stage.

Historical background and previous studies

It has been suggested, for example by Samuels (1972), that the eighteenth and early nineteenth century development of Middle English short *a* to long /a:/ rather than /æ/ before the fricative /f θ s/ (e.g. *bath, class*) as a reaction to the deconstriction of postvocalic *r*, preceded the development of /a:/ rather than /æ/ before a cluster of nasal plus obstruent (e.g., *dance*). The fact that Australian English varies, but tends more to /æ/ in the latter environment, as discussed below, is supportive of this view and may help to order and date the stages of lexical diffusion from /æ/ to /a:/ in England, as the koinéization (Trudgill 1986: 129–46) of Australian English probably took place, according to contemporary reports, in the very early nineteenth century. The phonetic similarity between a central to front /a:/ (as in current Australian English, as well as such regional varieties as Norwich in England) and front /æ/ would have facilitated the change; thus the backing of /a:/ to /ɑ/ in London and in RP is presumably a later development.[1]

227

The development of this particular split with merger is an excellent example of lexical diffusion, whereby a sound change spreads lexical item by lexical item, usually with phonological constraints as in this case.

Several scholars have noted the difference between RP and Australian English in this process; for example, Baker (1966: 442–43) writes: 'Australians show a general tendency to avoid the pure [ɑ]. There is, for instance, an increasing preference for the short [æ], especially before nasal consonants'. Mitchell and Delbridge (1965a: 53, 63–5) also suggest that the [æ] form is more widely heard in Australia, and on the increase; though they point out that the /a:/ form is the more conservative and educated alternative. Both sources give examples of words which vary, and suggest that words behave differently: Mitchell and Delbridge (1965a: 53) suggest that /a:/ in *plastic, lather, elastic, transfer,* is slightly ridiculous, while in *dance* or *demand* it is 'pedantry, snobbishness, or . . . undue striving for effect'. The claims that /æ/ is on the increase may reflect a reversal of the lexical diffusion process, but are more likely simply to imply a shift away from RP as the prestige norm in Australia.

Mitchell and Delbridge (1965a: 53) note the regional difference in the place name *Newcastle*, which is the subject of a regional stereotype, as will be noted below. This is also noted by Bernard (1981: 23). Laycock (1980: 2–4) gives much more on the regional distribution, but does not suggest that variation is involved.

Methodology and sample

A Labovian study[2] using interview data was carried out with a random sample of 40 speakers born in Melbourne, ten each from Sydney,[3] Brisbane and Hobart, and seven Adelaide speakers.[4] None of them had spent any substantial time away from the city of their birth; all were aged 18 or over; half were male, half female; half lived in a Working class (WC) suburb, and half in a Middle class (MC) suburb.[5] For this study a subsample of ten was selected from the Melbourne sample; thus it is based on interviews with a total of 47 speakers, distributed as shown in table 15.1.

Results

It should first be emphasised that most lexical items behave alike in RP and in Australian English. That is, most have the corresponding vowel in both; for example, *bat* and *bash* have /æ/ in both, while *bath* and *pass* have /a:/ in Australian and /ɑ:/ in RP. That the process has progressed further in RP is shown by the documented spread of /ɑ:/ in the recent past, as well as by those words which do differ: nearly all have a greater tendency to /ɑ:/ in RP but have /æ/ in Australian English; for example, words with the

Table 15.1. *Sex and class composition of the capital cities sample*

	MC area		WC area	
	male	female	male	female
Sydney	2	3	3	2
Brisbane	2	3	3	2
Hobart	3	2	2	3
Adelaide	2	3	–	2
Melbourne	3	2	2	3

Table 15.2. *Per cent /æ/ in all lexical items, reading styles*

	MC area	WC area	'Class' difference
Brisbane	45	48	3
Adelaide	6	29	23
Hobart	54	65	11
Melbourne	27	60	33

prefix *trans-* such as *transport* or *transfer* frequently have /ɑ:/ in RP but only very rarely have /a:/ in Australian English, where /æ/ is nearly universal for this prefix. There is some variation in RP as well, sometimes in words which also vary in Australia, for example, *graph*, but also in different words, such as *plastic* or *lather* which do not vary in Australia. Words which do not vary in Australian English will not be discussed further. Clearly there has been continuing contact with and influence of RP on Australian English; where this contact is more intensive, as in Adelaide, the pattern is more like that of RP – though still distinctively Australian.

Since the process involved is one of lexical diffusion, each word can be expected to behave differently. Thus a hierarchy or implicational scale can usefully represent the data, but an overall index may be misleading as different speakers happen to use different lexical items in interviews. What is most directly comparable is the formal reading tasks in the interview, where all speakers use exactly the same words in the same style (apart from misreadings). The most striking finding is the quantitative difference between cities in this comparable data. Social differences of speech within each city agree with previous observations that /a:/ is the prestige form, with residents of Working class suburbs and males using a higher proportion of /æ/ (see table 15.2).

Comparable Sydney results are not available, as a different, shorter

Table 15.3. *Per cent /æ/ in certain lexical items, reading styles*

Rank	Hobart	Melbourne	Brisbane	Sydney	Adelaide
1	*graph* 100	*graph* 70	*dance* 89	*dance* 60	*contrast* 29
2	*chance* 100	*castle* 70	*castle* 67	*graph* 30	*castle* 14
3	*demand* 90	*dance* 65	*graph* 44	*chance* 20	*dance* 14
4	*dance* 90	*chance* 40	*demand* 22	*grasp* 15	*chance* 14
5	*castle* 40	*demand* 22	*chance* 15	*demand* 10	*graph* 14
6	*grasp* 10	*grasp* 11	*grasp* 11	*castle* 0	*demand* 0
7	*contrast* 0	*contrast* 0	*contrast* 0	*contrast* 0	*grasp* 0

Table 15.4. *Per cent /æ/ by phonological environment*

	before nasal	before fricative	difference
Hobart	93	38	55
Sydney	30	11	19
Brisbane	42	31	11
Melbourne	42	40	2
Adelaide	9	14	–5

wordlist was used there. Using only the words in that wordlist, the overall results were Adelaide 9 per cent /æ/, Sydney 19 per cent, Brisbane 42 per cent, Melbourne 46 per cent and Hobart 72 per cent. The greatest social difference is seen in Melbourne, followed by Adelaide, Hobart, Sydney and nearly none in Brisbane. This pattern is in general accord with Australian perceptions of Adelaide and particularly Melbourne as sharply class-stratified, and Brisbane as much less so. Sabbadin (1985) found a similarly sharp social stratification for four varying words in Melbourne, with an average 43 per cent difference in Style C (reading passage) between speakers recorded in a Toorak (high-status area) milk bar and a Western suburb (low-status area) milk bar.

Also interesting are the different hierarchies observed in each city: the lexical diffusion appears to be operating separately in each centre, as shown in table 15.3.

It can be generally noted that the instances preceding nasals favour /æ/ more than those preceding fricatives: overall 44 per cent versus 27 per cent – the exceptions are Adelaide and perhaps Melbourne. The strength of this constraint differs, as shown in table 15.4.

This is, in fact, contrary to the pattern expected on historical grounds. However this is misleading as there are relatively few words in the fricative environment that differ from the RP pattern; most such words do not vary in either RP or Australian English. However there are many more words in the prenasal environment that vary in Australian English but show only /ɑ:/ in RP. For a partial list, see Bradley (1980: 86–7); examples include most of the words in prenasal environment cited here, such as *dance, chance* and so on, among many others.

For Melbourne, where the most data are available, results of this study combined with studies by McCann (1985) and Sabbadin (1985) show the following overall lexical hierarchy, from most to least /æ/; words containing the same stem were found to operate similarly: *castle* (*Castlemaine*); *graph* (*photograph*); *France*; *chant* (*enchant*); *dance*; *plant* (*plants, planted*); *answer*; *trance*; *chance*; *demand*; *grasp*; *contrast.*

Given that the lexical constraint is so strong, stylistic differences measured by a simple index may not reveal what is going on. It is necessary to look at stylistic variation virtually word by word, which limits the degree to which it can be quantified since not all speakers use the relevant lexical items outside the reading sections of the interview. Style shift towards /ɑ:/ in more formal contexts is observed in the data, especially for residents of Middle class suburbs, more so in Melbourne, Hobart and Adelaide. Bradley and Bradley (1991) discuss the pattern for the complete Melbourne sample in more detail. McCann (1985) also demonstrates a consistent style shift of 17 per cent on average between Style B (interview speech) and Style D (wordlists) for eleven varying lexical items in Melbourne.

Stereotyping

As noted above, several linguists have noted the regional distribution of /æ/-/ɑ:/ variation; they are simply reporting the most widely known regional stereotype about Australian English. Of the 47 interviewees, eight (17 per cent) spontaneously gave examples of this variation when asked about regional differences, more than for any other stereotype. They cited *castle* or place names containing it (*Newcastle, Castlereagh Street* in Sydney, *Castlemaine*); two speakers also cited *plant*, and one cited *dance*; in most cases they correctly attributed the /ɑ:/ form in *castle* to Sydney or New South Wales.[6] One speaker from Brisbane suggested that the /ɑ:/ form for *dance* and *plant* was a Victorian (Melbourne) and South Australian (Adelaide) form, with some justification as these words are much more likely to have /ɑ:/ there than in Brisbane – see table 3 above; one Hobart speaker who used /æ/ in the word attributed /ɑ:/ in *castle* to Queensland, where it occurs – but less frequently than in Hobart! Thus the perceptions of this variable were both fairly widespread and mostly accurate.

If the /ɑ:/ form is viewed negatively, this could support the suggestions by Baker (1966) and by Mitchell and Delbridge (1965a) that the /æ/

alternative is on the increase. There is evidence from associated comments that speakers reporting greater use of /a:/ elsewhere also view this as undesirable; this could be additional evidence for the increasing independence of Australian English from an RP-like norm.

What proportion of the population needs to comment on something variable for it to be considered a stereotype? Seventeen per cent may seem low; indeed some other speakers vigorously denied that regional differences exist in Australian English – which is in a sense an incompatible stereotype. It could also be argued that spontaneous reporting of stereotypes is uncommon. Bearing in mind that we are considering a portion of the population with relatively little exposure to the speech of other Australian cities due to the criteria for the sample, this seems strong evidence for stereotyping.

Further evidence is provided in an unpublished study by Lapidge (1983), in which Australians were asked to attribute speakers heard on tape to state of origin; the tape was a recording of a passage containing a large number of /a:/-/æ/ varying words. The rate of success was much better than chance, especially in the clearcut cases of South Australia (low /æ/), New South Wales (fairly low /æ/) and Victoria (high /æ/). So speakers can also recognise and identify based on the stereotype, to some degree.

Variation between /æ/, /a:/ and /eɪ/

As in other varieties of English, there are certain words which have /eɪ/ as an alternative to one or both of the two vowels considered here. Among these are *basic*, which has /eɪ/ for most speakers, but variably also /æ/, especially for older speakers and in Brisbane. Parallel is the past tense of *bid* (*bade*); for most speakers /eɪ/, but for a few /æ/. Other words showing this pattern include *sadist, patriot*, and a list of words cited by Baker (1966: 440); *matrix, data, status, gratis, apparatus*; some of these also have /a:/ as a possibility. The first two alternatives plus a third, /ə/, occur in the first syllable of *azure*. One word which shows all three alternatives is *pastie* (kind of pie); another is *lambaste*. The pattern observed for these is also regionally distributed, as shown in table 15.5. Some words show more categorical regional distribution than others; *cicada* has /a:/ in Sydney, but /eɪ/ in Melbourne. The distribution of vowels in these words differs from that of RP, generally in the direction of more /æ/ possibilities.

Unfortunately these words were not on the wordlist used in Sydney; but Laycock (1980) reports /eɪ/ for *pastie* there, and /a:/ in *Newcastle*. Baker (1966: 440–1) reports /eɪ/ more frequent than /æ/ for *basic* in Sydney, and gives all three forms of *azure* – though he characterises the schwa form as a spelling pronunciation. Variation in *bade* has been discussed in the literature on short versus long /æ/, and also occurs in Sydney. Overall, if

Table 15.5. *Vowels in four words which vary between* /eɪ/, /æ/ *and* /a:/: *per cent* /eɪ/, *per cent* /æ/, *per cent* /a:/ *(or per cent* /ə/ *for 'azure')*

	Hobart	Melbourne	Brisbane	Adelaide
basic	100/-/-	90/10/-	78/22/-	100/-/-
bade	10/-/-	75/25/-	89/11/-	71/29/-
azure	35/30/35	20/10/70	66/22/11	50/7/43
pastie	-/-/100	11/-/89	38/27/35	/-/-/100

anything, the phenomena with these words are less systematic than those relating to /a:/ versus /æ/.

Conclusion

Bradley (1980, 1989) and Bradley and Bradley (1991) give details of other regional phonological differences; as usual for dialects of English, most of these are in the vowel system. One such, the Adelaide backing of /u/ and /ou/ before /l/, has achieved the status of a stereotype, though not as well known as the one investigated here. Others have been noticed by a few non-linguists, but not by other linguists.

In this study a particular example of lexical diffusion has been investigated in detail, and shown to have interesting diachronic and synchronic ramifications.

NOTES

1. The related issue of long /æ:/ as in *bad* versus short /æ/ as in *bade* (for some speakers) will not be discussed here, though it is an additional type of phonetic similarity supporting the phonetic reasonableness of the change.
2. This study was funded at various stages by the University of Melbourne, by the Australian Research Grants Scheme, and by La Trobe University. I gratefully acknowledge the participation of my wife Maya Bradley in the design, data collection and analysis stages. Thanks are also due to Dr R. Huddleston and Dr D. Lee, Department of English, University of Queensland and to Dr P. Ball, Department of Psychology, University of Tasmania for provision of local assistance.
3. The Sydney interview was slightly different; in particular, the wordlist was shorter.
4. The Adelaide sample is smaller due to sampling problems: a high refusal rate. Completion of sampling in Adelaide and an extension of the survey to Perth will be carried out in the near future.
5. The suburbs were chosen from existing social surveys; for details, see Bradley

and Bradley (1991). The Adelaide sample lacks males from the Working class suburb.

6. It is also possible to hear the /a:/ form even for Victorian place names such as *Castlemaine* from Melburnians, in very formal contexts such as news broadcasts.

REFERENCES

Baker, S. J. 1945. *The Australian Language*. Sydney: Angus & Robertson. Second edition, 1966.

Bernard, J. R. L. 1969. On the uniformity of spoken Australian English. *Orbis* 18 (1): 62–73.

1981. Australian pronunciation. In Delbridge (ed.) 1981.

Bradley, D. 1980. Regional differences in Australian English phonology. *Working Papers in Linguistics, University of Melbourne* 6: 73–93.

1989. Regional dialects in Australian English phonology. In Collins, P. and Blair, D. (eds.) 1989. *Australian English: the Language of a New Society*. St Lucia: University of Queensland Press.

Bradley, D. and Bradley, M. 1991. *English in Australia*. Melbourne: Oxford University Press.

Delbridge, A. (editor-in-chief) 1981. *The Macquarie Dictionary*. St Leonards, NSW: Macquarie Library.

Hammarström, U. G. E. 1980. *Australian English: Its Origin and Status*. Hamburg: Buske.

Lapidge, C. 1983. Subjective reactions to Australian speech. MS, La Trobe University, Melbourne.

Laycock, D. 1980. Long 'short vowels' in Australian English – update. MS, Canberra.

McCann, E. 1985. Research project: (æ) and (h) in Melbourne English. MS, La Trobe University, Melbourne.

Mitchell, A. G. and Delbridge, A. 1965a. *The Pronunciation of English in Australia*. Sydney: Angus & Robertson. Second, revised edition.

1965b. *The Speech of Australian Adolescents*. Sydney: Angus & Robertson.

Sabbadin, V. 1985. Research project: (æ) and flaps in Melbourne English. MS, La Trobe University, Melbourne.

Samuels, M. L. 1972. *Linguistic Evolution with Special Reference to English*. Cambridge: Cambridge University Press.

Trudgill, P. 1986. *Dialects in Contact*. Oxford: Basil Blackwell.

Turner, G. W. 1966. *The English Language in Australia and New Zealand*. London: Longman.

16

Variation in subject–verb agreement in Inner Sydney English

EDINA EISIKOVITS

Like many other non-standard varieties of English, Inner-Sydney English (ISE) allows variation in its subject–verb agreement patterns, especially with the auxiliary verb DO (+ *not*), and the verb BE (as a copula and an auxiliary).

Such variation has been investigated in British English (Trudgill 1974; Cheshire 1982) and American English both in Black English (Labov *et al.* 1968; Wolfram 1969) and in various white varieties (Labov *et al.* 1968; Wolfram and Christian 1976; Feagin 1979). In Australian English, such variation has been noted by Eagleson (1976) in Sydney, Dines *et al.* (1979), Bradley (1979) in Melbourne, and Shnukal (1978) in Cessnock, but only Bradley and Shnukal provide any quantitative analysis.

This paper will attempt to explore systematically the factors which influence variation in subject–verb agreement patterns in Inner-Sydney English, focusing on the two variables, DO and BE, in order to determine the linguistic and non-linguistic constraints on the variation apparent.

Methodology of present study

This study is based on the speech of 40 adolescent residents of the Inner-City area of Sydney. All the informants were long-term residents of the area and were Australian-born of Australian-born parents. This was important, given the high migrant population of the Inner-City area of Sydney, in order to eliminate the possibility of language transfer.

Social class was not a strict criterion of selection but as this area of Sydney is to a large extent characterised as low status, the informants tended to be at the lower end of the social spectrum. Their parents were engaged in occupations relatively low in social status; for example, cleaner, truck driver, warehouse worker.

No attempt was made to produce a random sample; instead there was a focus on natural groups since, as Labov (1972: 256–7) points out:

> The vernacular is the property of the group, not the individual . . . the group exerts its control over the vernacular in supervision so close that a single slip may be condemned and remembered for years . . .

In all, 40 children were selected: 20 from Year 8 (average age 13 years, 11 months) and 20 from Year 10 (average age 16 years, 1 month). Within each group, half were males and half females.

The informants were interviewed in pairs with the view of obtaining as broad a picture of their natural language as is possible within the limitations of a tape-recorded situation. Interviews lasted from one-and-a-half to three hours depending on the involvement and interest of the informants. Many were spread over two sessions. In all, a total data base of more than 50 hours of recorded conversation was collected.

The data were analysed using the quantitative variationist approach pioneered by Labov (1966).

The variable (DO)

Although Inner-Sydney English does not generally allow -s deletion in third person present tense singular verbs, the auxiliary verb DO provides a special case in which such deletion may occur. However, such deletion only occurs in the presence of the negative particle, *not*, as in:

> Miss Sams don't even give me any marks. (3C/F/16–4)[1]
> It don't look all that good, does it? (6E/F/15–11)
> She works in a restaurant, don't she? (7A/F/14–4)

This environment favours -s deletion in other non-mainstream varieties of English as well as Inner-Sydney English. The frequencies of -s deletion for the auxiliary DO + *not* and for other third person singular present tense verbs in several varieties of English are presented in table 16.1.

It is interesting that both the other studies of Australian English listed in this table (Bradley 1979 and Shnukal 1978) show a lower frequency of occurrence of this form than is evident in this sample of ISE. Indeed, Shnukal (1978: 126) concludes:

> In Cessnock English, *be* is the only verb to show a consistent pattern of non-standard concord. There are no occurrences in the corpus of sentences like . . .
> 17.   It don't seem to make a difference.
> which are found in various British and American English dialects.

This conclusion is particularly surprising given the relatively high frequency of invariable *don't* used by this Inner-Sydney sample: 19.1 per cent – a frequency higher in fact that that of either invariable *is* or invariable *was*.

Bradley's (1979) results similarly suggest that invariable *don't* is not a

Table 16.1. *3rd singular -s deletion in several varieties of English*

	% *don't*/*doesn't*	% 3rd sing -*s*
Labov *et al.* (1968)	96.8	64.0
Fasold (1972)	87.5	65.1
Inwood males (Labov *et al.*, 1968)	64.3	0
Appalachian English	76.5	0
Alabama English (urban working class)	91.8	2.7
Norwich English (working class)	(?)	70.0
Reading English	95.2	[52.46[1]]
Inner-Sydney English	19.1	0
Melbourne Non-Standard	32.0[2]	0
Cessnock English	0	0

1. Reading English allows deletion of 3rd singular -*s* only with the verb DO; no figure is given for overall -*s* deletion.
2. This frequency given by Bradley (1979: 81) is not the overall frequency in her sample but the frequency among only those five speakers who use this form. Since 15 speakers in her sample evidence no occurrence at all of this form the overall frequency could be expected to be considerably lower. The frequency in this sample of ISE among a comparable group is 47.4 per cent.

central feature of her data; there are only seven occurrences in all, spread over five speakers, none of whom uses this form categorically. Such a conclusion is not borne out in this sample of ISE. Although the frequency of use of the form here is certainly lower than in the American and British varieties listed in table 16.1, its high frequency among the 17 speakers who evidence this form (47.7 per cent), three of whom use it categorically, would suggest that for some speakers at least this form is a central feature of this variety of English.

Variation in linguistic environments

Invariable *don't* may occur in Inner-Sydney English in either a negative statement or a tag question. In these contexts it may occur with three separate third person singular subjects:

(i) NP (singular) animate

> Mum don't like anyone calling anyone 'wog'. (7D/M/15–10)

(ii) 3rd person singular pronoun animate: *he/she*

> He don't belt us no more. (7B/M/14–3)

(iii) 3rd person singular pronoun inanimate: *it*

> It don't make no difference. (10D/M/15–8)

Table 16.2. Don't/doesn't *for subject type*

Name of Subject	Occurrences	% frequency
NP (sing) animate	15/26	57.7
3rd sing. pron. animate	32/69	46.4
3rd sing. pron. inanimate	5/14	35.7

No occurrences were noted of *don't* with an inanimate NP (singular) subject, though there was a small number of environments of this kind – an initially surprising absence, yet one consistent with the implicational scale below which suggests that invariable *don't* is more favoured by animate subjects than inanimate. Percentage frequencies for each of these subject types are given in table 16.2.

The data in this table suggest the following implicational scale:

> it *don't* > he/she *don't* > NP (sing) *don't*

That is, if a speaker occasionally uses *it don't*, then he or she is likely to use *he/she don't* and even more likely to use NP (sing) + *don't*. The converse, however, is not very likely.

Anecdotal evidence in support of this may be seen in the following examples, where a change of subject produces a change of form:

> My Dad don't hit me, he just talks to me. Like, if he hits me, I'd laugh at him, and then he'd get real angry. 'N 'en, 'n 'en, he'd know when he hits me, it doesn't hurt. (7B/M/14–3)
>
> Mum don't mind that but she doesn't like me getting drunk. (6C/F/16–9).

The pattern of individual speakers' usage supports this scale. Table 16.3 lists individual speakers' usage of these forms.

Variation in non-linguistic environments

Studies in the past have shown no correlation between the usage of non-standard agreement forms and either age or sex (see Wolfram and Christian 1976; Shnukal 1978; Feagin 1979). The results of this study, however, do suggest a relationship between the use of such forms and the variables of age and sex.

Table 16.4 shows the frequencies for invariable *don't* for the age and sex groupings in this study.

From table 16.4 it can be seen that males and females differ in their use of this variable. Invariable *don't*, although a significant feature of male speech, especially among the older age group, is hardly apparent among the female speakers. The low frequency of usage among the girls remains

Table 16.3. *Implicational scale for* don't

Speaker	*It don't*	*He/She don't*	NP (sing.) *don't*
7D	1	1	1
10D	1	1	1
6B	–	1	1
6D	–	1	1
5D	O	1	1
1D	O	1	1
8B	X	X	–
5B	–	X	1
7B	O	X	1
9D	O	X	1
5C	–	X	1
3C	O	X	–
6C	–	0	1
7A	–	0	1
4A	O	X	X
2A	–	X	O
6E	X	0	O

1 = categorical use
X = variable use
O = categorical absence
1 > X > O

Table 16.4. don't/doesn't *for age/sex*

Younger girls N = 10 Occurences 3/63 % = 4.8	Older girls N = 10 Occurences 5/77 % = 6.5
Younger boys N = 10 Occurences 13/78 % = 16.7	Older boys N = 10 Occurrences 31/60 % = 51.7

constant with age whereas the usage among the boys increases significantly.

This increase suggests that invariable *don't* has a strong status among the male groups as a marker of group identity, 'maleness' and working-class values. As the boys grow older and identify more strongly, perhaps,

Table 16.5. % don't/doesn't *for discourse type*

	Narrative	Conversation	Opinion
Younger girls N = 10	15.4	3.6	0.0
Younger boys N = 10	10.0	14.3	44.4
Older girls N = 10	0.0	10.2	0.0
Older boys N = 10	62.5	45.7	83.3

with males and as members of the working-class, their use of this form is favoured.

Among the girls, however, this form is never favoured. No female speaker evidences a frequency higher than 25 per cent whereas three males are categorical users of this form. Moreover, among the girls, usage remains relatively constant with age.

If the use of *don't* does carry strong 'male', working-class value for male speakers as has been suggested, we would expect this group's usage of this form to be sensitive to stylistic and contextual variation in line with this value. That is, the more 'formal' the situation, defined here either by the influence of the eliciting cue or the nature of the discourse context, the greater we would expect the use of this variable by the male speakers to be (see Eisikovits 1982a for further discussion of 'formality' in this sense). Similarly, we would expect the occurrence of this form in discourse in which the speaker is seeking to affirm his own identity as a working-class male. On the other hand, since this form is not much favoured by the female speakers and clearly has no equivalent value among this group, no such sensitivity would be anticipated in their behaviour.

These expectations are to a large extent borne out in the data. The data here are limited, especially among the female speakers, but among the male speakers there does appear to be a sensitivity to stylistic variation consistent with the patterns outlined above.

This trend is evident in the variation in usage of invariable *don't* by the various groups in different discourse contexts, as Table 16.5 shows.

In both age groups, males evidence the greater frequency of usage of the *don't* form in the most 'formal' context, that is, opinion, and among the younger boys, the lowest frequency in the least 'formal' context, that is, narrative. The relatively high percentage of occurrences of *don't* in the narrative context among the older boys is not inconsistent and may be explained as part of their expression of personal and social identity.

Some anecdotal evidence from the practice of individual male speakers supports the view that the invariable *don't* form is used to affirm the speaker's toughness and anti-establishment values.

For 5D, the expression of his toughness and growing independence of his family, especially his mother, is couched in the use of non-standard forms. Having just described how in his childhood he was severely disciplined for swearing, he concludes:

> If I swear in front of me mother now she don't say nothing.

Similarly for 6D, his attempt to assert himself in describing his relationship with his older sister is suggested in his comment:

> Me sister don't boss me around.

That his assertiveness is still tempered by some dependence is evidenced as he continues:

> Me brother, I don't worry about him much, but me Father is real strict. Doesn't like any bad manners or talking at the table . . .

For other male speakers, the 'Them and Us' attitude to society – school and teachers, employers and migrants – is suggested in their use of non-standard forms. 10D, for example, expresses his criticism of an authoritarian schoolmaster as follows:

> He's always patrolling round, seeing what you're doing. Like he don't trust us . . .

Later, describing an unpopular migrant group, he concludes:

> Everybody don't like 'em.

Similarly 1D, discussing the attitude of his peer group to work, comments:

> Half of em don't wanna work anyway. There's one kid, Roger, he don't wanna work so he told em all down at the Dole Office he wanted to be an elephant trainer.

The influence of eliciting cue also appears to support the view that the *don't* form is used by males to express solidarity with their own group and opposition to outsiders – in this case, the adult, female, middle-class Interviewer (see table 16.6).

The figures in table 16.6 are not decisive but do seem to point to a greater use of the *don't* form by the males when responding to a question from the Interviewer than a cue from a peer. The influence of the Interviewer appears to head them towards the use of this form while the influence of peers leans them in the opposite direction.

Table 16.6. *Influence of eliciting cue on* don't/doesn't

	Comment from peer	Question from Interviewer
Younger girls		
N = 10	7.4	2.8
Younger boys		
N = 10	14.3	19.5
Older girls		
N = 10	6.3	6.6
Older boys		
N = 10	42.9	54.3

The variable (BE)

As in many non-standard varieties of English, Inner-Sydney English allows alternative forms of BE in both the present and past tenses. That is, the forms *is* and *was*, reserved for use with a singular subject in standard English, may occur with a plural subject, for example:

> All the kids at school is calling me 'sissy' and that. (8D/M/15–4)
> Isn't there any girls going? (5A/F/14–7)
> We was lucky though cause there was five couches. (2C/F/15–11)
> I thought you was talking about Rhonda. (4B/M/14–11)

These forms do not occur categorically in ISE. Instead, variation is apparent both between and within speakers.

> We were little daredevils, we was. (6C/F/16–9)
> You're going, wasn't ya? (6F/M/16–8)
> There's only six children in the flats and they're all over fifteen. (2C/F/15–11)
> We got picked up for jigging school. We was walking down on the wrong side of the road and the ranger come up an says, 'Why aren't you kids at school?' and we says, 'Oh, we've moved,' you know, 'and we're allowed to come down here for the day'. There was five of us there. There was Penny an Stephen. They was there. An he took us down the ranger's station an they just sat there, an then he called the coppers. An they knew who we were. (5C/F/16–4).

Such forms have been found to occur in several other varieties of English. Table 16.7 shows the frequencies of occurrence of these forms for the varieties for which quantitative data are available.

From this table it is clear that while tense is an important factor with respect to agreement in several of these varieties of English, this is not as true of Inner-Sydney English. ISE does follow a similar pattern to that of other varieties described, in that variation in the past tense occurs more

Table 16.7. *Invariant* BE *in several varieties of English*

Variety	% invariant *is*	% invariant *was*
BEV	5	86.1
Inwood	0	12.1
Appalachian English	21	79.4
Alabama English	36.2	69.5
Cessnock English	24.1	30.4
Inner-Sydney English	19.5	24.5

Table 16.8. *Non-Agreement for present and past tense in 2 environments,* + there/ − there + *(sing)* BE + *NP (pl)*

	% invariant *is*	% invariant *was*	% total invariant *is/was*
(a) + *there*			
Younger girls			
N = 10	100.0 (20/20)	95.8 (23/24)	97.7 (43/44)
Younger boys			
N = 10	98.2 (53/54)	81.3 (13/16)	94.3 (66/70)
Older girls			
N = 10	97.7 (42/43)	83.3 (20/24)	92.5 (62/67)
Older boys			
N = 10	96.4 (53/55)	92.3 (24/26)	91.5 (77/81)
Total (N = 40)	97.7 (168/172)	88.9 (80/90)	94.6 (248/262)
(b) − *there*			
Younger girls			
N = 10	8.6 (15/174)	14.4 (16/111)	10.9 (31/285)
Younger boys			
N = 10	4.3 (8/184)	7.9 (11/139)	5.9 (19/323)
Older girls			
N = 10	0.8 (2/265)	12.1 (17/141)	4.7 (19/406)
Older boys			
N = 10	3.4 (8/234)	18.7 (20/107)	8.2 (28/341)
Total (N = 40)	3.9 (33/857)	12.9 (64/498)	7.2 (97/1355)

frequently than in the present, but this difference is not great. Instead, it is the nature of the subject which is of greater significance in ISE. That is, it is the structure *there* + singular BE + NP (pl) which sharply differentiates agreement/non-agreement, as table 16.8 shows.

From this table it is clear that while the use of a singular verb in the structure *There* + BE + NP (pl) is not categorical, it is nearly so. Indeed, for 30 of the 40 speakers in the sample, this form is used categorically in this structure. Only 10 speakers evidence variable usage.

Moreover, when the figures for the present and the past tenses are compared in the environments *There* + (sing) BE + NP (pl) and − *There* + (sing) BE + NP (pl) two different patterns emerge.

(i) In the environment *There* + (sing) BE + NP (pl), unlike the pattern outlined above, there does not appear to be a greater use of the invariable *was* form than the invariable *is*. Instead, there is a decline in use of the invariable form in the past tense compared with the present.

> present tense 97.7% : past tense 88.9%
> (+ *there*)   (+ *there*)
> $\chi^2 = 9.06$
> $p < 0.01$

(ii)   In environments other than *There* + (sing) BE + NP (pl), however, this pattern is reversed and indeed is in line with the trend in other varieties of English outlined above, that is, invariant *was* occurs more frequently than invariant *is*.

> past tense 12.9 : present tense 3.9%
> (− *there*)   (− *there*)
> $\chi^2 = 38.2$
> $p < 0.01$

The prevalence of the use of singular BE in the environment *There* + (sing) BE + NP (pl) with a frequency so much higher than in other environments suggests that it has become the local 'standard' form. Indeed, there is some evidence that this form has currency well beyond this sample of ISE and, in fact, does not carry the social marking of some of the other variables discussed in this study.

Shnukal, in her study of this variable in Cessnock English (1978: 134), argues that '*there* + *is/was* is accepted as the local standard and is not stigmatised in the way that other non-standard agreement is', pointing out that 'when the subject is expletive or 'dummy' *there*, the singular forms *is* and *was* alternate with *are* and *were* in the speech of even the most careful middle-class speakers'.

Furthermore, anecdotal evidence from media usage would suggest that the use of singular BE in this environment is widespread throughout Australian English − 'There's another four major changes in the Cabinet' (Australian Broadcasting Commission political reporter, 17/12/1980) − and, indeed, in American English (cf. Feagin 1979: 207) and informal British English (Quirk *et al.* 1972: 366, 958) as well.

Why should invariable *be* occur so frequently in the environment *There*

+ BE + NP (pl)? The most obvious answer is that in these sentences *there* is interpreted as a noun phrase and, because it directly precedes the verb phrase, as the subject of the sentence. Following the principle of proximity (see Quirk *et al*. 1972: 365), the verb then agrees with this surface subject rather than its plural 'notional subject' which occurs later in the sentence. As *there* is not marked for plural[2], a singular verb is used.

The problem with this explanation is the tenuous status of *there* as a noun phrase, and hence as a subject. Certainly, it does not embody the features used to identify most other noun phrases: it neither forms a plural nor allows a determiner. On the other hand, it does behave like a subject in some respects in that it inverts with the first auxiliary or the copula in the verb phrase to form a question:

> Is there any nets out there? (6A/F/13–11)

and may be copied in tag questions:

> There isn't any girls going, is there? (5A/F/14–7).

It is interesting, too, that such structures in which an 'empty' surface subject + singular verb may be followed by a plural noun phrase are also found in other languages. The French construction, *Il y a . . .*, and the German, *Es gibt . . .*, illustrate this.

Variation with social factors

Table 16.8 also evidences the age and sex differences in the use of *There* + (sing) BE + NP (pl).

In the present tense, its occurrence is almost categorical (97.2 per cent) and this usage is maintained over the four groups in the sample. Indeed, only four instances of *are* in this structure were noted.

In the past tense, the frequency is again high – 88.9 per cent – but there does appear to be some variation among the four groups in the sample, as table 16.9 shows.

As with *don't*, a difference in the usage of male and female speakers is apparent, but the difference is not altogether parallel. As with *don't*, the males increase their use of this form as they grow older, but here, the female speakers decline somewhat in their use of this form with age.

This patterning would suggest that two separate norms are operating for the two sex groups in this sample. In this case, as the girls grow older and become more conscious of external social and grammatical norms the use of *were* is favoured, whereas among the boys, increased age brings a different social awareness, perhaps a strengthening of working-class values, and an accompanying increase in the use of non-standard forms, in this case, *was*. The effect of other non-linguistic factors provides further support for the existence of these two normative patterns.

Table 16.9. There + was + *NP (pl) for age/sex*

Younger girls N = 10 Occurrences 23/24 % = 95.8	Older girls N = 10 Occurrences 20/24 % = 83.3
Younger boys N = 10 Occurrences 13/16 % = 81.3	Older boys N = 10 Occurrences 24/26 % = 92.3

The influence of the eliciting cue on the frequency of occurrence of *was* in this structure is different for males and females (see table 16.10). For the males the more 'formal' situation, that is, discourse initiated by a question from the Interviewer, brings an increase in the use of the *was* form, compared with its occurrence in discourse prompted by a cue from a peer. Among the females, however, the reverse is true. For them, the *was* form occurs more frequently in discourse prompted by a cue from a peer whereas the more formal context of the Interviewer's questions heads them towards the *were* form which, incidentally, is used consistently by the Interviewer throughout all interviews. No such variation is apparent in the use of *There + is + NP (pl)* (see table 16.11).

What this difference with respect to tense in the use of *there + sing* BE + NP (pl) would suggest is that the singular *is* form has become more accepted in this environment than has the *was* form.

Two interesting anecdotes from the practice of individual speakers among the older female group illustrate this. In response to the Interviewer's question:

Are there a lot of dances around here?

3C responds:

There is in the summer. They're all up Hurstville.

Similarly, when the Interviewer asks 6C:

Are there a lot of migrants round where you live? There are in the school.

6C replies:

Not in the area that I live, but further round in Enmore, round there, there's a lot of migrants, but not, you know round in the streets where I live there isn't. There's only bout one or two on our street.

– to which her companion, 5C, comments:

Table 16.10. *Effect of eliciting cue on* % was/were *in* There + BE + NP (pl)

	Comment from peer	Interviewer question
Younger girls N = 10	100	92.3
Younger boys N = 10	71.4	88.2
Older girls N = 10	85.7	77.8
Older boys N = 10	75.0	95.5

Table 16.11. *Effect of eliciting cue on* % is/are *in* There + BE + NP (pl)

	Comment from peer	Interviewer question
Younger girls N = 10	100	100
Younger boys N = 10	100	96.7
Older girls N = 10	100	95.7
Older boys N = 10	100	94.9

There is a lot in the school though.

With *there + was* + NP (pl), as with other variables examined, a prompt from the Interviewer was sufficient to lead the older girls away from the use of a non-standard form. Here, even the Interviewer's use of the *are* form does not influence the speakers in this direction.

Variation between *is* and *are* in other environments

Apart from the environment *There + is* + NP (pl) discussed above, there are very few instances of *is* with a plural subject in this sample of Inner-Sydney English. Indeed, the overall frequency of occurrence of this form (− *there*) is a low 3.9 per cent. With such a low frequency of occurrence it is perhaps tempting to disregard the examples which do occur as performance error; however it is important not to overlook any underlying patterning in this usage, despite its limited occurrence.

Table 16.12. is/are *for plural pronoun/non-pronoun subjects (N = 40)*

	Plural non-pronoun subject	Plural pronoun subject
is as auxiliary	Occurrences 12/44 % : 27.3	Occurrences 0/277 % : 0
is as copula	Occurrences 21/129 % : 16.3	Occurrences 0/407 % : 0
Total *is/are*	Occurrences 33/173 % : 19.1	Occurrences 0/684 % : 0

Examination of the data suggests that invariable *is* can occur with only three kinds of plural subjects:

(i)   with a plural noun phrase:

Is these rooms real soundproof? (7D/M/15–10)

(ii)   with a coordinated NP:

David and Doug's going to see Status Quo. (2A/F/13–11)

(iii)   with a relative pronoun in an embedded relative clause:

They try to help me, the kids that's with me. (6A/F/13–11)

Note that, as these examples illustrate, the *is* form with a plural subject may occur as either a copula or an auxiliary and in a question structure as well as a statement.

No occurrences were found with plural pronoun subjects. This non-occurrence accounts to some extent for the particularly low overall frequency of this form (see table 16.12). As table 16.12 shows, over the whole sample the frequency of *is* with a plural non-pronoun subject is 19.1 per cent.

In addition, the environments in which this form may occur in ISE are consistent with those allowing invariable *is* in other varieties of English[3], for example, Cessnock English, working-class Anniston English[4] and Appalachian English, suggesting that the occurrences here are not random and hence cannot be dismissed as performance error.

Instead, that this form occurs in such a limited number of environments suggests that invariable *is* is weakening in ISE compared with *was*. This has similarly been suggested of other varieties, for example Anniston English (Feagin 1979: 179).

Only 17 speakers in this sample evidence any occurrence at all of this

Table 16.13. is/are *for linguistic environments (N = 40)*

	NP (pl)	NP + NP	Relative pronoun
BE as auxiliary	Occurrences 6/32 % : 18.8	Occurrences 3/6 % : 50	Occurrences 3/6 % : 50
BE as copula	Occurrences 12/105 % : 11.4	Occurrences 5/8 % : 62.5	Occurrences 4/16 % : 18.8
Total is/*are*	Occurrences 18/137 % : 13.1	Occurrences 8/14 % : 57.1	Occurrences 7/22 % : 31.8

form in environments other than *There* + *is* + NP (pl). As would be expected, given the variation with tense outlined above, almost all of these speakers also evidence the use of *was* with plural subjects, suggesting that an implicational relationship exists between these two forms, that is, the use of invariable *is* implies the use of invariable *was*:

invariable *is* > invariable *was*

The frequencies of occurrence of *is* + plural subject in each of the linguistic environments in which it may occur are set out in table 16.13.

The data in table 16.13 seem to indicate the following implicational scale:

$$\begin{matrix} \text{NP (pl)} \\ + \text{ is} \end{matrix} > \begin{matrix} \text{relative} \\ \text{pronoun} \\ + \text{ is} \end{matrix} > \begin{matrix} \text{NP + NP} \\ + \text{ is} \end{matrix} > \begin{matrix} [\textit{There} + \textit{is} + \text{NP (pl)}] \\ \text{(See table 16.8 above)} \end{matrix}$$

That is, if a person uses *is* with a plural NP, he or she is also likely to use it with a plural subject in an embedded relative clause and with a coordinated NP subject. The converse however is not very likely.

Variation between *was* and *were* in other environments

It has already been shown (see table 16.8) that in environments other than *there* + *be* + NP (pl), the frequency of *was* with a plural subject is more than three times that of *is*. Moreover, *was* may occur in more linguistic environments, including pronoun subjects, than its present tense counterpart.

These environments are:
(i)   pronoun subjects:
    (a) *we*

Table 16.14. was + *plural subject in questions/statements*

Question	Statement
Occurrences	Occurrences
6/6	58/492
% : 100	% : 11.8

> We was driving a land rover; we wasn't supposed to be driving it. (10D/M/15–8)

　(b) *you*

> You felt like you was really in it. (5D/M/15–7)

　(c) *they*

> They was real friendly. (5C/F/16–9)

(ii)　non-pronoun subjects:
　　(a)　NP (pl)

> Two of them was trying to do it. (2B/M/13–11)

　　(b)　NP + NP

> Mary and Marion was there. (6E/F/15–11)

As these examples illustrate, the *was* form, like *is*, may occur with a plural subject as either a copula or an auxiliary.

As well, *was*, like *is*, may occur in either questions and question tags as well as in statements. For example:

> Who was you with? (6A/F/13–11)
> You're going, wasn't you? (6F/M/16–8)

Indeed, although it is difficult to generalise from the limited number of occurrences of past tense BE in questions, such a structure does appear to favour the use of the *was* form. Certainly, it can be said that among 40 speakers none used the *were* form with a plural subject in a question structure (see table 16.14).

This tendency is represented in a telling individual example (see speaker (6F/M/16–8) above) where a change of structure brings a change in the form of past tense *be*.

Because of this higher frequency and more widespread use of *was* compared with *is*, it has been suggested (see, for example, Fries 1940: 52; Wolfram and Christian 1976: 78; Feagin 1979: 201) that the verb BE is undergoing a process of levelling towards a single past tense form in line with that experienced by all other English verbs in the early Modern English period:

> This use of *was* is a carrying through of the levelling to a single form which affected all the preterits of strong verbs in Early Modern English. As a matter of fact, the verb *to be* with its preterit singular *was* and preterit plural *were* is the only verb left out of more than a hundred that had, up to the time of Shakespeare, distinct forms for singular and plural in the past tense. (Fries, 1940: 52)

The frequencies of occurrence of *was* + plural subject for each of the subject types with which it may occur are set out in table 16.15.

The data in table 16.15 seem to indicate the following implicational scale:

NP (pl)   *They   We   You*   NP+NP   (*There* + *was* + NP (pl)
+*was*   > + *was* > + *was* > + *was* > + *was*   (See table 16.8 above)

That is, if a person uses *was* with plural NP or with the pronouns *we/they*, he or she is also likely to use it with the pronoun *you* and even more likely to use it with a coordinated NP subject. The converse, however, is not very likely. The high frequency of *you* + *was* compared with other pronoun subjects is interesting in that since the *was* form already occurs with 1st and 3rd person singular pronouns (*I/he was*) this may indicate a levelling to a common singular past tense form:

I   *We*
You (sing)   } *was*   *You* (pl)   } *were*
He   *They*

Anecodotal evidence of this pattern may be seen in the following example from the speech of 5C, where a change of subject produces a change of form:

> I seed a car crash happen right in front of me. We was sitting there, you know, and we, the lights were just changing . . . and the bus come down . . . and there was three little kids in there. Everything was alright. The kids were alright. They was alright, none of em was hurt. The car wasn't really badly done either. (5C/F/16–4)

The pattern of individual speakers' usage supports this scale, as table 16.16 shows.

Conclusion

This analysis has produced a tentative hypothesis that two separate norms are operating among these speakers. Among the males, increased age brings about an increased use of non-standard forms, suggesting that for

Table 16.15. was/were *for linguistic environments (N = 40)*

	We	*You*	*They*	NP (pl)	NP + NP
was as copula	4/70	8/24	5/69	2/31	2/8
	5.7%	33.3%	7.3%	6.5%	25%
was as auxiliary	21/168	5/17	9/78	2/23	6/10
	12.5%	29.4%	11.5%	8.7%	60%
Total *was/were*	25/238	13/41	14/147	4/54	8/18
	10.5%	31.7%	9.5%	7.4%	44.4%

Table 16.16. *Implicational scale for* was/were

Speaker	NP (pl) We + *was*[5] *They*	*You + was*	NP + NP + *was*	*There + was +* NP (pl)
5D	X	1	–	1
1C	X	1	–	–
5C	X	X	1	1
10D	X	–	1	1
9D	O	O	1	1
6E	O	O	1	1
3D	X	X	–	1
5F	X	X	–	1
6F	X	X	–	1
7A	X	X	–	1
8B	X	–	–	1
5A	X	O	X	1
4F	X	X	O	–
4A	X	–	–	1
6C	X	–	–	1
2B	X	O	–	1
2C	X	O	–	1
7B	X	X	–	–
4B	O	1	X	X
8A	O	X	–	–
6A	X	X	X	X
7D	X	X	–	X
10A	X	–	–	–

1 = categorical use of *was* in this environment
X = variable use of *was* in this environment
O = categorical absence of *was* (i.e. use of *were*)
1 > X > O

this group such forms carry their own prestige as markers of gender and, perhaps, of class identity. For the females, the non-standard forms discussed here carry no such prestige. Where such forms are used to any degree by the younger females, increased age brings about a decrease in this usage, suggesting that as the girls grow older and become more conscious of external norms of 'correctness', they modify their usage in line with this perception. Different patterns of stylistic variation exhibited by the two sex groups provide support for this view.

To establish this hypothesis more firmly would require corroborative patterns of usage for other non-standard variables and for other speakers. Comparable patterns have been found to occur in this sample for several other non-standard variables: multiple negation, non-standard verb forms, perfective *have*, coordinated pronoun subjects, pronominal determiner *me/my* and *what* comparatives (see Eisikovits 1981, 1982, 1987a, forthcoming). Such evidence lends considerable weight to the hypothesis outlined above. Further investigations with other speakers of this and other varieties of Australian English are needed to determine the extent to which these patterns are widespread.

NOTES

1. The letters and numbers following quotations from transcripts identify the speaker and provide information about his or her age and sex. For example, 3C/F/16–4 indicates that the speaker 3C (C = older female group) is female and aged 16 years and 4 months.
2. Quirk *et al.* generalise the rule of plural concord as follows: 'A subject which is not definitely marked for plural requires a singular verb' (1972: 359).
3. The OED (1: 715) notes that in the northern dialect (ME and modern) *is* occurs for the plural when the subject is a noun or a relative, but not with plural pronoun subjects.
4. Working-class Anniston English allows some *they is*, but this is restricted to the speech of only two informants in the oldest age group (Feagin 1979: 199).
5. Because the frequencies of occurrence of *was* with these three subject types are so similar, these environments have been grouped together.

REFERENCES

Bradley, M. 1979. Negation. In Dines, E., Henry, P. and Allender, S. (eds.), 1979.
Cheshire, J. 1982. *Variation in an English Dialect*. Cambridge: Cambridge University Press.

Dines, E., Henry, P. and Allender, S. (eds.) 1979. *Formal and Functional Variation in Urban Children's Language*. Report prepared for Educational Research and Development Committee, Canberra, Australia.

Eagleson, R. D. 1976. The evidence for social dialects in Australian English. In Clyne, M. G. (ed.), *Australia Talks*. Canberra: Australian National University, pp. 7–27.

Eisikovits, E. 1982a. Inner-Sydney English: An Investigation of Grammatical Variation in Adolescent Speech. Unpublished PhD thesis, University of Sydney.

1982b. Cultural attitudes and language variation. *Australian Review of Applied Linguistics* 5: 129–42.

1987a. Sex differences in inter- and intra-group interaction among adolescents. In Pauwels, A. (ed.), *Language, Gender and Society in Australia and New Zealand*. Sydney: Australian Professional Publications.

1987b. Variation in the lexical verb in Inner-Sydney English. *Australian Journal of Linguistics* 7: 25–42.

1989. Girl-talk/boy-talk: Sex differences in adolescent speech. In Collins, P. and Blair, D. (eds.). 1989. *Australian English: the Language of a New Society*. Queensland: University of Queensland Press.

Fasold, R. 1972. *Tense Marking in Black English: A Linguistic and Social Analysis*. Arlington VI: Center for Applied Linguistics.

Feagin, C. 1979. *Variation and Change in Alabama English: A Sociolinguistic Study in the White Community*. Washington DC: Georgetown University Press.

Fries, C. 1940. *American English Grammar: The grammatical structure of present-day American English with especial reference to social differences or class dialects*. National Council of Teachers of English Monographs, 10, New York: Appleton-Century-Crofts.

Horvath, B. 1985. *Variation in Australian English: The Sociolects of Sydney*. Cambridge: Cambridge University Press.

Labov, W. 1966. *The Social Stratification of English in New York City*. Washington DC: Center for Applied Linguistics.

1972. Some principles of linguistic methodology. *Language in Society* 1 (1): 97–120.

Labov, W., Cohen, P., Robins, C. and Lewis, J. 1968. *A Study of the Non-Standard English of Negro and Puerto-Rican Speakers in New York City*. Vol. 1. Phonological and Grammatical Analysis. US Office of Education Cooperative Research Project No. 3288.

Oxford English Dictionary 1933. Murray, A., Bradley, H., Craigie, W. A. and Onions C. T. (eds.). Oxford: Clarendon Press.

Quirk, R., Greenbaum, S., Leech, G. and Svartvik, J. 1972. *A Grammar of Contemporary English*. London: Longman.

Shnukal, A. 1978. A sociolinguistic study of Australian English: Phonological and syntactic variation in Cessnock, NSW. Unpublished PhD thesis, Georgetown University.

Trudgill, P. 1974. *The Social Differentiation of English in Norwich*. Cambridge: Cambridge University Press.

Wolfram, W. 1969. *A Sociolinguistic Description of Detroit Negro Speech*. Washington DC: Center for Applied Linguistics.
Wolfram, W. and Christian, D. 1976. *Appalachian English*. Arlington VI: Center for Applied Linguistics.

17

Australian Creole English: the effect of cultural knowledge on language and memory

MARGARET S. STEFFENSEN

Introduction

Recent research in schema theory has demonstrated that background knowledge is a signficant factor in text comprehension. The theory proposes that schemata – dynamic abstract cognitive structures – are the basis of understanding. Comprehension is a constructive process integrating input from a message and the knowledge which is maintained in, and composes, schemata. It has been proposed that schemata contain slots or frames (Minsky 1975), which represent knowledge about a limited domain. These are instantiated with specific realisations as a text is comprehended (Anderson, Reynolds, Schallert and Goetz 1977), providing the reader the sense of having understood (Kuipers 1975). A schema also affects retrieval by providing a guide for the search process (Anderson and Pichert 1978).

The term 'schema' traces back to Bartlett (1932), who first demonstrated the effect of cultural membership on text recall. He had Englishmen read a North American Indian folktale, which was then recalled at increasing time intervals. From an English perspective, recalls were more coherent than the original story because subjects 'rationalised' exotic features of the text. Bartlett described remembering as an active process affected by 'an interplay of individual and social factors' (1932: 126).

Most recent work investigating the effect of cultural background knowledge on reading comprehension has focused on text structure. When Kintsch and Greene (1978) found that American college students read and recalled more of the propositions in a European fairy tale than an Apache folk tale, they proposed that there are cultural differences in story structure. They concluded that a match between a reader's culturally-based formal schema and that of the text increases comprehension. However, Mandler, Scribner, Cole and DeForest (1980) argued that the inherent difficulty of the structure of the Apache folk tale, not cultural differences, had caused these results. When text structure was controlled, they found similar recall patterns in Vai-speaking Liberians and Americans. This finding supported their claim that story structures are universal.

In a study of cross-cultural reading comprehension, Steffensen, Joagdev and Anderson (1979) demonstrated that content has significant effects when structure is controlled. Two letters describing an American and an Asian Indian wedding were read by Americans and Indians. Each group read its native text faster and understood it better. It was proposed that membership in a culture entails privileged information, which is subsumed by a rich system of schemata.

Steffensen and Colker (1982) replicated Steffensen *et al.* (1979) using an oral presentation. A balanced experiment was again used: subjects from two cultures listened to and recalled two culturally-based stories. Fifteen Aboriginal women living in an isolated federal settlement in the Northern Territory of Australia, near Katherine, and fifteen white American women living in central Illinois participated in the study. Subjects were roughly matched for age (17 to 61 years) and educational level (zero to grade twelve). The subjects heard texts describing illness and medical treatment from a Western and an Aboriginal perspective. In this paper, the Aboriginal recall protocols will be analysed to show the effect of background knowledge on language variation. A brief summary of that research follows.

Summary of recall study

Concepts of physical well-being, the causes of disease and treatment are facets of their culture with which all adults are familiar. Such concepts differ enormously between Western and Aboriginal society. Western medicine is based on germ theory and scientific methodology while in Aboriginal society, illness and treatment are facets of the metaphysical system. Disease and death may be attributed to sorcery or to the violation of a taboo. (See Maddock 1974; Hamilton 1972.)

Given these differences in conceptualisation, it was possible to show significant differences in the understanding of Western and Aboriginal texts. The Western text described a child's becoming ill from eating contaminated food; the Aboriginal text was a Walbiri account of illness told to Cawte (1974). The experimenter read one story, then asked the subject to retell it as close to the original version as possible. Aboriginal subjects were told to use either English or Creole. Every session was tape recorded in its entirety and transcribed.

Protocols were analysed for amount and quality of recall. It was found that, as in the case of reading, subjects elaborated their native text, adding information that was consistent with it but not actually stated. For example, the injunction in the original passage, *Watch out for animal dreaming*, was appropriately elaborated to *You don wanna go dere. Im dangerous place*. Distortions of the Western text by Aboriginal subjects reflected the accommodation of propositional content to the native schemata for illness and treatment. There was also some evidence of acculturation to Western health care, with which the subjects had some familiarity. Corresponding effects were found for American subjects: they remembered and elaborated more of the Western text, and distorted the Aboriginal text.

The linguistic context

Bamyili, the site of the research, was founded after World War II, when Aborigines from a number of tribal groups were relocated by the government. Virtually all the Aborigines were polylingual, speaking various combinations of a non-standard Aboriginal dialect of Australian English (NAE), Australian Creole English (ACE) as the lingua franca, and one or more Aboriginal languages. These languages included Ngalkbun, Dalabon, Rembarrnga, Djauan, Gunei and Maiali. While all the parents questioned expressed the desire that their children speak an Aboriginal language, interaction with them tended to be in ACE. In fact, parents would call and discipline their children in ACE while carrying on a conversation about the importance of maintaining the mother tongue.

Because Bamyili is near Katherine, the third largest town in the Northern Territory, the community was undergoing acculturation to the majority culture. The presence of 'European' teachers and government administrators (about 20 per cent of the population of 500) and the high level of interaction between them and the Aborigines, was accelerating this process. This is a classic situation for the formation of a creole continuum through decreolisation (Bickerton 1973; DeCamp 1971), and Bamyili Creole ranges from a basilect unintelligible to those who do not speak ACE to the acrolect, NAE. Each individual speaker occupied a place along this continuum, controlling a portion of the total range. Older informants generally spoke a basilectal variety with many Creole forms, the younger, an acrolectal form.

Aboriginal subjects were told that they could retell the stories in either English or ACE. On the basis of what is known about style shifting, whether it is attributed to topic or the speaker's perception of situation and the appropriate code, it was predicted that an acrolectal variety would be used for the Western text and a basilectal for the native text. Thus, those subjects at the acrolect end of the continuum would use either the acrolect or only a very limited number of Creole features in their recalls of the Western story. There would be a down-shifting, with more Creole features in the recall of the native text. For those whose speech fell closer to the basilect, there would be a proportionally higher occurrence of Creole features in both recalls.

Features analysed

Twenty features were chosen to sample a range of levels from the basilect to the acrolect. For example, the past tense particle *bin* occurs up to the acrolect, especially when it is contracted with the third person singular pronoun. Reduplication, which performs a number of functions (Steffensen 1979a), is found in basilectal styles (Steffensen 1979a). Vowel lengthening to intensify occurs only in the basilect.

Verb phrase markers

Past tense marker bin. Past tense is indicated periphrastically with *bin*, probably derived from the English *been*. It will contract with the third person singular pronoun, yielding *imin*.

1. Wi bin megim big ambi.
    we PAST make + TRANS big humpy (hut, shelter)
2. Imin gugum dad bib.
    she + PAST cook + TRANS that meat

Transitivity enclitic -im. This verbal enclitic, derived from English *him*, marks transitive verbs. The phonological variant *-um* occurs after back vowels. The verb *give* is an exception which takes the form *-id*.

3. Ai bin baindim im.
    I PAST find + TRANS him / her / it
4. Wi blandum mijelb.
    we plant + TRANS REFLEX
    Let's hide (ourselves).
5. Dad naib bin gadum mai bingga.
    that knife PAST cut + TRANS my finger

There is an optional rule which deletes the direct object. This results in sentences which are structurally quite different but which bear a superficial similarity to English because of the transitive enclitic:

6. Ai bin gilim garrim don.
    I PAST hit + TRANS with stone
    I hit (it) with a stone.

Continuous aspect enclitic, -bad. There are two means of marking continuous aspect. The form *-bad* is used with transitive verbs:

7. Im gugumbad dad ganggaru.
    he / she cook + TRANS + CONT that kangaroo

Reduplication. In the case of intransitives, continuous aspect is indicated through reduplication of the verb stem:

8.   *wagwag*, 'walking'; *bogibogi*, 'swimming'

Exceptions to this do occur, as in:

9.   Im geding mor fat, dad gel, imin olda taim itimitim.
       she getting more fat, that girl, she + PAST all + the time eat + CONT

Sentence 9 is an example of acrolectal Creole, as indicated by a number of features: *geding*, with the English continuous suffix, the comparative morpheme *more*, and a number of phonological features, including /f/ and /t/. *Geding* is a particularly significant form since the Creole typically does not have a surface reflex for the inchoative: Such sentences are translated by equational sentences:

10.   Mi taid na.
       I tired now
       I'm getting tired.

Reduplication is also used with adjectivals to denote a group of individuated objects. It does not intensify, as in many other European-based creoles (Steffensen 1979a):

19.   Jad lad gilaj, de jainijainiwan.
       that lot glass they shiny shiny + MOD
       Those glasses are shiny.
20.   *lilwanlilwan* (Used to describe a flock of small birds.)
       little + MOD + little + MOD

It can also be used to encode a condition repeated over time:

21.   Im drangdrangg.
       he drunk + drunk
       He's drunk now as he usually is.

Verbal enclitics. A number of English phrasal verbs have been reanalysed as verb plus enclitic. These include:

11.   *-ab* < 'up'
       jandab, 'stand up'; *logab*, 'close'; *jolab*, 'swollen, swell up';
       bilimab, 'fill' + TRANS 'up'
12.   *-aud* < 'out'
       waibimaud, 'destroy' < 'wipe' + TRANS 'out';
       gedaud, 'get out'
13.   *-ob* < 'off'
       gedob, 'get off'
14.   *in* < 'in'
       gwin, 'go in'

Adjective marker. There are two major adjectival markers in the Creole, *-wan* and *-bala*. Strict rules do not appear to exist regarding the distribution of these forms, but some tendencies emerge from the data. The marker *-wan* is probably related historically to what has been called the replacive *one* and is more commonly used, particularly with nonhuman nouns:

15.   *giniwan*, 'narrow' < 'skinny'; *gugwan*, 'ripe' < 'cooked.'

Derived from English 'fellow', *-bala* occurs most frequently on words modifying human nouns:

16.   *naigidbala*, 'naked'; *minbala*, 'stingy'.

The following pair demonstrates this distribution:

17.   Im blagbala.
      He's black / He's an Aborigine.
18.   Im blagwan iya.
      It's black here. (Referring to markings on bird.)

Prepositions. There is a system of prepositions derived from English. The locative *langa*, possibly derived from English 'along' is a generalised marker of location and covers a wide semantic range. It is frequently reduced to *la*:

22.   Mi na laigim go la gul.
      I NEG like + TRANS go LOC school
23.   la dij ga
      LOC this car
      in this car
24.   De baidim yu langa am.
      they bite + TRANS you LOC arm

This form sometimes occurs redundantly with verbal enclitics derived from English prepositions and phrasal verbs:

25.   Dad ga bin ranoba la im.
      that car PAST run + over LOC him

The genitive relationship is encoded by *blanga ~ bla*, 'belong.'

26.   Dad san bla mai sista im lib la Sydney.
      that son GEN my sister he live LOC Sydney
      My sister's son lives in Sydney.

Sentences do not usually begin with *bla*. However, if the possessive phrase modifies a noun phrase other than subject, it is common for the possessive phrase to precede its head noun:

27.   Nobadi sabi bla im nem na.
      nobody know GEN he name now
      Nobody knows his name now.

Pronouns. Pronouns include a singular, dual and plural. As in many Aboriginal languages, there is a distinction in the first person between inclusive and exclusive. Only a limited number of Creole pronouns occurred in the recall protocols. These included the invariant reflexive *mijelb* and the third person plural *alabad*:

28.   De bin megim mijelb don.
        they PAST make + TRANS REFLEX stone
        They turned themselves into stones.
29.   Alabad abi.
        they happy

Phonological Process. Vowel lengthening is a means of intensifying in the basilect:

30.   /imin gi : lim/
        he + PAST hit + INT + TRANS
        He beat him severely.

A limited number of lexical markers were counted, including:

31.   *nomo*, negative
        Nomo idim dad lad beri.
        NEG eat + TRANS that lot berry
        Don't eat those berries.
32.   *na* < 'now,' encoding present relevance.
        Imin go na.
        He has just gone.
33.   *ala* < 'always'
        Imin ala dringg.
        he + PAST always drink
34.   *binji*, 'stomach'
        bla im binji

The dubitative particle gen. This performs a number of pragmatic functions, encoding doubt and embarrassment, and marking false starts (Steffensen 1979b):

35.   Im – gen – dad debildebil.
        he DUB the devil

Tag question particle indid

36.   Imin go, indid?
        he PAST go TAG
        He went, didn't he?

As varieties approach the basilect, a greater number of Creole features are found throughout the phonological, lexical and syntactic systems. For example, implicational relationships exist between vowel lengthening and phonological characteristics such as the absence of sibilants and voiceless

Table 17.1. *Creole features in Aboriginal subjects' recalls of Western and Aboriginal texts*

Speaker	Number of features*		Percentage of features**	
	Western	Aboriginal	Western	Aboriginal
MB, #2	2	7	4	12
MyB, #5	4	11	12	26
LB, #8	1	5	0.8	2
MK, #9	7	5	20	18
RyB, #12	1	9	2	16
RB, #14	11	13	24	38

* Of a possible 20 selected for analysis.
** Based on total number of analysed features and words in protocol.

stops, and a five-vowel system. Similar changes occur in the morphology and syntax. Thus differences in the types and tokens analysed reflect striking differences in lects (see Sharpe 1976; Steffensen 1977; Sandefur 1979 for additional information on this creole.)

Results

Nine of the fifteen Aboriginal women used no Creole indicators in either recall. Table 17.1 presents the number of different Creole indicators (types) in the story protocols for the other six and the percentage of tokens to total words.

Due to the violation of the assumption of normal distribution, two-tailed t-tests for related samples were performed instead of one-tailed tests which could otherwise have been used. Results approached statistical significance for the number of Creole types (t (14) = 2.086, p = 0.0558). For percentages of Creole tokens found in the recall protocols, an arcsin transformation was applied. Results of the t-tests with these transformed data indicated that a significantly greater percentage of Creole tokens appeared in the recalls of the Aboriginal story (t (14) = 2.197, p < 0.05), than in the Western story.

Language variation

Nine of the fifteen subjects spoke NAE when recalling the two texts. They moved to the highest lect they commanded and used none of the scored features. Furthermore, there was essentially no difference between the Western and the Aboriginal protocols, supporting the observation that there is much more variation in a creole continuum than occurs in other codes (Bickerton 1975). This disjunctive shift from the speakers between ACE and NAE suggests that the context was one of diglossia (Ferguson 1964), with NAE identified as distinctive from the other lects along the continuum and filling different pragmatic functions. More formal, it was considered the appropriate code for the task involved – an educational study using the trappings of Western research, conducted by a 'European'. The fact that some of these subjects did not know whether the experimenter spoke ACE might have been an additional factor motivating the use of NAE, although such a consideration did not affect the other subjects.

Six women produced protocols with Creole features. Five sets show the predicted variation, with significantly more Creole features in the Aboriginal recall than the Western passage. This finding can be interpreted as showing an important aspect of cultural affiliation. Subjects were able to recall more of the native text, in spite of the fact that they denigrated native medical beliefs and practices, because they possessed the appropriate background knowledge, as shown by their unconscious but appropriate elaborations of the text. Similarly, they shifted toward the basilect for the native text because they recognised it as appropriate for the system of beliefs represented in the text. Although the setting and participants in the speech event remained the same, the content of the native story represented ingroup knowledge and appeared to override considerations of formality or intelligibility.

It was suggested (Penny Eckert, personal communication) that words in the Aboriginal text might have produced code switching. The word *dreamtime*, for example, might have prompted a change toward the basilect. An examination of the tapes did not show this to be a factor. Subjects appeared to have begun their recall at what they thought was the appropriate level and to have maintained that level throughout the recall.

Bickerton's observation that speed and vividness of expression helps identify the lect more natural for a speaker (1975) may provide some insight to this phenomenon. Because the speakers knew more about the native text and presumably had a stronger emotive response to it, they used a more basilectal form, with which they could more easily encode both propositional content and affect.

The one subject who showed essentially no linguistic variation across her two recalls also had the same recall scores for the two texts. It is tempting to propose that she was equally familiar with the two cultures (as indicated by the amount she recalled) and therefore did not feel that there was a difference in code suitability.

It has been demonstrated that Aboriginal children will draw pictures reflecting either the indigenous setting or the introduced setting depending upon whether instructions are given in an Aboriginal language or English (Cawte and Kiloh 1967). This study shows the reverse side of the coin: a story based on familiar concepts and assumptions causes subjects to shift toward the basilect. There is agreement between code, knowledge and group membership in both cases.

Conclusion

In the analysis of comprehension and recall based on these data (Steffensen and Colker 1982), it was assumed that there would be cultural differences in background knowledge concerning health and the treatment of illness. These differences were tapped through the two texts, which were based on cultural assumptions, beliefs and practices. Results showed that a match between the schemata underlying a text and those possessed by a listener is a significant factor in understanding and remembering.

The focus of the present analysis was the relationship between language, understanding, and pre-existing background knowledge. It was predicted that a basilectal variety would be used in the recall of the Aboriginal text and an acrolectal variety for the Western. This prediction was supported for the speakers who responded in Creole, showing a concordance between what the speaker knew, what she understood from the text, and what variety she used during recall.

It is accepted that the level of formality of language used in a given interchange is a function of aspects of the speech event such as setting, participants, and topic of discussion. In this study, the only aspect of the speech event which varied was the subject matter of the stories, representing a traditional and a modern version of medical beliefs and activities. More Creole features were used for the native story because it described deeply embedded, more completely understood cultural events. It may well be that language itself constitutes part of the dynamic schema for any particular event or object (Washabaugh, personal communication). This would entail that a speaker must repress the use of the 'schematic' code if it is inappropriate for the social context and must access one less fully integrated with the undergirding background knowledge.

In fact, the other subjects in the study did respond to more overt facets of the speech event, using a more formal code. This difference in behaviour may represent one intersection of social and psychological forces: the social individual decides what is appropriate but that decision may be based on individual factors which, at present, are not completely understood. The context provides the framework, but individual experience and assessment of the context may result in variation in the linguistic output.

NOTE

Many thanks to William Washabaugh, whose insightful comments and suggestions greatly improved the quality of this paper.

REFERENCES

Anderson, R. C. and Pichert, J. W. 1978. Recall of previously unrecalled information following a shift in perspective. *Journal of Verbal Learning and Verbal Behavior* 17: 1–12.

Anderson, R. C., Reynolds, R. E., Schallert, D. L. and Goetz, E. T. 1977. Frameworks for comprehending discourse. *American Educational Research Journal* 14: 367–82.

Bartlett, F. C. 1932. *Remembering.* Cambridge: Cambridge University Press.

Bickerton, D. 1973. The nature of a creole continuum. *Language* 49: 640–69.

    1975. *Dynamics of a Creole System.* London: Cambridge University Press.

Cawte, J. 1974. *Medicine is the Law.* Sydney: Rigby Limited.

Cawte, J. E. and Kiloh, L. G. 1967. Language and pictorial representation in Aboriginal children. *Social Science & Medicine* 1: 67–76.

DeCamp, D. 1971. Towards a generative analysis of a post-creole speech continuum. In Hymes, D. (ed.), *Pidginization and Creolization of Languages.* Cambridge: Cambridge University Press, pp. 349–70.

Ferguson, C. A. 1964. Diglossia. In Hymes (ed.), *Language in Culture and Society.* New York: Harper & Row.

Hamilton, A. 1972. Health in the Traditionally-Oriented Community. Paper presented at the Research Seminar, Aboriginal Health Services, Centre for Research into Aboriginal Affairs, Monash University, Melbourne.

Kintsch, W. and Greene, E. 1978. The role of cultural-specific schemata in the comprehension and recall of stories. *Discourse Processes* 1: 1–13.

Kuipers, B. J. 1975. A frame for frames: Representing knowledge for recognition. In Bobrow, D. G. and Collins, A. (eds.), *Representation and Understanding: Studies in Cognitive Science.* New York: Academic Press.

Maddock, K. 1974. *The Australian Aborigines: A Portrait of Their Society.* Harmondsworth: Penguin Books.

Mandler, J., Scribner, S., Cole, M. and DeForest, M. 1980. Cross-cultural invariance in story recall. *Child Development* 51: 19–26.

Minsky, M. 1975. A framework for representing knowledge. In Winston, P. (ed.), *The Psychology of Computer Vision.* New York: McGraw-Hill.

Sandefur, J. E. 1979. *An Australian Creole in the Northern Territory: A Description of the Ngukuur-Bamyili Dialects (Part 1).* Berrimah, NT: Summer Institute of Linguistics.

Sharpe, M. C. 1976. The creole language of the Katherine and Roper River areas, Northern Territory. *Pacific Linguistics* 23: 63–77.

Steffensen, M. S. 1977. *A Description of Bamyili Creole.* Report submitted to the

Department of Education, Darwin, Northern Territory, and the Australian Institute of Aboriginal Studies, Canberra, Australia.

1979a. Reduplication in Bamyili Creole. *Pacific Linguistics, Series A* 57: 119–33.

1979b. An example of lexical expansion in Bamyili Creole. Paper read at the Conference on Theoretical Orientations in Creole Studies, St Thomas.

Steffensen, M. S. and Colker, L. 1982. *Intercultural Misunderstandings about Health Care: Recall of Descriptions of Illness and Treatment* (Tech. Rep. No. 233). Urbana: University of Illinois, Center for the Study of Reading.

Steffensen, M. S., Joag-dev, C. and Anderson, R. C. 1979. A cross-cultural perspective on reading comprehension. *Reading Research Quarterly* 15: 10–29.

South Asia

18

South Asia

THIRU KANDIAH

Variation in society – the background and its impact

Differing perceptions of the language, different emphases

In all of the several countries of South Asia, the English language,
sustained by English-using élites of essentially the same kind, has continued, even after Independence, to play comparable crucial roles. In spite
of this, and in spite of the further relevant fact that these countries share a
great deal in the way of history, culture, interests and so on, and constitute
a natural 'linguistic area' (D'souza 1987; Masica 1976) within what,
moreover, is a natural geographical area, the attention paid within them
to the English language has varied greatly, both in depth of coverage as
well as in the range of issues looked at. India dominates the field in both
respects, with some contributions coming from Sri Lanka and considerably
fewer from Bangladesh and Pakistan.[1]

Evidently, the unique developmental processes within each of these
countries as they pursued their common task of post-colonial reconstruction have defined for them very different perceptions of the language and
of their relationship to it, perceptions that do not lead them all alike to
the kind of preoccupation with it that makes such obvious sense to the
increasing band of scholars studying New Varieties of English (NVEs).

The interests that the countries share are largely confined to the
'utilitarian' or 'instrumental' purposes English serves (Shaw 1981; Moag
1982). This is explained by the largely post-colonial measures taken within
all of them to throw open to the wider non-English using populace spheres
of activity previously dominated by English and its users. English, however, retained high significance in several of the most crucial of these
spheres as, among other things, an indispensable instrument of modernisation. This resulted in the exertion on decision makers of conflicting
linguistic pressures (of nationalism and egalitarianism, on the one hand,

271

and of modernisation and so on, on the other), a matter which language planners and scholars have devoted considerable attention to (Bhatti nd; Haque 1983; Kachru 1983: 89–93; Passé 1943.)

In addition, since the post-Independence social and educational structures could not guarantee, as the ones they replaced had done, that all those who entered the English-using spheres had the required command of the language, interest was widely generated in such practical problems as the 'maintenance of the standard of English' and the teaching of English. The several commissions appointed to go into these matters and the flood of publications dealing with them, both theoretical and practical, show the centrality of this interest.[2]

Some recent developments in Pakistan and their pragmatic focus

Pakistan has recently begun to concern itself with the different issue of its own distinct form of English (Saleemi 1985; Baumgardner 1987; forthcoming).[3] Stemming directly from a pragmatic concern with the teaching of English and the clarification of pedagogical norms, and significantly dependent on foreign initiatives, particularly from the British Council and the Asia Foundation,[4] this work shows a basic exonormative thrust, with the 'mother variety' of the language (British – more specifically, English – standard English) defining the model the local standard aspires to (Saleemi 1985: 18) or becoming, along the lines drawn by Nihalani, Tongue and Hosali (1978), the central point of reference against which Pakistani usage is described (Baumgardner forthcoming.)

These developments apart, Pakistan, like Bangladesh, has shown little interest in the English language beyond the practical considerations mentioned earlier, though the reasons for this have yet to be investigated.

The Indian situation

India's evident willingness to venture beyond such considerations, on the other hand, receives ready explanation in terms of that unique socio-political-linguistic psychology that reveals itself in the special place that, without the slightest damage to its national self-image, the country has accorded to English in its administrative and educational structures (Sridhar 1977; Kachru 1982a, 1983: 89–93). The conglomeration of diverse peoples who inherited the single administrative entity that the British had ruled over as India lacked a uniform set of linguistic and cultural symbols that could be ideologised for the purpose of creating an integrated national identity (Fishman 1968; Das Gupta 1968). English, therefore, the only language with 'an all-India circulation' (Narasimhaiah 1982), offered itself as a 'neutral link language' across the diversity (Kachru 1983: 1, 89–93; 1986: 8–9).

While confirming the place of the language within the emerging national infrastructure, this also caused it to be accepted into the national consciousness in a very organic manner, as something that helped maintain 'appropriate Indian patterns of life, culture and education' (Kachru 1983; see also Narasimhaiah and Srinath 1982). In fact, it enters freely into both public and personal domains and its functions extend far beyond the limits normally associated with an outside language, encompassing the instrumental, the regulative, the interpersonal and the self-expressive (Kachru 1981: 19; Sridhar 1985). Moreover, it has caused significant reallocations of roles and status in the verbal repertoire of its users (Sahgal this volume), not necessarily in a 'replacive' or, even, merely 'duplicative' way, but by equipping speakers with 'multiple codes' in certain domains where it 'overlaps' with local languages (Sridhar 1985; Sridhar and Sridhar 1986). The cost, though, has been the disturbance of the 'stable and balanced form' of Indian multilingualism that prevailed earlier (again, see Sahgal this volume).

While such matters have received considerable attention from scholars, there is one dimension that has remained neglected, notwithstanding its centrality to a proper understanding of English in India. This relates to the role of English as an instrument of power, the major linguistic means by which the dominant English-speaking élite secured their power base and social position across the whole nation, by forging unity among its widely dispersed and differentiated local representatives through an assurance of equal treatment for all of these representatives, based on their common linguistic possession.

The Lankan emphases – ambiguities, and issues of distinctiveness and identity

The Lankan work has paid some attention to this matter of power (Kandiah 1984) as well as to certain issues raised by the language acquiring, as in India, a wide range of local functions (Fernando 1982), in both public domains and personal interaction. Whether the Lankan situation in fact justifies the treatment of these issues in terms of domain shifts and code specialisation (that is, in replacive or complementary terms), as Fernando claims, rather than in terms of Sridhar's multiple codes (Sridhar 1985) remains, however, for further research to resolve.

The Lankan work, unlike the more wide-ranging Indian work, has generally tended to neglect such inquiry, focusing, instead, rather more exclusively on issues of distinctiveness and of identity (Passé 1948, 1955; de Souza 1969; Fernando 1973, 1982; Kandiah 1979/1981, 1981, 1987/90/ forthcoming).

The reasons for this are as follows. The smaller scales of the Lankan reality have permitted the majority group among the English-using middle class élite to define the national identity very exclusively, by ideologising their language, Sinhala, and their religion, Buddhism, for that purpose (Wijewardene 1953; Roberts 1979; Kandiah 1986). The inescapable practical value of English has, no doubt, prompted them to pay considerable attention to the teaching of the language and, even, to talk of making it a national language (Platt, Weber and Ho 1984: 199–200). Fearful of rendering suspect the intensely nationalist public image which their strategy for power obliges them to project to the non-English using masses, and reluctant to provide the non-Sinhala using minority with a 'neutral' linguistic tool that would restore equality to them, however, the leadership have been unable to take the decisive administrative and educational *action* that such positions entail. Rather, they have preferred a kind of surreptitious cultivation of the language that, under cover of their public nationalist front, has exploited existing social forces and mechanisms to maintain it, particularly among the élite.[5]

In the minds of those members of the English-using élite who tread outside the corridors of power, however, this ambiguous policy has generated genuine uncertainties that have challenged them to make sense, in their context, of their existence. It is largely out of this that the self-exploratory work mentioned above has emerged. Some of this work accepts the public nationalist assault on English and its users on its own terms, characterising its most regular users as 'marginal men', trapped 'between two worlds' (Fernando 1973, 1982; Ludowyk 1972). Other work, starting with the distinctive variety of English that has emerged in Sri Lanka, argues that it gives expression to the distinctive 'symbiotic personality' of its users, the personality that holds within itself in a unique relationship both Western and indigenous elements; that this symbiotic personality represents but a variation of the larger symbiotic personality that, through the dynamic interaction of foreign and local forces over the centuries, has replaced the original 'pure' indigenous personality across the *whole* nation; and that, because of this, as well as because English and its local users have a major role to play in the construction of a meaningful contemporary ideology/morality, nationalism is being challenged to redefine itself in more truthful and mature terms that allow it to accept English, divested of its potential for perpetuating inequalities, into itself (Kandiah 1979/81; 1981; 1987/90/forthcoming).

The emergence of a paradigm for the study of SAVEs

From these varied kinds of South Asian (SA) circumstances, there has emerged a not insubstantial body of work which has resulted in a new paradigm for the study of SA varieties of English (SAVEs) such as Indian English (IE), Lankan English (LE) and so on, as well as NVEs in general.[6] Looking at these varieties from the viewpoint of their own users rather than of users of older varieties of English (OVEs) such as British English (Kachru 1982c: 3–6), this paradigm has permitted them to be studied more revealingly than ever before.

It is now recognised, therefore, that these SAVEs, while acquiring 'new identities in new socio-cultural contexts' (Kachru 1985a: 222), and being, thus, 'nativised' (Kachru 1986: 120–22), have emerged as autonomous local varieties, 'self-contained system(s)' with their 'own set(s) of rules' (Verma 1982: 180) that make it impossible to treat their forms as 'mistakes' of 'deficient Englishes' (Kachru 1982a; see also Halverson 1966; Mehrotra 1982; Sridhar 1985; Kandiah 1979/1981; 1981). Sustaining these systems, moreover, are distinct speech communities (or 'fellowships'), whose members remain committed to shared sets of norms (Kachru 1985b; Sridhar 1985; Kandiah 1987/90/forthcoming).

Sociolinguistic variation

This paradigm has been established on the basis of an examination of the close systematic relationship that exists between the formal features of SAVE systems, their ranges of 'functional and communicative styles' and so on, on the one hand, and specific features (such as cultural, personal, regional, ethnic group, level of proficiency) of their local 'contexts of situation', on the other (Fernando 1982; Kachru 1965, 1976, 1981, 1982a, 1982b, 1983; Mehrotra 1982; Sridhar 1985). What is involved here is that canonical preoccupation of the sociolinguistic enterprise, the study of linguistic variation embedded in societal variation.

The work mentioned above has not analysed variation within the rigorous quantitative framework introduced by Labov (1964, 1966), preferring rather to use more informal models ('informality' *not* implying an absence of scholarly care and control), which have, nevertheless, allowed it to open valuable insights into the organic relationships between the forms of SAVEs and the social variables they interact with, insights without which rigorous quantitative studies could well flounder (see below).

Informed by the correct insights, quantitative studies do, of course, have a major contribution to make to the understanding of SAVEs, in confirming general perceptions and positions that the more informal work has helped define, and, above all, in permitting the convincing *demonstration* of the existence of generalised sociolinguistic patterns and of the speech communities that manifest them, as well as the discovery of directions of linguistic change (Labov 1964, 1966).

Agnihotri and Sahgal's work (1985) and the case study contributions to the South Asian section of this volume therefore assume a particular significance as being among the earliest work to study aspects of SAVEs quantitatively.

Khan (this volume), for instance, uses quantitative methods to demonstrate that there exists a consistent pattern of variation in IE usage with regard to the 'simplification' of consonant clusters, a pattern which correlates with sociological factors such as sex and age (women and younger people show greater deletion) and with styles of use (spoken styles show more deletion than reading styles). Agnihotri and Sahgal (1985) quantitatively demonstrate that there is a consistent pattern of variation in IE usage correlating with schooling, age and sex, that indicates the evolution of a set of norms by which the retroflexion of alveolar stops and the pronunciation of post-vocalic -r are becoming increasingly stigmatised.

These two studies show an interesting discrepancy with regard to the correlation of variation with sex. In Khan's study, the females show more of the non-prestigious usage than the males, while in Agnihotri and Sahgal's study, we see the opposite pattern. Khan's results, as she points out, only reflect the unequal position assigned to women in the Muslim culture from which her informants come. Agnihotri and Sahgal's pattern reveals a rather more complicated set of operative inequalities. Their female informants tended to come from the more privileged class, which in any event would, on account of its higher socioeconomic status and greater educational opportunities when compared with the less equal classes, be expected not just to reflect, but even to define, prestigious usage. The greater propensity that females showed for prestigious forms than males *within* this privileged class Agnihotri and Sahgal explain partly in terms of insecurities generated by male domination *within* the group, making it necessary for women to signal their status linguistically, and partly in terms of these women's notions of what is fashionable, and their greater susceptibility to Western influences (for discussion of the relationship between sex differences in language use and prestige, see Introduction, this volume; Milroy, this volume; cf. also Escure, this volume).

A further significant discrepancy in the two papers under discussion relates to their predictions of the direction of change in IE. The higher percentage of consonant cluster simplification shown by Khan's younger informants leads her to predict that IE is changing towards the use of the less prestigious variant, with the phonological system becoming more simplified when compared with the standard British English system. Agnihotri and Sahgal, on the other hand, predict, again partly on the basis of the behaviour of their younger informants, that IE is changing in the direction of the more prestigious variant, under what Sahgal (this volume) calls 'sociopsychological pressures towards standardisation' that 'favour the evolution of a single norm'.

The explanation for this discrepancy (which we shall return to later) lies largely in the different class membership and unequal educational backgrounds and opportunities of the two sets of participants involved in the studies, matters which are responsible for the attainment of different proficiency levels by them. On Kachru's 'cline of bilingualism', Khan's informants would belong closer to the monolingual end, Agnihotri and Sahgal's closer to the ambilingual. Sridhar (this volume) shows how facility in spoken English and sociocultural background are related to linguistic variation. Her paper represents a comparatively recent extension into the specific interactional, discourse-related dimension of variation, investigating speech acts (such as apologising and condoling) and thereby increasing our understanding of a neglected aspect of the communicative competence of speakers of varieties of Indian English.

Code switching and code mixing

A set of interactional matters that have begun to receive attention is code switching and code mixing. Kachru's discussion of these discourse strategies shows how IE users assign 'areas of function to each code' (1983: 193) and then exploit this in a 'rule-governed way' (1982b: 26) for specific communicative purposes such as, in the case of code mixing, style identification, elucidation, interpretation and neutralisation (1983: 197–8).

However, Sridhar and Sridhar's point (1986: 6) about the overlapping functions of the codes involved, together with Fernando's observation (1982: 200) that younger Lankan bilinguals code switch even when no code/interlocutor relationship of the kind that normally triggers the process can be demonstrated to exist, raises a further possibility. This is that at times these discourse strategies call for explanation not just in the usual gross functional terms, but in terms of the way in which they define an appropriate symbiotic code (what Saleemi 1985: 19 calls a 'bilect') for the expression of the particular variation of the symbiotic personality its users possess.

Attitudes

Clearly, much work remains to be done on sociolinguistic variation, in India as much as in the other SA countries, which have neglected the task almost completely. Nevertheless, even the little work that has been done has helped develop more comprehending local and international attitudes towards SAVEs by enhancing understanding of them.

Local attitudes towards usage

Attitudes among SA speakers to their own forms of English have always been 'self-annulling' (Sridhar 1985: 41; see also Kachru 1976; Kandiah 1981); and, with regard to the touchy question of norms that these attitudes involve, the scholars' views have invariably been in advance of those of the people whose usage they were studying. Partly, perhaps, as a result of the work of the scholars in calling the attention of these speakers to the norms that they actually follow, however, speakers of Indian English, at least, are now gradually coming to accept their usage as 'more respectable', as Sahgal (this volume) shows.

Attitudes towards classroom norms

A more complicated issue relates to Kachru's proposal that educated IE would define an appropriate endonormative model for learning and teaching the language in the local speech community (1976: 1982d). de Souza (1969) and Kandiah (1965, 1979/81) raise similar possibilities for Sri Lanka, while drawing attention to various educational and other issues that need to be considered in making decisions on the matter.

A major issue that the proposal raises is, of course, that of the intelligibility of these varieties to users of other varieties of English (see Prator 1968; Quirk 1981). Kachru's answer to this is that intelligibility is 'not an absolute criterion but participant and context dependent' (1986: 120); in local interaction among members of a SAVE community (which is what they most need that SAVE for), it is no problem.

While recognising that the problem is somewhat more complicated in the case of international interaction, where some form of 'linguistic engineering' (Quirk 1985) might be in order, Kachru even here expresses positive attitudes towards local usage, arguing that speakers of older varieties of English will have to learn to 'deEnglishise' or 'deAmericanise' themselves in order to participate in communication with speakers of new varieties of English (1983: 238).

What Kachru objects to here is the common assumption that the process of 'linguistic engineering' mentioned above involves an implicit reimposition in international communication of the older, standard British English or American English norms on interlocutors who speak a new variety of English (Nelson 1982). Baumgardner and Tongue (1987), for instance, define the international Standard Written English that they want taught to Lankans in remedial classes entirely in terms of traditional, native speaker, norms. This, however, is at variance with emerging South Asian attitudes, as expressed by Kachru (see above).

One elaboration of these attitudes, expressed by Kandiah (1987/90/ forthcoming) is that the people who, owing to their position, education and so on, occupy the centre of SA speech communities, define the norms of their SAVE linguistic systems through, among other things, the various acts of identity they carry out (Le Page and Tabouret-Keller 1985) and the related accommodation responses they make (Giles and Powesland 1975). In international communication (and it is these people who, more than most others in their communities, are likely to participate in such communication) their accommodation to users of other varieties does not necessarily involve an effort to make their speech converge towards that of their interlocutors, as Giles and Powesland (1975: 159) assume. Rather, it expresses itself in strategies such as slower and more deliberate delivery (Smith and Nelson 1985), strategies which acknowledge the right of the receivers to make sense of the communication while preserving the right of the speakers to say what they want to in essentially the way in which they want to say it.

To seek to alter their international medium beyond the limits to which they are willing to go, and in the direction of standard British or American usage, is to seek, too, to change their meanings and their message in the direction of what speakers of the older varieties say (or want them to say) – an impossible position to accept, given that, if English is important to speakers of SAVEs as an international medium, it is partly because it gives them a living means of expressing their *own* distinctive views and interests compellingly enough to win for themselves, and to maintain, in the international arena, the dignity and equality that, owing to the colonial interlude, they are still striving to achieve.[7]

The need for new models

These, as well as other statements expressing positions subversive of NVEs, are discussed in Kandiah (1979/81; 1981; 1987/90/forthcoming.) These papers define a further, more recent aspect of SA work on English, questioning the very model currently used for the study of SAVEs and making a plea for a radically new paradigm of thought. It is argued that, for all the achievements of the current paradigm, too much of its conceptual apparatus and methodology, borrowed, of necessity, from preceding work or from work in other areas of study, in other situations, is inadequate to the demands of the very special circumstances that surround SAVEs, leading it inevitably to positions, like those cited above, that undermine these varieties and obstruct the proper understanding of variation in them.

Briefly, it is argued that while the norms governing SAVE linguistic usage and behaviour were certainly based originally on those of the mother language, they have subsequently been influenced by their interaction with the local languages, as well as by the new contexts in which English has been used. These contexts include such elements as the functions that the language had for its users, the different acts of identity that they accomplished through it (see LePage and Tabouret-Keller 1985) and the nature of the social and linguistic convergence that they carried out (or, for good reason, in some cases, did *not* carry out) relative to their various interlocutors as part of the process of speech accommodation (Giles and Powesland 1975).

The resulting usage and behaviour naturally reflected the heterogeneity of the various factors involved. At the same time, there did seem to operate some abstract social mechanism or process that promoted integration on the basis of central or core values, implicitly uniting the members of the community by a commitment to a shared set of abstract norms of behaviour and usage (Labov 1964). These linguistic developments were, clearly, heavily influenced by the practice and precepts of the urban middle class élite (see also Agnihotri and Sahgal 1985), many of whom had learned the language in use and interaction, much like any first language, and used it habitually as one of their main languages for several important social and personal functions.

Among other things, this makes these speakers native users of their varieties of English, whose usage shows that 'unity and hierarchical superiority' (relative to the usage of other people) (Strevens 1982: 24) which provide the source of its validity in defining the norms of these varieties. Kachru (1985b) seems to acknowledge this, calling for a re-examination of the use of the native/non-native distinction in the literature. The problem, is, however, that neither the early nor the later work on English in South Asia projects this kind of picture of SAVE speech communities, where competent usage is clearly distinguished from incompetent or learner usage on the basis of an implicit set of shared norms. Not all proficiency-related usage constitutes usage that validly defines the system that the community uses. It is clearly important not to assume that any and every form that issues in the name of English from the mouths and pens of inhabitants of NVE-using countries, however incompetent they may be in the language, is a valid datum for the characterisation of these varieties. Kachru's cline of bilingualism, for example, incorporates this assumption and would accommodate every one of these forms, while Mehrotra (1982) insists that this is how it should be. This is understandable enough given the special proficiency-related issues that complicate English usage in these countries, and given the systematicity of a great deal of learner usage (see Corder 1981; Selinker 1972). However, as I argue in detail in Kandiah (1987/90/forthcoming), this is incorrect.

Defects such as this in the current paradigm are associated with a further, serious shortcoming in the study of SAVEs, namely, the quite inadequate understanding it often appears to show of the real nature of the linguistic *systems* that scholars routinely claim these SAVEs to possess. Instead of providing rigorous, systematic grammatical descriptions that seek to account for the *competence* of SAVE users, by formalising the productive rules they intuitively control, SAVE scholars have tended to support their claims about the systematicity of their varieties largely through lists and other taxonomic classifications of items. Worse, they have often presented these items less in terms of the *systems* they help define than in terms of their differences from (the original) older varieties of English (Passé 1948; Kandiah 1965; Kachru 1982a; Verma 1982). But this can only encourage their characterisation as 'interlanguages' (a notion that, even with its later enrichments – see Corder 1981; Pride 1979 – continues to remind us of the attempted rather than the successful learning of the target language) and allow them to be treated in such irrelevant terms as 'simplification', 'interference' and so on. Even more disturbingly, it permits them to be put down as 'semi-varieties' which are 'not amenable to the kind of idealised analysis that optimally stable and consistent languages are normally subjected to' (Saleemi 1985: 19).

As a corrective to some of this, I have, in Kandiah (1987/90/forthcoming) proposed a notion 'fulguration',[8] which attempts to wrest fundamental recognition for the all-important fact that out of the original interaction between the target and local languages, and beyond it, there have emerged self-contained new systems that incorporate, in addition to what was derived from the original interacting languages, new elements, combinations, meanings and so on, associated with new strategies and features that *have no direct pre-histories in any of the original systems*. Within the new system, all of these elements, old and new, cohere organically together in terms of their own internal logic, making reference to targets and sources synchronically irrelevant.[9]

There are signs, then, that work on SAVEs is moving in the direction of new models that will facilitate a more satisfying understanding of its objects of study. Kachru's own positions have been changing radically on such matters as the relative status of so-called 'first' and 'second' languages (compare, for example, chapter 3 of Kachru 1983 with the previous version in Kachru 1965), the 'native/non-native' distinction (Kachru 1985b) and 'deviance' (Kachru 1987). Similarly, Sridhar (1985: 55) demonstrates that NVEs are 'qualitatively different from the categories recognised in current sociolinguistic typology', while Sridhar and Sridhar (1986) and Mohanan and Mohanan (MS) point to the inadequacy of current theories of second language acquisition in accounting for the acquisition and nature of SAVEs. Many of the other works on SAVEs that have been mentioned in this paper also call for a redefinition or even a rejection of much of the current conceptual framework in the study of these varieties.[10]

Research on SAVEs has been pioneering in fostering an interest within the academic community in NVEs, due largely, as mentioned before, to the work of Braj Kachru. It continues to be pioneering today, in its efforts to encourage the development of new paradigms which, by facilitating a proper understanding of linguistic variation, among other things, will bring the study closer to the achievement of the sociolinguistic goal of promoting 'human self-understanding and thoughts about possible futures for the inhabitants of the planet' (Ferguson 1982: ix).

NOTES

1. No mention will be made below of Nepal, Bhutan and the Maldives, about which there is a great paucity of information.
2. Some of this work was highly original – indigenous, while remaining open to the best ideas on the international circuit. Consider N. S. Prabhu's 'procedural syllabus' in India, or the work done at the CIEFL or at the University of Bombay. In Sri Lanka, there was the *original* ESP notion, formulated in the late 'fifties by Doric de Souza, which combined with several other new ideas of his to issue in a bilingual methodology that was subsequently developed by others to exploit universals of language too (de Souza 1960, 1962, 1969; de Abrew and Kandiah MS; Kandiah 1971, 1971/72, 1978), in addition to Walatara's 'reconstruction method' (1974).
3. I am indebted to Robert Baumgardner for the information in this paragraph.
4. The strong academic influence of these institutions is, again, guaranteed by the objective, non-academic considerations relating to the international alignments Pakistan has formed to secure its position in the region.
5. The impossible national crisis created by their chauvinist policies has compelled the leadership, through the Indo-Lankan peace accord of July 1987, to contemplate giving some official recognition to English. Already, however, not four months after the accord (at the time of writing), there are second thoughts on the matter, and there is talk of making English simply a 'link' language rather than an 'official' language, as originally proposed.
6. The prolific writings of Braj Kachru have played a pivotal role in this task.
7. It is surprising that Kachru (1983) is able to accept Quirk's 'nuclear English' solution to the intelligibility problem (1981), a solution that runs counter both to his own views discussed above as well as the position just outlined in the main text, by both withdrawing from NVE users the freedom to use the standard versions of their own varieties and, also, foisting on them an attenuated form of a standard OVE that would put them at a permanent disadvantage in the international arena vis-à-vis the native users of its full form (see Kandiah 1987/90/forthcoming).
8. Borrowed from T. L. Markey, who used it in a talk on 'The Typology of Minority/Majority Languages' at the National University of Singapore (21/6/86).
9. A major significance of Mohanan & Mohanan's paper (MS) is that it is, perhaps, the first attempt to fill this gap and give a truly synchronic account of a SAVE system (the Phonology of Malayalee English (ME). In doing so, it provides strong support for the 'fulguration' notion, demonstrating formally and explicitly how the ME system resolves conflicts between the original interacting systems through the creation of specific new phonological structures by means of specific new strategies present in neither system.

A major problem with the paper, however, is that it focuses on what appears to be a none-too-competent usage, ignoring the more standard ME usage of its first author (its second author's usage betrays interference from a standard OVE).

10. One important development that the above discussion, particularly of the two empirical studies looked at, points to is the emergence of a fuller understanding of what constitutes data in the study of SAVEs. In addition to observed linguistic forms, the nature of their correlation with sociological variables and the empirically elicited patterns of variation they display, it appears that other matters too must be taken central notice of. Among these are the operative social forces, strategies of power, local and international self-perceptions and aspirations, ideologies and so on that play so important a role in defining the reality of SAVE communities. Far from providing the artillery for an insouciant and abstract polemics, these define matters that enter as much as the other matters mentioned into the characterisation of the data out of which a proper understanding of these varieties may be obtained.

REFERENCES

Agnihotri, R. K. and Sahgal, Anju. 1985. Is Indian English retroflexed and r-full? *IJOAL, XI* (Jan. 1985): 97–108.

Bailey, Richard W. and Görlach, Manfred (eds.), 1982. *English as a World Language*. Ann Arbor MI: University of Michigan Press.

Baumgardner, Robert J. 1987. Utilizing Pakistani newspaper English to teach grammar. *World Englishes* 6: 3.

Forthcoming. *Pakistani English: A Handbook for Teachers and Learners*. Karachi: Oxford University Press.

Baumgardner, Robert J. and Tongue, Ray. 1987. The problems and the potential of exploiting the English Language Press as an aid to language teaching in South Asia. In Chamberlain and Baumgardner (eds.) 1987.

Bhatti, Muhammad Ismail. n.d. Our multilingual heritage and English. *Journal of Research (Humanities)*. Punjab University.

Chamberlain, Dick and Baumgardner, R. J. (eds.). 1987. *ESP in the Classroom: Practice and Evaluation*. London: Macmillan.

Colin-Thomé, Percy and Halpé, Ashley (eds.). 1984. *Honouring EFC Ludowyk: Felicitation Essays*. Dehiwela: Tisara Prakasakayo Ltd.

Corder, S. Pit. 1981. *Error Analysis and Interlanguage*. Oxford: Oxford University Press.

Das Gupta, Jyotirindra. 1968. Language diversity and national development. In Fishman, *et al.* (eds.). 1968, pp. 17–26.

D'souza, Jean. 1987. South Asia as a Sociolinguistic Area. Unpublished PhD thesis, University of Illinois.

de Abrew, Kamal and Kandiah, Thiru. Themes in the teaching of English as a second language. MS, University of Peradeniya.

de Souza, Doric. 1960. The changing place of English in the educational system of Ceylon. In Sledd (ed.) 1960.

1962. English as a second language: some problems. *Changing Times* 2. 3.

1969. The teaching of English. *The Ceylon Observer*, 18–28 April.

Fernando, Chitra. 1973. Between two worlds: an examination of attitudes and language in Ceylonese creative writing. *New Ceylon Writing*: 31–46.

1982. English in Sri Lanka: a case study of a bilingual community. In Pride (ed.) 1982b, pp. 188–210.

Ferguson, Charles A. 1982. Foreword. In Kachru (ed.) 1982c, pp. vii–xi.

Fishman, Joshua A. 1964. *Readings in the Sociology of Language*. The Hague: Mouton.

1968. Sociolinguistics and the language problem in developing countries. In Fishman *et al*. (eds.) 1968, pp. 3–16.

Fishman, Joshua A., Ferguson, Charles A. and Das Gupta, Jyotirindra (eds.), 1968. *Language Problems of Developing Nations*. NY: Wiley.

Greenbaum, Sidney. 1985. *The English Language Today*. Oxford: Pergamon Press.

Giles, Howard and Powesland, Peter F. 1975. *Speech Styles and Social Evaluation*. London: Academic Press.

Halverson, J. 1966. Prolegomena to the study of Ceylon English. *University of Ceylon Review* 24 (1 and 2) : 61–75.

Haque, Anjum R. 1983. The position and status of English in Pakistan. *World Language English* 2 (1 and 2) : 6–9.

Hartford, B., Valdman, A. and Foster, C. R. (eds.). 1982. *Issues in International Bilingual Education: The Role of the Vernacular*. NY: Plenum.

John, V. V. 1969. *Education and Language Policy*. Bombay: Nachiketa Publications.

Kachru, Braj B. 1965. The *Indianness* in Indian English. *Word* 21: 391–410.

1976. Models of English for the Third World: White Man's linguistic burden or language pragmatics? *TESOL Quarterly* 10 (2): 221–39.

1981. The pragmatics of non-native varieties of English. In Smith (ed.) 1981. pp. 15–39.

1982a. South Asian English. In Bailey and Görlach (eds.), 1982, pp. 353–83.

1982b. The bilingual's linguistic repertoire. In Hartford *et al*. (eds.) 1982, pp. 25–52.

1982c. (ed.). *The Other Tongue: English Across Cultures*. Urbana: University of Illinois Press./1983. Oxford: Pergamon.

1982d. Models for non-native Englishes. In Kachru (ed.) 1982c, pp. 31–57.

1983. *The Indianization of English: the English Language in India*. Delhi: Oxford University Press.

1985a. Institutionalized second language varieties. In Greenbaum (ed.) 1985, pp. 211–26.

1985b. Standards, codification and sociolinguistic realism: the English language in the outer circle. In Quirk and Widdowson (eds.) 1985, pp. 11–30.

1986. *The Alchemy of English: The Spread, Functions and Models of Non-Native Englishes*. Oxford: Pergamon Press.

1987. ESP and non-native varieties of English: toward a shift in paradigm. In Chamberlain and Baumgardner (eds.) 1987.

Kandiah, Thiru. 1965. The teaching of English in Ceylon: some problems in constrastive statement. *Language Learning* 15 (3 and 4): 147–66.

1971. The transformational challenge and the teacher of English. *Language Learning* 15: 151–82.

1971/72. The teaching of English in Ceylon: some linguistic issues: a model-oriented discussion. *Journal of the National Education Society of Ceylon* 20: 52–92 and 21: 49–77.

1978. The notion of 'interference' and the universalist hypothesis: theory feeds into practice. In *Papers Presented at the Post-Plenary Session on Problems of Multi-Lingualism: Language Use in Education, Administration and Communication, Tenth International Congress of Anthropological and Ethnological Sciences, Mysore, 19–21, December, 1978*. Mysore: CIIL.

1979/1981. Disinherited Englishes: the case of Lankan English. *Navasilu* 3: 75–89 and 4: 92–113.

1981. Lankan English schizoglossia. *English World-Wide* 2 (1): 63–81.

1984. 'Kaduva': Power and the English language weapon in Sri Lanka. In Colin-Thomé and Halpé (eds.) 1984, pp. 117–54.

1986. Comment on David L. Marshall's *The Question of an Official Language: Language Rights and the English Language Amendment. IJSL* 60: 183–9.

1987/90/forthcoming. New varieties of English: the creation of the paradigm and its radicalisation. Sections I–III *Navasilu* 9: 31–42 and Sections V–VII *Navasilu* 10: 126–39. Concluding sections to appear in forthcoming issue of *Navasilu*.

Labov, William. 1964. The reflection of social processes in linguistic structures. In Fishman (ed.) 1964, pp. 240–51.

1966. *The Social Stratification of English in New York City*. Washington DC: Center for Applied Linguistics.

Le Page, R. B. and Tabouret-Keller, Andrée. 1985. *Acts of Identity*. Cambridge: Cambridge University Press.

Ludowyk, E. F. C. 1972. Writing in English in Ceylon. *Adam International Review* 367–9: 22–28.

Masica, C. P. 1976. *Defining a Linguistic Area: South Asia*. Chicago: University of Chicago Press.

Mehrotra, Raja Ram. 1982. Indian English: a sociolinguistic profile. In Pride (ed.) 1982b, pp. 150–73.

To appear. The language of Indian writing in English: some sociolinguistic evidence. *English World-Wide*.

Moag, Rodney. 1982. English as a foreign, second, native and basal language: a new taxonomy of English-using societies. In Pride (ed.) 1982b, pp. 11–50.

Mohanan, Tara and Mohanan, K. P. The lexical phonology of Malayalee English: towards a theory of morphogenesis in transplanted systems. MS.

Narasimhaiah, C. D. 1982. Introductory talk. In Narasimhaiah and Srinath (eds.) 1982, pp. 10–15.

Narasimhaiah, C. D. and Srinath, C. N. (eds.). 1982. *English: Its Complementary Role in India*. Mysore: Dhvanyaloka.

Nelson, C. 1982. Intelligibility and non-native varieties of English. In Kachru (ed.) 1982c, pp. 58–73.

Nihalani, Paroo, Tongue, R. K. and Hosali, P. 1978. *Indian and British English: A Handbook of Usage and Pronunciation*. Delhi: Oxford University Press.

Passé, H. A. 1943. The English language in Ceylon. *University of Ceylon Review* 1: 50–65. Reprinted in Passé 1948, ch. 1.

1948. The English Language in Ceylon. Unpublished PhD thesis, University of London.

1955. *The Use and Abuse of English*. Madras: Oxford University Press.

Platt, John, Weber, Heidi, and Ho, Mian Lian. 1984. *The New Englishes*. London: Routlege & Kegan Paul.

Prator, Clifford H. 1968. The British heresy in TESOL. In Fishman *et al.* (eds.) 1986, pp. 459–76.

Pride, John. 1979. Communicative needs in the use and learning of English. In Richards (ed.), 1979, pp. 33–72.

1982a. The appeal of the new Englishes. In Pride (ed.) 1982b, pp. 1–7.

1982b (ed.). *New Englishes*. Rowley MA: Newbury.

Quirk, Randolph. 1972. *The English Language and Images of Matter*. London: Oxford University Press.

1981. International communication and the concept of Nuclear English. In Smith (ed.) 1981, pp. 151–65.

1985. Natural language and Orwellian intervention. In Greenbaum (ed.) 1985, pp. 48–54.

Quirk, Randolph, Greenbaum, Sidney, Leech, Geoffrey and Svartvik, Jan. 1972. *A Grammar of Contemporary English*. London: Longman.

Quirk, Randolph and Widdowson, Henry (eds.). 1985. *English in the World: Teaching and Learning the Language and Literatures*. Cambridge: Cambridge University Press.

Richards, Jack C. (ed.) 1979. *New Varieties of English: Issues and Approaches*. Singapore: SEAMEO Regional Language Centre.

Roberts, Michael (ed.) 1979. *Collective Identities Nationalism and Protest in Modern Sri Lanka*. Colombo: Marga Institute.

Saleemi, Anjum P. 1985. English in non-native use: a second language view. *English Teaching Forum* 23(2): 16–20.

Schiffrin, Deborah (ed.) 1984. *Gurt '84. Meaning, Form and Use in Context: Linguistic Applications*. Washington DC: Georgetown University Press.

Selinker, L. 1972. Interlanguage. *IRAL* 10(3): 209–31.

Shaw, Willard D. 1981. Asian student attitudes towards English. In Smith (ed.) 1981, pp. 108–22.

Sledd, James (ed.) 1960. A Report of a Conference of Teachers of English held at the University of Ceylon, Peradeniya, Jan. 3–8, 1960.

1985. Layman or shaman; or, now about that elephant again. In Greenbaum (ed.) 1985, pp. 327–42.

Smith, Larry E. (ed.) 1981. *English for Cross-Cultural Communication*. Hong Kong: Macmillan.

Smith, Larry E. and Nelson, Cecil L. 1985. International intelligibility of English: directions and resources. *World Englishes* 4(3): 333–42.

Sridhar, Kamal K. 1977. *The Development of English as an Elite Language in the Multilingual Context of India: Its Educational Implications*. Ann Arbor MI: Xerox University Microfilms.

1982. English in a South Indian Urban Context. In Kachru (ed.) 1982d, pp. 141–53.

1985. Sociolinguistic theory and non-native varieties of English. *Lingua* 68: 39–58.

Sridhar, Kamal K. and Sridhar, S. N. 1986. Bridging the paradigm gap: second language acquisition theory and indigenized varieties of English. *World Englishes* 1(1): 1–13.

Strevens, Peter. 1982. The localised forms of English. In Kachru (ed.) 1982d, pp. 23–30.

Verma, Shivendra Kishore. 1982. Swadeshi English: form and function. In Pride (ed.) 1982b, pp. 174–87.

Walatara, Douglas, 1974. *Reconstruction: An English Technique for an Asian Context*. Kadawata: Virani Printers.

Wijewardane, D. C. 1953. *The Revolt in the Temple*. Colombo: Sinha.

19

Final consonant cluster simplification in a variety of Indian English

FARHAT KHAN

Previous sociolinguistic studies have indicated that consonant cluster simplification or, more specifically, deletion of the final stop (especially /t,d/) in a final consonant cluster, occurs to a greater or lesser extent in the speech of all native speakers of English. This paper presents an analysis of final cluster simplification in a non-native variety of English: Indian English. Simplification of final clusters is an important feature of Indian English, but it has been ignored by many Indian scholars working on this variety. Bansal (1972) noted final cluster simplification by Tamil, Telegu and Hindi speakers, but apart from this very brief analysis there are no quantitative analyses of this phenomenon.

For the present paper the data consist of tape-recorded face-to-face interviews with 40 adult bilingual speakers, aged from 16 to 42 years. The fieldwork was carried out in Aligarh in the state of Uttar Pradesh, in the northern part of India. Consonant cluster simplification was first analysed in different environments, according to the nature of the preceding and following segments, and was then correlated with the social variables of sex and age, and with style. Two types of clusters were examined: monomorphemic and bimorphemic. A preliminary analysis of the data led to the clusters being classified as follows:

$$
\text{preceding} \begin{cases} \text{spirant consonant} \\ \text{sonorant consonant} \\ \text{stop} \end{cases}
$$

$$
\text{following} \begin{cases} \text{consonant } /\text{-\#\#K/} \\ \text{pause } /\text{-\#\#P/} \\ \text{vowel } /\text{-\#\#V/} \end{cases}
$$

Linguistic constraints on final cluster simplification

Conditioning by following segment

Labov *et al.* (1968), Wolfram (1969, 1971), Fasold (1972) and Guy (1980) show considerable agreement as to the major conditioning effects on final stop deletion. They found that final /t,d,/ are deleted more often when they are part of a consonant cluster, and that an important constraint on cluster simplifcation was the nature of the following segment. In particular, these studies found that final /t,d/ were deleted more frequently when followed by a consonant than when followed by a non-consonant. Analysis of the present data similarly indicated that the major constraint affecting cluster simplification had to do with the nature of the environment following the simplified clusters, as shown in table 19.1

Table 1 shows the percentage frequency of final stop deletion in each of the three environments: thus, for example, 69.2 per cent of all clusters that occurred with a following consonant were simplified, and 30.1 per cent of all clusters that occurred with a following vowel were simplified. It can be seen that the highest percentage of deleted final stops is found when the next word begins with a consonant, and the lowest frequency when the next word begins with a vowel. This agrees with the findings of Labov *et al.* (1968), Wolfram (1969, 1971) and Fasold (1972), that a following consonant favours deletion of final /t,d/, whereas a following non-consonantal environment acts as a constraint inhibiting cluster simplification. Figure 19.1 is a graphic representation of the information contained in Table 19. 1.

The data were further subjected to an analysis of variance; this indicated that the difference in final /t,d/ deletion between consonantal and non-consonantal environments was highly significant ($p < 0.1$). However, the difference in final /t,d/ deletion between environment 2 (a following pause) and environment 3 (a following vowel) was not significant. The following conclusions can therefore be drawn:

1) The variability of final cluster simplification is not random. It is systematic, conditioned by linguistic factors.
2) A following consonantal segment favours deletion of final /t,d/.
3) Both vowels and pauses act as a constraint inhibiting final /t,d/ deletion.
4) As table 19.1 and figure 19.1 show, deletion of final /t,d/ occurs less frequently in bimorphemic clusters than in monomorphemic clusters.

Voicing agreement

In previous American studies on final cluster simplification, it was found that voicing agreement is an important restriction. Wolfram (1969), for

Table 19.1. *Effect of following segment on final stop deletion in monomorphemic and bimorphemic clusters*

	Environment 1 /-##K	Environment 2 /-##P	Environment 3 /-##V
Monomorphemic clusters: percentage frequency of deleted final stops	69.2	44.4	30.1
Bimorphemic clusters: percentage frequency of deleted final stops	51.7	27.8	15.6

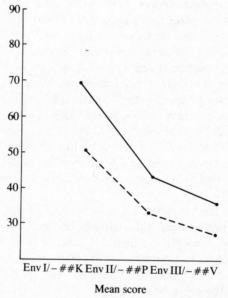

Env I/ – ##K Env II/ – ##P Env III/ – ##V

Mean score

Figure 19.1 Simplification of monomorphemic and bimorphemic clusters in 3 environments. Monomorphemic clusters (——); bimorphemic clusters (----).

example, claimed that final clusters can be reduced only when both consonants are voiced or when both consonants are voiceless, so that mixed voiced clusters in words like *belt, help* or *dent* never had reduced clusters. To investigate the phenomenon of mixed voice clusters, 25 occurrences of such clusters were analysed from each informant's speech. Table 19.2 shows the percentage frequency of final stop deletion in these clusters, with three different following segments.

The results in table 19.2 show that mixed voice clusters are frequently

Table 19.2. *Mixed voiced cluster simplification*

Clusters	Examples	Environment 1 /-##K/	Environment 2 /-##P/	Environment 3 /-##V/
-nt	rent, scent	67.5%	22.2%	10.2%
-lt	belt, melt	64.2%	20.0%	16.0%
-lk	silk, milk	55.4%	24.5%	20.4%

simplified in this variety of Indian English. Now the questions arise: is there any reason for this feature being common among these speakers of Indian English; and does it occur in other non-native varieties of English as well? The answer to the first question is that it is quite possible that the simplification of -*nt*, -*lt* and -*lk* are due to the process of convergence; that is, the converging influence of Indian languages and dialects on Indian English. Many Indian languages do not have final clusters, and most Indian speakers seem to find final consonant clusters difficult, often tending to break them either by inserting /ɪ/ or /ə/ in the middle of the cluster or by deleting the final stop completely. Due to the long contact which English has had with other Indian languages which do not have final clusters, Indian English may well have acquired some features of the local dialects which make it different from other varieties of English. The second question was, does mixed voice final consonant cluster simplification occur in other second language varieties of English? Unfortunately, it is difficult to answer this question at present, until further empirical research is carried out on other non-native varieties of English.

Conditioning by preceding segment

In the present study, the highest frequency of simplified final clusters occurred when the preceding segment was a spirant or a sonorant. The lowest frequency was found after a stop. Table 19.3 shows the percentage frequency of simplified spirant + stop, sonorant + stop and stop + stop clusters in the data. Two observations can be made from table 19.3: first, a preceding stop tends to act as a constraint on final stop deletion, whereas a preceding spirant or sonorant tends to favour deletion; secondly, bimorphemic (BM) clusters were more resistant to cluster simplification than monomorphemic (MM) clusters, as before. This is probably due to the grammatical function of the final stop in bimorphemic clusters. The presence or absence of a morpheme boundary within a cluster has been found to act as a grammatical constraint on final cluster simplification in previous studies (see, for example, Guy 1980).

So far I have been concerned with the linguistic factors affecting final

Table 19.3. *Effect of preceding consonant on final cluster simplification*

	Examples		% of final stop deletion
Preceding spirant	*fast, cost, just, mist*	MM	78.0
	missed, loved, amazed	BM	64.5
Preceding sonorant	*attend, blend, cold, gold, sold, bold*	MM	70.2
	called, rolled, opened, rained, happened	BM	54.3
Preceding stop	*act, fact, apt, sect*	MM	47.5
	robbed, stopped, talked	BM	30.0

consonant cluster simplification. In the next section I will examine the effect of social factors.

Variation by sex and age

Labov (1966) and Trudgill (1974) found that women used linguistic forms associated with the prestige standard more frequently than men, and suggested that social insecurity and societal expectations could partly account for this. Analyses of consonant cluster simplification in the USA found that women simplified clusters ending in /t,d/ less frequently than men (see, for example, Wolfram 1969; Neu 1980); that is, women used a higher proportion of what are assumed to be the prestige, unsimplified forms. The main question which will concern us here is: does the same pattern of sex variation occur in other, multilingual, communities where men and women may play different roles? In order to answer this question, one has to look at social and cultural factors, including the social conventions, traditions, attitudes, beliefs and religious values of males and females in these other communities.

In fact, the general accepted sociolinguistic finding that women tend to use prestigious forms more frequently than men is not reflected in the present study. The life of most women (especially Muslim women) in India is quite different from that of women living in England and America. Most of them have limited opportunities for participating in social and public life. They often feel tied to the religious and cultural traditions of their society. Social segregation of the sexes and strict religious norms restrict women's participation in intellectual activities. This often leads to conflicting situations, since the advancement of women's education is not compatible with the traditional views and social cultural norms of muslim culture.

These social and cultural barriers are reflected in women's linguistic

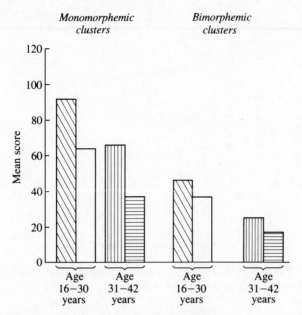

Figure 19.2   Final cluster simplification in men's and women's speech.
▨ = female (16−30 years);   ☐ = male (16−30 years);
▥ = female (31−42 years);   ▤ = male (31−42 years).

behaviour. In my study, female speakers deleted final stops more frequently than male speakers, who used a correspondingly greater proportion of unreduced clusters. The difference between final stop deletion in
men's and women's speech was significant for monomorphemic clusters
($p < 0.01$), but was not significant for bimorphemic clusters. Figure 19.2
shows the mean number of occurrences of final stop deletion in final
consonant clusters in men's and women's speech, for monomorphemic and
bimorphemic clusters. Figure 19.2 shows that in both age groups (16–30
years and 31–42 years) men have a lower mean score than women.

Other sociolinguistic studies in India have found a similar pattern in the
English used by men and women, with men using what can be interpreted
as prestige variants more frequently than women (see, for example,
Sawhney 1980 and Chaudhary 1981). A sociolinguistic study of the English
spoken in Delhi, however, shows a different pattern: Sahgal (1983) and
Agnihotri and Sahgal (1985) found that women used a higher proportion
of prestige variants than men. It must be noted, however, that Sahgal's
(1983) study deals with the more affluent sections of urban society, and
the female speakers who took part in her study were of a higher socioeconomic status than those in the present study, and hence are likely to
have accepted more easily the Western influence that is prevalent in most

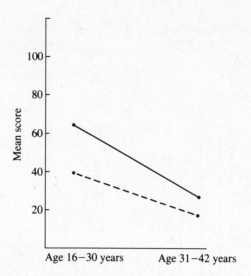

Figure 19.3   Simplification of monomorphemic and bimorphemic clusters by 2 age groups. Monomorphemic clusters (——); bimorphemic clusters (– – –).

urban societies. Most of my informants, on the other hand, were from a traditional Muslim society, where women have received little education compared to women from other ethnic groups in India. Due to their religious beliefs, they have less social mobility and less contact with the outside world. A similar situation was observed by Modarassi (1978) in Tehran. Modarassi found that young unmarried women from all social classes in Tehran used higher frequencies of stigmatised, low-prestige variants.

It should be pointed out that although the concept of 'prestige' has been used in previous studies to interpret sex differences in language use, there are several problems involved in the use of this concept (see, for discussion, Cameron and Coates 1985; Milroy 1987). Nevertheless, the following generalisation about men and women's speech could safely be made on the basis of the results discussed above: in countries where women have not traditionally played a role in public and social life, they are less likely to conform to the linguistic norms of the dominant (male) culture.

Figure 19.3 shows the mean scores for simplification of monomorphemic and bimorphemic clusters in two different age groups. Deletion of final stops occurs more frequently in the speech of the younger age group, and less frequently in the speech of the older age group, in both monomorphemic and bimorphemic clusters. The effect of age is very strong, with a statistically significant difference between the younger and the older age group ($p < 0.1$).

Table 19.4. *Mean scores for final cluster simplification in reading and interview styles*

Sex	Type of clusters	Reading style	Type of clusters	Interview style
Female	MM	51.7	MM	70.2
Female	BM	40.3	BM	55.1
Male	MM	20.5	MM	63.4
Male	BM	18.7	BM	36.2
Age	Type of clusters	Reading style	Type of clusters	Interview style
16–30 yrs	MM	48.1	MM	77.4
16–30 yrs	BM	45.2	BM	55.4
31–42 yrs	MM	25.0	MM	51.6
31–42 yrs	BM	22.8	BM	30.0

These findings raise at least two interesting questions. Firstly, is there a conscious effort on the part of older groups to retain final clusters? Secondly, why is there a big gap between the younger and the older speakers in the sample?

One possible answer to these questions is that there is a linguistic change taking place within this variety of Indian English. Most young speakers grew up in an environment where there exists a linguistic conflict between English and regional Indian languages. On the one hand, English is still seen as necessary for social prestige and advancement; on the other hand, strong positive feelings for the regional languages may result in correspondingly more negative attitudes towards English.

The older generation, however, grew up in a different political environment. Many of them were educated in private English schools, during the aftermath of the British Raj, and they still consciously try to retain some features of British English. Their attitude towards English is very different from young speakers, (see Sahgal, this volume) who sound increasingly less 'British' than their predecessors.

Stylistic variation

We have seen that this analysis of final cluster simplification revealed a clear pattern of variation based on sex and age. It also showed stylistic variation, between 'interview' style and 'reading' style. The range of stylistic variation was narrow for bimorphemic clusters but greater for monomorphemic clusters. Table 19.4 shows the mean scores for final cluster simplification for speakers of different sexes and then for speakers of different ages, in interview and reading styles.

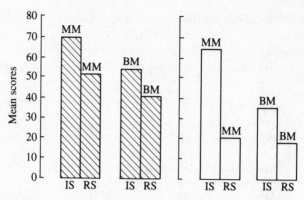

Figure 19.4   Variation by sex and style.   ▨ = female;   ☐ = male.
IS = Interview style; RS = Reading style.

The frequency of final cluster simplification is lower in reading style and higher for interview style, for all speakers. This is presumably due to the fact that while reading a passage and a word list, the speakers paid more attention to their speech, concentrating on every sentence and on every word. As a result, final stop deletion when reading is relatively low for both monomorphemic and bimorphemic clusters. In the interview style, the situation gradually changed, so that once the speaker got involved in the conversation, he or she became less conscious of their speech.

It was noted earlier that male speakers in this study deleted final stops less frequently than females. It can be seen from table 19.4 that this is so for both reading style and interview style ($p < 0.1$ in both cases). Mean scores for male speakers are particularly low in reading style, in bimorphemic clusters. It can also be seen that the older age group simplifies final consonant clusters less frequently than the younger age group in both styles. A further noteworthy point is that in reading style simplification of monomorphemic and bimorphemic clusters occurs to more or less the same extent in the speech of both age groups.

Figure 19.4 gives a graphic illustration of stylistic variation for men and women. It shows that men do more style shifting than women; the variation between reading style and interview style is much greater for men than it is for women, in both monomorphemic and bimorphemic clusters. One possible explanation for this could be, again, the public roles that men and women play in India, particularly in Muslim society. As mentioned earlier, most Muslim women do not have any social or public role to play compared to men, who depend on English for employment and other professional obligations. Perhaps, when they speak English, men are concerned to present a better picture of themselves more often than women are. It is interesting that Sahgal (1983) also found that men's use of 'non-standard' variants decreased more sharply than women's, in formal style.

Conclusion

The results of this study provide us with ample evidence of the correlation of final consonant cluster simplification with linguistic factors on the one hand, and with social and stylistic factors on the other hand. In the non-native variety of English analysed here, then, consonant cluster simplification is subject to similar linguistic and social constraints as it is in native-speaker varieties. However, although the linguistic constraints appear to be identical, for the most part, in native speaker varieties and in this non-native speaker variety, the social constraints differ, reflecting, it seems, differences in the social, cultural and political contexts in which English is used.

REFERENCES

Agnihotri, R. K. and Sahgal, A. 1985. Is Indian English retroflexed and r-full? *Indian Journal of Applied Linguistics* 11: 97–108.

Bansal, R. K. 1972. *The Sound System of Indian English*. Monograph no. 7, Hyderabad: CIEFL

Cameron, D. and Coates, J. 1985. Some problems in the sociolinguistic explanation of sex differences. *Language and Communication* 5: 143–51.

Chaudhary, S. C. 1981. A study of sociolinguistic factors affecting the second year intermediate tribal students' learning of English at Ranchi University. Unpublished MLitt. thesis, Hyderabad: CIEFL.

Fasold, R. 1972. *Tense Marking in Black English*. Washington DC: CAL.

Guy, G. 1980. Variation in the group and individual: the case of final stop deletion. In Labov, W. (ed.) *Locating Language in Time and Space*. New York: Academic Press, pp. 1–35.

Labov, W. 1966. *The Social Stratification of English in New York City*. Washington DC: CAL.

Labov, W., Cohen, P., Robins, C. and Lewis, J. 1968. *A Preliminary Study of the Structure of the English used by Negro and Puerto Rican Speakers in New York City*. Final report: Cooperative Research Project No. 3091. Washington DC: Office of Education.

Milroy, L. 1987. *Observing and Analysing Natural Language*. Oxford: Blackwell.

Modarassi, Y. 1978. A Sociolinguistic Analysis of Modern Persian. Unpublished PhD thesis, University of Kansas.

Neu, H. 1980. Ranking of constraints on /t,d/ deletion in American English: a statistical analysis. In Labov, W. (ed.), *Locating Language in Time and Space*. New York: Academic Press, pp. 37–54.

Sahgal, A. 1983. A Sociolinguistic Study of the Spoken English of the Delhi Elite. Unpublished MPhil thesis, University of Delhi.

Sawhney, S. K. 1980 Sociolinguistic Factors affecting Acquisition of English as a Second Language. Unpublished MLitt. thesis, CIEFL, Hyderabad.

Trudgill, P. 1974. *The Social Differentiation of English in Norwich*. Cambridge: Cambridge University Press.

Wolfram, W. 1969. *A Sociolinguistic Description of Detroit Negro Speech*. Washington DC: CAL.

1971. Black-white speech differences revisited. *Viewpoints: Bulletin of the School of Education*, Indiana University, 47; also in Wolfram, W. A., and Clarke, N. H. (eds.) 1971, *Black-white Speech Relationships*. Washington DC: CAL.

20

Patterns of language use in a bilingual setting in India

ANJU SAHGAL

Introduction

In the Indian urban context the use of English is becoming increasingly widespread, with English acquiring more functions now than ever before. This was not envisaged, however, by the framers of the Constitution before independence. The Indian Constitution recognises 15 national languages, with Hindi as the official language and English as the associate official language, with a directive that English was to be replaced by Hindi in a period of 15 years. However, this did not happen, for various social and political reasons, and English has flourished even more after independence.

The national impact of Hindi, on the other hand, has not been able to equal that of English and has led to English–Hindi rivalry, with each language continuing to compete for recognition as a pan-Indian language (Kachru 1979). Here, English has certain advantages over Hindi. Since it is not the language of any major group, it does not threaten any group's ethnic identity and hence is politically more acceptable. It is the main language of education, administration, the mass media, science and technology, and it has provided appropriate and stable registers in these areas. Hindi, despite government support, is still in the process of standardising and codifying the specific registers. Therefore, it cannot provide much professional and linguistic mobility to its users. Any language which aspires to replace English at the national level needs to acquire the functional load of English (Kachru 1979). Above all, English has tremendous prestige in India, and the members of the élite community often communicate amongst themselves only in English. Since they control political and social resources, the language they speak is treated as the language of upward mobility. Internationally, English has emerged as a world language, used increasingly in diplomacy, trade and

299

telecommunication, which again makes it useful for the tiny fraction of Indians who require it for such purposes.

There are several factors working against Hindi. It is the mother tongue of the largest group spread over a wide geographical area, hence the other Indian communities feel that they would be professionally, politically, and socially disadvantaged were Hindi permitted to assume the central role. Since the protest of these communities often takes a violent form,[1] the government has adopted a policy of maintaining the status quo. The greatest damage to the cause of Hindi, however, is being done by the protagonists of Hindi themselves. They have equated the question of national integration with Hindi and specifically with the 'pure', sanskritised variety of Hindi, which is not much understood even by educated native speakers of Hindi.

At the same time, the role of English has not been replacive and it has not succeeded in driving out any of the indigenous languages of India. In fact, in its long sojourn in India of over 300 years, it has been enriched by the Indian languages, and has enriched them in turn. Both attitudinally and linguistically, there is a growing awareness of the Indianness of English and a gradual distancing of Indian English from the native norms. The process of 'nativisation' of English in second language contexts is due not only to 'transfer' from local languages, but also to the pressures of a new cultural environment and fresh communicative needs. Other factors such as the absence of a native group, inadequate teaching and acquisitional limitations (such as lack of exposure and facilites, or learning under compulsion) could also lead to innovations in the course of time.

In this chapter, I attempt to describe the functional role of English vis-à-vis the other languages (mother tongue and Hindi as a second language) to see if the predominant status of English has caused a reallocation of the status of different languages in the verbal repertoire of some Indian communities. On the basis of the claimed preference of informants for the type of English they think should be spoken in India, it is empirically shown that people are now accepting and recognising their distinct variety of English.

Method of investigation

The sample consisted of 45 informants taken from three communities living in Delhi: Hindi speakers, Bengalis and Tamilians. They were randomly selected from the élite residential areas of Delhi. All of them belonged to the middle or upper strata of society. An interesting situation exists vis-à-vis these communities. It may be noted that the Hindi-speaking natives of Delhi speak only two languages, namely, mother tongue (Hindi) and English; while Bengalis and Tamilians, who are migrants from the East and South of India respectively, use three languages, namely, mother tongue (Bengali or Tamil), Hindi and English; both Hindi and English being second languages for them.

A questionnaire was given to the informants (see appendix 1). In part (A) of the questionnaire, they were asked to indicate what language(s) they would choose with various interlocutors. Eleven interlocutors were selected, five in the 'family' domain, three in the 'friendship' domain and three in the 'institutional' domain. The informants had to rate their language use with each interlocutor on the following scale:

Most of the time	:	5
Occasionally	:	3
Rarely	:	1
Never	:	0

The output of the analysis was in the form of scores indicating the degree of use of each language with each of the interlocutors. These were called dominance configuration[2] (DC) scores. If the DC score of a language was higher than the DC score of the other languages reported with that interlocutor, than the language scoring higher was considered dominant. After calculating the DC score of each language with each interlocutor, the mean score for each domain was calculated.

In part (B), the informants were asked to indicate the variety of English they had a preference for. Four choices were given: BBC English (a British variety); American English; English used by the newsreaders on All India Radio (AIR) / Television (which is considered to be the prestigious variety in India) and Ordinary Indian English, generally used by educated Indians in everyday conversation.

Patterns of language use in different domains

In order to describe the functional role of English in relation to the other languages in the verbal repertoire of the population, as well as to get some insight into trends in language maintenance and language shift, I decided to use Fishman's (1972) technique of domain analysis. Fishman defined domain in terms of 'institutional contexts or socio-ecological co-occurrences' (1972: 19) that attempt to designate the major clusters of interaction settings that occur in particular multilingual societies. The objective of such an analysis is to make predictions about the particular language likely to be used in a given role relation in a given domain. The domains to be investigated will vary from community to community, and so will the role relations within each community. The individual language choice is then related to the larger, stable, patterns of choices that exist in multilingual settings as a whole.

Table 20.1 shows the language use in the three domains of Family,

Table 20.1. *Patterns of claimed language use in different domains*

Languages	Family			Friendship			Institutional		
	H	B	T	H	B	T	H	B	T
Mother tongue	4.60	4.75	4.33	4.14	2.90	0.91	3.55	1.92	0.91
English	2.25	2.43	2.80	2.95	3.43	3.93	3.43	4.04	4.04
Hindi	NA	0.13	0.38	NA	1.06	2.22	NA	1.50	1.91

H = Hindi-speakers, B = Bengalis, T = Tamilians, NA = Not applicable

Friendship and Institution in terms of mother tongue (Hindi, Bengali and Tamil), English and Hindi (both as second languages).

Family Domain. Mother tongue stands out as the single dominant language of the family for all the communities. The Bengalis had the highest scores for the mother tongue, while the Tamilians had the lowest. The Hindi speakers used English the least, while the Tamilians used it the most. Regarding the use of Hindi (as a second language) by Bengalis and Tamilians, the scores are so negligible that one can safely say that Hindi has no place in the family domain. It thus appears that in this migrant situation, both Bengalis and Tamilians have resisted the pressures of the host society and maintained their linguistic identity. However, what is gradually causing a reallocation of languages in their verbal repertoire is the language of prestige i.e. English.

Friendship domain. Unlike the family domain, English emerges as the dominant language of the friendship domain for Bengalis and Tamilians. Hindi speakers, however, primarily use their mother tongue in this domain. One of the main reasons for the differential behaviour of the Bengalis and Tamilians could be that they often live in mixed neighbourhoods where they have to interact with several other Indian communities who do not share their mother tongue. What is again interesting is that while more Hindi is used by them in the friendship domain than in the family domain, it is still used less frequently than English.

Institutional domain. English is undoubtedly the dominant language of the institutional domain for all the communities. This is not surprising, as it is the main language of both administration and education. In the case of the two migrant communities, the Bengalis and the Tamilians, the differences between the English scores, and the mother tongue and Hindi scores, are even greater. The fact that Hindi speakers claim to use both

Hindi and English to an equal extent suggests that they frequently alternate between the two languages in this domain.

This study suggests that educated Indians are beginning to use English in the more intimate domains of family and friendship. At the same time, the predominance of mother tongue in the family domain suggests that English bilingualism in India is not replacive. What is interesting is the differential behaviour of the Hindi community and the two migrant communities, which reflects the different sociopsychological pressures operating on them. The Hindi speakers feel that Hindi should be the link language of India and assume the functions that English has. The non-Hindi communities prefer the more 'neutral' and prestigious language, that is, English. Hence, in the complex multilingual environment of Delhi, where the language of the host society (Hindi) and the language of prestige (English) are in 'a state of linguistic tension' (Kachru, 1975), it appears that the language that allows for the maximum advancement and mobility at the national and international level is more acceptable. As Srivastava (1977) points out, the increasing importance of English has 'forced the stable and balanced form' of Indian multilingualism into an 'uneven relationship'.

Choice of a model

English in India has not only acquired a wide range of functions, but in its process of Indianisation it has linguistically evolved its own characteristic features at the phonological, lexical, syntactic and even discourse level. While initially these innovations were rejected by purists, they are now becoming increasingly accepted, since English is treated not as a foreign language but as part of the cultural identity of India. These innovations have, however, led to new problems and anxieties which are primarily related to pedagogic standards, national and international intelligibility, as well as to technical problems of description and typology.

The question of a standard is still an oft-debated issue and the general consensus seems to favour a rather nebulous 'educated' Indian English variety, which is close to the native 'standard'. Both pedagogues and linguists often prescribe such a variety on the basis of ill-conceived empirical studies, or on just personal preference, taking no account of the sociolinguistic pressures operating in the society. As Kachru (1977) says, the universality of pedagogical models is suspect; it has to be sacrificed for local sociopolitical, educational and communicative needs. Kachru, therefore, rejects the didactic monomodel concept and suggests a more dynamic polymodel approach which recognises individual needs and pedagogical requirements as well as the social realities of the situation.

In most urban areas in India, the sociolinguistic situation is very complex, with various different cultural and linguistic groups interacting

Table 20.2. *Preferred models of English (N = 45)*

Models of English	Number of people	%
1. BBC English	11	24
2. American English	1	2
3. AIR/TV English	12	27
4. Ordinary Indian English	21	47

with each other. There is also considerable variation in the way, for instance, that educated Delhiites use English. They are faced with conflicting pressures: on the one hand, there exist the pressures of urbanisation, which bring in their wake literacy, education, mass media and westernization, all of which favour the evolution of a single norm; on the other hand, the diverse linguistic and cultural backgrounds of different groups in Delhi favour diversity, with Bengalis speaking a 'Bengali' English and Tamilians speaking a 'Tamil' English. It is natural that these different varieties of English should evolve their own distinct features in response to the needs and motivations of their users. At the same time, it is equally natural, perhaps, that sociopsychological pressures towards standardisation should level out just those features which mark out a variety most distinctively.

Since perceived models within a community influence linguistic behaviour considerably, I attempted to find out what variety of English was favoured by the informants. Four choices were given, ranging from the native varieties to 'Ordinary Indian English'. The results are given in table 20.2.

Table 20.2 demonstrates the low preference (26 per cent) for both the native varieties of English. My findings are contrary to those of Kachru (1976) where the first preference (66.66 per cent) was for the British model. The discrepancy between the two scores suggests that Indian English has become more respectable and that the prestige associated with native varieties of English (especially British English) is beginning to fade in a multilingual country like India. My findings also contradict Kachru's (1981) claim that American English is slowly becoming 'today's world language', its impact being 'all-pervasive on the English speaking world' (p. 39). Surprisingly, a low preference was shown for the English spoken by the AIR/TV announcers, who represent the 'educated' variety of English devoid of regional flavour. It was felt by some of my informants that AIR/TV announcers imitated the BBC pronunciation and had not evolved their own identity. This suggests that there is an increasing recognition and acceptance of the local varieties of English in this multilingual country.

To get a more realistic picture of the prevailing sociolinguistic situation,

Table 20.3. *Preference for models of English (revised scores)*

Models of English	Number of informants	%
Élite varieties of English	24	53
Ordinary Indian English	21	47

it would be useful, perhaps, to combine the scores of the native varieties of English and AIR/TV English as 'Élite' English. Table 20.3 furnishes the revised scores.

While the majority of the informants now appear to prefer 'élite' English, it is a thin majority. However, what is interesting is that the scores reflect the non-polarised sociolinguistic situation in India. In monolingual contexts, a certain dialect often becomes a model, for social and pedagogical reasons. In the more complex and fluid situations which obtain in multilingual countries, the perceived models are not so clearly polarised. My findings also reveal the gap that exists between the pedagogical norms (which normally tend to favour the 'élite' variety) and the people's desires.

Conclusion

In this study I have tried to show that English has acquired more functional roles, and is the main language of the friendship and institutional domain. It has even penetrated into the family domain, which suggests that domain separation is beginning to disappear, with English gradually becoming associated with intimacy, spontaneity and informality, along with its use in education, administration and the mass media. At the same time, the predominance of the mother tongue in the family domain does not permit us to say that English bilingualism in India is replacive in character. The study also demonstrates that in the linguistic rivalry that exists between English and Hindi, English is certainly more popular, especially among migrant populations in India. This suggests that English is part of the cultural identity of India, which is further emphasised by the fact that most of the informants preferred a 'local' variety of English, rather than an adherence to native-speaker norms.

NOTES

I thank Dr A. K. Sinha and Dr A. L. Khanna who very patiently read through the draft of this article. I am also grateful to Dr R. K. Agnihotri who guided me in my thesis 'A sociolinguistic study of the spoken English of the Delhi élite' (Sahgal, 1983), from which this article is extracted.

1. This refers primarily to the riots that took place in Tamil Nadu in May 1963, protesting against the imposition of Hindi.
2. My use of the term 'dominance configuration' is different from that of Fishman (1966).

REFERENCES

Fishman, J. A. 1966. *Language Loyalty in the United States*. The Hague: Mouton.
    1972. The relationship between micro and macro-sociolinguistics in the study of who speaks what language to whom and when. In Pride, J. B. and Holmes, J. (eds.), *Sociolinguistics*. Harmondsworth: Penguin, pp. 15–31.
Kachru, B. B. 1975. Linguistic roles and language function: multilingualism in the Indian context. *Studies in Language Learning* 1 (1): 182–85.
    1976. Models of English for the Third World: White Man's linguistic burden or language pragmatics? *TESOL Quarterly* 10 (2): 221–39.
    1977. The new Englishes and old models. *English Language Forum* 15: 29–35
    1979. The Englishization of Hindi: language rivalry and language change. in Rauch, I. *et al.* (eds.) 1979, *Linguistic Methods: Papers in Honour of Herbert Pensl*. The Hague: de Rider Press, pp. 199–211.
    1981. American English and other Englishes. in Ferguson, C. A. and Heath, S. B. (eds.), *Language in the USA*. Cambridge: Cambridge University Press.
Sahgal, A. 1983. A Sociolinguistic Study of the Spoken English of the Delhi Élite. Unpublished MPhil thesis, University of Delhi.
Srivastava, R. N. 1977. Indian multilingualism: myth and reality. Sharma, P. G. and Kumar, S. (eds), *Indian Bilingualism*. Agra: Kendriya Hindi Sansthan.

Appendix I

(A) Patterns of language use
Name of languages you use with:

	Interlocutors	Most of the time	Occasionally	Rarely
1.	Father			
2.	Mother			
3.	Wife or Husband			
4.	Children			
5.	Sibling			
6.	Best friends			
7.	Friends in the neighbourhood			
8.	Friends of the opposite sex			
9.	Colleagues at office or friends at school			
10.	Juniors/ Subordinates			
11.	Boss or teacher			

(B) What is the model of English that you think should be spoken in India? Tick your choice:

1. Model of the BBC newsreaders _____
2. Model of the AIR/TV newsreaders _____
3. Model of English in American movies _____
4. Ordinary Indian English _____

21

Speech acts in an indigenised variety: sociocultural values and language variation

KAMAL K. SRIDHAR

In studies of non-native varieties of English (hereafter NNVE's), with few exceptions (D'Souza 1987; Kachru 1982, 1983, 1986; Smith 1983),[1] not much attention has been paid to what may be called the pragmatic aspects of language use. By pragmatic aspects, I mean topics such as how certain speech acts, such as informatives, directives, commissives, etc. (cf. Austin 1962; Searle 1969) are performed in these varieties. Since NNVE's differ from native varieties in the performance of speech acts more than in formal properties, it is possible that the pragmatic approach may succeed in capturing the uniqueness of a NNVE where structural analyses fail to do so.

Recent studies have shown that there are important cross-cultural and cross-linguistic differences in the way the 'same' speech act is performed in different languages. For example, Olshtain and Cohen (1983) have pointed out that an apology in Hebrew is less likely to include a 'promise of forebearance' or 'an offer of repair' (for the damage) that is there in English. They also observe that the two languages differ in both the range of offences for which an apology is offered and the intensity of the expression of regret. (For other cross-cultural differences see Apte 1974; Loveday 1982; Sridhar and Sridhar 1986, Sridhar in press; Wolfson and Judd 1983).

As we shall see, such differences exist between varieties of the same language as well, especially between native and non-native varieties, and between one non-native variety and another. This study is an attempt to characterise some aspects of this variation with reference to the speech act of requesting in selected users of Indian English.

Data collection procedure

This study is based on an analysis of approximately 1100 examples of 'request' expressions collected in India in January 1988, using an elicitation technique in which people were asked to provide 'free responses to structured situations' given to them in the form of a questionnaire. A total of 164 undergraduate students from three different colleges in the cosmopolitan city of Bangalore, South India, took part in the study. They were presented with outlines of seven situations (described below) and asked to write down what they would say in each situation to request the service described. Their responses were analysed with reference to (1) the variables incorporated in the stimulus situations; (2) the sociocultural background of the students themselves; and (3) the conventions governing the performance of equivalent speech acts in their own languages. The characteristics of the language used by the Indian students were compared to the way requests are performed in a native variety of English, namely American English, as revealed in the judgements and comments on the acceptability of students responses by two native speakers of American English (experienced teachers of English as a second language). The questionnaire was divided into three parts. Part I elicited background information on the students' native language, area of study, earlier training and exposure to English, use of English, mother tongue and the regional language in the various utilitarian and affective domains, and how comfortable they felt in using English. Part II outlined seven discourse situations in which they were asked to request a service, favour, etc. The situations were constructed so as to incorporate a number of sociocultural variables, such as deference, Westernised versus traditional setting, differences in the social status of the requestee, etc. In part III, the respondents indicated whether they would use their mother tongue, English, or both languages in each of the seven situations presented in part II.

Subjects

The students all came from what is roughly described as a middle class background. However, their sociocultural backgrounds were interestingly different. Students of Mount Carmel College (MCC hereafter) typically came from more Westernised family and friendship backgrounds. These students tend to have greater facility in spoken English, having studied through the English medium practically from kindergarten and also having attended 'convent' schools where the use of the child's mother tongue is discouraged. Students from Vijaya College (VC, hereafter), on the other hand, come from a relatively more traditional background, with their culture rooted in the regional language. Students from the third campus, NMKRV college may be said to be somewhat in between the two clearly defined institutions, though they may be closer to MCC than to VC.

The study tested two hypotheses: (1) that the difference in socio-cultural background would affect the choice of verbal strategies in requesting: in the choice of language in a neutral encounter, in the choice of address

Table 21.1. *Mother tongues of students*

Language	No. of speakers	Percentage
Kannada	59	36.0
Tamil	30	18.3
Telugu	25	15.2
Hindi/Urdu	20	12.2
Malayalam	6	3.7
Konkani	8	4.9
Others	16	9.7
Total	164	100.0

forms, and in the choice of semantic formulae and lexical items; (2) that the MCC students would perform requests in a more native (English)-like manner, while those from VC would use strategies more closely reflecting those of Indian languages, and those from NMKRV would fall in-between.

The breakdown of the students from the three colleges is as follows: NMKRV College (65); MCC (49); and VC (50).

The majority of the students (73 per cent) are speakers of the four major Dravidian languages, Kannada, Malayalam, Tamil and Telugu, and of Hindi-Urdu (12 per cent). The other languages represented are Konkani, Gujarati, Sindhi, Marathi, Punjabi, and Tulu.

For almost all the students (97 per cent), English was the medium of instruction at high school and college levels. In other words, they had studied English for at least six years. Many had studied English as a subject and the other subjects through the medium of English for much longer. (However, as we shall see, having English as medium of instruction means different things in different settings.) Ninety per cent of the students claimed that they used English most often with their friends. An even higher number (98 per cent) claimed that they felt comfortable in using English. (This claim turned out to be interesting in the light of the data analyzed below). These claims reflect not only the multilingual, cosmopolitan nature of Bangalore city, where English often serves as a link language, but also the fact that it is prestigious to claim competence in English.

Results and discussion

In view of the limitation of space, I will cite, for each discourse situation, the three most frequently given responses along with the number and percentage of subjects who chose that response type. I will discuss the other, less common responses whenever they illustrate a noteworthy aspect of the socio-cultural context (i.e., those judged to be particularly 'deviant' or unusual by the two native speaker judges).[2]

> *Situation 1.* You are visiting your friend's house. Your friend is busy inside. Her/His mother comes out and asks you to sit down. You are very thirsty and need a glass of water. How would you ask her for a glass of water?

In Indian languages, it is customary to address elders with a kinship term. The addressee's proper name with title such as *Mr*, *Mrs* etc., is almost never used. (It would be considered 'uppity' or disrespectful.) With one's own relatives, the first name with the kinship term is used (as in the US). In the given situation, the friend's mother was addressed as *Aunty* by 92 of the respondents (56.1 per cent). Native speakers of English found the use of *Aunty* strange. Note that *Aunty* is an English word grafted on to a basically Indic semantic pattern, but it functions as a marker of Westernised sophistication among the upwardly mobile middle classes in urban India. This is seen clearly in the distribution of the use of *aunty* in table 21.2 for the three colleges; it is most frequently used by NMKRV students (64 per cent) and MCC students (57.1 per cent) and least frequently used by VC students (46 per cent).

Table 21.3 shows the choice of formulae used in requesting water. Indirect questions with modals *can, could*, or *may* (*Can I have a glass of water?, Could you please give me a glass of water?*, etc.) were most frequent. However, direct imperatives such as *Give me a glass of water, Get me some water* were also used (with or without *please* or *excuse me*). There is a distinct pattern in the distribution of these structures. Students from VC are more likely to use direct imperatives while students from the other two colleges use indirect questions.

> *Situation 2.* You are in the local Koshy's restaurant with some friends. You want to order some snacks. How would you ask the waiter for the menu?

This situation tested the effect of two variables: one was the Westernised setting, and the other the relatively low socioeconomic status of the addressee. Koshy's is a fashionable restaurant in the Westernised part of Bangalore, 'the Cantonment'. The responses included indirect requests (questions such as, *Could I have the menu, please?*) as well as statements (*Waiter, I want the menu (please)*) and imperatives (*Waiter, give us the menu*). The choice of sentence types is given in table 21.4.

Table 21.5 shows that the students, overall, chose a question pattern to request the menu. The more Westernised background of students from MCC is seen clearly in their overwhelming preference for indirect questions for requesting. The less frequent use of indirect questions in the

Table 21.2. *Distribution of* Aunty

College	No. of respondents	No. of subjects using *Aunty*	Percentage
Mount Carmel	49	28	57.1
NMKRV College	65	41	63.7
Vijaya College	50	23	46.0
Total	164	92	56.1

Table 21.3. *Choice of formulae in requesting water*

Structures	MCC	%	NMKRV	%	VC	%
Can/could/may I..	40	83.3	48	75.0	25	52.1
Can/would you give	1	2.8	7	14.2	2	4.1
Give/get me	5	10.4	5	8.0	17	35.4
I want/need	2	4.1	4	6.3	4	8.3

other two colleges is indicative of the students' reliance on Indian language strategies for making requests, which do not involve indirect questions.

The difference between the students from the three colleges in their use of polite expressions is also reflected in their use of *please* in requesting a menu. As table 21.6 shows, students from MCC are consistent in their use of the pragmatic convention of native English, namely, extending minimal courtesies such as the use of *please* regardless of the social or economic background of the addressee.

In contrast, the responses of students from Vijaya college more closely reflect the conventions of politeness characteristic of Indian languages: namely, the use of polite forms is more frequent with social superiors and nearly absent when the addressee is considered one's social inferior. Table 21.4 shows that eleven (22 per cent) Vijaya College respondents used 'invalid' forms. Some are requests that are direct translations from the native language; several students actually placed their order rather than requesting the menu. This response is understandable in view of the fact that in most traditional (non-Westernised) restaurants, the menu is recited orally by the waiter in response to the patron's question as to what is available.

> *Situation 3.* You are at the movie theater with some friends. You need 5 tickets. What will you say to the person in the ticket office?

Table 21.4. *Choice of semantic formulae in requesting menu*

Structures	MCC	%	NMKRV	%	VC	%
May I have	35	71.4	30	46.1	13	26.0
Can/could you	9	18.4	6	9.2	15	30.0
I want/give us (p1)	4	8.1	11	16.9	9	18.0
Invalid	0	—	4	6.1	11	22.0

Table 21.5. *Choice of sentence type in requesting menu*

College	Statement or imperative	%	Question	%
MCC	8	16.3	41	83.7
NMKRV	25	38.5	36	55.4
VC	14	28.0	25	50.0

Table 21.6. *Use of the politeness marker* please

College	Total	Please	%
Mount Carmel	49	41	83.7
NMKRV College	65	50	76.9
Vijaya College	50	25	50.0
All speakers	164	116	70.7

This situation also involved a low status addressee of whom a request is made, but unlike in the Westernised restaurant, the request is made to a clerk at a ticket counter in a movie theater. Given the social ranking of the addressees in the two situations, one would expect even fewer instances of polite forms here. As table 21.7 shows, the most common choice of request form in this situation was simply a noun phrase, for example, *5 tickets (please)*. However, once again, there was a difference between the three groups in their choice of direct versus indirect requesting strategies. There were more indirect requests from MCC students (51%) than from the other two colleges (NMKRV 31 per cent and VC 36 per cent).

As before, some of the students' awkwardness in the use of English in this context is evident from the choice of expressions such as *Would you like to give me, Please grant me*, or *Please would you grant me*, and *Excuse me, sir*, etc.

Table 21.7. *Requesting movie tickets*

Structures	MCC	%	NMKRV	%	VC	%
5 tickets (please)	23	49.3	41	68.7	25	50.0
Could you give me	13	26.5	10	15.4	15	30.0
Can I have . . . } May I have . . . }	12	24.5	10	15.4	3	6.0

Table 21.8. *Shopping*

Structures	MCC	%	NMKRV	%	VC	%
Can/could/would you	38	77.5	53	81.5	23	46
Will you show me	5	10.2	13	13.8	4	8
(Please) Show me	0	–	0	–	21	42

> *Situation 4.* You are on Commercial street, buying clothes (sarees, shirts, etc.) for yourself. You want the shop-keeper to show you the latest designs. What will you say to the shop-keeper?

Given the location of the shop (also in the 'Cantonment' area), this situation also involved a fashionable, Westernised context. The semantic formulae used for requesting in this situation are given in table 21.8.

Here one notices a clear difference between students of Vijaya College and those from the other two. Vijaya college students tended to use nearly as many direct imperatives (42 per cent) as indirect requests (54 per cent), while students from MCC and NMKRV overwhelmingly chose indirect requests (88 per cent and 95 per cent respectively). Interestingly, the direct imperative was not used by any student from either of these two colleges. The high frequency of the direct imperative in Vijaya College is to be explained with reference to two factors. First, the direct imperative is not an impolite form in Indian languages. (Politeness would be marked in an imperative by verbal suffixes which indicate deference and which do not translate into English.) Second, students of VC may have been thinking of a shop attendant rather than the shopkeeper as the addressee. Shop attendants in a clothing store occupy a fairly low rank on the social hierarchy, and do not receive extensive courtesy. Thus, the responses of VC students may have been influenced by mother tongue pragmatic conventions.

A noteworthy aspect of the requesting strategy, distributed fairly evenly among the subjects of the three colleges, is the use of the modal question *Will you . . . ?* While this expression would be regarded as petulant or rude in a native English context, it does not necessarily carry that social meaning in the Indian English context, mainly because it is a result of native language transfer. Indian students are genuinely confused about the distinctions between *can, could, will, would, will, shall, may*, etc., since no satisfactory grammatical account of these is available in pedagogical materials. When an Indian English speaker uses a *Will you. . .?* question, he or she is not necessarily being rude, but may be only using the equivalent of a question form in the native language.

> *Situation 5.* You are in the British Council Library and cannot find a particular book. You need it urgently. What will you say to the person at the desk (you want his help)?

The British Council library, which charges a membership fee and carries only English books, is also located in the Westernised part of Bangalore. Almost 80 per cent of the respondents are not members of this library, nor are they frequent users of this facility. It is used mainly by ambitious, upper middle class students. The specialised setting of the library contrasts with the anonymity of a movie theatre ticket counter. The library clerk is of a decidedly higher status than the restaurant waiter, the shop attendant or the clerk at the ticket counter. As expected, more indirect requests were found in this situation. The patterns of response are given in table 21.9.

Notice once again the difference between Vijaya College and the other two colleges. While about 70 per cent of MCC and NMKRV students use the polite *can/could/would you* request forms, only 44 per cent of VC students use them. One also notices the high percentage of use of *will you* as a request form, especially by students of Vijaya College (22 per cent).

> *Situation 6.* You are on your way to college and you are a bit late. You realise you have left your watch at home. A young school boy wearing a watch passes by. You really want to know how late you are. What will you ask the school boy?

The next situation involved a neutral setting with a child as the addressee and the content of the request the fairly mundane one of asking the time of day. The request strategy reported most often in this case was a direct question (*what's the time?*), without any preliminaries or embellishments.

In this situation, in Indian languages, a simple information question, with perhaps an attention getter or the vocative 'boy', will do, since the addressee is younger than the speaker. The responses (summarised in table 21.10) show that the single most frequently used structure is the direct information question. This is preferred by 40–50 per cent of students. The other half of the students use some form of an indirect question, though students from VC, once again, are less likely to use indirect questions for requests. The use of the *May I know . . .* question by a third of the MCC students is a little unexpected in that the structure would be regarded as overly polite when addressed to someone younger in the Indian context.

Table 21.9. *British Council Library*

Structures	MCC	%	NMKRV	%	VC	%
Can/could/would you	33	67.3	46	70.8	22	44
Will you help me	5	10.2	10	15.4	11	22
(Please) help me	0	–	2	3.0	8	16

Table 21.10. *Most commonly used structures in requesting time*

Structures	MCC	%	NMKRV	%	VC	%
Can/could/would you	10	20.4	23	35.4	8	16
May I know the time	17	34.7	9	13.8	10	20
What's the time	20	40.8	29	44.6	25	50
Time (please)	1	2.0	2	3.0	7	14

Table 21.11. *Requesting mark sheets*

Structures	MCC	%	NMKRV	%	VC	%
Can/could/may I have	17	34.7	22	33.8	9	18
Would/could/can you	7	14.3	10	15.4	8	16
I want to have + Q.	1	2.0	1	1.5	9	18
I need/want a copy	13	26.5	11	16.9	13	26

Situation 7. You need a copy of your mark sheets from the Registrar's office. What would you say to the person at the desk?

The most frequently used formulae were modal questions, followed by statements. The difference between MCC and NMKRV on the one hand and VC on the other shows up here again. Note that as many as 44 per cent of VC students use a statement, while the proportion is much less (though still high) in the case of students from MCC and NMKRV (28.5 and 18.4 per cent respectively). This is because a large number of students felt the need to explain their request with a statement of need, a fairly typical procedure in Indian languages. Note once again the difference among the three colleges in the choice of direct versus indirect strategies.

Significance and Conclusion

The major findings of this study could be summarised as follows:

First, it seems to be clear that the requesting strategy in Indian English is different from that in native varieties of English. This is seen most clearly in the less common use of indirect questions and more frequent use of direct questions and desiderative statements.

Second, many of the differences between native and non-native patterns of requesting have their source in the conventions of requesting in Indian languages. Thus, if variation theory is to include non-native varieties of language, the speaker's mother tongue has to be recognised as a major variable, analogous to factors such as class, region, and age, which are conventionally recognised in the paradigm.

Third, even when a non-native variety uses a structure that is apparently identical to one that may be employed in a native variety, the 'social meaning' of that structure may be different in the two contexts. This is illustrated by the use of the *Will you . . .* question in Indian English.

Fourth, variation studies must pay attention not only to the differences between native and non-native varieties, but also to variation within a non-native variety. In this connection, sociocultural factors such as *degree of Westernisation* and *stratification within the non-native society* function as variables differentiating one variety of non-native English from another.

Fifth, one of the most important differences between native and non-native varieties is that the latter involves 'partial linguistic/communicative competence'. The non-native speaker does not need English to perform a great many speech functions – his or her mother tongue is used for these purposes. Consequently, a number of speech functions are performed at best 'awkwardly' (from the point of view of the native speaker) but, in reality, in ways that involve a direct extension of either the limited L2 competence, or the speaker's mother-tongue competence.

To conclude, I wish to emphasise the fact that this has been a pilot study, and the results I have presented are only a 'first look' and need to be analysed carefully. Nevertheless, I hope that this little study demonstrates the research potential of the topic. A language like English, with its global spread and bewildering diversity of speakers and sociocultural contexts of use, poses special challenges to theories of language variation and change: non-native varieties have to be integrated into variation theory and the structural and pragmatic features of the speakers' mother tongues cannot be neglected. In the long run, pragmatic variation may well come to be seen as fraught with greater social consequences in interpersonal interaction.

NOTES

I am grateful to the following without whom this study would not have been possible: The teachers from the three colleges in Bangalore who collected the valuable data: Ms Yamuna Rao (NMKRV college), Ms Susheela Punitha (Mount

Carmel College), and Mr V. S. Sridhara (Vijaya College); Ms Lakshmi Murthy who provided crucial logistic support; Elaine Cromwell and Kathy Runchey, who gave their judgements on the NNVE data; the American Institute of Indian Studies and the State University of New York at Stonybrook for the awards that enabled me to work on this project; and Professors Yamuna Kachru, Braj Kachru, and S. N. Sridhar for their comments on an earlier version of this paper. None of the above is, of course, to be held responsible for the interpretations and conclusions contained in this paper.

1. For more references on NNVE, see Aggarwal 1982
2. It has not been possible to discuss the wealth of data on the use of attention getters, stylistic features of Indian English, and other related topics here. These issues are addressed in a forthcoming paper (Sridhar in press).

REFERENCES

Aggarwal, N. K. 1982. *English in South Asia: A Bibliographical Survey of Resources*. Gurgaon and Delhi: Indian Documentation Service.

Apte, M. L. 1974. *Thank you* and South Asian languages: a comparative sociolinguistic study. *International Journal of the Sociology of Language* 3: 67–89.

Austin, J. L. 1962. *How to do Things with Words*. London: Oxford University Press.

D'Souza, J. 1987. South Asia as a Sociolinguistic Area. Unpublished PhD thesis. University of Illinois.

Kachru, B. B. 1982. Meaning in deviation. In Kachru, B. B. (ed.) *The Other Tongue*. Urbana IL: University of Illinois Press, pp. 325–46.

1983. *The Indianization of English: The English Language in India*. New Delhi: Oxford University Press.

1986. *The Alchemy of English: The Spread, Functions and Models of Non-Native Englishes*. New York: Pergamon.

Loveday, L. 1982. *The Sociolinguistics of Learning and Using a Non-Native Language*. New York and Oxford: Pergamon Press.

Olshtain, E. and Cohen, A. 1983. Apology – a speech act set. In Wolfson and Judd (eds.) 1983, pp. 18–35.

Searle, J. 1969. *Speech Acts*. Cambridge: Cambridge University Press.

Smith, L. E. 1983. *Readings in English as an International Language*. Oxford: Pergamon Press.

Sridhar, K. K. In press. Pragmatics of South Asian English: An Empirical Study. In Baumgardner, R. J. (ed.) *English in South Asia: Structure, Use and Users*. Urbana, IL: University of Illinois Press.

Sridhar, K. K. and Sridhar, S. N. 1986. Bridging the paradigm gap: second language acquisition theory and indegenized varieties of English. *World Englishes* 5 (1): 3–14.

Wolfson, N. and Judd, E. (eds). 1983. *Sociolinguistics and Language Acquisition*. Rowley MA: Newbury House.

Southeast Asia

22

Southeast Asia and Hong Kong

MARY W. J. TAY

For the purposes of this article, Southeast Asia includes the following five countries: Indonesia, Malaysia, the Philippines, Singapore and Thailand. Apart from being members of the same political and educational organisations such as ASEAN (Association of Southeast Asian Nations) and SEAMEO (Southeast Asian Ministers of Education Organisation), all these countries have been studied *as a region* for the varieties of English spoken in them (Noss 1983; Llamzon 1983; Noss 1984). It seems reasonable, therefore, to include them as a single area. Hong Kong, consisting of the island of Hong Kong itself, Kowloon and the New Territories, fits less easily into the region although certain similarities and differences between Hong Kong, Singapore and Malaysia, have been pointed out by Platt (1982a: 384).

The aim of this article is to present an overview of the work done on selected sociolinguistic aspects of English in Southeast Asia and Hong Kong. This will be done by (a) highlighting common themes found in the published research on varieties of English in Southeast Asia; (b) discussing in greater depth the descriptions and analyses of the variety of English spoken in each of the countries mentioned above.

The focus throughout is on research already carried out rather than on what needs to be done. Accordingly, it is only in the conclusion that gaps in the current research are discussed and directions for future research on English in the region suggested. It is hoped that this approach will enable the reader to evaluate the research more objectively than if the writer's own views were given prominence throughout.

Common themes in research on English in Southeast Asia

A common theme studied in all Southeast Asian countries is the spread of English. Descriptions of the situation in Southeast Asia in general (Noss 1986; Llamzon 1983), Singapore and Malaysia (Bloom 1986; Platt and Weber 1980), Indonesia (Halim 1985), the Philippines (Sibayan 1985) and

Thailand (Sukwiwat 1985; Namtip 1980; Pornpimol 1984) provide the context needed to understand the research on English in these countries. Such research may be divided roughly into two main strands: the pedagogical and the sociolinguistic. As the pedagogical concerns fall outside the scope of this overview, they will be referred to only very briefly in this section, whereas the sociolinguistic themes will be further discussed in the section on individual countries that follows.

As one of the major concerns of the region has been the teaching of English (TESL in the Philippines and Singapore and, until very recently, Malaysia; TEFL in Indonesia and Thailand), there have been studies on the status and role (or functions) of the English language in these countries (Noss 1986; Halim 1985; Sibayan 1985; Sukwiwat 1985; Platt and Weber 1980; Tay 1979; and Asmah 1983). Other studies, more specifically pedagogical in orientation, include discussions about issues in language learning and language teaching, contrastive analyses done with a view to determining the extent of the influence of the first language on the type of English spoken, curriculum design and development, testing and evaluation, and teacher training (see, for example, Noss 1982; Halim 1985; Sadtono 1976; Sukwiwat 1985; Debyasuvarn 1981; Lee 1983; Wangsotorn 1980; Sibayan 1985; Gonzalez 1979). In the clearly EFL countries, that is, Thailand and Indonesia, research on English has focused almost exclusively on pedagogical issues. The only exceptions are Nababan's exploratory study on the phonological characteristics of Indonesian English (Nababan 1983), Lowenberg's discussion of nativisation in Indonesia (Lowenberg 1984: 151–77), and Pornpimol's (1984) description of the 'Thainess' of 'Thai English' in its sociocultural and discourse features. These will be discussed in greater detail under Indonesia and Thailand respectively.

In the research on sociolinguistic aspects of English in Southeast Asia, perhaps the only common thread running through all the countries is the discussion of nativisation, whether it be the influence of the first language (L1) on the variety of English spoken (Kreutrachu 1960; Chaiyaratana 1961; Rudhavanich 1967; Lekawatana et al. 1969; Thanyarat 1984), or the processes of indigenisation or nativisation (Lowenberg 1984; Pornpimol 1984; Llamzon 1983), or linguistic descriptions of the nativised code itself (Tay 1982a; Gupta 1986; Llamzon 1969; Nababan 1983). Studies on sociolinguistic variation such as the case studies by Platt and Gonzalez in this volume are fairly well-developed for Singapore (see, for example, Platt 1977a, 1979, 1980, 1982a; Tay 1982) and the Philippines (Gonzalez 1985), but noticeably lacking in the other countries. While the study of attitudes towards the type(s) of English spoken locally is of central concern to all the countries, large-scale studies are noticeably absent – existing studies take the form of impressionistic observations or are based on very small samples, mainly of teachers and students (see, for example, Shaw

1981; Goh 1983; Halim 1985; Sibayan 1985). Perhaps also arising out of pedagogical concerns are the studies on Standard Filipino English (Llamzon 1969) and Standard Singapore English (Tay and Gupta 1983; Tay 1982; Gupta 1986).

The paradigms and approaches used in the sociolinguistic research on English in Southeast Asia may be said to be based on, or at least influenced by, two main assumptions. The first is that by virtue of their non-native status, varieties of English in Southeast Asia should be studied in relation to native varieties. This explains why all studies so far, despite claims to independence, treat the 'nativised' varieties as 'deviant' from either British or American English (Gonzalez 1985; Platt and Weber 1980; Tay 1982). Closely allied to this assumption is the more subtle assumption that the native speaker is the sole arbiter of 'nativisation'. Thus, studies on standardisms and non-standardisms are often undertaken only from the native speaker's viewpoint, which may be far from being 'native' in the sociocultural and linguistic context of the country studied (Crewe 1977; Tongue 1974; Gupta 1986).

Second, there is the assumption that the 'nativised' varieties may be equated with one of the following: (a) 'second language' varieties (Gonzalez 1985, Platt and Weber 1980), (b) fossilised interlanguage (Platt 1977b); or (c) child language (Gupta forthcoming). These assumptions have tended to determine the direction of current research on English in Southeast Asia. The validity of these assumptions is discussed in the final section of this article where new directions for research are suggested.

As far as methodologies are concerned, there have been qualitative as well as quantitative studies, and impressionistic as well as objective analyses. While the importance of empirical data must always be recognised in sociolinguistic research, the value of introspection and observations in the work of scholars native to the region (as, for example, in the work of Gonzalez, Llamzon, Halim, Sadtono, Nababan, Debyasuvarn, Sukwiwat, Wong, and Tay) needs to be recognised as well. Undoubtedly, there is a place for quantitative analysis of the Labovian/Trudgillian type (see, for example, Platt's case study in this volume), but it would be unfortunate if these were considered the only insightful studies. In the opinion of this writer, studies on varieties of English which do not merely replicate those done in other parts of the world but which, by taking careful cognisance of 'local' considerations including 'local' sensitivities, arrive at new typologies (as exemplified by Gonzalez' paper in this volume) are the ones that are most likely to make a lasting contribution to the field.

Singapore and Malaysia

Like all the other countries in Southeast Asia, research on the variety of English spoken in Singapore and Malaysia may be said to have begun with a pedagogical orientation. Thus, Tongue's pioneering work (1974) was intended for English Language teachers rather than specialists in linguistics. Crewe's book of exercises (1977a) aims to give educated Singaporeans an awareness of the extent to which they personally are able to distinguish the Singaporean local usage from Standard English. It was only in the late 1970s and early 1980s when Platt and Weber, Tay, Lowenberg, Wong, Gupta and others started publishing on English in Singapore and Malaysia that a more sociolinguistically oriented approach became evident.

The status of English in Singapore is that of an official language, along with three other official languages – Mandarin, Malay and Tamil (Tay 1979). It has also been described as a *de facto* national language (Llamzon 1977) and an ESL variety (Platt and Weber 1979). While English appears to be increasing in importance in Singapore (Tay 1984), its status in Malaysia is clearly second to the national language and may in due course become more like a foreign than a second language (Platt and Weber 1979).

Of all the varieties of English spoken in Southeast Asia, Singaporean English performs the widest range of uses. Six characteristic uses of English have been described (1) official language, (2) language of education, (3) working language, (4) language of inter- and intra-ethnic communication, (5) language for the expression of national identity, (6) international language (Tay 1979). To these, Bloom (1986: 388) adds (7) language of religion and (8) home language. It is significant that, in Singapore, English is used not only in the public domains of transactions, employment, education, media, government, law and religion, but also in the more private domains of family and friendship (Platt and Weber 1980).

Describing the distinctive characteristics of a variety of English which performs so many functions is not an easy task. Although Singaporean/ Malaysian English is neither a classic creole continuum nor a classic diglossic community (Gupta forthcoming), it has been described as polyglossic (Richards and Tay 1977; Platt 1980) and as a 'creoloid' (Platt 1977b). However, it is within the lectal continuum paradigm that the features of Singaporean English have been described (Tay 1979; Platt and Weber 1980; Lowenberg 1984). The suitability of the lectal continuum framework has been questioned (Le Page 1984; Tay 1985, 1986; see also Platt, this volume) and a more dynamic, multidimensional model might be more appropriate in describing the characteristic features of Singaporean English. Wong's (1981) classification of the varieties of Malaysian English into (a) the wider speech form and (b) the local dialect, has definite advantages not present in the lectal continuum paradigm.

Variation in Singaporean English has been the focus of a number of papers. Richards (1977) describes Singaporean English in terms of a Low-Mid-High speech continuum which allows both for distinctions between formal and informal registers and for the expression and identification of social position. Richards and Tay (1981) describe variation in terms of well-formedness (which includes not merely grammatical well-formedness but speech act rules as well) and functional elaboration. They are careful to distinguish between a learner variety (or a developmental continuum) and a non-learner variety (or a non-developmental lectal continuum). Tay (1979) describes variation not only along use variables but also user variables such as age, sex, proficiency, attitudes, role and linguistic background. These descriptions are based on observations and experience as a native Malaysian and a nativised Singaporean. Platt's analysis of variation in Singaporean English is a quantitative analysis, following the methodology used by Labov and Trudgill. Phonetic, phonological, morphosyntactic and syntactic variables have been investigated (Platt and Weber 1980) and a certain degree of systematicity is indicated. In his case study in this volume, Platt discusses variables such as the indefinite and definite article, BE as copula and auxiliary, the third person singular present tense and the plural.

Although there is now a significant body of research on Singaporean/ Malaysian English, certain gaps are evident. It is hoped that future research will focus on these neglected areas: discourse features, code mixing, Singaporean/Malaysian literature, and attitudes towards varieties of English.

The Philippines

Of the Southeast Asian countries, the Philippines has perhaps produced the most comprehensive research on an indigenised variety of English. While there are noticeable gaps in the research on Singaporean English, as mentioned above, there is an impressive breadth in the research on Philippine English.

Many different themes are covered in the research: theoretical and methodological issues in the study of new varieties of English (Llamzon 1984), the status of English (Pascasio 1984; Sibayan 1985), discourse patterns in Philippine fiction and poetry in English (Gonzalez 1985), stylistic under-differentiation and insecurity in written Philippine English (Gonzalez 1983, also this volume), structural features and styles of written and spoken Philippine English of the mass media (Gonzalez 1985, also this volume), and code-mixing (Bautista 1974; Marasigan 1983), to name but a few areas.

Three themes which should be of methodological interest have been selected for analysis in this overview: attempts to characterise a distinct Philippine variety of English, variation in Philippine English, and code-mixing.

The existence of an autonomous indigenised variety of English in the Philippines was first documented by Llamzon (1969) who defined the emerging or emergent characteristics of English spoken by the educated élite of the Philippines as Standard Filipino English. Gonzalez (1972) questions Llamzon's use of the word 'standard' as well as his assumptions that a large enough group of first language speakers exists in the Philippines (see also Gonzalez 1985; Llamzon 1984). He points out that even among the élite, the substratal first language of a speaker is almost always recognisable, so that one could speak of a Bisayan or Ikokan or Tagalic variety of English rather than a standardised Philippine variety. Gonzalez, however, does not deny the existence of distinctive characteristics in the Philippine variety of English and in his own research (Gonzalez and Alberca 1978; Gonzalez 1985) he recognises that local features of pronunciation and grammar which have become common are no longer construed as errors (Gonzalez 1983), but have become legitimised features of Philippine English. Gonzalez defines 'standard' more rigorously than Llamzon: features of written and spoken Philippine English have to recur several times in the speech of several people to qualify as standard and only the mass media are chosen for analysis. Detailed characteristics of the phonological, lexical, morphological, syntactic and stylistic features of written and spoken Philippine English in the mass media are discussed in Gonzalez and Alberca (1978), Gonzalez (1985, this volume).

Variation in Philippine English has been studied in terms of stylistic variation (Gonzalez 1985, also this volume) and significant differences between generations have been observed with regard to the mastery of English phonology (Gonzalez 1984a). Gonzalez' definitions of formal versus informal writing and casual versus careful speech are methodologically important. For example, his criteria for informality are: use of nickname, a series of sentences and phrases separated by three periods, contractions and code-switching to establish familiarity and rapport. The study of variation across generations (Gonzalez 1984a) is important for the light it sheds on how to determine whether the standard of English has been deteriorating, a concern shared by all countries in Southeast Asia.

Of the studies on code-mixing, Bautista (1974) and Marasigan (1983) are methodologically significant. Bautista provides a typology of Tagalog-English code-switching (Mix-mix), establishes patterns and constraints in code-switching and indicates the main similarities and differences between Tagalog and English structure that facilitate or inhibit code-switching. Marasigan (1983) offers for the first time a quantitative metric for classifying the features of Mix-mix and highlights some characteristics of what might aptly be called 'Philippine creole'.

Indonesia

Unlike Singapore, Malaysia and the Philippines, English in Indonesia is not a second but a foreign language. This partly explains why so little research has been carried out on the sociolinguistic aspects of English in Indonesia. Whatever relevant research there is covers the following themes: status, domains of use, attitudes towards English, and nativisation.

The status of English in Indonesia is that of a foreign language (Halim 1985; Sadtono 1976). Sadtono shows from historical evidence how the status of English has progressed from just one of those foreign languages into the first foreign language. The 'foreignness' of English is explained by both Halim and Sadtono as follows: it is not part of the linguistic repertoire of Indonesia and Indonesians (Halim 1985: 20); and it does not occupy a position in most respects equal to the first language (Sadtono 1976:5). Halim (1985:20–21) even predicts that it is unlikely that English will ever gain second-language (L2) status because the Indonesians in general feel that the Indonesian language fully serves all the functions of language in Indonesia.

The domains in which English is currently used in Indonesia are typically public domains: government, training and learning especially in science and technology, international and business transactions and the mass media (Halim 1985: 8–11, 21–4). However, English is also used as a language of wider communication and it is very likely that the use of English in Indonesia will expand to include four additional directions: as a *lingua franca* between Indonesians and foreigners and among foreigners in Indonesia, as a *lingua franca* in Southeast Asia, as a means of career development, and as an alternative source of information. Most of the subjects in Halim's study agreed with the opinion that the use of English in Indonesia is at present increasing and also that it has been increasing in the last five to ten years.

Most of the motivating factors for learning English in Indonesia as reflected in the objectives of the teaching of English in the high school curriculums are said to be 'instrumental', that is, a means of achieving goals which are more economic than sociocultural in nature. In Halim's small empirical study, very few teachers considered their English proficiency to be very good.

Nababan's exploratory work on the nativisation of English in Indonesia has already been mentioned. Although some of the assumptions he makes are controversial, they are important because only further research can prove them to be valid or otherwise. Two such assumptions are: (1) non-native English consists of only one variety, whereas native English displays a complete range of varieties (dialects, sociolects, functiolects and chronolects) (Nababan 1983: 114); (2) pidgin and creole Englishes are not varieties of English but separate codes of language. Lowenberg (1984: 151–177) studies nativisation in Indonesia in terms of form and function and concludes that even in a performance variety, English undergoes considerable nativisation in the contexts of the culture and situation in which it is used. Such nativisation is generally restricted to certain domains in which English is in complementary distribution with other foreign languages, especially Sanskrit.

Thailand

The pedagogical motivation behind most of the research on English in Thailand has already been mentioned. It was only in the 1970s that sociolinguistic considerations found a place in studies of English in Thailand. Thus Phinit-Aksorn (1973) in a tagmemic contrastive analysis of English and Thai question constructions points out differences arising not just from the code itself but also from sociocultural considerations; for example, a Thai child asking an adult a question must use an indirect form because of politeness constraints which require the choice of appropriate words and structures. In the 1980s greater awareness of the sociolinguistic aspects of English led researchers to discuss the following themes: the status of English, the domains of its use, attitudes towards English, the relationship between language and culture, and nativisation.

The status of English in Thailand has always been that of a foreign language; in the 1980s its importance as an international language for Thailand has also been recognised. (Pornpimol 1984; Debyasuvarn 1981). If the findings of Shaw (1981) are correct, it would appear that English has gained considerable prestige in Thai society, in addition to being a tool for higher education.

Pornpimol (1984: 93–8) lists six domains in which English is currently used in Thailand: (1) the educational system: most textbooks in higher education are still published in English; (2) government agencies; (3) the private sector; (4) the élite community in Thailand; (5) the media; (6) publications. It is significant that these are all public domains and there apears to be little English used in the more private domains such as the home or in personal interaction (see also Shaw 1981: 113).

Studies on the attitudes of Thai speakers towards English have been few and far between and the sample sizes are not large enough to be representative of all Thai speakers of English. Sindhavananda et al. (1980), in a study of first-year students at Thammasat University in Bangkok, found that 97 per cent believe English to be essential for upward mobility in Thailand. Shaw (1981), in a study of 313 final-year Bachelor of Arts degree students in Bangkok also found positive attitudes towards English. However, when asked to describe the English used by their educated speakers as akin to British English, American English, Australian English, or a variety unique to Thailand, the students were quite divided (Shaw 1981: 119).

Studies by Warie (1979) and Sukwiwat (1981, 1983) show the interrelatedness of language and culture by documenting misunderstandings between Thai and other speakers of English arising not so much from lack of proficiency in English but from cultural differences. These studies, however, lack a proper theoretical framework and no attempt is made at a typology of these cultural differences. Warie (1977) also discusses code-mixing between Thai and English and the nativisation of English lexemes.

The existence of a unique Thai variety of English is hinted at in Sukwiwat (1983) and fully developed in Pornpimol (1984). The latter discusses nativisation by (a) examining the specific characteristic of Thai English resulting from direct influence of the native language, Thai and (b) discussing Thainess in Thai English in terms of style and discourse. Pornpimol's conclusions are that the Thainess in Thai English includes transfer, shifts, lexical borrowing, hybridisation and reduplication. In terms of style and discourse, the Thainess in Thai English is seen in the use of pretentious words, wordiness and modes of address. Examples are taken from novels, short stories and newspaper articles.

Hong Kong

Like Indonesia and Thailand, studies on the sociolinguistic aspects of English in Hong Kong are few and far between. Four themes will be reviewed very briefly here: the status of English in Hong Kong, the domains in which English is used, the features of English spoken in Hong Kong, and code-mixing.

The status of English in Hong Kong is unique in that it does not correspond strictly to either a second or foreign langue model (Luke and Richards 1982). Although both English and Chinese have equal official status (Luke and Richards 1982; Platt 1982a), English is clearly the language of power while Cantonese is the language of solidarity (Cheung 1984) or a powerful symbol of ethnicity (Luke and Richards 1982).

English is used mainly in the public domains: English-medium schools; employment, especially in the higher paid jobs; media and entertainment; and the legal system. In transactions there is more Cantonese than English (Platt 1982a). Using English in intra-communication, that is, within the fairly homogeneous Chinese community, is regarded as being in very bad taste, culturally speaking (Cheung 1984).

It should be clear from the preceding paragraphs that there is no social motiviation for the indigenisation of English in Hong Kong. Thus, English spoken in Hong Kong has been considered either a learner's language, a developmental rather than a lectal continuum (Platt 1982a), or is described in terms of a cline of bilingualism (Luke and Richards 1982). The only attempt to characterise the phonetic and morphosyntactic features of English spoken in Hong Kong (Platt 1982a) does not appear to capture the most essential characteristics of this variety of English, which are register underdifferentiation and code-restrictiveness (Luke and Richards 1982).

Perhaps the most important area of research on English in Hong Kong, however, is the study of code-mixing. The frequent mixing of English and Cantonese in the speech of Hong Kong Chinese is well attested but disliked by the speakers themselves and the education authorities alike. Gibbons (1979a, 1979b, 1983) indicates that an ambivalent attitude towards this code-mixed variety known as 'Mix' appears to exist among its users. There is expressed hostility towards 'Mix' but there appears to be evidence that it is a useful, culturally-neutral choice falling between English and Cantonese and that it may in fact, therefore, have covert status in the community. The educational authorities, however, appear to be anxious to discourage the use of this mixed code, especially by teachers. For example, the Curriculum Development Committee of the Hong Kong Educational Department is in the process of preparing an English–Chinese glossary of terms commonly used in the teaching of various subjects in secondary schools, so that teachers can teach in Cantonese rather than in a mixed code in Cantonese-medium schools. The effect of this on code-mixing will be evident only in due course.

Future directions for research on English in Southeast Asia

From the case studies in this volume by Platt, Gonzalez and Lowenberg, and from the works cited in this article it is evident that much research has already been carried out in the region. However, it should be equally evident from this overview that we are still a long way from meeting what Tay (1985, 1986) calls the 'minimum requirements' in the study of new Englishes. For instance, the following questions central to the study of New Englishes remain largely unanswered: What are the discoursal features characteristic of each of the varieties of English in Southeast Asia? What are the linguistic and communicative characteristics of code-switching and code-mixing in Southeast Asia and how can these be integrated into the study of varieties of English? What is a suitable framework for describing the bilingual's creativity if it is not to be treated simply as 'fossilised interlanguage' or 'discourse accents' (Kachru 1986)? What framework is powerful enough to account for differences in English arising from differences in style and medium (formal and informal, spoken and written)? What does intelligibility mean when applied to new varieties of English and how can it best be measured? How does one compare varieties of English if it is inadvisable to describe non-native varieties in terms of native ones? How can sociolinguistic research be made relatable and more relevant to the pedagogical norms of English which, after all, must be the most important question for educators in developing countries such as the Southeast Asian countries covered in this overview?

If these important research questions are to be given insightful answers, it would seem that the first step to take is to question existing paradigms and to evolve new typologies, as Gonzalez has done in his case study in this volume. In particular, we need to re-examine pet assumptions about the relationship between native and non-native varieties of English, the relevance and adequacy of the lectal continuum approach, and the differences between adult, stable varieties of English in Southeast Asia and their less stable manifestations in genuine interlanguage and child language. Along with a re-examination of these assumptions, a more balanced view of the methods used in sociolinguistic research would seem essential, a view which recognizes the value not only of empirical and quantitative research but also of the intuitions and observations of scholars native to the region. All these call for better team work, the kind of team work that recognises equal partnership not only between native and non-native speakers of English but, perhaps even more importantly, between specialists in language and specialists in literature (see, for example, Thumboo 1985).

The study of English is bound to be much richer if it combines the insights of both those who use it as their only code as well as those who use it as only one of several codes, those who are adept at analysing the language and those who, by their literary creativity, are particularly aware of the finer subtleties of the language.

REFERENCES

Asmah, O. 1983. The roles of English in Malaysia in the context of national language planning. In Noss (ed.) 1983.

Bautista, L. 1974. *The Filipino Bilingual's Competence: a Model Based on an Analysis of Tagalog – English Code-Switching*. Unpublished PhD thesis, Ateneo de Manila University – Philippine Normal College Consortium.

Bloom, D. 1986. The English Language and Singapore: A Critical Survey. In Kapur, B. K. (ed), *Singapore Studies: Critical Surveys of the Humanities and Social Sciences*. Singapore: Singapore University, pp. 337–458.

Chaiyaratana, C. 1961. *A Comparative Study of English and Thai Syntax*. Unpublished PhD thesis, University of Indiana.

Cheung, Y. S. 1984. The uses of English and Chinese languages in Hong Kong. *Language Learning and Communication* 3 (3): 273–83.

Crewe, W. J. 1977a. *Singapore English and Standard English: Exercises in Awareness*. Singapore: Eastern Universities Press.

(ed.) 1977b. *The English Language in Singapore*. Singapore: Eastern Universities Press.

Debyasuvarn, M. L. 1981. Will EIIL succeed where ESL and EFL fail? In Smith (ed.) 1981, pp. 83–93.

Gibbons, J. 1979a. Codemixing and Koinéising in the speech of students at the University of Hong Kong. *Anthropological Linguistics* 23 (3): 113–23.

1979b. U-gay-wa: a linguistic study of the campus language of students at the University of Hong Kong. In Lord, R. (ed.) 1979, *Hong Kong Language Papers*. Hong Kong: Hong Kong University Press, pp. 3–43.

1983. Attitudes towards language and codemixing in Hong Kong. *Journal of Multilingual and Multicultural Development* 4 (2 and 3): 129–47.

Goh, Y. T. 1983. Students' perception and attitude towards the varieties of English spoken in Singapore. In Noss (ed.) 1983, pp. 251–77.

Gonzalez, A. B. 1972. Review of Teodoro A. Llamzon's *Standard Filipino English*. *Philippine Journal for Language Teaching* 7 (1 and 2): 93–108.

1979. Cultural content in English language materials in the Philippines: A case study of linguistic emancipation. *Philippine Journal of American Studies* 1(1): 98–107.

1983. When does an error become a feature of Philippine English? In Noss (ed.) 1983, pp. 150–72.

1984a. Philippine English across generations: the sound system. *DLSU Dialogue* 20 (1): 1–23.

(ed.). 1984. *PANAGANI: Essays in Honor of Bonifacio P. Sibayan on His Sixty-Seventh Birthday*. Manila: Linguistic Society of the Philippines.

1985. *Studies on Philippine English*. Singapore: Regional English Language Centre Occasional Papers no. 39.

Gonzalez, A. B. and Alberca, W. 1978. *Philippine English of the Mass Media*. Manila: Research Council, De la Salle University.

Gupta, A. F. 1986. A standard for written Singapore English? *English World-wide* 7 (1): 75–99.

Forthcoming. *Acquisition of Diglossia in Singapore English*.

Halim, A. 1985. *The Status and Role of English in Indonesia*: A Report Prepared for the United States Information Service, Jakarta.

Kachru, B. B. 1986. The bilingual's creativity and contact literatures. In Kachru, B. B. (ed.) 1986, *The Alchemy of English: The Spread, Functions and Models of Non-Native Englishes*. Oxford: Pergamon, pp. 159–73.

Kreutrachu, F. L. 1960. Thai and English: A Comparative study of Phonology for Pedagogical Applications. Unpublished PhD thesis, University of Indiana.

Lee, K. C. 1983. *Language and Language Education*. Singapore: Singapore University Press.

Lekawatana, *et al.* 1969. *A Contrastive Study of English and Thai*. Ann Arbor MI. [Contrastive Analysis Project].

Le Page, R. B. 1984. Retrospect and prognosis in Malaysia and Singapore. *International Journal of the Sociology of Language* 45: 113–26.

Llamzon, A. 1969. *Standard Filipino English*. Manila: Ateneo University Press.

1977. Emerging patterns in the English language situation in Singapore today. In Crewe (ed.) 1977b, pp. 34–45.

1983. Essential features of new varieties of English. In Noss (ed.) 1983.

(ed.) 1983. *Varieties of English and Their Implications for ELT in Southeast Asia*. Singapore: SEAMEO RELC. [Occasional Papers No. 29].

1984. The status of English in metro Manila today. In Gonzalez (ed.) 1984, 106–21.

Lowenberg, P. H. 1984. English in the Malay Archipelago: Nativisation and Its Functions in a Sociolinguistic Area. Unpublished PhD thesis, University of Illinois.

Luke, K. K. and Richards, J. C. 1982. English in Hong Kong: Function and Status. *English World-Wide* 3 (1): 47–64.

Marasigan, E. 1983. *Code-switching and Code-mixing in Multilingual Societies.* Singapore: Singapore University Press.

Nababan, P. W. J. 1983. The non-native variety of English in Indonesia. In Noss (ed.) 1983, pp. 113–24.

Namtip, A. 1980. EFL Planning in Thailand: a Case Study in Language Planning. Unpublished PhD thesis, Georgetown University.

Noss, R. B. (ed.) 1982. *Language Teaching Issues in Multilingual Environments in Southeast Asia.* Singapore: Singapore University Press. [RELC Anthology Series, No. 10].

(ed.) 1983. *Varieties of English in Southeast Asia.* Singapore: Singapore University Press. [RELC Anthology Series No. 11].

(ed.) 1984. *An Overview of Language Issues in Southeast Asia: 1950–1980.* Singapore: Oxford University Press.

1986. *The Status and Role of English Language in ASEAN Countries: a Regional Assessment.* Research Report Prepared for the US Information Agency.

Pascasio, E. M. 1984. Philippine bilingualism and code-switching. In Gonzalez (ed.) 1984, pp. 122-34.

Phinit-Aksorn, V. 1973. *Tagmemic Contrastive Analysis of Some English and Thai Question Constructions.* Unpublished PhD thesis, Univeristy of Pittsburgh.

Platt, J. T. 1977a. The sub-varieties of Singapore English: their sociolectal and functional status. In Crewe (ed.) 1977, pp. 83–95.

1977b. The Creoloid as a special type of interlanguage. *Interlanguage Studies Bulletin* 2 (3): 22–38.

1979. Variation and implicational relationships: copula realization in Singapore English. *General Linguistics* 19 (1): 1–14.

1980. Multilingualism, Polyglossia and code selection in Singapore. In Afendras, E. A. and Kuo, E. C. Y. (eds.), *Language and Society in Singapore.* Singapore: Singapore University Press, pp. 63–83.

1982a. English in Singapore, Malaysia and Hong Kong. In Bailey, R. W. and Görlach, M. (eds.), *English as a World Language.* Ann Arbor MI: University of Michigan Press, pp. 384–414.

1982b. The Singapore English speech continuum: system in the acquisition of morpho-syntax. *Australian Review of Applied Linguistics* 5 (1): 1–8.

Platt, J. T. and Weber, H. K. 1979. The position of two ESL varieties in a model of continuity and tridimensionality. In Richards (ed.) 1979, 112–30.

1980. *English in Singapore and Malaysia: Status, Features, Functions.* Kuala Lumpur: Oxford University Press.

Pornpimol, C. 1984. A Sociolinguistic Study of an Additional Language: English in Thailand. Unpublished PhD thesis, University of Illinois.

Richards, J. C. 1977. Variation in Singapore English. In Crewe (ed.) 1977b, pp. 68–82.

Richards, J. C. and Tay, M. W. J. 1977. The *la* particle in Singapore English. In Crewe (ed.) 1977b, pp. 141–56.

1981. Norm and variability in language use and language learning. In Smith (ed.) 1981, pp. 40–56.

Rudhavanich, P. 1967. Comparative Study of English and Thai Suprasegmental Phonemes. Unpublished PhD thesis, Columbia University, NY.

Sadtono, E. 1976. Problems and Progress in Teaching of English as a Foreign Language in Indonesia. Paper read at International Reading Association Sixth World Congress on Reading. Singapore: August 17–19, 1976.

Shaw, W. D. 1981. Asian Student Attitudes Towards English. In Smith (ed.) 1981, pp. 108–22.

Sibayan, B. P. 1985. Status and Role of English and Filipino. MS Manila.

Sindhvananda et al. (eds.) 1980. English and the Social Needs at the University Level. Bangkok: Thammasat University Press.

Smith, L. E. (ed.) 1981. English for Cross-Cultural Communication. Hong Kong: Macmillan Press.

Sukwiwat, M. 1981. Crossing the cultural threshold: a challenge to users of EIL. In Smith (ed.) 1981, pp. 216–24.

1983. Interpreting the Thai variety of English: a functional approach. In Noss (ed.) 1983, pp. 190–210.

1985. The Status and Role of English in Thailand. A Report Prepared for the United States Information Service.

Tay, M. W. J. 1979. The uses, users and features of English in Singapore. In Richards (ed.) 1979, pp. 91–111.

1982. The phonology of Educated Singapore English. English World-Wide 3 (2): 135–45.

1984. Trends in Language, Literacy and Education in Singapore. Singapore: Department of Statistics. Census Monograph No. 2.

1985. Comments and replies (about the lectal classification of non-native varieties of English). World Englishes 4 (3): 387.

1986. Lects and institutionalised varieties of English: the case of Singapore. Issues and Developments in English and Applied Linguistics 1: 93–107.

Tay, M. W. J. and Gupta, A. F., 1983. Towards a description of Standard Singapore English. In Noss (ed.) 1983, pp. 173–89.

Thanyarat, P. 1984. Thai students' encounters with English: two common situations conducive to improper response. PASAA 14 (2): 20–31.

Thumboo, E. 1985. English literature in a global context. In Quirk, R. and Widdowson, H. G. (eds.) English in the World: Teaching and Learning the Language and Literatures. Cambridge: Cambridge University Press, pp. 52–60.

Tongue, R. K. 1974. The English of Singapore and Malaysia. Singapore: Eastern Universities Press.

Wangsotorn, A. 1980. UNESCO-RELC Conference on Language Teaching Issues in Multilingual Environments in Asia and Oceania. Mysore.

Warie, P. 1977. Some aspects of code-mixing in Thai. Studies in the Linguistic Sciences 7 (1): 21–40.

1979. Some Sociolinguistic Aspects of Language Contact in Thailand. Unpublished PhD thesis, University of Illinois.

Wong, I. F. H. 1981. English in Malaysia. In Smith (ed.) 1981, pp. 94–107.

23

Stylistic shifts in the English of the Philippine print media

ANDREW GONZALEZ

Background

Philippine English, as one of the New Englishes, has been carefully studied in terms of its structural features (Llamzon 1969; Alberca 1978; Gonzalez and Alberca 1978). Llamzon studied oral and written varieties, while Alberca concentrated on oral and written varieties in the mass media, using data from radio and TV and from print (newspapers and weekly periodicals). Llamzon compared different styles of oral English (formal, i.e., the equivalent of a formal reading style; and informal); so did Alberca in drawing a distinction between newscasts and talk-shows on TV as oral varieties, and between different journalistic styles as written varieties. Newscasts were considered to be formal oral varieties (equivalent to careful reading style) and talk-shows to be informal oral varieties. Of the written varieties, news stories were considered to be formal varieties, whereas feature articles and columns[1] were considered to be informal varieties.

In these seminal works on style, some attempt was made at frequency counts of the incidence of certain features, to demonstrate stylistic differences empirically. Subsequently, Gonzalez (1982) reported a more careful study of style, pointing out qualitative differences and using examples from different types of journalistic writing.

In an attempt to examine features of Philippine English at the discourse level, I also examined different works of Philippine literature in English, using samples of major authors (Gonzalez 1983). I came to the conclusion that because of the academic roots of Philippine literature in English and the influence of British and American literature, little if any of the discourse conventions or other linguistic features from traditional folk (oral) literature in the first language remained, so that, at least in this genre, the domination of the second (colonial) language was complete.

In the stylistic study reported in Gonzalez (1982), only two styles were differentiated: formal and informal. Code-switching was subsumed under the informal style, since one of the main functions of code-switching in social usage (especially among well-educated Filipinos who are competent in both Filipino and English) is to establish rapport with the interlocutor and to render the situation informal. In this same study, I likewise called attention to the 'stylistic underdifferentiation' of the Philippine English of the print media. In other words, because of the way that Filipinos have acquired English (in a formal school setting) and the content of the English syllabi throughout their schooling in English, the style they are most familiar with and have mastered is what I called the classroom variety of English or, more properly, the 'compositional' style of Philippine written English, with its characteristic features of lexis, phraseology, syntactic constructions and discourse patterns. A corollary was what I called the 'stylistic insecurity' of educated Filipino writers, in the sense that when they attempt writing of a less formal nature, they often switch styles within the same discourse. The shift is often from informal to formal, the latter being the style that they are most comfortable with. One is thus confronted with the phenomenon in Philippine life where people speak as if they were reading a formal essay. An extreme example of this style of speaking occurs when someone giving an oral presentation refers to himself or herself as 'the undersigned' or, semi-facetiously, as 'yours truly'.

In this essay, I have focused exclusively on stylistic shifts in the Philippine printed media, to discover the incidence of such shifts in different types of journalistic writing and to arrive at a typology of shifting as it actually occurs in contemporary Philippine English. In the process, I decided that it was necessary to posit more than two styles (i.e., more than simply 'formal' and 'informal' styles) in order to account for the data.

Methodology

Sources

Since the change of government in the Philipines in February 1986, there has been a proliferation of daily newspapers, in addition to weekly periodicals of a popular nature, which continued even during the period when there was control of the press.

One issue each of 14 daily newspapers was examined (during the period from 23 December 1986 to 22 January 1987), and 12 weekly periodicals of a popular nature were likewise included in the data base.[2] Since I was interested only in Philippine English, I excluded from the data to be examined all foreign-authored news stories, and all articles which were either releases from agencies or reprints of articles which had already appeared abroad. All types of journalistic writing were included in the analysis, including letters to the editor and advertisements; in what follows, they will all be referred to as 'articles', for convenience.

Procedure

The individual articles were read carefully to discover, first of all, the general style of the article, initially using Joos' (1969) five-point scale, which defines style in terms of varieties arising from solidarity relations between interlocutors. The five styles moved along a cline of assumed nearness to or distance from the interlocutor on the part of the speaker: intimate, casual, consultative, formal and frozen. The identification of the general style of the article was made on the basis of the researcher's native speaker intuition of Philippine English, as well as his knowledge of different styles of British and American English in literature and the mass media. Then examples of shifting were identified, again on the basis of the researcher's intuitions. Finally, a series of quantitative analyses were performed on the data.[3]

Results

Towards a typology

As the analysis proceeded, it soon became evident that Joos' stylistic categories had to be changed in order to take account of the specific sociolinguistic situation in a multilingual community such as the Philippines. The formal colonial language still prevails in certain domains but, on the other hand, the national language is extending its domains beyond its traditional ones. Moreover, in this multilingual situation, a number of vernaculars are still used in the home, according to the native or first language of non-Tagalogs or immigrants into the Tagalog-speaking areas. Thus, the Filipinos are 'intimate' in the vernacular, or home language, or in Filipino[4] if they are speaking to someone not of the same ethnolinguistic group as they are. Most likely, they will be 'casual' in the vernacular or in Filipino; usually they will be 'consultative' in Filipino. Only when they are normal or 'frozen' do they switch to English. This behaviour is characteristic of spoken language use in the Philippines. Since the focus in this study is on the use of English in the printed media, the styles are even more limited; really only relatively formal and relatively informal, at least on initial inspection. Within the formal style, however, two degrees of formality could be identified, and there were likewise two degrees of relative informality. Moreover, in journalistic writing, which calls for certain conventions to be followed, there is a variety of frozen writing which accords with specific canons. Thus, it was felt that a different nomenclature would be more suitable: Formulaic (equivalent to Joos' 'frozen'), Formal 1 and Formal 2 (equivalent to Joos' 'formal'), and Friendly 1 and Friendly 2 (with features in common with Joos' 'consultative' and 'casual' but not quite the same, as the examples that follow will show). Moreover, because of the educated Filipino's mastery of both Filipino and English, there is a code-switching variety with specific uses, especially for friendly purposes; in Philippine journalistic practice, this code-switching variety occurs even in formal writing. Code-switching was thus included in the categorisation that was arrived at, as will be illustrated below.

Table 23.1 contains a grid laying out the possibilities of stylistic shifts; an *x* within a cell indicates that the type of shift actually occurred in the data; a blank within the cell indicates that the shift posited did not occur in the data. Further investigation in the future should indicate whether or not this non-occurrence is a typical characteristic of Philippine English or merely a reflection of the limitations of the data used for the study.

In addition, the possibilities of shifting from one style to another were determined *a priori* and then tested. Table 23.2 shows which shifts actually occurred in the data.

Exemplification

From outstanding examples of the more frequent kinds of shift, a simple characterisation of the types of shifts and of their directionality will be exemplified. However, before this characterisation of shifts, the five styles themselves will be illustrated.

Formulaic

Example 1 (News Story)

> Manila, January 12. An Air Force light plane carrying 12 people crashed into the Sulu Sea Saturday evening after developing engine trouble, leaving two dead and five missing, authorities said yesterday. Five others were rescued.
>
> Air Force chief Brig. Gen. Antonio Sotelo said in a statement the BN Islander plunged into waters in the vicinity of Pilas Island about 70 kilometers southwest of Zamboanga City.
>
> Killed were Col. Ramon Fabie, the 3rd Air Division commander based in Zamboanga, and S/Sgt. Teofilo Gabriel. Sotelo said fishermen rescued five and five others were missing . . .
>
> (Colonel dies in crash; five others missing. *Philippine Daily Inquirer*, 12 January 1987, p. 1.)

As example 1 demonstrates, news stories are characterised by objectivity, and in the opening paragraph they answer the questions WHO,

Table 23.1. *Types of possible stylistic shifts according to level and solidarity*

Grammatical levels	Styles (according to cline of distance between speaker and interlocutor)				
	Friendly 1	Friendly 2	Formal 1	Formal 2	Frozen
Lexical	x	x	x	x	x
Phrasal	x	x	x	x	
Clausal	x			x	
Sentential	x	x		x	
Paragraph	x			x	x

Table 23.2. *Style shifts*

	Formulaic	Formal 1	Formal 2	Friendly 1	Friendly 2
Formulaic		→		→	→
Formal 1			⇄	⇄	⇄
Formal 2	→	→		⇄	→
Friendly 1		⇄	⇄		→
Friendly 2		⇄			

The arrow head indicates the direction of the shift; ⇄ indicates shifting in both directions.

WHAT, WHERE, WHEN and HOW. Details are furnished in diminishing order of importance, to give the editor leeway in cutting certain stories short.

However, it should be mentioned that the formulaic style is typical not only of news stories but even of other types of story which in journalism follows certain rather rigid conventions; for example, sports stories follow similar conventions and are especially characterised by sports jargon.

A relatively recent development, not noted earlier, is the use of direct quotations in Filipino in sports stories, often quoting a celebrity or the subject of a story to explain reasons for certain actions. The reasons for this switch are not to establish rapport, but to give local colour to the interview.

Similarly formulaic are advertisements, obituaries, and classified advertisements which all follow certain well-established conventions.

Formal 1

Example 2 (Editorial)

> The negotiators have agreed to adopt the Diokno plan, which asks the negotiators to concentrate on 'food and freedom, jobs and justice'. The plan, formulated by Jose W. Diokno, one of our great thinkers, from his sick bed, assumes a Filipino solution.
>
> What is implied in a Filipino solution? Many things. For example, it implies a government that abjures tyranny and abides by the rule of law.
>
> A Filipino solution to the present conflict cannot accept tyranny in all its forms. As we all know, the NPA gained strength during martial law and the former régime met its fate at EDSA. Tyranny whether from the right or the left is the same and nobody can deny that communism, once it is in power, is tyrannical.
>
> The rule of law follows from the absence of tyranny. The trouble is that while the rule of law is in place, it is often violated, and this has been one of the causes of the insurgency.
>
> A Filipino solution to the problem must never be taken for granted. It must be kept in mind all the time because to adopt a non-Filipino approach is tempting. It would be un-Filipino to liquidate all suspected communists or to round them all up and put them in a concentration camp. It would un-Filipino to use foreign advisers in the campaign against the enemy. Since the causes of the trouble were of Filipino origin, the solution must be Filipino in nature.
>
> (The Filipino solution. *Manila Bulletin*, 14 January 1987, p. 6.)

The style labelled Formal 1 comes closest to the well-written classical essay using the standard principles of rhetoric. It has a good beginning, middle, and end, and is usually expository or hortatory in purpose. Its vocabulary is not that of every day and it is rich in Latinate vocables – and Victorian vocabulary, for it follows the nineteenth-century models of prose on which the average well-educated Filipino has been raised, including the writings of Newman, Carlyle, Ruskin, Arnold and, among Catholics, Belloc and Chesterton. It comes closest to what I earlier (Gonzalez 1982) called the Philippine classroom compositional style, which was taught by presenting students with models for imitation.

In the Philippine printed media, the daily editorial comes closest to this formal style. Published speeches delivered on formal occasions and printed as special features in the editorial page also exemplify this style.

What is interesting in Philippine writing is that this same formal style, which of course is used extensively as a model in thesis and dissertations, as well as in report writing, finds its clearest exponent in legal writing, for which many Filipinos have a special predilection. Thus, once Filipinos begin explaining a point of law, they fall into the legal jargon similar to that used in writing legal briefs. Their writing approaches the formulaic style exemplified earlier, but tempered by the facts of the case, which prevent too much reliance on the formulae. What is interesting, and often amusing, is that even Letters to the Editor manifest the characteristics of this formal style.

Formal 2

Example 3 (Feature Article)

> The Daily Express is screaming bloody murder all the way to its inky grave. Since the PCGG ladled out a death sentence to the daily just after the New Year, scheduling its closure for the end of January, the publication has puffed itself to its full twelve pages to invoke the name of press freedom in its bid to survive.
>
> 'The primary consideration for the closure,' claims Melanio Mauricio, president of the Philippine Daily Express Employees Union (PDEEU), 'is being hurt by the critical stance of the paper. Our criticisms hurt a sensitive agency in the new government and this agency is now hitting back.'
>
> Interviewed at the PDEEU offices near Intramuros, Mauricio went on to stress that a history of articles and columns in the Express had headlined PCGG 'wrongdoings' since the Commission's creation. As he spoke, a man in one corner of the room moved back from a poster he had just completed to admire its crimson and black message: 'PCGG, Killer of Press Freedom.'
>
> Mauricio was not daunted by the suggestion that the concept of press freedom was a touchy one for the Express to latch on to in its hour of need, given the crony reputation that so often propelled copies of the paper on to the bonfires of anti-Marcos boycotters. 'We don't deny,' he said, 'that the Express was not exactly an independent paper during the Marcoses' time. We're trying to shake off that crony image . . .'
>
> And yet, is it all that easy to overlook the days when, as Mauricio himself admitted, the paper was less than independent? The record of how the Express comported itself throughout the Marcos years dies hardest of all.
>
> (Francisco Joaquin. The Daily Expres Grinds To A Halt. *Mr & Ms*, 16–22 January 1987, p. 14.)

Less classical in structure, less characterised by complex syntactic parallelism and balance, but nevertheless using Latinate vocabulary and the jargon of a specific formal register (not merely that of law), Formal 2, although less distant from the interlocutor than Formal 1, is still quite objective and scholarly in tone.

This style is best exemplified by feature articles, even articles dealing with less weighty matters, such as romance and cuisine. These, too, are characterised by the typical classroom composition style of the Philippine school and vary from the more formal style (Formal 1) only in degree of formality of vocabulary and complexity of sentence structures. A serial pattern of simple sentences or, at most, compound sentences, prevails, rather than the classical manifestations of parataxis and protasis-apodosis that are typical of Formal 1 style.

This type of style may use direct quotations in Filipino, or even phrases in Filipino, by way of explaining local reality, but not to establish rapport as in the oral code-switching variety.

Friendly 1

Example 4 (Column)

> Hawaiian resident Ferdinand Marcos denies that he secretly owns five properties in New York. He is right – he actually owns eight properties.
>
> *****
>
> The Japanese Broadcasting Corp. (NHK) also named President Cory as their 'Woman of the Year.' She is the first non-Japanese to receive this award. To the Japanese people we say Banzai! Arigato Gozaymaska.
>
> ******
>
> Idi Amin stated in his will that he wants to be cremated. I guess he wants to get used to the place where he is going.
>
> *****
>
> They say that President Cory is losing her popularity. That's right, only half of the people in Sweden, Tibet, Bermuda, Norway and Istanbul know her.
>
> *****
>
> Filipino boxing great Pancho Villa was inducted into Boxing's Hall of Fame. FM will also be inducted into the Political Hole of Fame.
>
> ******
>
> My date last night said she was on a diet. She ordered a diet Tab, lasagna and 3 orders of halo-halo.
>
> *****
>
> KMU is staging protest strikes again – most of them are Protestants.
>
> *****
>
> At the Ateneo alumni homecoming, I saw so many old faces and new teeth.
>
> *****
>
> FM is being eyed as the next talent for an ad agency. He would be ideal for the 'Ibalik Ninyo Ako sa Pilipinas' commercial.
>
> *****
>
> There is a restaurant in Ongpin that specializes in noodles with American flavor. It is called Mami Vice.
>
> *****
>
> The Land Transportation Commission (LTC) wages war on smoke belchers. Riding in a smoking car is hazardous to your health. Smoking in a car is even more dangerous.
>
> (Gary Lising. Cory is losing popularity – only half of Tibet knows her. *The Manila Chronicle*, 15 January 1987, p. 12.)

Clearly different in tone is the type of writing exemplified above, with its mainly simple monosyllabic/disyllabic vocabulary (the non-learned vocabulary of Anglo-Saxon), the attempt to establish closer social relations, to be friendly without resorting to code-switching.

This kind of style is best exemplified by columns in non-entertainment domains. It is not above gossip, but without teasing or familiar attempts to make comments as asides and to editorialise. It is likewise used for more serious columns of a political or business nature, letters to the editor when the letter writer is not trying to be pompous and learned, and in most advertisements.

Friendly 2

Example 5 (Letters to the Editor)

> Dear Editor,
> That's Entertainment is the most popular TV show these days to young people like me who, whenever we see a young showbiz personality in person, experience a sort of beatific vision. We look at them as if they were saints or gods and goddesses who have descended from Mount Olympus to see what is happening in this ill-fated country of ours which, in spite of the horrible economic crisis, is trying its best to prove that life is, indeed, worth living. Please publish articles about them.
> I am having sleepless nights just thinking about Ronel Victor, Gary 'Boy' Garcia, Jojo Alejar and that new delectable morsel Jovit Moya. How I wish I could have a date with each one of them!
> Well, as the song went in the beautiful Walt Disney full-length cartoon, Cinderella – A Song is a Wish Your Heart Makes.
> > Forlorn,
> > MA. BEATRIZ R. LINDAYA

> We'll try to accede to your request one of these days. A bit of advice to you, my dear Ma. Beatriz. Try to control your excessive day-dreaming about these young showbiz personalities. Force yourself to come down from your ivory tower of treating life as if it were a fairy tale. Try to concentrate on your studies. Judging from your letter, you have an adequate grasp of the English language. Don't you have any inclination of becoming a journalist? Who knows, you may follow the footsteps of Julie Yap-Daza or Kerima Polotan-Tuvera. Ed.
> (TV Fan-Atic. *TV Guide*, 16 January 1987, p. 31.)

Perhaps closest to Joos' (1969) 'casual' is this type of style, which clearly attempts to adopt a conspiratorial tone with the reader, a sharing of secrets, in order to establish rapport and familiarity. It may or may not code-switch, but if there is code-switching, this is definitely intended to heighten the efforts at rapport. It is best exemplified by gossip columns on personalities in society, by the entertainment page and, occasionally, by advertisements.

Shifts in style

Space does not permit an illustration of each one of the different shifts that occurs in the data; the following, however, provide some exemplification.

Friendly 1 to Formal 1

Example 6 (Word level)

> The five Commissioners of the Philippine Racing Commission – all of whom were reportedly recommended by a presidential relative (yes, it's Peping) have changed the whole perspective of racing in the country, and even athletics. The Commissioners are all horse owners, who at the same time will appoint the racing stewards who will *adjudicate* disputes involving horses. Neat no?
> (Luis D. Beltran. Where have all the bright young Filipinos gone? *Philippine Daily Inquirer*, 12 January 1987, p. 4.)

The style of the entire paragraph is Friendly but the use of legalese *adjudicate* shifts the style momentarily to Formal 1.

Friendly 1 to Formal 2

Example 7 (Phrase level)

> This Marine officer was involved up to his eyeballs in what is now known as Irangate or Iranscam or Iranamok. Earlier, Ollie was described by Mr Reagan as 'National hero'. Not very long ago thereafter, however, he was bitterly unburdening himself for having been 'abandoned'. This 'abandonado' *found solace* as a devout Catholic, in the Psalms.
> (Rene Saguisag. President Aquino and Col Oliver North. *Mr and Ms.*, 13 January, 1987. p. 12.)

The Friendly 1 style shifts to Formal 2 *found solace* at the phrase level.

Friendly 1 to Formal 1

Example 8 (Clause level)

> New Year's resolution by this time would seem a little late since we are almost halfway through January. But *we beg the kind indulgence of the readers* as we make New Year's resolutions for our two favourite

government officials: Manila acting Mayor Mel Lopez, Jr and Tourism
Minister Jose Antonio Gonzalez.
(Rowena Macatangay. New Year's resolutions for Lopez Jr, Gonzalez.
The Manila Times, 13 January, 1987, p. 5.)

The Friendly 1 style shifts to Formal 1, *we beg the kind indulgence of
the readers*, at the clause level.

Formal 2 to Friendly 1

Example 9 (Sentence level)

It is possible that the virus is found in the soil. In that case, it may not
be advisable to plant in the soil you are using now. *If you are just growing
a few for your own consumption, maybe you should get uninfected garden
soil and use a drum or some other container for growing your favorite
ampalaya.*
(Zac Sarian. Shall I remove the dead fronds of Staghorn Fern? *Women's
Home Companion*, 14 January 1987, p. 26.)

The Formal 2 style using the impersonal *it* shifts to Friendly 1 at the
sentence level – note the direct address *you* in spite of the Latinate words
consumption, uninfected, container.

Friendly 1 to Formal 2

Example 10 (Paragraph level)

Hers was a behavior admirable and truth would only be hidden by her
statements, something like, 'I never regretted my being a mother, but I
think I would have waited a little longer. Yes, I would still marry the
same person, but not this early . . .'
Recent events, however, changed that perspective. I felt I was caught
into the trap behooving every big star's life. Am I again taken into a
ride?
Sharon Cuneta, in answer to a question about the alleged illicit relations
of her husband with constant co-star Vilma Santos, a more senior star
than her husband, remarked with something like, 'Bahala sila. Buhay nila
'yon, buhay ko ito . . .' What was that? It was a well-thought-answer, at
the height of the promotions of her latest movie, Nakagapos na Puso. A
more well-meaning star would have answered discretely like, 'hindi ako
naniniwala sa mga tsismis na 'yan' to offset the myriad implications of the
statement. It was clear she did not want to kill the rumor.
(Mike Feria. Sharon-Gabby Marital Woes, For Sale?, *Miscellaneous*, 23
December 1986 – 5 January 1987, p. 41.)

The first two paragraphs are in Friendly 1 style, except for the archaic
word *behooving*. The idiom *being taken into a ride* is a Filipinism for

Standard American English *being taken for a ride*. However, the third paragraph switches to Formal 2, with its use of legal *alleged illicit relations* and formal *myriad implications of the statement*. The code-switching to Tagalog is in quotation marks and hence does not break the formality.

Formal 1 to Friendly 2

Example 11

> When confronted about the star status of the kids in That's Entertainment, German Moreno is non-committal. Meaningfully, he smiles and unlike an oracle, he disappoints. At last, he cryptically says, 'I don't want to mention names. But if they persevere, they will succeed. *May kanyakanyang suwerte at panahon 'yan*. How to maintain the public interest is the key to the whole thing.' With this statement, visions of images and youth linger in the popular imagination. In wonder and delight, the public awaits the next star.
>
> (Henry C. Fejero. Showbiz Workshop, *TV Guide*, 16 January 1987, p. 10.)

The paragraph shows Formal 1 style especially in its choice of vocabulary – *non-committal, confronted, cryptically*. Even the quotation is Formal, *persevere*, but shifts to Friendly 2 in code-switching to Filipino.

Formal 2 to Friendly 1

Example 12

> The coming New Year has a very special significance for Mr and Mrs Martin Nievera and Bong Revilla and wife Lani Mercado – being their first celebration as married couples with both Martin and Bong having boys as their first-born thereby gratifying their manhood and certifying the continuity of their respective bloodline. The celebrity mothers had their *date with the stork* last November at the same hospitals (Makati Medical Center), Pops after Lani just as they *trekked the aisle* mid-1986 (Lani in the States last May and Pops at the Santuario de San Antonio in Forbes Park in June). The Nievera's babe has been named Roberto Martin in honor of his paternal *grandpa* and his father and will be christened come February when Mrs Nievera will have recuperated from her caesarian operation. That of the Revillas, or rather the Bautistas (Bong's real surname), will be baptized Bryan.
>
> By this time, Gigi de la Riva, cousin of Marianne, will have *tied the knot* with Marlon Bautista, thus adding another beauty to Ramon Revilla's clan. We understand that the young *starlet* has decided to give up her career to become a full-time housewife. *Wonder if Lani will do otherwise*.
>
> (Y. Cora Pastrana. Showbiz kids and couples in the news at year's end, *Miscellaneous*, 23 December 1986–5 January 1987, p. 42.)

The citation shows Formal 2 style but shifts to Friendly 1 with the choice of friendly words and collocations *date with the stork, trekked the aisle,* paternal *grandpa, tied the knot, starlet,* and in the use of a subjectless sentence as the last one.

Formal 2 to Friendly 2

Example 13

> The Cory leaders in Quezon are legion: Philippine Coconut Authority chairman Oscar 'Oca' C. Santos, deputy Natural Resources Minister Benny Marquez, deputy Local Governments Minister Hjalmar Quintana, provincial board member Federico Agcaoili. There was really no rhyme or reason behind the appointment of somebody with dubious political loyalties.
>
> *****
>
> In Pampanga, former MP Rafael 'Peleng' Lazatin, the UNIDO chairman for Central Luzon, was virtually shoved aside in the campaign for the draft Constitution. Of course, 'Peleng' was given the *consuelo de bobo* in the form of a formal invitation, but he was not really given a role worth his position in UNIDO and Pampanga. Lazatin may be an old man, but nobody can question the intensity of his efforts against the deposed regime of Ferdinand Marcos.
> (Art A. Borjal. Coryista out in the cold, *The Philippine Star*, 12 January 1987, p. 4.)

The first paragraph illustrates Formal 2 style and the second exemplifies Friendly 2 style, especially in the use of nicknames in quotation marks (see also the first paragraph), and a term like *consuelo de bobo* ('a sop', literally, 'consolation of an idiot').

Friendly 1 to Formal 1

Example 14

> Pretty soon the AWF will branch out into stage and film production – not on a commercial basis, mind you, but only to provide their graduates the required *exposures* to be truly *professional*. Johnny and Laurice's efforts are dictated by the *norms of their own environment* – Johnny comes from a highly *motivated* and missionary family, *steeped in social activism* while Laurice's background has been *primarily academic*. Now the tandem is making its dreams come true, so it's not Goin' Bananas forever for Johnny nor Danny Zialcita forever for Laurice.
> (Oscar Miranda. The movies make television viable, *Philippine Daily Inquirer*, 12 January 1987, p. 11.)

Friendly 1 style characterises the paragraph with shifts to Formal 1 in the italicised lexical items and collocations.

Friendly 1 to Formal 2

Example 15

> Remember when rumors spread that even his San Miguel contract was almost 'sequestered'? *Well, his recent TV ad with the APO Hiking Society with the 'reconciliation' theme is proof enough that his affiliation with the company is still as is.*
>
> At the moment, your guess is as good as mine. The most popular Seee baby, Charlie Arceo, has received four offers (repeat . . . four, apat) from independent producers and at his price pa raw. Before the month ends, Charlie must have made up his mind already which to choose and God knows what happens next. *What's ironic is Charlie is also Inday's protege.*
>
> (M. L. Celestial. Strictly Showbiz, *Woman's Home Companion*, 14 January 1987, p. 32.)

The whole passage of two paragraphs is clearly Friendly 1, even bordering on Friendly 2 with the code switching *apat*, Tagalog for 'four', and the Tagalog clitics *pa raw* 'even at his price, according to reports'. However, the first italicised sentence shifts style to Formal 2 and even borders on the legalese language associated with Formal 1. Moreover, except for the contraction *What's,* usually associated with Friendly 1 or 2, the second italicised sentence is also Formal 2.

Quantitative analysis

Various counting procedures were used in order to go beyond mere impressions and to give the investigation a sounder empirical basis. Thus, not only is the occurrence of a particular style or shift indicated by a simple yes or no, as indicated by the xs in table 23.1 or as a mere categorisation (as shown by the arrows in table 23.2) but the frequency of occurrence of all forms of shifting at all linguistic levels was analysed. The results are displayed in table 23.3. In addition, for each of several different types of newspaper article, the average number of sentences in which shifts occurred was calculated, for each linguistic level, as well as the average number of shifts per sentence. Tests of statistical significance were performed where relevant (chi-square and Cramer's V). Only some of the results can be discussed here, due to limitations of space.

Overall frequency of shift type

Table 23.3 shows that, overall, the most frequently occurring shift of style was from Friendly 1 to Formal 2 (39.8 per cent), with shifts from Friendly 1 to Formal 1 occurring with the next highest frequency (18.4 per cent). This was closely followed by shifts from Formal 2 to Friendly 2 (18 per cent).

Table 23.3. *Frequencies of shifts per article at the different grammatical levels, and frequencies and percentages of shift types. (For. = formal, Fr. = friendly)*

	SHIFT-TYPE															
	Formulaic				Formal 1			Formal 2				Friendly 1			Friendly 2	
	For. 1	2	Fr. 1	2	For. 2	Fr. 1	2	For. 1	Fr. 1	2	Formulaic	For. 1	2	Fr. 2	Fr. 1	2
Lexical																
News stories	3		3		16			17				12	19			67
Features			1		36			42				65	147			294
Columns					8			29		2		49	110	5		203
Editorials								16								16
Letters to the editor								12					2		4	18
Captions													3			3
Advertisements													2			2
Programme schedules													4			4
Phrasal																
News stories	1				3			1	1			2				7
Features	12				11	1		7	4			19	6			61
Columns					4			3	3			1	12			24
Editorials								2								2
Letters to the editor															5	5
Captions														1		
Advertisements																1
Programme schedules					1											1

Table 23.3. *Continued*

	SHIFT-TYPE									
	Formulaic		Formal 1		Formal 2			Friendly 1		Friendly 2
	For. 1 2	Fr. 1 2	For. 2	Fr. 1 2	For. 1	Fr. 1 2	Formulaic	For. 1 2	Fr. 2	Fr. 1
Clausal										
News stories										
Features			3		1			1		2
Columns			4		2			1		3
Editorials										
Letters to the editor										
Captions										
Advertisements										
Programme schedules								1		1
Sentence										
News stories	8				1			1		18
Features			10		2		8		5	20
Columns			4		3			4		15
Editorials										
Letters to the editors										
Captions										
Advertisements										
Programme schedules										

Table 23.3. *Continued*

	SHIFT-TYPE														
	Formulaic			Formal 1			Formal 2			Formulaic	Friendly 1		Friendly 2		Total
	For. 1	2	Fr. 1	For. 2	Fr. 1	2	For. 1	Fr. 1	2	Formulaic	For. 1	2	Fr. 2	Fr. 1	
Paragraph															
News stories														2	
Features	2						9			19	1			30	
Columns					1				1			5		6	
Editorials															
Letters to the editors															
Captions															
Advertisements															
Programme schedules															
Total frequency	3	19	8	10	87	1	2	145	19	19	148	319	16	9	805
Percentage	0.37	2.4	1.0	1.2	11.0	0.12	0.25	18.0	2.4	2.4	18.4	39.8	2.0	1.0	100

Table 23.4. *Frequencies and percentages of style-shifts*

Shift From		Shift to:					
		Formal 1	Formal 2	Friendly 1	Friendly 2	Formulaic	Total
Formulaic	Frequency	3		19	8		30
	Row %	10		63	27		4
	Column %	2		7	18		
	Total %	0.4		2	1		
Formal 2	Frequency	2		145	19	19	185
	Row %	1		78	10	10	23
	Column %	1		58	43	100	
	Total %	0.2		18	2	2	
Formal 1	Frequency		10	87	1		98
	Row %		10	89	1		12
	Column %		3	35	2		
	Total %		1	11	0.1		
Friendly 1	Frequency	148	319		16		483
	Row %	31	66		3		60
	Column %	91	97		36		
	Total %	18	40		2		
Friendly 2	Frequency	9					9
	Row %	100					1
	Column %	6					
	Total %	1					
Total	Frequency	162	329	251	44	19	805
	Percentage	20	41	31	5	2	100

The majority of shifts, that is to say, were from a Friendly style to a Formal style.

Table 23.4 shows, more simply, the origin and direction of shifts in the total data. It can be seen that most shifts (60 per cent) came from Friendly 1. They went primarily to Formal 2 (66 per cent), and to Formal 1 (31 per cent). It should also be noted that shifts from Friendly 1 to Formal 1 made up 91 per cent of all shifts to Formal 1, and that shifts from Friendly 1 to Formal 2 made up 97 per cent of all shifts to Formal 2. The second most frequent style shifts (a relatively small percentage, however, i.e., 23 per cent) were those from Formal 2. 78 per cent of them went to Friendly 1. The shifts from Formal 1 to Friendly 1 made up 35 per cent of all the shifts to Friendly 1. The third most frequent shifts (12 per cent) came from Formal 1. 89 per cent of them went to Friendly 1. The shifts from Formal 1 to Friendly 1 made up 35 per cent of all the shifts to Friendly 1.

By destination (i.e., shift to), the largest group of shifts (41 per cent) were to Formal 2. 97 per cent of these shifts came from Friendly 1. Conversely, the second largest group (31 per cent) went to Friendly 1; of these, 58 per cent were from Formal 2 and 35 per cent from Formal 1. The third largest group (20 per cent) went to Formal 1; 91 per cent of these came from Friendly 1.

Overall frequency of linguistic level of shift

Table 23.5 shows the level of shift in each of the different types of journalistic articles that were examined. It can be seen that the highest percentage of shifts occur at the lexical level (75.4 per cent) and that other linguistic levels show remarkably low percentages. Table 23.6 presents the results in a simplified form, which makes it easier to compare the percentage of shifts that occur in each type of article. It should be noted that although the percentage of shifts is high for captions, advertisements and programme schedules, letters to the editor and editorials, these figures result from a relatively low number of occurrences of these types of article, as Table 23.5 shows. Nevertheless, it is interesting that in many of these types of article the shifts occur at only two linguistic levels (lexical and phrasal). The differences between the percentages of shifts at the different linguistic levels was statistically significant ($p < 0.00003$; Cramer's $V = 0.1149$).

News stories, feature articles and columns

News stories, feature articles and columns comprised the largest part of the data. A fuller analysis of the shifts that occurred in each of these types of article was therefore carried out. Tables 23.7, 23.8 and 23.9 show the relative frequencies of shifts for each of these three types of article, together with the percentages of shift that occurred at each linguistic level.

Table 23.7 shows that in news stories, style shifts occurred most frequently at the lexical level (71.28 per cent of the total number of shifts). The next most frequent level at which shifts occurred was the sentence level, though there was a big drop (19.5 per cent). Table 23.7 also shows that the most frequently occurring direction of shift was from Formal 1 to Friendly 1 (23.4 per cent of the total number of shifts in news stories were of this type). Shifts from Friendly 1 to Formal 2 were the next most frequent (21.8 per cent) and the third and fourth most frequent types were from Formal 2 to Friendly 1 (18.19 per cent) and from Friendly 1 to Formal 1 (14.89 per cent). News stories, in other words, have a dual pattern of shifting, both from a more friendly style to a more formal style and from a more formal style to a more friendly style.

Table 23.8 indicates that, as for news stories, shifts occurred most

Table 23.5. *Frequencies and percentages of shifts (per article type) by grammatical level.* (Freq. = frequency)

| | LEVELS | | | | | | | | | | |
| | Lexical | | Phrasal | | Clausal | | Sentence | | Paragraph | | Total |
	Freq.	Column %	Freq.	Column %	Freq.	Column %	Freq.	Column %	Freq.	Column %	Freq.
News stories	67	71	7	7			18	19	2	2	94
Features	294	72	61	15	2	0.49	20	5	30	7	407
Columns	203	81	24	9	3	1	15	6	6	2	251
Editorials	16	89	2	11							18
Letters to the editor	18	78	5	22							23
Captions	3	100									3
Advertisements	2	67	1	33							3
Programme schedules	4	67	1	17	1	17					6
Total frequency	607		101		6		53		38		805
Percentage of total no. of shifts by level	75.4		12.55		0.75		6.58		4.72		100

Table 23.6. *Percentages of shifts (per article type) by grammatical level*

| | LEVELS | | | | | |
	Lexical (%)	Phrasal (%)	Clausal (%)	Sentence (%)	Paragraph (%)	Total (%)
News stories	71			19		100
Features	72	18		5	7	100
Columns	87	10		6		100
Editorials	89	11				100
Letters to the Editor:	78	22				100
Captions	100					100
Advertisements	67	33				100
Programme schedules	67	17	17			100
Percentage of the total shifts by level	75	12.55	0.75	6.58	4.72	100

frequently at the lexical level in feature articles (77.24 per cent); in this type of article, however, the level at which the second highest frequency of shift occurred was the phrasal (14.99 per cent), again with a big drop between the highest and the second highest levels. The most frequently occurring direction of shift was, this time, from Friendly 1 to Formal 2 (38.08 per cent), with a shift from Friendly 1 to Formal 1 occurring with the second highest frequency (20.64 per cent), followed by a shift from Formal 2 to Friendly 1 (14.99 per cent) and from Formal 1 to Friendly 1 (11.79 per cent). In feature articles, therefore, a shift from a more formal style to a more friendly style occurs more frequently than a shift in the reverse direction.

Columns, similarly, had by far the greatest number of shifts occurring at the lexical level. Table 23.9 shows that 80.88 per cent of shifts occurred at this level, followed, after a big decrease, by shifts at the phrasal level (9.55 per cent). Here the most frequently occurring directions of shift were identical to those that occurred in feature articles.

The results were highly significant for news stories and feature articles ($p < 0.001$ for news stories; $p < 0.0000001$ for feature articles), though not for columns.

Average number of shifts in different types of article

The total number of articles examined was 968; of these, 196 exhibited style shifts, leaving 772 articles that did not. Certain types of article occurred relatively infrequently in the data and were therefore omitted from subsequent analysis: these were comic strips, announcements, public service announcements, obituaries, programme schedules and editorials.

Table 23.7. *Percentage of shifts in news stories.* (Freq. = frequency)

Grammatical levels shift-types	Lexical Freq.	%	Phrasal Freq.	%	Clausal Freq.	%	Sentence Freq.	%	Paragraph Freq.	%	Total Freq.	%	Rank order
Formulaic-Formal 1													
-Formal 2													
-Friendly 1	3	3.19	1	1.06					2	2.13	6	6.38	
-Friendly 2							8	8.15			8	8.51	
Formal 1 -Formal 2													
-Friendly 1	16	17.02	3	3.19			3	3.19			22	23.4	1
-Friendly 2													
Formal 2 -Formal 1							1	1.06			2	2.13	
-Friendly 1	17	18.09	1	1.06							17	18.09	3
-Friendly 2													
-Formulaic													
Friendly -Formal 1	12	12.77	2	14.29							14	14.89	4
-Formal 2	19	20.21					1	1.06			20	21.28	2
-Friendly 2							5	5.32			5	5.32	
Friendly 2-Formal 1													
Total	67	71.28	7	7.45	0	0	18	19.15	2	2.13	94	100	

Table 23.8. *Percentage of shifts in feature articles.* (Freq. = frequency)

Grammatical levels / shift-types	Lexical		Phrasal		Clausal		Sentence		Paragraph		Total		Rank order
	Freq.	%	Freq.	%	Freq.	%	Freq.	%	Freq.	%	Freq.	%	
Formulaic-Formal 1	3	0.74									3	0.74	
-Formal 2													
-Friendly 1	1	0.25	12	2.95							13	3.19	
-Friendly 2													
Formal 1 -Formal 2							10	2.46			10	2.46	
-Friendly 1	36	8.85	11	2.7					1	0.25	48	11.79	4
-Friendly 2			1	0.25							1	0.25	
Formal 2 -Formal 1			1	0.25							1	0.25	
-Friendly 1	42	10.32	7	1.72	1	0.25	2	0.49	9	2.21	61	14.99	3
-Friendly 2			4	0.98			8	1.97			12	2.95	
-Formulaic									19	4.67	19	4.67	
Friendly 1-Formal 1	65	15.97	19	4.67							84	20.64	2
-Formal 2	147	36.12	6	1.47	1	0.25			1	0.25	155	38.08	1
-Friendly 2													
Friendly 2-Formal 1							5	5.32			5	5.32	
Total	249	72.24	61	14.99	2	0.49	20	4.91	30	7.37	407	100	

Table 23.9. *Percentage of shifts in columns.* (Freq. = frequency)

Grammatical levels shift-types	Lexical		Phrasal		Clausal		Sentence		Paragraph		Total		Rank order
	Freq.	%	Freq.	%	Freq.	%	Freq.	%	Freq.	%	Freq.	%	
Formulaic-Formal 1													
-Formal 2													
-Friendly 1													
-Friendly 2													
Formal 1 -Formal 2													
-Friendly 1	8	3.19	4	1.59			4	1.59			16	6.37	4
-Friendly 2													
Formal 2 -Formal 1													
-Friendly 1	29	11.55	3	1.2	2	0.8	3	1.2	1	0.4	38	15.14	3
-Friendly 2	2	0.8	3	1.2							5		
-Formulaic													
Friendly -Formal 1	49	19.52	1	0.25							50	19.92	2
-Formal 2	110	43.82	12	4.78	1	0.4	4	1.59	5	1.99	132	52.59	1
-Friendly 2	5	1.99	1	0.4			4	0.4			10	3.98	
Friendly 2-Formal 1													
Total	203	80.88	24	9.55	3	1.2	15	5.98	6	6	251	100	

Table 23.10. *Average number of shifts in 6 different types of article*

Article type	No. of shifts	Total number of articles	Average number of shifts
Features	407	210	1.938
Columns	251	140	1.793
Letters to the editor	23	34	0.676
News stories	94	463	0.203
Advertisements	3	38	0.079
Captions	3	42	0.714

Table 23.11. *Percentage occurrence of shifts per sentence in news stories, feature articles and columns*

Article type	Percentage occurrence of shifts per sentence
News stories	0.273
Features	0.171
Columns	0.111

The average number of shifts for each of the remaining types of article was calculated by dividing the total number of shifts per article type by the total number of articles of that type. Thus, for features, the average number of shifts was 407/210 = 1.938. The figure of 1.938 means that in feature articles, on average, a shift occurred approximately 1.9 times in each article. The average number of shifts for each type of article is shown in table 23.10.

The percentage occurrence of shifts per sentence in the three most frequently occurring types of article was also analysed, that is, in news stories, feature articles and columns. The results of this analysis are shown in table 23.11. The differences between the different types were statistically significant ($p < 0.0006$).

Summary

The findings discussed in this paper may be summarised thus:

1. Five types were needed to distinguish the different styles of Philippine English in the printed media. These were termed Formulaic, Formal 1, Formal 2, Friendly 1 and Friendly 2.

2. The following types of shift occurred in the data:
   Formulaic to Formal 1, Friendly 1 and Friendly 2

Formal 1 to Formal 2, Friendly 1 and Friendly 2
Formal 2 to Formal 1, Friendly 1, Friendly 2 and Formulaic
Friendly 1 to Formal 1, Formal 2 and Friendly 2
Friendly 2 to Formal 1

Although shifts occurred both from a relatively more Friendly style to a relatively more Formal style and vice-versa, a higher proportion of shifts were from a more Friendly style to a more Formal style.

3. Shift types of all kinds and at all levels occur most frequently in the following types of journalistic writing: Features (1.94 shifts per article), Columns (1.79), Letters to the Editor (0.68), News stories (0.20), Advertisements (0.08) and Captions (0.07). Considering the large corpus, the average frequencies are quite small. By and large, then, the present group of journalists in the Philippines (all in Metro Manila) are 'secure' in their abilities to maintain style consistently, albeit with occasional lapses. However, when the corpus is narrowed down to the main article types, the shifts are more frequent (see 4 below).

4. The average number of occurrences of shifts per sentence in the main article types is:

News stories 0.27
Features   0.17
Columns   0.11

In other words, shifts occur on average 27 times in 100 sentences of news stories, 17 times in 100 sentences of features, and 11 times in 100 sentences of columns. At this relatively low level, the stylistic 'insecurity' is more pronounced.

5. By grammatical level, the most frequent occurrence of style shift is at the lexical level (75 per cent) and the phrasal level (12.55 per cent) and the least frequent is at the clausal level (0.75 per cent).

Conclusions

An investigation of this type yields both methodological and substantive insights which may be used for further research and theory building.

Methodologically, in research of this type, as Richard Noss (personal communication) suggests, we must go beyond impression and qualitative description to more rigorous counting and, where applicable, testing for significance and measuring magnitudes of significant differences, to see which occurrences of style shifts are more frequent, and why.

Frequency counting may be done in various ways, the 'delicacy' of counting depending on what we are looking for. Thus, if we are looking at journalistic types (news stories, features, editorials, columns, letters to the editor, advertisements) to see in which types shifts occur most frequently, then a simple count of incidences per article type might be sufficient. If we are likewise interested only in the type of stylistic shift (formulaic to formal or friendly, formal to friendly, friendly to formal, etc.), then a simple counting of incidences of such shift per article might also be sufficient. However, if we are after more refined occurrences within each article, then we must compute the average number of occurrences per 100 sentences of an article out of the total number of sentences in that article and then come up with a percentage; subsequently we must do a summation of averages from article type to article type and then test for statistical significance. Under this average, we would count incidences at all levels and of all types of style shifts.

Substantively, the typology of style shifting looks promising. The question of the non-occurrence of certain types of style shift is interesting. This could be a function of the limitations of the data, or it could mirror reality, showing the systematic nature of different styles and the shifts that are possible. The typology may be used to explain various rhetorical effects. For example, humour may achieve its effect by sudden and unexpected style shifts. Some illustrations of this are given weekly by Derek Davies in his column in the *Far East Economic Review*, which cites gaffes in Asian English, some of which are manifestations of large shifts (jumping two or more 'steps' along the cline rather than merely one). More frequently, perhaps, the more common occurrences of shifting from one style to the next is a result of the non-mastery of the different lects of a second language. It is also possible that the typology is more finely discriminating than is, in fact, necessary. The two Formal styles (Formal 1 and Formal 2), and the two Friendly styles (Friendly 1 and Friendly 2) are quite close to each other, and the differences between 1 and 2, in each case, may be too subtle to really cause any kind of surprise in the native speaker-listener.

Most interesting is the occurrence of certain style shifts as opposed to the non-occurrence of others, in terms of directionality. Why is it that it is more common to shift from a friendly style to a formal, even formulaic style? Why is it that in the Philippines, writers seem to be able to hold a consistent formulaic or formal tone better than a friendly one? As we have seen, shifts from friendly styles to formal styles are far more frequent than shifts from formal styles to friendly ones. Is it because Filipino writers feel most secure with the formulaic (and stereotyped) and the formal, since these are the styles they have most competence in, as a result of their schooling? As pointed out earlier, English is learned in the Philippines for the most part in a classroom setting, and mostly for academic purposes. Does the stylistic insecurity of the Filipino, especially with the friendly styles, indicate a lack of real training and practice in this style? Is the aetiology, then, of this insecurity due more to educational gaps than to sociolinguistic reasons?

The dynamics of code-switching have been studied elsewhere (see

Pascasio 1978; Marasigan 1981; Gonzalez 1985; Barrios *et al.* 1977) and the reasons for such code-switching amply documented. Undoubtedly, the same reasons that account for this phenomenon in oral communication apply in written communication as well except, that the audience is larger and invisible. A new phenomenon, however, is the use of quotation marks or long quoted statements in Filipino even in the formal or formulaic style (in sports stories); this is a recent development. In these features, and sports stories, one suspects that the extended quotations in Filipino are not intended so much to establish rapport with the reader as to capture the 'tone' of the interview and to give insight into the speech repertoire and speech uses of the person being interviewed or featured. Code-switching is thus finding new uses in Philippine society.

Where a second language has been learned through a colonial educational system and in a school setting, for school use, its domains and uses are bound to be limited, especially when, during the post-colonial period, there has emerged a competing indigenous language which is expanding its domains, as is the case with Filipino at present.

In such a situation, the stylistic repertoire of the second language speaker becomes quite limited, to really only one or two types of style (of the formulaic and at best the formal type) with little or no opportunity to master the friendly style or even slang and argot, unless the learner has spent some time abroad or unless the learner is widely read in the literature where these different, more informal, casual and even intimate styles are exemplified, either in novels, short stories, or on radio and TV.

Obviously, at higher levels of literary study, syllabi will have to include familiarisation of the learner with these other styles, not so much in order to use them as to be, at least, conscious of them. In this way learners will appreciate better the semiotics of reading novels and literature, or that of watching TV and plays in the second language. As long as English in Philippine life becomes narrowed down to its uses as an international language (a language of wider communication) for diplomacy and for international negotiations, and its use as an academic tool for science and technology, the mastery of only the formulaic and formal styles is more than sufficient for the Filipino. There is little need for the friendly style or the intimate or familiar style in English since he or she has other linguistic resources to call on (in Filipino and the vernacular) for these other styles.

On the other hand, for the printed media, as long as Filipino writers judge it good for their markets and their publications to adopt a more friendly style, then it behooves the writers to become aware of their limitations with this style and either refrain from attempting it or learn to do it well.

Actually, when I did my earlier study on 'stylistic underdifferentiation' (see Gonzalez 1982) and called attention to the linguistic insecurity of most Filipino writers of the printed media, it was a period of relative press control, a period when serious and talented writers more or less absented themselves from writing and when mediocre writers dominated the media. This may explain the distinctly negative impression created by the press then on the seemingly frequent occurrence of these shifts among some second-rate writers. With the political situation significantly changed, and with a proliferation of newspapers and periodicals as a result of the new press freedom and the return of many talented writers to journalism – both those who stayed in the country and those who have now returned from exile – the quality of writing in the Philippine printed media is now good, in spite of the recorded shifts, which are really quite few, relatively speaking, and then confined only to the friendly (non-formal) writing characteristic of features and columns. Actually, as long as the Filipino writers stay with the formal and formulaic style, they do quite well and make themselves free from communication miscues and therefore capable of reaching a larger audience outside of the Philippines through their writing. Perhaps, after all, given the difficulty of mastering these special styles in a second language, the Filipino writer has done relatively well.

The stylistic shifting of Filipino journalists would be typical of any sociolinguistic situation similar to that of the Philippines where the use of the second language is restricted to certain domains and where its learning, of necessity, has had to be limited to one, or at most two, styles. One suspects that as the shifts become institutionalised by becoming widespread, and by not being corrected by copy-editors and proof-readers who themselves are unconscious of the shifts, these will become features of Philippine English. In other words, one cannot expect second language learners of English, no matter how intelligent, to be as sensitive as native speakers are to such shifts, since their exposure to models has been different.

Hence, the stylistic level of words and collocations will become different for each New English, since the speakers of the New English will usually not be conscious of these shifts nor of movements from one level to another. Not only do these 'shifts' (in the eyes of the first language speaker) become characteristic features of the variety, but as they are spread among the users of the second language in the post-colonial situation, then these features become accepted and institutionalised and become part of the New English of the society. This is therefore another area where the New Englishes will become different from the 'Old' English variety.

NOTES

1. The term 'columns' is used in the Philippines as it is in US English, to refer to gossip columns and also to recurrent (sometimes daily) features written by an

acknowledged opinion-maker who makes comments about sundry things, including politics. The usual form is a series of thematically unconnected paragraphs separated by three asterisks.

2. The study is based on a longer and more detailed manuscript which contains details of the printed materials and their sources as well as many more examples of stylistic types and shifts and their tabulation and frequencies. The author may be contacted for copies of this longer study.

The titles of the newspapers/magazines used and their dates of issue are: *Philippine News and World Report* (9–15 January 1987), *The Guardian* (10–16 January 1987), *Malaya* (12 January 1987), *Philippine Daily Inquirer* (12 January 1987) *The Philippine Star* (12 January 1987), *The New Daily Express* (12 January 1987), *We Forum* (12–18 January 1987), *Tempo*, (13 January 1987), *The Manila Times* (13 January 1987), *People's Journal* (13 January 1987), *The Philippine Tribune* (14 January 1987), *Manila Bulletin* (14 January 1987), *The Manila Chronicle* (15 January 1987), *Mr. and Ms.* (16 January 1987), *Miscellaneous* (23 December 1986–5 January 1987), *Prime* (8–14 January 1987), *Women's Journal* (10 January 1987), *Glitter* (10–23 January 1987), *Mr. and Ms. Magazine* (13 January 1987), *Sensation* (13 January 1987), *Woman Today* (14 January 1987), *Women's Home Companion* (16 January 1987), *Mod* (16 January 1987), *TV Guide* (16 January 1987), *Extra Hot* (16 January 1987), and *Kislap* (19 January 1987). Fourteen newspapers and 12 magazines were used; there were a total of 463 news stories, 210 feature stories, 140 columns, 10 editorials, 34 letters to the editor, 42 captions, 38 advertisements, 9 comic strips, 7 programme schedules, 10 announcements, 3 public service notices, and 2 obituaries.

3. I am grateful to Corazon Tiqui, my research assistant, who did the laborious task of counting after I marked incidences of style-shifting in the data and characterised their styles and the shifts in style. With the help of my colleague Luke Moortgat, CICM, director of De La Salle University's Statistical Assistance for Research (STAR) office, she likewise prepared the raw data for statistical treatment and analysis. To them both, my sincere appreciation.

4. Tagolog was made the official language of the Philippines in 1952 and given the new name of Pilipino; since 1987 it has been referred to (in official quarters, at least) as Filipino. Tagalog, or Filipino, is the mother tongue of about 10 million people living in the Philipines, mostly in southern Luzon in an area that includes the capital, Manila.

REFERENCES

Alberca, W. L. 1978. The Distinctive Features of Philippine English in the Mass Media. Unpublished PhD thesis, University of Santo Tomas, Manila.

Barrios, Mary Angela, Castillo, Emma S., Galang, Rosita G., Santos, Pauline C., Tiangco, Norma G., Vergara, Elvira C. and Villamor, Esperanza O. 1977. The Greater Manila speech community: bilingual or diglossic? In Pascasio, Emy M. (ed.), *The Filipino Bilingual: Studies on Philippine Bilingualism and Bilingual Education*. Quezon City: Ateneo de Manila University Press.

Gonzalez, A. B. (FSC) 1979. Becoming bilingual in English in a Philippine setting. A partial report of a Manila sample. In Boey, L. K. (ed.), *Bilingual education.* RELC anthology series no. 7. Singapore: Regional Language Centre, pp. 177–206.

1982. English in the Philippine mass media. In Pride, J. B., (ed.), *New Englishes.* Rowley MA.: Newbury, pp. 211–26.

1983. On English in Philippine literature in English. *Solidarity* 3 (96): 29–42.

1985. *Studies on Philippine English.* Occasional Papers No. 39. Singapore: Regional Language Centre.

Gonzalez, A. B. and Alberca, W. L. 1978. *Philippine English of the Mass Media* Preliminary edition. Manila: Research Council, De La Salle University.

Joos, M. 1969. *The Five Clocks.* New York: Harcourt Brace.

Llamzon, T. A. 1969. *Standard Filipino English.* Manila: Ateneo de Manila University Press.

Marasigan, E. 1981. Creolized English in the Philippines. Paper given at SEAMEO Regional Language Centre, 16th Regional Seminar, 20–24 April.

Pascasio, E. M. 1978. Dynamics of code-switching in the business domain. *Philippine Journal of Linguistics* 9 (1 and 2): 40–50.

24

Variation in Malaysian English: the Pragmatics of languages in contact

PETER H. LOWENBERG

Recent research on the forms and functions of English in Malaysia has tended to focus on the changing status of English there, particularly since the late 1960s, when Malay, renamed 'Bahasa Malaysia', became Malaysia's sole official language and began replacing English as the predominant medium of instruction in the schools. As a result, most analyses of Malaysian English (e.g., Platt and Weber 1980; Wong 1982) have concentrated on a predicted 'deterioration' in the English proficiency of younger Malaysians, which has accompanied diminishing needs to use English. In so doing, these studies have often ignored another outcome of this change in the relative status of English and Malay: the many domains of language use in which these two languages are now coming into increasing contact.

After a brief review of the history of English in Malaysia, this chapter will examine patterns of lexical borrowing from Malay into English and of code mixing and switching between English and Malay by the current Malaysian élites, who still use and set the standards for English usage in Malaysia. It will be shown that an analysis of the forms and functions of these borrowings, mixes, and switches can enhance our understanding of variation in contemporary Malaysian English.

The development of English in Malaysia

English during the colonial period

The sociolinguistic setting of Malaysian English began to develop during the British colonisation, from the late eighteenth until the mid twentieth centuries, of the Malay Peninsula and of present-day Sabah and Sarawak on the island of Borneo. The British established schools, especially in the urban trading centres on the west coast of the Malay Peninsula, where English was first taught and then used as the medium of instruction and of other school activities (Platt, Weber, and Ho 1983). The students in these

364

schools came from the more prosperous families of the indigenous Malays and of the large Chinese and South Asian (Indian and Ceylonese) populations who had been immigrating to the region since before the colonial period.[1] The privileged recipients of this education came to use English increasingly in their daily affairs, with the result that when the British began to withdraw from the area in the late 1950s, English had become the dominant language of the non-European élites, both as a language of power and prestige and as an inter-ethnic link language (see Platt and Weber 1980; Lowenberg in press).

English since the colonial period

At the time of its independence in 1957, the Federation of Malaya, consisting of the Malay Peninsula except for Singapore, adopted as official languages not only English but also Malay. The official rationale for this policy was to solidify the national aspirations of the new nation (Hassan 1975); however, an equally important goal was to improve the status of the Malays, the largest and politically most powerful ethnic group, in their economic competition with the descendants of the Chinese and South Asian immigrants (Le Page 1962; Hua 1983).[2] These non-Malays, especially the Chinese, had during the colonial period gained a significant economic advantage over the Malays, in part due to their concentrations in the urban centres, where they had access to the English-medium schools (Hirschman 1984).

The second half of the 1960s brought implementation of a more radical policy to replace English with Malay as sole official language of the expanded nation of *Malaysia*, established in 1963, and consisting of the previous Federation of Malaya, Sabah and Sarawak and, until 1965, Singapore.[3] In order to promote it as a truly national language, Malay was renamed a more ethnically neutral *Bahasa Malaysia* (literally, the 'Malaysian language'). In 1969, the Ministry of Education initiated a policy whereby all English-medium schools were to become Malay-medium, a process which by the early 1980s was virtually completed nationwide at the primary through tertiary levels of education (Le Page 1984; Watson 1984). English has been retained as the compulsory second language throughout all levels of primary and secondary school, and it still figures prominently as a reading language in higher education, but it now serves as the medium of instruction in extremely few settings (Platt and Weber 1980; Augustin 1982; Le Page 1984).

Variation in educated Malaysian English

One result of this language policy has been a dramatic increase in Malaysians' study and use of Bahasa Malaysia and a corresponding decrease in their use of English, particularly in rural areas (Platt and Weber 1980). This diminishing use of English, especially in the schools, has produced widespread popular concern that the general level of English proficiency among Malaysians is in decline, a concern frequently reflected in English language newspaper headlines such as 'First Aid Needed for Our English' (*New Sunday Times*, 21 April 1985) and 'Decline and Fall of the English Language' (*New Straits Times*, 11 May 1985).

As they have less exposure to English and fewer occasions to use it, many Malaysians' proficiency in standard English does appear to be declining (Platt and Weber 1980; Asmah 1983).[4] Examples (1) and (2) are taken from compositions written in 1985 by graduate linguistics students in the United States soon after their arrival from Malaysia, where their education had been entirely in the medium of Bahasa Malaysia.

(1)   For example, *when the first time I came here*, I did not have enough *vocabularies* . . .

(2)   *One of my instructor in George Mason University* said that when a person learns a language he also learns the culture of the language.

However, preoccupation with an overall decline in English proficiency among Malaysians obscures the fact that English is still widely used by the current Malaysian élites, who were educated in English-medium schools during the colonial or initial post-colonial periods and are still quite proficient in it. Augustin (1982) reports that of the 1.1 million Malaysians who completed secondary school between 1956 and 1970, almost 70 per cent had an English-medium education: 'The educated peninsular Malaysians now in the prime of life and who play leadership roles in government and trade are fairly competent in the use of English for intergroup communication.' These English-educated élites are concentrated in the urban centres of Peninsular Malaysia, where approximately 25 per cent of the population (about one million people) use English 'to communicate among themselves' (Augustin 1982: 251–2), with the result that English remains 'the most indispensible requirement in the achievement of social and economic status' (Asmah Haji Omar, in Platt and Weber 1980: 159). It is these élites who set the norms for English usage as reflected in the major English language textbooks used in the schools (see, for example, Devi 1973; Koh and Leong 1981; Tan 1982).

Nevertheless, the increasing use and status of Bahasa Malaysia is having a marked impact on the English of these élites. The following examples illustrate the variable degrees of contact between these languages along the stylistic continuum of English as used by these speakers, from lexical borrowings in the 'standard' subvariety of Malaysian English,[5] as used in the major English language newspapers, to code-mixing and code-switching in the informal letters and casual conversation of the colloquial subvariety. As will be demonstrated, the pragmatic functions of this borrowing, mixing, and switching likewise vary along this continuum, in all cases reflecting not a decline in English usage, but the adaptation of the norms of English to the political, economic, and sociocultural contexts of contemporary Malaysia.[6]

Standard English: lexical borrowings

Lexical transfer from Malay has been noted in most analyses of standard Malaysian English (Tongue 1979; Platt and Weber 1980; Wong 1981), but it has generally been attributed to the filling of lexical gaps, for which other varieties of English have no denotatively equivalent terms. Examples of such borrowings occur in examples (3), (4), and (5).

(3)   The residents will repair the roofs on a *gotong-royong* basis.
        (*The Malay Mail*, 12 January 1988)
(4)   'I have often been criticised by my friends for easily bowing down to apologise, but I will always do so – it is required by both our religion and *adat*.'
        (quote from political speech, *New Straits Times*, 27 April 1987)
(5)   A carpenter was jailed for five years and ordered to be given six strokes of the *rotan* by the Sessions Court today for possession of heroin. (*New Straits Times*, 5 March 1987)

All of the borrowed terms in these sentences refer to institutions unique to Malay-speaking Southeast Asia: *gotong-royong* is a form of communal cooperation, *adat* is a body of traditional law, and the *rotan* is a rattan cane used in officially sanctioned and administered punishments.

However, the impact on English of the ascending status of Bahasa Malaysia is more evident in 'lexical shifts' (Richards 1979: 14), where Malay words replace English words or phrases which are denotatively, but not connotatively, equivalent. The most striking of these lexical shifts are what Paine (1981: 14) has called 'banner words': 'single words or phrases . . . that are likely to induce a proposition by inference.' Examples of such words in American English are *democracy* and *freedom fighters*, which trigger in most Americans a complex set of values and associations that politicians repeatedly appeal to when seeking support for their positions from the electorate (Parkin 1984; Geis 1987).

In Malaysian English, banner words are frequently borrowed from Bahasa Malaysia, the national language. An example occurs in (6), where the writer supports his opinion regarding broadcast programming by associating it with the popular slogan *Majulah Malaysia!*, or 'Let's advance Malaysia!'

(6)   Well, with the video craze in full swing, I believe RTM [Radio and Television Malaysia] just has to to loosen its belt and start investing

wisely in local programmes to attract viewers. This new path might just
prove its saviour. *Majulah Malaysia!*
(letter to the editor, *New Straits Times*, 11 June 1983)

A more striking use of a Malay banner word transferred to English is
the frequently occurring *bumiputera* (sometimes *bumiputra*) which literally
means 'son of the soil'. This term refers to people considered indigenous
to Malaysia, predominantly the ethnic Malays, but also including other
ethnic groups, especially in Sabah and Sarawak, who are neither Malays
nor descendants of Chinese and South Asian immigrants. It is used in the
context of a large number of economic, political, employment and
educational programmes which favour these indigenous peoples in order
to elevate their socioeconomic status to parity with Chinese and South
Asian Malaysians. The word *Bumiputera*'s roots in Sanskrit, long considered the most classical and scholarly language of the Malay Archipelago
(Alisjahbana 1976), tend to neutralise this deliberate inequity in official
policy while lending it nationalistic legitimacy. Examples occur in the news
report in (7), in the employment advertisement in (8), and in the
newspaper headline in (9), the last of which demonstrates adaptation of
the term to the abbreviations common to Malaysian English (see Tongue
1979; Platt and Weber 1980).[7]

(7)   The special issue of 12.85 million shares to *Bumiputera* investors approved
        by the Trade and Industry Ministry at $1.40 per share is to increase
        Bumiputera shareholders to about 20 per cent of the enlarged capital.
        (*New Straits Times*, 22 July 1983)

(8)   The Company is seeking a qualified and experienced *Bumiputra* executive
        to fill this newly created position based in the Head Office in Petaling
        Jaya . . . Candidates must be *Bumiputras* with good educational back-
        ground . . . (classified advertisement, *The Straits Times* [Singapore], 25
        June 1980, for a position in Malaysia)

(9)   *Bumis* need to have more initiative.
        (*New Straits Times*, 5 December 1985)

The semantic range of *Bumiputera* can vary. Although, as just noted,
the term officially includes not only Malays but also many other ethnic
groups, in the political speech reported in (10) the title of *Bumiputera* is
apparently being restricted to just the Malays.

(10)   Deputy Prime Minister Ghafar Baba has been appointed the head of a
        high-powered committee to review the New Economic Policy (NEP) and
        formulate a new policy to help *Bumiputeras* own 50 per cent of the
        nation's wealth by the year 2000 . . . Encik Ghafar said the new policy
        was expected to 'give *Malays* equality with the other races in the real
        sense of the word'. . . 'I need the support and prayers of all *Bumiputeras*
        in this venture to improve the well-being of *the race*,' he added.
        (*New Straits Times*, 23 March 1987)

Also significant is the official designation of all other Malaysians as *non-Bumiputera*, as in (11), which institutionalises their distinct status in many avenues of economic advancement.

(11)   These studies also cover *non-Bumiputeras* and foreigners in Malaysia.
         (*New Straits Times*, 5 December 1985)

In essence, Malaysians of Chinese and South Asian descent are here being defined in the language of the politically dominant ethnic Malays, illustrating an observation made by Trömel-Plötz (1981, quoted in Kachru 1986: 133) that 'only the powerful can define others and make their definitions stick. By having their definitions accepted they appropriate more power.'

In contrast to this exclusionary force of *Bumiputera*, another Malay banner word often borrowed in English, *rakyat*, has a more inclusive function, especially in the press, where Kachru (1987: 14) observes, 'the aim is to establish, contextually speaking, an identity with the readers.' In traditional Malay, *rakyat* meant 'the rural ethnic Malay population', but in contemporary Bahasa Malaysia it refers to 'the Malaysian people,' as in (12) and (13).

(12)   Reaching out and touching the hearts of the *rakyat*.
         (*New Straits Times*, 1 June 1983)

(13)   Datuk Taib thanked the gathering for supporting him and his policies and urged all to work for the *rakyat* to ensure the Fifth Malaysia Plan was successfully implemented.
         (*New Straits Times*, 24 January 1985)

This extended semantic range of *rakyat* is noteworthy in (13), which reports on a political address given by an ethnic Malay in Sarawak, where in 1980 only 19.8 per cent of the population were Malays (*Europa Yearbook 1987*: 1,801). As with *non-Bumiputeras* above, the Malay borrowing in this context defines a largely non-Malay population in Malay terms.

Though not employing banner words, (14) from neighboring Sabah, where in 1978 only 5.1 per cent of the population were ethnic Malays (*Europa Yearbook 1987*, 1,801), similarly demonstrates the use of Malay borrowings for promoting an identity.

(14)   A night to remember. '*Mengalai begitu dong!*' says the expert to one of the *makchiks*. The sporting *neneks* sang and '*mengalaid*' through the night.
         (*Sabah Times*, 20 June 1980, p.13)

This is the caption to a photograph accompanying a feature article in the women's section of a major newspaper in Kota Kinabalu, the capital of Sabah. The article describes an in-service training course for elderly midwives from remote villages in Sabah. Of particular interest here are the words *nenek* and *makchik*, affectionate Malay terms for 'grandmother' and 'older woman,' respectively. In this article, these Malay words refer to women who are not ethnically Malay, thereby defining them in the terms of the nationally dominant Malays.[8]

Colloquial English: code-mixing and code-switching

In the more colloquial subvariety of Malaysian English, transfer from Malay expands from lexical borrowings to more extensive code-shifts with a broader range of pragmatic functions. In (15) and (16), a popular syndicated cartoonist examines the 'ups and downs of married life' (Lat 1978: 116).[9]

(15)   *bila saya bilang* . . . DARLING I LOVE YOU! *Tapi dia jawab* OH, SHUT UP YOU! Somebody told me *dia ada lain perempuan.*
        I said DARLING I LOVE YOU! But she answered OH, SHUT UP YOU! Somebody told me you have another woman.

(16)   And about the husband who asked for trouble . . . *Saya pulang ke rumah cukup senang hati, but* my *ternampak* lipstick on my *pipi.*
        And about the husband who asked for trouble . . . I came home feeling happy, but my, there was lipstick on my cheek.

In these cases, the primary intent of the shifts appears to be one of engaging the reader's involvement in the episode by conveying the humour through a shared bilingual repertoire.

In the examples in (17), from informal letters written between English-medium-educated ethnic Malay students attending universities in the United States, the reason for code-shifts is to foreground feelings of friendship, rapport, and intimacy.

(17)   I'm trying to study, *tapi tak boleh.*
                                (but I can't.)
        Charleston is so boring *kalau you tak ada.*
                                (when you're not here)
        (Meedin 1985:18)

The extended dinner-time conversation in (18) also occurred among English-medium-educated ethnic Malay university students in the United States.

(18)   Shah: *Apa you tengok tu?* ('What are you watching?')
        Zainal: 'Airwolf'.
        Shah: Ah, *sudah* ('It's over'). . . News in five minutes . . . News *sekarang?* ('now'). Oh, I'm sorry. See, in Texas it's different. Uh, prime time starts at seven.
        Zainal: Seven?
        Shah: And then, you know, the news is at ten, and then they have 'Night Line', and then they have Johnny Carson show at ten-thirty.

> Zainal: I haven't been to Texas.
> Shah: Texas is a very simple state. Very, very wealthy state . . . extremely wealthy . . . Well, to me, anyway, I can see the wealth . . . *Sana macam* ('There is a type of') shopping mall . . . they've got exclusively *orang kaya punya* ('rich people'), and uh, parking, valet parking . . . when you *masuk* ('enter'), red-carpet . . . you *masuk ke dalam* ('go inside'), my God, they, that's expensive place *lah* (emphatic particle), and, see there, in Texas, even the rich people there *pakai* ('wear') jeans and cowboy shirt, but then they wear custom-made cowboy shoes, you know. To have a cowboy boot custom-made costs you about $1,500, $1,800.
> Liza: Why is it so expensive?
> Shah: Custom-made.
> Liza: Yeah . . . but in Malaysia . . .
> Shah: *Itu janganlah* compare! *Janganlah gitu!* ('Don't compare like that! Don't do that')

(Unpublished data collected by Noor Liza Mohd. Isa, Department of Linguistics, Georgetown University)

Shah's initial contribution in this exchange is a question asked in Malay. He then switches to English, occasionally mixed with Malay, in his descriptions of prime time television and shopping malls in Texas. However, when shifting from this narrative to an admonishment to Liza not to compare the prices of boots in Texas with those in Malaysia, Shah switches back into Malay, with the English borrowing *compare*. Shah's switches in this conversation demonstrate how variation in the type of transfer and shifting between English and Malay can coincide with changes in speakers' pragmatic intentions.

Conclusion

The examples in this chapter only hint at the numerous patterns of borrowing, mixing, and switching occurring in Malaysian English. Similar analyses of additional data should reveal how other groups, including the large populations of Chinese and South Asian Malaysians, combine elements of their ethnic languages with English to accomplish diverse pragmatic ends. Also awaiting rigorous investigation is a growing body of Malaysian English literature, which not only mirrors much of the English usage in Malaysian society, but also illustrates the creative potential of the types of language transfer and shifting discussed here.

Nevertheless, the data presented here indicate at least three dimensions of variation that should be considered in future analyses of Malaysian and other non-native varieties of English. The first of these dimensions concerns the variable proficiency in English among the Malaysian population. As opportunities to use English in Malaysia diminish, the competence in English of most Malaysians may well include numerous deficiencies, as reflected in examples (1) and (2) above. However, such deficiencies do not portend an inevitable decline in English proficiency among those Malaysians most proficient in English – the current English-medium-educated élites, who still establish the norms for English usage in Malaysia. Consideration of this continuum of proficiency will prevent researchers from confusing variable acquisition of English with the model which serves as the target of that acquisition.[10]

A second dimension of variation results from the fact that these élites do not use English in a predominantly monolingual speech community, as is the case with most speakers of British, American, and other 'native-speaker' varieties of English. Rather, these norm-setters of Malaysian English use English as part of an extremely complex verbal repertoire (Hymes 1984), consisting of several languages from a number of language families. Largely as a result of language policy decisions, in the verbal repertoire of the Malaysian élites a decreasing role of English has been balanced by the increasing use of Malay in many domains of language use. This shift in relative status is marked linguistically by increasing lexical transfer from Malay into English, and by code-mixing and switching between English and Malay.

The third dimension of variation is in the amount and type of transfer and code-shifting between English and Malay according to speakers' communicative purposes along the stylistic continuum of Malaysian English. In the standard English of the major English language newspapers, lexical items and phrases are frequently borrowed from Malay, not only to fill lexical gaps but also to foreground or neutralise national and ethnic identities. At the more colloquial level, code-mixing occurs to enhance rapport and familiarity and code-switching to mark changes in pragmatic intentions.

Attention in future research to these variable parameters of proficiency, verbal repertoire, and pragmatic intent will enhance our understanding not only of Malaysian English, but also of English as a world language and of the basic dynamics of language spread, variation, and change.

NOTES

1. Detailed information on immigration patterns is in Le Page (1962) and Hua (1983). By the time of its first census in 1911, the population of colonial Malaya included 1.5 million Malays, over 900,000 Chinese, and 267,000 Indians. The predominant languages spoken by these ethnic groups were Hokkien, Teochew, Cantonese, Hakka, and Hainanese as the primary Chinese languages; Tamil as the most widely used South Asian language, in addition to Malayalam, Telugu, and Punjabi; and Malay as both the primary language

of the ethnic Malays and the most widely used lingua franca for inter-ethnic communication (Platt and Weber 1980; Asmah 1985).

2. In 1980, the population of Peninsular Malaysia, corresponding geographically with the previous Federation of Malaya, was just under eleven million, of whom approximately 54.6 per cent were Malay, 35.0 per cent were Chinese, and 10.4 per cent were South Asian (*Europa Year Book 1987*: 1,801).

3. Singapore, with its predominantly Chinese population – 76.4 per cent by 1985 (Encyclopedia Britannica 1987: 744) – withdrew from Malaysia due to political problems resulting from Chinese-Malay tensions (Hua 1983; Lowenberg in press).

4. However, Abdullah Hassan (personal communication) points out that many young Malaysians with only limited proficiency in English come from rural areas, where until a recent expansion in the provision of universal education, little if any instruction in English was available. Therefore, the 'deterioration' in the Malaysian population's proficiency in English may not be as severe as some observers lament.

5. Standard English in any variety of English – native or non-native – is here functionally defined as the linguistic forms of that variety that are normally used by speakers who have been educated in that variety for government, business, academic and journalistic writing, and for public speaking before an audience on radio or television (Wong 1981; Tay and Gupta 1983, Trudgill 1983).

6. The style range of Malaysian English has been described in diverse ways by Tongue (1979), Platt and Weber (1980), Augustin (1982), and Wong (1983). However, these studies have all concentrated on the degree of structural divergence at each stylistic level between the formal features of Malaysian English and those of standard British English. Deviations discussed have included those attributed both to language contact and to other processes of language change, including strategies of second language acquisition. In contrast, this analysis focuses on the variable pragmatic functions of lexical borrowings, code-mixing, and code-switching along the stylistic continuum.

7. These examples also reflect adaptation of Malay borrowings to English morphology. Rules of Malay morphology would form the plural of *Bumiputra* by reduplication (*Bumiputra Bumiputra*). The use of the shorter plural suffix from English occurs with *Bumiputras* in (8), *Bumis* in (9), *Bumiputeras* in (10), *non-Bumiputeras* in (11), and *makchiks* and *neneks* in (14).

8. The word *mengalai* is glossed in the article as meaning 'to disco' in this context. *Mengalai begitu dong* can be translated as 'Dance like this.'

9. The colloquial tone of these passages is marked by the use of the informal Malay constructions, including *tapi* ('but') instead of standard *tetapi*, and *jawab* ('answer') instead of *menjawab*. The code-mixing in (15) is also marked by the construction *lain perempuan* ('another woman'), which appears to be influenced by English syntax; this phrase would be *perempuan lain* in standard Malay.

10. The likelihood of this model being maintained by the next generation is enhanced by the continuing importance of English in obtaining prestigious and highly paid employment. Le Page (1984: 118) observes that 'the urban middle classes of all ethnic groups try to retain English' by sending their children

abroad or to private schools. Even the urban middle class Malays, who in their economic competition with the Chinese stand to benefit most from the shift to Bahasa Malaysia, 'may go to some lengths to ensure that their children are bilingual [in English] too, since a good command of English is still an advertised requirement for highly paid jobs, at least in the commercial sector'.

REFERENCES

Alisjahbana, S. Takdir. 1976. *Language Planning and Modernization: The Case of Indonesian and Malaysian*. The Hague: Mouton.
Asmah Haji Omar. 1983. The roles of English in Malaysia in the context of national language planning. In Noss (ed.) 1983, pp. 229–50.
1985. Patterns of language communication in Malaysia. *Southeast Asian Journal of Social Science* 13(1): 19–28
Augustin, John. 1982. Regional standards of English in Peninsular Malaysia. In Pride (ed.) 1982, pp. 248–58.
Devi, Sarojini. 1973. *Dewan's New Primary English, Course Book 6*. Kuala Lumpur: Dewan Bahasa dan Pustaka.
Encyclopedia Britannica. 1987. *Britannica Book of the Year 1987*. Chicago: Encyclopedia Britannica, Inc.
The Europa Year Book 1987. 1987. Vol. 2 London: Europa Publications Ltd.
Geis, Michael L. 1987. *The Language of Politics*. New York: Springer-Verlag.
Hassan, Abdullah. 1975. The standardisation and promotion of Bahasa Malaysia. Paper given at Regional English Language Centre Conference, January, Bangkok, Thailand.
Hirschman, Charles. 1984. The society and its environment. In Bunge, Frederica M. (ed.), *Malaysia, A Country Study*. Washington DC: The American University, pp. 69–127.
Hua Wu Yin. 1983. *Class and Communalism in Malaysia*. London: Marram Books.
Hymes, Dell. 1984. Sociolinguistics: stability and consolidation. *International Journal of the Sociology of Language* 45: 39–45.
Kachru, Braj B. 1986. The power and politics of English. *World Englishes* 5(2/3): 121–40.
1987. World Englishes and applied linguistics. Plenary paper presented at Eighth World Congress of Applied Linguistics, August 16–21, Sydney, Australia.
Koh, Judy and Leong Suat Chin. 1981. *Dewan's New Comprehensive Secondary English, Book 3*. Kuala Lumpur: Dewan Bahasa dan Pustaka.
Lat. 1978. *Lat's Lot*. Kuala Lumpur: Berita Publishing Sdn. Bhd. 2nd edition.
Le Page, Robert B. 1962. Multilingualism in Malay. In *Symposium on multilingualism*. Proceedings of the second meeting of the Inter-African Committee on Linguistics, July 16–21, 1962, Brazzaville. London: Committee for Technical Cooperation in Africa.
1984. Retrospect and prognosis in Malaysia and Singapore. *International Journal of the Sociology of Language* 45: 113–26.
Lowenberg, Peter H. In press. Malay in Indonesia, Malaysia, and Singapore:

Three faces of a national language. In Coulmas, Florian (ed.), *With Forked Tongues: What are National Languages Good For?* Ann Arbor: Karoma Publishers.

Meedin, Hafriza. 1985. Code-switching, Malaysian style. MS, Department of Linguistics, Georgetown University.

Noss, Richard B. (ed.) 1983. *Varieties of English in Southeast Asia.* Anthology Series 11. Singapore: SEAMEO Regional Language Centre.

Paine, Robert. 1981. When saying is doing. In Paine, Robert (ed.), *Politically Speaking.* Philadelphia: Institute for the Study of Human Issues, pp. 9–23.

Parkin, David. 1984. Political language. *Annual Review of Anthropology* 13: 345–65.

Platt, John and Weber, Heidi. 1980. *English in Singapore and Malaysia.* Kuala Lumpur: Oxford University Press.

Platt, John, Weber, Heidi, and Mian Lian Ho. 1983. *Singapore and Malaysia.* Volume 4 in *Varieties of English around the World.* Amsterdam and Philadelphia: Benjamins.

Pride, John B. (ed.). 1982. *New Englishes.* Rowley MA: Newbury House.

Richards, Jack C. 1979. Rhetorical and Communicative styles in the new varieties of English. *Language Learning* 29(1): 1–25.

Tan Chor Whye. 1982. *The New Communication English, Subject 122.* Kuala Lumpur: Pustaka Sistem Pelajaran Sdn. Bhd.

Tay, Mary W. J. and Gupta, Anthea Fraser. 1983. Towards a description of Standard Singapore English. In Noss (ed.) 1983, pp. 173–89.

Tongue, R. K. 1979. *The English of Singapore and Malaysia.* Singapore: Eastern Universities Press. 2nd revised edition.

Trömel-Plötz, Senta. 1981. Languages of oppression (review article). *Journal of Pragmatics* 5: 67–80.

Trudgill, Peter. 1983. *Sociolinguistics: An Introduction to Language and Society.* Harmondsworth: Penguin. Revised edition.

Watson, J. K. P. 1984. Cultural pluralism, nation-building and educational policies in Peninsular Malaysia. In Kennedy, Chris (ed.), *Language Planning and Language Education.* London: George Allen and Unwin, pp. 132–50.

Wong, Irene F. H. 1981. English in Malaysia. In Smith, Larry E. (ed.), *English for Cross-Cultural Communication.* New York: St Martin's Press, pp. 94–107.

1982. Native speaker English for the Third World today? In Pride (ed.) 1982, pp. 261–86.

1983. Simplification features in the structure of colloquial Malaysian English. In Noss (ed.) 1983, pp. 125–49.

25

Social and linguistic constraints on variation in the use of two grammatical variables in Singapore English

JOHN PLATT

Singapore English is probably the classic case of the indigenisation of English as it performs such a wide range of functions, not only internationally but intranationally, not only interethnically but intraethnically, not only in the more public domains but increasingly in the more private domains of family and friendship as well. This does not, of course, mean that it has supplanted the various local languages: Chinese dialects, Malay and the various languages of the Indian communities. However, its use in various domains has been increasing annually.

English came to Singapore with the establishment of a trading centre by Sir Stamford Raffles in 1819. The functions of English increased quite rapidly, and with the establishment of English-medium schools came the beginnings of Singapore English.

Although a pidginised form of Malay, Bazaar Malay, was the general lingua franca throughout the colonial period and was used not only for interethnic communication between Chinese, Malays and Indians but also by Europeans communicating with the majority of the local population, English gradually became a kind of prestige lingua franca among the small but increasing English-medium educated section of the population.

As pointed out in Platt (1975: 365, 1977a: 83) and Platt and Weber (1980: 17–22), it was through English-medium education that an indigenised variety of English developed. A kind of fossilised interlanguage became a lingua franca in the English-medium schools among students whose home language might be one of the Chinese dialects (not all of them mutually intelligible), an Indian language or Malay.

With independence and a great increase in educational opportunity, English continued to spread. At first, the main medium of education was Chinese (Mandarin) but over the years the proportion of students of all ethnic backgrounds attending English-medium schools has increased and now virtually all education is English-medium, although Chinese (Mandarin), Malay and the southern Indian language, Tamil, are compulsory second languages.

As could be expected, a speech continuum has developed as in post-creole situations such as Jamaica (De Camp 1971) or Guyana (Bickerton 1975). Naturally, the concept of a speech continuum should not be taken absolutely literally. It would be ridiculous to consider that for a continuum to exist each speaker should be in the same relative position to every other speaker in regard to every linguistic variable. Le Page (1984: 121), in criticising Platt (1977a) and Tay (1982a, 1982b), states that both

> attempt to describe the 'subvarieties' of Singapore English in terms, borrowed from creole studies, of a linear continuum from 'basilect' to 'acrolect'. I would very much doubt, however, whether this is an appropriate model; a multidimensional model is more likely to be useful as more detailed sociolinguistic studies are made . . . since there can be no single 'farthest from Standard' variety in a community in which 'English' of different kinds is being learned as second, third or fourth language by speakers of a wide variety of other languages and under varied circumstances; nor is there in effect any single standard.

Le Page conveniently ignores the sentence in Platt (1977a: 83) on the first page of the article referred to: 'Henceforth, I shall use 'Singapore English' to refer to the English of the typical product of English medium education but I shall assert that not all speakers of Singapore English have a command of all its sub-varieties.' Furthermore, as pointed out in Platt and Weber (1980: 46) 'What is perhaps surprising is the amount of system to be observed within Singaporean English and the increasing similarity of Singapore English as spoken by those of different ethnic backgrounds.' As the ethnically Chinese majority constitutes 76 per cent of the population, the influence of Chinese dialects, especially of the dominant dialect, Hokkien, is the main one. Many features of colloquial and basilectal Singapore English strongly suggest a Chinese influence although, as will be shown later, not everything can be convincingly explained by substratum influence.

Interestingly too, the influence of Hokkien was not always direct but through Baba Malay, the creole spoken by the Peranakan or 'Straits-born' Chinese. As pointed out in Platt and Weber (1980: 30–31), the Peranakan Chinese took up English-medium education very enthusiastically and it is apparent that many of those at English-medium schools in the earlier days were of Peranakan background (cf. also Chia 1980, 1983). This partly explains why Malay lexical items such as *makan* 'eat, food' became a part of colloquial Singapore English along with Chinese influenced morpho-syntactic structures and semantics as in verbs of direction (Platt, Weber and Ho 1983).

Quantitative investigation of spoken Singapore English has revealed considerable systematicity. Before considering two variables in greater depth, I shall make brief mention of some other morpho-syntactic variables which have been investigated.

Indefinite and definite article

The indefinite and definite articles are variable in Singapore English in that they do not always occur in environments where they would be expected in Standard English, for example:

> My paren' have (a) flat in Geylang.
> You see (the) green shop house over t'ere? (from Platt, 1977b)

Comparative frequencies for the occurrence of the indefinite article (*a/an*) and the definite article (*the*) are given in Platt (1977b). For 14 Chinese-medium educated speakers, the scores for the definite article were higher in 13 cases and for 20 English-medium educated speakers they were all considerably higher for the definite article. To what extent this can be attributed to substratum influence and to what extent to universals of a 'bioprogram' type (Bickerton 1981) is arguable as both Chinese and Malay appear to have a system of nominal reference which is closer to a specific–nonspecific than to a definite–indefinite system. Interestingly, a similar trend was found in an investigation of the English compositions written by ethnically mixed groups of students at three Malaysian secondary schools (Zahariah Pilus 1986).

BE as copula and auxiliary

The variable occurrence of BE as copula and auxiliary is a well known phenomenon of Black English Vernacular (e.g., Labov 1969) and it has been reported for British Black English (Edwards 1986). Examples in the speech of Australian Aboriginal children are given in Eagleson *et al.* (1982: 93). It is also a well known feature of English-based pidgins and creoles to have no copula-like verb in certain environments where 'native speaker' English usually has BE. Examples of non-occurrence in the speech of educated speakers from East Africa, Ghana, India and The Philippines are quoted by Platt, Weber and Ho (1984: 78–79).[1]

In Platt (1979), variation in the occurrence of BE in the speech of 59 Singaporeans was explained mainly by influence from the substratum languages: Chinese dialects, Malay and Tamil. In these languages, there is typically no copula-like verb in pre-adjective position, at least in the spoken varieties, and it is variable in spoken Malay (including Bazaar Malay and Baba Malay) before a predicate nominal or a locative.

It was found that the lowest mean score (75.0 per cent) was for the occurrence of BE preceding an adjective. Furthermore, no speaker had categorical BE occurrence in this environment. For the pre-locative environment, the mean score was 86.5 per cent and 35 of the 56 speakers using such a structure (58.9 per cent) had categorical occurrence of BE.

For the pre-predicate nominal environment, only 16 of the 56 speakers using such a structure (58.9 per cent) had categorical occurrence and for the pre-verb+*ing* environment 26 out of the 54 speakers using this type of structure (48.1 per cent) had categorical occurrence of BE.

In a more detailed investigation by Ho (1986) of BE occurrence in the speech of 100 ethnically Chinese Singaporeans, all English-medium educated, and of 5 different educational level sub-groups, over 10,000 potential tokens of BE were examined. It was found that only 4 of the 100 speakers had categorical BE occurrence preceding an adjective whereas in the pre-locative environment 47 of the 98 speakers using such a structure (48 per cent) had categorical occurrence. There was a particularly high occurrence of BE in the environment preceding a clause as in:

Dat is *what dey are trying to do.*

Overall occurrence was 97.9 per cent and 78 of the 94 speakers who used this type of structure (83 per cent) had categorical occurrence.

It was also found that there was a relationship between preceding environment and BE occurrence. The highest occurrence was after a clause, as in:

We work here is not bad lah.
'Working here isn't bad at all.'

The overall occurrence was 96.1 per cent with 69 of the 75 using this type of structure (92%) having categorical occurrence. The lowest occurrence, 80.3% overall, was after a pronoun other than *I*, *he* or *she*, as in:

We waiting for de flight to come in.

with only 9 of the 100 speakers having categorical occurrence.

Ho's investigation covers various other factors related to the degree of BE occurrence. These include the influence of Chinese syntax and of English BE-less structures in subordinate clauses. What is clear is that BE occurrence in Singapore English is far from random but is related to the combined influences of various syntactic, semantic and phonetic factors.

Third person singular present tense and noun plural

In an investigation reported in Platt (1977b), it was found that all 32 speakers who used third person singular present tense marking at all, whether English-medium or Chinese-medium educated, had a higher degree of noun plural marking than third person singular marking. For a

Table 25.1. *Noun plural marking*

	Overall percentage of noun plural marking	Percentage of those with scores of 70 per cent or higher for noun plural marking
Group I	82	92
Group II	60	22

group of 15 English-medium educated Singaporeans, Ho (1981) found that noun plural marking was higher than third person singular marking in each of 10 phonetic environments.

Obviously, there cannot be a phonetic explanation for this difference between third person singular and noun plural affixation as, except in the case of some irregular noun plurals, the form of affixation is the same, the addition of /s/, /z/ or /ez/.[2] In Chinese, plural is not marked on the noun and verbs are not marked for person or number. In Malay, reduplication of the noun occurs when there is no numeral or other quantifier and it is not obvious from the wider context that there is reference to more than one. Thus:

> orang-orang   'persons, people'

but

> lima orang   'five people'
> banyak orang 'many people'

and there is no reduplication of *pisang* 'banana' in:

> Saya pergi ke pasar untuk membeli pisang.
> 'I'm going to the market to buy bananas'.

as one would hardly go to the market to buy one banana. In Malay, too, verbs are not marked for person or number.

However, it would seem that the concept of plural is generally meaningful to those being taught English, in the sense that they are aware of the difference between a single item and more than one of the same item. On the other hand, the marking of only the third person singular of the present tense of verbs with an affix which has the same form as that for noun plural is far less meaningful. Surprisingly, however, Ho (1986) found that verbs with past reference were sometimes marked for third person singular, particularly when referring to repeated events or to states. The marking of verbs for past tense is discussed in the next section.

Of course, there is variation in the degree of noun plural marking according to educational level. Table 25.1 (from Platt and Weber 1980: 70) gives figures for noun plural marking for 42 English-medium educated

Singaporeans. Group I had more than four years of secondary education and Group II had four years or less.

What is particularly interesting about noun plural marking in Singapore English is the extent to which the syntactic-semantic environment affects it. In Platt and Weber (1980: 176) it was stated of Malaysian English 'In general, percentages for noun plural marking *after* numerals were higher than if no numeral preceded the noun.'

In Ho's investigation (Ho 1981) of noun plural marking in the speech of 50 English-medium educated, ethnically Chinese Singaporeans of 5 different educational levels (10 in each sub-group), 8 environments were analysed according to what preceded the head noun in the noun phrase. It was found that the highest degree of plural affixation was after a quantifier such as a number other than one, *several, many, (a) few, both*, for example:

> a few dollars, three months.

Not only was plural affixation highest in this environment (1,419/1,822 = 77.9 per cent) but it was highest for each of the 5 educational level sub-groups except in the case of those with 1–3 years of secondary education, in which case it was slightly lower than when a noun was simply preceded by the definite article (58.85 per cent as against 59.02 per cent). In fact, marking of noun plural was higher when preceded by a quantifier than for any other environment for 30 of the 50 speakers.

On the other hand, in the zero determiner environment, for example:

> We may get project( ) of similar size and magnitude

(this from a graduate speaker), noun plural affixation was lower: 1155/1701 = 67.9%. Furthermore, whereas 14 speakers had categorical noun plural marking in the post-quantifier environment, none had this in the zero determiner environment.

This is clearly not a case of L1 influence but rather of an underlying semantic influence.

> Where there is a strong semantic relationship, nouns are more likely to be marked for plural. It is precisely the lack of this semantic unity that causes scores for the Third Person Singular Present Tense marking to be lower than Noun plural marking (Ho 1981: 117).

That the influence of a quantifier is not peculiar to Singapore English is shown in Budge's study of spoken English in Hong Kong (Budge 1986). She found that 61 out of 75 speakers (81.1 per cent) marked plural more when the noun was preceded by a quantifier than when preceded by a modifier that was neutral with respect to plurality.

That the higher degree of noun plural marking when preceded by a quantifier is not peculiar to the acquisition of English by speakers with a Chinese language background is shown in Sudipa's investigation (Sudipa 1986) of essays written in English by students at Udayana University, Bali.

Table 25.2. *Past tense marking by 2 sub-groups of Singaporeans*

	C+/d,t/	V+/d/	Vowel change	C+*ed*
Above 4 years secondary schooling	19/35 54.3%	17/25 68.0%	80/89 89.9%	17/17 100.0%
4 years secondary schooling or less	15/93 19.4%	40/82 48.8%	160/272 58.8%	33/54 61.1%
Whole group	34/128 26.6%	57/107 53.3%	240/361 66.5%	50/71 70.4%

For each year level, the degree of noun plural marking was higher when preceded by a quantifier than when not and yet in neither Bahasa Indonesia nor Balinese are nouns marked in any way for plural when preceded by a quantifier.

Past tense marking

In an investigation of past tense marking in the recorded speech of 42 English-medium educated Singaporeans (Platt 1977c), it was found that there were considerable differences according to phonetic type and, not surprisingly, according to level of education. There were 10 speakers with over 4 years of secondary education, including some with tertiary education, and 32 with 4 years of secondary education or less. The verb types were classified into:

> Consonant+/d,t/ e.g. *pass, work,* where past tense affixation produces a consonant cluster;
> Vowel+/d/ e.g. *try, play,* where the vowel stem ends in a vowel sound;
> Consonant+/d/ e.g. *started, wanted,* where the affix is typically -*ed* in Singapore English;
> Vowel change e.g. *break – broke, come – came.*

Four verbs, GET, BE, GO and HAVE, were considered separately but for present purposes GET and BE will be excluded while GO will be included under the Vowel change type and HAVE under the Vowel+/d/ type because of its past tense form HAD.

As can be seen from table 25.2, verbs forming their past tense with a consonant cluster have the lowest degree of past tense marking. This is clearly because in the L1s of the speakers there are no consonant clusters in word final position. The next lowest group is the Vowel+/d/ group. Here, although there is no consonant cluster problem, there is still the need to add a dental/alveolar stop to form the past tense. In the Southern Chinese dialects it appears that a stop does not occur after a diphthong. However, many of the Vowel+/d/ verbs do have a diphthong preceding the final stop in their past tense forms, for example, *tried, followed, paid*. Scores for the Vowel Change type were higher. In fact 6 of the 10 speakers in the upper group had categorical past tense marking for this type. However, of those in the lower educational group, only 4 of the 31 using such a verb type did (12.9 per cent). It would appear that once the past tense forms of these irregular verbs have been acquired there is a high degree of past tense marking because there is no final consonant problem. Even if the final consonant in a past tense form such as *bought* or *broke* is omitted, the verb is still marked for past tense by the vowel change. This is also true of the Consonant+*ed* type as marking involves the addition of an extra syllable.

In Ho's investigation (1986), however, it was found that for her 100 English-medium educated, ethnically Chinese speakers of five different educational levels the Vowel change type had the overall highest degree of past tense marking (57.3 per cent), followed by Consonant+*ed* (40.6%), Vowel+/d/ (36.2 per cent) and Consonant+/d,t/ (3.9 per cent). A possible reason for differences in the ordering of the environments as regards Vowel change and Consonant+*ed* is that 40 per cent of the speakers in Ho's corpus had above 4 years of secondary education whereas in Platt (1977c) only about 24 per cent had. At the other end of the scale, 20 per cent of Ho's interviewees had no secondary education at all whereas in the group investigated for Platt (1977c) only 2 interviewees had – approximately 5 per cent. The fact that Ho is herself a Singaporean would also have had an effect as many speakers would have monitored their speech less and not added the -*ed* suffix.

What is more interesting than phonetic conditioning of past tense marking, however, is underlying semantic influence. Bickerton (1981) claims that a punctual-nonpunctual distinction is basic and part of the 'bioprogram' and he gives figures to show this in two decreolising situations: Guyana Creole and Hawaiian Creole English.

> When all past-reference verbs were divided into two categories – those that referred to SINGLE, PUNCTUAL EVENTS, and those that referred to iterative or habitual events – insertion rates (for past tense marking) were shown to vary between the two (Bickerton 1981:104)

and he gives figures:

		Punctual	Nonpunctual
Past-marking rates	GC	38%	12%
	HCE	53%	7%

In Platt (1977c) it was suggested under 'Problems for further research' that 'variation in past tense marking in stative as opposed to non-stative verbs' should be investigated. In recordings of speakers of other indigenised varieties of English as part of research for Platt *et al.* (1984) it was found that verbs used non-punctually appeared to be less frequently marked for past tense. In Ho's investigation (1986) it was found that 8,725 verbs should, prescriptively, have been marked for past tense. These verbs were subdivided into three categories:

(a) verbs used punctually in the sense that they refer to a single event;
(b) verbs used statively, e.g., *love* as in 'She loves music';
(c) verbs which are not used statively but which are used non-punctually as they refer to habitual or iterative events.

It was found that for all educational levels there were considerable differences in the degree of past-tense marking. The overall degree of marking was:

punctual	57.3%
stative	36.9%
non-punctual	14.7%

What is even more striking is the variation in the degree of past tense marking for verbs according to the proportion of tokens used punctually or non-punctually. Verbs for which 85 per cent or more of the tokens were used punctually received a high degree of past tense marking, for example:

	Proportions of punctual tokens	Past tense marking
leave	96.2	87.6%
lose	93.3	86.7%
tell	89.2	74.6%
meet	85.3	80.3%

What is equally striking is the degree of past tense marking for these verbs according to whether they are used punctually or non-punctually:

	Punctual	Non-punctual
leave	91.1%	0.0%
lose	92.9%	0.0%
tell	79.7%	32.0%
meet	90.4%	22.2%

For example, a speaker who had completed 6 years of secondary education and passed the Advanced level examinations did not mark *leave* for past tense when speaking about someone's habitual behaviour in the past:

. . . whenever he *leaves* his place he'll switch off de switch.

whereas another speaker with three years or less of secondary education referring to a single event said:

I *left* for Hong Kong.

With some verbs, more than 50 per cent of the tokens were used non-punctually and with these there was generally a low to very low degree of past tense marking. Three examples are:

	Proportions of non-punctual tokens	Past tense marking
eat	100.0	16.7%
keep	100.0	21.6%
teach	89.2	33.9%

In the case of *teach*, 71.4 per cent of the punctual tokens were marked whereas only 29.3 per cent of the non-punctual tokens were.

The evidence for underlying semantic distinctions being a major factor in the degree of past tense marking is therefore very strong. For every educational level, for every phonetic subgroup of verbs and for every one of 26 vowel change verbs examined, there is a higher degree of past tense marking of punctual than non-punctual tokens.

Is this an influence from Chinese or is it a universal in the acquisition of English? It is true that in Chinese a perfective or completive particle (*le* in Mandarin) may co-occur only with verbs used punctually but not with verbs expressing habitual actions or continuing states. However, it would seen unlikely that there is a direct influence from Chinese. Research is needed in other areas where there are different L1 influences so that it may be determined how general is the relationship between the punctual-nonpunctual distinction and the marking of verbs for past tense marking. A similar trend has been found in the English of Singapore Tamils, especially among those with lower levels of English-medium education (Saravanan 1986).

From the data presented it will be seen that variation in Singapore English is far from random. Besides the expected differences related to level and medium of education and type of employment, and to phonetic problems, as in the case of the Consonant+/d,t/ type verbs, there are deeper semantic influences as in the case of noun plural marking and the past tense marking of verbs. It has been possible here to deal with only some of the variables in Singapore English but a fuller discussion and exemplification of these and other variables is presented in Platt and Ho (in press).

NOTES

1. These speakers were interviewed and recorded in Australia. Research by Platt has been supported by Australian Research Grants Scheme grants A68/16801, A77/15355, A28015239 and A58515856.
2. In Singapore English, the affix after a sibilant is typically [-ez].

REFERENCES

Bickerton, D. 1975. *Dynamics of a Creole System.* Cambridge: Cambridge University Press.
1981. *Roots of Language.* Ann Arbor: Karoma.
Budge, C. 1986. Variation in Hong Kong English. Unpublished PhD thesis, Monash University, Melbourne.
Chia, F. 1980. *The Babas.* Singapore: Times Books International.
1983. *Ala sayang!* Singapore: Eastern Universities Press.
De Camp, D. 1971. Toward a generative analysis of a post-creole system. In Hymes, D. (ed.) *Pidginization and Creolization of languages.* Cambridge: Cambridge University Press.
Eagleson, R. D., Kaldor, S. and Malcolm, I. G. 1982. *English and the Aboriginal Child.* Canberra: Curriculum Development Centre.
Edwards, V. 1986. *Language in a Black Community.* Clevedon: Multilingual Matters.
Ho, M. L. 1981. The Noun Phrase in Singapore English. Unpublished MA thesis, Monash University, Melbourne.
1986. The Verb Phrase in Singapore English. Unpublished PhD thesis, Monash University, Melbourne.
Labov, W. 1969. Contraction, deletion and inherent variability in the English copula. *Language* 45(4): 715–62.
Le Page, R. B. 1984. Retrospect and prognosis in Malaysia and Singapore. *International Journal of the Sociology of Language* 45: 113–26.
Platt, J. T. 1975. The Singapore English speech continuum and its basilect 'Singlish' as a 'creoloid'. *Anthropological Linguistics* 17(7): 363–74.
1977a. The sub-varieties of Singapore English: their sociolectal and functional status. In Crewe, W. (ed.), *The English Language in Singapore.* Singapore: Eastern Universities Press.
1977b. The 'creoloid' as a special type of interlanguage. *Interlanguage Studies Bulletin* 2(3): 22–38.
1977c. English past tense acquisition by Singaporeans – implicational scaling versus group averages of marked forms. *ITL* 38: 63–83.
1979. Variation and implicational relationships: copula realization in Singapore English. *General Linguistics* 19(1): 1–14.
Platt, J. T. and Ho, M. L. In press. *Dynamics of a Contact Continuum.* Oxford: Oxford University Press.
Platt, J. T. and Weber, H. 1980. *English in Singapore and Malaysia.* Kuala Lumpur: Oxford University Press.

Platt, J. T., Weber, H. and Ho, M. L. 1983. Some verbs of movement in Standard British English and Singapore English. *World Language English* 2(3): 156–60.

(1984) *The New Englishes*. London: Routledge and Kegan Paul.

Saravanan, V. 1986. Variation in the English spoken by English-Tamil bilinguals in Singapore. Unpublished PhD thesis, Monash University, Melbourne.

Sudipa, I Nengah 1986. The Acquisition of English by Balinese students. Unpublished MA thesis, Monash University, Melbourne.

Tay, M. W. J. 1982a. The phonology of educated Singapore English. *English World-Wide* 3(2): 135–45.

1982b. The uses, users and features of English in Singapore. In Pride, J. B. (ed.) *New Englishes*. Rowley MA: Newbury House.

Zahariah Pilus 1985. Acquisition of the English Noun Phrases by Malaysian Secondary School Students: An Error Analysis of Written Compositions. Unpublished BA Honours minor thesis, Monash University, Melbourne.

East Africa
(Tanzania and Kenya)

26

East Africa (Tanzania and Kenya)

MOHAMED H. ABDULAZIZ

Background

In the East African region of Kenya and Tanzania, a complex multilingual situation exists. It comprises nearly 140 indigenous languages, over 100 in Tanzania and about 40 in Kenya, spoken by over 40 million people. These languages belong to four major African language families: Bantu, Nilo-Saharan, Cushitic and Khoisan. The Khoisan family is represented by tiny remnants spoken by a few thousand speakers in central Tanzania. In Tanzania more than 90 per cent of the languages and speakers belong to the Bantu group, a linguistic fact that has made the acceptance of Kiswahili as the national and official language there relatively easier than in Kenya. In Kenya over 75 per cent of the population speak languages belonging to the Bantu family, about 20 per cent speak Nilo-Saharan languages, which include Luo, Maa and Kalenjin, and the rest speak Cushitic languages which include Somali, Oromo and Rendille. These ethnic languages serve as languages of group identity at the subnational level, as Schmied observes in his paper in this volume.

This paper focuses on English in Kenya and Tanzania, which are the subjects of the case study papers in this volume. For discussion of English in other East African countries, see Hancock and Angogo (1984).

Status of English

Kiswahili is the lingua franca, national language and the wider language of communication in both countries. In addition, it is the main official language in Tanzania (with English functioning as official in some peripheral areas), and a co-official language in Kenya being, with English, an official language of parliamentary debates and the predominant language of politics. Then there is English, the language of instruction in post-primary education in Tanzania, in all subjects except Kiswahili, Political

391

Education and Religious Education, and the language of most of the education system in Kenyan education (with the possible exception of the first three primary years in ethnic areas). In Kenya, English is also the official language of civil service correspondence and of the legal system (together with Kiswahili), as well as the language of the armed forces and the police, and generally of all modern sectors of socioeconomic activity, · including the commercial and industrial sectors. The leading newspapers are published in English. Of the two prominent radio channels, one is in English; the only television channel is dominated by programmes in English. In Tanzania, in contrast, there are several Kiswahili newspapers, though the two English language papers, the *Daily News* and *Sunday News*, seem to have the most detailed coverage. In both Tanzania and Kenya, English is the language of diplomacy and of all international communication, and it is generally the language through which modern styles of life, science and technology are introduced. However, due to different colonial situations and the emergence of divergent sociopolitical, economic and cultural policies after independence in the early 1960s, English has fared differently in these two countries.

In Tanzania, English during the British rule and up to the end of the 1960s played a very important role as the language of higher education (at secondary and tertiary levels), as well as of the higher levels of administration, of legal and commercial activities and of international communication. Although Kiswahili had long been established as a lingua franca in what was formerly Tanganyika, English had developed into a crucial second language at Independence in the early 1960s, existing in a stable form of diglossia with Kiswahili, on the one hand, and in a triglossic situation, on the other hand, with Kiswahili and the mother tongues (Abdulaziz 1972). The mother tongues have always functioned as languages of primordial ethnic identity, with Kiswahili as the language of social, cultural and business interaction between members of different ethnic and racial groups, and English as the efficient language of education and formal business. The English that was used, however, was a restricted, formal variety of the language, for reasons to be discussed later. The Arusha Declaration of 1967, ushering in egalitarian socioeconomic policies and the ethos of self-reliance, altered this diglossic balance. Kiswahili was now made the only medium of instruction at the primary level, the sole official language of administration, the forces, the civil service, parliamentary debating and The Hansard (the official parliamentary gazette) and the language of political and social organisation. English has continued to be the official language of instruction at secondary level and above, including university level, and it is the language of international communication. It is, to some extent, still an official language, together with Kiswahili, in a number of domains, such as banking, insurance, international travel, tourism and commerce. There are still a number of domains, however, where language policy is not clearcut, and where it is possible for Tanzanians to use either or both of the languages, creating areas of functional overlap. In Kenya, on the other hand, the importance of English increased after independence and it occupies as a second language a secure role as the language of education, administration, commerce and modernisation in general.

Literary writing in English began in East Africa after the Second World War and increased significantly during the 1960s. Those who disapprove of writing in English have always argued that it is élitist, alienating, European culture-bound and inimical to the growth of indigenous African writing. Supporters of writing in English emphasise the practical problems of publishing, the benefit of an international readership and the fact that English is historically part of the African linguistic experience (see Schmied 1985a). Literary writers such as Ngugi wa Thiongo, Grace Ogot and Meja Mwangi use formal English even in dialogue. Their writings lack the literary usage of idiom, imagery, colloquialisms and metaphor typical of native writers of English. Instead, they use African themes, metaphor and imagery, since they consider their literature as basically African, despite the English medium in which it is written.

Attitudes to English differ markedly. In Kenya there is positive acceptance by the authorities and the general public. In Tanzania attitudes vary between very warm acceptance by some Tanzanians and indifference from others. The issue of attitudes towards English must be seen in the context of societal complexities, in the sense of attitudes of governments and the ruling parties, of the various linguistic communities, of the functionaries who implement language policies, of the various socioeconomic classes as well as of individuals. Individual variation in the use of English to a large extent depends upon the quality and quantity of exposure to the language, plus the attitude of the speaker towards English and how much effort he or she is prepared to make to improve their usage.

Variation in English

Objective, systematic study of English in East Africa has yet to be done, at both macrolevel and microlevel, to ascertain if a distinct variety can be said to exist and, if so, what its linguistic features are. It appears, however, that a form discernable as East African English has emerged on the phonological level, due to mother tongue interference, a factor that is well illustrated in the case studies by Kanyoro and Schmied in this volume. At the regional level, there are also features of pronunciation that identify Kenyan from Tanzanian speakers of English. A legitimate question is, since the mother tongues themselves exhibit significantly different interference features, why is it still possible to recognise Kenyan English from Tanzanian English, and East African English from the English spoken in the other regions of the world? The answer is that attitudinal factors concerning the use of English have led to strong tendencies for the levelling of national forms in each of the two countries, as well as in the region as a whole.

East African English

For most of this century, and especially up to about 1970, Kenya and Tanzania were exposed to similar educational, socioeconomic, cultural and linguistic experiences. Secondary and tertiary educational institutions, whether government, private or missionary, have always admitted students from all linguistic and ethnic backgrounds (with the exception of European and Asian children, before independence). The wider mass media, printing presses and publishing houses were run on a regional, East African basis. During the 1930s, 1940s and 1950s there was a single University College in Uganda which served the whole region. Major services and institutions like Railways and Harbours, the Post Office and Telecommunications, the Income Tax Department, Customs, Airlines and the territorial armed forces were all run on an East African basis, and there was free transfer of officials and workers within the whole region. Furthermore, there was free movement and trade across the borders; these, in any case, artificially divided the ethnic communities.

Also, teachers who were expatriate native speakers of English tended to be transferred to various areas, and to have similar attitudes towards the variety of English to be taught to Africans. They insisted on a limited formal variety close to standard Southern British English and RP. The main purpose, it would seem, was to teach a formal literary variety which would produce civil service functionaries and professionals capable of communicating orally and of writing in formal domains with other speakers of English, particularly with senior European officials, Asians and those Africans who did not share a common African language. This form of English lacked the colourful English idiomatic expressions which are an important feature of the relaxed, everyday social use of the language. Even simple contractions such as *don't*, *can't* or *isn't* were not allowed in school, to avoid the growth of a habit that might influence written formal English. Since East Africans were exposed mainly to the English of the school and the office, they had little chance to learn the relaxed, affective, idiomatic and conversational forms of the language. It was Kiswahili that took over this function.

Unlike the French and the Portuguese in their colonies, the British never aimed at teaching English to Africans within its wide cultural context, because of their belief in separate social and cultural development for people of different races. In any case, there was very little opportunity for Africans in East Africa during the colonial period to interact socially with Europeans. This made it unnecessary for them to acquire anything other than the formal official variety of English which they learned at school and practised at their places of work. British settlers were most reluctant to use English with their native servants and with Africans in general, as they believed that this knowledge might 'spoil' them in the master-servant relationship that existed. British officials, including teachers, civil servants, police officers and professionals, would use formal English to 'educated' Africans at their place of work, and simplified Kiswahili in other contexts. In fact, all British civil service officers had to learn Kiswahili before they went out to East Africa, and their promotion to some degree depended on passing tests in the more advanced forms of the language. Unlike in the French colonial territories, there was an almost deliberate attempt in the decades before independence not to develop English as a lingua franca, in fact to encourage the promotion of Kiswahili for this role (see, for Tanzania, Schmied 1985b).

Another levelling factor is the fact that in schools and universities people have always joked about those who speak English with mother tongue interference. It was common to imitate each other's 'mistakes', such as devoicing the voiced English sounds, or using pre-nasalisation phenomena (see Kanyoro, this volume). This had a tremendous effect on every student and speaker of English to try hard to approximate to the East African norm, or to what they considered to be the national norm. A further factor is that no pidginised or creolised form of English emerged, as it had in West Africa, since Kiswahili, as the interethnic and interracial lingua franca, adequately provided for all those functions that might have required an English-based pidgin or creole.

All these factors contributed to a considerable levelling of differences caused by mother tongue interference, and gave rise to a recognisable East African usage of English. Cursory observation shows that these levelling tendencies did not only concern phonological features, but also discourse strategies, idiomatic expressions, and general handling of the syntax (see Angogo and Hancock 1980; Zuengler 1982; and Hancock and Angogo 1984, for descriptions of some of these characteristics). One feature that distinguishes East African English from RP is intonation: a great deal of research needs to be done on this. It appears to be largely due to this feature that East African English is easily distinguished from the West African variety. A great deal of general research, in fact, still needs to be done on the linguistic features that distinguish East African English from both standard Southern British English and from other standard varieties of English.

National varieties of English

Kiswahili, as we have seen, has always been an important factor in the levelling of subnational varieties of English and, more recently, in the emergence of national varieties. In Kenya and Tanzania, Kiswahili has always been an intermediate language between English and the mother tongues. In the period before independence Kiswahili, in most African schools, was used as the medium of instruction in intermediate classes, the mother tongue being used in the lower ones, and English in the higher levels of education. The first levelling exercise, therefore, was towards approximating the Kiswahili standard. When pupils transferred to the English medium the Kiswahili standard was the base of reference for the acquisition of English. There was a belief that Kiswahili, of all the African languages of this region, was closest to English with respect to its phonemic system. Although Kiswahili has only five open vowels (/i, e, a, o, u/) and no diphthongs, it is true that all the English consonants have their basic Kiswahili counterparts. There are allophonic variations in Kiswahili involving phonetic oppositions such as dental versus non-dental, aspirated versus non-aspirated or plosive versus implosive consonants, but these are not apparent in print or on typewriter keyboards. Also, Kiswahili, like English, has no lexical or grammatical tones. To establish this belief further, European writers of earlier Kiswahili grammars unwittingly described Kiswahili phonemes in terms of their nearest English ones, writing, for example, '*b* as in English *bin*, *ch* as in *chin*', or '*j* as in *judge*'. Standard Kiswahili grammars have always been based on English-Kiswahili equivalents for morphological and syntactic categories, including tense and aspect, much as English grammars used to be based on the syntactic categories that had previously described Latin.

Kiswahili is still an important factor in the development of English in East Africa. To some extent, the ease with which one can distinguish Kenyan English from Tanzanian English today is due to the different roles that Kiswahili now plays in the two countries, as a reference language for learning English. Kanyoro's paper, in this volume, examines the different linguistic features that have resulted from the different roles that Kiswahili and English now play in Tanzania and Kenya.

Schmied's paper in this volume is probably the first systematic study of the phonological features of Kenyan English. Although his data sample is necessarily limited (since his paper is a 'feasibility' study), his conclusions nevertheless support the impressionistic observations of educationists and linguists in Kenya. It is interesting to note that some of the features that are listed in teachers' books in Tanzania as needing remedial treatment (see Kanyoro, this volume) in fact function as markers of subnational identity, according to Schmied. It would be interesting to study linguistic variation in data obtained from face to face conversations, as there appears to be a tendency in Kenya to make a deliberate attempt to come as close as possible to what is perceived as RP when one is reading a text aloud. This is particularly true in contexts like the Teacher Training Colleges where there is high sensitivity towards 'correct' pronunciation and usage, a tendency that often leads to hypercorrection.

Neither Schmied nor Kanyoro has looked at syntactic variables. These are much more difficult to analyse systematically, for various reasons (see Schmied 1988a), not the least of which is that there is wide individual variation. However, certain features of syntax seem to recur among groups of speakers from similar socioeducational backgrounds. No systematic research has been done on this, though some educators have written unpublished pamphlets on common syntactic 'errors' among Kenyan speakers of English (see, for example, Hocking 1978).

Social correlates of variation

Unfortunately no systematic research has been carried out on this topic. Impressionistic observation suggests that English varies in relation to social factors such as the sociocultural and educational background of the speaker, and the quality and intensity of exposure to standard British English and RP. It would seem that in Kenyan English there is much greater variation between individual speakers than there is in Tanzanian English. This is due to the fact that Kenyan society is more cosmopolitan, and more stratified in socioeconomic terms. In addition, in Kenya there is a much larger number of high cost private and international schools where many of the teachers are expatriate native speakers of English. Children who go to these expensive schools come from the rich, Western educated élite, normally with both wife and husband possessing high competence in the English language. Such homes are usually bilingual with English often as the primary language in the family. The children live in exclusive and expensive multiracial and multinational suburbs where the primary language of the playground, shopping centres, schools, places of entertainment, churches and hospitals is English. These households are likely to have facilities such as television, radio, a household library, and other household items typical of the life style of a Western middle class family.

At the other extreme is the typical peasant or pastoral life style of the African village or the over-crowded working class urban estates, where the primary languages of socialisation are the mother tongues and Kiswahili. In between these two extremes are various other socioeconomic groups whose competence in English varies widely, as does the frequency of its use and exposure to standard forms. It is in this last group in Kenya that a new in-group jargon called 'Sheng' has emerged among children. It is an urban in-group language which is a mixture of mother tongue, Kiswahili and English. This, too, has yet to be studied in any linguistic detail.

In Tanzania there were until recently few private schools, and the egalitarian socioeconomic policies have to a large degree levelled out socioeconomic and socioeducational differences. The primary language of socialisation and of day-to-day business is Kiswahili here, and therefore sociolinguistic variation in the use of English is much less noticeable than in Kenya.

Among middle class teenage groups in Kenya a new variety of English seems to be emerging, which is influenced by American English. This variety of English is slowly gaining prestige among this peer group, apparently as a result of the influence of popular music and of American films, video movies and discotheque jargon. There is a great deal of use of colloquial English with teenage idiomatic expressions, reminiscent of those heard in native English-speaking countries. As mentioned above, collo-quial English is rarely heard among older generations, who were mainly exposed to school varieties of formal English.

Among middle class and upper class children there seems to be a gradual shift to English from the mother tongues and Kiswahili. This has been widely noticed, and comments are often heard in the mass media and during political rallies that young people, especially in Nairobi, are losing their African cultural heritage. Again, very little research has been done as to the nature of this shift and the groups it is affecting most.

There is a great deal of apparently random and unrestrained code-switching between English and Kiswahili on the one hand and between English and the mother tongues on the other hand, among all generations (see Parkin 1977). Such code-switching, even within a sentence, seems to be socially acceptable, and even fashionable. Such unconscious code-switching is brought about partly by this unstable multilingualism, and by the now overlapping functional roles of English, Kiswahili and the mother tongues. For many urban groups it is no longer very clear what language should be used to say what to whom, and since there is free tolerance of code-switching in conversation, this language behaviour is very common.

In Tanzania there appears to be much less code-switching between English and Kiswahili among the younger generations, who have been brought up with Kiswahili as the primary language of socialisation at the national level. And given the pride with which one shows off one's competence in the national language, there are considerable social con-straints on code-switching. There is a clearly discernable shift in favour of Kiswahili, to the extent that the government is somewhat alarmed that the current low level of competence in English is lowering general standards of education in Tanzania. It requested support in English language teaching in secondary schools, in order to improve the situation. The British Overseas Development Agency has undertaken to supply Tanza-nian secondary schools with English textbooks for forms 1 to 4, with easy readers for class libraries and with reading kits and teachers' materials. In addition Key English Language Teaching (KELT) officers are posted to the different zones in order to conduct in-service courses, mainly to improve teaching methods and to ensure the effective use of the limited materials available (Schmied 1988b).

Language attitudes

There has been very little research on language attitudes in any of the East African countries. The only systematic research that has been carried out is Schmied's research in Tanzania (Schmied 1985a, 1985b). Schmied underscores the difficulties of conducting research of this kind in Third World countries where statistical data are often unreliable, and where people are not used to questionnaire techniques. He devised his attitude tests to elicit reactions to English, Kiswahili, French and Arabic. Attitudes were found to vary along three main dimensions: socioeducational, linguistic-ethnic and geographical – that is, urban versus rural. His main conclusion was that there is no uniform, monolithic attitude towards English among Tanzanians. However, his tests showed that English enjoys a very high prestige nowadays as a language of education and economic opportunity, Kiswahili as a national language of intimacy and socialisation, French as a pan-African language, and Arabic, which scored least highly, as an important language among Muslims.

Although no research other than Schmied's has been carried out into language attitudes in East Africa, Kanyoro (this volume) rightly stresses that the development of two different socioeconomic and language policies in Kenya and Tanzania since independence has led to different attitudes towards English and Kiswahili. In Tanzania attitudes towards English and the mother tongues are derived from the uncompromising situation of Kiswahili as the national and official language, with all the prestige that goes with it. The mother tongues are considered important subnational heritages, but they have no official place in the education system nor in any other sphere of public life. Attitudes towards English have varied with the sociopolitical fortunes of Tanzania. Before independence English had very high prestige as the language of education, modernisation and as the gateway to economic opportunities. Then came the period between independence and the mid-1970s when an antagonistic relationship between English and Kiswahili existed, to the detriment of the standards of English in the education system and a general decline in its use in public life. This was the period when English had the lowest prestige in Tanzania. Attitudes towards English began again to change in its favour from the mid 1970s. In 1974 President Nyere declared:

> Tanzanians would be foolish to reject English. We are a small country.
> English and French are African languages . . . It is a very useful language.
> (*The Times*, 9 December 1974. See Kihore 1976: 50).

This public statement had a profound effect. Apparently the drive towards using Kiswahili in public life began to slow down, especially with regard to the development of materials for using Kiswahili as the medium of instruction in secondary schools. The period between the mid-70s to the present day has been one of continued economic decline in Tanzania, which has meant the abandonment of many plans, including the plan to use Kiswahili in education, that were conceived in the late 1960s and early 1970s. The idea of Kiswahili as the medium of instruction in secondary schools seems to have been forgotten, at least for the present. English is likely to remain for the foreseeable future the language of post-primary education, though this brings many problems in its wake (see Schmied 1985a). Children who succeed in being accepted for secondary education have been educated in Kiswahili and their level of competence in English language does not make it easy for them to follow instruction in English. The situation is compounded by a lack of books in English for the various secondary school subjects, and a lack of teachers who have an adequate enough command themselves of English to teach it confidently. Attempts at introducing crash courses in English language skills often meet similar problems of lack of materials and teachers.

In Kenya attitudes towards the mother tongue, Kiswahili and English are based on how speakers perceive the sociocultural and, perhaps, the economic advantages attached to each language. In a situation of sensitive ethnic susceptibilities, the mother tongue functions as the language of identity and solidarity at the subnational level, being associated with personal friends, family, clan and ethnic group. In a situation of linguistic and cultural shifts, maintaining the home language is perhaps the most important recognisable feature of 'belonging'. Knowing Kiswahili, and a national variety of that language, as opposed to the Tanzanian or Ugandan variety, is likewise establishing one's identity at the national level. The use of English in Kenya is a marker of good education and of modernity. The level of competence and style of use of English helps to identify a person's level of education: primary, secondary, or tertiary, including University. It also marks the speaker's degree of modernisation and Westernisation – often, these days, regardless of the speaker's manner of dress. Recently there has been great emphasis on the need for Kenyans to be proud of their cultural heritage. Western dress, which until very recently was one of the symbols of modernisation, is no longer as important as it used to be, although it is still significant, especially where expensive sartorial taste is involved. It is still the case, however, that if one is well dressed, in Western fashion, one is expected to speak English well; whereas in other African countries, such as Nigeria, Ghana and Senegal, this is not necessarily the case. Another superficial feature of linguistic identity is the assumption of certain airs. Walking smartly, briskly and confidently in the manner attributed to British people during the colonial days, especially when combined with Western dress, usually gives rise to the idea that that person needs to be addressed in English, on the often mistaken assumption that they might be annoyed or upset if their linguistic identity is overlooked.

These cultural pointers are important to highlight, as they relate closely to the use of English and to attitudes towards English and the other languages that are spoken in the East African region. As mentioned above, in Kenya people in Western dress and with Western airs may be addressed in English; they may be objects of admiration, seen as having 'made it' in life. In Tanzania, on the other hand, they may well be considered ridiculous, or stupidly arrogant, aping the exploiting classes of the colonialists. They might be deliberately addressed in Kiswahili, to upset them or shame them. In other words, in East Africa, as elsewhere, it is impossible to consider the use of English without at the same time considering the social, cultural and social psychological contexts in which English and the other languages of the region are embedded.

REFERENCES

Abdulaziz, M. H. 1972. Triglossia and Swahili-English bilingualism in Tanzania. *Language in Society* 1: 197–213.

Angogo, Rachel and Hancock, Ian F. 1980. English in Africa: Emerging standards or diverging regionalisms? *English World-wide* 1: 67–96.

Hancock, Ian F. and Angogo, Rachel. 1984. English in East Africa. In Bailey, R. W. and Görlach, M. (eds.), *English as a World Language*. Cambridge: Cambridge University Press, pp. 306–23.

Hocking, Brian D. W. 1978. *All what I was Taught and other Mistakes*. Nairobi: Oxford University Press.

Kihore, Y. M. 1976. Tanzania's language policy and Kiswahili's historical background. *Kiswahili* 42(2).

Parkin, D. 1977. Emergent and stabilized multilingualism: polyethnic peer groups in urban Kenya. In Giles, H. (ed.), *Language, Ethnicity and Intergroup Relations*. London: Academic Press, pp. 185–209.

Schmied, J. 1985a. *Englisch in Tansania. Sozio-und interlinguistische Probleme*. Heidelberg: Groos.

1985b. Attitudes towards English in Tanzania. *English World-wide* 6: 237–69.

1988a. Recognizing and accepting East African English grammar. In Williams, H. (ed.), *The Role of Grammar in the Teaching of English*. Proceedings of the British Council Conference, Nairobi 1988.

1988b. English in East Africa: theoretical, methodological and practical issues. *Bayreuth African Studies* Series 14.

Whiteley, W. H. (ed.). 1974. *Language in Kenya*. Nairobi: Oxford University Press.

Zuengler, J. E. 1982. Kenyan English. In Kachru, B. B. (ed.), *The Other Tongue: English across Cultures*. Oxford: Pergamon, pp. 112–24.

27

The Politics of the English language in Kenya and Tanzania

MUSIMBI R. A. KANYORO

Introduction

In a previous publication, (Angogo and Hancock 1980) we[1] traced the history of the English language in Africa and established that there were specific phonological and idiomatic features which distinguished East African English from West African English. In another publication (Hancock and Angogo 1982) we took a detailed look at the so-called Anglophone Eastern Africa, and attempted to give a sociolinguistic description of speakers of East African English. We proposed a breakdown of four varieties of English registers in East Africa. This paper continues along similar lines. My focus will be on the politics of the English language in Kenya and Tanzania. In other words, the question that the paper seeks to explore is whether different political systems necessarily cause differences in the variety of language use. To put it another way, is the English spoken in Tanzania different from that spoken in Kenya because the two countries have pursued different political systems?

Background

Kenya and Tanzania share a common border. They also share a history of British colonisation and the introduction of the English language (Hancock and Angogo 1982: 309). Alongside English, Kiswahili is the lingua franca of both countries. The politics and the use of the one language is inseparably linked to those of the other. Following independence, Kenya and Tanzania each adopted politics and language policies which differed radically from each other. Language, like choice of an economic system, was based on the country's politics. While Kenya opted for capitalism and English as the most practical medium for business communication,

Tanzania adopted a policy of *Ujamaa* – socialism – and chose Kiswahili as the language of the people.

The border between Kenya and Tanzania was closed between 1977 and 1985. During this entire period, there was very little contact between the two countries. It was during this period that Tanzania was very busy developing Kiswahili. As a result, a gulf developed between the Kiswahili spoken in Kenya and that spoken in Tanzania. For example, in Kenya a dictionary entry for the word *ndugu* ('brother') would gloss it only in its kinship sense, i.e., 'male sibling'; but in Tanzania, while it means that too, it would be necessary to add 'one who is part of the sociopolitical life of Tanzania, male or female'.

Until 1984, Kenya and Tanzania followed the same educational system: seven years of primary school, four of secondary school and then two years of high school after which successful candidates were eligible for university entry.

Despite the emphasis on Kiswahili, Tanzania did not altogether drop the teaching of English in its schools. The question then is, what happened to English in Tanzania during those years of Kiswahili emphasis? Did Kenya develop a variety of English different from that of Tanzania?

I set out to find the answers to these questions by examining the English used in primary and secondary school textbooks written and published in Kenya and Tanzania after 1964. For Kenya, I chose the books prepared by the Ministry of Education through the Kenya Institute of Education. Similarly, for Tanzania, I chose those books prepared by the Tanzania Institute of Education, which, too, is an arm of the Ministry of Education. The composition of the two Institutes and the methods each used to prepare the textbooks share many common features. Both Institutes reflect the thinking of their respective governments. The books were usually prepared by a group of not less than ten scholars with representation from educators, language teachers, linguists and government administrators. Both Institutes developed English syllabi and textbooks for primary and secondary school instruction leading students to prepare for examinations.

I expected to find definite linguistic features which would distinguish Kenyan English from Tanzanian English. Instead I found that the English in the Kenyan and Tanzanian textbooks is basically the same. Both teach English based on British usage and spelling. The books have been so carefully prepared that even the accepted East Africanisms which we commonly found in recorded speech in our earlier research (Hancock and Angogo 1982) had been sieved. This phenomenon suggests that both Kenya and Tanzania, despite political pronouncements on adapting the English language to the local usage, still consider British English as the ideal for school textbooks. The only departure from British English was the use of Kiswahili words which have now been adopted into East African English. This includes such words as *safari* for 'journey', *sufuria*, 'a cooking pan', *Ujamaa*, the Tanzanian form of 'socialism' and others. There was no difference in the use of these words in the textbooks. They are simply chosen for appropriateness of context.

There were differences, however, in the volume of English textbooks prepared by each country and in the instructions provided in the teachers' handbooks or the syllabi for the English language. In addition to textbooks, Kenya prepared up to twelve supplementary readers for each level of education. Tanzania prepared only one textbook and a teacher's handbook at each level.

Although I could not identify from textbooks the specific language features that were peculiar to each country, my experience in both countries still convinced me that there was a difference in English usage between Kenya and Tanzania. However, students' textbooks prepared by government institutions are not the place to find the differences. Rather, the teachers' handbooks and syllabi reflect the politics of the English language in each country, and provide information which can shed some light on the possible differences. The following sections examine the politics of the English language in each country as it is perceived by the government's Ministry of Education. The instructions to the teachers form the basis for my conclusions about the differences between Kenyan and Tanzanian varieties of English.

Kenya

English is the official language in Kenya. Abdulaziz (this volume) describes the many domains in which English is used, and the extensive role that English plays in education. Clearly, in Kenya English is associated with socioeconomic prestige. In fact, some of the best educated people in the country who also command a high socioeconomic status are the least fluent in other languages, especially Kiswahili, the national language. Until recently, certain classes of people, especially front-desk office workers, were offended whenever they were addressed in Kiswahili.

English in Kenya therefore is exclusively a high status language. It is associated with white collar jobs and major responsibilities within the government and the private sector. Mastery of English is a ladder to success. Therefore, there is motivation for learning the English language.

The Kenya Government and the English language

The Ministry of Education, more than anyone else, realises that it holds the key to the acquisition of English language skills. Kenya syllabi state the following objectives for primary school English (1977a: 1):

all children should acquire a sufficient command of English in spoken and written form, to enable them to communicate freely, follow subject courses and textbooks, and read for pleasure in the language . . . It is necessary also to meet the needs of those children – the majority – for whom formal education terminates when they leave primary school . . . The seven years of Primary schooling should provide leavers from Standard VII with:

(a) a pronunciation of international intelligibility,
(b) a good ear for language
(c) working command in the necessary skills of words and phrases (including idioms) of general serviceability, and
(d) working command in the necessary skills of grammatical items (often referred to as 'Sentence Pattern') of general serviceability; the essential needs of Primary School leavers will have been met, whether they leave for the Secondary School or for employment involving the use of English.

The introduction to *Teaching English in Kenya Secondary Schools* also emphasises these same criteria:

How important is English in the Secondary Schools and beyond?. . . First, the question on the importance of English. The answer must be that English is very important, and for a variety of reasons. The most obvious one is that English is a service subject, in that fluency in all aspects of the English language will undoubtedly enable the student to perform better in all other subjects. A perhaps less obvious reason is that in the last few years Kenya has become a centre for service that extends over the whole of Eastern Africa and beyond, to Ethiopia, Somalia, Zambia and even further. All these services, ranging from technology and management to agricultural and environmental concerns, have made Kenya international in a way that countries such as Uganda and Ethiopia are not; and the importance of English, as the most widely used international language in the world has increased so much that ability in English is often the yardstick by which young Kenyans are judged.

As a statement from the government, it is a clear indication that English is held with much esteem. Indeed Kenya hosts many international conferences of every kind, including political, economic, religious and many others. Moreover, two United Nations Commissions have their headquarters in Nairobi. Many international bodies with Africa sections have regional offices in Nairobi. In addition, Kenya's economic policy encourages foreign investment and tourism. To promote all the above, Nairobi has become an important air connection. Many flights from Europe to Eastern, Southern, Central Africa and the Indian Ocean Islands have stop-overs in Nairobi. It is on this basis that Kenya interprets and justifies its policy for the promotion of the English language.

Teaching of English in Kenyan schools

English language instruction constitutes the largest segment of the curriculum in Kenyan Schools. Depending on the needs of each school, eight 25-45 minute lessons per week are allocated to English language instruction. Rural schools require more English lessons than urban schools.

The objectives of English instruction in Kenyan schools are to assist the pupil to master four basic skills: (1) listening, (2) speaking, (3) reading, and (4) writing. The first two skills are taught through drills and oral work. Reading is taught through comprehension passages, literature and library work, while writing is taught through composition.

Oral work

Oral work presents a good starting point, for identifying specific patterns which might be labelled as Kenyan English. Both primary and secondary school syllabi stress the importance of developing oral fluency through such activities as speech drills, drama, debates, riddles, proverbs, story telling and poetry reading. Besides building the students' confidence of self expression through oral exercises, teachers are told to use those lessons for identifying specific language errors which need remedial work. *The Progressive Peak English, Standard One Course for the Teacher* (1977b: 1) cautions the teachers:

> Pupils will learn their spoken English by imitating that of their teacher. It is therefore your duty to speak a kind of English that can be safely imitated . . . a regional colouring to a pronunciation, provided it is not so strong as to cause misunderstanding is altogether acceptable. It is as right and natural for a citizen of this country to sound Kenyan as it is for an Irishman to sound Irish, or a Frenchman to sound French . . . What however is not acceptable in any speaker of English as an international language is a pronunciation which cannot be understood by an educated speaker of English. Your pronunciation must set a model of Spoken English that is internationally intelligible.

To help ensure that students will learn a kind of English which can be understood by the international community, all course books for teachers of English provide guidance in English pronunciation by giving both the orthographic representation and phonetic transcription. Stress and intonation are also indicated. In the *Standard One Course Book for the Teacher* (1975) detailed notes on the phonetic transcription, based on the IPA system, are given. English vowels, for example, are presented with all details of length, height and quality.

Many teaching drills and remedial work are based upon the expectations that Kenyans should speak a kind of English that will be internationally intelligible. However, faced with a greater range of varieties of pronunciation, Kenyans are tolerant of each other's lack of oral purity. A number of comedies on radio, television, and theatre are based on linguistic errors resulting from first language interferences or transfer of local phonology to the English language.[2] The Ministry of Education is aware that Kenyan English is tainted with local usage. In the ministry's *Teaching English in Kenyan Secondary Schools* (1980: 37) English teachers are told:

> Almost all pupils are in need of remedial English owing to low standards of English in primary schools which in turn are due to primary English teaching having to be entrusted to teachers who have had no training, insufficient training under inadequate tutors or insufficient learning experience of English before having to start teaching it . . . therefore the secondary English teacher has to realise that it is necessary for him to do a great deal of remedial work in the time allocated to him for English teaching.

In the pages that follow on remedial work, teachers are required to address errors which are seen specifically as Kenyan errors. Muchiri and Muthiani (1980:137–46) give a long list of the type of errors made by Kenyans. The list may be summarised under two categories:

1. Mother tongue interference
2. Incorrect usage of English

Mother Tongue Interference

This is perhaps the most conspicuous element that identifies a Kenyan variety of English. If the Ministry of Education indeed meant that it was acceptable for Kenyans to sound Kenyan, they might not have addressed this element in the Kenyan textbooks. However, it is mother tongue interference that makes Kenyan oral English unintelligible to non-Kenyans. Hence, teachers are encouraged to provide remedial work for mother tongue interference with a focus on phonology and incorrect usage of the English language due to literal translations of local vocabularies or idioms from local languages.

In Hancock and Angogo (1982: 313), we gave several examples of East African phonological interferences. Hocking (1978) among others also addressed the subject of phonological errors made by Kenyans.

Although Kenyans are tolerant of each other's lack of oral purity, teachers are cautioned against letting students lapse into pronunciation that makes communication impossible. They are reminded about the tonal nature of various languages in Kenya, and about how tone may be carried over to English. Kiswahili intonation, for example, is often carried over to the English language. The illustrations below show some aspects of Kenyan phonology upon which remedial work is built.

1.   Stress

English Stress	Kenyan Stress
'execute	exe'cute
pho'tography	photo'graphy
'demonstrate	demon'strate
'argument	argu'ment
'convict (n)	con'vict (n)
'present (n)	pre'sent (n)
'progress (n)	pro'gress (n)

2.   Vowels not found in Kenyan languages. For example:

/ə/   as in RP *bacon*
/ɜ:/   as in RP *bird, herd, turn*
/æ/   as in RP *bad*

3.   Vowels not distinguished for length in Kenya:

Front vowels:
Short   /ɪ/   as in RP *hit, list, this, live*
and long   /i:/   as in RP *heat, least, these, leave*
Back vowels:
Short   /ɒ/   as in RP *pot, stop*
and long   /ɔ:/   as in RP *port*

4.   Vowels not distinguished for quality:

/æ/	/ɑ:/	/ʌ/
back	bark	buck
cap	carp	cup
cat	cart	cut
bad	bard	bud
lack	lark	luck
stack	stark	stuck

Diphthongs:

/ɒ/	/ou/		/ɛ/	/eɪ/
not	– note		let	– late
cot	– coat		bet	– bait
got	– goat		get	– gate
cock	– coke		pen	– pane
cost	– coast		met	– mate
rob	– robe			

5.   Consonants which present problems to particular mother tongue speakers:

a. Kalenjin speakers use the following interchangeably:

/tʃ/ ch	⟷	/dʒ/ j
/b/ b	⟷	/p/ p
/k/ k	⟷	/g/ g

cheer	⟷	jeer
bakery	⟷	pakery
cocacola	⟷	gogakola
cake	⟷	gake

b. Luo speakers do not have /ʃ/ (voiceless palato-alveolar fricative):

/ʃ/ sh	⟷	/s/ s

sugar	⟷	sugar
shirt	⟷	sat

c. Central Kenya Bantu use the following sounds interchangeably:

/l/ l	⟷	/r/ r
/ʃ/ sh	⟷	/tʃ/ ch

lorry	⟷	rorry
rice	⟷	lice
land	⟷	rand
lost	⟷	rost
show	⟷	chow
chariot	⟷	shariot

These languages also pre-nasalise the voiced stops /b/, /d/, /g/:

bad	→	mband
red	→	rend
had	→	hand
sad	→	sand
lad	→	land
goat	→	ngoat

Hypercorrection within this group of languages usually results in nasal sounds being deleted before voiced stops:

language	→	laguage
distinguish	→	distiguish
land	→	lad
band	→	bad

d. Western Kenya Bantu:
The Luyia languages of Western Kenya do not have voiced stops and fricatives:

bible	→	piple
drive	→	trife
give	→	kife
jet	→	chet
guest	→	kest

Teachers are expected to provide assessment and remedial English tutelage for each student after identifying his or her particular problem.

Incorrect usage of English

It was interesting to note that most of what the textbooks treat as incorrect usage covers carry-overs of idioms and vocabulary from other Kenyan languages. Story telling reflects one of those areas. In many African narratives repetition is a discourse marker. For example:

> The fox ate the chicken. After eating the chicken, the farmer killed the fox. After the fox was dead, the farmer buried it.

Another area is literal translation. Many local idioms translated literally have become part of Kenyan English. Additionally, Kenyans' use of certain English words differs in meaning from that of native English speakers. For example, the word *spoil* can refer to: 'spoilt fruit' – meaning 'rotten or damaged'; 'spoilt car', meaning 'having mechanical problems'; 'spoilt language' – meaning 'imperfect language' etc. The word *miss* may be used in the context of 'miss to come' meaning 'fail to come' or 'miss food' meaning 'lack food'. These usages are literal translations from local languages. Textbook English for Kenyan schools does not allow any of the above local usages.

Comprehension and writing

The teaching of comprehension is carried out by means of comprehension passages given in each book. In the early years of education, children are given pictures to interpret. In that way they learn the language in context.

The syllabi require that the student is exposed to many different types of literature. In higher classes, Forms 3 and 4, each student is required to read a minimum of 20 library books in a year, in addition to the class-readers. The class-readers are specific, carefully selected books which are meant to be used for intensive comprehension skills and for teaching literary criticism. They are studied under a teacher's supervision. The library time aids the students' self-paced reading ability, knowledge of the language, and fosters the habit of reading for pleasure.

Writing is taught mainly through composition. The students are encouraged to compose essays on subjects of their own interest as well as on prescribed subjects. Original composition of poetry is highly encouraged.

In addition to the teaching of language *per se*, teachers of English in Kenya have to teach study drills, since English is seen as a service subject. The lessons include note-taking, study habits, use of encyclopaedias, use of dictionaries, library references and etiquette. This latter is such an obvious remnant of British influence that anyone can see through it. The lessons here include phrases such as:

> How do you do?
> Thank you, sir.
> No, thank you madam.
> You are welcome.
> Will you please pass the salt?

To summarise, both primary and secondary school English textbooks provide extensive and intensive exposure to the English language. Clearly, Kenya's politics have encouraged the development of English among its students.

Tanzania

English is an official language in Tanzania, a fact that has been over-shadowed by the emphasis on Kiswahili. English is taught as a subject from primary school, and is officially used as a medium of instruction for most secondary school subjects (though actual practice does not always coincide with the official rule) and at university.

The Tanzanian Government and the English language

It is next to impossible to discuss English in Tanzania without reference to Kiswahili (see Abdulaziz 1971, this volume). Kiswahili has been well-established in Zanzibar and the Tanganyikan coast and urban centres since the 1800s. Prior to World War 1, the colonial German administration provided the impetus for the dissemination and development of Kisawahili in the Tanganyikan interior. This process was reinforced through the intervention of the churches. Missionaries studied Zanzibar's form of Kiswahili and produced written studies on it. With the availability of Kiswahili textbooks, it was possible to incorporate the language into Tanganyika's educational system long before it was used in the same way elsewhere in East Africa.

Before independence English was associated with prestige and with the chance for better jobs and personal advancement, and it was given a predominant role in education (again, see Abdulaziz, this volume). This changed after the Arusha Declaration of 1967. The Declaration argued that anything that promoted a few people to be the 'bosses' was contrary to the ideals of equality. Tanzania decided that its first goal was the education of its citizens to be self-reliant. The role played by the English language was minimised in status, use and instruction.

During the 1970s, Tanzania revised its syllabi for primary and secondary schools as well as teacher training institutions. The grade A English syllabus, for example, stated that the aim of teaching English in Tanzania was to increase the students' ability to understand and interpret materials written in English and to train students to write their own materials in English which incorporate principles of *Ujamaa*. The syllabus stated that the ultimate goal for learning English in Tanzania was to help students acquire functional English.

There were some problems right from the time the change-over was initiated. In teacher training colleges, for example, both the Standard VII and Form IV leavers were put together in the grade C syllabus. The Form IV leavers who had studied more English, among other things, than the Standard VII had to do less challenging work as the training of teachers of English was lowered to accommodate Standard VII school leavers. Yet to separate the two classes was seen as being discriminatory on the basis of a foreign language.

Reading materials in English became scarce as Tanzania concentrated on developing Kiswahili materials. Most *Ujamaa* propaganda materials produced at that time were not yet translated into English. Since it was more important to be involved in building socialism and developing the Kiswahili language, the motivation for studying English decreased.

The teaching of English in Tanzanian schools

Tanzanian textbooks and teachers' handbooks prepared by the Institute of Education emphasise comprehension and composition over oral fluency. Unlike the Kenyan books, there were no notes for the teacher to watch out for regional variations and mother tongue interferences in the students' English. I do not think that this was an oversight. Rather, it is a deliberate support for the government's emphasis on functional proficiency.

Likewise the Tanzanian textbooks incorporated no introductions stating the importance of the English language in that country. The books go directly to the subject matter, which is composed of comprehension, grammar and vocabulary-building. While the comprehension passages in these books cover a wide range of subjects, local as well as international, the Tanzanian books have more passages that address the Tanzanian political system. This aspect is remarkably absent in the Kenyan texts. Note, for example, the contents of a Tanzanian textbook entitled *Post Primary English Stage I*.

1. Introduction
2. Unit One: The Great Friends
   From the Classroom to the Village
3. Unit Two: Our National Language
   Traditional Methods of Communication
4. Unit Three: Giving Culture Its Due Respect
   Old but Hard Working

5. Unit Four: Quality not Quantity
    Chakula Ni Uhai and Agriculture
6. Unit Five: Good for Us but Not for Plants
    Fishing in Tanzania
7. Unit Six: *Chakula Bora*
    Poultry Keeping in Tanzania
8. Unit Seven: Dressing the Colonial Wounds
    The Game is Too Expensive
9. Unit Eight: Pleasing Identical Twins
    The Fruits of *Ujamaa*

It was also interesting to note how Tanzania disseminates the concepts of *Ujamaa* through the teaching of the English language. For example in teaching the calendar months to beginners in primary school, the following associations were used:

January — We open school. (Picture showing school children outside a school building)

February — We have CCM holiday. (Picture showing a group of boys and girls with placards in Kiswahili: *Tujitegemee* (let us be self-reliant), *CCM – Chama Cha Mapinduzi* (i.e. the party), *Vijana Oyee* – (Hail the Youth)

June — We have school holiday. We help our mother and father. (Picture showing a boy working on a maize plantation)

July — We have Saba-Saba Day. (Picture of celebrations with drums)

December — We have Independence Day. (Picture of soldiers in socialist march style)

(Incidentally Kenyan textbooks illustrate December with Christmas). Supplementary reading is recommended by the textbooks. In *Tanzania, Pupils Book VII*, after every series of comprehension passages, the pupils are asked to request their teacher for a book to read for pleasure. However, the Institute did not prepare any supplementary readers. I was told by the teachers in Tanzania that supplementary English readers are very scarce. Even the propaganda materials on *Ujamaa* are too limited to meet the needs of the students of English language. The absence of books of varying difficulty in the English language for different levels of students may have greatly reduced the quality of English used, especially among young Tanzanians of the post-Arusha Declaration.

By the time young Tanzanian students enter secondary school, they are expected to have had reasonable exposure to both oral and written English. They will have been introduced to simple structures of language such as basic grammar and sentence construction. Theoretically, they will have a limited but sufficient vocabulary for communicating simply but intelligently and with confidence.

The same is expected of Kenyan students. However, in many cases that

I have encountered, Tanzanian students lack the confidence to express themselves in English due to the fact that they have had fewer opportunities to read extensively in the language and to hear it spoken. However, when asked to address the same subject in Kiswahili, Tanzanian students may express themselves more confidently than Kenyan students do in English.

Varieties of English in Kenya and Tanzania

In Angogo and Hancock (1980:71), we proposed a breakdown of English in Africa which we saw as consisting of four types:

I   The native English of expatriates and locally-born whites;
II   The native English of locally-born Africans;
III Non-native English spoken fluently as a second language in several styles; and
IV   Non-native English spoken imperfectly as a foreign language in several styles.

We did not concern ourselves with Type I, as we were interested in African English. For Type II, we classified it as the English of those Africans of Westernised backgrounds, due either to marriage, location, or other circumstances that made English their mother tongue. We observed that a number of African children born in many cities become members of this group. We saw Type III as the model for African English. It is the English spoken comfortably by people who have learnt an African language first, but who because of their education or profession have grown up hearing and using English daily and therefore speak it as well, or even better, than their ancestral language.

We classified Type IV speakers as people who have acquired imperfect English by virtue of lacking sufficient exposure to the language to have mastered it. English therefore remains a foreign language to such people. Depending on their motivation, social position and opportunities for further education, they may or may not eventually acquire Type III English.

I see the Kenya – Tanzania differences in the use of English through the above definitions. Due to the position that the English language occupies in Kenyan politics, Kenya is likely to produce more speakers of types II and III than Tanzania. Although both countries aim at producing speakers of Type III, Kenya stands a better chance of achieving that goal. The majority of English speakers in East Africa might fall in Type IV, because many students leave the school system before they have achieved fluency in English. But given the political systems of Kenya and

Tanzania, Tanzania is likely to produce more speakers of Type IV than Kenya.

The future of English in Kenya and Tanzania

It is noteworthy that although English is still taught and studied at University level, the English departments at all three East African universities have been replaced by departments whose main concern is Linguistics and African Languages and Literature. Debates on the issue of English language continue to surface from time to time in both Kenya and Tanzania. Letters from the public discussing the issue also appear frequently in national dailies. The East Africa Center for Research in Oral Traditions and African National Languages situated in Zanzibar recently composed a list of articles on language in Tanzania published between 1982 and 1986. In the appendix of this paper we reproduce a list of those articles which specifically address the subject of the English language in Tanzania.

Kenya's capitalistic system, whose success depends on foreign investment, creates a climate for dependence on the English language. However, its pro-English policy has not been without challenge. In Kenya it is widely felt that English should not receive special attention or be promoted over any other language, but rather it should be on an equal footing with other languages in the country. It is also sometimes heard from this or that group, 'why can't Luo or Kipsigis or Kamba or Gikuyu etc. be a national language?' or 'why can't we have several Kenyan languages promoted to national status?' The argument made is that, after all, the number of speakers of any one of these languages equals or surpasses the number of English speakers in the country. The argument continues further that those unfamiliar with any of the regional languages would need to expend no more effort to learn any other local language than they would to learn English. On the other hand, those who prefer English to Kiswahili or indigenous languages point out that English is neutral, with no ethnic or emotional attachments and, in addition, it provides a link to the world beyond East Africa. Opponents counter that English is a language foreign to Africa and to African thought, and carries the stigma of colonialism. Because English is acquired only through the educational system, it excludes the majority of Kenyans from participating in the development of their own country. The debate continues and still the English language continues to thrive!

As for Tanzania, if letters to the newspapers are any indication of people's attitudes towards English, then the pendulum is likely to swing in favour of expanding English instruction in schools. During my frequent visits to Tanzania, I meet many teachers who would like to see the

teaching of English intensified. However, it is unlikely that English will
retrieve its former status of prestige and privilege, unless the political
system were to change drastically.

NOTE

1. Musimbi R. A. Kanyoro previously published under the name Rachel Angogo.
2. Students of English, however, are apparently less tolerant of variation in
   pronunciation (see Abdulaziz, this volume) [Ed].

REFERENCES

Abdulaziz, M. H. 1971. Tanzania's national language policy and the rise of Swahili
   political culture. In Whitely and Forde (eds.) 1971, *Language Use and Social
   Change: Problems of Bilingualism with Special Reference to Eastern Africa*.
   London: Oxford University Press.
Angogo, Rachel. 1978. Language and politics in South Africa. *Studies in African
   Linguistics* 9: 211–21.
Angogo, Rachel and Hancock, Ian F. 1980. English in Africa: emerging standards
   or diverging regionalism. *English World-wide* 1(1): 67–96.
Hancock, Ian F. and Angogo, Rachel. 1982. English in East Africa. In Bailey,
   Richard W. and Görlach, Manfred (eds.), *English as a World Language*. Ann
   Arbor: University of Michigan Press, pp. 306–23.
Hocking, B. D. W., 1978, *All what I was Taught and other Mistakes* Nairobi:
   Oxford University Press.
Kenya Institute of Education.
   1972 *Teaching Written English*. A Method Handbook.
   1975. *The Progressive Peak English Course*. Book for the Teacher STD 1.
   1976. *The Progressive Peak English Course*. Book for the Teacher STD II.
   1977a. *Kenya Syllabus for Primary Schools*.
   1977b. *The Progressive Peak English Course*. Book for the Teacher STD III.
   1980. *Teaching English in Kenya Secondary Schools*.
   1982. *The Progressive Peak English Course*. Book Two.
   1983a. *The Progressive Peak English Course*. Book One.
   1983b. *The Progressive Peak English Course*. Book Three.
   1983c. *Regulations and Syllabuses*. KCE.
Muchiri, Mary and Muthiani, Joseph. 1980. Remedial and Practical Language
   Work. *Teaching English in Kenya Secondary Schools*.
Tanzania Institute of Education.
   1967. *English for Tanzanian Schools. Book 6*.
   1973. *English for Tanzanian Schools. Teachers' Book Five*.
   1977a. *Post-Primary English Stage One. A Course for Adults*.
   1977b. *Learning Through Language*.

1981. *English for Tanzanian Schools. Book 7.*
1982a. *Primary English for Tanzania. Book 1.*
1982b. *Primary English for Tanzania. Book 2.*
1983. *Primary English for Tanzania. Book 3.*
1985. *Primary English for Tanzania. Book 4.*

Appendix

Letters to the press on the English language in Tanzania

Serial	Issue	Date	Title
		Sunday News	
		1982	
1)	1546	11 Oct.	The role of language in society
2)	1548	31 Oct.	The English language
		1983	
3)	1593	11 Sept.	Kiswahili or English?
4)	1594	18 Sept.	The Minister is right
5)	1594	18 Sept.	We need English
6)	1595	25 Sept.	We need both languages
7)	1595	25 Sept.	Importance of English
8)	1596	2 Oct.	What are we debating about?
9)	1596	2 Oct.	What's in a language?
10)	1596	2 Oct.	Does education mean language?
11)	1596	2 Oct.	English is vital
12)	1598	16 Oct.	English still vital
13)	1502	13 Nov.	English
14)	1502	13 Nov.	English is medium of instruction
15)	1504	27 Nov.	English, English, English
16)	1607	18 Dec.	Student's views on English
		1984	
17)	1649	7 Oct.	Whither English?
		1985	
18)	1702	13 Oct.	In Love with English

Letter continued

Serial	Issue	Date	Title
		1986	
19)	1720	23 Feb.	Clearing the language barrier
20)	1722	16 Mar.	English must be revived
21)	1724	30 Mar.	Re-introduce oral English Exams
22)	1724	30 Mar.	(Deterioration of Standard)
23)	1728	27 Apr.	How to improve English?
24)	1730	11 May	English on a stretcher
25)	1730	11 May	New drive to improve English
26)	1733	1 June	Give English top priority
27)	1733	1 June	Problem calls for dynamism

Daily News

Serial	Issue	Date	Title
		1982	
1)	3027	23 June	Comment
2)	3130	15 Nov.	Encourage English
		1983	
3)	3190	21 May	Candidates must know English
4)	3192	14 May	Teaching English
5)	3310	10 Oct.	Language
6)	3310	10 Oct.	Issue is lack of books
7)	3317	18 Oct.	Stick to English
8)	3328	31 Oct.	Kiswahili is appropriate
9)	3343	17 Nov.	English has problems
10)	3371	20 Dec.	Comments
		1985	
11)	3786	18 Apr.	English textbooks scarce
12)	3858	13 July	A world language
13)	3259	11 Aug.	Teaching English in Primary Schools
14)	3286	12 Sept.	Is Kiswahili inadequate?
15)	3292	19 Sept.	Debate on English, Kiswahili
16)	3299	27 Sept.	English is dominant language
17)	3303	1 Oct.	Newfoundland English
		1986	
18)	4043	14 Feb.	Poor English affects exam
19)		17 Feb.	Poor English not the only cause
20)	4085	5 Apr.	Teach English from
21)	4110	6 May	Problems in teaching English
22)	4126	24 May	English
23)	4136	5 June	How to improve English

28

National and subnational features in Kenyan English

JOSEF J. SCHMIED

The following analysis is a feasibility study for a research project on 'English in East Africa: an independent African means of communication?', which is the contribution of English Linguistics to the Special Research Programme (SFB) on 'Identity in Africa' carried out at the University of Bayreuth.[1] I will therefore briefly explain the background to this study in relation to the notion of identity, before explaining the methodology and problems of the analysis and the results of this micro-sociolinguistic study on the co-variation of pronunciation, social and contextual variables.

English and Kenyan identities

The basic assumption of this research project is that attempts to define specific African national identities must rest on various distinct concepts of cultural identity as well as on various overlapping regional identities. In this overall framework language is seen as a means of expressing, together with a message, a personal and/or a group identity, which is chosen by the speaker and interpreted by the hearer. In modern ethno-psychology personal identity is often seen as the sum of heterogeneous identities. Thus if a market woman in a market in Nyeri responds in English to a white man's question in Swahili, she expresses part of her identity, just as when she talks in Kikuyu to her market neighbours. Similarly, a Luo hotel manager may talk in basilectal English to his Kikuyu cleaners and in acrolectal English to his foreign guests. Here, language, and a particular variety of language, is seen as a marker, used (within a certain repertoire even deliberately) by the speaker to suggest a distinct identity to the hearer and/or interpreted by the hearer as signalling a particular speaker identity. English is unique in East Africa as it may signal international, national and subnational identities.[2]

In this analysis I investigate which features in the pronunciation of

Kenyan English (KenE) may be interpreted as sociolinguistic signals of national (all-Kenyan) or subnational (ethnic) identities. Such signals, or markers, are defined as variants that are constantly used (and clearly perceived) by one group of speakers rather than another. As nation-building is generally considered of prime importance in Africa, ethnic background was examined as the basic nonlinguistic variable, the dimensions of sex and linguistic context and style later. Although some notions about linguistic markers are commonly held impressionistically by educated and linguistically conscious people in Kenya, they have not been subjected to rigorous analysis before (Zuengler 1982, for instance, does not mention pronunciation in 'Kenyan English'). The basic hypothesis of this study was that the pronunciation of vowels (levelling of quantitative distinctions between vowels, monophthongising diphthongs and avoiding central vowels) systematically differentiates KenE from 'Standard English', that is, southern British standard English (including RP), whereas the pronunciation of consonants ('r/l problems' for the Bantu, 'alveolar fricative problems' for the Luo – see Kanyoro, this volume) expresses differentiations within KenE.

Research methodology and problems

The research methodology of this analysis was guided by the basic principle of recording not only which features occur, as in traditional dialectology, but also how consistently they are used. From previous studies (for example, Hancock and Angogo 1982 and Schmied 1985) the basic patterns of 'Africanisation' were well-known, especially for the more obvious vowel system (see figure 28.1), but it was not clear what the relative importance of these features was. Thus the methodology used in our analysis had to be quantitative; that is, structured data had to be elicited, which could later on be coded and analysed statistically.[3] Generally, the research methodology was inspired by Johnston (1983) and Jibril (1986), who investigated similar processes that occur when a pronunciation standard independent of RP develops.

The selection of informants for the three comparable studies was different. Whereas Johnston used a random sample of (29) mother-tongue speakers, Jibril and I selected second-language speakers (45 and 44, respectively). Like Jibril, I selected English language 'promoters', but I chose a more homogeneous socioeducational group, namely trainee teachers, who were mainly between 20 and 25 years old and had studied English for 13 to 15 years at school and college (which places them somewhat lower on the socioeconomic scale than Jibril's informants). There were 18 male and 25 female informants in the sample.

Due to the low number of informants (and to avoid data interpretation when there were less than 5 members in a cell) only language groups were

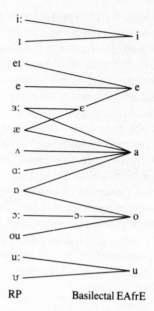

Figure 28.1   The vowel systems of RP and EAfrE compared.

analysed (this excluded the Teso and Taita informants). The informants' mother tongues (and birthplaces) fall into four groups: 19 Central Bantu, that is, mainly Kikuyu, but also Meru, Embu and Kamba, 9 Western Bantu, that is Luhya, Maragoli and Gusi, 6 Kalenjin (Southern Nilotes), that is Kipsigis, Nandi, Sabaot and Pokot, and 8 Luo (Western Nilotes). The distribution of this sample over the four language groups roughly reflects the ethnic distribution over the whole of Kenya, with the exception of the Coastal Bantu and the Cushitic sections.

The language data was not selected from free or structured conversation, as by Johnston and Jibril, but only from a reading list, which consisted of a continuous text (a slightly adapted version of Henry Sweet's 'Arthur the rat', which has often been used in English dialect studies) and a list of isolated words and word pairs specifically put together to elicit typically East African pronunciation features. Although this reading list may have caused a more formal interview situation, even though most of the recordings were made by Kenyans, it was the only way to ensure absolute qualitative and quantitative comparability.

Altogether about 110 sound units in different places in the text were selected as pronunciation variables, but only variables with more than 3 clearly identifiable variants from the standard norm were included in the statistical analysis. These remaining 72 variables were also marked according to three types of context variation, as text variables (names coded plus a prefix T), pair variables (plus a prefix P) and isolated word variables (plus a prefix I). This made it easy to recognise the context of individual features as well as to calculate aggregated context variables.

The coding system was developed to record qualitative and quantitative deviations from the English norm (RP), which theoretically is still regarded as *the* standard norm among Kenyans (see Abdulaziz, this volume). The general scale from acrolectal to basilectal variation can be represented by a cline from 0 to 3, with 1 and 2 representing mixtures or transitional forms between the extremes. For some features additional values were necessary: for long vowels and diphthongs 4 represents quantitative, 5 qualitative and 6 quantitative + qualitative differences from the basic variant 3; for short vowels and consonants 4 to 6 represent qualitative differences from 3 (for some quantitative procedures the values 4 to 6 had to be collapsed into 3). Thus the pronunciation of [ɜ:], as in *heard* or *further*, was recorded as 0 = [ɜ:], 3 = [a:], 4 = [a], 5 = [e:] and 6 = [e]. The values 7, 8 and 9 were reserved for hypercorrect, deviant and missing items, respectively.

Some coding problems were connected with listening comprehension, since only listeners with some experience in East African pronunciation proved to be reliable for coding (these were two German and two English mother-tongue speakers). Another (technical) problem is connected to the cline from 1 to 3. Although some 'East Africanisms', for example, [a:] or [e:] for [ɜ:], are much more salient, with larger distances between the extremes, than others, for example, [o:] for [ou], all pronunciation variables were coded according to the same scale. Thus similar numerical values for Africanisation may conceal quite different perceptual impressions of 'Africanness'.

Results

General features of KenE pronunciation

A wide range of pronunciation variables was examined in order to gain as complete a picture of (segmental) pronunciation features as possible. Figure 28.2 summarises 21 features of KenE: long vowels, short vowels, diphthongs and consonants.

Figure 28.2 can be compared with Jibril's Figure 2 (1986: 57), reprinted as Figure 28.3 below, bearing in mind that Jibril records 'typical' representations of YorubaE and IgboE, whereas this figure shows aggregated means. An important difference between West and East African English is the pronunciation of the RP *but* sound, [ʌ]. In general it becomes manifest that some vowels (including diphthongs) clearly and consistently mark KenE, whereas the consonants, in general, show less difference from the maintained RP model.

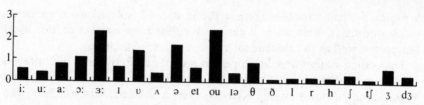

Figure 28.2   'Africanisation' of 21 RP phonemes in KenE.

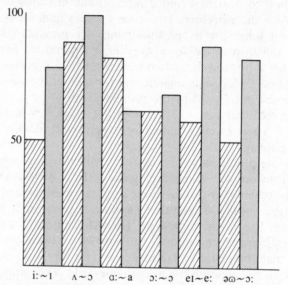

Figure 28.3   Some typical Igbo/Yoruba realisations of some RP vowels (from Jibril 1986). ⧄ = speaker 10, Igbo; ▦ = speaker 21, Yoruba.

This general rule, however, conceals an important difference between four types of variables. Some are salient and used consistently, such as [a:] for [ɜ:], some are less salient and still used consistently, such as [o:] for [ou] or [dj] for [dʒ] and some are salient but used inconsistently, such as [r] for [l] (the fourth group, which is neither very salient nor consistently used, is of course not examined here).

These three groups of features pose different problems as far as intelligibility and acceptability are concerned. Less salient and less consistent features are easily understood and accepted. They include most of the rising diphthongs (mainly /eɪ/ and /ou/ and, though less so, /aɪ/ and /ɔɪ/, which tend towards double monophthongisation), with a reduced glide or even levelling to monophthongs (/e/ and /o/ respectively), as well as the centring diphthongs (mainly /ɪə/, /ɛə/ and /ɔə/), which tend to become double monophthongs, with a final [a] element. Salient and consistent features of pronunciation pose a problem of intelligibility when they merge

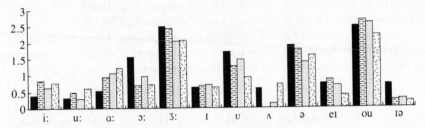

Figure 28.4 'Africanisation' of vowels by four Kenyan language groups.
■ = Central Bantu; ▤ = Western Bantu; ☐ = Kalenjin; ▨ = Luo.

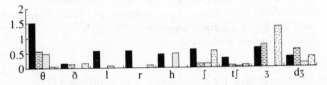

Figure 28.5 'Africanisation' of consonants by four Kenyan language groups.
■ = Central Bantu; ▤ = Western Bantu ☐ = Kalenjin; ▨ = Luo.

with other phonemes. This is certainly the case with the frequent levelling of differences between long and short vowels in KenE, but this seems to be much less of a problem for East Africans themselves than for foreigners unaccustomed to this language behaviour (for problems of mergers see Milroy and Harris 1980). The most salient and consistent case is [ɜ:]. In this case most East Africans would shrug off the obvious discrepancy between the theoretical (RP) norm [ɜ:] and the actual language behaviour [a:] or occasionally [e:]. 'I don't want to strain myself so much to say [fɜːst] (first) only to sound British' or 'This would seem snobbish to my colleagues' would be typical reactions. Obviously the vernacular forms have covert prestige. They seem to function as a symbol of group identity, which is used to signal national solidarity even by those who have, through study and travel, clear links with standard English speakers, but who do not necessarily want to be associated with them in the national context. These salient and consistent features are clearly markers of the developing national variety of KenE (or EastAfrE). Salient and inconsistent features include most of the fricatives and were further analysed to find out whether they showed a more consistent pattern on the subnational level.[4]

Subnational features of KenE pronunciation

Figures 28.4 and 28.5 show the pronunciation of vowels and consonants broken down into the four language groups analysed. Due to sample restrictions single results can only be interpreted tentatively, but again a difference between the vowels and the consonants can be seen.

In a rigorous statistical analysis with ONEWAY (using the fairly conservative Scheffé method) the following features showed significant differences at the 0.05 level between our four language groups:

- the pronunciation of RP voiceless *th* [θ] as voiced [ð] by the Central Bantu differs from that of all the other groups,
- the pronunciation of RP [l] as an [r]-like sound by the Central Bantu differs from that of the Western Bantu and of the Luo,
- the pronunciation of [i:] by the Central Bantu again differs from the Luo and the Western Bantu, as they tend not to keep the length distinction,
- generally diphthongs as pronounced by the Central and the Western Bantu differ from those of the Kalenjin and Luo; whereas the former tend to monophthongise diphthongs the latter are somewhat 'better' at maintaining the second element.

This means, on the whole, that our hypothesis that the four language groups are distinguished by consonants was confirmed, but it raises new questions as far as the diphthongs are concerned. The occasionally expressed opinion that 'the Luo maintain the vowel distinctions better than the Kikuyu' was not confirmed.

Other features that were not analysed quantitatively but that certainly occur (inconsistently) in rapid or basilectal speech are insertions of nasals before alveolar plosives, as in *sala(n)d* or *foo(n)d*, and the related hypercorrect omissions in *hand*, pronounced as *had* or even *ad* (then it may become a homophone with *and*), by the Kikuyu and Meru; or unreduced unstressed final vowels, particularly by the Luo. Some features even identify only specific mother-tongue speakers and not the whole language group, for example, dropping initial [h] is fairly consistently heard from the Kamba, but only inconsistently from the Kikuyu.

Towards these subnational pronunciation features Africans express a less 'generous' attitude. The pronunciation of RP [l] as [r], for instance, is clearly stigmatised, even by those who use it themselves ('You know, we Kikuyu have this *r/l* problem'). Thus, although this feature is quite common and serves as a social marker for certain groups, it is not an acceptable one. Here no covert prestige is attached to vernacular forms. This may be explained by the fact that in the multilingual context in Kenya, English does not function as a means of communication to express intra-ethnic solidarity, as here ethnic languages, the mother tongues, are used.

Contextual and other influences

An analysis of all 'deviations' in the three context styles – text, word pairs and isolated words – shows that 'Africanness' is more clearly marked in

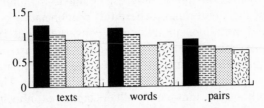

Figure 28.6 'Africanisation' of variables in reading texts, isolated words and word pairs by four Kenyan language groups. ■ = Central Bantu; ▦ = Western Bantu; ▤ = Kalenjin; ▨ = Luo.

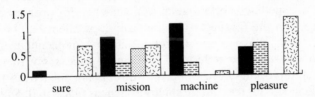

Figure 28.7 The pronunciation of the alveolar fricatives in *sure, mission, machine* and *pleasure*. ■ = Central Bantu; ▦ = Western Bantu; ▤ = Kalenjin; ▨ = Luo.

the text than in the word list, but that the differences between the context styles are not significant (see figure 28.6 for the four language groups). This may mean either that all three interview styles are rather formal or that English in general is a rather formal language. In view of this the general level of 'deviation' seems rather high.

The narrow context, in the sense of variable position within the word, plays a much more decisive role for some variables. Figure 28.7 shows the pronunciation of some variables containing alveolar fricatives. This example shows that the pronunciation of [ʃ] as [s] is partly, that is, in word-initial position, a marker for the Luo, partly a more general phenomenon, that is, in central positions. 'Common' modifications of [ʃ], for example, a slightly voiced pronunciation, are often accepted, yet modifications 'in the Luo way' are stigmatised.

Other subnational features related to the word context, for instance the tendency towards the lenition of voiceless plosives in final word position by the Luhya ([send] for *sent*), and other fortis-lenis differences, are related to phonotactic rules of the first language. In many cases, particularly with Coastal Bantu, intrusive vowels are prominent. For Bantu generally, these include final -*i* added to words ending in alveolar or palatal consonants and final -*u* added to those ending in labial consonants; furthermore intrusive -*i*- occurs in consonant clusters, as in *against them* [agenisti ðem].

The high rate for the voiced instead of voiceless pronunciation in

Arthur, even by the non-Bantu, may also be due to the immediate context, that is, the vocalic environment where this pronunciation is more normal. Here inter- and intralinguistic influences converge. Similarly the affricate instead of the fricative in *machine* may reflect hypercorrection or a more 'normal' pronunciation. The tendency seems to be not to make exceptions to the general pronunciation rules for specific words. This tendency is related to another important factor influencing the pronunciation of KenE, that is, the spelling.

Since in many ESL countries the written form of English is (through education and documents) considered more important and prestigious than the spoken version and since few native speakers are available as models, the spelling is often taken as a guideline for pronunciation. This can be seen in the (basilectal) pronunication of 'silent letters', as in *half* and *calf*, and in hypercorrect pronunciations, for example, of the full vowel in *said* and the reduced vowels in *let us/let's say* (here 'spelling pronunciation' occurs even when the vowel is not spelled). Some special words included in the questionnaire, such as *juice* and *Southern*, are pronounced as they are written even by highly educated East Africans. Other reflections of spelling pronunciation are the variants chosen to avoid the central vowels. The unstressed [ə] in *horror* and *pilot* is likely to be pronounced as [o], although the more likely KenE pronounciation of [ə], as in *angrily* and *figure*, is [a]. The same applies to long [ɜ:] in *word* occasionally, which can become a homophone with *ward*.

Differences between the sexes

An analysis of male–female differences in pronunciation reveals, as in most comparable studies, that women are more 'conservative', closer to the overt norm. A comparison of Figure 28.8 and Figure 28.9 shows that the differences between vowels are less striking than between consonants. As women tend to avoid salient features more than men, differences between the sexes are most striking where men use more vernacular forms. This is certainly the case when variants are stigmatised, such as the subnational forms of *th*, *r/l*, *h* and *sh*, but it is also so for variants that seem to have covert prestige, such as the Kenyan pronunciation of the national features [ɜ:] and possibly [iə]. The only variants that are used more often by women than by men are the less salient features [i:], [u:], [ɔ:], [ɪ], [ʒ] and [dʒ].

This difference between the sexes is also visible in the comparison of the stylistic contexts (see Figure 28.10). The 'Africanisation' is, in all three styles, more noticeable with the men than with the women, and the differences between the three styles are more extreme for the men than for the women.

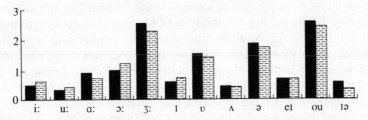

Figure 28.8 'Africanisation' of English vowels by male and female Kenyans.
■ = male; ▨ = female.

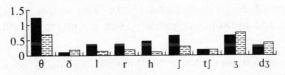

Figure 28.9 'Africanisation' of English consonants by male and female Kenyans.
■ = male; ▨ = female.

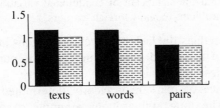

Figure 28.10 'Africanisation' of variables in reading texts, isolated words and word pairs by male and female Kenyans. ■ = male; ▨ = female.

Reasons for national and subnational features

For an explanation of national and subnational features in KenE it is important to consider two aspects, their origin and their persistence.

The influence of the mother tongue certainly plays a decisive role. Since the mother tongues often belong to different language families they explain many subnational features, for example, the Kikuyu have only one sound for *r* and *l*, only voiced *th* and nasalised plosives in their mother tongue; the Luo have no alveolar fricatives [ʃ,ʒ], only affricates [tʃ,dʒ]. There are, however, also areal features of KenE, for example the lack of certain consonants, that are surprising because they do occur in the respective mother tongues, at least as peripheral phonemes. In Kisii, where Luo and Gusi groups overlap, some Luo occasionally have 'r/l problems', whereas many Gusi replace [ʃ] by [s] (even in African languages, e.g. [samba] for *shamba*). On the national level it is interesting in this context that the pronunciation of [ɜ:] in Kenya strongly tends towards [a:] and in Tanzania towards [e:]. The second possibility would be parallel exposure to the non-standard English of colonial administrators, settlers and missionaries. Here the sheer quantity of native speakers does not seem sufficient (as there were, for instance, fewer settlers than in South Africa and fewer missionaries than in Malawi, both possibly with some influence on the English spoken there; see Hancock and Angogo 1982). A third factor is teaching methods, which often do not reflect specific learning problems sufficiently and the efficiency of which must be seen in the context of local development problems (see Schmied 1986). Finally I want to mention a fourth factor, namely general language learning strategies in relation to the structure of English. Gimson (1980: 306) writes of RP, which he considers as the appropriate model (even if only to measure deviances from it):

> the full systems (20 V and 24 C) must be regarded as complex compared with the systems of many other languages. In particular, the opposition of the close vowels /i:/–/i/, /u:/–/u/, the existence of a long central vowel /ɜ:/ and the delicately differentiated front vowel set of /i:/–/i/–/e/–/æ/+/ʌ/, together with the significant or conditioned variations of vowel length, will pose problems to many foreign learners.

Thus he almost predicts the lack of vowel distinctions in 'New Englishes'. The acquisition of these and other sounds may be particularly difficult, because they are less universal.

The maintenance of markers is clearly determined by the attitudes towards them. The long and arduous attempts of traditional school-teachers[5] to eradicate some of the (national) features of KenE may have been in vain, because they are not considered as 'bad enough' mistakes in relation to the overt prestige norm, having acquired some covert prestige of Kenyan solidarity, which signals an African identity independent of European prescriptivism (see the attitudes towards [a:] instead of [ɜ:] above).

There are, however, many more questions concerning the variation of KenE, particularly socioeconomic and age variation. If national features are gradually accepted, then younger informants should use them more often than older informants; similarly informants higher on the socioeconomic scale should switch regularly between covert and overt prestige variants in certain circumstances, in order to deliberately express certain identities. Another question concerns syntactic variables. Is it really the case that 'syntax is the marker of cohesion in society', whereas 'pronunciation reflects the permanent social group with which the speaker indentifies' (Hudson 1980: 48)? This analysis has shown that some pronunciation features in KenE do identify groups at an intra- and an international level. Whether syntax really unites them will have to be shown in future studies.

NOTES

1. This project is sponsored by the German Research Association (DFG). The first field trip and basic data collection was carried out in March and April 1986. It is partly modelled on my PhD dissertation, 'English in Tanzania' (Schmied 1985) and was supplemented and expanded in 1987 and 1988. The main aspects of English in East Africa analysed are:

   a) the use of English as opposed to Swahili and other languages (see Schmied forthcoming a, b)

   b) attitudes towards English in general (Schmied forthcoming a, b)

   c) attitudes towards East African varieties of English,

   d) pronunciation features of EAfrE (as reported in this analysis),

   e) grammatical features of EAfrE in writing (particularly by students and teachers),

   f) the acceptability of these features by teachers (see Schmied 1988).

   I have to thank many officials and friends for discussion and assistance in many ways. In particular I wish to thank Jane and Kembo Sure from Kisii TC, where the recordings were made and the Computer Centre of Bayreuth University for their kind assistance with several 'minor problems'.

2. Much in the same way as Swahili may signal different identities, as it covers a wide intralingual spectrum from coastal to up-country varieties.

3. I used SPSS/PC+, a 'Statistical Package for the Social Sciences for Personal Computers', which is available and used world-wide, so that the methodology and results may be comparable to other studies. It allows a wide range of statistical procedures and at present up to 200 variables per active file, which is satisfactory for normal sociolinguistic purposes. In connection with MS-CHART it also produces simple graphs used for summary and illustrative purposes in this study.

4. Besides these phonetic features, prosodic features are striking. These include relative syllable length and prominence, voicing, devoicing before plosives and (post-)aspiration; the supraphonemic tendency in general is towards a syllable-timed, not a stress-timed pronunciation. This accounts for the general tendency to give too much weight to the unstressed syllables and weak forms of English, and helps to avoid consonant clusters, as in *difficult*.

5. An important factor in the persistence of subnational features is school background. In secondary schools with a nation-wide intake or with teachers from different ethnic groups these features will be stigmatised and levelled down after some years. This is normally not the case where students and teachers come from the same ethnic group. Children from the (few) English-medium missionary schools will develop only a few national features and hardly any subnational ones.

REFERENCES

Gimson, A. C. 1980. *An Introduction to the Pronunciation of English*. London: Edward Arnold.

Hancock, I. and Angogo, R. 1982. English in East Africa. In Bailey, R. and Görlach, M. (eds.), *English as a World Language*. Ann Arbor: University of Michigan Press, pp. 306–23.

Hudson, R. 1980. *Sociolinguistics*. Cambridge: Cambridge University Press.

Jibril, M. 1986. Sociolinguistic variation in Nigerian English. *English World-wide* 7: 47–74.

Johnston, P. A. 1983. Variation in the Standard Scottish English of Morningside. *English World-wide* 4: 133–85.

Kachru, B. B. 1986. *The Alchemy of English. The Spread, Functions and Models of Non-native Englishes*. Oxford: Pergamon.

Milroy, J. and Harris, J. 1980. When is a merger not a merger? The MEAT/MATE problem in a present-day English vernacular. *English World-wide* 1: 199–210.

Schmied, J. J. 1985. *Englisch in Tansania. Sozio- und interlinguistische Probleme*. Heidelberg: Groos.

1986. English in Tanzanian education. *Bayreuth African Studies Series* 5: 63–114.

1988. Recognizing and accepting East African English grammar. In *The Place of Grammar in the Teaching of English. An International Conference held at the British Council*. Nairobi: British Council, pp. 94–101.

1989. English in East Africa: theoretical, methodological and practical issues. In Schmeid, J. (ed.) *English in East and Central Africa 1*. Bayreuth African Studies Series 15, pp. 7–37.

Forthcoming a. The status of English in Kenya and Tanzania. In Bammesberger, Alfred and Kirchner, Teresa (eds.), *Language and Civilisation*. Frankfurt: Lang.

Forthcoming b. *English in Africa An Introduction*. Harlow: Longman.

Zuengler, J. E. 1982. Kenyan English. In Kachru, B. B. (ed.), *The Other Tongue: English across Cultures*. Oxford: Pergamon, pp. 112–124.

Southern Africa

29

Southern Africa

MAURICE M. CHISHIMBA

Introduction

The term Southern Africa is in fact primarily a political rather than a geographical description of the countries south of the Equator which have a historical link with white South Africa. Traditionally, Southern Africa has included English-speaking countries (South Africa, Lesotho, Swaziland, Botswana, Zimbabwe, Zambia and Malawi) which are former colonies of Britain, and the Portuguese-speaking countries of Angola and Mozambique, which are former colonies of Portugal. Namibia, which was a mandated territory of South Africa, is also English-speaking.

Needless to say, the linguistic geography of Southern Africa is such a complex phenomenon that it would take a paper of its own for it to be treated with justice. Despite that complexity, however, Southern Africa – with the exception of Angola and Mozambique – enjoys language unity through English. This point is important in understanding the context in which the case study papers in this section are set. Apart from perhaps Lesotho, Swaziland and Botswana, all the countries in the region are multi-ethnic and multilingual. In each country, there are serious clashes of interest when the question of local languages is at issue. Yet, for some reason, solace is often found in the fact that English is there to act as a common language.

Part of the reason for the dominance of English as a common language is that all language policies in the region recognise and promote English as the official language. The one exception is South Africa, where Afrikaans is a co-official language with English. Another feature is worth mentioning with regard to Sesotho, Seswati and Setswana, languages spoken in Lesotho, Swaziland and Botswana respectively. In these countries, perhaps because of the existence of only one dominant local language, the local language is competing with English very effectively as the official

435

language. Elsewhere in English-speaking Southern Africa, English enjoys
unparallelled importance in comparison with the local language.

Status of English in Southern Africa

This section will discuss the different functions that English fulfills in the
different 'societies' of Southern Africa. It should be noted, however, that
there is a sense in which the term 'societies' is misleading. As will become
clear later, the politically separate nations of Southern Africa are plural
nations, each comprising differing societies and speech communities. It
should not be construed, therefore, that there is a correlation between,
for example, the reality of the term 'Zimbabwe' and the concept 'society',
as that concept is commonly understood. The phenomenon of linguistic
variation also has to be seen against this pluralistic background.

Except in South Africa, English is spoken as a first language by only a
small percentage of the population of the countries of Southern Africa.
Few studies have tried to establish the numbers of people who speak
English as a first language in these countries; of these Ohanessian and
Kashoki (1978) for Zambia, and Lanham (1978, 1982) for South Africa,
are probably the most serious attempts. However, Lanham's report does
not give a proper quantitative distribution of speakers, but simply points
to indicators of the size of each of the different English and Afrikaans
speech communities, paying particular attention to the English speech
communities. In South Africa, English is a first language of a large
percentage of the more than five million whites, and also of coloured and
Indian communities. But South Africa is essentially a bilingual country in
that almost half or more of those who speak English natively also have to
speak Afrikaans. Both Afrikaans and English are used as official languages
and are used in trade and business. In addition, Afrikaans functions as a
national language for those South Africans who regard themselves as
Afrikaaners (i.e. white people who are by descent Dutch but who are now
Africans and subscribe to the ideology of keeping themselves distinct and
African).

In the rest of the English-speaking Southern African countries, English
is a second and an official language for the majority of its speakers. To say
this, however, is not to imply that the status of English as an official
language is the same in all of the non-white Southern African countries.
There are basically two tendencies which can be differentiated. The first is
to be found in Botswana, Lesotho, Swaziland and black South Africa. The
second is in Zambia, Malawi and Zimbabwe. Perhaps we should add that
if it were possible to determine the sociolinguistic situation of English in
Namibia, that would be likely to constitute a third tendency. Each of these
tendencies is sketched below.

Although English is a second language for most of its speakers in Botswana, Lesotho, Swaziland and black South Africa, there is a sense in which 'secondness' does not properly reflect attitudes towards English. In these countries, communication normally takes place in the local lingua franca or vernacular. In Botswana, Lesotho and Swaziland the vernaculars are, respectively, Setswana, Sesotho and Seswati, as mentioned earlier. These are spoken as a native language by the majority of the population of these countries, except perhaps in Botswana, where Sesarwa, Karanga and Setswana are also spoken as native languages. The vernaculars are standardised and are used with English in all areas of business, government and the mass media. Radio and television stations operate with equal weighting in English and the vernaculars. The sequence is always the vernacular first, followed by English. Here, then, English is truly a 'second' language, in that the need to use English comes only after the local vernacular has been used. In other words, it is failure to operate in the vernacular that would bring about the use of English as an alternative.

One conclusion that can be drawn about the status of English in Botswana, Lesotho, Swaziland and black South Africa, then, is that it is a second language that is used strictly as an official language. Setswana, Sesotho and Seswati are national languages, used in politics, government, the public media and also in other strictly official domains. A follow-up to this is that the attitude to the local vernacular in these countries also indicates people's attitudes towards English. Although English is an international language, people in these countries prefer to use their vernaculars (unless English is necessary) in official and national contexts. Those who use English instead of the vernacular are regarded as members of the 'out-group'.

The status of English as an official and second language in Zambia, Zimbabwe and Malawi is rather different from that of the other countries mentioned above. Firstly, because these countries are bilingual or multi-lingual in the local languages, language policy has favoured English as a compromise, to avoid possible language conflict. Secondly, partly because of this policy and the efforts made to sustain it, people have to use English in a greater number of domains than is the case in the other countries. A larger proportion of the population, therefore, have to acquire English as a necessary means of communication. As in the rest of the region, English is learnt mainly through school. However, whereas in other countries this is done by gradually increasing exposure to English as pupils progress through the grades, in Zimbabwe, Malawi and, particularly, in Zambia, there is almost total exposure in the earliest grades and in nursery school. Except in Malawi, where Chewa is the national language, and, to a lesser degree, in Zimbabwe, where Shona enjoys near national dominance, the local languages feature very insignificantly as official languages.

Domains of use

As is the case in other English-speaking African countries, English is used in most public domains in English-speaking Southern Africa. However, as mentioned above, there are cases in which both English and another language are used almost interchangeably. The most obvious such case is South Africa, where both English and Afrikaans are used in the printed media, business, politics, law and government. This bilingualism is not very much in evidence, however, amongst the different non-white groups, particularly in the domains of politics and education. Blacks, coloureds and Indians normally conduct their political activities in English. In the majority of cases, they would rather send their children to English-medium schools where Afrikaans is only a taught subject. The majority of South Africans, however, acknowledge that Afrikaans is an important competitor to English, particularly in the mass media, business, law and government. For the South Africans who speak different Bantu languages (mainly Sesotho, Zula and Xhosa), these languages enjoy almost equal prominence in television and radio, business, advertising, employment and, to a lesser degree, in the printed media. Among those who regard themselves as Afrikaaners, political activity mostly goes on in Afrikaans, with some use of English. But in spite of the increased use of Afrikaans in public domains in South Africa, it is still second to English in these domains. It is still used as a local vernacular or lingua franca and thus faces some of the same problems other languages elsewhere face against the predominance of English in public domains.

In the other countries of the region, English is predominantly the language used in public domains. However, as mentioned earlier, there are important variations in its use and importance in certain domains in the almost monolingual nations of Botswana, Lesotho and Swaziland. Although English is the official language and is used in the media, business, law, government, education and politics, the local language is also used wherever possible. In education, it is not the medium of instruction until the fourth grade (10–11 years of age), when it is mixed with the local language. It does not become the sole medium of instruction until secondary school (at age 13–14 years). In politics, it is officially compulsory only in parliament; outside parliament much political activity goes on in the local language, with occasional use of English.

In Zimbabwe, Malawi and Zambia, English is the only language in public domains. In education, English is the medium of instruction in Zambia from pre-school grades up to university. In Malawi and Zimbabwe it becomes the medium of education mainly after grades three and four. Before that it is a very important subject. In the case of politics, again Malawi and Zimbabwe allow limited use of Chewa (in Malawi) and Shona and Ndebele (in Zimbabwe), but only in relatively informal political activity and by relatively low-level politicians. In parliament it is strictly English that is used, unless translation for readers or listeners is required.

In each of these countries, there are domains where the local languages are allowed to operate, for certain clearly specified reasons. Due to high rates of illiteracy, most people cannot read or speak English. As a result, radio and newspapers provide information in selected languages. This practice is true also for Botswana, Lesotho and Swaziland. In some cases local government activities are carried out in local languages in the remote and peripheral urban area. However, in all cases where records should be kept, this is done in English.

English in Southern Africa, then, excluding English-speaking South Africa, is mainly used in official and semi-official situations. However, English is also used in other situations and contexts where speakers deem it necessary. For example, as Siachitema (this volume) shows, English may be used in the home, to a limited extent. When that is the case it is mainly an instance of code-switching away from the preferred vernacular that is normally used at home. More commonly, English is used between any two strangers or persons who do not share a common language. Even this is not always the case, however, where a lingua franca has developed. For example, in Zambian towns any two Zambians are likely to speak Nyanja if in Lusaka, Bemba if on the Copperbelt and Lozi if in Livingstone. Otherwise they will use English, or switch to English. In Malawi any two Malawians will use Chewa and optionally switch to English if there is no other language which they share. The situation is somewhat different in Zimbabwe, where Shona and Ndebele are the principal regional languages. It is possible that a Ndebele speaker will have to speak in Shona to a Shona speaker if he or she is outside the Ndebele-speaking region. However, in most cases such interaction will take place in English. Official policy, however, treats Shona and Ndebele as equal, and limited recognition of this has been given by way of allowing both of them to be used in a few selected official domains.

In Botswana, Lesotho and Swaziland, one has to be clearly a foreigner to expect to be spoken to in English. The test is the failure of the foreigner to respond to conventional greeting expressions, which then normally gives the local person a clue as to the identity of the other as a foreigner. On that basis, conversation can then proceed in English. Most interpersonal verbal interaction, however, takes place in Setswana, Sesotho and Seswati. This is so in all non-official domains, unless there is optional code-mixing or code-switching with English.

It might be said, then, that English is used in many non-official domains, including the home, drinking-places, and during cultural activities. However, these are areas where the local lingua francas are very dominant. Resort to English, as mentioned above, is governed by factors such as whether the interlocutor shares the speaker's language, and whether he or she is a stranger or a foreigner. In addition, there are sociolinguistic constraints on the use of English which are mainly culturally determined. For example, a wife may not talk in English to her husband if both of them speak the same local language; a young person may not use English while talking to an elder if there is a local language available to them; however learned one is, one cannot go to the in-laws, the home village, the local authorities and other similar groups of people and expect to speak in English. The social marking and cultural expectations associated with English in these situations are stereotypical and governed by custom and tradition. There are cultural constraints on the use of English in non-official domains which support the assertion that English in this region is strictly an official language and not a national language.

There is a further sense in which it can be said that English in Southern Africa is used for purposes which do not form part of the core of valued cultural activities or beliefs. As happened to other imposed languages elsewhere in the world, English is the preferred language for public and interethnic ceremonial activities, commercial magic and sports activities; and also for vulgarisms. Most of the popular swear words and insults are in English. If not, then the local lingua franca caters for that. Similarly, those parts of ceremonies which have no African cultural tradition are conducted in English. For example, at weddings the church service and ceremony are often in English; at funerals the church service and memorial service are often in English; even the ordaining of a priest will be in English, although subsequent religious activities carried out by that priest, as well as by laypeople, will take place in the vernacular. In short, all conventionalised non-local or Western ceremonies are conducted mainly in English. So also are those activities in trade, commerce and elsewhere which have, at least in part, some Western origins; examples are bidding, auctioning, going to concerts and taking part in picnics.

Autonomy of English

Having said this, we must ask whether there is a clearly definable distinctive variety of English in Southern Africa. As can be seen from the discussion so far, English is spoken natively by a large community in only South Africa. Lanham (1978, 1982) and Lanham and Macdonald (1985) have described this sociolinguistic phenomenon. Although they do not give a thorough description of the use of English in South Africa, it is clear from their concern with English as a standard variety in South Africa that a 'focused' variety (Milroy 1982) of South African English exists. A further attempt to describe South African English as a distinctive variety has been made by Beeton and Dorner (1975) and by Branford (1978). Branford has compiled a dictionary of South African English on the strong assumption that such a variety indeed exists. Branford's attempt is purely lexicographical, but there are many other indications from the research on South African English that it is considered to be a variety distinct from other varieties of English that are spoken natively (see, for example, Lanham 1978, 1982; Lass and Wright 1986). However, this is so only for white, coloured and Indian native speakers of English. Other speakers of English in South Africa show similar tendencies in their use of English to those found among other speakers in the rest of Southern Africa.

Of particular interest is the English spoken by native English-speaking coloureds in South Africa. The existence of the concept of a South African standard of English has led researchers such as Malan (1981) to refer to this as non-standard English, by analogy with the non-standard English that is said to be spoken in Britain, Australia, New Zealand and the USA. Like other 'non-standard' varieties, its use expresses group identity and solidarity; and variation in the use of specific linguistic features, such as non-standard present tense verb forms and auxiliaries (see Malan 1981) is governed by linguistic and social constraints.

Mesthrie's work on South African Indian English (Mesthrie 1987, 1988, and this volume) is also of great interest. There are people who consider the Indians of South Africa as still having strong roots in the former home country, India. On the contrary, however, they appear to be very different from other people of Indian origin who are resident in Malawi, Zambia and East Africa. Mesthrie's work testifies to the fact that the Indian community in South Africa is an English-speaking community, using English as the primary means of communication; and he assumes that South African Indian English is a distinct, language shift variety of English.

However, it is neither easy nor correct to consider the English that is spoken in the rest of Southern Africa as a distinct variety of English. The kind of research that is currently going on in different countries of the region shows that there are tendencies towards defining varieties of English as part, or as product, of nation. For this reason, there has been talk of 'national' or 'territorial' Englishes such as 'Zambian', 'Malawian' and 'Zimbabwean' Englishes. At the moment, however, it is completely counter-intuitive to consider these as varieties, for there is no logical correspondence between 'nation' and 'English' in this region of Africa, in the sense in which there is a correspondence between 'England' and 'English' (see Chishimba, 1984, 1985).

Nevertheless, a number of empirical studies have been undertaken on English as a national variety, particularly in Zambia. This development is very interesting. Research into English in South Africa is to be expected; and it is necessary, if only because English in that country has become a variety spoken natively by a large proportion of different and unrelated racial communities. One would expect that the impact of English on other countries in the region would spark off an interest in studying its status and functions in these countries. However, to date this interest has surfaced mainly in Zambia, as mentioned above, where numerous unpublished university-based studies and several PhD dissertations have been written on various aspects of 'Zambian' English (see, for example, McAdam 1973; Chishimba 1979; Africa 1980; Chisanga 1987; Siachitema 1987). A number of scholars have studied formal changes in the morphology, syntax and phonology of English in Zambia (see, for example, Simukoko 1977, 1981; Haynes 1982, 1984; Lawrence and Sarvan 1983; Africa 1983; Moody 1985). The results of these studies are in terms of observed tendencies, and they do not describe or predict linguistic change. Unlike English in, say, some West African countries, English in Zambia does not appear to be undergoing noticeable linguistic change towards any forseeable norm. There are no comparable studies for the rest of the black African states of Southern Africa, as far as I know, but the analytical stalemate reached in Zambia suggests that similar problems of identification and description may exist in the other countries of the region.

English in interpersonal interaction

Although there has been an interest in English as a distinct variety, very little research has been done on the use of English in interpersonal interaction. In South Africa, studies by Chick (1985, and this volume) illustrate an approach to the analysis of verbal interaction which is lacking in the rest of the region. The only comparable study is Moody (1985), which discusses how Zambians use English in conversation, and which shows the significance and social use of code mixing and code switching. The use of verbal cues which mark social distance is illustrated in considerable detail, and Moody reaches the same general conclusions as Chick on the linguistic marking of respect, deference and status, as well as of social characteristics such as the sex of the speaker. The work of Siachitema (this volume) can also be mentioned from this perspective. Siachitema investigates the way in which social meanings such as respect and deference are expressed by alternation in the use of English and a vernacular language.

Variation in English

In the Southern African context it is pointless to discuss variation in English from the point of view of large-scale social factors such as regional variation, social class variation or variation on a standard–non-standard dimension. We can only discuss variation in terms of communities. By communities is meant those groups who share a common culture, ancestry, race or tribe.

Variation of this kind between different tribes/ethnic groups and races has been informally observed in terms of 'accent'. In Southern Africa it is popularly supposed that there are ways of speaking English which are characteristic of certain tribes (or ethnic groups) and certain racial groups. For example, Nguni-speaking people are said to have an 'accent' which is distinct from that of Sotho-speaking people. Coloured people are said to speak a variety of English which black and white people feel is distinct and which appears to trigger certain social stereotypes. However, although these distinctions may be appealing, they have not yet been empirically investigated and they have no scholarly value. They are socially interesting but cannot be said to be reliable indicators of the existence of sociolinguistic variation.

Attitudes

There have been no studies of language attitudes in the region, but personal observation suggests that the promotion of the vernaculars in Botswana, Lesotho, Swaziland and black South Africa has had some impact on the relationship between language and ethnic loyalty. As in other countries where a sense of personal national identity stems from the use of a single common language, there appear to have been two attitudinal consequences: firstly, imposition of any foreign language is received with mixed feelings and even abhorrence; secondly, the common, vernacular, language becomes a mark of identity without which nobody can claim access to power or status, nor even, sometimes, to residence. One has to speak the local language to be considered a national. Failure to speak the language, and especially insistence on speaking English, gives a very negative impression.

Conclusion

An attempt has been made in this paper to sketch the sociolinguistic status of English in Southern Africa. It should be clear that few significant studies have been carried out with the aim of providing quantitative data on different aspects of the use of English.[1] However, some tentative research findings have emerged from a number of studies; and there are some accounts that are based on either observation or introspection. It is hoped that future empirical research will advance our understanding of the complex linguistic situation in Southern Africa.

NOTE

1. Some additional relevant studies and papers are: Chishimba 1980; Essillfie 1983, 1987; Magura 1984, 1985; Ngara 1974, 1975, 1982.

REFERENCES

Africa, H. P. 1980. Language in Education in a Multilingual State; A Case Study of the Role of English in the Educational System of Zambia. Unpublished PhD thesis, University of Toronto.

1983. Zambian English: myth as reality. MS. Lusaka, University of Zambia.

Beeton, D. and Dorner, Helen. 1975. *A Dictionary of English Usage in South Africa*. Cape Town: Oxford University Press.

Branford, J. 1978. *A Dictionary of South African English*. Cape Town: Oxford University Press.

Chick, J. K. 1985. The interactional accomplishment of discrimination in South Africa. *Language in Society* 14: 299–326.

Chisanga, T. 1987. An Investigation into the Form and Function of Educated English in Zambia as a Possible Indigenized Non-native Variety. Unpublished PhD dissertation, University of York.

Chishimba, M. M. 1979. A Study of the Zambia primary English Course. Unpublished EdD dissertation, Teachers' College, Columbia University.

1980. Observations on the English language component of the Zambia primary course. *Zambia Educational Review* 2: 32–48

1984: African Varieties of English: Text in Context. Unpublished PhD thesis, University of Illinois.

1985. *Deviation and Innovation in English: Zambian Examples*. Lusaka: University of Zambia.

Essilfie, T. 1983. English in multilingual countries: problems of pedagogy and acquisition – the case of Botswana. *Proceedings of UNESCO Conference on English in Southern Africa, Lusaka, December 1983*. Gaborone: University of Botswana.

1987. The African linguist and his chores: language teaching programmes in SADUCC universities and the philosophy behind them. *Proceedings of ATOLL Conference on Language and Literature in Liberation and Development. Harare, August 1987*. Gaborone: University of Botswana.

Haynes. R. 1982. The emergence of an English based creole in Zambia: possibilities and implications. *English Teachers' Journal* 6: 2–13.

1984. *A Pilot Study into the Emergence of a Non-Standard Dialect of English in Zambia. Part 1: Possibilities*. Lusaka, University of Zambia.

Lanham, L. W. 1978. South African English. In Lanham, L. W. and Prinsloo, K. P. (eds.), *Language and Communication Studies in South Africa*. Cape Town: Oxford University Press.

1982. English in South Africa. In Bailey, R. W. and Görlach, M. (eds.), *English as a World Language*. Ann Arbor: University of Michigan Press, pp. 324–52.

Lanham, L. W. and Macdonald, C. A. 1985. *The Standard in South African English*. Heidelberg: Groos.

Lass, R. and Wright, S. 1986. Endogeny vs. contact: 'Afrikaans influence' on South African English. *English World-wide* 7: 201–24.

Lawrence, L. and Sarvan, C. 1983. Zambian English: an enquiry. *Zambia Educational Review* 4 (1): 27–39.

McAdam. B. H. G. 1973. The Effectiveness of the New English Medium Primary

School Curriculum in Zambia. Unpublished PhD thesis, University of Manchester.

Magura, B. J. 1984. Style and Meaning in Southern African English. Unpublished PhD thesis, University of Illinois.

1985. Southern African Black English. *World Englishes* 4: 251–6.

Malan, K. C. 1981. An investigation of non-standard English syntax in 12-year-old coloured children. *The South African Journal of Communication Disorders* 28: 68–80.

Mesthrie, R. 1987. From OV to VO in language shift: South African Indian English and its OV substrates. *English World-wide* 8 (2): 263–76.

1988. Toward a lexicon of South African Indian English. *World Englishes*

Milroy, L. 1982. Social network and linguistic focusing. In Romaine, S. (ed.) 1982. *Sociolinguistic Variation in Speech Communities*. London: Edward Arnold, pp. 141–52.

Moody, J. A. 1985. Zambians talking: twenty-five English conversations. Mimeograph. Lusaka, University of Zambia.

Ngara, E. A. 1974. A redefinition of the role of the English language in African universities. *Bulletin of the Association of African Universities* 1 (2): 35–42.

1975. Comments on the teaching of English in Botswana, Lesotho and Swaziland. *Education in Botswana, Lesotho and Swaziland* 9: 4–14.

1982. *Bilingualism, Language Contact and Planning: Proposals for Language Use and Language Teaching in Zimbabwe*. Gwelo: Mambo Press.

Ohanessian, S. and Kashoki, M. E. 1978. *Language in Zambia*. London: 1A1.

Siachitema, A. K. 1987. Use and Attitudes towards the English Language in Lusaka. Unpublished PhD thesis, University of Edinburgh.

Simukoko, Y. T. 1977. A Preliminary Investigation into some features of a Zambian Variety of English with Particular Reference to Bemba Speakers. Unpublished MSc thesis, University of York.

1981. Some Aspects of the English of Bantu Speakers in Urban Primary Schools in Zambia. Unpublished PhD thesis, University of Edinburgh.

30

Sources and consequences of miscommunication in Afrikaans English – South African English encounters

J. KEITH CHICK

Introduction

This paper reports on research involving the fine-grained qualitative analysis of interactions between Afrikaans and English speakers in South Africa, in the medium of English. The goal of this research is to see whether the explanation of the sources and consequences of miscommunication between Zulu and English speakers offered in Chick (1985) holds for Afrikaans and English speakers as well. The essence of this explanation is that a mis-match of culturally-preferred interactional styles contributes to asynchrony (see Erickson 1975, 1976, 1978), in the context of which participants misinterpret and misevaluate one another, and that repeated miscommunication of this sort generates negative cultural stereotypes. Asynchrony is the antithesis of conversational synchrony which, Erickson (1975) explains, is the rhythmic patterning of conversationalists' coordinated behaviour that enables them to judge the occurrence in real time of significant 'next moments'. This information they need in order to accomplish conversational inferencing. As a great number of studies have shown (e.g. Gumperz 1982a, 1982b; Pride 1985), intercultural communication is frequently characterised by asynchrony in which the participants look, sound and feel clumsy, and often miss one another's signals because they occur at unexpected moments. In this paper I present evidence which suggests that, indeed, a mismatch of interactional styles is partly responsible for the asynchrony in the encounters analysed, and I suggest what some of the distinctive features of these putative styles are.

By style, here, I do not mean a distinct code or even a variety distinguishable by means of statistical counts of key items. Rather I mean predispositions to behave communicatively in certain 'targeted' ways rather than in others, and therefore the tendency to see certain features of the surface form of messages (contextualisation cues – see Gumperz 1982a) rather than others as having signalling value. Such predispositions are largely the product of previous interactive experience, but are to some extent renegotiated in the course of each interaction. In this paper the putative styles are distinguished in terms of the schemata (see Tannen 1979; Fillmore 1975, 1976, and 1977, Chafe 1977a, 1977b) and contextualisation cues the participants rely on in establishing what activity they are engaged in, and the ways of presenting self (politeness stragegies) they prefer in negotiating the relationship between them (see Brown and Levinson 1978; Lakoff 1973, 1979; Scollon and Scollon 1982, 1983).

Methods of data collection and analysis

The opportunity to collect data was provided by English language courses which, together with two colleagues, I designed and conducted for an Afrikaans banking organisation. Data collection would, ideally, have taken the form of video recordings of interactions between the bankers and their South African (henceforth SA) English speaking clients in the banks, but because, for various reasons, this was not possible, we chose the option of video recording simulated banker–client interviews.

Elsewhere (see Chick 1987) I discuss whether simulated interviews are acceptable sources of data, and how authentic the banker–client data is. I conclude that, although some of the data collected (32 interviews in all) are inauthentic, there is sufficient similarity between interviews that observers judged as authentic and real interviews, for at least tentative generalisations about how the participants behave interactionally in real situations, to be based on them.

Initially questionnaires were used to elicit the participants' perceptions of the general level of synchrony/asynchrony, of how successful the interviews had been, of whether they had achieved their goals or not, and of how the interviews affected their views of the other participant's attitudes, motives and abilities.

At a later stage, certain of the interviews were selected for transcription and closer analysis using elicitation techniques developed by Gumperz and associates (see Gumperz 1982a, 1982b). They attempt to 'obtain convergence between researchers' and participants' perspectives' (Mehan 1979: 37) by eliciting participants' and independent listeners' interpretations of and judgements about progressively finer details of the discourse.

Culturally-specific styles as sources of asynchrony

An interview which appears to provide some support for the hypothesis that a mis-match of interactional styles is a source of asynchrony is one involving an academic, Mark, and one of the bankers, Kallie. Only a portion of this interview is examined here, although, to contextualise this, and to allow the reader to search for an alternative interpretation, a description is given of the part of the interview which precedes it.

The interview opens with informal discussion about the academic's disciplinary affiliation, and the bank's interest in doing business in the Durban area. Kallie then asks Mark how he can help him, and Mark talks at some length about his need for investment advice. Kallie advises fixed interest investments with the bank. Mark queries the wisdom of this, suggesting that the tax may be punitive. He asks whether the share market would not be a better investment, and is warned against it on the grounds that as a layman he would be out of his depth. Mark then suggests unit trusts, and is warned against that, too. The interview continues:

```
121.  MARK: Is that not safe
122.                     KALLIE: no it is safe but a I think you have
123.  more flexibility if you stay with the more (unclear) . . .
124.                     MARK: I mean are you not a a is
125.  your bank into the share the share market at all I mean are
126.  you not advising me to to avoid that because (smiling) that's
127.  no business for your bank
128.         KALLIE (smiling): no certainly I'd like
129.  to keep your business with myself
130.              MARK: ya
131.                     KALLIE: so I must bring you
132.  back into a fixed interest investment with ourselves
133.                              MARK: I see . . .
134.  but I (quickening up) mean are you thinking principally
135.  of your interest of my interest in this (unclear) . . .
136.         KALLIE (smiling): no obviously
137.  the client's interest is paramount so I must give
138.  you the best package which I believe is a . . .
```

An examination of the politeness strategies employed by the participants and the contextualisation cues by which these are signalled and interpreted, give some hint as to the source of the asynchrony in this extract (which was commented on by Mark). In lines 124–7 and 134–5 Mark challenges the soundness of Kallie's advice, which is face-threatening behaviour. That he is aware of the potential for face-loss and attempts to off-set this, is evident from his action of smiling, an expression of solidarity, and his choice of interrogative form, an indirect, deference strategy. Although Kallie seems to interpret the significance of the cue, smiling, accurately (for he responds to it by smiling himself), he apparently fails to see the cue of the interrogative form as salient. Brown and Levinson (1978: 253) explain that 'the fact that indirect acts are highly conventionalised in English means that in most circumstances using an indirect act implicates that the speaker is trying to respect the hearer's negative face'. If Kallie's behaviour here is typical, and the other data suggest that it is, then one of the culturally-distinctive characteristics of Afrikaans English is that, in it, indirectness is not a conventionalised means of expressing politeness. To return to this extract, the interrogative form serves as a face-saving strategy by leaving Kallie the face-saving option of interpreting the utterance as a question rather than an accusation, the speech act which SA English-speaking informants felt Mark intended to imply. The options open to someone accused are to admit guilt or deny it, and at face value Kallie seems to accept guilt (lines 128–9):

128.   KALLIE (smiling): no certainly I'd like
129. to keep your business with myself

and then, when pressed further, deny it (lines 136–9).

136.   KALLIE (smiling): no obviously
137. the client's interest is paramount so I must give
138. you the best package which I believe is a . . .

Significantly though, in both cases, he does so while smiling which means that either he is showing a callous disregard of the face-threat involved in accusations, denials and inconsistency of responses to repeated accusations, or he feels that less loss of face is involved than most SA English-speaking informants feel there is. That Kallie saw neither his nor Mark's behaviour as face-threatening is evident from his observations: 'I allowed the client to feel comfortable and that he was in charge of the conversation, that is, to freely challenge me' and 'The client did not become agitated when I disagreed with his views and ultimately accepted my views'. This perception is at odds with Mark's observations that he was completely unconvinced by Kallie's argument, and that he was offended by what he saw as an attempt to force him into an investment which was in the bank's interest rather than his own.

The role of politeness behaviours in the miscommunication here suggests what may be partly responsible for the asynchrony of this extract, the differences in the interpretations of the participants, and Mark's negative evaluation. This is a mismatch in their perceptions of the relationship between them, and an inability to negotiate a mutually acceptable definition of that relationship, because they do not share preferences for particular kinds of politeness behaviours, and do not always recognise the cues which signal such behaviours.

What the analyses of the banker – client interviews reveal is that, in those situations at least, SA English speakers display a mixture of solidarity *and* deference politeness, and that the deference strategy of indirectness is particularly favoured. This is brought into sharp focus by its apparently being dispreferred by Afrikaans English speakers. Such a mismatch could account for the negative cultural stereotypes of SA English speakers referred to by one Afrikaans English informant, namely 'that they don't say what they mean' and that in conversation 'hulle loop met a draai' (literally, 'they walk an indirect route'). On the basis of this and other data (see Chick 1985) I hypothesise that the interactional ethos of the SA English speaking group is in a state of transition, with a movement from a preference for what Brown and Levinson (1978) refer to as a symmetrical deference politeness system in which differences in status are de-emphasised (−power) but maintenance of distance is valued (+distance), to a preference, in at least some situations, for symmetrical solidarity politeness (−power; −distance). To represent this diagrammatically, the movement is from

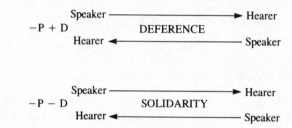

to

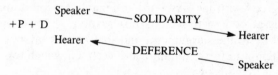

The interviews suggest, further, that, by contrast, the targeted politeness system for Afrikaans English speakers, at least when communicating with strangers (+distance), is an asymmetrical one (+power) with solidarity behaviour preferred by higher status participants and deference behaviour by lower status participants. This can be represented as follows:

Support for the notion that English speakers and Afrikaaners typically or conventionally treat the factor of power differently, comes from Odendal (1976). He notes that, by comparison with American English norms, there is within the Afrikaans-speaking community a wider range of situations where 'status is clearly specified, speech style is rigidly prescribed, and the form of address of each person is derived from his social identity' (Ervin Tripp 1972: 227). One way in which status differences and specifically deference to persons of high status is signalled in Afrikaans, is the honorific *u*, an option which is not available in English, except in conservative religious discourse, for example, *thee* and *thou*. Another way of showing deference is the use of what Odendal refers to as 'sydelingse aanspreekwyse' (lateral address forms), namely, the use of family and formal titles, sometimes repeated in the same utterance, in referring to the speaker, where, in English, the second person *you* would be used. For example,

'Goeie more *oom*, kan ek *oom* help?' (Good morning uncle can I help uncle?)

'Kan *buurman* vir my se . . .?' (Can you tell me neighbour . . .)

What apparently contributes as much to the distinctive Afrikaans interactional style, is how distance is treated. In many situations Afrikaaners apparently emphasise distance much less than English speakers do. This could account for the extension of kinship terms such as *oom* ('uncle') and *tannie* ('auntie') well beyond those with whom the speaker has blood ties (see also Sridhar, this volume). It could also account for the fact that while in most of the interviews the bankers seem to behave in a manner consistent with the putative interactional style sketched above, they do not do so in all. Prompted by what I observed in these exceptions, I hypothesise that the preferred style for the Afrikaans-speaking community when communicating within the group (with 'volk' rather than strangers) is one in which status differences are emphasised but distance minimised. In this politeness system, higher status participants express solidarity not baldly (as in the first Afrikaans English putative style), but softened by teasing, joking and what Wolfson and Manes (1980) refer to as 'terms of endearment', such as the wide use of diminutives: *kindjie* ('little child'): *liefie* ('little love'). The use of these diminutives sometimes appears to be a way of emphasising status differences (+power) while, at the same time, signalling protectiveness, that is, the implied message seems to be something like: 'I am big and powerful – you are small and vulnerable – I undertake to look after you.' Terms of endearment such as *dear* or *sweetie* are also used by English speakers speaking 'downwards', but apparently less frequently, especially by men. Since 'softened' forms of solidarity politeness are highly conventionalised in Afrikaans, their use implies that the speaker is trying to respect the hearer's need to be accepted and appreciated, that is, to belong. In this system lower status participants use a mixture of solidarity and deference politeness. This system can be represented diagrammatically as follows:

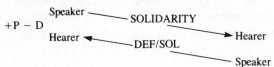

Elsewhere (see Chick 1987) I present evidence which suggests that higher-status Afrikaans English speakers sometimes use this form of solidarity behaviour when interacting with strangers, that is, they treat them as if they were members of the in-group even though they are not. This would account for the behaviour of the bankers, which is not consistent with the first of the Afrikaans English interactional styles described above.

To return to the analysis of the Mark – Kallie encounter, Kallie, according to Afrikaans informants, would have perceived Mark, who is older and better educated, as the superior, and as 'out-group'. He would, therefore, probably have expected Mark to use predominantly bald-on-record strategies. Instead we note that, even where he feels himself imposed upon, Mark adopts such deferential strageties as the use of the interrogative form in accusing, and such neutral feedback as *I see* (line 13). By this response he apparently means 'I hear you but am not convinced', but the banker probably interpreted it as acceptance. Kallie's consistent failure to interpret the meanings implicit in the deferential (off-record/indirect) politeness employed by Mark, could account for Kallie's perception that, despite some asynchronous phases, the interview had been a mutually satisfactory one.

By contrast, Mark did not see himself as significantly older than Kallie, and saw any difference in education as being offset by Kallie's relevant experience. In terms of how Mark perceived their relationship, and what he saw as an appropriate interactional style, Mark probably expected a mixture of deferential and solidarity politeness, and moderate volubility from both participants, and equal rights to hold the floor. Consistent with his view of how a lower-status participant should behave, Kallie probably saw his allowing Mark 'to feel that he was in charge of the conversation' as appropriate deference behaviour on his part. However, because such deference is excessive in terms of his expectations, Mark interpreted this not as face-saving behaviour, but, ironically, as face-threatening behaviour. Mark saw Kallie's failure to make suggestions for different avenues of investment, and not building on Mark's suggestions, as restricting his freedom of choice (not respecting his negative face needs) and not respecting his need for appreciation and acceptance (not respecting his positive face needs).

There is internal evidence in the extract above that these were indeed Mark's expectations. As McDermott, Gospodinoff and Aron (1978) note, one of the ways of ensuring that the analyst's interpretation coincides with that of the participant, is by noting what the participants do (and this subsumes what they say) in the absence of expected behaviour. I suggest that what Mark is implying in what he says in lines 124–7

124.   MARK: I mean are you not a a is
125.   your bank into the share market at all I mean are
126.   you not advising me to avoid that because (smiling) that's
127.   no business for your bank

and 134–5

134.   but I (quickening up) mean are you thinking principally
135.   of your interest or my interest in this

is that Kallie is not conforming to his expectation that he would appear (even if only hypocritically) to put Mark's interests before those of the bank. One possible explanation of why Kallie failed to meet Mark's expectations, is that he is incompetent. However, such an explanation is at odds with the unanimous positive evaluation Kallie received from his peers, when they viewed the recordings.

This points to another possible explanation, in terms of culturally-specific schemata. I hypothesise that Mark's expectations, described in the previous paragraph, reflect culturally-specific schemata. One such schema includes the expectation that an investment advisor is expected to suggest a number of possible investment options and, together with the client, to work out the advantages and disadvantages of each in terms of the client's specific circumstances and needs. This is a schema which Kallie apparently does not have access to. Another such schema includes expectations about how people establish their credibility. In the light of what takes place in a number of the interviews and of observed differences between business correspondence emanating from Afrikaans-orientated and English-orientated banking institutions (see Adendorff, Chick and Seneque 1985), I hypothesise that Afrikaans English speakers tend to try to establish their credibility by being *emphatic* and consistent, while SA English speakers tend to do so by presenting themselves as *empathetic*. This might also explain why Kallie does not suggest a number of different investment options, why his response to Mark's suggestions is to briefly point out one or two negative features of them, why he does not compare different options, why he does not attempt to relate the various options to Mark's particular circumstances and needs, and, above all, why he does not shift his position at all in response to Mark's queries and arguments. This analysis suggests a partial explanation for the negative cultural stereotypes of Afrikaans English speakers as conservative, authoritarian, inflexible and dogmatic.

Further support for the hypothesis that mis-match of culturally-specific interactional styles is the source of some of the asynchrony experienced in the interviews, and that the distinguishing features of these styles are as described, comes from an interview between Bob, who is in his early thirties, and Johan, a banker in his late forties:

1. BOB: ya no I've . . . just go some questions about a um a portfolio I'm
2.   member of staff in the university and I never seem to find enough money
3.   to be able to save and (speeding up) I'm just getting a little
4.   concerned about it so what I . . . what I'd like to get from you is a
5.   some advice on organizing my investment portfolio at the moment I
6.   don't have one . . . I don't I don't manage to put aside any money at
7.   all to save so what I am looking at is all the different
8.   possibilities that are open to me
9.   JOHAN: so at this stage you've got no

10.   savings account no nothing at all
11.   BOB: nothing at all
12.   JOHAN: so you work
13.   on a current account on a creditor basis
14.   BOB: yes . . . an I am putting in a
15.   voluntary contribution into my because that's subsidized by the
16.   government . . . so . . . I'm paying an extra R200 into my into my bond
17.   which will pay off the bond in 7 years so . . . in a sense I would regard
18.   that as an investment . . .
19.   JOHAN: (starts to speak)
20.   BOB: other than that I'm I'm not saving anything
21.   JOHAN: are you having a budget every month do you work on a budget
22.   BOB: no not
23.   really
24.   JOHAN: ja
25.   BOB: jus work on a month to month basis (continues,)
26.   JOHAN: ja I think that it is
27.   very much important especially f'r I I presume if you you are married
28.   BOB: yes ya
29.   JOHAN: you wife does the budget I believe . . . and a . . . the best
30.   thing is to do is to have a budget every month
31.   BOB: ya
32.   JOHAN: an to see what amount you can save
33.   BOB: right
34.   JOHAN: and . . . open a
35.   savings account w w w with a with an amount that is R50 is the new
36.   amount at the moment and a save ev every month sign a stop order from
37.   the current account
38.   BOB: ya
39.   JOHAN: to to the savings account every month and when
40.   when when it's accrued to about a agh at least about R100 R200 or
41.   something
42.   BOB: m
43.   JOHAN: just put that into fixed deposit
44.   BOB: ya
45.   JOHAN: for about a year
46.   or two years
47.   BOB: m
48.   JOHAN: where you your rates are 14 14,5 at the moment
49.   BOB: ya
50.   JOHAN: and then I would also advise a you can g- you income tax
51.   your income tax problems
52.   BOB: m
53.   JOHAN: any income tax problems
54.   BOB: m
55.   JOHAN: there's annuity

56.		BOB: ya
57.	JOHAN:	(lower volume) dealing kind of you know a substantial amount to annuity
58.		for 10 years (volume rises) that is also tax free
59.		BOB: right
60.		JOHAN: they deduct it
61.		from your income tax
62.		BOB: yes . . . do you think its a good or a bad thing
63.		that I'm putting R200 into my bond do you think it would be wise
65.		JOHAN: I I I think
66.		it's actually it's I won't say it is unwise but actually it is
67.		yes a you can take that R200 and put that in an annuity maximum is
68.		BOB: ya
69.	JOHAN:	750 per annum you can deduct that monthly from or yearly from your
70.		income tax . . . because because . . . your your bond is secure
71.		BOB: m
72.	JOHAN:	you got got a insurance on the bond
73.		BOB: right
74.		JOHAN: when you pass
75.		away
76.		BOB: ye
77.		JOHAN: that property is paid for
78.		BOB: yes
79.		JOHAN: so actually its its worth
80.		more to your wife and an your kids to have the house paid with a
81.		bigger bond than a lesser amount still owed to the bond
82.	BOB:	ah thinking about the you know tax free subsidy you know because
83.		I'm paying an extra R200 per month into my bond but R160 or no sorry
84.		R140 approximately R140 is subsidized
85.		JOHAN: (nod)
86.		BOB: so I get R140 tax free
87.		as an allowance from the central government
88.		JOHAN: ah yes I see ya ya ya
89.		BOB: so the only
90.		real deduction I have from my salary is R60
91.		JOHAN: is a actually a sixty rand
92.		yes . . . no I I would also also a good investment if there's income
93.		tax problems if there any problems is this . . . a a post office
94.		certificates
95.		BOB: I see
96.		JOHAN: 6 6 month 9,5 percent also also income tax
97.		free that's paid after 6 months you can draw as and so forth you get
98.		interest every 6 months so I I would advise you to open a savings account
99.		you must have that

As with the Mark–Kallie encounter, there was a mis-match in the
perceptions of the participants as to how synchronous and how satisfactory
the outcome of this interview was. Johan reported that he experienced the

interview as comfortable, that he felt that there was some chance that Bob would do business with the bank again, and that he believed that Bob was reasonably satisfied with the services he had provided. By contrast, Bob reported that he found the interview stressful at times, and that he would not do business with the bank again, and criticised the banker for not initiating enough and for being too reliant on himself for ideas.

Part of the explanation for this mis-match of perceptions, I suggest, relates to culturally-specific schemata. Bob apparently relies on much the same schematic knowledge as Mark in the first interview; knowledge that Johan, like Kallie in his interview with Mark, does not seem to have access to. In lines 1–8 we get some idea of what Bob's overall goals are for the interview, and what his expectations and assumptions are about the activity they are to engage in. I suggest that 'advice on organising my investment portfolio' is intended to serve as a contextualisation cue which will activate in the mind of the hearer much the same schema as is signalled by Mark in the first interview analysed, that is, one in which the expectation is that the participants will engage in a problem-solving exercise in which the advantages and disadvantages of various investment opportunities are examined together with the circumstances, needs and goals of the client, and decisions made about how to invest available funds in an investment package (portfolio) which will best assist the client to satisfy his needs and reach his goals.

Either this cue is not salient for Johan, or he does not have access to the schema described, for, rather than engage in the expected behaviour, he builds on what is apparently merely a subordinate theme for Bob, namely the fact that he has no funds presently available for investment because he is using surplus funds to accelerate his bond repayment. Accordingly Johan proceeds to give Bob advice on how to save (lines 29–48). Bob's comment after viewing this part of the tape was that, here, Johan fails to answer the central question. What becomes apparent as the interaction unfolds, at least to SA English observers, is that Bob would like the accelerated repayments of the bond to be considered as one of a number of options, in arriving at the best investment package, with possibly the amount used for this purpose being reduced, or this option being abandoned altogether in favour of an investment better suited to Bob's needs, goals and circumstances. However, when Bob attempts to make this point (lines 14–20), Johan does not build on this contribution, probably because he does not see it as very relevant to the activity he assumes they have agreed to engage in, namely, one in which Johan provides advice on how to save and Bob checks to see that he has understood adequately. After listening at some length to such advice Bob (lines 62–63) attempts, as he sees it, to get the discussion 'back on track' by asking Johan to evaluate the accelerated bond repayment as an investment. This time Johan does build on Bob's contribution, but not in the manner in which the schema described above would lead Bob to anticipate. Johan does compare accelerated bond repayments as an investment with an annuity investment, and presents reasons for preferring the latter. However, he does so without establishing, for example, how much of the additional R200 repayment is coming out of Bob's own pocket, what size the bond is, what size the annuity would be on maturity, how inflation might affect both types of investment and so on. That Bob anticipated such behaviour is evident from his observation that Johan 'threw out the suggestions in a vacuum' and from his subsequent supplying of some of this information himself without the prompting of Johan (lines 82–90), a sequence in which he also implicitly calls on Johan to reconsider his evaluation in the light of this further information. Johan signals explicitly that he understands what Bob says here:

88.   JOHAN: ah yes I see ye ya

and

91.   JOHAN: is a actually R60 yes

However, probably because such an interpretation is inconsistent with the schema he has accessed, and because he starts coming in before Bob has finished speaking (see lines 87–8):

87.   as an allowance from | the central government
88.   JOHAN: |ah yes I see ye ya ya

Johan apparently fails to interpret Bob's utterance as an invitation to reconsider. This is apparent from the fact that rather than do so, he suggests another investment (Post Office savings certificates). Thus, as much as five minutes after the start of the interview, the participants show little evidence of having constituted a mutually acceptable definition of what activity it is that they are engaged in, such that they can make better sense of their individual moves in that activity.

The fact that Johan does not shift his position about what is Bob's best course of action, in response to further information supplied by Bob, suggests that we have here further evidence of a mis-match of culturally-specific schemata, again of the sort observed in the Mark – Kallie encounter, namely whether credibility is established by being empathetic or emphatic. Bob's complaints that Johan 'was not concerned with saving me money' and that 'he was reeling off suggestions that were in a vacuum without contextualising them into my situation and my problem', show that he expected Johan to be empathetic.

As with the first interview, there is evidence that a further source of the asynchrony was a difference in the participants' perceptions of what their relationship was, what politeness behaviours were appropriate, and a failure to negotiate in the interaction a mutually acceptable definition of that relationship. According to Afrikaans English informants, Johan, who is significantly older than Bob, would have considered Bob junior to him in status and out-group. In terms of the first of the putative culturally-specific styles described above, he would, therefore, have regarded appropriate politeness from himself as solidarity (and predominantly bald-on-record) strategies and from Bob deference strategies. By contrast, Bob reported that he saw himself as senior in status, which means that, in terms of the putative SA English interactional style described above, he would have regarded appropriate politeness behaviour as a mixture of solidarity and deference strategies from both participants.

An examination of the transcript reveals that Bob and Johan do behave, for the most part, in ways consistent with their perceptions of the relationships between them and the putative culturally-specific styles described above. From Bob's perspective, appropriate deference behaviour from Johan would have involved inviting Bob to explain his circumstances and needs and giving him ample opportunity to do so, while appropriate solidarity behaviour from Johan would have involved him being sufficiently empathetic. Instead Johan displays what he sees as appropriate (bald-on-record) solidarity behaviour: shortly after the start of the interview he starts suggesting a solution (line 29):

29.   JOHAN: your wife does the *bùd*get I believe . . . and a . . . the best
30.   to do is to . . .

before, as Bob sees it, he has established what the problem is, thus threatening Bob's face. Significantly, rather than inquire how the household finances are handled in Bob's home, Johan states what his assumptions about this are. This he does using a falling tone on the tonic syllable *bud* in the word *budget*, rather than a rising tone which, in terms of Afrikaans English norms, would have signalled that he was requesting confirmation of his assumptions rather than merely stating them. This interpretation is confirmed by the judgements of Afrikaans English informants that they did not perceive Johan as asking a question here, and the observation that in line 21 he uses a rising tone on the same syllable on two occasions, apparently to invite confirmation of an assumption. Of significance, also, is Johan's response (lines 65–6) to Bob's inquiry (lines 62–3) as to whether he has acted wisely or not in accelerating his bond repayment. In the SA English-speaking community it is very face-threatening to tell someone they have acted foolishly, or to be told that one has acted foolishly even if you have invited such an evaluation. Johan seems to recognise the potential for face-loss, for he hesitates, seems to be opting for the deference strategy of euphemism:

I won't say it's unwise

but finally opts for the bald-on-record strategy:

but actually it is

A possible explanation for this choice is that he could not think of a suitable euphemism, but equally plausible is that, after careful consideration, he decided that bald-on-record was the most appropriate choice of strategy.

To explain why, although Bob's feelings about the interaction were so negative, Johan's were generally positive, we need to examine the politeness strategies used by Bob. Significantly, when Johan threatens Bob's face by imposing his perception of the arrangements for household financial management in Bob's home, Bob responds by using the extreme deference strategy of not saying anything. The offence experienced by Bob is, thus, not signalled overtly, and can only be inferred, something that Johan, given his assumption that bald-on-record behaviour on his part is appropriate, would be unlikely to do. In lines 82–4 Bob feels constrained to perform a face-threatening act himself, namely a challenge to the argument against accelerated bond repayments supplied by Johan. Significantly, again, he employs here a mixture of solidarity and deference strategies. In addition to the solidarity strategy of appearing to assume that his hearer's knowledge is the same as his own (*you know*), he employs the off-record, deference strategy in which the face-threatening challenge is left implicit (*ah thinking about . . .*). Since Johan did not feel constrained by what Bob said here to defend his position, he apparently did not interpret this as a challenge. In the short term, therefore, the effects of this misinterpretation were positive. However, in the long term, misinterpretations which lead to erroneous positive evaluations (such as those of Kallie and Johan) are potentially as harmful for future relations between the participants as misinterpretations which lead to negative evaluations (such as those of Mark and Bob). There is the danger that when, subsequent to what Afrikaans English speakers perceive to be relatively successful interactions, SA English speakers avoid future contact or behave hostilely in encounters, Afrikaans English speakers will perceive them as cold, inconsistent, unreliable and so on.

Summary and conclusion

The fine-grained analyses of parts of two Afrikaans English–SA English encounters which the participants perceived as asynchronous reveal evidence to support the hypothesis that the asynchrony can be explained, in part, in terms of a mis-match of culturally-preferred interactional styles. They also reveal some of the characteristics of these putative styles. In addition, the analyses suggest how, in such asynchronous encounters, negative cultural stereotypes of SA English speakers as 'not saying what they mean', 'being cold and aloof', and 'unreliable and inconsistent', and of Afrikaans English speakers as conservative, authoritarian, dogmatic and inflexible, are generated and reinforced. To date most of the explanations offered for the prejudice and conflict between members of these groups, and between other groups of South Africa, tend to be given in terms of the psychology of individuals or, more frequently, historically-given structural features of the wider social context. This study suggests that such explanations need to be supplemented by explanations in terms of what takes place in the micro contexts of countless everyday interactions.

Key to transcription conventions

⌐__ = latch mark, indicating no gap or overlap
└__   in speech between turns
⌐__ = overlapping speech /
         two people talking at the same time
. . . = noticeable pause (+0.5 second)
underline = accentuation (nucleus or accent placement)
(brackets) = information about paralinguistic (e.g. laughter) and kinesic features
         (e.g. smiles)
'   = rise tone
`   = fall tone
^   = rise/fall tone
ˇ   = fall/rise tone

REFERENCES

Adendorff, R. D., Chick, J. K., and Seneque, M. B. 1985. Negotiating meaning in an English cultural environment. In *Journal of Language Teaching*. Johannesburg: Rand Afrikaans University.

Brown, P. and Levinson, S. L. 1978. Universals in language usage: Politeness phenomena. In Goody, E. N. (ed.), *Questions and Politeness*. (Cambridge Papers in Social Anthropology 8). Cambridge University Press, pp. 56–289

Chafe, W. 1977a. The recall and verbalization of past experience. In Cole, R. W. (ed.), *Current Issues in Linguistic Theory*. Bloomington: Indiana University Press, pp. 215–45.

1977b. Creativity in verbalization and its implications for the nature of stored knowledge. In Freedle, R. D. (ed.), *Discourse Production and Comprehension*. Vol. 1. Norwood NJ: Ablex, pp. 41–55.

Chick, J. K. 1985. The interactional accomplishment of discrimination in South Africa. *Language in Society* 14(3): 299–326.

1987. Interactional sociolinguistics: insights and applications. Unpublished PhD dissertation, University of Natal, Durban.

Erickson, F. 1975. Gatekeeping and the melting pot: Interaction in counselling encounters. *Harvard Educational Review* 45(1): 44–70.

1976. Gatekeeping encounters: A social selection process. In Sanday, P. (ed.), *Anthropology and Public Interest*. New York: Academic Press, pp. 111–45.

1978. Timing and context in everyday discourse: Implications for the study of referential and social meaning. Paper delivered at the Conference on Children's Oral Communication Skills, University of Wisconsin.

Ervin Tripp, S. M. 1972. Sociolinguistic rules of address. In Pride, J. B., and Holmes, J. (eds.), *Sociolinguistics*. Harmondsworth: Penguin, pp. 225–240.

Fillmore, C. J. 1975. An alternative to checklist theories of meaning. In *Proceedings of the First Annual Meeting of the Berkeley Linguistic Society*. University of California, Berkeley, pp. 123–31.

1976. Frame semantics and the nature of language. In Harnad, S. R. *et al.* (eds.), *Origins and Evolution of Language and Speech*. New York: Academy of Science, pp. 20–32.

1977. Scenes-and-frames semantics. In Zampoli (ed.), *Linguistic Structures Processing*. North Holland, pp. 55–81.

Gumperz, J. 1982a. *Discourse strategies*. (Studies in Interactional Sociolinguistics 1.) Cambridge University Press.

1982b. *Language and Social Identity*. (Studies in Interactional Sociolinguistics 2.) Cambridge University Press.

Lakoff, R. 1973. The logic of politeness: Or minding your p's and q's. In Corum, C., Smith-Stark, T. C., and Weiser, A, (eds.), *Papers from the Eighth Regional Meeting of the Chicago Linguistics Society*, pp. 292–305.

1979. Stylistic strategies with a grammar of style. In Oraisainn, J., Slater, M. and Loeb Adler, L. (eds.), *Annals of the New York Academy of Sciences* 327. New York: Academy of Sciences, pp. 53–78.

McDermott, R., Gospodinoff, K., and Aron, J. 1978. Criteria for an ethnographically adequate description of concerted activities and their contexts. *Semiotica* 24(3,4): 245–75.

Mahan, H. (1979). *Learning Lessons*. Harvard University Press.

Odendal, E. F. 1976. Oor die aanspreekvorme in Afrikaans. In De Klerk, W. J. and Ponelis, F. A. (eds.), *Gedenkbundel H. J. J. M. van der Merwe*. McGraw Hill, pp. 105–13.

Pride. J. B. (ed.). 1985. *Cross-Cultural Encounters*. Melbourne: River Seine.

Scollon, R., and Scollon, S. 1982. *Narrative, Literacy, and Face in Interethnic Communication*. Norwood NJ: Ablex.

1983. Face in interethnic communication. In Richards, J. C. and Schmidt, R. W. (eds.), *Language and Communication*. London and New York: Longman, pp. 156–88.

Tannen, D. 1979. What's in a frame? Surface evidence for underlying expectations. In Freedle, R. (ed.), *New Directions in Discourse Processing*. (Advances in Discourse Processes II.) Norwood, NJ: Ablex, pp. 127–181.

Wolfson, N. and Manes, J. 1980. Don't 'dear' me!. In McConnell-Ginet, Borker, R. and Freeman, N. (eds.), *Women and Language in Literature and Society*. Praeger, pp. 79–92.

31

Syntactic variation in South African Indian English: the relative clause

RAJEND MESTHRIE

Introduction

South African Indian English (SAIE) illustrates the rich syntactic variation characteristic of an English dialect that has arisen from a process of language shift. Once a second or third language spoken by a group of indentured and merchant Indians in Natal, SAIE is today, 125 years after the first immigrations, a first language sharing a great deal with other English varieties of South Africa (SAE), while having a host of linguistic features of its own. Despite many features in common with the English of India, SAIE has, on the whole, the characteristics of a new dialect born on South African soil, rather than those of a transplanted Indian English variety (Mesthrie 1988).

Sources of variation in SAIE

The following typology of Englishes according to the (decreasing) degree of variability in syntax can be posited:[1]

> Creole/post-creole Englishes – Language shift Englishes – L2 Englishes – English and American dialects/Colonial Standards

The break in tradition between ancestral languages and the new variety of English is less rapid in language shift than in pidginisation, and one may consequently expect less variation than that reported for creole and post-creole Englishes. I believe that the transfer of terms like basilect, mesolect, acrolect from creology is, however, appropriate in the study of language shift varieties, perhaps more so than for L2 Englishes, to which the extension was first made by Platt (1977).

Specific factors resulting in internal variation within SAIE are of a sociohistoric nature. One can reasonably expect that for the oldest speakers – one generation removed from the experience of indentureship, or, less commonly, immigrant trade – the amount of exposure to English both at school and outside school is a significant determinant. Other possible determinants include the ancestral language, gender, level of education, and social class. The various ancestral languages have a slightly differential effect on the phonetics (Bughwan 1970) and lexis (Mesthrie: 1988) of subgroups of SAIE speakers, but whether syntax is affected in similar ways has still to be ascertained.

The other major determinant of variation, not surprisingly, centres around discourse factors, different styles correlating with the degree of formality of the situation, one's acquaintance with the interlocutor, and judgement of the interlocutor's social standing. Language shift Englishes appear to differ from other varieties of English in the greater degree of style-mixing and the greater predilection for such shifting among younger speakers. Older speakers of SAIE, for example, tend to be bilingual but monostylistic with respect to English.

Aims and methodology

This case study is based on 24 SAIE speakers, residing either in the city of Durban or the rural districts of Umkomaas on the South Coast of Natal. It is part of a larger study, in progress, of 200 SAIE speakers chosen from various areas of Natal. For the larger study a representative selection of areas set aside for Indian housing in Natal was made, and within each area a random selection of interviewees made, on the basis of valuation rolls obtained from district councils.

This study reports on one area of syntactic variation – the relative clause. The working assumptions which the study hoped to illuminate were as follows:

a) that the syntactic structures of SAIE were furthest removed from standard South African English (see Trudgill and Hannah 1982, 1987)[2] in interesting ways in the speech of those older speakers who had the least education, even in their careful style;

b) that younger educated speakers tend to approximate standard English syntax, except in informal speech, which shows the influence and covert prestige of basilectal speech;

c) that there is a continuum of usage between the most basilectal style and the most acrolectal, similar to those reported for Jamaican English (DeCamp 1971) and Guyanese English (Bickerton 1975).

The method of eliciting data involved informal tape-recorded interviews, conducted by me – a member of the community under study – using the by now 'classic' Labovian techniques for eliciting the vernacular. In addition, I was able to take advantage of kin and friendship networks available to me in the rural parts of Umkomaas to gather data in a non-interview situation. This was done in two ways. The first involved use of a hidden tape recorder to record acquaintances who, it was felt, would not object to the procedure when disclosed later. The resulting disadvantage of lack of optimal quality of tape was easily made up for by the participant-analyst's ability to decipher whispers, fast speech, etc. The second resource involved the immediate jotting down of vernacular features whenever possible, without offence or embarrassment to speakers.

It was not desirable in this study to extend the use of network contacts beyond the neighbourhoods in which one was known. To attempt to establish networks via friends of friends (as described in Milroy 1980) would seem less natural than simply approaching people in their homes, as membership of this minority group within the South African spectrum is, for the purposes at hand, *bona fides* in itself. The network approach, of course, carries the further disadvantage of limiting one to a particular geographical area over a long period of time. I was still able to benefit from its great advantage of affording the researcher spontaneous data of natural groups *in situ*, because of my own networks in both areas of study.

Topics that usually elicited unselfconscious discussion related to interviewees' families, their ancestors, elementary politics, and danger of death stories, usually – it turned out – involving motor accidents, illness or occasional mishaps at sea. The interviews and other tape recordings were very successful in eliciting informal conversational style, as can be gauged from channel cues like laughter, occasional bits of anger, tears, the use of slang and occasional obscenities by some speakers, questions directed at the interviewer, and conversations carried on simultaneously on tape. Using this abundance of natural data, two areas of syntax were investigated, relative clause strategies (RCs henceforth) and topicalisation; their occurrence was subsequently correlated with the use of two morphological endings: the third person -s for regular present verbs, and the plural -s for regular nouns. It is only possible, however, within the limitations of space, to report in detail on the relative clause here, and to summarise the other findings insofar as they lend themselves to comparison with relativisation strategies in SAIE.

Variation in the Relative Clause

A wide array of relative clauses is to be found in SAIE, some no different from modern standard southern British English usage, others clearly derived from English usage, with minor differences in detail, and still others based on substratal analogies or having their origins in discourse organisation. In the following exemplification of SAIE relatives those corresponding to standard English constructions are excluded:

a) *Restrictive versus non-restrictive*: The majority of relatives in the corpus fell into the class of restrictive RCs, with only 4 being properly non-restrictive. Sixteen sentences, discussed below as 'near-relatives', provided a problem for this restrictive/non-restrictive dichotomy.

b) *'Near-relatives'*: Hypotaxis is not favoured in most SAIE lects, preference being given to the paratactic arrangement of clauses, with both syndetic (i.e. with conjunctions) and asyndetic (without conjunctions) arrangements. The following is an illustrative basilectal fragment, chosen at random. (Short pauses are indicated by /, longer ones by //.)

> Ey so hot it was today man can't sit inside can't sit by the tree too man/ you know 'specially me I got the wheezing/ can't keep using the pump too you know // that thing dries you up you know what that pump is// Father had you should know about it// I got pump you know I got mentholyn/ I got viroid/ you know they gave me in hospital/ I can't keep using that too// use it too much too you know it'll finished no good // I go sit by the tree can't do it/ come an' sit here can't do it/ took cold water too had a bath today too/ what else you going to do?

This means that the usual English relatives making recourse to 'equivalent NP deletion' with accompanying relative pronouns are rare in the basilect. Yet in many instances the demands of fluent discourse come close to producing RCs. These I call 'near-relatives', which, though they have a 'full' NP or pronoun and no special relative particle, come close to subordination in terms of intonation patterns and occasional placement within a matrix sentence.

1. You get carpenters, they talk to you so sweet.
2. I got viroid, they gave me in hospital.
3. And you know that cook, she was cooking over there, she fell on one big big thorn tree.
4. One faller, I don't think you know that faller,[3] one faller was staying here, outside the shop here.
5. The old man gave it to his stepson, he was a alcoholic, sold that for six hundred rand without telling us.

It is clear from these examples that fluent basilectal speakers are on the way to forming relative clauses from full sentences, with a pronoun used as an intermediate type of relative particle. The substitution of a relative marker *who* or *that* for the pronoun in the (apparently) subordinate clauses in 1, 3 and 5, above, would render them as 'standard'. The use of a pronoun instead of a range of relative particles is a useful step in an emergent dialect which has no problems with gender differentiation of pronouns (i.e. in the appropriate selection of *he, she* or *it*), but some difficulty (see g below) with the selection restrictions governing relative pronoun choice. There is a parallel in the development of RCs in Hawaiian Pidgin English where, according to Bickerton (cited by Romaine 1982:

59), there are (similar) difficulties in deciding whether we are dealing with subordination or loose conjoining, and where simple pronouns are used as an intermediate stage between zero forms and a full range of English relative pronouns. The following example is from Bickerton (1977: 126):

6.   Da boi jas wawk aut fram hia, hiz a fishamaen.
        'The boy who just walked out of here, he's a fisherman'

c) *Correlatives*: Also found in basilectal SAIE is a modified correlative construction, in which the relative clause, usually introduced by *which*, precedes the main clause. The head noun of the sentence usually surfaces in the preposed clause and an anaphoric pronoun replaces the NP in the main clause. Where discourse context makes the referent clear, both NPs may be replaced by relative particle constructions *(which one . . . that one* or some close equivalent, as in 8 and 9).

7.   But now, which one principal came here, she's strict just like the other faller. 'The principal who has just joined the school lately is as strict as her predecessor.'
8.   Which one haven' got lid, I threw them away. 'I threw the bottles that don't have caps away.'
9.   Who get education they get two standard, three standard, finished. 'Those who received an education only went up to standard two or three.'

SAIE correlatives are described in further detail in Mesthrie (1987).

d) *Compound relatives*: Older speakers, bilingual in SAIE and an Indic or Dravidian language, occasionally use compounded forms in place of full relatives. Like the correlative construction, these involve a preposed RC:

10.   That Sally's-baked-cake you like? 'Do you like that cake which Sally has baked'.
11.   At least that light-peoples' house, comes late too, at least they can sleep and put it on. 'People who have electricity in their homes can at least watch late night T.V. in bed.'

e) *Contact relatives*: Jespersen (cited by Romaine 1982: 74) uses the term 'contact clause' for sentences in which a subject NP is relativised without an overt relative pronoun:

12.   There is a man wants to see you.

Such Janus-like clauses, with the relative NP facing both clauses, *there is a man*, and *a man wants to see you*, usually occur in locative or existential sentences. The following examples from SAIE illustrate this tendency, but 15 and 16 show further possibilities for the use of contact RCs.

13.   And there's so many qualified teachers haven't got nice jobs.
14.   He's got one boy is twelve, and the other is nine.

Table 31.1. *Relative frequencies of RC types in SAIE*

Near Relatives	25%	
that Relatives	21%	(20% standard, 1% *that-one* RC)
Contact Relatives	14%	
what Relatives	7%	
who Relatives	7%	(standard)
ø relatives	7%	(standard – object NP in RC deleted)
where relatives	5%	(standard locative RCs)
Correlatives	5%	
which Relatives	4%	(2% std, 2% with [+human NPs]
Compound Relatives	3%	
pronoun-retaining RCS	2%	
which-one Relatives	1%	
when Relatives	1%	(standard)

15. You know who's that – Ntuli's son, you know the litee should row the boat an' all. *(litee* = slang for 'boy'; *should* = 'used to')
16. For function, for any wedding anniversary carries on, anything, he used to come here.

f) *Pronoun retaining relatives*: These involve the retention of a 'shadow' pronoun in the RC, which is introduced by an appropriate relative pronoun:

17. Starter is a thing that it gets hot quickly.
18. You know the people who, you know, they saved you know, somehow or other they built their farm and they stayed.

This type of relative, though common in some Northern varieties of British English, is rare in my corpus, and uncharacteristic of the dialect; it is probably a function of spontaneous pragmatic factors which have not stabilised in the dialect.

g) *Other RCs with non-standard relative pronouns*: Unlike the others above, a last group of SAIE RCs are structurally similar to those of standard English except for the selection restrictions governing the choice of relative pronoun. These include *what* as [-animate] relative pronoun, *which* with [+human] nouns, and *that one* with apparently any noun.

19. Let's get most of the things what we can.
20. First time I saw the clothes what she was wearing.
23. This is my daughter which left school.
24. How's your sister, that one was sick just lately.

Table 31.1 furnishes the percentage occurrence of different types of relatives, from the total of 102 relative or near-relative clauses, in order of decreasing magnitude.

With the number of non-standard RCs in a majority (58 per cent), one would expect to find some interesting sociolinguistic patterning. One of the first issues to be resolved is whether these constructions lend themselves to sociolinguistic comparison. The debate regarding the nature of the linguistic variable on the syntactic level is an important one, but out of the scope of this case-study. For the New Englishes, as with creoles and post-creoles (Winford 1984), there seems to be significant variation, which patterns with external parameters in similar ways to phonological and morphological variables.[4] I shall assume, with Cheshire (1987), that although the concept of the linguistic variable should not necessarily be used to analyse variation in syntax, the attempt to quantify syntactic features in discourse can nevertheless provide us with valuable insights.

Table 31.2 gives the number and types of RCs used by individual speakers, the subscripts denoting numbers assigned to speakers in the order in which tapes were transcribed. The speakers were ranked in terms of percentage values of the number of non-standard RCs to the total number of RCs used. As can be seen, the spread was from 0 to 100. The ranking also took into account the number of RCs used, in order to separate speakers bunched at 0 or 100. The speaker with a score of 100 based on 4 RCs was, for example, ranked higher than one with a score of 100 based on less than 4 RCs. The column 'Other' denotes problematic cases, where a RC was involved, but where it was left incomplete or where a slip of the tongue had occurred, and so on. These were left out of the calculation of the percentages in table 31.2.

Table 31.3 indicates the percentage of speakers who used only standard RCs, only non-standard RCs, or both.

Table 31.4 ranks the 24 subjects on a basilectal-mesolectal-acrolectal scale, and provides a social profile of individual speakers. The terms *basilect*, *acrolect* etc are not rigorously defined ones (see Bickerton 1971: 464), since they involve an impressionistic scaling of speech repertoires. The basilect is simply the (creole) variety furthest away from the colonial language which formed the original superstrate, the acrolect the variety closest to the colonial language, differing mainly in phonological details, and the mesolect a cover term for a host of sub-varieties in between. For SAIE we can assume for the time being that having a basilectal syntax entails using only 'exotic' RCs, such as correlatives or compounds far removed from the standard forms; that acrolectal syntax involves only standard RCs; and mesolectal syntax makes some use of both standard and non-standard types. On the whole the distribution of other morphological and syntactic features in SAIE does not seem to be as clear-cut as this; for example, the range of variation for the -*s* endings on present tense verbs and for the use of various topic-forming strategies does not reach the outer limits of 0% or 100%, and the mesolectal limits are more arbitrary.

Table 31.2. *RCs used by 24 SAIE speakers*

Rank order	Speaker	Near-rel.	Correl.	Compound	Contact	Pro. Ret.	Non-std part.	Std	Other	Total	%
1	S18	5			3				1	9	100
2	S3	3	1		1					5	100
3	S2	1		2	1					4	100
4	S4			1	1		1			3	100
5	S15	1			1					2	100
6	S14		1							1	100
6	S13				1					1	100
8	S5	5	1			1	1	1		9	89
9	S7	5			2			2		9	78
10	S9	3			2			2		7	71
11	S21				1		1	1		3	67
12	S19	1					2	3	1	7	50
12	S10					1		1		2	50
12	S6		2				2	4		8	50
15	S12						2	3	1	6	40
16	S11	1			1			4		6	33
16	S17	1						2		3	33
18	S22							3		3	0
18	S24							3		3	0
20	S23							4		4	0
21	S20							7		7	0

No data: S1; S16; S8.

Note: correl. = correlative, pro ret. = pronoun retaining RC, part. = particle, std = standard

Table 31.3. *Standard/non-standard use of RCs according to individual speakers*

% with only standard RCs			16.6
% with some standard RCs	(> 50%)	25 ⎱	41.6
	(< 50%)	16,6 ⎰	
% with no standard RCs			29.1
% no data			12.5

Table 31.4. *The social profile for RCs in SAIE*

	Speaker	Rural/ Urban	Age	Gender	Educ- ation	Home lang.	Profi- ciency	Inter- view	Income
Bas.	S18	U	30+	M	6	Ur	P	O	M
	S3	R	60+	F	7	Te	P	O	L
	S2	R	60	F	3	Hn	P	C	L
	S4	R	50	F	6	Te	P	O	L
	S15	U	50+	F	5	Ta	P	O	M
	S14	U	70+	M	0	Ur	P	O	M
	S13	U	50+	M	7	Ta	P	O	L
Mes.	S5	R	60+	M	4	Ta	P	O	L
	S7	R	70+	M	4	Ta	P	O	M
	S9	R	20+	M	12	Hn	NP	C	H
	S21	U	70+	M	10	Hn	P	O	M
	S19	U	30+	M	8	Ta	P	O	L
	S10	R	30+	M	12	Hn	NP	C	M
	S6	R	20+	F	8	Hn	P/NP	C/O	L
	S12	R	50+	M	10	Hn	P	C	H
	S11	R	50+	M	8	Ur	P	C	L
	S17	U	50+	F	6	Hn	P	O	H
Acr.	S22	U	20+	F	12	Gu	P	O	H
	S24	U	20	F	12	Gu	P	O	H
	S23	U	40+	F	10	Ta	P	O	H
	S20	U	50+	M	9	Hn	P	O	L
No data:									
	S1	R	40+	F	8	Te	P	O	L
	S16	U	40+	F	8	Hn	P	O	H
	S8	R	20+	M	11	Hn	NP	C	H

Note: Bas. = basilectal, Mes. = mesolectal, Acr. = acrolectal, U = urban, R = rural, M = male, F = female, Ur = Urdu, Te = Telugu, Hn = Hindi/Bhojpuri, Ta = Tamil, Gu = Gujarati, P = proficient in an Indian language, NP = not actively proficient, P/NP = some proficiency, O = overt interview, C = covert recording, C/O = both overt interview and covert recordings, L = low, M = middle, H = high. Education given in number of years in English schools.

Some patterns emerge clearly in table 31.4. The group that uses only standard RCs consists of middle class young female urban speakers, except for one 55-year-old working class male.[5] Another group, which used only non-standard RCs in the interviews, comprises elderly women with little formal education (with one glaring exception, once again). The middle group with a mixed repertoire, drawing from a variety of sources including the standard, is the most heterogeneous, drawing on young and old, educated and less educated alike.

A summary of the main social variables and their influence with respect to RCs follows:

a) *Urban vs Rural networks*: No patterns among the basilectal and mesolectal varieties; but the acrolectal end comprises only urban speakers.

b) *Age*: The basilectal end comprises (with one exception) speakers over 50; the mesolectal middle has no age correlates; the acrolectal end has, with one exception, no speakers above the age of fifty.

c) *Gender*: The basilectal end is mixed, but with one exception has females bunched at the extreme; the mesolectal middle is mixed; the acrolectal end comprises females, with the one exception.

d) *Education*: The basilectal end comprises speakers with less than eight years of schooling (the limit of primary education); the mesolectal end is mixed; the acrolectal end comprises speakers with more than eight years of schooling.

e) *Proficiency in an Indian language from birth*: The basilectal end comprises speakers with at least equal proficiency (in terms of fluency) in English and an Indian language; the mesolectal middle has no such correlation; the acrolectal end does not exclude proficiency in an Indian language, but has speakers whose competence in an Indian language does not exceed that in English.

f) *Ancestral Language*: Does not correlate with any particular type of relative, or with standard or non-standard tendencies.[6] Although substratal influences might originally have differed according to whether speakers were of an Indic or Dravidian background (as these language families present different types of relatives; see Mesthrie 1987), such influence appears to have been levelled out.

g) *Style of Interview*: The basilectal end produces non-standard RCs even in instances when the speaker is aware of being taped; the acrolectal end produces only standard RCs in (informal) interviews; the mesolectal middle is variable in this regard, but no other conclusions can be drawn until further study of the interplay between covert and overt recording situations has been undertaken.

h) *Income Group*: As social class is not clearly defined for the community under study, it seemed safer to examine the (relative) income group to which the speaker has belonged for much of his or her life. Lower and middle income groups tend to fall into the basilectal or mesolectal levels; and higher income groups fall into the mesolectal or acrolectal levels.

It is a matter for future investigation whether the group of younger middle-class females is really in the vanguard of syntactic assimilation with the standard, as table 31.4 suggests and if so by what means. As apartheid legislation limits contacts between young South Africans of all groups, it is a possibility that the 'Indian' variety used at the 'Indian' school plays a bigger role in influencing the direction of language change than the potentially prestigious standard variety of South African English. It would appear that young men generally are less affected than middle-class young women by standard models potentially available in schools. Put another way, it seems that the distance between middle-class and lower-class speech is greater for women than men.

There are several shortcomings in this survey, notably in the lack of information, at this stage, on younger male urban speakers. Secondly, the mix between covert recordings for some speakers and overt ones for others raises some problems of classification which can, however, be partly remedied at a later stage of data collection, by reversing the procedures where possible. The diverse range of syntactic forms that young people have in their repertoire needs to be studied under a variety of conditions, as SAIE is not simply a 'focused' vernacular, but a continuum incorporating the standard, which speakers can shift along.

The findings for RCs correlated very well with two other areas of variation (the use of topicalisation, and -s endings for 3rd person singular present tense verbs and plural nouns – too detailed to be reported on here). It therefore seems eminently possible that for 'New English' varieties one can speak of the possibilities of doing social syntax.

NOTES

I wish to acknowledge my indebtedness to the Human Sciences Research Council for funding this project. Thanks are also due to Roger Lass for comments on an earlier draft.

1. This typology can be sharpened by differentiating between English as a second language and English as a foreign language; and between language shift involving several languages (for example, SAIE) and language shift involving a single ancestral language (for example, Welsh English in some parts of Wales).
2. The syntactic differences between standard South African English and standard southern British English are thought to be very few (see Trudgill and Hannah 1982: 26).
3. *That faller*, reduced to *daffale* in fast speech, is used as a pronoun in basilectal SAIE.

4. For a contrary view, and discussion of how syntactic variation in Guyanese Creole differs from 'Labovian' patterning, see Bickerton (1975: 17–18).
5. The present sample does not, unfortunately, include any young urban male speakers.
6. The occurrence of English – Gujarati bilinguals only under the acrolect is an accident arising from the small size of the corpus reported on here. There certainly are older basilectal speakers in this subgroup.

REFERENCES

Bickerton, D. 1971. Inherent variability and variable rules. *Foundations of Language* 7: 457–92.

1975. *Dynamics of a Creole System*. Cambridge: Cambridge University Press.

1977. *Change and Variation in Hawaiian English, Vol 1: General Phonology and Pidgin Syntax*. Social Sciences and Linguistics Institute, University of Hawaii.

Bughwan, D. 1970. An Investigation into the Use of English by the Indians in South Africa, with Special Reference to Natal. Unpublished PhD thesis, University of South Africa.

Cheshire, J. 1987. Syntactic variation, the linguistic variable, and sociolinguistic theory. *Linguistics* 25: 257–82.

DeCamp, D. 1971. Toward a generative analysis of a post-creole speech continuum. In Hymes, D. (ed), *Pidginization and Creolization of Languages*. Cambridge: Cambridge University Press, pp. 349–70.

Mesthrie, R. 1987. From OV to VO in language shift: South African Indian English and its OV substrates. *English World-Wide* 8(2): 263–76.

1988. Toward a Lexicon of South African Indian English. *World Englishes* 7(1): 5–14.

Milroy, L. 1980. *Language and Social Networks*. Oxford: Basil Blackwell.

Platt, J. T. 1977. The Singapore English Speech Continuum and its basilect 'Singlish' as a 'Creoloid'. *Anthropological Linguistics* 17(7): 363–74.

Romaine, S. 1982. *Socio-Historical Linguistics: Its Status and Methodology*. Cambridge: Cambridge University Press.

Trudgill, P. and Hannah, J. 1982. *International English: A Guide to Varieties of Standard English*. London: Arnold. 2nd edition 1987.

Winford, D. 1984. The linguistic variable and syntactic variation in creole continua. *Lingua* 62: 267–88.

32

The social significance of language use and language choice in a Zambian urban setting: an empirical study of three neighbourhoods in Lusaka

ALICE K. SIACHITEMA

The social setting

In the urban centres of most of post-colonial Africa, Western languages have become permanently associated with those domains or spheres of social activity which symbolise Western influence, while the indigenous languages remain as symbols of family ties and ethnic identity.

In most monolingual communities, different varieties of a single language are employed to express every aspect of life; in post-colonial Africa, however, speakers generally use two or three different languages to express different aspects of their social identities. Research conducted in Kenya, notably that of Parkin (1977) and Scotton (1982), shows that ethnic identity in that country is expressed in one's mother tongue, trans-ethnic solidarity (as Africans) in Swahili, and power, education and high economic status in English. In the Zambian urban setting, where both Western and traditional institutions are present, the choice of English rather than a local language, or vice-versa, in a given situation, carries certain habitual value connotations. These, in the long run, regulate the way in which the languages are used within the community. The aim of the present paper is to illustrate how the position of the mother tongue in the households of Lusaka is being encroached upon by the two major lingua francas, namely English and Nyanja. The paper also attempts to explain the social significance of language choice in the home domain.

It is first necessary to clarify the use of the terms 'mother tongue' and 'assumed first language' in this paper. In fact, Davies' observation that the notion 'mother tongue' is problematic, avoiding as it does difficult questions of language loss and attrition, of switching and shifting, of dual first language, of intelligibility between languages, of claimed status and the reflection of status in the claimed 'mother tongue' (1986: 9), cannot be applied to a more appropriate context than that of language use in Lusaka.

It is estimated that about 40 per cent of the population of Zambia currently lives in the urban areas. Lusaka, being the capital city and the centre of all national and international activities, has naturally received more than its fair share of rural-urban migration, which began immediately after independence in 1964. Apart from the voluntary movement of people from rural to urban centres, there has been a deliberate Government policy since independence to post civil servants away from their home areas to other parts of the country, to discourage ethnic cleavage and to foster a new consciousness based on the country's motto 'One Zambia One Nation'.

The consequences of the movement of people from one part of the country to another are many. Firstly, in order to perform their duties effectively and to be accepted by the locals, many people have found it necessary to learn the language of their new area of residence on top of what they claim to be their mother tongue. Secondly, depending on their age, the offspring of such people have tended to acquire mother-tongue fluency in the language of the new area at the expense of the original one, so that the new language may now be spoken more frequently in the household than the former language. Thirdly, the further people move away from their area of origin, either as civil servants or in search of new job opportunities, the less likely they are to marry someone from their own ethnic group; as a result, inter-ethnic marriage is a common feature of most Zambian urban centres. Many couples in this situation compromise by adopting one of the lingua francas of the town they live in for speaking to their children. These children, therefore, are likely to grow up speaking neither of their parents' languages, unless an opportunity presents itself for learning one of them, such as a spell in the village with one of the grandparents. This then complicates further the meaning of the term 'mother tongue'.

The 'boarding school' experience is another factor which deserves mention here. This involves leaving one's home area to board at a school in another part of the country, where a completely different language may be spoken. This phenomenon started during the colonial period and continued at an increased pace after independence. Apart from learning English, which is an inevitable part of the school process, the boarding school experience has also enabled many people to learn languages which they would otherwise not have learnt, and has further encouraged intermarriage as people from different linguistic and cultural backgrounds intermingle in the environment of the school.

The extended family system, which encourages close ties between members of a large number of inter-related families, also contributes to language additions and language shift in individuals. For instance, a civil servant from the western Province who is posted to the eastern Province might decide to include a niece or nephew, or even a distant cousin, among the members of his family. Members of such a family are likely to add Cewa, Tumbuka or other languages to their linguistic repertoire. With intermarriage on the increase, the extended family now embraces families from very different linguistic backgrounds, adding a new dimension to the already complex language scene. Members of two families who are united through marriage in this way may try to converge by learning each other's languages, thereby adding another language to their linguistic resources. To this list of factors we must add another. All of Zambia's local languages belong to the Bantu language family; consequently they share a number of structural and lexical features, although, of course, some languages are more closely related to each other than others (Kashoki 1978). This being the case, it is relatively easy for Zambian people to learn each other's language, provided that there is sufficient motivation.

It is in this context, then, that the terms 'mother tongue' and 'assumed first language' should be understood. The term 'mother tongue' is used here to refer to the language people claim to have spoken first as children in the home. In most cases, this coincides with the ethnic group people consider themselves to belong to. So, in fact, for a number of people in this study, the term 'mother tongue' may simply be interpreted in a sentimental way, as a symbol of ethnic identity, and may not be the language that is actually used in the household. However, as the study on which this paper is based aimed to investigate not only language use but also attitudes towards language[1] we tried not to tamper with people's sentiments. Instead we decided to use the term 'assumed first language' to refer to the language which is claimed to be used more frequently in the household.

Language use and language choice in Lusaka

The study on which this paper is based investigated the use of English and attitudes towards the English language in the home, work and public spheres. It was conducted among 352 respondents residing in three socially differentiated neighbourhoods of Lusaka. The three neighbourhoods, Kalingalinga (a shantytown), Libala (medium cost housing) and Kalundu (high cost housing) were chosen mainly because they were seen as being roughly representative of the social structure of Lusaka, where an individual's socioeconomic status is to a large extent evaluated on the basis of a formal education and on a degree of proficiency in the English language.

A questionnaire was administered orally to the 352 selected respondents. Apart from basic personal information from each respondent on their age, sex, marital status, education, occupation and mother tongue, the questionnaire required the respondents to name the language(s) they speak in a given situation to a specified person, and sometimes on a given topic. Respondents were also asked to name the language(s) they speak at home and to rank them according to frequency of use.

The results, summarised in tables 32.1–32.4, show that there are three major languages used in most verbal interactions in the home, namely the mother tongue[2], Nyanja (functioning in its own right as a mother tongue for a large group of people as well as a local lingua franca), and English. Most of the code-switching patterns that people claimed to use also involved various combinations of the same three languages.

Table 32.1 summarises the general pattern of language use in the home according to neighbourhood. It can be seen from this table that most households in all three neighbourhoods claim the mother tongue as the most frequently spoken language in the home. Note that where Nyanja functions as mother tongue for respondents, it has been included in the 'mother tongue' category. However, 65 households (18% of the sample) claim Nyanja as the most frequently spoken language in the home, and 27 households (8% of the sample) claim English as the most frequently used language. Table 32.1 also shows that although the mother tongue is generally dominant in households in all three neighbourhoods, mother-tongue maintenance is nevertheless strongest in the neighbourhood of Libala, where 70% of respondents claim the mother tongue as the most frequently spoken language in the home, and weakest in the neighbourhood of Kalundu, where only 61% of households make this claim.

Bilingualism and even trilingualism in the home seems to be a common phenomenon; 56% of the total sample claim to speak a second language in the home and 18% claim to speak a third language. The same three languages – the mother tongue, Nyanja and English – are found alternating as either first, second or third most frequently spoken language in the home. Bilingualism, and trilingualism, seems to be more common in the neighbourhoods of Libala and Kalundu, where two languages are spoken in 68% and 75% of the households respectively, and where three languages are said to be spoken in 24% and 27% of the households. In Kalingalinga only 32% of the households claim to speak two languages and only 5% claim to speak three.

Tables 32.2–4 summarise the pattern of language use among various members of the family on a number of given topics. The tables show that there are some topics for which those who are bilingual in the mother tongue and English tend to use the mother tongue more, and others for which the reverse is true (compare, for example, topics 1, 2 and 6 in table 32.2 with topics 3 and 5, for respondents living in Kalundu).

Overall, however, the mother tongue dominates in the home and in those situations which involve interaction with family members; but the other two languages, namely Nyanja and English, are not excluded from

Table 32.1. *Language used in the home according to neighbourhoods*

	Neighbourhoods	MT	%	Nyan	%	Eng	%	Other	%	Code-s	%	Total	%
First most frequently used language	Kalingalinga (Shanty)	87	67	38	30	0	0	4	3	0	0	129	
	Libala (Medium cost)	107	70	23	15	10	7	12	8	0	0	152	
	Kalundu (High cost)	43	61	4	5	17	24	7	10	0	0	71	
% Total sample		237	67	65	18	27	8	23	7	0	0	352	
Second most frequently used language in the home	Kalingalinga (Shanty)	17	13	13	10	1	1	11	8	0	0	42/129	32
	Libala (Medium cost)	18	12	38	25	25	16	23	15	0	0	104/152	68
	Kalundu (High cost)	11	16	8	11	23	32	11	16	0	0	53/71	75
% Total sample		46	13	59	17	49	14	45	13	0	0	199/352	56
Third most frequently used language in the home	Kalingalinga (Shanty)	4	3	2	2	0	0	0	0	0	0	6/129	5
	Libala (Medium cost)	4	3	7	4	15	10	7	4	4	3	37/152	24
	Kalundu (High cost)	7	10	7	10	4	6	2	3	0	0	20/71	29
% Total sample		14	4	16	5	19	5	9	3	4	1	63/352	18

Note: MT = mother tongue, Nyan = Nyanja, Eng = English, Code-s = code-switching, ('Other' includes Bemba, Tonga and Lozi)

Table 32.2. *Languages used in the home between spouses according to neighbourhoods*

Spouse to Spouse		Neighbourhoods		
		Kalingalinga (Shanty)	Libala (Medium cost)	Kalundu (High cost)
Topic 1	MT	66 = 63%	41 = 40%	17 = 28%
Re: work at the	Nyan	26 = 25%	10 = 10%	1 = 2%
office	Eng	0	24 = 23%	24 = 39%
	Others	4 = 4%	5 = 5%	5 = 7%
	Code-s	9 = 8%	23 = 22	15 = 24%
Total		105	103	62
Topic 2	MT	64 = 61%	42 = 41%	18 = 29%
Re: Children's	Nyan	25 = 24%	12 = 12%	1 = 1%
school work	Eng	2 = 2%	23 = 22%	24 = 39%
	Others	5 = 5%	5 = 5%	6 = 10%
Total		105	103	62
Topic 3	MT	65 = 62%	48 = 47%	27 = 44%
Re: Children's	Nyan	26 = 25%	13 = 13%	3 = 5%
discipline	Eng	0	11 = 10%	12 = 19%
	Others	5 = 5%	7 = 7%	7 = 11%
	Code-s	9 = 8%	24 = 23%	13 = 21%
Total		105	103	62
Topic 4	MT	66 = 63%	43 = 42%	22 = 36%
Re: House-keeping	Nyan	25 = 24%	12 = 12%	2 = 3%
money	Eng	1 = 1%	15 = 14%	15 = 24%
	Others	4 = 4%	6 = 6%	6 = 10%
	Code-s	9 = 8%	27 = 26%	17 = 27%
Total		105	103	62
Topic 5	MT	66 = 63%	49 = 48%	28 = 45%
Re: Strange	Nyan	25 = 24%	15 = 14%	3 = 5%
behaviour of	Eng	1 = 1%	11 = 11%	11 = 18%
Neighbours	Others	4 = 4%	6 = 6%	6 = 10%
	Code-s	9 = 8%	22 = 21%	14 = 22%
Total		105	103	62
Topic 6	MT	65 = 62%	44 = 43%	14 = 22%
When annoyed with	Nyan	24 = 23%	6 = 6%	1 = 2%
spouse	Eng	1 = 1%	21 = 20%	22 = 35%
	Others	4 = 4%	4 = 4%	6 = 10%
	Code-s	1 = 1%	28 = 27%	19 = 31%
Total		105	103	62

* Only married respondents answered this part of the questionnaire.

Table 32.3 *Languages used in the home by parents to children according to neighbourhoods*

Parent to Child*		Neighbourhoods		
		Kalingalinga (Shanty)	Libala (Medium cost)	Kalundu (High cost)
Topic 1	MT	75 = 62%	42 = 30%	11 = 16%
Re: School work	Nyan	29 = 24%	13 = 9%	2 = 3%
	Eng	6 = 5%	55 = 39%	34 = 49%
	Others	2 = 2%	5 = 3%	3 = 4%
	Code-s	8 = 7%	27 = 19%	19 = 28%
Total		120	142	69
Topic 2	MT	77 = 64%	62 = 44%	22 = 32%
Re: Friends	Nyan	31 = 26%	19 = 13%	2 = 3%
	Eng	2 = 2%	30 = 21%	19 = 28%
	Others	2 = 2%	7 = 5%	5 = 7%
	Code-s	8 = 6%	24 = 17%	21 = 30%
Total		120	142	69
Topic 3	MT	77 = 64%	79 = 55%	29 = 42%
Helping with House	Nyan	33 = 28%	20 = 14%	2 = 3%
work	Eng	1 = 1%	11 = 8%	12 = 17%
	Others	3 = 2%	7 = 5%	7 = 10%
	Code-s	6 = 5%	26 = 18%	19 = 28%
Total		120	142	69
Topic 4	MT	80 = 67%	66 = 46%	28 = 41%
When annoyed with	Nyan	32 = 27%	11 = 8%	1 = 1%
child	Eng	0	25 = 18%	19 = 27%
	Others	2 = 1%	7 = 5%	6 = 9%
	Code-s	6 = 5%	33 = 23%	15 = 22%
Total		120	142	69

* Only those involved with children either as parents or as guardians answered this part of the questionnaire.

these situations. On the contrary, they too are employed in conjunction with the mother tongue and with varying degrees of frequency in over half of the households involved in the study. It is normal for people to hold a conversation in the mother tongue on one topic and to change to English or Nyanja on another, or to switch from one language to another within the same topic (though it was clear from discussions about the

Table 32.4 *Languages used by children to parents according to neighbourhoods*

		Neighbourhoods		
		Kalingalinga (Shanty)	Libala (Medium cost)	Kalundu (High cost)
Child to parent	MT	109 = 84%	132 = 87%	62 = 88%
	Nyan.	12 = 9%	7 = 4%	3 = 5%
	Eng.	0	4 = 3%	0
	Others	6 = 5%	9 = 6%	5 = 7%
	Code-s	2 = 2%	0	0
Total		129	152	71

questionnaire that respondents felt self-conscious about what they considered to be their inability to stick to one language during a conversation).

Tables 32.5–7 show that bilingualism and trilingualism are related to education, age and sex. They are higher among members of the educated groups 'ED2' and 'ED3' (those who have had 12 or more years of formal education), among age groups 2 and 3 (26–35 and 36–45 years) and among males. This seems to agree with Kashoki's findings (1978) on the degree of multilingualism in Zambia. Whether English or Nyanja is chosen to function in conjunction with the mother tongue in a given household, then, depends on a number of factors; but the major factor is the overarching influence of education. This is not surprising, proficiency in English being a privilege of the few who manage to go through at least twelve years of formal education. Not only does education tend to group people of similar educational levels in the same neighbourhood, thereby encouraging the use of a particular lingua franca in that neighbourhood, but its socioeconomic implications affect the lifestyle of the residents of the neighbourhood. Whereas the informality of atmosphere in neighbourhoods such as Kalingalinga and, to a large extent, Libala, means that residents can interact freely with each other, learning and using Nyanja in the process, the atmosphere in Kalundu, where there are often physical barriers such as high walls separating one neighbour from another, encourages people to interact mainly with members of their own family and with a particular set of friends with whom they exchange visits. As these friends would most likely be in the same socioeconomic bracket and would share English as a lingua franca, contact with them need not involve using Nyanja. In addition to this, the working lives of this group of people would often be conducted in English; as a result members of this group often learn only just enough Nyanja to be able to buy their vegetables at

Table 32.5. *Language used in the home according to education*

	Education	MT	%	Nyan	%	Eng	%	Other	%	Code-s	%	Total	%
First most frequently used language in the home	ED1	148	72	45	22	1	1	10	5	0		204	
	ED2	31	62	9	18	3	6	7	14	0		50	
	ED3	58	59	11	11	23	24	6	6	0		98	
% of Total sample		237	67	65	18	27	8	23	7	0		352	
Second most frequently used language in the home	ED1	23	11	29	14	13	6	20	10	0		85/204	42
	ED2	7	14	13	26	11	22	9	18	0		40/50	80
	ED3	16	16	17	17	25	26	16	16	0		74/98	75
% of Total sample		46	13	59	17	49	14	45	13	0	0	199/352	56
Third most frequently used language in the home	ED1	4	2	4	2	2	1	3	1	0		13/204	6
	ED2	3	6	1	2	8	16	2	4	2	4	16/50	32
	ED3	7	7	11	11	9	9	7	7	0		34/98	34
% of Total sample		15	4	16	5	19	5	15	4	0	0	63/352	18

Note: MT = mother tongue, Nyan = Nyanja, Eng = English, Code-s = code-switching, ('Other' includes Bemba, Tonga and Lozi)
ED1 = 0–10 years of education, ED2 = 12 years education, ED3 = 12 years of education + college or University training

Table 32.6. *Language used in the home according to age*

	Age		Languages									
		MT	%	Nyan	%	Eng	%	Other	%	Code-s	%	Total	%
First most frequently used language in the home	Age 1	59	66	20	22	3	3	8	9	0		90	
	Age 2	100	72	16	11	16	11	8	6	0		140	
	Age 3	42	61	15	22	7	10	5	7	0		69	
	Age 4	36	68	14	26	1	2	2	4	0		53	
% of total sample		237	67	65	18	27	8	23	7	0		352	
Second most frequently used language in the home	Age 1	11	12	16	18	7	8	9	10	0		43/90	48
	Age 2	22	16	26	18	24	17	22	16	0		94/140	67
	Age 3	8	12	13	19	10	14	10	14	0		41/69	59
	Age 4	4	8	4	8	8	15	5	9	0		21/53	40
% of total sample		45	13	59	17	49	14	46	13	0		199/352	56

Table 32.6. *Continued*

	Age	Languages											
		MT	%	Nyan	%	Eng	%	Other	%	Code-s	%	Total	%
Third most frequently used language in the home	Age 1	2	2	3	3	5	6	5	6	0		15/90	17
	Age 2	8	6	7	5	7	5	2	1	3	2	27/140	19
	Age 3	3	4	4	6	6	9	2	3	0		15/69	22
	Age 4	2	3½	2	3½	1	2	0		1	2	6/53	11
% of total sample		15	4	16	5	19	5	9	3	4	1	63/350	18

Note: MT = mother tongue, Nyan = Nyanja, Eng = English, Code-s = code-switching, ('Other' includes Bemba, Tonga and Lozi)
Age 1 = 18–25 years, Age 2 = 26–35 years, Age 3 = 36–45, Age 4 = 46 & above

Table 32.7. *Language used in the home according to sex*

Situation	Sex	Languages											
		MT	%	Nyan	%	Eng	%	Other	%	Code-s	%	Total	%
First most frequently used language in the home	Female	121	27	27	16	8	5	12	7	0		168	
	Male	116	63	38	21	19	10	11	10	0		184	
% of total sample		237	67	65	18	27	8	23	7	0		352	
Second most frequently used language in the home	Female	18	11	27	16	20	12	19	11	0		84/168	50
	Male	28	15	32	17	29	16	26	14	0		115/184	62
% of total sample		46	13	59	17	49	14	45	13	0		199/352	56
Third most frequently used language in the home	Female	5	3	4	2	7	4	7	4	0		23/168	13
	Male	10	5	12	7	12	7	2	1	4	2	40/154	22
% of total sample		15	4	16	5	19	5	9	3	4	1	63/352	18

Note: MT = mother tongue, Nyan = Nyanja, Eng = English, Code-s = code-switching, ('Other' includes Bemba, Tonga and Lozi)

Table 32.8. *Language used to parents*

Language	ED1	%	ED2	%	ED3	%
MT	177	87	45	90	82	84
Nyanja	17	8	1	2	5	5
English	1	1	1	2	3	3
Other	9	4	3	6	8	8
Code-s	0	0	0	0	0	0
Total	204	100	50	100	98	100

ED1 = 0–10 years of education
ED2 = 12 years of education
ED3 = 12 years of education and college or university training

the market, unless other extraneous factors exist which create the need for frequently speaking Nyanja in the house.

The social significance of language use and language choice

We have so far established that most people are bilingual in the mother tongue and in either English or Nyanja, and sometimes in all three. It now remains to determine what factors influence bilinguals to choose one language rather than the other in a given situation. The results of the study suggested that the use of the languages at the bilingual's disposal seem to be determined by certain social factors. For instance, it was found that most bilingual respondents claimed that they communicated in the mother tongue, and no other language, with their parents (see table 32.8), while the same respondents felt free to switch from one language to another when speaking to their spouses and their children. It was also found that when people were annoyed with their spouses, many of them expressed this emotion in their mother tongue, but many of those with a high level of education expressed it in English or in code-switching (between English and the mother tongue). However, when this same emotion was directed against children, both English and the mother tongue were employed equally (see table 32.9). What seems to regulate language choice in these situations is the nature of the role relationship between the interlocutors (Bell 1976; Scotton 1982).

The predominant use of the mother tongue when communicating with parents could be explained on the basis of it being the only language the parents may have in common with their child. This is particularly true of those respondents who are bilingual in the mother tongue and in English, which many elderly parents do not speak. It would therefore be considered an insult to one's parents if one addressed them in English, if the parents

Table 32.9. *Language used when annoyed*

Situation	Language	Education of speaker					
		ED1	%	ED2	%	ED3	%
Between spouses,	MT	98	61	13	44	16	20
when annoyed with	Nyanja	27	17	3	10	1	1
spouse	English	5	3	4	13	31	39
	Code-s	21	13	8	27	29	36
	Other	9	6	2	6	3	4
Total		160	100	30	100	80	100
Parent to child,	MT	124	65	19	42	31	33
when annoyed with	Nyanja	35	18	5	11	4	4
them	English	7	4	8	18	29	31
	Code-s	18	9	10	22	26	27
	Other	7	4	3	7	5	5
Total		191	100	45	100	95	100

do not speak English or understand it themselves. Even if one's parents did speak and understand English, it would be socially more acceptable to use the mother tongue, or at least another African language known to them, rather than English. For a start, the cultural values associated with the relationship between child and parent in the Zambian context demands a high degree of respect on the part of the child towards the parents; this same behaviour should extend to one's elders in general. Most Bantu languages have in-built structures which express this deferential relation-shiip, which English has not. So from this standpoint alone, it seems objectionable to use English. Another factor which militates against the use of English in this situation is the social significance assigned to the English language, which makes it a language associated with the expression of one's superiority over others. This makes its use socially intolerable where one's parents are concerned, and still more so in situations like the one noted above where the parents themselves do not speak the language. It gives the impression that one is looking down on one's parents.

Although this seems to be an accepted norm regulating the use of the mother tongue and English towards one's parents and towards elders in general, it must be cautioned that many educated young parents do speak English to their children, and vice versa. This is particularly true of households involved in intermarriage where sometimes one of the lingue is adopted as a common language to bridge the differences between the couple. It is likely that such parents may not themselves hold strong views as to which language their children should address them in, but it is probably true to say that they themselves would be careful in their language selection when communicating with their own parents. Although it is rather difficult to generalise with the few situations shown in this paper about the nature of code-switching patterns, the results of the main study showed that there is a relationship between the rate of code-switching and the nature of the relationship between interlocutors. Thus the rate of code-switching was found to be higher among bilingual friends with the same mother tongue and between spouses than it was between parent and child when it was the parent addressing the child, and almost non-existent when the child addressed the parent. In work situations, it was also found that code-switching was higher among equals than among members of different ranks, and that juniors rarely switched codes when addressing their superiors. This seems to imply that code-switching is related to the degree of formality of the relationship between interlocutors.

The concept of role-relations runs through the situation which involves the expression of anger or annoyance. The fact that respondents who are bilingual in English and the mother tongue tended to express their anger more in English than in the mother tongue when their anger was directed against their spouses, and in English and the mother tongue equally when it was directed against children, has implications concerning the role-relations between the interlocutors; the languages involved assume a special significance in these circumstances. If, for instance, a couple communicated in the mother tongue in normal circumstances, the choice of English in moments of anger by one partner could have different connotations, depending on a number of factors. The immediate implication of a switch from the language of normal, everyday interaction is that of distancing oneself from the object of one's anger. However, depending on whether the partner against whom the anger is directed also speaks and understands the chosen language, the choice could have additional implications from that of mere distance in intimacy. For instance, if the recipient partner does not speak English or if their level of proficiency is lower than that of the initiator of the switch, the choice of English in these circumstances would not only imply distancing oneself from one's partner, but the other connotations associated with the language in the society as a whole come into play. In this case one is not only declaring hostility but also saying 'I am your superior'.

If on the other hand, both partners speak the language equally well, while the choice of English would still imply distance, it may also serve to define the role relations between the interlocutors in terms of equality.

For the couples who are bilingual in English and the mother tongue, but who choose to express their anger for each other in the mother tongue, the implications could be that the partner who initiates the choice has opted to maintain the role-relationship between husband and wife, as defined by the cultural context expressed by that language.

The use of English and the mother tongue to express anger to children seems to have similar connotations. The use of the mother tongue has the significance of an appeal on the part of the parent to the traditional role relationship between parent and child, under which the parents' authority over the child is absolute and cannot be challenged. The use of English, on the other hand, seems to be an appeal to a new order of things under which the role relations between parent and child seem to take a new direction. Private observations on the use of English or mother tongue between parents and children in Zimbabwe by Makoni (1986, personal communiqué), suggest that the choice between the two languages is crucial to the outcome of an argument between parent and child. The choice of the mother tongue has an inhibiting effect on the child, so that he or she cannot answer back; the argument therefore swings in the parents' favour. The choice of English, on the other hand, lowers the parents' defences and exposes their authority to challenge, by putting the parent on an equal footing with the child.

Code-switching between English and the mother tongue, and vice-versa, is also used by a substantial number of respondents to express anger. It is not clear whether code-switching in these circumstances serves as a means of appealing to both value systems, as represented by the two languages, or simply for communicational efficiency between the interlocutors.

As regards the significance of topic to language use, it was observed that some topics seem to trigger the use of English more than the mother tongue, and vice versa. Topics associated with traditional aspects of behaviour, such as the discipline of children, the expectation that children, especially girls, should help their mother with housework, matters relating to one's village and light gossip about one's neighbours are expressed more frequently in the mother tongue than in English. On the other hand, those topics which have to do with that aspect of life associated with the English language in society, such as work at the office, children's school work, films or, to put it more succinctly, those expressing modernity, tend to have more respondents claiming to use English than the mother tongue.

Conclusion

The discussion has attempted to establish what languages are used in interactions involving members of the family in the home. It has further tried to clarify the social significance of language use and language choice in this domain.

Language use between members of the family was found to involve the mother tongue, including Nyanja in that capacity, and English. The mother tongue in these interactions serves to express and maintain the traditional status quo between members of the family. It takes the form of recognising the authority of elders and the adoption of an appropriate behaviour of deference, which regulate relationships between young and old people. English, on the other hand, signifies status in the modern sense, which is based not on the central concept of age, but instead on education and material success. It provides an escape for the young people from their traditional obligation of deference towards people older than themselves and often sets them in a position of superiority over their elders. Predictably, this order of things is resented by the old people and this gives rise to the social conventions which regulate who speaks English to whom in interactions involving members of the family in the home.

NOTES

1. This paper is based on research conducted in Lusaka and supervised at the University of Edinburgh, UK, for the degree of PhD.
2. 'Mother tongue' here refers to a number of different languages spoken in Lusaka as mother tongues among in-group members.

REFERENCES

Bell, R. 1976. *Sociolinguistics*. London: Batsford.
Davies, A. 1986. Introduction. In *Language in Education in Africa*. Centre for African Studies, University of Edinburgh: Seminar proceedings no. 20.
Kashoki, M. 1978. The language situation in Zambia. In Ohanessian, S. and Kashoki, M. (eds.), *Language in Zambia*. International African Institute.
Parkin, D. 1977. Emergent and stabilized multilingualism: polyethnic peer groups in urban Kenya. In Giles, H. (ed.), *Language, Ethnicity and Intergroup Relations*. London: Academic Press, pp. 185–209.
Scotton, C. M. 1982. The possibility of code-switching: motivation for maintaining multilingualism. *Anthropological Linguistics* 24: 434–44.

West Africa

33

West Africa

EYAMBA G. BOKAMBA

Introduction

Background

It is generally acknowledged that the duration of the contact between English and West African languages on a sustained basis is essentially coterminous with the colonial era, namely circa 1880–1960 (cf. Kirk-Greene 1971; Angogo and Hancock 1980; Bokamba 1984a). During much of that period and up to the late 1960s English was, as Spencer (1971) notes, an institutional link rather than a community language: It was primarily learned in school and used in educational, administrative, and commercial institutions.

While this institutional character remains largely true today, the development of Sierra Leonean Krio (*c.* 1800) and that of other more recent Pidgin English varieties (e.g., Cameroonian, Liberian, Nigerian), combined with the phenomenal expansion of pre-university education into rural areas in the 1970s, have significantly extended the domains of English in the region. In particular, established West African Pidgin Englishes have become the link languages *par excellence* for many communities in the region (cf. Shnukal and Marchese 1983; Jones 1987; Faraclas 1984 and this volume). 'Educated West African English' or the variety of English spoken by educated West Africans, has itself assumed an increasingly preponderant role as the intra-African and inter-continental language of communication for the sub-region. In view of these functional roles, it is reasonable to assume that the increased contact between West African languages and English in the past century or so has had important structural effects on the latter.

This paper provides an overview of the varieties of English used in West Africa, commonly referred to as West African (Vernacular) English or WAVE (Spencer 1971; Angogo and Hancock 1980). In addition to the

493

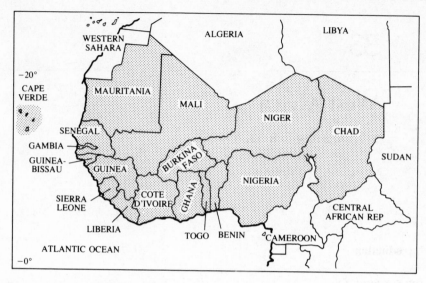

Figure 33.1   Map of West Africa.

general background and sociolinguistic profile presented in this section, the paper reviews many of the salient features of WAVE and discusses the sociolinguistics of English that has led to the development of this variety.

English-speaking West Africa.

The geographical designation *West Africa* refers to a culturally, historically, and linguistically diverse region north of the Equator on the western coast of Africa. The region includes the seventeen countries indicated by shading in the map above, and had an estimated population of 196,500,000 in 1986 (cf. *Africa Today* 1987: 7)

Most of the countries in the region were colonised by Britain and France but achieved their political autonomy at the beginning of the 1960s, as table 33.1 indicates.

The region covers an area of 7,927,244 square miles (including the Cameroon). A third of these nations, whose use of English is the subject of the present study, comprises English-Speaking West Africa (henceforth, ESWA): Cameroon, Gambia, Ghana, Liberia, Nigeria, and Sierra Leone.

ESWA states are interspersed between and surrounded by the French-speaking West African countries identified in table 33.1 below. This checkered location of the countries in the region reflects the arbitrary partition of Africa by European colonial powers during the scramble for Africa in the nineteenth century. As will be seen later (table 33.2), it is a well-known fact of African political history that the creation of colonies

Table 33.1. *Historical and demographic facts about West Africa*

Country	Former colonial ruler	Independence date	population (in millions) (1986)
Benin	France	1 August, 1960	4.1
Burkina Faso	France	5 August, 1960	7.1
Cameroon	Germany, France, Britain	1 October, 1961	10.0
Cape Verde	Portugal	5 July, 1975	0.3
Chad	France	11 August, 1960	5.2
Côte d'Ivoire	France	7 August, 1960	10.5
Gambia	Britain	18 February, 1968	0.8
Ghana	Britain	6 March, 1957	13.6
Guinea	France	2 October, 1958	6.2
Guinea-Bissau	Portugal	24 September, 1973	0.9
Liberia	(United States of America)[1]	26 July, 1847	2.3
Mali	France	22 September, 1960	7.9
Mauritania	France	28 November, 1960	1.9
Niger	France	3 August, 1960	6.7
Nigeria	Britain	1 October, 1960	105.5
Senegal	France	20 August, 1960	6.9
Sierra Leone	Britain	27 April, 1961	3.7
Togo	France, Britain	27 April, 1960	3.0
Total Population			196.5

* Source: *World Bank* (1983: 148) and *Africa Today* (1987: 7, 9)

failed to take into consideration ethno-linguistic factors. Individuals belonging to the same ethnic group and speaking the same language often found themselves divided into different colonial territories and imposed different European languages as official media of vertical communication. What is particularly interesting about this geopolitical situation for our purpose here is the fact that many of the so-called West Africanisms in English result not only from African languages, but also from the French that is spoken in a neighbouring country or within the same country. This is especially true of states such as the Cameroon, Gambia, and Ghana, as will be seen in the following section.

A sociolinguistic profile of ESWA.

While the contact between English and West African languages during the mercantile/colonial era was admittedly shorter than that involving English and Indian languages (e.g., Hindi-Urdu, Kashmiri, Kannada, Persian), the resulting variation exhibited in English has been no less interesting. As in any other language contact situation, to appreciate the various phenomena which underly this variation and, in some cases, linguistic changes, one must first examine and understand the sociolinguistic context(s) under which English was and is used in West Africa. The significance of such a consideration is aptly pointed out in the following statement by Kirk-Greene (1971: 126):

> in the context of English in West Africa, sociolinguistic considerations must be given high priority in examining the direction and causes of change and development. Only by understanding both the structure of the first language and the method by which English is acquired as well as the purposes for which it is used can we account for the deviant forms in bilingual usage, for these are often conditioned by non-linguistic factors.

Among these non-structural factors are language spread, extent of multilingualism, and functional allocation of the languages spoken in the given society.

Even though English-based pidgins (such as Krio and Nigerian Pidgin) may have been used as trade languages as early as the eighteenth century (Angogo and Hancock 1980; Agheyisi 1984), the actual implantation and systematic extension of English in West Africa appears to have been initiated on 6 May, 1882. On that date the British colonial government passed its first colonial educational ordinance in the region to regulate educational practices in the Gold Coast (now Ghana) and Lagos, Nigeria (Adesina 1977). According to Awoniyi (1976:36), this ordinance provided for, among other things, grants-in-aid to voluntary agency schools where English was used as a medium of instruction; such support was denied to schools in which African languages were utilised as media of instruction. Subsequent educational reforms, resulting in part from the visits of the Phelps-Stokes Commission on African Education to West Africa (1920–21) and East Africa (1924), and in part from the introduction of public education by the colonial administration, strengthened considerably the English language policy. The policy received further support with the advent of political independence and the generalisation of education in the 1960s and 1970s when the language policies of the ESWA countries mandated the use of English as the sole medium of instruction at all levels.

In summary, the spread of English in ESWA occurred in three phases: (1) the development of English-based pidgins and creoles during the precolonial period; (2) the introduction of Western education by missionaries in the 1880s; and (3) the post-independence generalisation of education and adoption of English as an official language (Spencer 1971). Trade, religion, administration (both colonial and post-colonial), and education served characteristically as the agents of the spread of English in the region.

The expansion of English in ESWA has occurred in a highly multilingual communicative context: It is estimated that there are at least 700 languages, of which about twenty are recognised as national languages or lingua francas, which are spoken in the region (UNESCO 1985). Table 33.2 below provides a sociolinguistic profile of the sub-region. It will be noticed from this table that except for Nigeria, and to a limited extent Ghana and Sierra Leone, the use of the national languages (column 3) in administration (A), education (E), written press (P, column 6), radio and television (R and T) broadcasting, and literacy education (L), is highly restricted even though these are the inter-ethnic community languages. English is the predominant, in some cases (such as Gambia and Liberia) the exclusive, medium of instruction in the sub-region, with the national languages being restricted to adult literacy programmes and to the first three years of primary education. In the Cameroon the two official languages, English and French, serve as the exclusive media of all formal education.

Liberia, which has a unique settlement history and relationship to English, has, of all the African countries, the highest estimated number of speakers of English (40%) outside of South Africa. Statistics on the number of speakers of English in other ESWA states are not available, but it can be estimated on the basis of data from countries such as Kenya, Malawi, Uganda, and Zambia that this figure falls between 10–20%. Since 'educated West African English' (WAVE) is learned almost exclusively through formal education, it is reasonable to assume that the actual number of speakers in these countries does not exceed that of elementary and post-secondary school enrollees and graduates. And these statistics are low for the countries concerned (cf. Bokamba 1984a).

In addition to the facts given in table 33.2, it is to be noted here that youth (+15 years) and adult illiteracy in the region is extremely high, ranging from 66 to 90 percent as of 1980 (cf. Bokamba 1984a). Ghana, which had a literacy rate of 66 percent in 1980, is an exception to this characterisation. Illiteracy interacts with sociolinguistic factors in the sense that it affects both the acquisition and the use of an institutional language like English. In particular, non-literates residing in urban centres are expected to learn street or non-educated varieties of English that they in turn spread to other residents. These varieties form the continua of pidgin Englishes (from basilectal to accroletal English) which serve as the community link languages (see both Faraclas and Singler, this volume). And as a number of previous studies (e.g., Spencer 1971; Kirk-Green 1971; Agheyisi 1971; 1984) and Faraclas and Singler, this volume, have observed, pidgin Englishes and 'standard' English mutually affect each other.

Table 33.2. *A sociolinguistic profile of English-speaking West Africa*[2]

Country	No. of languages	National languages (percentage of speakers)	Other nations where spoken	Official language(s)	Functional allocation in country
Cameroon	237	Basa			PRL
		Beti-Fang	Equatorial Guinea, Gabon, Congo		PRL
		Duala			RL
		Fulfulde	Senegal, Sudan		RL
		Pidgin English (20%)		French/ English	AEPRTL
Gambia	??	Mandinka (42%)	Côte d'Ivoire, Senegal, Mali		R
		Pulaar (18%)	Guinea, Guinea Bissau		R
		Wolof (16%)	Senegal, Mauritania		R
		Dyola (9.5%)	Côte d'Ivoire, Guinea		R
		Soninke (8.7%)	Mali		R
				English	AEPRL
Ghana	46	Akan (6 M)	Côte d'Ivoire		EPRTL
		Ewe (2 M)	Togo, Benin		ERTL
		Ga (1 M)			ERTL
		Dangme (1.5 M)			EL
				English	AEPRTL
Liberia	25	Kpelle (23%)	Guinea		PRT
		Kru/Grebo (22%)			RT
		Bassa (16%)			RT
		Loma (6.6%)			PRT
				English (40%)	AEPRTL
Nigeria	390+	Hausa (32%)	Niger, Ghana, Chad, Cameroon		AEPRTL
		Yoruba (25%)	Benin, Togo		AEPRTL
		Ibgo (22%)			AEPRTL
		Fulfulde (8.6%)	West African states		EPRL
		Efik/Ibibio (5.3%)		English	EPRL
					AEPRTL
Sierra Leone	18	Mende (31%)	Guinea, Liberia		AEPR
		Temne (30%)	Guinea, Liberia		AEPR
		Limba (8.4%)			R
		Krio (1.9%)			R
				English	AEPRT

A = administration, E = education, P = written press, R = radio, T = television,
L = literacy education

To summarise this section, three major conclusions can be drawn from the preceding discussion. First, English, inherited about a century ago from the British colonial era, has remained an institutional and minority language that is largely learned through formal education. Second, it has been adopted in all six ESWA states as the official language for administration, education, trade and diplomacy, and other related governmental activities such as radio and television broadcasting, the written press, and literacy education. These *de jure* and *de facto* functional allocations have placed English in a uniquely privileged position in the hierarchy of co-existing code repertoires in the sub-region, thus making it an enviable investment.

Third, in its horizontal communicative function English is one of at least four choice languages in the multilingual functional hierarchy. Depending on the context of the situation, the selection of the code to be used in a conversation would be made from, in order of preference, the following sets: (1) local languages; (2) national languages; (3) Pidgin Englishes; and (4) English. For instance, if the conversation involves interlocutors from the same ethnic group, a local or ethnic language will be used. However, if the speakers come from different linguistic groups, the preferred choice would be a regional or national language, if they share one; if not, pidgin English would be selected. English is generally utilised in horizontal communication as the 'default' code: when there is no other alternative because of the dictates of either the individuals' linguistic repertoires or other factors in the context of the situation (e.g., topic and setting). Polyglossia, rather than diglossia, is the norm and code-switching and code-mixing are typical phenomena in the daily speech of ESWA inhabitants. This is part of the sociolinguistic background that underlies the structural phenomena surveyed below and discussed in some detail in the West African case study contributions to this volume (Faraclas, Jibril, Singler).

Characteristics of WAVE

The question of whether there is an educated West African variety of English or the so-called WAVE remains unsettled. The reasons for this uncertainty have much less to do with the nature of structural linguistic evidence, as they do with linguistic attitudes: speakers of English in West Africa, most of whom consider themselves the proud recipients of the Cambridge certificates of education and are in many cases direct beneficiaries of British education, do not perceive their English to be different from that of their mentors (Angogo and Hancock 1980; Bamgbose 1982). Such denials are characteristic in the emergence of speech varieties throughout the world (Pride 1981; Kachru 1982, 1986). A cursory examination of the structural evidence, however, will convince any skeptic that there is indeed a variety of English which is characterizable as WAVE. The evidence can be deduced largely from phonetics/phonology, the lexicon and to a certain extent, syntax. Space restrictions allow me to do no more than highlight a few of these features.

Pronunciation

Anecdotal data indicate that WAVE is first and foremost discernible from other varieties of African English (e.g., East African and Southern African) at the phonetic and phonological levels, with the most salient differences being observed in the realisation of vowels (Angogo and Hancock 1980; Bamgbose 1982) and prosodic features.

A selected set of consonants present certain difficulties for a number of WAVE speakers; these include /θ/,/ð/,/g/, and the distinction between /l/ and /r/ (Tregidgo 1987:187). Tregidgo (1987) notes further that there is a tendency to simplify word-final consonant clusters, thus resulting in the pronunciation of *next* as *nest*, and *needs* as *knees*. The existing scanty evidence in this area, however, permits only a very tentative and speculative characterisation of WAVE phonetics and phonology at this point in time.

Lexicon and semantics

In contrast to the phonetic and phonological dimensions of WAVE, its lexical and semantic characteristics have been relatively well-documented. A number of studies have shown the lexicon to be the most interesting area of WAVE in that it reflects at its best the creativity and dynamism of this dialect (Kirk-Green 1971; Sey 1973; Angogo and Hancock 1980; Tingley 1981; Bamgbose 1982; Bokamba 1982; Adegbija 1988). WAVE exhibits considerable morphological variation resulting from what appear to be lexical formation rules. For example, several studies have noted the occurrence of plural mass nouns such as *furnitures, properties, noises, chats, correspondences*, as in the following examples (Kirk-Greene 1971; Sey 1973; Bokamba 1982):

(1)   a. I lost all my *furnitures* and many valuable *properties*.
        b. There were thunderous *noises* of laughter and *chats*.
        c. I was in charge of all *correspondences*.

These examples suggest a paradigm regularisation by essentially ignoring the 'count' vs. 'non-count' semantic dichotomy established in British and American Englishes.

Viewed from a second language acquisition perspective it might be inferred here that the pluralisation of non-count nouns results either from ignorance of semantic (rule) restrictions or interference from the speakers' mother tongues. The former case represents a straightforward instance of over-generalisation in any aspect of language learning; whereas the latter implies the process of language transfer. The language transfer hypothesis would also be consistent with explanations of language contact phenomena advanced in the literature (e.g., Weinreich 1953; Romaine 1988). The difficulty with taking the language transfer hypothesis alone as a possible explanation for the pluralised non-count nouns in (1), however, is that the application of the rule of pluralisation in WAVE is not as consistent as these facts might suggest. Singler (this volume) notes that some of the speakers of 'Liberian English' that he surveyed with regard to the use of plural marking express the plural of regular nouns variably, both in terms of the frequency and choice of markers. Singler, who assumes his sample population to be representative of the speakers of Liberian English, attributes this variation to social, phonological, and syntactico-semantic factors: it is governed, that is to say, by social and linguistic constraints.

Similar evidence of sporadic pluralisation is reported in Tingley (1981: 50) from a survey of the English used in Ghanaian newspapers (in 1976–77).

A close examination of the data presented in the literature (e.g., Spencer 1971; Kirk-Greene 1971; Sey 1973; Chinebuah 1976; Tingley 1981; Singler, this volume) and evidenced in the writing of educated West Africans suggest that deviations involving number agreement extend beyond the lexicon: they also affect subject-verb concord and the selection of personal and possessive pronouns in the third person in syntax (cf. Tingley 1981: 51–2)

The most interesting aspect of the lexicon that shows the dynamic nature of WAVE, however, is word-formation through coinage and semantic changes of various sorts. Coinage in WAVE exploits the processes of prefixation, suffixation, reduplication, and compounding in the production of lexical items of different categories: verbs, nouns, adverbs, and adjectives. Common derivations of this type include *enstool* 'crown a traditional monarch', *destool* 'to dethrown a traditional monarch', *manage with* 'live with', *be on seat* 'be in/present', *bush-meat* 'game', *chewing stick* 'toothbrush', *gate fee* 'admission fee', *known faces* 'acquaintances', *European appointment* 'high-level white-collar position', *been-to* (someone who has been to United Kingdom or elsewhere outside of Africa), *serviceable* 'a person or animal that is always willing to serve', *quick quick* 'quickly', and *slow slow* 'slowly' (Kirk-Greene 1971; Bamgbose 1971, 1982; Sey 1973; Bokamba 1982; Adegbija 1988). Many of these lexical items are analogical formations from British English (e.g., *enstool(ment)*, *destool*, *been-to*, *serviceable*), while others are loan-translations from West African languages (*chewing-stick, quick quick*). Adegbija (1988) provides several such terms from Nigerian English.

Regardless of their sources, however, what is most interesting in the occurrence of such words in institutionalised varieties of English (Kachru 1986) in West Africa is that they introduce into the English language and characterise what has come to be known as WAVE. The distinctiveness of this variety is further highlighted through the process of semantic contextualisation/nativisation that basic English lexical items undergo. There are three main strategies adopted to achieve this: (1) semantic extension; (2) semantic shift; and (3) semantic transfer (for further discussion, and examples, see Kirk-Greene 1971; Sey 1973; Bamgbose 1982; Bokamba 1982; Adegbija 1988).

Of all the verbal strategies employed thus far, outright coinage, in all its dimensions (analogical, calques, neologism, euphemistic constructions) appears to be the most productive strategy that distinguishes and characterizes WAVE. Expressions such as *to put in the family way*, 'to make a woman pregnant', *to put to bed*, 'to deliver a baby', *bottom power*, 'favours obtained by a woman through the use of her body', *national cake*, 'rights, privileges, and items to be shared by states or citizens', *khaki boys*, 'a derogatory name for soldiers or uniformed men in general', *son of the soil*, 'a native of a particular place', *portable*, 'a slender, small body (usually used in reference to ladies)', *go slow*, 'a traffic jam or unexpected delay', *small boy/girl*, 'an inexperienced, naive person', *tight friend*, 'a close, intimate friend', *cash madam*, 'an excessively rich woman socialite who flaunts her wealth', and *to smell pepper*, 'to face a tough time or be given a rough deal', cited in Adegbija (1988 13–30) as representing aspects of the creativity of Nigerian English which contributes to variation in English, are very representative of WAVE (cf. Spencer 1971; Sey 1973; Angogo and Hancock 1980; Tingley 1981; Bamgbose 1982; Bokamba 1982). It is this kind of lexicon, more than any other area of the grammar (i.e. language structure), that gives WAVE its distinctive 'flavour', because it reflects the sociolinguistic milieux in which English is spoken.

Syntax

A number of studies have claimed that WAVE distinguishes itself from native varieties of English (namely, British and American varieties) through its syntax (Kirk-Greene 1971; Sey 1973; Chinebuah 1976; Tingley 1981; Bokamba 1982; Bamgbose 1982). Four syntactic features are often cited as typifying this variety of English. The first is the omission and misuse (viewed from the perspective of standard southern British English) of function words, such as articles and prepositions (see Kirk-Greene 1971; Sey 1973; Chinebuah 1976; Hakatua 1978; Tingley 1981; Bokamba 1982; Jibril, this volume). According to Jibril (this volume), apparent inconsistencies and variation in the use of prepositions in Nigerian English can be accounted for by various social factors, especially levels of formal academic achievement and socioeconomic standing.

A second feature is the occurrence of resumptive pronouns, especially in object and locative positions. Chinebuah (1976: 75–6) states that sentences such as the following are widespread in WAVE and specific to speakers of languages from the Kwa and Gur sub-families:

(2) a. The guests whom I invited them have arrived.
     b. Taking a course in a country which her language you did not know is a big problem.
     c. You are going to do your course [i.e. studies] in a country where you have never been there before.

Another important aspect of WAVE but one that has thus far received little attention is grammatical agreement. In addition to the noun pluralisation patterns noted in the section on the lexicon and semantics, above, it has been observed that subject-verb concord and the selection of personal and possessive pronouns in the third person differ from native speaker varieties of English (see, for example, Bamgbose 1971: 37; Tingley 1981: 522–53). These three features of WAVE also occur, to one degree or another, in many other non-native varieties of English, including African, Indian and Singaporean English, and in learner's English (see Bokamba, 1982; Zuengler 1982; Kachru 1982; Wolfram et al., 1986; Swan and Smith 1987). A fourth characteristic – comparative constructions – is perhaps more uniquely characteristic of WAVE. Chinebuah (1976) gives the following examples of the omission of the comparative or the correlative element in the construction:

(3) a. It is the youths who are skilful in performing tasks *than* the adults.
     b. They would have *more* powder on the hand and in their faces.

Sentences such as these are commonly found in other varieties of African English, and seem to reflect the structure of comparatives in African languages, where comparative elements are generally incorporated (semantically) into the verbs *exceed* or *surpass* (see Bokamba 1982; Grant 1987).

It should, however, be pointed out that few, if any, of the so-called typical syntactic deviations are unique to WAVE; as mentioned above, they occur in many other institutionalised and learner's varieties of English. What actually distinguishes WAVE from other non-native varieties of English is its lexicon, including the occurrence of certain types of code-mixing and regionally-bound idiomatic expressions.

The existence of Pidgin Englishes (i.e., Cameroonian, Liberian, Nigerian and Krio), which are increasingly becoming the inter-ethnic media of oral communication in the region contributes further to the differentiation of WAVE from other African Englishes. Because of the wide-spread practice of code-switching and code-mixing in the region due to pervasive multilingualism, there has been a strong and mutual influence between

WAVE and the pidgin Englishes. Consequently, certain aspects of the syntax of these otherwise distinct varieties have become undistinguishable for certain classes of speakers; grammatical agreement and tense-aspect modality are two such aspects. As pidgin Englishes, with their strong African languages substratal influences, become increasingly the common link languages and thereby creolised (Shnukal and Marchese 1983; Agheyisi 1984; Faraclas 1987), the degree of convergence will eventually expand to other areas of the grammar.

Conclusion

It is now commonly acknowledged that language variation is inherent and that certain psycholinguistic and sociolinguistic variables feed into this process (cf. Weinreich et al., 1968; Labov 1972; Cooper 1982, Kachru 1982, 1986, Trudgill 1984; Obeidat 1986). The emergence of WAVE, whose salient features have been reviewed here and discussed further in other contributions in this volume, is a typical case of language variation resulting from language spread. Some of the sociolinguistic and psycholinguistic factors involved in the devlopment of WAVE have been outlined and hinted at in the introductory section. To gain a better understanding of the structural properties presented in the preceding section, one must take into account the sociolinguistics of English in West Africa. The relevant questions to be addressed in this regard are: who speaks English in West Africa and for what purpose? These questions have been essentially answered in the introduction, but some of the points made there deserve special attention here.

WAVE initially evolved out of the teaching and learning of English as a foreign language during the colonial era, when grammar-translation was the predominant approach to foreign language instruction. During much of that period English was taught to multilingual speakers of West African languages by British speakers of English, who may well have spoken different varieties of British English. Variation may thus have been initially introduced by the instructors and then expanded through the multilingual contact situation and the teaching method. Multilingualism and the difficulty of establishing a single national African language for any of the countries concerned during the colonial era contributed to the imposition of English as the official language for education and 'national' administration (Bokamba 1984a, 1984b). In view of these functions, English became the medium par excellence of communication between the colonial administration and its educated subjects, as well as the prized vehicle for educational development and socioeconomic upward mobility. Formal education, therefore, served as the primary agent of the spread of English in each of the countries concerned; those colonial subjects who had no opportunities to enter the golden gates of formal education were practically barred from acquiring the so-called educated English used as the contact language between the British and the educated African élite.

Fortunately, however, the emergence of West African pidgin Englishes as trade languages in the eighteenth century, prior to the implantation of educated English, offered needed communication links to the masses (Agheyisi 1984). In particular, Pidgin Englishes (including Krio) in the Cameroon, Gambia, Liberia, Nigeria, Sierra Leone, became the link languages within and across national boundaries. Their rapid expansion under this function eventually led to an intersection of roles with educated English both during and after decolonisation. In the mid-1950s and throughout the 1960s, for example, there merged important segments of the population that acquired Pidgin English as a second language in the region before being exposed to educated English. Today, according to some estimates (see Shnukal & Marchese 1983, Agheyisi 1984, Faraclas 1984, and this volume), Pidgin English appears to be the most widely spoken non-ethnic language in Nigeria. I suspect similar estimates can be made for the other ESWA states.

It is interesting to note here that a high percentage of speakers of educated English also speak Pidgin English, but the converse is not true. This bidialectal situation has increased considerably with the expansion of formal education into the rural areas, especially since the 1970s, thus making educated English and Pidgin English part of the linguistic repertoire of English-speaking West Africans. This co-existence of the dialects, where mutual structural influence is unavoidable, constitutes the third major source of the birth of WAVE. A fourth factor is the use of West African speakers of English as teachers of the language to other West Africans. This situation provides for the transmission of WAVE, not British English upon which the textbooks are based, to the new learners.

The fifth and final major contributing factor to the development of WAVE is creative writing. Indigenisation of the type described above is very common in former colonial societies where a link language has become the vehicle of creative expression (cf. Kachru 1982, 1986). In attempting to convey West African sub-cultures through their literary works in English, West African writers have found it necessary to adapt and indigenise certain aspects of the English language, including the lexicon and narrative style (cf. Bokamba 1982, Goke-Pariola 1987). Chinua Achebe, who is often quoted in this regard and widely recognised for his imaginative indigenisation of English in his writing, sums up eloquently the attitude that motivates nativisation (Achebe 1966: 21):

> . . . my answer to the question, can an African ever learn English well enough to be able to use it effectively in creative writing? is certainly yes. If on the other hand you ask; Can he ever learn to use it like a native

speaker? I should say: I hope not. It is neither necessary nor desirable for him to be able to do so. *The price a world language must be prepared to pay is submission to many different kinds of use. The African writer should aim to use English in a way that brings out his message best without altering the language to the extent that its value as a medium of international exchange will be lost* . . . (emphasis added,)

Thus Achebe, like many other African writers who use English, French, and Portuguese for their creative works, *bends* the language to accommodate the African cultural experience. This conscious nativisation, combined with the unconscious structural adjustments due to language contact and foreign language acquisitional considerations, account for the emergence of WAVE.

In a society that is pervasively oral and where varieties of Pidgin English (including Krio) remain the dominant link languages and where code-mixing is a common phenomenon, the rate and degree of variation in a language such as English is likely to be much more rapid and extensive than in societies with a strong written tradition. In the latter types of societies, variation emanating from the spoken language is blunted by the written language where the extensive written and broadcasting media (such as newspapers, magazines, books, radio, television) provide a strong standardising influence. WAVE, therefore, is more likely to continue its course towards divergence from, rather than convergence into, what I have referred to as an educated native variety of English.

NOTES

1. Strictly speaking, Liberia was never a colony of the United States. Instead, it was settled by blacks from the New World under the auspices of the American Society for Colonizing the Free People of Colour in the USA.
2. This table is adapted from the UNESCO's (1985) survey of the language situation in Sub-Saharan Africa.
3. Liberian English, as already mentioned, has a different and unique history. Educational, cultural and economic ties with the USA means that the English spoken in Liberia has been influenced to a marked extent by American English (Todd 1984: 284).

REFERENCES

Achebe, C. 1966. The English language and the African writer. *Insight* October/December.
Adegbija, E. 1988. Lexico-semantic variation: A study of nativization of English in Nigeria. *World Englishes*.

Adesina, S. 1977. *Planning and Educational Development in Nigeria*. Lagos: Educational Industries of Nigeria Ltd.

Africa Today: An Atlas of Reproducible Pages. 1987. Wellesley MA: World Eagle. Revised edition.

Agheyisi, R. N. 1971. West African Pidgin English: Simplification and Simplicity. Unpublished PhD thesis, Stanford University.

1984. Linguistic implications of the changing role of Nigerian Pidgin English. *English World-Wide* 5(2): 211–33.

Angogo, R. and Hancock, I. 1980. English in Africa: Emerging standards or diverging regionalisms? *English World-Wide* 1(1): 67–96.

Awoniyi, T. A. 1976. Mother tongue education in West Africa: A historical background. In Bamgbose, A., (ed.), *Mother Tongue Education: The West African Experience*. Paris: UNESCO, pp. 27–42.

Bamgbose, A. 1971. The English language in Nigeria. In Spencer John, (ed.), *The English Language in West Africa*. London: Longmans, pp. 34–48.

1982. Standard Nigerian English: Issues of identification. In Kachru, B. B. (ed.), *The Other Tongue: English across Cultures*. Champaign, IL: University of Illinois Press, pp. 99–111.

Bokamba, E. G. 1982. The Africanization of English. In Kachra (ed.), 1982, pp. 77–98.

1984a. Language and literacy in West Africa. In Kaplan R. B. (ed.), *Annual Review of Applied Linguistics 1983: Literacy Issues*. Rowley MA: Newbury House, pp. 40–74.

1984b. French colonial language policy in Africa and its legacies. *Studies in the Linguistic Sciences* 14(2): 1–36.

Chinebuah, I. K. 1976. Grammatical deviance and first language interference. *West African Journal of Modern Languages* 1: 67–78.

Cooper, R. L. 1982. A framework for the study of language spread. In Cooper, R. L. (ed.), *Language Spread: Studies in Diffusion and Social Change*. Bloomington IN: Indiana University Press, pp. 5–36.

Faraclas, N. 1984. Rivers Pidgin English: Tone, stress, or pitch-accent language? *Studies in the Linguistic Sciences* 14(2): 67–76.

1987. Creolization and tense-aspect-modality system of Nigerian Pidgin. *Journal of African Languages and Linguistics* 9: 45–59.

Goke-Pariola, B. 1987. Language transfer and the Nigerian writer of English. *World Englishes* 6(2): 127–36.

Grant, N. 1987. Swahili speakers [of English]. In Swan, M. and Smith, D. (eds.), *Learner English: A Teacher's guide to Interference and other Problems*. Cambridge: Cambridge University Press, pp. 194–211.

Hakuta, K. 1978. A report on the development of grammatical morphemes in a Japanese girl learning English as a second language. In Hatch, E. M. (ed.), *Second Language Acquisition*. Rowley MA: Newbury House.

Jones, F. C. 1987. Some lexico-semantic characteristics of English-derived words in Sierra Leone Krio. MS.

Kachru, B. B. (ed.). 1982. *The Other Tongue: English across Cultures*. Champaign IL: University of Illinois Press.

1986. *The Alchemy of English: The Spread, Functions and Models of Non-native Englishes*. Oxford: Pergamon Press.

Kirk-Greene, A. 1971. The influence of West African languages on English. In Spencer, J. (ed.), *The English Language in West Africa*. London: Longmans.

Labov, W. 1972. *Sociolinguistic Patterns*. Philadelphia: University of Pennsylvania Press.

Obeidat, H. A. 1986. An Investigation of Syntactic and Semantic Errors in the Written Composition of Arab EFL Learners. Unpublished PhD thesis, University of Illinois, Urbana.

Pride, J. B. 1981. Native competence and the bilingual/multilingual speaker. *English World-wide* 2(2): 141–53.

Romaine, S. 1988. *Pidgin and Creole Languages*. London: Longman.

Sey, K. A. 1973. *Ghanaian English: An Exploratory Survey*. London: Macmillan.

Shnukal, A. and Marchese, L. 1983. Creolization of Nigerian Pidgin English: A progress report. *English World-wide* 1(1): 17–26.

Spencer, J. (ed.). 1971. *The English Language in West Africa*. London: Longmans.

Swan, M. and Smith, B. (eds.). 1987. *Learner English: A Teacher's Guide to Interference and other Problems*. Cambridge: Cambridge University Press.

Tingley, C. 1981. Deviance in the English of Ghanaian newspapers. *English World-wide* 2(1): 39–62.

Todd, L. 1984. The English Language in West Africa. In Bailey, R. W. and Görlach, M. (eds.), *English as a World Language*. Cambridge: Cambridge University Press, pp. 281–305.

Tregidgo, P. 1987. Speakers of West African languages. In Swan and Smith (eds.). 1987, pp. 185–93.

Trudgill, P. 1984. *On Dialect: Social and Geographical Perspectives*. New York: New York University Press.

UNESCO. 1985. *La définition d'une stratégie relative à la promotion des langues africaines*. Paris: UNESCO.

Weinreich, U. 1953. *Languages in Contact*. New York: Publications of the Linguistic Circle of New York.

Weinreich, U., Labov, W., and Herzog, M. I. 1968. Empirical foundations for a theory of language change. In Lehmann, W. P. and Malkiel, Y. (eds.), *Directions for Historical Linguistics: A Symposium*, pp. 95–195. Austin TX: University of Texas Press.

Wolfram, W., Christian, D. and Hatfield, D. 1986. The English of adolescent and young adult Vietnamese refugees in the United States. *World Englishes* 5(1): 47–60.

Zuengler, J. E. 1982. Kenyan English. In Kachru, B. B. (ed.), *The Other Tongue: English across Cultures*. Champaign IL: University of Illinois Press, pp. 112–24.

34

The pronoun system in Nigerian Pidgin: a preliminary study[1]

NICHOLAS FARACLAS

Background

Demography

Nigerian Pidgin (hereafter NP) is spoken as a second language in all parts of Nigeria and as a first language by a growing number of people in the southern part of the country (and perhaps in the urban centres of the North as well). Although no official figures are available, a conservative estimate of the number of speakers of NP at present would fall somewhere between 30 and 35 million, a number which can be expected to rise significantly in the near future, due to the rapid spread of NP among young adults and children, who together constitute well over 50 percent of the national population.

History

About 400 languages are spoken in Nigeria. Historical researchers are uncovering more and more evidence indicating the existence of a complex network of very vibrant mercantile (and often highly urbanised) cultures in all parts of the country. This linguistic diversity, alongside the need for interethnic communication in societies where speakers of different languages are in constant contact with one another due to geographic proximity, intermarriage, trade, travel, and the growth of cities and towns, makes it very likely that pidginised languages, learned as a common second language by people of different linguistic backgrounds who need to communicate with one another, have existed in Nigeria since ancient times.

While pidginised forms of Hausa are still in use in non-ethnically Hausa areas of the North, and pidginised Igbo can still be heard in some Niger Delta markets, these varieties must certainly have been in existence before the first maritime contacts were established with the Europeans in the late fifteenth century. In fact, much ongoing linguistic research suggests that NP could be (at least in part) the descendant of a pidginised Nigerian language which was spoken along the coast before the coming of the Europeans whose vocabulary (rather than the phonology, grammar, or semantics) was eventually replaced largely by words of European origin, sometimes via other Afro-English varieties, such as Sierra Leone Krio and Cameroonian Pidgin.

Geographic variation

While no systematic attempt has yet been made to identify different geographic dialects of NP, at least four regional varieties exist, whose boundaries coincide roughly with the former Midwestern, Eastern, Western, and Northern Regions of Nigeria. NP is most widely spoken in the Midwest (Bendel State) and in the East (especially Rivers State), and has become a first language (and in some cases the mother tongue) of a significant number of people in Warri, Sapele, and Port Harcourt.

Socially conditioned variation

Socially conditioned variation is substantial in NP, and may be broken down for convenience of description into three sets of social dialects. Firstly, those who have had little or no formal schooling and who use NP mainly in markets or in brief exchanges with strangers typically speak *basilectal varieties* of NP. Basilectal varieties of NP often display features found in the mother tongue of the speaker but not in other varieties of NP. Secondly, those speakers of NP who are able to read, write, and/or speak Nigerian standard English (NSE) typically speak *acrolectal varieties* of NP, which often display features found in NSE but not in other varieties of NP. Finally, those who use NP as their principal means of communication in a multi-ethnic family or workplace or for whom NP is the mother tongue or a first language typically speak *mesolectal varieties* of NP, whose features are normally found to some degree in *all* varieties of NP. Many speakers command a full range of social dialects and vary them according to the social context, using basilectal varieties in the market, mesolectal varieties at home, acrolectal varieties in government offices, etc.

Nigerian Pidgin and Nigerian standard English

NP is by no means a 'simplified' or 'broken' version of standard English. For the great majority of NP speakers who have learned NP as a second language, NP represents a 'bridge' between the mother tongue and Nigerian standard English (hereafter NSE). The most serious problem with NP in relation to NSE, then, is a political one. As long as NP is not accorded the place it deserves in Nigerian education, an invaluable tool for the teaching of English will continue to lie wasted and unused. Official recognition should be extended to NP as a major Nigerian language. A standardised scientific orthography should be adopted to facilitate its use in written communication.

The sample[2]

For the general sample, tape recordings of conversations, narratives and other relatively spontaneous speech (at least one hour per speaker recorded over several sessions) were made in the markets and working-class neighbourhoods of urban Port Harcourt from each of some 50 individuals chosen on the basis of age, sex, socioeconomic level, ethnolinguistic background and educational history to represent a cross section of the city's NP speaking population. After the recordings were transcribed a panlectal grid (as illustrated in Rickford 1980) was applied to the data to reveal patterns of socially conditioned variation.

Orthography

The orthography used in this paper is that recommended by Faraclas et al. (1984). Vowels are nasalised before syllabic final nasal consonants, which are often either homorganic to a following consonant or deleted. A vowel marked ' bears a high tone, while a vowel marked ` bears a low tone. Subdots indicate 'short' (narrow pharynx) vowels.

The pronoun system of Nigerian Pidgin

Previous descriptions

Previous works on NP (see Agheyisi 1971; Faraclas et al. 1984; Elugbe and Omamor forthcoming) divide the non-possessive pronouns into three categories, which correspond very closely to the categories used for the description of pronouns in many Benue-Congo languages: (1) neutral or non-emphatic subject pronouns (SP); (2) accusative or object pronouns (OP) and (3) pronominals or emphatic pronouns (EP). Non-emphatic pronouns occur in the same phonological phrase or stress group as the verb for which they serve as arguments, while emphatic pronouns normally form the nucleus of a separate stress group, independent of any verb with regard to the rules of stress assignment (Faraclas 1985). In the example below, *mì* is the first person singular emphatic pronoun, *à* is the 1st person singular non-emphatic subject pronoun and *yù* is the second person

Table 34.1. *Pronouns in NP*

Person	Subject pronoun	Object pronoun	Emphatic pronoun
1st sing.	à	mì	mí
2nd sing.	yù	yù	yú
3rd sing.	i/í(m)	àm	ím
1st plu.	wì	wì/ọ̀s	wí
2nd plu.	ùnà	ùnà	ùnà
3rd plu.	dẹ̀m	dẹ̀m	dẹ́m

singular non-emphatic object pronoun; *o* is a particle (/ marks stress boundary):

> Mí, à láyk yù o
> //EP /SP OP //
> '(As for) me, I (really) like you'

The above mentioned authors list the pronouns for NP as in table 34.1.

Pronouns in the target sample

The phonetic form of every unambiguous instance of pronoun usage in the initial 3,500 words (minus the very first 200) realised by each of 17 speakers was noted and classified according to person, gender, and the three pronoun categories outlined above: subject, object, and emphatic. The 17 target speakers for this pilot study represent the entire set of individuals recorded in one of three urban compounds where the majority of the data in the general sample were collected. The adult members of the target compound speak NP as a second language and work as traders or labourers or are unemployed. Most of the children in the compound speak NP as a first language and all attend school except for the youngest ones, who are not yet old enough to be admitted. Because this compound is the most diverse of the three compounds included in the general sample (in terms of socioeconomic level, amount of formal schooling, and history of NP use), it was selected to illustrate the broadest range of socially conditioned variation.

A listing follows showing, for each member of the target sample, their age (in years), their sex (M=male, F=female), formal education (in years) and whether NP is spoken as a first language (L1) or as a second language (L2):

speaker	age	sex	education	first or second language
A	53	M	5	L2
B	37	F	1	L2
C	36	M	0	L2
D	23	M	6	L2
E	22	F	6	L2
F	20	M	11	L2
G	13	F	9	L1
H	13	F	8	L1
I	12	F	5	L2
J	11	M	6	L1
K	10	F	5	L1
L	10	F	3	L1
M	10	M	3	L1
N	9	F	3	L1
O	8	F	1	L2
P	6	F	0	L1
Q	5	F	0	L1

Table 34.2 lists all of the realisations attested for each type of pronoun among the 17 target speakers. Because emphatic subject pronouns sometimes differ from emphatic object pronouns, each is listed separately.

The data in table 34.2 show that there are some subject and object pronoun forms that do not vary, and that correspond to the forms given in previous descriptions of Nigerian Pidgin (see table 34.1). For the object pronouns these are the second person singular, third person masculine singular, and first and second person plural forms; for the subject pronouns it is the first person plural form. Note that earlier descriptions (see table 34.1) give both *wì* and *ọ̀s* as first person plural object pronoun forms; this pronoun is always realized as *ọ̀s* in the data from the target sample (though *wì* does occur in the speech of some elderly speakers in the general sample who have learnt Nigerian Pidgin as a second language). All the other subject and object pronoun categories show variation, as do some of the emphatic pronoun categories. Note also that a formal distinction exists for some categories between the emphatic subject pronoun and the emphatic object pronoun.

Patterns of variation

Most of the patterns of variation which occur in the sample are not random. Some forms occur only in the speech of those with extensive

Table 34.2. *Realisation of pronouns by target speakers*

Person	Subject pronoun	Emphatic subject pronoun	Object pronoun	Emphatic object pronoun
1 singular	à/áy	mí	mì/à	mí
2 singular	yù/í	yú/í	yù	yú
3 singular (neuter)	í(m)	í(m)/hí(m)	àm/í	ám
(masculine)	í(m)	í(m)/hí(m)	àm	ám
(feminine)	í(m)/shì	í(m)/shì	àm/hà	ám/há
1 plural	wì	wí	ọ̀s	ọ́s
2 plural	ùnà/yù	ùnà	ùnà	ùnà
3 plural	dèm/í	dém	dèm/àm	dém

exposure to acrolectal varieties of Nigerian standard English (NSE), while other forms are found only in the speech of those who speak NP as a second language and who use the language only in a limited number of contexts (in other words, who use basilectal varieties). The forms which are found in the speech of all 17 speakers are almost without exception the very same forms which are invariable in the speech of children for whom NP is a first language, especially those children who have never attended school. These children are considered to speak mesolectal varieties. The patterns of variation which typify the speech of preschool age children who speak NP as a first language may therefore be said to represent a common or core system, which is reflected in the speech of all other speakers in the sample, but which is modified in the direction of NSE in acrolectal varieties and in the direction of other Nigerian languages in basilectal varieties.

Table 34.3 traces how the mesolectal forms (marked by the number 2 in the matrix) gradually begin to vary with more acrolectal forms (marked by the number 3 in the matrix) as the degree of exposure to NSE (mainly via formal schooling) increases. The affected categories are (in order of their susceptibility to acrolectal variation): third person singular neuter subject, third person singular feminine subject, third person singular feminine object, second person plural subject and third person singular masculine subject. Each line of the matrix represents the pronoun use patterns found in the speech of one or more of the individuals in the target sample (i.e. in a single isolect). The age, sex and number of years of schooling completed are listed for one or two speakers of each isolect in the column to the far right. First language speakers of NP are marked L1 while second language speakers are marked L2.

Table 34.4 shows how certain pronoun categories are increasingly affected by variation between mesolectal forms (marked 2 in table 34.4)

Table 34.3. *Acrolectal (isolect A5) to mesolectal (isolect MØ) grid*

Isolect	1st sing. subj.	3rd sing. neuter subj.	3rd sing. fem. subj.	3rd sing. fem. obj.	2nd plu. subj.	3rd sing. masc. subj.	Example Speaker	age/sex/ ed./NP
	3-*a* 2-*ay*	3-*hi*(*m*) 2-*i*(*m*)	3-*shi* 2-*i*(*m*)	3-*ha* 2-*am*	3-*yu* 2-*una*	3-*hi*(*m*) 2-*i*(*m*)		
A5	3/2	3/2	3/2	3/2	3/2	3/2	H	13/F/8/L1
A4	3/2	3/2	3/2	3/2	3/2	2	G	13/F/9/L1
A3	3/2	3/2	3/2	3/2	2	2	M	10/M/3/L1
A2	3/2	3/2	3/2	2	2	2	D	23/M/6/L2
A1	3/2	3/2	2	2	2	2	L	10/F/3/L1
MØ	3/2	2	2	2	2	2	P	6/F/Ø/L1

and basilectal forms (marked 1), as the age of a speaker of NP as a second language increases, and as her/his reliance on NP as the principal language used in daily activities decreases. These categories, in order of increasing susceptibility to basilectal variation, are: first person singular object, third person singular neuter object, third person singular neuter object used as a marker of transitivity (discussed below), second person singular subject, third person plural subject, third person plural object and first person singular subject (reading from right to left across the table). As in table

Table 34.4. *Basilectal (isolect B6) to mesolectal (isolect MØ) grid*

Isolect	1st sing. subj.	3rd plu. obj.	3rd plu. subj.	2nd sing. subj.	Transitivity marker	3rd sing. neuter obj.	1st sing. obj.	Example Speaker	age/sex/ ed./NP
	1-*ay* 2-*a*	1-*am* 2-*dẹm*	1-*i* 2-*dẹ*(*m*)	1-*i* 2-*yu*	1-3NOP* 2-ø	1-*i* 2-*am*	1-*a* 2-*mi*		
B6	1/2	1/2	1/2	1/2	1/2	1/2	1/2	A	53/M/5/L2
B5	1/2	1/2	1/2	1/2	1/2	1/2	2	B	37/F/1/L2
B4	1/2	1/2	1/2	1/2	1/2	2	2	E	22/F/6/L2
B3	1/2	1/2	1/2	1/2	2	2	2	C	36/M/Ø/L2
B2	1/2	1/2	1/2	2	2	2	2	D	23/M/6/L2
B1	1/2	1/2	2	2	2	2	2	I	12/F/5/L2
MØ	1/2	2	2	2	2	2	2	P	6/F/Ø/L1

* NOP = neuter object pronoun

34.3, the right hand column gives a profile of one or two speakers of each isolect.

As shown in both table 34.3 and table 34.4, the first person singular subject pronoun *a* varies with *ay* in all isolects. This pattern of variation is extremely stable across all socially defined groups and indicates that this feature is not undergoing linguistic change, thereby providing support for Rickford's suggestion (1980: 176) that the relationship between diachronic language change and synchronic variation is not completely symmetric. It should be noted, however, that the great majority of variation patterns exhibited in the use of pronouns in the sample may indeed be analysed as instances of language change in progress.

A re-examination of table 34.2 in the light of the data provided by tables 34.3 and 34.4 reveals that variation patterns which tend to increase the number of semantic distinctions marked by pronouns in mesolectal varieties seem to establish themselves first in focused, or emphatic, environments (that is, the usage patterns of the emphatic pronouns tend to introduce further complexity into the mesolectal system). This is illustrated by the third person singular neuter and masculine subject pronouns in acrolectal varieties. They then spread to nonfocused, non-emphatic environments (see the acrolectal use of the third person singular feminine subject and object pronouns). Variation which tends to decrease the number of semantic distinctions marked by pronouns in the mesolects appears, on the other hand, to start in nonfocused environments (see the acrolectal second person plural subject pronoun, and the basilectal third person plural subject and object pronouns) before affecting the emphatic pronouns (see the second person singular subject pronoun in the basilects). In other words, the usage patterns of the non-emphatic pronouns tend to simplify the mesolectal system.

Towards an adequate description of the pronoun system of NP

An adequate description of the nonpossessive nonreflexive pronoun system of NP must include an account of patterns of variation as well as of areas of stability. I propose the following amendments to the set of pronouns posited by my predecessors and shown in table 34.1, above. The pronoun system which typifies the mesolectal varieties of the language and which is found to one degree or another in all varieties of NP is quite stable and may be summarised as in table 34.5.

The patterns of variation in pronoun usage exhibited by speakers of a full range of NP social lects are summarised by the following rules, assuming the mesolectal forms to be the underlying forms. Each rule is variable and each is weighted, with higher numbers indicating greater distance from mesolectal varieties. A more heavily weighted rule may not apply where a less heavily weighted rule has not already applied:

Table 34.5 *The pronoun system of Nigerian Pidgin*

Person	Subject pronoun	Emphatic subject pronoun	Object pronoun	Emphatic object pronoun
1 sing.	à(y)	mì	mì	mì
2 sing.	yù	yú	yù	yú
3 sing.	ì(m)	ì(m)	àm	àm
1 plu.	wì	wì	ọ̀s	ọ̀s
2 plu.	ùnà	ùnà	ùnà	ùnà
3 plu.	dẹ̀m	dẹ́m	dẹ̀m	dẹ̀m

ACROLECTAL RULES

<3rd sing. neuter subject →	hi(m)>₁
<3rd sing. fem. subject →	shi>₂
<3rd sing. fem. object →	ha>₃
<2nd plu. subject → 2nd sing. subject>₄
<3rd sing. masc. subject →	hi(m)>₅

BASILECTAL RULES

| <3rd plu. object → 3rd sing. object>₁ |
| <3rd plu. subject → 3rd sing. subject>₂ |
| <2nd sing. subject → 3rd sing. subject>₃ |
| <3rd sing. neuter object → TRANS>₄ |
| <3rd sing. fem. object →3rd sing. subject>₅ |
| <1st sing. object → 1st sing. subject>₆ |

NOTES

1. A shorter version of this work first appeared in *Journal of West African Languages* 16,2 (1986): 3–8 and was presented at the WALS Congress at Ibadan in March, 1986.
2. The study on which this work is based was made possible by a Fulbright-Hays grant (GOO8540643-US Dept. of Education) and the invaluable help of Mr Magnus Igwe, my assistant. Thanks are also due to Mr S. Adewole for his helpful comments.

REFERENCES

Agheyisi, R. N. 1971. *West African Pidgin: Simplification and simplicity*. Unpublished PhD dissertation, Stanford University

Bokamba, E. (ed.). 1985. Language in African Culture and Society. *Studies in the Linguistic Sciences* 14, 2.

Elugbe, B. O. and Omamor, A. P. Forthcoming. *Nigerian Pidgin (NP): Background and Prospects*.

Faraclas, N. 1985. Rivers Pidgin English: Tone, stress, or pitch-accent language? In Bokamba, E. (ed.). 1985, pp. 67–76.

1986a *Reading and Writing Nigerian Pidgin*. Rivers Readers Project. University of Port Harcourt.

1986b. Pronouns, creolization, and decreolization in Nigerian Pidgin. *Journal of West African Languages* 16(2):3–8.

1987. Creolization and the tense-aspect-modality system of Nigerian Pidgin. *Journal of African Languages and Linguistics* 9: 45–59.

1988. Nigerian Pidgin and the languages of southern Nigeria. *Journal of Pidgin and Creole Languages* 3(2): 177–97.

1989. *A Grammar of Nigerian Pidgin.* Unpublished PhD dissertation, University of California, Berkeley.

1990. From Old Guinea to Papua New Guinea: A comparative study of Nigerian Pidgin and Tok Pisin. In Verhaar, J. (ed.), *Proceedings of the 1st International Tok Pisin Conference. Studies in Language. Supplement series.* Amsterdam: Benjamins.

Faraclas, N., Ibim, O., Worukwo, G., Minah, A. and Tariah, A. 1984. Rivers State Pidgin English. *Journal of the Linguistic Society of Nigeria* 2: 187–98.

Rickford, J. 1980. Analyzing variation in creole languages. In Valdman and Highfield (eds.) 1980, pp. 165–85.

Rotimi, O., and Faraclas, N. Forthcoming. *A Dictionary and Grammar of Nigerian Pidgin.* Port Harcourt: University Publications.

Valdman, A. and Highfield, A. (eds.). 1980. *Theoretical Orientations in Creole Studies.* New York: Academic Press.

35

The sociolinguistics of prepositional usage in Nigerian English

MUNZALI JIBRIL

Introduction

Although sociolinguistic studies of syntactic variation are quite common (see, for instance, Bickerton 1975; Labov 1972; Akere 1977; and Cheshire 1982), little attention appears to have been paid to the sociolinguistics of prepositional usage. In Nigerian English, previous studies of sociolinguistic variation have concentrated on phonology to the exclusion of syntax (Jibril 1982, 1986; Awonusi 1985). Since prepositions, even in ENL (English as a Native Language) settings, are known to be highly variable, it was decided to investigate the sociolinguistics of prepositional usage in Nigerian English for the present study.

Methodology

The instrument used for the generation of data was a 50-item linguistic questionnaire (see appendix). Each item on the questionnaire is a sentence which contains a blank space to be filled by a preposition. Three choices of preposition are then provided, only one of which is appropriate in standard (southern English) English.

The 50 sentences were not artificially constructed, nor were the prepositions arbitrarily chosen. Instead, authentic Nigerian texts provided the models on which the items were based. For example, Amos Tutuola, the Nigerian novelist, provided the frame for Variable 17 in his *My Life in The Bush of Ghosts* (1954: 117) with this sentence: 'Even these evil works will appear as well on my "Will" . . .' A Government document signed by a very senior official provided the frame for Variable 3 with this sentence: 'The responsibility for running secondary schools lies on the Federal and State Governments.' Undergraduate student essays and dissertations from students at Bayero University provided the models for many of the sentences, for example, numbers 2, 13, 18, 20, 21, 22. Although it is quite obvious that owing to the heteregeneity of their sources, the sentences fail to be stylistically homogeneous, it was decided that the need for authenticity should take precedence over the need for stylistic consistency.

The draft of the 'standard' forms of the 50 sentences was checked for correctness by a native speaker of English who had been born in London and educated at Cambridge and Essex Universities. His suggestions were incorporated into the final version of the questionnaire. This final version was also sent to Leeds University and was checked by three postgraduate students of the University who are speakers of standard British English, with Received Pronunciation (Andrew, 22, from London, Rachel, 23 from Brighton and Cheryl, 22 from Bristol). According to my 'field assistant' in Leeds, 'All three quibbled with 3 of the offered alternatives and agreed absolutely on the others'. The three items on which they offered their own preferred choices are 18 (*by* in place of my *to*), 25 (*from, for*, in place of my *off*) and 28 (*of* in place of my *for*). However, by the time this report arrived from Leeds, it was too late to revise the questionnaire. In fact, a careful check on the three items confirmed that the original alternatives do sometimes occur in 'educated' southern English English – although no. 25, in particular, is typical of colloquial usage – and this suggests that perhaps the quibbles of the three young native speakers might have been sociolinguistically, rather than grammatically, motivated.

The questionnaire also includes a section which elicits personal information from each respondent. About 200 copies of the questionnaire were produced and distributed, out of which about 120 were completed and retrieved. I distributed and retrieved many of the questionnaires myself but I also received help from friends and other volunteers who made special efforts to get female respondents and low income workers, among other groups, to complete the questionnaire.

The completed questionnaires were then edited and 14 of them were rejected, either because they had been improperly completed or because they had been completed by non-Hausa speakers. It had been decided at the planning stage to restrict the study to native speakers of Hausa so as to keep the ethnicity variable constant.

The edited completed questionnaires were then coded and analysed by the Bayero University Computer Centre. Cross-tabulation analysis was carried out using the SPSS package. The interaction between five social variables (education, occupation, income, sex and age) and each of the 50 linguistic variables was tested for statistical significance.

Although a linguistic questionnaire measures usage only indirectly, it was chosen as the main instrument here because the time and resources needed to elicit more authentic data were simply beyond the scope of the present study.

The sample

The sample consists of 105 'educated' Hausa speakers who live in Kano. In spite of efforts made to recruit informants from all social groups, the sample group turned out to be skewed in many respects. In terms of educational qualifications, for instance, while only 8.6 per cent had primary education only, 32.4 per cent had Bachelor's degrees as table 35.1 shows. Table 35.1 also shows that in terms of occupation 56.3 per cent belong to the professional and prestigious groups (groups 1–18) while 4.9 per cent belong to the semi-professional group (groups 19–21) and 38.8 per cent belong to the auxiliary and manual groups (22–29). Table 35.2 shows that the distribution of income is also skewed in favour of the low-income group (35.6 per cent) and the middle income group (48.1 per cent) with the high-income group accounting for only 16.4 per cent of the sample. In terms of gender, too, the sample is skewed in favour of males who constitute 65.7 per cent of the sample (see table 35.3). It is, of course, possible to argue that in this particular case, the proportion of females (34.3 per cent) represents their true relative proportion to educated males in the society. According to the *National Integrated Survey of Households 1983–84* Nigerian urban males had a literacy rate of 64 per cent while urban females had one of only 38 per cent in 1983/84. Similarly, table 35.3 shows that the distribution of age among the sample is skewed in favour of young people who are below 30 (who constitute 61.9 per cent). Indeed, people aged 39 or less constitute 90.5 per cent of the sample.

The linguistic variables

The 50 linguistic variables show varying degrees of 'difficulty' (as reflected by the percentages of the sample who selected the standard variants) as well as sensitivity to the social variables.

As can be seen from table 35.4, standard English variants of the 50 variables exhibit an elicitation range of between 18.8 per cent (variable 5) and 98.1 per cent (variable 49). Overall, none of the 105 respondents selected fewer than 19 standard variants out of the 50 available and, although no one selected all 50 standard variants, 87.9 per cent of the sample selected between 26 and 49 standard variants. This indicates that not all of the 50 variables selected were equally difficult or sociolinguistically variable.

Table 35.5 gives a detailed breakdown of the relative degree of sensitivity of each of the 35 sensitive variables. It shows that 16 of the variables are sensitive to one social variable each, 8 are sensitive to two each, 9 are sensitive to 3 each and 2 are sensitive to 4 each. A close examination of table 35.5 also reveals that 7 linguistic variables are sensitive to education and sex simultaneously. This shows a moderate

Table 35.1. *Summary distribution of sample by social factors (highest educational qualification; occupation)*

Highest educational qualification	(No.)	Percentage of sample	Cumulative frequency
1. Primary school certificate	(9)	8.6	8.6
2. WASC/GCE 'O' level	(15)	14.3	22.9
3. HSC/GCE 'A' level	(9)	8.6	31.4
4. OND	(6)	5.7	37.1
5. NCE	(7)	6.7	43.8
6. HND	(1)	1.0	44.8
7. Bachelor's degree	(34)	32.4	77.1
8. Master's degree	(9)	8.6	85.7
12. PhD	(4)	3.8	89.5
13. Others	(11)	10.5	100.0

Occupation	(No.)	Percentage of sample	Cumulative frequency
1. Politician	(1)	1.0	1.0
2. In business	(3)	2.9	3.9
4. Public administrator	(9)	8.6	12.6
5. Medical doctor	(3)	2.9	15.5
6. Company executive	(1)	1.0	16.5
7. University lecturer	(6)	5.7	22.3
8. Educational administrator	(2)	1.9	24.3
9. College lecturer	(5)	4.8	29.1
10. Lawyer	(5)	4.8	34.0
13. Accountant	(2)	1.9	35.9
15. Engineer	(1)	1.0	36.9
17. Journalist	(6)	5.7	42.7
18. Secondary school teacher	(14)	13.3	56.3
19. Nurse	(2)	1.9	58.3
20. Confidential secretary	(1)	1.0	59.2
21. Technician	(2)	1.9	61.2
22. Primary school teacher	(2)	1.9	63.1
23. Clerk	(4)	3.8	67.0
24. Police officer	(1)	1.0	68.0
25. Soldier	(1)	1.0	68.9
26. Trader	(1)	1.0	69.9
27. Tailor	(1)	1.0	70.9
28. Labourer	(1)	1.0	71.8
29. Others	(29)	27.6	100.0

Table 35.2. *Summary distribution of sample by social factors (income)*

Income level	(No.)	Percentage of sample
Grade-levels 1–6	(37)	35.2
Grade levels 7–8	(39)	37.1
Grade levels 9–11	(11)	10.5
Grade levels 12–14	(8)	7.6
Grade levels 15–17	(6)	5.7
Others	(3)	2.9

Table 35.3. *Summary distribution of sample by social factors (sex and age)*

Sex	(No.)	Percentage of sample	Age	(No.)	Percentage of sample
male	(69)	65.7	15–19	(8)	7.6
female	(36)	34.3	20–24	(29)	27.6
			25–29	(28)	26.7
			30–34	(21)	20.0
			35–39	(9)	8.5
			40–44	(5)	4.8
			45–49	(3)	2.9
			50–59	(2)	1.9

correlation between the two social variables; in other words it suggests that perhaps female members of the sample are better educated than their male counterparts.

Education and income are fairly well correlated in that they share sensitivity to 10 of the linguistic variables. This correlation is quite natural as income depends largely on education. However, income and occupation share sensitivity to only 4 of the linguistic variables while education and occupation share sensitivity to only 6 of the linguistic variables.

It is, of course, difficult to explain why individual linguistic variables are sensitive to some social variables but not to others. But in general, the 35 sensitive linguistic variables can be grouped into four categories: (i) those which include among their variants stable Nigerianisms which are different from the standard southern British English variants; (ii) those which include among their variants forms which are closer to mother-tongue (i.e., Hausa) patterns; (iii) those which include among their variants British colloquialisms which are unfamiliar to the majority of respondents; and (iv) those which include among their variants forms which are based on analogy with other usages in the English language.

Table 35.4. *Percentage of standard variant responses by variable*

Variable no.	'Correct' responses (%)	Variable no.	'Correct' responses (%)
1	82.9	26	45.7
2	60.6	27	81.9
3	63.8	28	75.2
4	89.3	29	76.2
5	18.8	30	69.5
6	75.2	31	81.0
7	81.9	32	85.7
8	71.2	33	76.5
9	93.3	34	90.5
10	88.5	35	76.9
11	37.5	36	65.4
12	93.3	37	33.0
13	84.3	38	84.8
14	71.8	39	89.2
15	83.7	40	90.3
16	66.7	41	66.7
17	67.3	42	76.0
18	63.1	43	45.2
19	87.6	44	20.4
20	79.8	45	60.6
21	84.5	46	85.7
22	86.7	47	63.1
23	75.0	48	73.3
24	70.5	49	98.1
25	36.2	50	95.2

Stable Nigerianisms Since Nigerian English is a stable variety of English with its own distinctive linguistic features, many usages which are not acceptable in standard British English are found quite frequently, often in the speech of educated Nigerians. These I refer to as 'stable Nigerianisms', as distinct from less stable forms which would be labelled as erroneous even by relatively unsophisticated Nigerian users of English. Two examples of such stable Nigerianisms can be found in items 6 and 37 of the questionnaire. The most obvious choice for the average Nigerian user of English for item 6 is *The policemen were put at alert*, a form that may have originated by analogy with *at attention*. Similarly, for item 37, the most obvious choice is *I am applying for casual leave to enable me visit my aged father*. Again, the omission of *to* is probably based on analogy with such verbs as *help*, where *to* is optional in similar constructions (for example, *please help me clean the house*).

Table 35.5. *Linguistic Variable Sensitivity Index*

Variable no.	Occupation	Education	Income	Sex	Age	Total
2	–	Yes	Yes	–	–	2
4	Yes	–	–	–	Yes	2
5	–	–	Yes	–	–	1
6	–	Yes	Yes	–	Yes	3
7	–	Yes	–	–	–	1
9	Yes	Yes	Yes	–	–	3
10	Yes	–	–	–	–	1
15	Yes	–	–	–	–	1
16	–	–	Yes	–	–	1
17	Yes	Yes	Yes	–	–	3
19	Yes	Yes	–	Yes	–	3
20	Yes	Yes	–	–	Yes	3
21	Yes	–	–	–	–	1
22	Yes	–	–	–	–	1
23	–	Yes	–	Yes	–	2
25	–	Yes	Yes	Yes	Yes	4
26	–	–	–	Yes	–	1
28	Yes	–	–	–	–	1
29	–	Yes	Yes	Yes	Yes	4
31	–	–	–	Yes	–	1
32	Yes	–	–	–	–	1
33	–	–	Yes	Yes	–	2
34	Yes	–	–	Yes	–	2
35	–	Yes	Yes	Yes	–	3
37	–	Yes	Yes	–	–	2
38	Yes	–	–	–	–	1
40	Yes	–	–	–	–	1
41	–	Yes	–	–	–	1
42	–	Yes	Yes	Yes	–	3
43	Yes	Yes	Yes	–	–	3
45	Yes	Yes	–	Yes	–	3
46	Yes	–	–	–	–	1
47	–	Yes	Yes	–	–	2
48	Yes	–	Yes	–	–	2
50	Yes	–	–	–	–	1
Total	35	19	17	15	11	5

Mother-tongue-like forms　Hausa, like many African languages, does not have prepositions which correspond to the English ones. Instead, it makes do with a few general purpose particles which are less specific in their reference to temporal and spatial relations than the English ones. For example, the Hausa particle *da* ('with') translates into several English prepositions/conjunctions, as illustrated below:

> Yaa zoo da saafe
> (literally, 'He came in with morning')
> He came *in* the morning

> Yaa tafi da akuyaa
> (literally, He went with goat)
> He went *with* the goat

> Musa da Audu sun zauna
> (literally, Musa with Auda they sat down)
> Musa *and* Auda sat down

Similarly, the Hausa particle *a* overlaps with a number of English prepositions, as illustrated below:

> Na ganshi a gida
> I saw him *at* home

> Na ganshi a mota
> I saw him *in* (a) car

> Na ganshi a babur
> I saw him *on* (a) motorcycle

Consequently, Hausa speakers, like many other Nigerians, have difficulty mastering the subtleties of English prepositions. Whenever one of the options offered by the questionnaire corresponds in meaning to a mother-tongue particle that could be used in the same context, it tends to attract the respondents. Examples include item 17, where the mother-tongue-like choice is *My decision will appear on my Will*, owing to the blurring of the distinction between *on* and *in* in Hausa (both being roughly translatable as *a*) and item 34, where the mother-tongue would pull the respondent towards choosing *We arrived safely with night*.

Analogy Many deviations from standard British English in Nigerian English usage are due to analogy with other forms in English. For example, in standard British English *according*, the *-ing* form, takes as its preposition *to*, but *accordance*, the noun, takes as its preposition *with*. The second language learner would often generalise one of the two prepositions and use it for both forms of the word; hence the tendency for many respondents to select *to* as the appropriate preposition to go with *accordance* (item 7). Similarly, *to result* is often treated as meaning the same thing as *to turn into* or *to amount to*; hence the tendency to select as the most appropriate, the form *Her illness resulted to her having a miscarriage* (item 43).

Table 35.6. *List of variables sensitive to education with χ^2 and levels of significance*

Variable no.	Context and variants	ch sq/d.f	Significance
2	Limit to/on/for	24.751/9	0.0033
6	on/to/at the alert	23.882/9	0.0045
7	accordance with/to/∅	27.286/9	0.0013
9	charge of/with/for	18.571/9	0.0291
17	in/on/for my will	20.135/9	0.0171
19	for/in/to/a walk	18.186/9	0.0331
20	think/of/to/∅	24.149/9	0.0041
23	provision for/to/of	18.508/9	0.0297
25	bought off/to/by	34.476/9	0.0001
29	addicted to/with/by	34.848/9	0.0001
35	among/∅/with/of	24.956/9	0.0030
37	enable me to/∅/with visit	18.365/9	0.0312
41	in/on/to/this regard	19.420/9	0.0218
42	underneath ∅/of/to	23.761/9	0.0047
43	resulted in/to/on	22.605/9	0.0071
45	congratulation on/for/in	21.311/9	0.0113
47	left ∅/since/before three hours ago	22.727/9	0.0068

Colloquialisms Certain idiomatic expressions such as *to buy something off someone* (item 25) and *to have a drink on someone* (item 26) are unfamiliar to many respondents; hence their tendency to select variables other than the appropriate ones in such cases.

Correlations between the social and the linguistic variables

The degree of association between each linguistic variable and each social variable was analysed. Chi square tests of significance were applied, and levels of significance of $p < 0.05$ or below were accepted.

Education and prepositional usage

Of the variables, 17 are sensitive to education; of these, only one (42) is not sensitive to any other social variable. This means that education is a very reliable social correlate of sociolinguistic behaviour as measured by prepositional usage.

Table 35.6 lists the variables that are sensitive to education along with the levels of significance, which in each case are below $p < 0.05$. A careful analysis of these variables shows that their variability can be explained in one of four ways: (i) there are stable Nigerianisms which compete with the

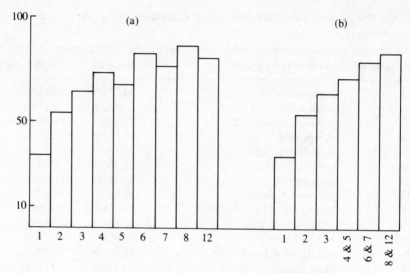

Figure 35.1 (a) Percentage of group scores by educational qualification. For key, see table 35.1. (b) New percentages of group scores by educational qualification.

standard southern British English variants (e.g., nos. 6, 35, 37, 42, 45 and 47); (ii) there are variants based on analogy with other usages which also compete with the standard variants (e.g., 7, 9, 19, 23, 41 and 43); (iii) there are mother-tongue-like variants which are different from the standard variants (e.g., 2, 17, 20 and 29); and (iv) the standard variant is a colloqualism unfamiliar to many of the respondents (25).

Figure 35.1a illustrates the relationship between education and these variables. The vertical axis reflects the average percentage of informants in each educational category who chose the standard variants of the 17 variables. In other words, the vertical axis represents group scores for the 17 variables.

Informants who have had only primary school education score the least; those who have had both primary and secondary school education score more; those who have acquired GCE 'A' levels or the equivalent score even more; and those who have obtained an Ordinary National Diploma score even more. Holders of the Nigerian Certificate in Education (which is, in reality, equivalent to the OND) score less than OND holders, but the rising pattern is restored by Higher National Diploma holders who score even more than their counterparts, university graduates who hold first degrees. Again, the rising pattern is restored by holders of the Master's degree, who score even more than PhD holders.

However, if we re-classify respondents so that people who hold equivalent educational qualifications (e.g. OND/NCE, HND/Bachelors degree) are grouped together we obtain a neater picture, as in figure 35.1b where

Table 35.7. *List of variables sensitive to occupation with* χ^2 *and levels of significance*

Variable no.	Context and variants	ch sq/d.f	Significance
4	on/at/with/arrival	43.623/23	0.0058
9	charge of/with/for	60.537/23	0.0000
10	placed on/in/at	47.992/23	0.0011
15	died at/by/with 5.am	48.191/23	0.0016
17	in/on/for/my will	38.536/23	0.0223
19	for/in/to/a walk	35.714/23	0.0441
20	think of/∅/to	39.196/23	0.0134
21	danger to/of/∅	44.362/23	0.0032
22	apart from/of/to	37.101/23	0.0317
28	basis for/to/on	42.421/23	0.0081
32	one of/in/inside	39.107/23	0.0193
34	at/in/with night	37.981/23	0.0256
38	responsible for/to/of	36.813/23	0.0340
40	running after/behind/beside	51.107/22	0.0004
43	resulted in/to/on	46.418/22	0.0017
45	congratulations on/for/in	36.884/23	0.0334
46	attached to/with/in	41.805/23	0.0096
48	on/in/for/page 19	36.692/23	0.0350
50	laughed at/for/on	54.285/23	0.0002

not only the four categories listed above are merged but also the categories of Master's degree and PhD holders. The merger of the last two categories is based on the assumption that after the Master's degree education ceases to have any effect on sociolinguistic behaviour.

Occupation and prepositional usage

Although up to 19 variables are sensitive to occupation, it is still a less reliable indicator of sociolinguistic behaviour as measured by prepositional usage in this study than education. To begin with, up to 8 of these 19 variables are sensitive to no other social parameter (10, 15, 21, 22, 32, 40, 46, 50), which indicates the possibility of the relationship being merely accidental (although each of the 19 cases of relationship has been found to be statistically significant at the 5 per cent level, as can be seen from table 35.7)

Variability can be explained in terms of the categories earlier set up: that is, (i) some of the variables contain mother-tongue-like variants (4, 10, 17, 20, 32, 34, 46, 48, 50); some contain variants which, based on analogy, would appear to fit the given context (9, 19, 21, 22, 28, 38, 40,

43) while some of the variables contain stable Nigerianisms as variants (15, 45).

Since there is no ready-made index of the relative prestige of different occupations in Nigeria, I made a crude impressionistic list of 28 occupations for inclusion as an item in the questionnaire (see appendix). This crude ranking proved largely irrelevant, since the relative prestige of an occupation does not appear to correlate with prepositional usage. However, the statistical analysis did establish that as far as the 19 variables are concerned, there are significant differences between respondents based on their occupational grouping, though not necessarily on the relative prestige of their occupations.

Differences between the occupational groups become consistent when we classify them into two broad categories: those who belong to the élite group (professionals and semi-professionals, i.e., groups 1–21) and those who belong to the sub-élite/masses group (auxiliary and manual workers, i.e. groups 22–28). Figure 35.2a shows group scores based on the classification of occupations in the questionnaire in relation to the 19 variables. These do not appear to correlate with any objective ranking of the relative status of these occupations. However, if we aggregate the scores of respondents in groups 1–21 on the one hand and 22–28 on the other, we get the picture represented in figure 35.2b. Here the manual and auxiliary workers show a remarkably lower score than professional and semi-professional respondents.

This result appears to reinforce the widely-held view that in Africa, social classes in the Western sense have not yet emerged and that society can be profitably viewed as consisting of two or three broad groups: the élite, the sub-élite and the masses (cf. Plotnicov 1970).

Income and prepositional usage

Of the 15 variables which are sensitive to income, only 2 (5 and 16) are not sensitive to other social parameters. This ranks income next to education as a reliable correlate of sociolinguistic behaviour as measured by prepositional usage.

Table 35.8 lists the 15 variables which are sensitive to income along with chi square and levels of significance. An analysis of the probable causes of variability shows that in six cases, the variables contain mother-tongue-like variants (2, 16, 17, 29, 33, 48); in five cases, the variables contain variants which are analogous to other forms (19, 43, 47) and one variable contains an unfamiliar colloquialism (25).

In all but one variable, scores rise with income except that the highest income group scores, on average, less than the two groups immediately below it, as can be seen from figure 35.3a. However, when the income groups are re-classified so that they fall into two broad groups of 'junior'

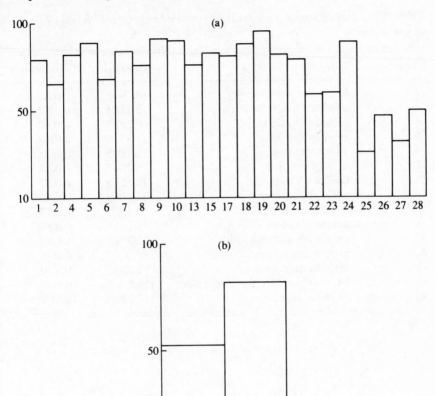

Figure 35.2 (a) Group scores based on occupation. For key, see table 35.2. (b) Percentage of scores by groups of occupation.

and 'senior' staff (i.e., low and high income earners), we obtain a tidier picture of the difference between them as in figure 35.3b. It appears that this is a more natural division than the finer one envisaged in the questionnaire.

The case of variable 37, which is an exception in that scores for it *fall* with income, deserves some discussion. The zero variant of this variable (*to enable me visit*, for instance) is a widespread Nigerianism. It is used regularly in the national news bulletins (both radio and television) and also in the written speeches of the political élite. This appears, therefore, to be a case of linguistic change initiated from the top of the social

Table 35.8. *List of variables sensitive to income with χ^2 and levels of significance*

Variable no.	Context and variants	ch sq/d.f	Significance
2	limit to/on for	18.560/5	0.0023
5	in/with/through the hope	12.181/5	0.0324
6	on/to/at the alert	16.227/5	0.0062
9	charge of/with/for	13.590/5	0.0184
16	on/by/with foot	11.489/5	0.0425
17	in/on/for/my will	18.484/5	0.0024
25	bought off/to/by	18.622/5	0.0023
29	addicted to/with/by	24.250/5	0.0002
33	use/Ø/with/on	12.558/5	0.0279
35	among/Ø/with/of	15.213/5	0.0095
37	enable me to/Ø/with visit	12.340/5	0.0304
42	underneath/Ø/of/to	15.667/5	0.0079
43	resulted in/to/on	12.538/5	0.0281
47	left Ø/since/before three days ago	16.547/5	0.0054
48	on/in/for page 19	14.096/5	0.0150

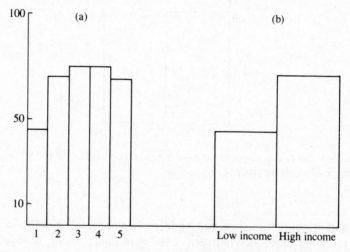

Figure 35.3 (a) Percentage of group scores by income. For key, see table 35.3. (b) Percentage of group scores according to the junior/senior dichotomy.

hierarchy which has not yet permeated down to the bottom. For this reason, members of the élite group (the higher income earners) deviate more from the standard variant than do lower income earners who still prefer the standard British English variant.

Table 35.9. *List of variables sensitive to sex with χ^2 and levels of significance*

Variable no.	Context and variants	ch sq/d.f	Significance
19	going for/to/in a walk	4.657/1	0.0309
23	provision for/to/of	5.664/1	0.0173
25	bought off/to/by	10.092/1	0.0015
26	drink on/to/in	6.566/1	0.0104
29	addicted to/with/by	7.233/1	0.0072
31	aware of/with/Ø	3.146/1	0.0022
33	use Ø/with/on	4.768/1	0.0290
34	at/in/with night	5.766/1	0.0163
35	among Ø/of/with	6.742/1	0.0094
42	underneath Ø/of/to	10.300/1	0.0013
45	congratulations on/for/in	10.965/1	0.0009

Sex and prepositional usage

As established by other sociolinguistic studies (e.g., Trudgill 1974; Schmied, this volume) women's speech tends to approximate more to the standard than men's. Although the differences between male and female scores in this study reach significance at the 5 per cent level in only 11 cases, women consistently score higher than men in a total of 37 of the 50 variables. In only 10 variables are the men's scores slightly higher, while the scores are equal in one case.

As in the three previous subsections, we are concerned with the 11 variables for which the differences in scores reach significance at the 5 per cent level. These are listed in table 35.9. Of these, variability appears to be ascribable to mother-tongue-like forms in 4 cases (29, 31, 33, 34), to stable Nigerian variants in 3 cases (35, 42, 45), to analogy in 2 cases (19, 23) and to an unfamiliar colloquialism in 2 cases (25, 26).

Like education and income, sex is also a reliable correlate of sociolinguistic behaviour as measured here by prepositional usage. Out of the 11 sensitive variables, 10 are shared with other social parameters and only one (26) is not.

As can be seen from figure 35.4, there is a clear difference between the average male score (62.88 per cent) and the average female score (86.8 per cent) as far as the 11 sensitive variables are concerned.

Age and prepositional usage

Like education, income and sex, age is also a reliable correlate of sociolinguistic behaviour in Nigerian English. Although only 5 variables

Table 35.10. *List of variables sensitive to age with* χ^2 *and levels of significance*

Variable no.	Context and variants	ch sq/d.f	Significance
4	on/at/with arrival	17.903/7	0.0124
6	in/with/through the hope	24.323/7	0.0010
20	think of/∅/to	22.624/7	0.0020
25	bought off/to/by	18.367/7	0.0104
29	addicted to/with/by	14.267/7	0.0466

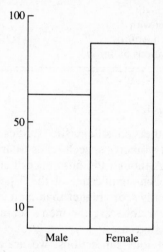

Figure 35.4   Percentage of group scores by sex.

show sensitivity to age at the 5 per cent level, all 5 are also sensitive to at least one other social parameter. The small number of variables sensitive to age is probably due to the skewness of the sample in the direction of people aged below 40 years.

As with education and income, scores for these five variables rise with age. Table 35.10 gives a list of these variables and the chi square and level of significance in each case. A careful analysis of the possible causes of variability suggests that mother-tongue-like forms are responsible for triggering variability in three of the cases (4, 20, 29), analogy is responsible in 1 case (6) and an unfamiliar colloquialism is responsible in the fifth case (25).

The significance of the mother tongue as a major determinant of age differences in prepositional usage lies in the fact that younger people are, as would be expected, less able than older users of English to cast off its influence.

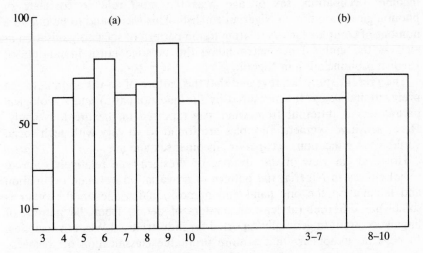

Figure 35.5 (a) Percentage of group scores by age. For key, see table 35.3 and appendix. (b) Aged 15–39, aged 40–59.

Figure 35.5a illustrates the differences in score among 8 age-groups represented by the sample. It shows that there is a significant rise in score between people aged 15–19 on the one hand and 20–24 on the other. This rising pattern is also maintained between this latter group on the one hand and those aged 25–29 on the other. The pattern is continued between this latter group and those aged 30–34. However, the pattern is then broken because there is a drop of some 16 percentage points between the 30–34 group and the 35–39 group. Although the 40–44 group scores higher to resume the rising pattern, its score is still some 13 points below that of the 30–34 group. The rising pattern is fully restored by the 45–49 group but the score drops sharply again when we get to the oldest group, the 50–59 group.

As with education and income, in order to capture sensitively the underlying generalisation involved, we have to redefine our groups. In figure 35.5b groups 3, 4, 5, 6 and 7 (people aged 15–39) are classified together while groups 8, 9 and 10 (people aged 40–59) are classified together. This gives the young group an average score (over the 5 variables) of 61 per cent and the older group an average score of 72 per cent.

Conclusion

My earlier studies of the sociolinguistics of spoken English in Nigeria (Jibril 1982, 1986) found that speech training, rather than education, income, occupation, sex or age, was the most reliable correlate of phonological variation in Nigerian English. This was found to be due to a number of complex factors relating to the pattern of social organisation as well as the ambivalence surrounding the prestige norm in matters of English pronunciation in Nigeria.

The present study has revealed that the pattern of co-variation between prepositional usage (as measured by the questionnaire) and sociological parameters is different from what was reported in the previous study. Here, sensitive syntactic variables are found to co-vary with such social variables as education, occupation, income, sex and age.

However, in view of the absence of Western-type relatively discrete social classes in Nigeria, the pattern of co-variation between occupation and income on the one hand and prepositional usage on the other is somewhat different (at least in matters of detail) from the pattern of linguistic variation generally reported for industrialised Western societies. In Nigeria, it appears that a more profitable classification of socioeconomic groups is one that consists of two or three broad categories (corresponding to the masses/sub-élite/élite classification) rather than the more complex classification that is typically used in research carried out in Western societies (e.g., Trudgill (1974) used a five-point classification into lower working class, lower middle working class, upper working class, lower middle class and middle middle class). As this study has shown, the co-variation of linguistic behaviour and social status becomes more meaningful if the social grouping follows the broader categorisation.

Interestingly, the study has provided additional evidence for the tendency of female speakers to approximate more to the prestige norm in language than male speakers.

Finally, the study has given us new insights into linguistic change in progress in Nigerian English. Seven of the variables which have been found to be highly sensitive to social factors contain, among their variants, stable Nigerianisms. These are prepositional usages which are commonly found in the speech of educated Nigerians such as (5) *with the hope that*, (6) *at alert*, (37) *to enable me visit him* and (45) *congratulations for your promotion*. An interesting relationship is found between usages that result from analogy and mother-tongue interference on the one hand and stable Nigerianisms on the other. The latter are the mature descendants of the former. From the results of the present study we can confidently predict that more stable Nigerianisms will emerge out of those variables which contain mother-tongue-like and analogical forms. We can also infer that prepositional usage is an area in which there is, and will continue to be, great divergence between Nigerian English and other varieties of World English because, as this study reveals, 70 per cent of the prepositional variables, which were *not* pre-tested for their sensitivity, proved to be highly variable when analysed in relation to social variables.

REFERENCES

Akere, F. 1977. 'A Sociolinguistic Study of a Yoruba speech Community in Nigeria: Variation and Change in the Ijebu Dialect Speech of Ikorodu'. Unpublished PhD thesis, University of Edinburgh.

Awonusi, V. A. 1985. Sociolinguistic Variation in Nigerian (Lagos) English. Unpublished PhD thesis, University of London.

Bickerton, D. 1975. *The Dynamics of a Creole System*. Cambridge: Cambridge University Press.

Cheshire, J. 1982. *Variation in an English dialect: A Sociolinguistic Study*. Cambridge: Cambridge University Press.

Jibril, M. M. 1982. Phonological Variation in Nigerian English. Unpublished PhD thesis, University of Lancaster.

1986. Sociolinguistic Variation in Nigerian English. *English World-wide* 7(1):47–74.

Labov, W. 1972. *Sociolinguistic Patterns*. Philadelphia: University of Pennsylvania Press.

Federal Office of Statistics. 1986. *National Integrated Survey of Households 1983–84*. Lagos.

Plotnicov, L. 1970. The modern elite of Jos, Nigeria. In Tuden, A. and Plotnicov, L. (eds.), *Social Stratification in Africa*. London: The Free Press.

Tutuola, A. 1954. *My Life in the Bush of Ghosts*. London: Faber and Faber.

Trudgill, P. 1974. *The Social Differentiation of English in Norwich*. Cambridge: Cambridge University Press.

Appendix: Bayero University, Kano Faculty of Arts & Islamic Studies Research into English usage in Nigeria

Section One: English Usage

Kindly fill in this section by ticking off the most appropriate of the three choices given to fill the blank space in each sentence.

Please note that 'nil' means that no word is required to fill in the blank space.

1. Garba now lives ----- Lagos.

<u>for</u>
<u>in</u>
<u>at</u>

2. I have decided to limit my study ----- a few areas.

<u>foe</u>
<u>on</u>
<u>to</u>

3. The responsibility for running secondary schools lies ----- the Federal Government.

<u>on</u>
<u>with</u>
<u>nil</u>

4. He went straight home ----- arrival.

<u>on</u>
<u>at</u>
<u>with</u>

5. I am writing ----- the hope that you will respond.

<u>with</u>
<u>in</u>
<u>through</u>

6. The policemen were put ----- the alert.

<u>to</u>
<u>at</u>
<u>on</u>

538

7. In accordance ----- the terms of the agreement, you are
   required to pay compensation to the other party.

   to
   nil
   with

8. This should prove better ----- the long run.

   in
   on
   for

9. The Headmaster is in charge ----- the school.

   with
   for
   of

10. The economy should be placed ----- a sound footing.

    on
    in
    at

11. He started drinking ----- his old age.

    on
    in
    at

12. Mallam Dauda goes to work----- bus.

    with
    by
    in

13. There is no need to explain ----- the reason.

    of
    nil
    on

14. The amount of money spent on tobacco is ----- the
    increase.

    at
    in
    on

15. The man died ----- 5.am.

    by
    at
    with

16. Safiya went to market ----- foot.

    by
    with
    on

17. My decision will appear ----- my will.

    on
    in
    for

18. Some smokers appear to be enslaved ----- smoking.

    to
    with
    on

19. I'm going ----- a walk.

in
for
to

20. People who think ----- the injury caused by smoking avoid it.

nil
of
to

21. One of the disadvantages of smoking is the danger it poses ----- the smoker.

of
nil
to

22. Apart ----- being injurious to health, smoking is also an expensive habit.

of
from
to

23. Provision has been made ----- contingencies.

for
to
of

24. In his capacity as Secretary ----- the Association, Mallam Tukur delivered the vote of thanks.

for
nil
of

25. I bought this car ----- my brother-in-law.

to
of
by

26. Please have a drink ----- me.

to
on
in

27. The supply ----- brown sugar has decreased.

of
on
for

28. What is the basis ----- the decision?

to
on
for

29. He is addicted ----- heroin.

to
with
by

30. The demand ----- flour has gone up.

of
for
on

31. I am aware ----- its existence.

<u>of</u>
<u>with</u>
<u>nil</u>

32. Choose one ----- the two.

<u>in</u>
inside
<u>of</u>

33. I'll use ----- what I have to get what I want.

<u>with</u>
<u>nil</u>
<u>on</u>

34. We arrived safely ----- night.

<u>at</u>
<u>in</u>
<u>with</u>

35. I don't think you'll find him among ----- them.

<u>with</u>
<u>of</u>
<u>nil</u>

36. I categorically dissociate myself ----- the petition.

<u>from</u>
<u>with</u>
<u>against</u>

37. I am applying for casual leave to enable me ----- visit my aged father.

<u>nil</u>
<u>to</u>
<u>with</u>

38. You will be responsible ----- your feeding and accommodation.

<u>to</u>
<u>of</u>
<u>for</u>

39. Please don't come ----- tomorrow.

<u>unless</u>
<u>until</u>
<u>except</u>

40. The minister is busy running ----- money.

<u>after</u>
<u>behind</u>
<u>beside</u>

41. ----- this regard, it should be noted that she was not the only candidate affected by the Board's decision.

<u>on</u>
<u>in</u>
<u>to</u>

42. When he came, he found the paper underneath ----- the table.

<u>of</u>
<u>nil</u>
<u>to</u>

43. Her illness resulted ----- her having a miscarriage.

to

on

in

44. It comprises ----- six units.

of

nil

in

45. Please accept my congratulations ----- your promotion.

on

for

in

46. The relevant letter is attached ----- this one.

with

to

in

47. I left my home for the wedding ----- three hours ago.

since

nil

before

48. The information may be found ----- page 19.

in

for

on

49. He said ----- me 'Go away!'.

with

to

for

50. He also laughed ----- me.

at

for

on

Section Two: Personal Information

Would you be kind enough to provide information on yourself by ticking off the appropriate box in each item below?

1. Name:..

2. Age: Below 10   _____   1 ☐
         10–14   _____   2 ☐
         15–19   _____   3 ☐
         20–24   _____   4 ☐
         25–29   _____   5 ☐
         30–34   _____   6 ☐
         35–39   _____   7 ☐
         40–44   _____   8 ☐
         45–49   _____   9 ☐

50–59	____	10 ☐
60–69	____	11 ☐
70 and above	____	12 ☐

3. *Sex*:

   Male   ____ 1 ☐

      Female ____ 2 ☐

4. *Place of birth*

    Town/village...

    Local government..

    State..

5. *State of origin* ....

6. *Native language* ....

7. *Other languages spoken*

   (i) ....

  (ii) ....

 (iii) ....

 (iv) ....

8. *Occupation*

1	____	Politician	☐
2	____	Businessman/businesswoman	☐
3	____	Traditonal ruler	☐
4	____	Public administrator	☐
5	____	Medical doctor	☐
6	____	Company executive	☐
7	____	University lecturer	☐
8	____	Education administrator	☐
9	____	College lecturer	☐
10	____	Lawyer	☐
11	____	Pharmacist	☐
12	____	Banker	☐
13	____	Accountant	☐
14	____	Architect	☐
15	____	Engineer	☐
16	____	Librarian	☐
17	____	Journalist	☐

18 ____ Secondary school teacher   ☐
19 ____ Nurse   ☐
20 ____ Confidential secretary   ☐
21 ____ Technician   ☐
22 ____ Primary school teacher   ☐
23 ____ Clerk   ☐
24 ____ Policeman/policewoman   ☐
25 ____ Soldier   ☐
26 ____ Trader   ☐
27 ____ Tailor   ☐
28 ____ Labourer   ☐
29 ____ Other (please specify) ....

9. *Highest educational qualification attained*

1 ____ Primary School Leaving Certificate   ☐
2 ____ West African School Certificate/GCE 'O' level   ☐
3 ____ Higher School Certificate/GCE 'A' level   ☐
4 ____ OND   ☐
5 ____ NCE   ☐
6 ____ HND   ☐
7 ____ Bachelor's degree   ☐
8 ____ Master's degree   ☐
9 ____ ACIS   ☐
10 ____ ACCA   ☐
11 ____ AIB   ☐
12 ____ PhD   ☐
13 ____ Others (please specify) ....

10. *Income*

1 ____ GL 1–6 (N1,500 – N2,994) per annum)   ☐
2 ____ GL 7–8 (N3,174 – N4,824) per annum)   ☐
3 ____ GL 9–11 (N5,112 – N7,860) per annum)   ☐
4 ____ GL 12–14 (N8,034 – N12,078) per annum)   ☐
5 ____ GL 15–17 (N12,354 – N15,084) per annum)   ☐
6 ____ Above N15,500 per annum   ☐
7 ____ Other/equivalent (please state).............................

36

Social and linguistic constraints on plural marking in Liberian English

JOHN VICTOR SINGLER

Plural marking in Liberian English

Liberian English, the range of English from pidgin to standard spoken in Liberia, is characterised by vast variation in the marking of semantically plural nouns. Some speakers never mark the plural, while others mark it most of the time. Of the 21 speakers examined in the study that forms the basis for the present article, three of them mark the plural 2 per cent of the time or less, while two others mark it 70 per cent or more. Speakers also vary as to how they mark the plural, whether by a postposed free morpheme, *dɛn* (as in 1 and 2), or by an allomorph of suffixal -*z*.[1]

(1)   ma frɛn dɛn
        'my friends'
(2)   di gɛ dɛn
        'the girls'

This variation, both in frequency and choice of markers, is subject to disparate factors: social, phonological, and syntactico-semantic.

The impact of these factors on the frequency of plural marking was analysed by use of the VARBRUL programme. The data comprised 2,039 semantically plural nouns drawn from sociolinguistic interviews and conversations, with a maximum of 100 tokens taken from any one speaker.[2]

Social factor groups

Singler (1984) has as its central point that Liberian English – as it extends from pidgin to Liberian standard English – is a continuum of the type proposed by De Camp (1971).[3] The position of the speaker's output along the Liberian continuum correlates with the speaker's background. In

545

particular, Singler (1984, 1987, 1988a) links the following factors to position on the continuum:

Age at acquisition of Liberian English
  child (less than 12 years old)
  adult (older than 12 years)
Amount of Western education
  0–3rd grade
  4th–9th grade
  10th grade or beyond
  (Liberia uses American school designations)
Site of acquisition
  Monrovia
  elsewhere along the coast
  the interior

Earlier age at acquisition, greater amount of education, and proximity to Monrovia (the capital of Liberia) all correlate with a higher range along the continuum. Those speakers whose output lies at the basilectal extreme are adult learners from the interior with no Western education, while those speakers whose output lies at the acrolectal extreme are child learners (i.e., those who began learning Liberian English as a child) who have attended high school, particularly those from Monrovia. The social factors being referred to are not entirely independent of one another. For example, the only speakers in the study who had acquired English as children yet had never gone to Western schools were people who had grown up in Monrovia. Given this interdependence, a single factor group was constructed that combined age at acquisition and amount of Western education and the hypothesis was advanced that earlier age at acquisition and greater amount of Western education would favour greater frequency of plural marking. (Phenomena pertaining to site of acquisition were made note of but were not incorporated into the statistical analysis.[4])

Semantic factor groups

Two semantic factor groups were tested. The first is humanness/nonhumanness, with [+human] hypothesised as being the favouring factor.

The second involves individuation, definiteness, and overt plural marking elsewhere in the NP. Such a framework – or one similar to it – has been advanced in several cases as being the principal constraint on plural marking in Atlantic pidgins and creoles (Alleyne 1980; Dijkhoff 1983; Mufwene 1986). The present study draws in particular on the work of Mufwene, who links plural marking to referentiality and then characterises referentiality in terms of individuated/nonindividuated, the crux of this distinction being whether the entities in question are considered denumerable or not.

According to Mufwene, 'INDIVIDUATED nouns refer to their denotations or subsets thereof as consisting of denumerable individuals' (1986: 39). In contrast,

> NONINDIVIDUATED subsumes both traditional count and mass nouns when these are used as 'ensembles' without reference to the fact that their denotative classes may consist of several denumerable members (1986: 37).

Mufwene further employs a definite/indefinite distinction. With specific reference to plural marking, Mufwene states that creoles, for example, Jamaican, mark plural overtly only on those individuated nouns for which plurality is not marked elsewhere within the NP. Ordinarily this is restricted to NPs marked by a definitiser or a possessive.

Mufwene's model, then, divides semantically plural nouns into seven categories. These categories are outlined in table 36.1 below, with overt plural marking expected only on those individuated nouns that do not show number elsewhere in the NP, that is, (1) and (2) in table 36.1. (The other individuated NPs – those that fit into (3)–(5) in table 36.1 – are all overtly marked for number; for that reason, plural marking on the head noun is predicted not to occur.) Strictly speaking, Mufwene's model excludes generics; he argues that in the creole system such nouns have no number, neither singular nor plural. In the present study generics have been included in order to allow for the possibility that Liberian English may be like standard English in assigning overt number to generics.

The examples, which are consistent with Mufwene's predictions, are drawn from the Liberian corpus.

The seven factors outlined in table 36.1 form the second semantic factor group in the present study.

1. A phonological factor group

The phonological factor group consists of the segment immediately preceding the plural marker, that is, the final segment of the noun. The allomorphs of suffixal -z are [-ɛz], [-s], and [-z], and their distribution corresponds to plural distribution in standard English: -ɛz (< -iz) after sibilants, -s after voiceless nonsibilants, and -z after all other segments. The irregular plurals of standard English are also present in Liberian English. For example, irregular nouns such as *man* and *fut*, 'foot', if marked morphologically, show up as *mɛn* and *fit*. The factors in the phonological factor group, then, are ones that correspond to standard English plural marking: preceding sibilant, preceding nonsibilant consonant, preceding vowel, and irregular noun. Liberian English displays an

Table 36.1. *Plural nouns in Mufwene's schema*

A. INDIVIDUATED, DEFINITE.
  i. Not marked for number elsewhere in the NP
    1. Possessive NPs
      wia o fada dɛn 'our old fathers'
    2. Definitiser NPs
      di wuman dɛn 'the women'
  ii. Marked for number elsewhere in the NP
    3. Demonstrative NPs
      doz nyamanyama wɔn 'those insignificant ones'

B. INDIVIDUATED, INDEFINITE
  Marked for number elsewhere in the NP
    4. Numeral NPs
      tu mun 'two months'
    5. Nonnumeral individuating quantifier NPs e.g.
      sɔn 'some', *ɔ* 'all'
      sɔn gɛ frɛn 'some girl friends'

C. NONINDIVIDUATED
  i. Not marked for number elsewhere in the NP
    6. Generics and other unmarked NPs
      dɔg 'dogs'
  ii. Marked for number elsewhere in the NP
    7. Partitive quantifier NPs e.g. *plɛni* 'plenty'
      plɛni wuman 'many women'

---

extremely strong push towards the canonical CV syllable structure. It is frequently the case that the *-ɛz* allomorph (for sibilant-final nouns) is realised as -[ɛ]; in such cases, the presence of the suffix actually 'improves' the syllable structure of the noun. Where the suffix is a consonant, adding it to a noun either leaves a word with a final consonant (in the case of vowel-final nouns) or creates a highly disfavoured final consonant cluster (in the case of nonsibilant-consonant-final nouns), though the latter situation can be resolved by the deletion of the final consonant(s) of the noun stem. Thus, the prediction is that plural marking is most likely when the stem ends with a sililant, and least likely when it ends with a nonsibilant consonant.

The examination of possible phonological impact upon plural marking follows Rickford (1986). While other studies of Atlantic pidgins and creoles have argued for the primacy of semantic factors, Rickford asserts instead that phonological factors determine the distribution of plural marking in Gullah. The speaker who is the focus of Rickford's study uses *dem* only once, *-z* being the primary plural marker. In analysing variation

Table 36.2. *Probabilities for plural marking (dɛn and -z) for all speakers according to phonological, semantic, and social factor groups*

Age at acquisition/amount of education			
adult, 0–3	0.26	child, 0–3	0.42
adult, >4	0.29	child, 4–9	0.64
		child, >10	0.85
Humanness			
[+human]	0.67	[−human]	0.33
Preceding segment			
sibilant	0.79	vowel	0.37
nonsib. cons.	0.28	irregular noun	0.54
Individuation/number			
possessive	0.70	numeral	0.40
definitiser	0.52	sɔn, etc.	0.52
demonstrative	0.53	generic	0.35
		plɛni, etc.	0.48

$p. = 0.000$

in plural marking, Rickford posits phonologically conditioned rules of -*z* deletion. He uses a VARBRUL analysis to establish that preceding and also following phonological environments – but not semantic factors – are statistically significant.[5]

Plural marking in the speech community as a whole

When all 21 speakers in the sample are considered as a group, the results in table 36.2 obtain. The factor groups are listed in order of statistical significance; here and throughout this study statistical significance is determined using a threshold for *p* of 0.05. The results in table 36.2 are for all markings of the plural, whether by suffixal -*z* or free morpheme *dɛn*. (Of the 571 nouns marked for the plural, 118 are marked by *dɛn*, 467 by suffixal -*z* or the irregular form; 14 nouns are doubly marked, e.g., *doz bɔz dɛn* 'those boys'. The frequency of plural marking is broken down by individual factor in the appendix.[6]

Probabilities are presented in order of statistical significance of the factor group, from more to least. Individual probabilities greater than 0.5 favour plural marking, while those less than 0.5 disfavour it. The further a value is from 0.5, the stronger that factor's effect is.

The results presented in table 36.2 confirm the hypothesis that child learners are more likely to mark the plural than adult learners, that those with Western education are more likely to mark plurals than those without, and that [+human] nouns are more likely to be marked than [−human] ones. The results also show that sibilant-final nouns are by far the most likely to show plural marking. With regard to individuation/number, the results are less clearcut, but they do reveal strong tendencies for possessive nouns to be marked for the plural and for generic nouns not to be marked. The strongest individual factors favouring plural marking involve the speaker (child learner with ten or more years of Western education, .85) and the phonological form of the noun (sibilant-final, .79), while the strongest factors disfavouring plural marking involve the same two factors, the speaker (adult learner, little or no Western education, 0.26; adult learner, some Western education, 0.29) and the phonological form of the noun (nonsibilant-consonant-final, 0.28).

A comparison of ranges of the continuum

If age at acquisition and amount of Western education are seen as indices of position on the Liberian continuum – and several previous studies provide strong support for this assertion – then position on the continuum itself is the single factor most significant for determining frequency of plural marking. (The two extremes cited earlier – a rate of 2 per cent or less for some speakers, more than 70 per cent for others – make two points about Liberian English: first, in other Atlantic continua, the basilectal extreme involves use of creole marking, for example, dɛn, but in Liberia it involves use of no plural marking whatsoever; and second, even among the most acrolectal of speakers, the plural is marked only three-quarters of the time or less.)

Subsequent analysis shows the distinction within the group of adult learners as to amount of education not to be statistically significant. However, both the distinction between adult and child learners and also the distinction among child learners as to amount of education are significant. Clearly the results reinforce the links between these two social factors and position on the continuum. Given the strong range in frequency of plural marking among speakers (from 0 per cent to 75 per cent) and given the strong correlation between social factors and position on the continuum with regard to plural marking, the likelihood is raised that semantic and phonological factors will exert themselves to differing extents over different parts of the continuum. To test this, the continuum was broken down into four subsets according to age at acquisition and amount of Western education:

      adult learners;

    0–3 child learners, that is, those child learners whose Western education did not extend beyond the third grade;

Table 36.3. *Statistically significant factor groups when the corpus is divided by age at acquisition/amount of education*

Adult	Child		
	0–3	4–9	>10
Humanness	Humanness	Preceding seg.	Humanness
Individuation	Preceding seg.	Humanness	Preceding seg.
Preceding seg.			Individuation

Probabilities for each subset are presented in order of statistical significance of the factor group, from most to least.

> 4–9   child learners, that is, those child learners whose Western education extended at least as far as fourth grade but did not extend beyond ninth grade;
>
> \>10   child learners, that is, those child learners whose Western education extended beyond ninth grade.

Parallel VARBRUL analyses were undertaken for each of the four subsets; table 36.3 indicates for each the factor groups that were found to be statistically significant.[7]

As table 36.3 indicates, [+human]/[−human] and the preceding phonological segment are significant for all groups, with [+human]/[−human] the single most significant factor group for all but one group.

The interaction of the humanness and preceding segment factor groups is skewed: virtually all sibilant-final nouns in the corpus are [−human] (111/114, 97.4 per cent), and most irregular nouns are [+human] (163/189, 86.2 per cent). Further, there is a sharp difference between adult and child learners both with regard to the marking of sibilant-final nouns and with regard to the marking of irregular ones; the figures in tables 36.4 and 36.5 attest to this.

Tables 36.4 and 36.5 establish that child learners mark irregular and sibilant-final nouns for plural far more often than adult learners do.[8] Indeed, the primary difference in plural marking between adult learners and 0–3 child learners lies in the treatment of irregular and sibilant-final nouns.[9] When irregular and sibilant-final nouns are removed from consideration, the differences between adult learners and 0–3 child learners largely disappear. Table 36.6 gives the distribution by acquisition/education for nonsibilant-final regular nouns, while table 36.7 compares probabilities for the acquisition/education factor groups. When all nouns are considered, the difference in probabilities between adult learners and

Table 36.4. *Frequency of plural marking in [+/− human] sibilant-final regular nouns according to speaker's age at acquisition/amount of Western education*

	Sibilant-final regular nouns					
	[+human]			[−human]		
	%	Total	%	%	Total	%
Adult	−	0/0	−		21/78	27
Child, 0–3	−			2/2	(100)	
Child, 4–9	−			12/13	92	
Child, >10	3/3	(100)		16/18	89	
Child, total		3/3	(100)		30/33	91

Percentages in parentheses indicate cells with five or fewer tokens.

Table 36.5. *Frequency of plural marking in [+/− human] irregular nouns according to speaker's age at acquisition/amount of Western education*

	Irregular nouns					
	[+human]			[−human]		
	%	Total	%	%	Total	%
Adult		30/96	31		1/9	11
Child, 0–3	23/29	79		−		
Child, 4–9	15/17	88		9/12	75	
Child, >10	18/22	82		3/4	(75)	
Child, total		56/68	82		12/16	75

Percentages in parentheses indicate cells with five or fewer tokens.

0–3 child learners is 0.15; when irregular and sibilant-final nouns are removed from the sample, the difference shrinks to 0.04.

dɛn

The discussion thus far has shown age at acquisition and amount of Western education to be the strongest influences on frequency of plural marking. In turn this factor group has been shown to exert its strongest effect on the marking of irregular and sibilant-final nouns. The remainder of the discussion is concerned with nonsibilant-final regular nouns only: once irregular and sibilant-final nouns have been removed from consideration, a correlation emerges between particular factor groups and the form of the plural marking, that is, *dɛn* or *-z*.[10]

For the adult learners in the corpus, *dɛn* is the primary marker of nonsibilant-final regular nouns, accounting for 71 per cent (72/101) of plural marking for these nouns.[11] (*dɛn* is not found at the basilectal extreme, but that is because no plural marking is found there.) Less basilectally, the amount of *dɛn* use as a fraction of total plural marking drops, accounting for 50 per cent (14/28) of the plural marking among 0–3 child learners (i.e. with Western education not extending beyond 3rd grade) and 15 per cent (15/99) of the marking among 4–9 child learners. Finally, *dɛn* does not occur at all among > 10 child learners in the corpus.

It is not the case, however, that *dɛn* and *-z* are identical in distribution within a particular speaker's output or that progression along the continuum from basilect to acrolect is characterised by a simple and ever-increasing substitution of *-z* for *dɛn*. The distribution of *dɛn*, but ordinarily not that of *-z*, is constrained by syntactico-semantic factors. To begin with, the use of *dɛn* is highly sensitive to humanness, while the use of *-z* is not. Table 36.8 illustrates this.

Furthermore, within the group of [+human] *dɛn*-marked nouns, there is great sensitivity to the factors outlined in Mufwene's framework (table 36.1) though not necessarily in the way that he predicts. Adult learners use *dɛn* frequently with possessive and demonstrative [+human] NPs, somewhat less frequently with definitiser and nonnumeral individuating quantifier (*sɔn*, etc.) [+human] NPs, and infrequently with all other NPs. In contrast, the two groups of *dɛn*-using child learners narrow their use of the marker, using it frequently with possessive and demonstrative [+human] NPs and infrequently with all others.[12] This distribution is spelled out in table 36.9.

Mufwene predicts plural marking on possessive and definitiser NPs and not elsewhere. The Liberian *dɛn* data depart from this in that frequent marking is confined to [+human] nouns. Moreover, while frequent marking is associated with possessive NPs, it is also tied to demonstrative rather than definitiser NPs. Perhaps the higher rate of marking on possessive and demonstrative NPs is to be explained by the fact that they are the most definite of all individuated plural NPs (with 'most definite' here meaning 'most specific'). The high rate of *dɛn* plural marking for [+human] demonstrative NPs establishes that overt marking of number elsewhere in the NP does not in Liberian English make marking on the noun itself less likely.

While the use of *dɛn* correlates with semantic features, the use of *-z* among the groups of speakers examined in table 36.9 correlates with the

Table 36.6. *Frequency of plural marking in nonsibilant-final regular nouns according to speaker's acquisition/education*

	Nonsibilant-final regular nouns			
	[+human]	%	[−human]	%
Adult	74/210	35	26/646	4
Child, 0–3	18/50	36	10/119	8
Child, 4–9	38/88	43	61/270	23
Child, >10	61/82	74	130/271	48

Table 36.7. *Probabilities for acquisition/education for the complete corpus compared to probabilities for acquisition/education when restricted to nonsibilant-final regular nouns*

	All nouns	Nonsibilant-final regular nouns only
Adult	0.22	0.27
Child, 0–3	0.37	0.31
Child, 4–9	0.58	0.56
Child, >10	0.81	0.82
	$p = 0.00$	$p < 0.001$

Table 36.8. *Distribution of* dɛn *and* -z *by humanness and acquisition/ education*

	dɛn				-z			
	[+human]	%	[−human]	%	[+human]	%	[−human]	%
Adult	66/210	31	6/646	1	8/210	4	20/646	3
Child, 0–3	14/50	38	0/119	0	4/50	8	10/119	8
Child, 4–9	13/88	15	2/270	1	25/88	28	59/270	22

phonological factor group if it correlates with anything at all. Table 36.10 illustrates this.

The 10 child learners, the ones with extensive Western education, show no use of *dɛn* in the corpus. However, unlike all the other speakers under study, these speakers display semantically conditioned -z marking. For

Table 36.9. *Distribution of* dɛn *marking according to individuation and acqusition/education*

	Adult	%	Child, 0–3	%	Child, 4–9	%
[+human]						
possessive	29/46	63	12/25	48	7/14	50
demonstrative	4/6	67	1/3	(33)	1/3	(33)
Total	33/52	63	13/28	46	8/17	47
definitiser	13/34	38	1/9	11	1/23	4
sɔn, etc.	13/33	39	0/6	0	1/9	11
Total	26/68	38	1/15	7	2/32	6
generic	5/56	9	0/5	0	1/27	4
numeral	2/30	7	0/2	(0)	0/9	0
Total	7/86	8	0/7	0	1/36	3
plɛni, etc.	0/4	(0)	0/0	–	2/3	(67)
[−human]	6/646	1	0/119	0	2/270	1

Percentages in parentheses indicate cells with five or fewer tokens.

these speakers, as table 36.11 shows, humanness is the most significant of factor groups, followed by individuation, and then by preceding phonological segment. In other words the use of -*z* is affected by the same semantic constraints as *dɛn*.

Bickerton (1975) notes that a pattern characteristic of continua is for creole forms in the basilect to give way in the mesolect to target language forms while the underlying creole *system* persists. (Then in the acrolect the target language system supplants the creole one.) Singler (1984 and elsewhere) confirms this pattern for Liberian English. To some extent, the results with regard to the semantics of -*z* for > 10 child learners suggest that for these speakers target language forms express the creole system: the creole sensitivity to semantic factors is now reflected not in the creole plural marker but in the standard English marker. Inasmuch as these speakers represent the Liberian acrolect, this reckoning places the distribution of plural marking in this acrolect as intermediate between creole and target, not yet wholly reflective of standard English. There are limits, however, as to how far one can go in making the claim. In particular, the *extremes* of *dɛn* marking in all nonacrolectal groups are not replicated in

Table 36.10. *Probabilities for -z plurals, nonsibilant-final regular nouns only, for groups that also use* dɛn

Adult	(No groups selected)	
Child, 0–3	Preceding segment	
	vowel	0.74
	nonsib. cons.	0.26
	$p < 0.003$	
Child, 4–9	Preceding segment	
	vowel	0.57
	nonsib. cons.	0.43
	$p < 0.024$	

Table 36.11. *Probabilities for -z plurals among >10 child learners, nonsibilant-final regular nouns only*

Child, >10	Humanness	
	[+human]	0.60
	[−human]	0.40
	Individuation	
	possessive	0.64
	demonstrative	0.50
	definitiser	0.55
	sɔn, etc.	0.61
	numeral	0.35
	generic	0.36
	Preceding segment	
	vowel	0.57
	nonsib. cons.	0.43
	$p < 0.014$	

Probabilities are presented in order of statistical significance of the factor group, from most to least.

-z marking in the acrolectal group. In separate VARBRUL analyses of *den* marking among adult learners, 0–3 child learners, and 4–9 child learners, most of the semantic factors in each analysis are 0.25 or more away from the neutral point (0.5), an indicator of powerful constraints. In contrast, the strongest single factor in the analysis of -z marking among >10 child learners is only 0.15 from 0.5 (numeral NPs, 0.35). Simply put, while the factors constraining -z marking among > 10 child learners are statistically significant, none approach the power of the factors that constrain *dɛn* marking among any of the less acrolectal groups of speakers.

Conclusions

With a range of frequency of plural marking from 0 per cent to 75 per cent among individual speakers, the question arises as to whether it is more appropriate to speak of the insertion or the deletion of plural markers. Throughout the continuum, semantic factors would seem to be more appropriately expressed as constraints on an insertion rule. Phonological factors, on the other hand, might be expressed either by a deletion rule (operating on forms that are either underlyingly present or the output of an insertion rule) or might be themselves constraints on an insertion rule. For regular nouns, for example, operation of a deletion rule would be promoted by a preceding nonsibilant consonant; conversely, operation of an insertion rule would be favoured by a preceding sibilant. (Irregular plurals are probably governed by individual lexical rules, with such a rule occurring early along the continuum for *chedren*, 'children', and late for *wumen*, 'women'.) Finally, for those speakers who use both *den* and *-z*, it would seem to be the case that a rule of *den* insertion would operate prior to any rule involving *-z*.

This investigation of plural marking on the Liberian continuum has shown the most important constraint to involve the speaker's age at acquisition of Liberian English and amount of Western education, with age at acquisition the more important of the two. Given the importance of age at acquisition, the question arises as to what support such findings offer for a critical age theory and for a theory that would see nativisation as crucial to creolisation. In the present case, such support would have to be seen as premature. Age at acquisition in Liberia ties in to a wide range of socioeconomic and geographical factors. Thus, 'adult learner' and 'child learner' designate speakers displaying certain patterned backgrounds. It is rarely the case in Liberia that, for an adult learner and a child learner, all other social factors are identical or equivalent. Still, even without the greater implications that one might look for in the case of age at acquisition, the well-established link between acquisition/education and position on the Liberian continuum establishes in the present case a fairly straightforward relationship between position on the continuum and frequency of plural marking.

NOTES

Part of the data upon which this study is based were collected under a New York University Research Challenge Fund grant. I am grateful to the following for their assistance in the collection, transcription, and interpretation of these data: Samson Tiklo, Sumoyea Guluma, Boakai Zoludua, Boima Barclay, Samuel Dweh, Dubel Nyankun, David Peewee, and John Mason. I am also grateful to Arthur Spears and, especially, to Salikoko Mufwene for their discussion with me of the issues addressed in this article.

1. The orthography used here is that found in Fyle & Jones (1980) and Todd (1982). The syllable-final sequence ⟨Vn⟩ represents [Ṽ]. As in other Atlantic English-lexifier creoles, there is also an associative morpheme *dɛn*, whose meaning is roughly 'and the others', e.g., *do dɛn* 'Doe and the other leaders'. Instances of this associative use of *dɛn* have not been included in the present study.

2. These speakers were chosen from a larger pool of speakers. The selection from the larger group was nonrandom in that an effort was made to obtain a cross-section of social attributes. With regard to the speakers selected, almost all of them had been interviewed for between 40 and 60 minutes. As a rule, the search for tokens began with the 31st minute of the interview, proceeded to the end of the interview (or until 100 tokens had been found), and – if necessary – continued from the beginning of the interview. Only nouns whose pluralness was unambiguous were counted. Such nouns occur less frequently in the most highly basilectal range of speech. The speakers for whom fewer than 100 tokens were obtained were all highly basilectal. Given the necessity of restricting inclusion of tokens in the sample to those that were unambiguously plural and given the greater amount of ambiguity in this regard in basilectal speech, the likelihood exists that the rate of plural marking is even lower than reported here.

3. The Liberian continuum does depart from the standard model in that, for geographical and historical reasons, there is more than one basilect. These basilects converge to form a single mesolect. At its extreme one basilect, Liberian Interior English, is the speech of rubber tappers and soldiers whose first language is a Mande language. The extreme of the second basilect, Kru Pidgin English, is the speech of the 'Krumen', those first-language-Kru speakers who participated in work gangs on board ships or in Kru enclaves in Ghana, Nigeria, or Sierra Leone. For reasons of space, it has been necessary to confine the present study to a continuum that excludes Kru Pidgin English and extends from Liberian Interior English to Liberian standard. (The basilect referred to subsequently in the text is Liberian Interior English.) It should be noted that plural marking in Kru Pidgin English is by no means identical to plural marking in Liberian interior English. Kru Pidgin speakers mark the plural more frequently than do Liberian Interior speakers, they do not use *dɛn*, and their plural marking is sensitive (at a statistically significant level) to phonological factors only. Because of the removal of the Kru Pidgin speakers from consideration, a discussion of substratal impact on plural marking in Liberian English has also been omitted. Also omitted from the present study because of space limitations is an examination of plural marking in Settler English, the variety spoken by those whose ancestors were Black American immigrants to Liberia in the nineteenth century. Kru Pidgin plural marking is the subject of Singler (1988b), and Settler plural marking is the subject of Singler (1989).

4. The reliability of geographical assessments is complicated by the mobility of individual Liberians; most of the speakers in the sample had lived in more than one region of the country.

5. Rickford's results (adjusted to show rate of the *presence* of plural marking) are the following:

Preceding phonol. segment		Following phonol. segment	
Vowel _____ :	0.729	_____ Vowel:	0.703
Sib. Cons. _____ :	0.413	_____ Pause:	0.396
Nonsib. Cons. _____ :	0.346	_____ Cons:	0.391

$p = 0.032$

In the Liberian case, following phonological segment was also considered as a factor group, and Rickford's distinctions were employed. (Irregular nouns were not included.) In fact, the factor group of following phonological segment emerges as statistically significant in one instance only, in an analysis of plural marking by those who acquired Liberian English as adults. In this subgroup, all other factor groups (humanness, individuation, and preceding phonological segment) have greater statistical significance than does the following segment. For reasons having to do with the strong Liberian push towards CV syllable structure, it was hypothesised that the results would be comparable to Rickford's. When following segment is statistically significant (in the speech of adult learners), the probabilities that obtain are essentially the opposite of what had been hypothesised (Vowel, 0.38; Pause, 0.49; Consonant, 0.63). (More acrolectally, values in line with the original hypothesis do prevail but not at a statistically significant level.)

6. In the Liberian English speech community, there are ample numbers of adult learners with no Western education and ample numbers of child learners with Western education. Also, in Monrovia, there are child learners with no Western education. The fourth permutation – adult learners with Western education – is the one that obtains least frequently. In the present sample there are two speakers of this type. Because there are only two, the distinction between them with regard to amount of Western education (4th grade–9th grade vs. 10th grade or more) has been collapsed.

7. In carrying out the analyses of the subgroups, factors with five or fewer tokens were removed. Thus, sibilants were removed from consideration for 0–3 child learners, and the semantic category of nonindividuated partitive quantifier NPs (*pleni*, etc.) was removed from each of the child learner groups.

8. The irregular nouns are *chad* 'child', *man*, *wuman* 'woman', *tut* 'tooth', and *fut* 'foot'. Their distribution by acquisition/education is the following:

	chad	%	*man*	%	*wuman*	%	*tut*	%	*fut*	%
Adult	21/22	95	4/23	17	5/51	10			1/9	11
Child, 0–3	18/18	100	1/7	14	4/4	100				
Child, 4–9	15/15	100	0/2	0			8/9	89	1/3	33
Child, >10	12/12	100	1/4	25	5/6	83			3/4	75
Total	66/67	99	6/36	17	14/61	23	8/9	89	5/16	31

The primary difference between adult and child learners with regard to irregular nouns involves the noun *wuman*, for which the adult learner frequency is 10 per cent while the child learner frequency is 90 per cent (9/10).

9. In the corpus, as indicated in table 4, there are only two sibilant-final nouns among 0–3 child learners. However, an examination of all sibilant-final plural nouns for these speakers (and not just those found in each speaker's first 100 plural nouns) turns up a total of five such nouns; the plural is marked in four of the five.

10. Subsequent discussion establishes a strong correlation between [+human] and the use of *dɛn* marking. Given the correlation between [−human] and sibilant-final nouns, it is not surprising that only three sibilant-final nouns show *dɛn* marking. On the other hand, 14 irregular nouns are marked by *dɛn*; of these, eight are instances of the doubly marked *chedren dɛn* 'children'.

11. Four speakers account for the bulk of the uses of *dɛn* (81/118, 68.7 per cent) in the corpus. They are all adult learners whose first language is a Mande language, but no clearcut social distinction distinguishes the frequent *dɛn* users from other first-language-Mande adult learners.

12. The sole exception to the characterisation of *dɛn* use among child learners involves partitive quantifier (*plɛni*, etc.) [+human] NPs in the speech of 4–9 child learners. In this instance but more generally as well, there are too few tokens of this type to support any conclusions about them.

REFERENCES

Alleyne, Mervyn C. 1980. *Comparative Afro-American: An Historical-Comparative Study of some Afro-American Dialects in the New World*. Ann Arbor: Karoma.

Bickerton, Derek. 1975. *Dynamics of a Creole System*. Cambridge: Cambridge University Press.

DeCamp, David. 1971. Toward a generative analysis of a post-creole speech community. In Hymes, Dell (ed.), *Pidginization and Creolization of Languages*. Cambridge: Cambridge University Press, pp. 349-70.

Dijkhoff, Martha B. 1983. The process of pluralization in Papiamentu. In Carrington, Lawrence D. (ed.), *Studies in Caribbean Language*. Saint Augustine, Trinidad: Society for Caribbean Linguistics, pp. 217-29.

Fyle, Clifford N. and Jones Eldred D. 1980. *A Krio-English Dictionary*. London: Oxford University Press.

Mufwene, Salikoko S. 1986. Number delimitation in Gullah. *American Speech* 61: 33-60.

Rickford, John R. 1986. Some principles for the study of Black and White speech in the south. In Montgomery, Michael B. and Bailey, Guy (eds.), *Language Variety in the South*. University AL: University of Alabama Press, pp. 38-62.

Singler, John Victor. 1984. Variation in Tense-Aspect-Modality in Liberian English. Unpublished PhD, thesis, University of California at Los Angeles.

1987. The city, the mesolect, and innovation. *Journal of Pidgin and Creole Languages*. 2: 119–47.

1988a. The homogeneity of the substrate as a factor in pidgin/creole genesis. *Language* 64 (1): 27–51.

1988b. The place of variation in the formal expression of inflectional processes: Evidence from Kru Pidgin English. In Ferrara, K., Brown, B., Walters, K., and Baugh, J. (eds.), *Linguistic change and contact: Proceedings of the Sixteenth Annual Conference on New Ways of Analyzing Variation in Language*. Austin: University of Texas Department of Linguistics, pp. 345–53.

1989. Plural marking in Liberian Settler English. *American Speech* 64: 40–64.

Todd, Loreto. 1982. *Cameroon*. (Varieties of English Around the World, T1.) Heidelberg: Groos.

Appendix

Frequency of plural marking (dɛn and-z) for all speakers according to phonological, semantic, and social factors

	Applications	Totals	Percentage
Preceding segment			
Sibilant	54	114	47
Nonsibilant cons.	193	980	20
Vowel	225	756	30
Irregular noun	99	189	52
Individuation/number marking			
Individuated, definite			
Possessive	120	264	45
Definitiser	128	396	32
Demonstrative	23	61	38
Individuated, indefinite			
Numeral	100	534	19
sɔn, etc.	88	228	39
Nonindividuated			
Generic	103	523	20
plɛni, etc.	9	33	27
Humanness			
Human	280	596	47
Nonhuman	291	1443	20
Age of acquisition/amount of Western Education			
Adult learners			
0–3rd grade	105	839	13
>4th grade	47	200	23
Child learners			
0–3rd grade	53	200	26
4th–9th grade	135	400	34
>10th grade	231	400	58
Totals	571	2039	28

The Caribbean

37

The Caribbean

DONALD WINFORD

Introduction

The islands of the Caribbean stretch over a thousand-mile arc from the top of the Florida archipelago to the mainland of South America. They are usually classified according to their (latest) affiliation to the European powers that colonised them from the fifteenth century onwards, and also in terms of the official languages they recognise. For the most part, these two criteria coincide. The major groupings include the Spanish-speaking nations, the French-official (francophone) Caribbean, the Dutch-official territories, and the English-official (anglophone) Caribbean. The largest group of islands belongs to the last of these categories.

The English-official Caribbean countries together have a total population of about five and a half million speakers. They include the vast majority of the islands outside of the Greater Antilles group (see figure 37.1), as well as two mainland nations – Belize in Central America, and Guyana in South America. These communities differ substantially in their sociolinguistic structures and particularly in terms of the relationship that English bears to the other varieties of language in use.

The vast majority of these countries are communities in which English as the official language coexists side by side with a lexically related creole language as the vernacular,[1] with other varieties either non-existent or severely restricted in use. Such communities make up the so-called creole continua of the Caribbean. A list of the countries, their area, population and languages is provided in table 37.1.

A much smaller group of English-official countries consists of communities where English coexists not only with a lexically-related creole variety, but also with at least one other unrelated vernacular. These include the islands of Dominica and St Lucia where a French-lexicon creole is widely used, as well as Belize, where several ethnic languages are in everyday use.[2]

In all of the above communities, standard British English has long

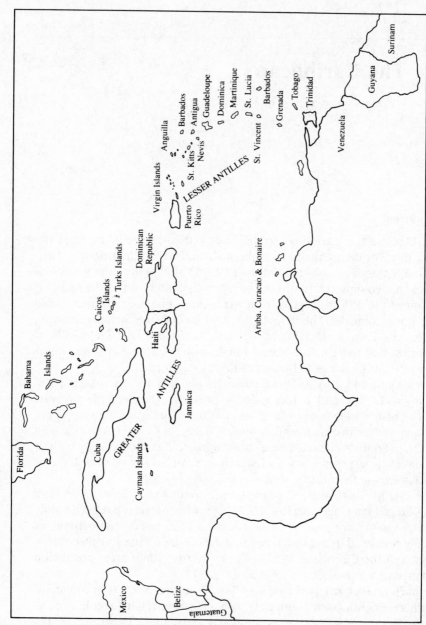

Figure 37.1 Map of the West Indies.

Table 37.1. *Populations and languages of the anglophone Caribbean*

Country	Area	Population (census year)	Major vernacular(s)	Other vernacular(s)
Anguilla	35 sq ml	6,519 (1974)	English Creole	–
Antigua and Barbuda	170 sq ml	72,355 (1977)	English Creole	–
Bahamas	5,000 sq ml	222,000 (1983)	English Creole	–
Barbados	166 sq ml	252,700 (1985)	English Creole	–
Belize	8,866 sq ml	140,000 (1980)	English Creole, Spanish	Garífuna (Carib) Mopan, Kekchi
British Virgin Islands	59 sq ml	10,030 (1976)	English Creole	–
Cayman Islands	100 sq ml	14,800 (1977)	English Creole	–
Dominica	289½ sq ml	73,795 (1981)	French Creole	–
Grenada	133 sq ml	111,184 (1977)	English Creole	Hindi/Bhojpuri;
Guyana	83,000 sq ml	758,619 (1980)	English Creole	Amerindian languages
Jamaica	4,411 sq ml	2,109,400 (1977)	English Creole	–
Montserrat	39 sq ml	12,160 (1977)	English Creole	–
St Kitts-Nevis	101 sq ml	42,000 (1975)	English Creole	–
St Lucia	238 sq ml	134,066 (1984)	English Creole, French Creole	–
St Vincent (and The Grenadines)	150 sq ml	127,883 (1982)	English Creole	–
Trinidad & Tobago	1,978 sq ml	1,132,700 (1978)	English Creole	Hindi/Bhojpuri, French Creole
Turks and Calcos Islands	166 sq ml	7,650 (1977)	English Creole	–
US Virgin Islands	136 sq ml	101,130 (1978)	English Creole	Spanish, French Creole

Sources: Caribbean Yearbook 1979/80. Caribook Ltd., Toronto, Canada. Where possible, population figures were taken from *The Annual Digest of Statistics* for several countries.

served as the official language, and even in those nations that are now independent, it continues to exercise considerable influence over the local forms of standard English that have evolved (see below).

Before I begin to explore the anglophone Caribbean in greater detail, some mention should be made of the communities in which American English serves as an official language and a model of linguistic behaviour. On the one hand, there are the US Virgin Islands where the vernacular is a creolised form of English which stands in much the same relationship to the official language as that which obtains in other anglophone territories. On the other hand there is Puerto Rico, where both English and Spanish are official languages, but the vast majority of the population use Spanish as their vernacular (see Dillard 1973; Lawton 1971; McCroskey *et al.* 1985; Nash 1982 and bibliography therein). These American-influenced communities are not normally included within the anglophone Caribbean in the socio-linguistic literature, though they offer valuable insights into the effects of linguistic imperialism – this time from another direction – on the social habits and culture of the peoples concerned.

The status of English

It should be made clear from the start that the anglophone Caribbean is anything but a linguistically homogeneous area. Indeed, the brief picture painted above oversimplifies the situation, particularly in the case of the creole continua, which involve quite different kinds of sociolinguistic situation, depending chiefly on the degree of distance between the creole and English extremes of the continuum, and the degree of social uniformity in the community as a whole.

As the sole official language in the anglophone Caribbean, English is used as the medium of public communication in such areas as the state bureaucracy, the legal system, the mass media and other areas normally associated with official languages. It is also the vehicle of literacy, and the medium of education at all levels of the education system.

As an official language, English enjoys considerable prestige, and is associated with the upper echelons of Caribbean society. Competence in English is acquired for the most part in the school systems; very few West Indians learn the official language as a native tongue. Consequently, command of English is to a large extent an index of educational achievement and high social status.

For the vast majority of the population, whose native language is some form of Creole, English remains a distant target. The sociolinguistic situation may demand that they shift their speech in the direction of English on formal occasions, but the nature and extent of such shifting is dependent on the social background of the speakers.

Local varieties of English

In its written form, the offical English of the Caribbean differs little, if at all, from international standard English. In its spoken form, Caribbean English consists of a range of localised forms of English which differ from one community to the next.

Some work has been done on the linguistic features that distinguish West Indian localised forms of English from other varieties. Craig (1982) discusses some of the phonological and lexical features shared in common by some varieties of Caribbean English. Williams (1985, 1986) has documented some of the characteristics of (native-born) white speech in several communities. Also of interest is the work being done by Richard Allsopp and his associates in the Caribbean Lexicography project (Allsopp 1971a, 1971b, 1972, 1978). This project is concerned with codifying the lexicon of those varieties of English spoken by educated West Indians. Its aim is to define a standard Caribbean English as a prestigious standard in its own right, distinct from standard British American, Canadian and other forms of standard English throughout the English-speaking world.

There is still, however, a great deal of work to be done before the basic features of educated Caribbean English can be specified and codified.

The autonomy of creole

The question of the autonomy of creole vernaculars has been a persistent theme of the literature on Caribbean English. Some conceptions of creole continua have led to the view that the creole varieties in such situations are heteronomous to a very considerable extent, with respect to English (see Chambers and Trudgill 1980: 12). This view is not in fact accepted by most Caribbean linguists, who argue that there are sound linguistic grounds for treating the creole varieties in creole continua as autonomous systems (Devonish 1978; Haynes 1973; Alleyne 1980; Gibson 1982; Edwards 1983; and Escure 1983). Essentially these scholars argue that it is possible to describe creole continuum situations as involving at least two coexistent systems – the standard language and the Creole. Most scholars also make a distinction within the creole between the basilect, or extreme creole variety, and the mesolect, or intermediate varieties.

A large part of the debate on the autonomy of creole has centred on just one or two situations, for example, Guyana and Jamaica, and for that reason one has to be careful about generalising any conclusions reached to the rest of the Caribbean. In the first place, not all communities have a basilectal variety as conservative as Guyana's or Jamaica's. This applies to Barbados, the Bahamas and Trinidad, for example, and these communities are often cited as cases which call for a redefinition of the vernacular variety as a dialect of English rather than a creole (see Alleyne 1980:

Ch.7). Secondly, there are wide difference in social organisation among those communities which do have a basilect. There is a need for much more research on the various creole continuum situations in the Caribbean before a more accurate picture of the degree of homogeneity and autonomy of their creole varieties can emerge.

Sociolinguistic variation

Models of variation

The range of variation in creole continua has provided a fruitful basis of research for sociolinguists who seek to uncover the systematicity of patterning that underlies it. Several models of variation have been applied to this task. Among them is the implicational model, developed by Bickerton (1975) on the basis of work done by De Camp (1971b) and C. J. Bailey (1973). Since this makes no attempt to include social or other extra-linguistic factors as an integral part of the analysis, it will not be considered here.

Research using the Labovian model has been done by Winford, on Trinidad, and by Rickford, on Guyana. Winford's earlier work (1972, 1980) suggests that patterns of variation in creole continua are similar in many respects to the types of correspondence between linguistic and sociological phenomena which have been shown to exist by Labov and others in more 'typical' dialect situations. However, Winford (1984) points to a variety of problems involved in attempting to apply the fully-developed quantitative model, including variable rules, to the description of creole continua.

Rickford (1979) represents a more up-to-date application of the fully-developed quantitative model to analysis of a creole continuum, offering, in addition, an insightful comparison of the quantitative and implicational models. He suggests that the former is superior in the handling of phonological variables, which tend to display gradient stratification, and that by contrast the implicational model seems better suited to the analysis of grammatical variables showing sharp stratification, such as his morphological pronoun variables (1979: 513).

There are several other quantitative studies of sociolinguistic variation in other Caribbean communities, including Minderhout (1977) on Tobago, Young (1973) on Belize, Christie (1969) on Dominica and Cooper (1979) on St Kitts. These studies again do not employ the fully developed Labovian model and they have not been followed up by continued research and publication on the communities concerned. Other quantitative studies, including the work of Edwards on Guyana and of Escure on Belize, will be discussed below.

Le Page's acts of identity model (see Le Page 1978; Le Page and Tabouret-Keller 1985) is particularly significant to Caribbean sociolinguistics because it in fact grew out of attempts to come to terms with the social and linguistic processes at work in the Caribbean (as well as other) communities. The model has so far been applied to Belize and St Lucia by Le Page and Tabouret-Keller (1985). It differs from Labovian-type and other variationist studies primarily in not taking concepts such as 'a language' and 'a group or community' as givens, but rather exploring the ways in which such concepts come into being through the acts of identity which people make within themselves and with each other. However, Le Page and Tabouret-Keller acknowledge a link between their model and Labov's, which lies in the fact that both see linguistic behaviour as symptomatic of social groups. This is the theme of the work done by Edwards on Guyana (1975, 1983, 1985, 1986).

Another highly attractive alternative to the Labovian model is the social network model, developed in Milroy (1980). Milroy's approach is quite compatible with the acts of identity model, as Le Page and Tabouret-Keller themselves point out (1985: 116). It is unfortunate therefore that the social network model has not so far been applied to Caribbean communities. One apparent exception is Edwards (1984). But this is based on hindsight and relies on data drawn from Edwards (1975) and reinterpreted so as to fit the social network model.

There is a need for sociolinguistic studies which apply both the acts of identity model and the social network framework to the analysis of Caribbean communities. The Labovian model has come in for a great deal of criticism with respect to its assumption of fixed categories of socioeconomic status and social role which do not always reflect the reality of social organisation in these communities. As a result, several questions remain unanswered as far as the social organisation of Caribbean language is concerned – for example, how to explain the fact that persons of similar social background will demonstrate very different linguistic behaviour, with no apparent motivating factor; or how the same individual will use quite different speech varieties in different social contexts, with different types of interlocutors.

In the following section, I will attempt to provide a brief description of the contribution that the studies referred to above have made to our understanding of the social functions of language in Caribbean communities.

Socioeconomic status

Most studies of Caribbean situations concentrate on factors related to socioeconomic status. While social class differences are by no means uniform across Caribbean communities, we can still acknowledge a surprising degree of similarity in the patterns of relationship between differences in social role and rank on the one hand, and differences in language choice on the other.

A general pattern of correlation between creole and lower status on the one hand, and acrolect (English) and higher status on the other, is a fairly common feature of all the communities reported on in the literature. In the case of Trinidad, which is characterised by a quite fluid social structure, these correlations take the form of fine distinctions among the four social groupings identified in Winford (1972, 1980). The Bahamas and Barbados appear to be similar to Trinidad in these respects, but sociolinguistic studies of these communities are rare (see Roy 1984 on Barbados).

In the case of communities like Guyana and Belize, which are far more heterogeneous both linguistically and socially, patterns of gradient stratification along socioeconomic lines also emerge for the phonological variables. Rickford (1979) reports on social class differences in the use of vowel laxing (a phonological variable) and singular pronominal forms (morphological variables). His study, however, is restricted to one rural community, so we obtain a rather limited picture of social differentiation in Guyana. His sample is divided into only two social classes: EC (Estate Class – labourers etc) and NEC (Non-estate class – supervisors, shopowners, tradesmen etc). According to Rickford, these groups can be considered as corresponding roughly to the 'working class' and 'lower middle class' groups of Guyanese society. (1979: 121).

Rickford's analysis indicates that 'social class is the single most powerful constraint on the variation, the EC members overwhelmingly favouring the basilectal variants, and the NEC members overwhelmingly favouring acrolectal ones' (1979: 510). A brief synopsis of these findings is contained in Rickford's contribution to the present volume.

His findings are somewhat at variance with those of Edwards (1975, 1984) whose investigations are based on an urban sample in Georgetown, the capital, and a complex of three small rural villages – Ann's Grove, Two Friends and Clonbrook. Edwards studied a far wider range of grammatical variables (15 in all), but pays little or no attention to phonological variables. Edwards finds community (i.e., urban vs rural provenance) to be the most powerful variable. As far as socioeconomic status is concerned, however, he comments that 'education and occupational status are only weakly significant determinants of linguistic choice' (1984: 4). Indeed, he points to cases where informants of similar education and status show widely differing behaviour, while informants of higher education actually use more creole variants than less educated ones (see below).

Apart from the studies just discussed, there are relatively few detailed analyses of social class differences in language in Caribbean communities.

Akers (1981) investigates two phonological variables – final consonant clusters and use of /r/ in Jamaica, but his analysis provides little information on extralinguistic conditioning, concentrating instead on the purely internal (linguistic) constraints on production of acrolectal variants.

Other studies which provide a smattering of information on social class differences include Minderhout (1977) on Tobago. Christie (1969) on Dominica, Young (1973) on Belize, Cooper (1979) on St Kitts and Roy (1984) on Barbados.

Ethnicity

Most Caribbean communities are more or less ethnically homogeneous. However there are several in which ethnic differences play a major role in the social structure. They include Belize, Guyana and Trinidad.[3] No sociolinguistic analysis of these communities can ignore the role of ethnicity.

Belize is easily the most heterogenous of the three, containing five major ethnic groups that have preserved distinct native languages. In her (1982) study, Escure investigates ethnic differences in language use in the village of Placencia, located in an area where Creoles and Black Caribs are in frequent contact. Her analysis of five morphological variables leads her to conclude that

> the interlocutor's ethnic membership has been shown to narrow down a creole speaker's choices. The observed selection of the mesolect is determined by a combination of linguistic insecurity and of social dominance relative to the neighbouring Carib group. (1982: 258)

Le Page and Tabouret-Keller (1985) investigate language use in the Western Cayo district of Belize, an area in which the Mestizo and Creole populations mostly balance out, so that Spanish and Creole English have roughly equal status in the community at large. They demonstrate that children in these communities have a choice of ethnic identities which is reflected in their choice of language. Both Escure and Le Page and Tabouret-Keller focus on the emerging role of Creole as a symbol of Belizean identity.

The ethnic factor has also been shown to be significant in Guyana (Edwards 1975) and Trinidad (Winford 1972) which are remarkably similar in having an almost equal balance of Africans and East Indians in their populations. It is interesting that rural Trinidadian East Indians display a predilection for creole variants similar to that reported by Edwards for their Guyanese counterparts. Indeed, several of the stereotypes of East Indian speech in both communities are actually very conservative features of creole which have been lost in urban varieties. It would be well worth investigating how extensive such linguistic differences are, and to what extent they reflect an attempt on the part of either group to preserve a distinct identity.

Age

Studies of phonological variation which pay attention to age differences in Caribbean communities are relatively few. They include Rickford (1979) and Winford (1972, 1979). Other studies such as Akers (1981) pay little or no attention to age.

Rickford's (1979) study investigates the distribution of vowel laxing in three age groups in a rural Guyanese community – under 18, 18–55 and over 55. The pattern of distribution of vowel laxing shows no evidence of change in progress, though analysis of careful and casual styles shows that the youngest members of the community have acquired a higher degree of stylistic differentiation (i.e., a greater ability to approximate acrolectal norms) than their parents and grandparents. The relative similarity among the various age groups in their use of this phonological feature is rather surprising. One suspects that a quite different picture would emerge from an investigation of other types of phonological variable similar to those discussed by Winford (1972, 1979) for Trinidad. Unfortunately no studies of such variation (e.g., among vowels) in Guyanese speech are available.

Winford's studies in fact demonstrate that there are significant differences in the use of certain vowel variants among different age groups in the rural community of Mayo, in Trinidad. Younger rural speakers tend to reflect urban patterns of usage far more than older ones. The differences in usage may be seen as representing, at least partially, the processes of change that lie behind the structure of variation in the vowel system of Trinidadian English.

Rickford (1979) also investigates age differences in the use of morphological pronoun variables. The picture that emerges here is quite different from the patterns of distribution of vowel laxing. There is a noticeable decrease in the frequency of basilectal pronouns among the younger age-levels – a distribution which matches Labov's (1966: 325) model of 'a stigmatized language feature showing change in progress'. Some of these findings are given in Rickford's contribution to this volume. These results may be profitably compared with those of Edwards (1975, 1985) who touches rather incidentally on age differences in the use of several morphological variables. The age factor is however closely tied up with ethnicity and geographical location. Edwards finds that age differences are far more pronounced in the rural than in the urban community, and much more evident among Blacks than Indians.

Apart from Rickford's and Edward's work on Guyana there appear to be no studies which focus attention on age differences in the use of grammatical variables in any other Anglophone Caribbean community.

Sex

Very little work has been done on sex differentiation in language in the anglophone Caribbean. Most of the primary sociolinguistic studies of the area, such as Winford (1972) or Edwards (1975), confine their sample populations to men, while others, such as Akers (1981), treat sex-based variation as incidental to other concerns, or rely on rather limited data.

Given the dearth of studies in this area, Escure's paper (this volume) is a welcome contribution. She discusses patterns in the use of the copula in a variety of grammatical environments, and concludes that such linguistic differences as emerge between men and women are not uniquely correlated with sex, but rather with the intersection of sex and other variables.

Escure's paper provides a good basis on which to extend this neglected area of Caribbean sociolinguistics. It is instructive in the way it attempts to sort out the factor of sex from other possible influences such as age, topic and occupational status. Like Rickford's study (1979 and this volume), this one focuses on a rural community, with its own distinct patterns of social organisation and interaction. One suspects that very different pictures of sexual differentiation in language will emerge from an investigation of urban communities, or more fluid societies such as Trinidad or Barbados where the old stereotypes of women's roles are fast being eroded by the expanding consciousness of the new Caribbean woman.

Functional or stylistic differentiation

It seems clear from the sociolinguistic literature as a whole that situational variation in language use has received far less attention than social differentiation. Moreover, the factors involved in situational variation have been less precisely defined, and the descriptive frameworks not clearly developed. This imbalance is also true of sociolinguistic studies of the Caribbean. Most of the studies already referred to make little or no attempt to elicit a truly representative range of informants' stylistic repertoires, limiting themselves instead to the division of single-interview data into the artificial 'contextual' styles first proposed by Labov (1966) – sometimes with some modifications.

Rickford (1979), Edwards (1975, 1985) and Winford (1972) represent the Labovian method best. In spite of the obvious limitiation of the methods they employ, these studies offer some indication of the nature and range of style shifting in creole continua. All of them demonstrate that there are clear distinctions between more casual and more formal style in interview speech. These distinctions are generally equivalent to

creole/English differences, and they apply to all levels of linguistic structure, including phonology. A general pattern that emerges is that higher
status speakers tend to display much bigger differences between styles
than lower status ones, usually indicating that the former are able to
approximate the English end of the continuum more closely than the
latter.

Winford (1972) and Escure (1982) record informants in more natural
situations. Winford (1972) investigates the language of 22 urban and 21
rural informants in two lower status groups (Upper Working and Lower
Working Class) interacting with their peers in natural situations. Much of
his data is drawn from surreptitious recordings. His analysis shows that,
for all variables, an already high incidence of creole variants in the most
'casual' interview style is further increased in peer-group style. Rickford
(1979, 1987) also attempts to explore the fullest possible range of his
informants' stylistic repertoire by eliciting spontaneous interview style as
well as data recorded in peer group sessions and re-interviews conducted
by expatriates.

There is still a great deal of work to be done in this area, particularly in
the case of higher status groups whose vernaculars have tended to be
neglected in studies of this type.

Intra- and inter- group behaviour

Another area of situational variation that is hopelessly under-researched
in the Caribbean is style shifting arising from differences in intra-group
and inter-group interaction. Edwards (1983, 1985, 1986) and Escure (1982)
have made valuable contributions in this area. Edwards finds that the
behaviour of rural East Indian Guyanese differs significantly in urban
contexts where they are removed from contact with their own community.

Escure (1982) examines the behaviour of Belizean Creoles in two kinds
of interaction – with members of their own group, and with Black Caribs
– in the rural village of Placencia. She finds that Creoles produce a wide
range of varieties in intra-group sessions, but reduce this range to a
relatively homogeneous mesolectal variety when interacting with Black
Caribs. Both Escure and Edwards point to cases of individual speakers
who vary significantly in their linguistic outputs despite the similarity in
their social characteristics. Indeed, Edwards cites cases of informants with
higher educational achievement who use more creole variants than their
less educated peers. Behaviour such as this must be explained in terms of
factors such as reference group membership, power relationships between
groups, and the values associated with sub-cultures within the community.
Such findings provide a clear challenge to Labovian-type approaches
which expect to find neat patterns of correlation between linguistic
behaviour and extralinguistic factors such as education and occupational

status in Creole continua. They also suggest that the continuum model itself is misleading in suggesting that the acrolect is always the target of the language-conscious and in failing to recognise that the basilect is an equally important focal point of linguistic loyalty.

Speech events

Another area of stylistic variation about which we know all too little involves the nature and types of speech events in creole communities. Escure (1982) offers a sketch of salient speech events in the Belizean speech community which call for different styles of speaking.

Rickford (1979: 153) also refers to a number of structured speech events in the rural Guyanese community of 'Cane Walk'. They include *rowing* (loud quarrelling); *tanlize* (< *tantalize*, i.e., playful teasing among friends); *talking nancy* (telling traditional folk tales or Anansi stories); and *rhyming* (narrative jokes or ritual insults). Speech events such as these are an integral part of the vernacular culture and find their best expression through the medium of creole. In this respect, there are marked similarities among Caribbean communities, all of which have speech events corresponding to these.

Another significant contribution to the study of the ethnography of speaking in Caribbean communities is the work of Abrahams, most of which has been collected in Abrahams (1983). His theme is the 'man-of-words' in West Indian societies – the good talker who functions in traditional performances like toasts, speeches or recitations at wedding receptions, parties, funerals and the like, as well as the good arguer whose colloquial invective occurs at less solemn occasions. Abrahams also emphasises the links between Black American and Caribbean communities in the roles played by speakers who have mastered the intricate verbal dexterity associated with different kinds of performance. His work indeed represents the only substantial attempt at chronicling this area of Caribbean folk culture and at tracing its connections with Afro-American folklore traditions as a whole.

There is enormous room for further investigation of these and other aspects of the ethnography of speaking in the West Indies.

Attitudes

The only systematic studies of language attitudes in the English-speaking Caribbean are those of Rickford (1983), Winford (1976) and Haynes (1973). However, there are several other discussions of attitudes in a variety of communities which are based on observation and impressionistic judgement, rather than on direct systematic investigation.

Typically, the standard variety of English in these communities is associated with high status and prestige. It is also the yardstick by which other varieties are judged. Attitudes towards creole, on the other hand, have traditionally been negative, or at best ambiguous. This evaluation is referred to by Rickford (1983: 2) as the 'standard' attitude, in the sense that it is the orthodox one, and also because 'it assumes a positive orientation toward the standard variety alone'. The sociolinguistic literature on the Caribbean is replete with references to this 'standard' view; see, for example, De Camp (1971a); Rickford and Closs-Traugott (1985); Stewart (1962).

More systematic investigation of attitudes in creole continua, however, has revealed that the orthodox view is only part of the picture, and that there are also positive values associated with the use of creole. Reisman's (1970) study of Antiguan creole was one of the first to point out the duality of attitudes which pervades Caribbean communities. While overt recognition is withheld from Creole, and English appears dominant in terms of social prestige, Creole culture and language are characterised by 'a hidden, underlying set of values and cultural patterns'.

Haynes' investigation of Barbados and Guyana (1973) reveals a positive evaluation of creole also. These positive evaluations of creole are confirmed in Winford's (1976) study of Trinidadian attutides and Rickford's (1983) study of Guyanese attitudes, both of which employ more established techniques of attitude measurement.

Both reveal a tension between 'public' or 'standard' attitudes which extol English while denigrating Creole, and more 'private' attitudes which bear testimony to a sense of pride and joy in Creole. This tension continues to be a defining characteristic of Caribbean creole communities, but is slowly being resolved – more so in some societies than in others – in favour of a more tolerant view of creole and its place in Caribbean cultures. This is especially true of public, official attitudes toward creole in societies such as Belize, Jamaica and Trinidad.[4]

The changes in attitudes have been due to several factors, not the least being the attainment of political independence by most Caribbean states within the last 30 years, and the growing sense of nationalism that this has engendered. Adjustments in the social structure of the communities, and in the avenues to social advancement, particularly among educated sectors of Caribbean populations, have also contributed to the growing acceptability of Creole. This has been further aided by the emergence of recognised literary figures who use the vernacular in their work. Rickford and Closs-Traugott (1985) point out that 'more and more writers have been using pidgins and creoles . . . as a vehicle for the presentation of the cultures and rich communities in which these languages flourish, often as the voice of reality, truth and genuineness in a world otherwise largely destructive (the colonial world) or corrupt (the go-getting, often fraudulent world of post-colonial governments)'.[5]

Finally, of course, the growing status of Caribbean creoles has been reinforced by the emergence of a body of scholarship which treats these languages as worthy of study in their own right. According to Carrington (1979) this continuing re-evaluation of creole has resulted in:

1. Lowering of self-consciousness about the use of Creole.
2. Expansion of the cultural domains in which the creole is acceptable.
3. Reduction in the tendency to make automatic class membership judgements based on a speaker's use of Creole.
4. Rapid spread into the youth culture of all societal classes of the creole as the common bond of the sub-culture. (1979: 10)

Instrumentalisation

This reappraisal of the place of Creole in the culture of Caribbean nations is also having a significant impact on both popular and official views on the possible instrumentalisation of Caribbean vernaculars. There is already a substantial literature on language policy and language planning in West Indian communities, and, although, as usual, official reaction and implementation lag far behind the recommendations of scholars, the academic research of the last two decades has finally begun to influence policy making in several communities, particularly in the area of education (see Carrington, 1976, 1982; and Craig 1976, 1977, 1980; and the bibliographies therein).

More recently, researchers have begun to see the language problems of Caribbean schools as only a part of the language problems of the societies at large. Devonish (1986) adopts a radical position on the question of language reform:

> It seems, therefore, that a reform in language education policy cannot take place outside of a more general reform in the roles and functions of the various languages used within the society as a whole. (1986: 119).

Devonish's work on this question of language reform represents an important contribution to the literature on language planning in general, and on language policy in the Caribbean in particular. His (1978) thesis is an attempt to select a variety of Guyanese creole which might be codified and assigned special status, to function as a standard language. Such a variety would consist of features shared by both urban and rural varieties of creole, which show the widest co-occurrence distribution across the range of the Guyanese continuum. His contribution to the present volume is a condensed discussion of the principles which he applies to the selection of the variant features which should constitute this standard variety. It provides a thought-provoking basis on which the task of standardisation might proceed in creole continua generally, as well as in other situations where the vernacular consists of a range of overlapping varieties. In other publications (1983, 1986), Devonish has endeavoured to broaden the scope of his discussion to examine problems of status planning (code selection, assignment of new functions), corpus planning (codification, elaboration), and the implementation of new policy, as all of these relate to creole vernaculars in the Caribbean as a whole.

Conclusion

The language situations of the Caribbean have provided an extremely rich source of data for the investigtion of language from a variety of different perspectives. Since they exemplify so well the mutual interaction of social context and language use, they have offered particularly fruitful grounds of research in every area of sociolinguistic investigation. The data gathered from creole situations have forced researchers to rethink and reformulate the principles of linguistic theory and methodology itself (see, for example, Bickerton 1973a, 1973b; Labov 1972, 1980; Rickford 1980; Winford 1984, 1988). The study of such situations demands some grasp of social history, and familiarity with social systems and relationships. The study of Caribbean languages cannot be divorced from questions of social structure, politics, education and national identity. Finally, such situations offer a unique opportunity for the interaction between theory and practice, a link between the goals of linguistics on the one hand, and practical concerns such as literacy, language planning, language development and social change, on the other.

And yet the surface has barely been scratched. We are still a long way from a taxonomy of sociolinguistic situations in the Caribbean. Many communities are still untouched, most under-researched. After several decades of intense activity in the field, we can still assert with Hymes (1980: 390) that 'the inescapable embedding of pidgin and creole languages in social history remains a theme to be argued for, a topic to be rediscovered'.

NOTES

1. I use the term 'vernacular' here in the sense intended by Labov (1972), to refer to the most natural and spontaneous form of speech produced by members of a community in everyday interaction.
2. There are also several Amerindian languages in use in Guyana, but they are confined to small isolated tribes in the jungle interior of the country. Hindi/ Bhojpuri is also used to some extent among East Indians, but most if not all use Creole English as their everyday vernacular.
3. There is also some degree of ethnic diversity in islands such as St Vincent and St Lucia (East Indian and African) and Dominica (African and 'Caribs'). As

far as I know there are no studies of the relationship between language and ethnicity in these communities.
4. Moves towards standardisation of non-English creoles are well on their way in communities such as Aruba and Haiti and even in St Lucia. On the whole, though, the English-speaking Caribbean still lags far behind in this respect.
5. For further discussion of the use of Creole in Caribbean literature, see Rickford and Closs-Traugott (1985), and references there.

REFERENCES

Abrahams, Roger D. 1983. *The Man-of-Words in the West Indies: Performance and the emergence of Creole Culture.* Baltimore: The John Hopkins University Press.

Akers, Glenn A. 1981. *Phonological Variation in the Jamaican Continuum.* Ann Arbor: Karoma.

Alleyne, Mervyn C. 1980. *Comparative Afro-American.* Ann Arbor: Karoma.

Allsopp, Richard A. 1971a. Some problems in the lexicography of Caribbean English. *Caribbean Quarterly* 17 (12): 10–24.

1971b. What dictionary should West Indians use? *The Journal of Commonwealth Literature* 6: 12.

1972. The problem of acceptability in Caribbean creolized English. Paper presented at the UWI/UNESCO Conference on Creole Languages and Educational Development, The University of the West Indies, Cave Hill, Barbados.

1978. Washing up our wares: towards a dictionary of our use of English. In Rickford, J. (ed.) *A Festival of Guyanese Words.* University of Guyana, Georgetown.

Bailey, Charles-James. 1973. *Variation and Linguistic Theory.* Arlington: Center for Applied Linguistics.

Bailey, R. W. and Robinson, J. (eds.) 1973. *Varieties of Present-Day English.* New York: MacMillan.

Bickerton, Derek. 1973a. The structure of polylectal grammars. In Shuy, R.W. (ed.) *Report of the 23rd Annual Round Table Meeting on Linguistics and Language Studies* (Monograph Series on Language and Linguistics, No.25). Washington DC: Georgetown University Press, pp. 17–42.

1973b. On the nature of a creole continuum. *Language* 49: 640–69.

1975. *Dynamics of a Creole System.* Cambridge: Cambridge University Press.

Carrington, Lawrence D. 1976 Determining Language Education Policy in Caribbean Sociolinguistic Complexes. *International Journal of the Sociology of Language* 8: 27–44.

1979. Linguistic Conflict in Caribbean Education. Paper presented at the International Congress of the Psychology of the Child, Paris.

1982. Rational language policy decisions for the Creole-speaking Caribbean States. Faculty of Education, The University of The West Indies, St Augustine, Trinidad.

(ed.). 1983. Studies in Caribbean language. Society for Caribbean Linguistics, The University of the West Indies, St Augustine, Trinidad.

Chambers, J. K. and Trudgill, P. 1980. *Dialectology*. London: Cambridge University Press.

Christie, Pauline. 1969. A Sociolinguistic Study of Some Dominican Creole Speakers. Unpublished DPhil thesis, University of York.

Cooper, Vincent. 1979. Basilectal Creole, Decreolization and Autonomous Language in St Kitts-Nevis. Unpublished PhD thesis, Princeton University.

Craig, Dennis R. 1976. Bidialectal education: Creole and Standard in the West Indies. *International Journal of the Sociology of Language* 8: 93–136.

1977. Creole languages and primary education. In Valdman A. (ed.), *Pidgin and Creole Linguistics*. Bloomington: Indiana University Press, pp. 313–32.

1980. Models for educational policy in Creole-speaking Communities. In Valdman and Highfield (eds.) 1980, pp. 245–65.

1982. Toward a description of Caribbean English. In Kachru, Braj (ed.), *The Other Tongue: English Across Cultures*. Urbana: University of Illinois Press, pp. 198–209.

De Camp, David. 1971a. Introduction: The Study of Pidgin and Creole Languages. In Hymes (ed.), pp. 13–39.

1971b. Toward a Generative Analysis of a Post-creole continuum. In Hymes (ed.) 1971, pp. 349–70.

Devonish, Hubert. 1978. The Selection and Codification of a Widely Understood and Publicly Useable Language Variety in Guyana, to be used as a vehicle of National Development. Unpublished DPhil thesis, University of York.

1983. Toward the establishment of an Institute for Creole language standardization and development in the Caribbean. In Carrington (ed.) 1983, pp. 300–26.

1986. *Language and Liberation: Creole Language Politics in the Caribbean*. London: Karia Press.

Dillard, J. L. 1973. Standard Average Foreign in Puerto Rico. In Bailey and Robinson (eds.) 1973, pp. 77–99.

Edwards, Walter. 1975. Sociolinguistic Behaviour in Rural and Urban Circumstances in Guyana. Unpublished DPhil thesis, University of York.

1983. Code Selection and Code Switching in Guyana. *Language in Society* 12 (3): 295–311.

1984. Socializing the continuum: Guyanese sociolinguistic culture as social networks. Paper read at the March 1984 Meeting of the International Linguistics Association (ILA).

1985. Intra-style shifting and linguistic variation in Guyanese speech. *Anthropological Linguistics* Spring 1985.

1986. Morpho-syntactic acculturation at the rural urban interface in Guyana. Paper presented at the Sixth Biennial Conference of the Society for Caribbean Linguistics, the University of the West Indies, St Augustine, Trinidad.

Escure, Genevieve. 1982. Contrasive patterns of intra-group and inter-group Interaction in the Creole continuum of Belize. *Language and society* 11 (2): 239–64.

1983. The use of Creole as interlanguage by the Black Caribs of Belize. In Ingemann, Frances (ed.), *1982 Mid-American Linguistic Conference Papers*. University of Kansas, Lawrence, pp. 217–82.

Gibson, Kean. 1982. Tense and Aspect in Guyanese Creole. Unpublished DPhil thesis, University of York.

Haynes, Lillith. 1973. Language in Barbados and Guyana: Attitudes, Behaviours and Comparisons. Unpublished PhD thesis, Stanford University.

Hymes, Dell. (ed.), 1971. *Pidginization and Creolization of Languages*. Cambridge: Cambridge University Press.

1980. Commentary. In Valdman and Highfield (eds.) 1980, pp. 389–423.

Labov, William. 1966. *The Social Stratification of English in New York City*. Washington DC: Center for Applied Linguistics.

1971. The notion of 'system' in Creole languages. In Hymes (ed.) 1971.

1972. *Sociolinguistic Patterns*. Philadelphia: University of Pennsylvania Press.

1980. Is there a Creole speech community? In Valdman and Highfield (eds.) 1980, pp. 369–88.

Lawton, David. 1971. The question of creolization in Puerto Rican Spanish. In Hymes (ed.) 1971. pp. 193–6.

Le Page, R. B. 1978. Projection, Focussing, Diffusion, or, Steps Toward a Sociolinguistic Theory of Language, illustrated from the Sociolinguistic Survey of Multilingual Communities, Stage 1: Cayo District Belize and II: St Lucia. *Society for Caribbean Linguistics Occasional Paper 9*. The University of the West Indies, St Augustine, Trinidad. Reprinted in *York Papers in Linguistics* 9 (1980).

Le Page, R. B., Christie, P., Jurdant, B., Weeks, A., and Tabouret-Keller, A., 1974. Further report on the Sociolinguistic Survey of Multilingual Communities: Survey of Cayo District, British Honduras. *Language in Society* 3: 1–32.

Le Page, R. B. and Tabouret-Keller, Andrée. 1985. *Acts Of Identity: Creole-Based Approaches to Language and Ethnicity*. London: Cambridge University Press.

McCroskey, James, C., Fayer, Joan and Richmond, Virginia. 1985. Don't speak to me in English: communication apprehension in Puerto Rico. *Communication Quarterly* 33(3): 185–92.

Milroy, Lesley. 1980. *Language and Social Networks*. Oxford: Basil Blackwell.

Minderhout, David. 1977. Language variation in Tobagonian English. *Anthropological Linguistics* 19: 167–79.

Nash, Rose. 1982. Pringlish – still more language contact in Puerto Rico. In Kachru, Braj (ed.), *The Other Tongue: English Across Cultures*. Urbana: University of Illinois Press.

Reisman, Karl. 1970. Cultural and linguistic ambiguity in a West Indian village. In Whitten, Norman E. and Szwed, John F. (eds.), *Afro-American Anthropology*. New York: The Free Press, pp. 129–44.

Rickford, John R. 1979. Variation in a creole continuum: quantitative and implicational approaches. Unpublished PhD thesis, University of Pennsylvania.

1983. Standard and non-standard language attitudes in a creole continuum. *Society for Caribbean Linguistics Occasional Paper* No.16. The University of the West Indies St Augustine, Trinidad.

1987. The haves and have-nots: sociolinguistic surveys and the assessment of speaker competence. *Language in Society* 16 (2): 149–78.

Rickford, John R. and Closs-Traugott, Elizabeth. 1985. Symbol of powerlessness and degeneracy, or symbol of solidarity and truth? Paradoxical attitudes toward pidgins and creoles. In Greenbaum, S. (ed.), *The English Language Today*. Oxford: Pergamon Press, pp. 252–61.

Roy, John D. 1984. An Investigation of the Processes of Language Variation and Change in a Speech Community in Barbados. Unpublished PhD thesis, Columbia University.

Schumann, John H. 1978. The relationship of pidginization, creolization and decreolization to second language acquisition. *Language Learning* 28: 367–79.

Stewart, William A. 1962. Creole languages in the Caribbean. In Frank A. Rice (ed.), *Study of the Role of Second Languages in Asia, Africa and Latin America*. Washington DC: Center for Applied Linguistics, pp. 34–53.

Strevens, Peter. 1982. The localized forms of English. In Kachru, Braj (ed.), *The Other Tongue: English across Cultures*. Urbana: University of Illinois Press, pp. 23–30.

Valdman, A. and Highfield, A. (eds.). 1980. *Theoretical Orientations in Creole Studies*. New York: Academic Press.

Williams, Jeff. 1985. Preliminaries to the study of the dialects of White West Indian English. *Nieuwe West Indische Gids* 59: 27–44.

1986. White West Indian English: A Comparative socio-historical Study. Unpublished PhD thesis, University of Texas, Austin.

Winford, Donald. 1972. A sociolinguistic description of two communities in Trinidad. Unpublished DPhil, thesis, University of York.

1976. Teacher Attitudes Toward Language Varieties in a Creole Community. *International Journal of the Sociology of Language* 8: 45–75.

1979. Phonological Variation and Change in Trinidadian English – the evolution of the vowel system. *Society for Caribbean Linguistics Occasional Paper No.12*. The University of the West Indies, St Augustine, Trinidad.

1980. The creole situation in the context of sociolinguistic studies. In Day, R. (ed.), *Issues in English Creoles – Proceedings of the 1975 Hawaii Conference*. Heidelberg: Gross, pp. 51–76.

1984. The Linguistic Variable and Syntactic Variation in Creole Continua. *Lingua* 62: 267–88.

1985. The Concept of 'Diglossia' in Caribbean Creole Situations. *Language in society* 14: 345–56.

1988. The creole continuum and the notion of the community as locus of language. In Rickford, J. R. (ed.), *Sociolinguistics and Pidgin-Creole Studies*. *International Journal of the Sociology of Language* 71(3): 1988.

Young, Colville. 1973. Belize Creole: A Study of the Creolized English Spoken in the City of Belize, in its Cultural and Social Setting. Unpublished PhD thesis, University of York.

38

Standardisation in a Creole continuum situation: the Guyana case

HUBERT DEVONISH

Introduction

Descriptions of the language situation in Guyana have tended to treat it as being made up of two maximally distinct language varieties, standard Guyanese English, on one hand, and Guyanese Creole, on the other, linked by a series of intermediate varieties (Allsopp 1958; Bickerton 1975). This kind of description, while capturing a particular aspect of the language situation, misses others. One such is the diglossic nature of the Guyana language situation. Varieties approximating to standard Guyanese English tend to be employed in the more public and formal situations of interaction. This contrasts with the more private and informal situations in which varieties approximating to Guyanese Creole tend to be employed. Another aspect not captured by an analysis which treats the Guyana situation as one involving a Creole-to-English continuum, is that speakers normally control more than one language variety. Such persons code-switch between the language varieties within their linguistic repertoires, depending on the social factors present within the speech event and the social functions associated with each of these varieties.

Standard Guyanese English operates as the sole official language of the country. What this means is that those speakers who do not have this variety within their repertoires or whose competence in the variety is limited, are effectively excluded from all forms of official communication. In these circumstances, it is clear that an alternative official language policy is necessary if one is to avoid the continued exclusion of non-English speakers from official communication. This would have to involve the granting of official status to some language variety or varieties other than English.

The question arises as to which non-English language variety or varieties should be selected to function as official language. Two quite different options are available. Firstly, one could select a particular variety along

585

the continuum to perform the role of official language. This could be either the variety of Guyanese Creole maximally different from English, or an intermediate variety along the continuum. Edwards (1975), in a detailed study of Creole language use in Guyana, finds that the urban–rural factor is the most significant factor affecting language use in the society. The rural population tends to speak basilectal or 'deep' varieties of Creole; on the other hand, the urban population mainly use mesolectal or intermediate varieties. Guyana is a country with a primarily rural population, with 74 per cent of its people residing outside of the major towns. One could, based on the sheer numerical dominance of the rural population, propose the selection of a basilectal variety of Guyanese Creole as an official language. This would, however, have the effect of ignoring the language behaviour of the urban population. Although making up only a minority of the total population, the people of the urban areas in Guyana, like in many other societies, have prestige and influence far exceeding their numerical strength. In these circumstances, therefore, selection of a single variety along the continuum, be it basilectal or mesolectal, would serve to exclude an important section of the population.

What the option discussed above fails to take into account is the fact that speakers within the speech community do not possess linguistic repertoires made up of a single variety. Rather, the linguistic repertoire of an individual speaker consists of a span of varieties along the Creole-to-English continuum. What this suggests is that there is some overlap between the repertoires of speakers who might be designated 'basilectal' and those who could be described as 'mesolectal' speakers. The second option and the one advocated in this study involves exploiting this overlap in the linguistic repertoires of these two broad types of speakers. Such an overlap would provide the basis for the identification and description of a variety of Guyanese Creole which would have features familiar to the widest cross section of the Guyanese population possible. It is such a variety which could, with the minimum inconvenience to the speech community as a whole, be made to function as an official language in Guyana.

Co-occurence rules and language standardisation in Guyana

A linguistic variable can be conceived of as a set of different ways of saying the same thing (Labov: 1972:94) Or, it can be thought of as simply a category which can have different manifestations. The variable is made up of variants, that is, features which can alternate within the variable. A language variety can be said to be made up of a series of mutually co-occurring variants. Within the variables which coexist in the same utterance, there is a selection in each case of the variant associated with the particular language variety. Let us examine what happens in a situation where two distinct language varieties coexist without any intermediate varieties developing in-between. In such a situation, linguistic variants associated with a particular language variety co-occur exclusively with each other and never with variants associated with the other language variety. Where two varieties are part of the linguistic repertoire of a single speaker, however, this kind of mutual exclusiveness between the variants associated with each of them becomes impossible. When several speakers within a speech community, even though only a tiny minority, have command of two distinct language varieties, the conditions are ripe for the development of linguistic convergence. It is this which we argue has given rise to the Creole-to-English continuum in the Guyana language situation.

The major way in which this convergence develops involves variants associated with one language variety, Guyanese Creole, being able to co-occur with variants identified with the other variety, standard Guyanese English. If this mixing of variants were free and ungoverned by co-occurrence rules, what would exist in Guyana would be a single language variety made up of variants which were historically of either English or Creole origin. There would be no basis, synchronically, for positing the existence of separate language varieties. Variation would exist purely at the level of the linguistic variable, with a speaker able to select any variant, irrespective of the selections made for other variables within the utterance. This situation, however, does not exist in Guyana. Even though variants associated with English and with Creole are allowed to co-occur, such co-occurrence is rule governed. A variant of one variable will be allowed to co-occur with certain variants of coexisting variables, but will be blocked from co-occuring with others. Co-occurrence rules serve the function of allowing for convergence between the two language varieties whilst preventing them from fusing into one single variety.

It might be noticed in the last paragraph that it was stated that we were looking at 'the major way in which convergence develops'. There is, of course, another aspect of convergence. This involves the development, among intermediate varieties, of structures and forms peculiar to themselves and in no way directly related to those found in the two extreme varieties. It is being suggested here, however, that this is a secondary feature of the development of linguistic convergence in a situation such as that existing in Guyana.

The question arises as to what the syntactic units are within which co-occurrence rules apply. As we shall see, such rules seem to operate amongst variables within individual constituents of the sentence such as the Noun Phrase (NP) and Verb Phrase (VP). In addition, certain co-occurrence rules operate from variables in one constituent across to variables in another. However, there is no evidence in the Guyana Creole-to-English continuum situation of co-occurrence rules operating from one sentence across to the the other. The sentence appears to be the largest syntactic unit over which co-occurrence rules can operate. Beyond the boundary of a particular sentence, the speaker is free to select variants based on his or her perception of their social significance, constrained only by the co-occurrence rules involving variants within the new sentence.

The Creole-to-English continuum in Guyana is made up of a series of language varieties. Within the terms of our approach, each such variety could be regarded as being made up of a cluster of linguistic variants which can co-occur within the sentence or within one of its constituents. We can also look at the variation from the point of view of the linguistic variable and its individual variants. One variant of a variable may be employed in several varieties along the continuum. Another may be used in fewer such varieties and a third may appear in only one. The first would be the one with the widest powers of co-occurrence and, therefore, would have the ability to appear in the widest range of language varieties along the continuum. It is this variant of the particular variable which, as a result, would be the one most familiar to the widest cross-section of speakers within the community. This, in turn, would make it the most suitable variant of the variable for use in a standardised variety of Guyanese Creole.

The proposal here is to identify the linguistic variables existing within the sentence and its constituents. As a further step, the particular variants of each variable are identified. Next, their powers of co-occurrence with variants of other variables within the sentence is arrived at. With this information now available, it is possible to find out which variant has the widest powers of co-occurrence, and to select it as the variant to be employed in a standardised variety of Guyanese Creole.

Data and methodology

The data consists of transcriptions of tape-recordings of conversations. The material was taped and transcribed by Walter Edwards as part of his own research work (Edwards 1975). He kindly made his material available to me.

In each of Edwards' interviews, each informant (all were male) was asked to talk about his job or occupation, the games he played as a child, tell any traditional Nansi story which he remembers, and give an account of an experience of being in danger of death. The last is intended to put the informant in a state of mind where he pays minimal attention to the language structures being produced. The aim was to try to get the informant to produce uninhibited speech.

As can be seen from the table below, the sample which I select from the body of Edwards' data is evenly balanced in terms of factors such as age, ethnic origin, and urban vs. rural background. The fact that the informants are all male is the major problem with the data.

Table 38.1. *(Total informants = 47)*

	Urban	Rural
Indians		
21–30	5	6
45+	7	6
Africans		
21–30	6	5
45+	6	6

Another aspect of the data which is significant is the socioeconomic background of the informants. The bulk of Edwards' sample was made up of people who could be classified either as members of the working class or as small farmers. There was, however, a small number of informants who came from other social backgrounds. This suited my own purpose well since co-occurrence rules are a feature of the language behaviour of the entire speech community and not simply of the most disadvantaged sectors. Since the sample is weighted heavily in favour of the social groups which stand to benefit the most from Creole language standardisation, the inclusion of data from other social groups adds some needed variety.

The task was to identify (i) the linguistic variables within the data, (ii) the variants of these variables, and (iii) the relative powers of co-occurrence of the variants making up a particular linguistic variable. There was, however, a problem with regard to (iii) which the extensive nature of the data (over 500 pages of transcription) reduced but did not solve. Even in such a large body of data, all the possible combinations of variants of different variables did not appear. Absence of a particular combination from the data could mean either simply an accidental gap in the material or the existence of a co-occurrence restriction rule. I used my intuition as a native speaker of the language varieties involved to distinguish between these possibilities.

Analysis and selection

The exercise of standardising Guyanese Creole is, by definition, a very complex one. What we will attempt to do here is simply demonstrate, using a small number of examples, the process by which the relative powers of co-occurrence among competing variants can be determined. This information is then used as a basis for selecting standard Guyanese Creole variants for the variables concerned.

The continuative aspect variable in the Guyanese Creole-to-English continuum has the variants presented below. Examples of sentences in which they occur are also given.

Variant 1: *a*

(1)   dem *a* pich marbl   'they are (in the state of) throwing marbles'

Variant 2: *-in*

(2)   hii beg*in*   'he is (in the state of) begging'

The variant *-in* occurs with a wider range of variants from other variables within the VP than does *a*. We will look at a few of the more important cases which point to the difference in co-occurrence powers between these two variants.

Let us first examine the ability of variants of the continuative aspect variable to co-occur with variants of the past tense variable. This variable has variants *woz*, *did* and *bin*. The continuative aspect variant *a* can only occur with the past tense variant *bin*, whereas *-in* can co-occur with all three past tense variants, as demonstrated below.

(3)   awii *bin a* plee   'we were playing'
(4)   *awii/wii *did a* plee
(5)   *awii/wii *woz a* plee

But

(6)   hii *bin* duu*in* konstrokshon wok   'he was doing construction work'
(7)   a *did* wok*in*   'I was working'
(8)   di maan *woz* taak*in*   'the man was talking'

The superior powers of co-occurrence of *-in* over *a* were also shown when these variants were examined in relation to variants of a series of other variables within the VP. One such variable is the negative, consisting of variants *na*, *-nat*, *-nt* and *een*. This is illustrated by the following examples.

(9)   yu *na a* ge di ookroo fortilaiza   'One is not getting fertilizer for ochroes'
(10)   *yu *nat a* ge di ookroo fortilaiza
(11)   *yu *a nt* ge di ookroo fortilaiza
(12)   *yu *een a* ge di ookroo fortilaiza

But

(13)   yu *na* get*in* am   'you are not getin it'
(14)   dee ar *nat* yuuz*in* it   'they are not using it'
(15)   it *eent* distorb*in* os   'it is not disturbing us'

This is the kind of evidence which is available to support the assertion that *-in* has much wider powers of co-occurrence than does *a*. Against this background, therefore, *-in* would be selected as the variant of the continuative aspect variable to be employed in the standardised variety of Guyanese Creole.

The past tense marker is the other variable within the VP which we will examine.

Variant 1: *bin*
(16)   dee *bin* gyaafin   'they were chatting'

Variant 2: *did*
(17)   a *did* tel yu   'I had told you'

Variant 3: *woz*
(18)   it *woz* tof   'it was tough'

In relation to the variants of the continuative aspect variable already discussed, let us examine the relative powers of co-occurrence of the variants of the past tense variable. The variants *woz* and *did* show themselves capable of co-occurring only with *-in*, whereas *bin* co-occurs with both *a* and *-in*.

(19)   awii *bin a* plee   'we were playing'
(20)   a puulis *bin* paas*in*   'a policeman was passing'

But

(21)   ai *did* go*in*   'I was going'
(22)   *ai *did a* go

And

(23)   ai *woz* luk*in* owt   'I was looking out'
(24)   *ai *woz a* luk owt

In relation to the variants of the negative variable, *bin* again turns out to have superior powers of co-occurrence when compared with the competing variants within the past tense variable. The past tense variant *bin* is the only one able to co-occur with all four negative variants. For example, no past tense variant other than *bin* can co-occur with the negative variant *een*, as can be seen in the examples below.

(25)   wii *een bin* swimin   'we have not been swimming'

But

(26)   *wii *een did* swimin

And

(27)   *wii *een woz* swimin

Against the background of this kind of evidence, the only choice of variant of the past tense variables is *bin*.

What we have done, up to now, is to briefly look at the kinds of co-occurrence rules which exist among grammatical variables within the VP. Since the VP lies at the core of any sentence, it seems logical to establish co-occurrence rules within the VP first. The variants of these variables within the VP can, in turn, be regarded as providing an environment within which co-occurrence rules of variants elsewhere in the sentence could operate.

The first person plural pronoun variable is the non-VP variable which we will briefly examine in this discussion. The variants of this variable are *awii* and *wii*.

Variant 1: *awii*
(28)   *awii* na a get stoon marbl   'we are not getting stone marbles'

Variant 2: *wii*
(29)   *wii* na kuulii   'we are not East Indians'

Let us first explore the co-occurrence powers of these two variants in the environment of variants of the continuative aspect variable. In relation to this variable, *wii* has equal powers of co-occurrence with *awii* in the environment of the variants *a* and *-in*.

(30)   *awii a* kech maan   'we are catching men'
(31)   *awii* fish*in*   'we are fishing'

And

(32)   *wii a* tell am   'we are telling him'
(33)   *wii* wash*in* kyaar   'we are washing cars'

What makes a difference, however, is the behaviour of these personal pronoun variants in the environment of the past tense variable variants *bin*, *did* and *woz*. The variant *wii* emerges as having wider powers of co-occurrence, being able to co-occur with *woz* where *awii* is blocked.

(34)   *awii bin* wan said   'we were on the sidelines'
(35)   *awii did*n get a chaans   'we did not get a chance'
(36)   **awii woz* pleein it

But

(37)   *wii bin* get di monii   'we had gotten the money'
(38)   *wii did* mek wud baal   'we had made wooden balls'
(39)   *wii woz* pleein it   'we were playing it'

An examination of the co-occurrence possibilities of *wii* and *awii* with variants of a wide range of other variables within the sentence confirms the impression that *wii* has superior powers of co-occurrence. The variant *wii* is the one which would be selected as the standard form of the first person plural pronoun variable.

The question might very well arise in the mind of the reader as to whether the language variety produced by the procedures employed here would not be artificial. In fact, however, what is being done is to select a variety which naturally occurs within the Creole-to-English continuum from a range of other naturally occurring varieties. In order to demonstrate this, we will present a diagram which will show the co-occurrences possible among the variants of the three variables discussed in this paper. The line connecting one variant of a variable with a variant of another variable represents the co-occurrence relationships within a single language variety. The standard variant selected for each variable is presented in capital letters, and the lines connecting such variants are marked with the symbol >.

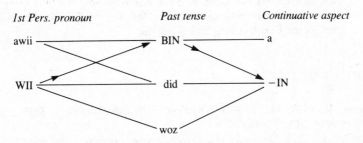

The combination of the selected variants *wii*, *bin* and *-in* is, as can be seen from the diagram, one of seven possible combinations of variants of the variables involved. Each of these combinations could be said to constitute a language variety within the terms of our approach. The combination of selected variants, therefore, only constitutes a language variety which already exists within the speech community, and which is being given a special status and set of functions.

Conclusion

In a much longer and detailed work (Devonish, 1978), the principles outlined in this paper were applied to the data. A wide range of variables were examined, both within the VP and within the NP, and co-occurrence powers were identified for each variant of the variable under study. Based on this information, standard variants were selected for each of these variables, the variant with the widest powers of co-occurrence being the one normally selected. What follows is a brief text using the variants thus selected, accompanied by an English translation.

Wii Langgwij

Wii Kriiyoliiz langgwij mos ton nashanal langgwij. Wa di ardinerii maan mos trai fo larn Ingglish taak fo? Aftaraal, di kontrii, di govament, di aafisiz-dem, di skuulz-dem, dong to di reejoo steeshon an aal, iz di piipl oon. Le dem yuuz langgwij wa di piipl kyan andastaan. Wan-wan piipl se how Kriiyoliiz taak een prapa langgwij an how it gon kyarii wii bak, bak. Bot wii gon shoo dem. Suun, aal di nyuuzpeepa gon de in wii langgwij, tiicha gon tiich in wii langgwij, an gon bii ploor Kriiyoliiz pon di reejo. Kriiyolliz taim komin.

Our Language

Our Creolese language must become the national language. Why should the ordinary need to learn English? The country, the government, the offices, the schools and even the radio station all belong to the people. Let them all use the language which the people can understand. A few people say that Creolese is not a proper language and that it would carry the country backwards. We, however, are going to show them. Soon, all the newspapers are going to be in our language, teachers are going to teach in our language and only Creolese will be used on the radio. The day of the Creolese language is coming.

REFERENCES

Allsopp, R. 1958. The English language in British Guiana. *English Language Teaching* 12(2): 59–66.

Bickerton, D. 1975. *Dynamics of a Creole System*. London: Cambridge University Press.

Devonish, H. 1978. The Selection and Codification of a Widely Understood and Publicly Useable Variety in Guyana, to be Used as a Vehicle of National Development. Unpublished DPhil thesis, University of York.

Edwards, W. 1975. Sociolinguistic Behaviour in Rural and Urban Circumstances in Guyana. Unpublished DPhil thesis, University of York.

Labov, W. 1972. *Language in the Inner City*. Philadelphia: University of Pennsylvania Press.

39

Gender roles and linguistic variation in the Belizean Creole community

GENEVIEVE ESCURE

Previous studies of the sex variable

Few linguistic studies have dealt systematically with sex differentiation in language use, and none in the context of Creole societies, even though the latter provide ideal terrain for this type of research because of recent changes in gender roles. The following claims have been made in respect to men and women's use of language, and their roles in the diffusion of linguistic change.[1]

(1) Women are more likely to use standard or prestige forms, and to upgrade their speech patterns in formal situations than men of the same age, social class and education level. This appears to hold true for all social classes, and is interpreted as a strategy to compensate for the general subordination to which women are subjected in social structures (see, however, Milroy, this volume).

(2) Men's speech patterns are more directly related to their socioeconomic status. Nonstandard speech has positive connotations of masculinity and signals male solidarity, mostly for working classes, but for others as well. Thus, in formal situations working class men do not deviate from low status variants as much as women do. But lower middle class men are so conscious of the social value of standard speech that they often hypercorrect, a sign of linguistic insecurity, according to Labov (1972).

(3) Women are innovators in linguistic change, but only in the direction of standard speech, whereas men lead in the use of new vernacular forms.

(4) Men speak more than women, and often interrupt women.

These claims will be tested in the context of the Creole continuum spoken in Belize, Central America, with detailed reference to the copular morphosyntactic variable.

The Creole continuum and the sex variable

In the creole context, a wide range of linguistic variability derives from the co-occurrence of at least two distinct systems, one standard and the other nonstandard. In Belize as in other Caribbean communities, the English-based Creole is the native vernacular widely used in ingroup communication. In addition, Belizean standard English is also present in the community as the official language heard on the radio, and the prescribed educational medium in schools.

It has been widely assumed that a movement towards the standard variety, and away from the vernacular (decreolisation) is occurring in West Indian linguistic communities.[2] If this is true, then the general claims outlined above would predict that women as promoters of prestige varieties, as stated in claim (3), spearhead this process by eliminating basilects from their repertoire, and would turn out to be primarily acrolectal speakers, whereas men would be mostly basilectal speakers because of the positive values they associate with the vernacular within the same social class and age group.

However, such claims are not supported by this study of the Belizean Creole community. Crucial evidence is derived from two observed aspects of language behaviour: first, the extensive repertoire available to both men and women, and second, the role played by women in maintaining the vernacular.

First, the repertoire of Creole speakers is being extended because of the increased accessibility of the standard which enables more speakers to control a broad range of varieties, without necessarily causing the loss of basilects (Mufwene, 1987). There is constant fluctuation between the Creole and the standard, with the significant presence of intermediate forms (Escure 1982, 1983). Linguistic multidirectionality is thus a function of the community as well as of the individual. The same speaker may control the whole linguistic spectrum (basilects, mesolects and acrolects), or at least a broad crosslectal section of it. Although the single-lect speaker is a theoretical possibility, repeated investigations of the Belizean community reveal that each individual has the ability to shift 'up' or 'down', adopting different varieties according to context. This is found to apply to both men and women, but especially to women.

Secondly, certain women appear to play an important role in the maintenance (or perhaps the revival) of the Creole vernacular; that is, the variety which has been traditionally stigmatised. This phenomenon will be analysed within the context of the Placencia fishing community which presents an interesting re-analysis of the social roles traditionally assigned to men and women, in part because of specific features of the local economic situation.[3]

Table 39.1. *Overall distribution of three copular variants in Placencia (Belize) (N = 2,995)*

be occurs 51.4% of the time		(1,541 tokens)
Ø	34.3%	(1,030)
de	14.1%	(424)

Lectal identification and the copular variable

The speech data used in this study were collected between 1979–85, and field methods are fully outlined in Escure (1982). The respondents cover a wide age spectrum, from 11 to 78 years, and include 14 women and 19 men. The data base consists of 37 speech samples recorded exclusively in spontaneous contexts, with the help of a local assistant, in the village of Placencia (Stann Creek District of Belize). The common occurrence of extensive individual repertoires, as discussed above, explains why in the corpus presented the number of lects (37) is greater than the number of speakers (33).[4]

In order to identify accurately the role of sex as a social variable in linguistic performance, a specific morphosyntactic feature (the copula and its variants) was selected as linguistic variable because it had previously been found to be representative of the variety intended by a Creole speaker. The copula has three subvariants spanning the continuum, and their distribution patterns mirror individual choices from among the available gradatum. Those three copular variants include (see appendix for data):

1) *de*, strictly basilectal, which functions as continuative aspect marker as well as locative verb,
2) a zero form (represented as Ø) in basilects and mesolects,
3) inflected forms of the English verb *be* which start appearing in mesolects.[5]

The corpus analyzed consists of 2,995 copular tokens which appear in the community at large in the proportions shown in table 39.1.

The figures in table 39.1 indicate that the community favours the English *be* variant, which might lead to the conclusion that vernacular forms (as represented by *de*) are not in active usage at the moment. This type of generalised data has no doubt been the basis for claims that the continuum is 'postcreole' or 'decreolised'. However, such claims are meaningless unless the lectal level is taken into account, since the relative proportions

Table 39.2. *Distribution of copular variants in 14 basilectal samples (N = 1,131), and 23 mesolectal samples (N = 1,864). Total number of copular tokens is N = 2,995.*

	de	*Ø*	*be*
Basilects	12.7% (381)	22.6% (678)	2.4% (72)
Mesolects	1.4% (43)	11.7% (352)	49.0% (1,469)

of the three morphemes differ according to the variety selected. The samples have therefore been separated for analysis into two major segments – namely, a set of 14 basilects and a set of 23 mesolects. The basilectal group represents the most vernacular forms found in the sample whereas the mesolectal group includes those varieties which represent a shift away from basilects, yet indicate avoidance of acrolectal behavior. Acrolects are rarely found in intragroup situations.

Table 39.2 shows that basilects can be identified through the complementary use of *de* and *Ø* (*be* hardly occurs), and mesolects through the complementary incidence of *Ø* and *be* (with the virtual absence of *de*). This patterning reflects decreasing use of creole features and concomitant increase in standard features when shifting up.

Sex and lectal separation

The role of the sex variable in linguistic differentiation is best identified in terms of the lectal repertoires displayed, respectively, by men and women, as represented in the distribution of copular variants in the two groups of lects.

Amount of speech and prestige variants without lectal separation

Comparing the distribution of a single linguistic feature in two gender groups, but *without* lectal separation yields interesting but misleading results, both in terms of the amount of speech produced by each sex group, and in terms of the actual distribution of variants. For example, both claim (4) 'men speak more than women', and claim (1) 'women are more likely to use standard forms' appear to be confirmed by table 39.3, which is a sex-sensitive version of table 39.1.

Table 39.3 confirms claim (4) because of the discrepancy in the amount of copular data produced respectively, by men (2,034 tokens), and women (961 tokens). The apparent conclusion is that men speak overall more than twice as much as women.[6]

Table 39.3. *Relative incidence of three copular variants in men and women's speech (total N = 2,995)*

	Women	Men
be	63.5% (611)	45.7% (930)
Ø	27.3% (263)	37.7% (767)
de	9.0% (87)	16.5% (337)
	(961)	(2,034)

Table 39.4. *Women's and men's average copular output*

	Basilects	(N of samples)	Mesolects	(N of samples)
Women	23.7	(8)	85.6	(9)
Men–	136.8	(6)	78	(14)

On the other hand, the stereotype of women as users of prestige forms is supported by the fact that they produce in their overall speech a greater incidence of the English variant *be*, and a lower incidence of the Creole marker *de*.

Amount of speech with lectal separation

Very different results emerge if basilects are separated from mesolects for both men and women: a comparison of men's and women's average copular output in each group of lects (see table 39.4) shows that the discrepancy is highly marked in basilects (women speak about six times less than men), but negligible in mesolects (in fact in such contexts, women speak more than men).

This difference in speech output depending on the context points again to the unreliability of claims based on one single speech style. The difference is all the more striking because more women (8) than men (6) are represented in the basilectal corpus, whereas the opposite applies in the mesolectal corpus, in which more men (14) than women (9) are represented. One reason for such discrepancies lies in part in the conversation patterns observed in the Belizean community: in informal, playful contexts (which typically yield basilects) involving two or three individuals, women are more likely to interrupt each other, with short, overlapping sentences, than men, who generally take longer turns (see below, note 3). On the other hand, mesolects are usually produced in more formal, serious

Table 39.5. *Lectal variations in the use of three copular variants in men's and women's speech (the same 3 women and 1 man are represented in both groups)*

	Basilects		Mesolects	
	Women = 8	Men = 6	Women = 9	Men = 14
be	10.5% (21)	5.5% (51)	76.5% (590)	80.5% (879)
Ø	54.2% (103)	61.1% (575)	20.7% (160)	17.5% (192)
de	34.7% (66)	33.4% (315)	2.7% (21)	2.0% (22)
Total N =	190	941	771	1,093

contexts, and at a slower tempo, and often occur in monologues, such as speeches at village council meetings, or discussions of topics affecting community life, whether past or present.

Use of prestige variants with lectal separation

Table 39.5, which takes into account both gender and style in showing the relative incidence of each of the three variants (*be*, Ø, and *de*) provides a more accurate insight than either tables 39.2 or 39.3 into the potential significance of the sex variable in matters of language use and, in particular the selective usage of prestige variants.

With lects separated, it is now clear that men and women broadly agree on the overall combination of the three copular variants in both groups of lects. It is no longer evident that women favour prestige variants (claim 1). In fact, they use slightly less of the morpheme *be* than men in mesolects, though somewhat more of it in basilects. Women also display a slightly higher incidence of the stigmatised variant *de* in basilects. In terms of lectal selection, men are indeed the ones who favour more prestigious forms (as represented in mesolects) since they perform at the mesolectal level more than twice as often as they produce basilects (14: 6). As to women's samples, they are equally divided between the two varieties (8: 9).

Individual repertoires and context

The extensive range of individual linguistic repertoires (especially women's) is well represented in the fact that three women and one young man perform competently at both levels in different contexts. The copular frequencies of those four speakers are shown in table 39.6, and reflect individual choices in the combinations of variants.

Table 39.6. *Use of copular variants by four polylectal speakers*

			Basilects			Mesolects		
Speaker	Age	Sex	*de*	Ø	*be*	*de*	Ø	*be*
J	15	M	.61	.37	.02	.17	.45	.38
D	55	F	.53	.34	.13	.13	.29	.59
S	52	F	.41	.45	.14	.00	.16	.84
A	15	F	.23	.74	.02	.02	.20	.78

A brief outline of the contexts in which those samples were recorded helps understand how linguisitic choices are effected by members of the community. The two younger speakers (J and A) yield quite distinct versions of both lects, although the contexts of their conversations were similar. Their basilects occurred in interactions with same-sex peers: J told two other boys (14 and 15) Anansi stories, and various horror stories, which elicited laughter and jeers. A gossiped with three other women (age 15 to 22) about boys and men, with assorted jokes, innuendoes, and giggling. J's basilect has a higher incidence of the Creole morpheme *de* than A's, which gives preference to the Ø variant. Similar selective frequencies occur in similar proportions in the other boys' and girls' samples.

Mesolects for both J and A occurred in natural conversations with adults (including the creole male fieldworker) and at least one other youth. The topics discussed were mostly serious or neutral (fishing, life in Belize, goals in life, emigration to the USA). Thus, in the same context type, the young woman shifts up to a high mesolect with a high 78 per cent incidence of *be*, whereas the young man merely moves to a low mesolect with an average 38 per cent of *be*, and still 17 per cent of the Creole variant *de*.

The two middle-aged women (D and S) appear to be primarily sensitive to their interlocutors' age groups, using generally mesolects with their peers, and basilects with younger members of the community. D's mesolect was produced in a conversation with neighbours on traditional forms of entertainment (dances, stories) that seem to be no longer appreciated by young people. But S's mesolect is closer to an acrolect in an informal report of a recent meeting to the vice-chairman of the village council who had just returned from a fishing trip. Both women use basilectal varieties when discussing community issues (job opportunities, economic situation of the village, marriage and women's roles in the village) with the 26-year-old fieldworker.

Such contextual information indicates that linguistic choices in the Creole community are in part determined by extralinguistic variables such as topic, age, status and occupational patterns. Clearly, the function of sex

Table 39.7. *Incidence of* de *and* be *in two groups of lects, with age/sex reference (N = number of speakers; n = number of tokens)*

Age group	*de* (Basilects)			*be* (Mesolects)		
	N	%	n	N	%	n
I (10–30)	M = 5	0.33	(298/896)	M = 4	0.55	(90/164)
	F = 6	0.28	(37/130)	F = 1	0.59	(29/449)
II (31–45)	M = 0			M = 6	0.86	(599/696)
	F = 0			F = 2	0.85	(159/186)
III (46–60)	M = 1	0.38	(17/45)	M = 2	0.81	(150/185)
	F = 2	0.48	(29/60)	F = 2	0.75	(186/249)
IV (61 up)	M = 0			M = 2	0.79	(38/48)
	F = 0			F = 4	0.72	(207/287)

in linguistic choice cannot be identified independently of the psychosocial features of the community, if gender is defined as the social interpretation of sex roles.

Sex and age-grading

The interaction of sex, age and occupation offers the most revealing clues to the use and development of language in the Placencia community.

Apparent time with its reference to crossgenerational differences appears to be a relatively accurate indicator of the directionality of change, although real time (longitudinal) studies are more reliable. The age-grading represented in table 39.7 suggests that mesolectal usage has a stable position in intra-community interactions for both men and women. Mesolects do not correspond merely to a temporary interlanguage in the acquisitional process, as claimed by those who view second dialect or second language acquisition as unidirectional; they seem, on the contrary, to have a sociopsychological value of their own which is distinct from that of the acrolect (indeed, no speaker produces a categorical percentage of *be*).

In contrast, among the four age groups represented in table 39.7, only two (I and III) use basilects, and the women in Group III, in the 46–60 age range, function differently than other men and women in the community.

Group IV

The oldest generation (both men and women) clearly avoids the vernacular and overtly values nonbasilectal varieties (which of course does not necessarily mean that they are not used in unobserved contexts). This generation is still attached to British traditions[7] and acceptance of ex-colonial values is aptly reflected in their predominant choice of the acrolectal variant.

Group III

This group displays great linguistic flexibility (as shown in table 39.6), which reflects their awareness of changing social and political patterns (Belize's independence was declared in 1981), and a reassessment of the local values reflected in the Creole vernacular. Women in this group are especially aware of the psychological erosion of Creole values, the result of colonisation, but also of the increasing prestige of American values, especially reflected in the mass emigration of Group II to the USA, or to Belize City. Group III women stand out in the village as the most active participants in its administration, contrary to younger women who prefer not to get involved. In fact, Placencia is a covert matriarchal society, in spite of the fact that status positions are officially occupied by men (chairman and vice chairman of the village council, school principal, policeman). The local fishing economy keeps the men away for extensive periods of time, and consequently wives are fully in charge of community affairs (rules of governance, fund-raising, correspondence with officials, etc.). They view their role as one of mediators between generations, maintaining cohesion in the community as well as in the home. Avoiding language polarisation in one single direction is a politically astute step towards keeping good relations with all members of the community. This may account for their shifting ability, and in particular their display of basilectal competence, which under appropriate circumstances matches the choices effected by the youngest generation (Labov 1972 and Trudgill 1972 also found that women often control a wider range of varieties than men).

Group II

The 31–45 generation has developed a more materialistic approach, and has turned its hopes away from the village and towards the values associated with the American way of life. English acrolects are perceived as a desirable replacement for the vernacular, as many plan to join spouses or siblings already living in the USA. The highest percentages of *be* are found among members of this group, men and women.

Group I

But the youngest generation, both men and women, seem satisfied with village life, and the positive value they associate to their Creole identity is reflected in their increasing use of basilects, even though they have had earlier and more extensive access to acrolects than any other age group. Rastafarian values have penetrated even as far as distant rural areas, and no doubt contributed to the reinforcement of local values.

Conclusion

Most of the findings emerging from this study suggest that there is no consistent difference between women's and men's speech patterns: women do not overwhelmingly use more prestige variants than men; men do not especially favour vernacular forms; men and women do not systematically differ in the quantity of speech they produce. Such results are indeed interesting in that they reflect a society in which gender roles are less polarised than, say, in a white middle class context. Indeed, the Placencia community is not divided along class lines, although status differences do exist. This explains why linguistic hypercorrection (typically associated with the lower middle class; see, for example, Labov 1972) is not found in the Belizean fishing community under investigation. Nichols (1983) pointed out that linguistic choices are constrained by the options available to men and women: she found that young and middle aged black women in rural South Carolina use 'the least creolized speech' because of their recent access to white-collar jobs outside the community, which require the use of English. In the Belizean rural context, women's increased participation in local administration *within* the village entails just the opposite, namely a greater usage of the Creole vernacular, because it reinforces the bonds that they are striving to maintain.

It thus appears that the sex variable has an impact on language development, provided other social factors are taken into consideration. Observations of change in apparent time indicate that the Placencia community favors the overt recognition of the status of the Creole vernacular as a symbol of ethnic identity. Middle-aged women involved in community governance are clearly instrumental in this development. In this sense, they can be termed innovators of linguistic change, and if the Creole is now overtly defined as prestigious, then they indeed spearhead linguistic change, though not just 'in the direction of the standard'. Instead, they actually promote a bi-polar repertoire which can incorporate the multiple values of the new society, and which can, in particular, assign prestige to local ethnic values (as represented in the Creole) beside the traditional educational and cultural values associated with English. This trend is increasingly observable in the process of nativisation taking place in many developing countries.

NOTES

This research was supported by the University of Minnesota Graduate School.

1. For example, Fisher 1958, Gauchat 1905; Labov 1972; Levine & Crockett 1966; Milroy 1980; Trudgill 1972; and Thorne, Kramarae & Henley 1983 for an overview. See Cameron and Coates (1989) for a critique.

2. Claims in support of decreolisation (whether initiated by men or by women) are mostly unfounded due to the absence of diachronic data documenting earlier stages of the continuum. As suggested by Mufwene (1987) the continuum as it is now may have existed from the very beginning, which does not exclude the possibility of regular linguistic change.

3. Data were collected in the village of Placencia (Stann Creek District), a small fishing community (population 400) with the help of a local Creole fieldworker. Typically, men go fishing at sea for one or two weeks, then return to the village for ten days to rest, drink and talk. Between trips, men are therefore eager conversationalists. On the other hand, women are constantly busy cooking, washing, taking care of the children and, for some of them, managing village affairs. Conversations with them are always interrupted by some urgent business.

4. Four speakers (three women and one man) are each represented twice in the corpus, in basilects and in mesolects.

5. The realisation of copular variants is influenced by grammatical subcategorisation in Belizean Creole (Escure MS) as well as in Black English (Labov 1972, Baugh 1980)) and other creoles (Holm 1980). The changing semantactic function of copular variants is discussed in Escure 1984.

6. In Swacker (1975) men were found to speak about four times more than women. This was based on an analysis of word output in the specific context of description tasks assigned to white middle class young men and women.

7. The official photograph of Queen Elizabeth II and Prince Philip is prominently displayed in many Creole homes.

8. A morpheme *da* (or its occasional variant *a*) occurs in a potential copular position, and has indeed been treated as copula in most studies of Caribbean creoles. This interpretation would raise to four the number of copular variants in this study. However, arguments have been presented in support of the claim that *da* in present-day Belizean Creole functions as a focusing device, and has lost all copular value (Escure 1984). This constitutes the basis of my analysis of the copular variable into three variants rather than four.

REFERENCES

Baugh, J. 1980. A reexamination of the Black English copula. In Labov, W. (ed.), *Locating Language in Time and Space*. New York: Academic Press, pp. 83–106.

Cameron, D. and Coates, J. 1989. Some problems in the sociolinguistic explanation of sex differences. In Coates, J. and Cameron, D. (eds.), *Women in their Speech Communities*. Harlow: Longman, pp. 13–26.

Escure, G. 1982. Contrastive patterns of intragroup and intergroup interaction in the creole continuum of Belize. *Language in Society* 11: 239–64.

1983. The use of creole as interlanguage by the Black Carib of Belize. In Ingemann, F. (ed.), *1982 Mid-America Linguistics Conference Papers*. University of Kansas, pp. 271–82.

1984. The Belizean copula: a case of semantactic shift. In Carrington, L. (ed.), *Studies in Caribbean language*. Trinidad: Society for Caribbean Linguistics, pp. 190–202. (Also in Dascal (ed.), *Dialogue: An Interdisciplinary Approach*. Benjamins, pp. 265–81.)

1983. Grammatical constraints on copular distribution. MS.

Fischer, J. L. 1958. Social influences on the choice of a linguistic variant. *Word* 14: 47–56.

Gauchat, L. 1905. L'unité phonétique dans le patois d'une commune. In *Aus Romanischen Sprachen und Literaturen Festschrift Heinrich Mort*: Halle: Max Niemeyer, pp. 175–232.

Holm, J. 1980. The Creole copula that highlighted the world. In Dillard, J. L. (ed.), *Perspectives on American English*. The Hague: Mouton, pp. 367–75.

Labov, W. 1972. *Sociolinguistic Patterns*. Philadelphia: University of Pennsylvania Press.

Levine, L. and Crockett, H. J. 1966. Speech variation in a Piedmont Community: postvocalic *r*. In Lieberson, S. (ed.), *Explorations in Sociolinguistics*. The Hague: Mouton.

Milroy, L. 1980. *Language and Social Networks*. Oxford: Blackwell.

Mufwene, S. 1987. Review article of Montgomery and Bailey (eds.), *Language Variety in the South: Perspectives in Black and White*. In *JPCL* 2(1): 93–110.

Nichols, P. 1983. Black women in the rural South. In Thorne, Kramarae and Henley (eds.), 1983, pp. 54–68.

Swacker, M. 1975. The sex of the speaker as a sociolinguistic variable. In Thorne, B. and Henley, N. (eds.), *Language and Sex: Difference and Dominance*. Rowley MA: Newbury House, pp. 76–83.

Thorne, B., Kramarae, C. and Henley, N. (eds.). 1983. *Language, Gender and Society*. Rowley MA: Newbury House.

Trudgill, P. 1972. Sex, covert prestige and linguistic change in the urban British English of Norwich. *Language in Society* 1:179–95.

Appendix: Data sample

(The three major copular functions – attribution, equation and duration – are illustrated below, with specific reference to the variants *de* or zero used in basilects and mesolects. When nearing acrolects, some form of *be* may replace any variant):

a. Attribution is marked by zero-copula with adjectives (stative verbs). Creole passive equivalents are placed in this category:

   (1) *dat izi fu mek*
       'That's easy to make'
   (2) *i sopoz tu don, tu finish lang taim*
       'It should have been done, it should have been finished a long time ago'
       it (Ø)suppose to (Ø)done, to (Ø)finish long time/

b. Equation or class membership is marked by Ø with nominal predicates and possibly by *da* or *a* in basilects[8]:

   (3) *dat da di hadas ting, da fu tek op yu ruts*
       'That's the hardest thing, take up your roots' /That that(is) the hardest thing, that to take up your roots/
   (4) *bot di jaj an di dakta, da gud fren*
       'But the judge and the doctor are good friends' /But the judge and the doctor, those(are) good friends/
   (5) *no a wan mata a we i chipa*
       'It's not a question of price' /not that a matter of whether it cheaper/

c. Location is marked either by *de* or Ø:

   (6) *unu me stil de in de wen a kum bak*
       'You were still there when I came back' /You(pl) Past still there in there when I come back/
   (7) *di baj me don de ina wata aredi*
       'The barge was already in the water' /The barge-Past-finish there in the water already/

d.　Duration is marked by the preverbal continuative morpheme *de* or by Ø:

(8)　*B. ina fi im bonk de slip*
　　　'B. was in his bunk sleeping' /B. in his bunk Cont-sleep/
(9)　*Dat da we dei me de du riper pan, we dei neva du gud*
　　　'That that(is) what they-Past-Cont-do repair on, which they never do good/

40

Sociolinguistic variation in Cane Walk: a quantitative case study

JOHN R. RICKFORD

Introduction

Cane Walk is a pseudonym for a Guyanese village within half an hour's drive of Georgetown, the capital. In the mid 1970s, when the data for this study were collected, approximately 3,650 people lived there. About 97 per cent of these were East Indian, descendants of indentured labourers brought from India between 1838 and 1917 to replace and supplement Africans (emancipated in 1838) as the sugar industry's labour force. The Cane Walk community was created by the nearby LBI (La Bonne Intention)/Ogle Sugar estate in the 1950s to provide alternative housing for its workers, after the barrack-like 'logies' in which they had housed them, on the estate itself, were condemned. The community's stratification into two classes, which we will refer to as 'Estate Class' (EC) and 'Non-Estate Class' (NEC), reflects in part a sugar industry distinction between 'labourers' and 'junior class' employees (see Jayawardena 1963: 28–52). Most EC members work as cane-cutters, weeders and in other labouring capacities in the canefields behind the village. Some NEC members are junior supervisors on the estate, but most work as shopowners, contractors, clerks and in similar 'lower middle class' jobs off the estate, some in Georgetown.

Data

In this paper, I will summarise some of the key findings about sociolinguistic variation in this community, drawing on an earlier study of pronominal usage in a judgement sample of 24 Cane Walkers (Rickford 1979). We have about 70 hours of recorded speech from these individuals, most of it in 'spontaneous' interviews, but some in controlled interviews in which intuitions were elicited (Rickford 1987). Our linguistic variable will be

609

Table 40.1. *Characteristics of the Cane Walk sample*

1. Derek EC Male <18 (575)	13. Mark NEC Male <18 (305)
2. James EC Male <18 (445)	14. Magda NEC Female <18 (458)
3. Florine EC Female <18 (236)	15. Katherine NEC Female <18 (488)
4. Reefer EC Male 18–55 (344)	16. Kishore NEC Male 18–55 (645)
5. Sultan EC Male 18–55 (446)	17. Sheik NEC Male 18–55 (445)
6. Raj EC Male 18–55 (292)	18. Seymour NEC Male 18–55 (650)
7. Irene EC Female 18–55 (812)	19. Radika NEC Female 18–55 (208)
8. Rose EC Female 18–55 (433)	20. Claire NEC Female 18–55 (273)
9. Sari EC Female 18–55 (269)	21. Bonnette NEC Female 18–55 (805)
10. Ajah EC Male >55 (405)	22. Ustad NEC Male>55 (885)
11. Darling EC Female >55 (478)	23. Oxford NEC Male >55 (562)
12. Nani EC Female >55 (498)	24. Granny NEC Female >55 (466)

morphological variation between basilectal (deep Creole) and non-basilectal variants of singular personal pronouns, which alternatively encode or neutralise various case and gender distinctions (Bickerton 1973: 657–60; Rickford 1979: 336–41). Nine pronoun subcategories have such variants, three with mesolectal (intermediate) variants as well as acrolectal or standard English ones:[1]

	BAS	ACR			BAS	ACR			BAS	MES	ACR
1 Subject	mi	ai	3 Feminine Subject		hi	ʃi	3 Masculine Object		am	hi	hɪm
1 Possessive	mi	mai	3 Neuter Subject		i	ɪt	3 Feminine Object		am	ʃi	hʌr
3 Masculine Possessive	hi	ɪz	3 Neuter Object		am	ɪt	3 Feminine Possessive		hi	ʃi	hʌr

Table 40.1 provides, for each of the 24 individuals in the sample, information about their social class, sex and age-group, and the number of pronoun tokens recorded from them in spontaneous speech (i.e., excluding elicited forms) across all nine subcategories.

Sociolinguistic variation

Social class

Figure 40.1, which shows the relative frequency of basilectal (Creole) forms across all nine subcategories by individual and social class, provides a dramatic demonstration of the saliency of class membership as a sociolinguistic constraint in this community. Except for Florine and Granny, EC and NEC members occupy different areas of the scale

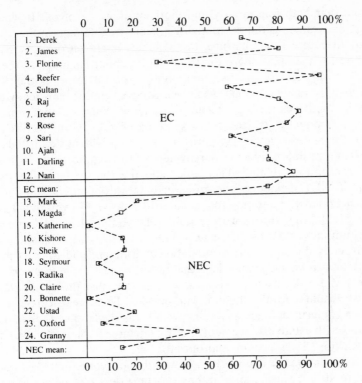

Figure 40.1   Basilectal singular pronoun usage by individual and class.

altogether, the former overwhelmingly favouring basilectal pronoun forms (using them, on average, 75 per cent of the time), the latter overwhelmingly disfavouring such variants (using them only 13 per cent of the time). Other variables – plural marking, negation, pronominal vowel laxing – provide similar evidence that the EC speakers tend to stick closer to the basilectal or Creole end of the continuum than the NEC speakers do.

Why should this be so? When the indentured predecessors of the current Cane Walk population came into Guyana, what they learned was not standard English, but the basilectal Creole of the African labourers among whom they lived and worked. EC members, like their forefathers, continued to work as estate labourers, in the company of other fieldworkers, and consequently had little opportunity or motivation to modify their creole speech in the direction of the standard. NEC members, however, found jobs and social contacts off the estate, particularly in Georgetown, went further in school, and had increased opportunity and motivation to acquire the mesolectal and acrolectal varieties of English spoken by teachers and other high-status individuals.

Note that both opportunity and motivation are involved. It would be wrong to assume, as the functionalist models predominant in the sociolinguistic literature (see Cheshire, this volume) might encourage us to do, that the EC members share the same values about language as the NEC members do, and would use more non-basilectal forms if they could. Although formal elicitation reveals that some EC individuals really do not have productive control over some acrolectal variants, and that some NEC individuals equally lack control of some basilectal variants (see Rickford 1987), the recorded/everyday performance of individual Cane Walkers in general represents a selective deployment of their competence in line with their conceptions of the social order and the role of language variants within it. NEC members, who are already upwardly mobile, tend to have the functionalist orientation that standard English helps you to get ahead, while Creole, in Oxford's words, 'don't take you nowhere.' EC members, for whom movement off the sugar estate or up its occupational hierarchy is extremely difficult, tend to be anti-establishment and Marxist in their orientation to language and the social order, using Creole to assert that it is the social order itself which must change, and that the use of standard English would not take them ahead anyway. This is particularly true of militant cane cutters such as Reefer, who leads the field workers in labour disputes with estate management. For EC members, then, a conflict model (see Rickford 1986) is more appropriate.

A comment on the two individuals who do not typify their class patterns in figure 40.1 – Florine and Granny – is in order. Florine is exceptional among EC members insofar as her closest friends at the time were NEC members, specifically Mark and Magda, her neighbours. She was often at their home (she was even recorded there), and her lower than usual basilectal pronoun use reflects that association, since it is closer to their more standard-like language use. Granny, on the other hand, runs a rum shop at the back of the village which is frequented by estate labourers, has little contact with higher status Georgetown types, and seems quite uninterested in mimicking their language or behaviour. Her higher than usual basilectal pronoun use reflects these NEC-atypical associations and orientations.

Sex

Figure 40.2 indicates that while basilectal pronoun usage in Cane Walk is strongly correlated with social class, it is almost completely unaffected by sex membership. NEC men and women use basilectal pronoun variants equally often (mean = 0.13), while EC women use them only slightly more often (mean = 0.77) than EC men do (mean = 0.74).

Although this particular variable shows no male-female differentiation, other variables might confirm the general impression one derives from

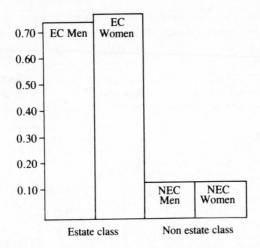

Figure 40.2   Basilectal singular pronoun usage by class and sex.

talking to husband-wife pairs that middle-aged and older women are more comfortable at the basilectal/Creole end of the continuum, while their husbands can operate equally comfortably in the mesolectal to acrolectal range. This may be partly because older men have generally gone further in school than older women, and have had more contacts with standard English speakers outside of the home and village than older women have.

Age

Figure 40.3 shows the relative frequencies of basilectal singular pronoun variants by social class and age. The age levels themselves were chosen to represent the primary distinctions which community members consider significant, the under-18 group representing 'young people' who cannot vote and are generally in school, the 18–55 group representing 'big people' who constitute the bulk of the labour force and enjoy political and social adult privileges, and the over-55 group representing 'old people,' many of them retired (since 55 was, until recently, the retirement age for the average estate field worker). Between the oldest and youngest age-levels in each social class, there is a noticeable decrease in basilectal pronoun use, equal to 0.16 in the EC, and 0.12 in the NEC. This distribution closely matches Labov's (1966) model of 'a Stigmatised language feature (showing) change in progress.' As Labov (1966: 325) suggests, a distribution of this type is symptomatic of a recent increase in the social stigmatisation of the variable, so that 'older speakers will show greater use of the newly stigmatised feature, and the younger groups less.'

The position of the intermediate age group differs, however, for each

Table 40.2. *Mean education levels by social class and age*

	Over 55	18–55	Under 18
EC	Elementary	Elementary	Secondary
NEC	Elementary	Secondary	Secondary

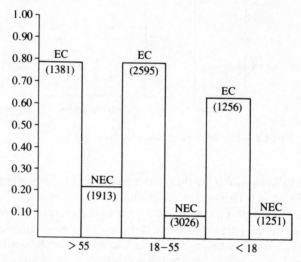

Figure 40.3   Basilectal singular pronoun usage by class and age. Note: N's in parentheses.

social class. It is on par with the oldest group within the EC, but on par with the youngest group within the NEC. This suggests that the increase in the social stigmatisation of basilect forms comes earlier for NEC members than for EC members because of some other factor. Table 40.2 suggests that this factor is the level of education which the various age groups within each social class were able to obtain.[2] It is only the youngest EC group which has had access to secondary or high school education, while the intermediate and youngest NEC age-groups have both had some secondary education. There is no class-independent correlation between education and basilectal usage, but a secondary education (usually acquired outside the village) seems to lead both EC and NEC members to lower their basilectal usage below the level characteristic of older members of their class, whatever that level may be.

Other data which space prevents us from introducing here (see Rickford 1979: 371–74) indicate that the age differences depicted in figure 40.3 are most marked in the first person, third feminine and third neuter subject subcategories, which together account for two thirds of all pronoun tokens recorded in the nine subcategories (7,526/11,424). Other subcategories reveal little or no general movement towards non-basilectal norms, or slightly different tendencies for the EC and NEC.

Pronoun subcategory

Although it is convenient and valid to combine basilectal frequencies across the nine pronoun subcategories as an index of basilectal usage overall, as we have been doing up to this point, it is worth noting that pronoun subcategory is itself a significant internal constraint. Basilectal variants are much more frequent in the third masculine possessive and first person possessive subcategories (EC means of 1.0 and 0.99, NEC means of 0.43 and 0.40 respectively, and least frequent in the third feminine subject and object subcategories (EC means of 0.34 and 0.33, NEC means of 0.04 and 0.01 respectively). One possible reason for this is that the basilectal variants in the former subcategories pose no referential or communication difficulties because the case marking offered by the acrolectal variants e.g., (*his book*, *my sister*) is redundant, the possessive relation between pronoun and noun already reflected by word order. In the latter subcategories, however, the fact that the basilectal variants do not mark referents as male or female, and that the syntax does not provide any help in this respect, offers real potential for referential confusion in a community where many speakers do morphologically encode this distinction. Interestingly enough, when we look at actual stretches of discourse, it turns out that the unmarked use and interpretation of *(h)i* by basilectal speakers is masculine, as it is with mesolectal and acrolectal speakers; *(h)i* tends to be used with feminine reference only when its feminine reference is unambiguous from the sentential or real world context (see Rickford 1979: 361–5).

Style

Finally, there is considerable evidence that basilectal pronoun usage in this community, like Creole usage in Guyana more generally, is sensitive to stylistic constraints, particularly the nature of the addressee and the occasion. To cite only one example: Reefer used the basilectal variant in the third masculine object subcategory (*am*) 100 per cent of the time (n = 8) when he was recorded in interaction with his peers, 82 per cent (n = 17) in spontaneous interviews with me, a fellow Guyanese, and only 53 per cent (n = 17) when he was reinterviewed by three expatriates (two Englishmen and an American). Similarly Ustad used the basilectal variant in the first person subject subcategory (*mi*) 26 per cent of the time (n = 74) at an informal party in his home, 13 per cent (n = 344) in spontaneous interviews with me, and not at all (n = 30) in the expatriate reinterviews. These results are characteristic of a general tendency to use more basilectal or Creole speech in more informal, in-group contexts.

Conclusion

As we have seen from looking at morphological variants of the personal pronouns, linguistic variation in Cane Walk is jointly constrained by both internal and external factors, its structure neatly revealed by quantitative distributions of basilectal and non-basilectal forms. Similar systematic non-qualitative variation has been revealed by other linguists, using other variables and constraints, elsewhere in Guyana and the Caribbean (see Winford's overview paper in this volume). Caribbean linguistic situations, particularly those which involve creole continua, offer rich exemplifications of sociolinguisitic principles, and fertile opportunities for testing and extending sociolinguistic theory.

NOTES

I'm grateful to Angela Rickford, Bill Labov, Dell Hymes, Gillian Sankoff, Derek Bickerton and John Fought for encouragement and feedback when I was preparing the dissertation on which this paper is based.
1. The *h* in *hi, him, hiz* and *hʌr* is often absent in casual speech.
2. 'Elementary school' means 'completed elementary school,' except for some of the oldest EC members, who only reached grade 3 or less. 'Secondary school' means forms 1–3; more of the youngest NEC group have gone on to forms IV–V (finishing high school) than any other group.

REFERENCES

Bickerton, D. 1973. The nature of a creole continuum. *Language* 49: 640–69.
Jayawardena, C. 1963. *Conflict and Solidarity on a Guyanese Plantation*. London: Athlone Press.
Labov, W. 1966. *The Social Stratification of English in New York City*. Washington DC: Center for Applied Linguistics.
Rickford, J. R. 1979. Variation in a Creole Continuum: Quantitative and Implicational Approaches. Unpublished PhD thesis, University of Pennsylvania.
  1986. The need for new approaches to social class analysis in sociolinguistics. *Language in Communication* 6: 215–21.
  1987. The haves and have nots: Sociolinguistic surveys and the assessment of speaker competence. *Language in Society* 16: 149–77.

The Pacific

41

The Pacific

SUZANNE ROMAINE

Introduction

The Pacific is a vast area containing a large number of indigenous languages, Asian mainland languages, half a dozen European languages and a number of pidgins and creoles. Here I will take the Pacific to include the island nations and territories of Micronesia, Melanesia and Polynesia (excluding Australia and New Zealand). These three areas are taken by geographers and others to comprise Oceania. Micronesia includes the island groups east of the Philippines and north of the equator. They include, for example, the Mariana, Marshall, Caroline and Gilbert Islands and have a land area of about 1,335 square miles. Melanesia comprises the island groups in the southwestern Pacific extending southeastwards from the Admiralty Islands to Fiji and includes such nations as Papua New Guinea, the Solomon Islands, Vanuatu, and New Caledonia. Polynesia consists of a group of islands in the eastern and southeastern Pacific extending from New Zealand north to Hawaii and east to Easter Island.

This section includes papers representing two of the areas of Oceania, namely, Melanesia (Mühlhäusler on Tok Pisin, and Siegel on English in Fiji) and Polynesia (Sato on English in Hawaii). Despite the considerable interest in Oceania on the part of anthropologists and linguists (see Watson-Gegeo 1986 for an overview of research on the use of indigenous languages), to my knowledge no systematic studies have been done on the history and use of English (or any other European language such as German) in Micronesia, so this area is not represented here. There is, however, much scope there for further sociohistorical work on such topics as the pidgin English spoken by Gilbertese plantation workers and the lingua francas of the mining industry on Nauru (see Siegel 1988). I will first give brief consideration to linguistic diversity in the Pacific before turning specifically to the position of English.

Linguistic diversity in the Pacific

The Pacific Islands are thought to be the most recently peopled part of the globe. It is generally estimated that the Austronesians left their homeland in southern China 6–7,000 years ago. Some settled in Micronesia and parts of Melanesia. Others went as far as Easter Island, off the coast of Chile. Still others travelled as far as Madagascar, off the coast of Africa.

These migrants brought many varieties of Austronesian languages, which may ultimately be related to the Tai language family of Southern China and continental Southeast Asia. As a result of the great distances separating the Pacific Islands and their sparse population, the linguistic diversity of Austronesia is high. Cavalli-Sforza and Wang (1986: 41) estimate that island Southeast Asia and Oceania contain some 1,400 indigenous languages, out of some 7,000 estimated for the world (see Wurm 1982 on the Papuan languages of Oceania). The total number of speakers inhabiting this area is some 150 million out of a world population of four billion. This means that roughly 4 per cent of the world's population speak 20 per cent of its languages.

The greatest linguistic diversity is found in Melanesia. In Papua New Gunea alone estimates of the number of languages vary between 700 and 750 (see Foley 1986, Wurm 1982 for a survey of the Papuan languages; and Wurm 1976 on Austronesian). There are around 105 languages spoken in Vanuatu, and as many as another 700 in other parts of Melanesia. Polynesia and Micronesia are less diverse. On the basis of lexicostatistical investigations Mühlhäusler estimates (1987:1) that the former area contains 40 and the latter 50 languages. Any estimate of the number of languages spoken in such an area is fraught with difficulties due to the problems inherent in defining terms like language and dialect. Mühlhäusler (1987: 1) in fact says that the very concept of a language may turn out to be a European cultural artefact. In many parts of the Pacific there are extensive chains of interrelated languages and dialects with no clear internal boundaries. Laycock and Vorhooeve (1971), for example, say that it is rare for speakers of Papuan languages to have a name for themselves, in their own language, as a linguistic unit.

There can be no doubt, however, that since contact with Europeans and the imposition of colonial administrations in various Pacific islands there has been a decline in the number of languages, and drastic changes have taken place in those which survive. Westernisation of the Pacific languages has brought them closer semantically and grammatically to the standard European languages which prevail in metropolitan centres, such as Port Vila in Vanuatu. Europeans also introduced their own nomenclatures and classifications of indigenous languages, at the same time that they imposed their own languages as a means of social and economic control. In a great number of cases the newly independent nations, like Papua New Guinea, which have emerged out of former colonial rule, have simply perpetuated langauge policies that reflect colonial practices and attitudes. For example, in Papua New Guinea and the Solomon Islands, the official medium for education is English, rather than Solomon Islands Pijin or Papua New Guinea Tok Pisin (see, for example, Watson-Gegeo 1987). At the moment, English is the official language of all the Pacific island nations except those under French control (i.e., French Polynesia and New Caledonia).

Language contact in the Pacific: European languages and pidgins and creoles

Of the European languages (see further below) which have been brought to the Pacific, none has had the impact that English has. However, before I consider specifically the role of English, I will take a brief look at some of the other European languages and contact languages which have played a part in linguistic history.

Linguistic history in the Pacific is intertwined with political history and economics. Colonisation and trade have left their mark on the indigenous languages of the Pacific. For example, the area now known as the Trust Territory of the Pacific Islands has been subjected to a series of influences from Spanish, German, Japanese and English (see Laycock 1971: 884–5). The main languages of colonial influence other than English in the area under consideration here are German and French. I will make some brief remarks about each of these.

German in the Pacific

The first German trading depot was established on Samoa in 1856. Trading activities emanated from this base throughout much of Micronesia, and also in Fiji and Tonga. However, German influence in the Pacific dates officially at least from 1884 with the annexation of northeast New Guinea and the Bismarck archipelego. Samoa, the Carolines, the Marianas, Nauru and Bougainville were acquired in the following two decades. All of these possessions were, however, lost during World War I after less than 30 years of German administration. Nevertheless, some Germans, particularly missionaries, who remained in the islands, continued to have some linguistic influence.

Laycock (1971: 878–9) says that the amount and type of German contact was not sufficient to have much of an impact on indigenous languages of the Pacific, apart from a few loanwords, for example, in Buin (Bougainville) *arapait* (German *Arbeit*, 'work'). Some of the Catholic missions in northern New Guinea gave instruction in German, and remnants of pidgin German still exist today in various parts of Papua New Guinea (see, for example, Volker 1982 on Rabaul Creole German; Mühlhäusler 1984; and Romaine 1988: 122–3). The language policy of the German administration was opposed to pidgin English; however, it was used in daily dealings with the inhabitants.

It is in Tok Pisin that the greatest German influence can be found. Mihalic (1957) lists about 80 words of German origin, or about 5 per cent of the total entries. Many of these words have also entered native languages via pidgin. Some of the etymologies are however, problematic and not unequivocally traceable to German origin. Pidgin etymology is a risky business anyway (see Mühlhäusler 1982), particularly in cases where closely related langauges such as English and German, which share a high percentage of cognates, are involved. It is difficult to argue unique sources for words like *gaden* in Tok Pisin (cf. German *Garten* and English *garden*). Another problematic example is *maski*, which Mihalic derives from German *machts nichts* '(It) makes no difference', but which other creolists derive from the Portuguese/Spanish *mas que* because it can be found in Atlantic creoles too. It is in the nature of pidgins to have convergent etymologies.

French in the Pacific

The French were relative latecomers to the Pacific. French traders appear to have operated mainly on the eastern fringes of the Pacific, especially along the South American coast. Pidgin English was already an established and essential means of communication in the Pacific by this time. The effects of the expansion of French in the Pacific have to be considered in relation to a number of other languages with which it came into contact, for example, Chinese, Japanese, Indonesian, Vietnamese, but particularly English. Where the French annexed an area or declared it a protectorate, the status of French in relation to pidgin English and English underwent change. The island territories controlled by France are for the most part demographically Polynesian. In all of them education, law, administration, radio and television (where it exists) are carried out in the medium of French. The majority of the population is multilingual or bilingual, speaking at least French and a Polynesian language. Even in Tahiti, however, where French influence is perhaps at its strongest, borrowings from English are almost twice as great as those from French.

In Melanesia too, French faced competition from Engish and pidgin English, in this case from Beach-la-Mar, now Bislama. The latter, however, became progressively more English in lexicon (see below). Much more work needs to be done on pidgin French in the Pacific (see Hollyman 1971; Baker 1943; O'Reilly 1953; and Charpentier 1983).

English in the Pacific

A number of varieties of English can be found in the Pacific: Australian, American and British varieties in addition to English-based pidgins and creoles. The various islands which make up the area referred to as Polynesia have various political affiliations today. However, they share in common the fact that the first European language they came into contact with was the English brought first by Captain Cook, spread by whalers and traders and later consolidated by missionaries. The words introduced by English-speaking missionaries into Polynesian languages are almost all that remains of English influence in the islands which later came under French control.

In areas that remained or came under British or American control a new wave of borrowing began and is still continuing as part of increasing urbanisation and westernisation (see Laycock 1971: 887, and later in this chapter). The best documented case of English language influence in Polynesia is in Hawaii, as discussed by Sato in this volume. Had there been more space, the case of Pitcairn and Norfolk islands could have been included. Pitcairnese developed on Pitcairn Island from contact between Tahitian and the varieties of English spoken by the mutineers of *HMS Bounty* and their descendants.

Prior to 1790 Pitcairn Island was uninhabited. The conditions under which Pitcairnese developed were exceptional since more is known about the details of the linguistic input than in most other cases of language contact in the Pacific (or indeed elsewhere). We know, for example, that there were 28 original inhabitants of the island, which included nine mutineers from HMS *Bounty*, six Polynesian men, twelve Polynesian women and one small child. The birthplace of most of the settlers and details of the education and background of some of the Englishmen are known. For the first 33 years the settlers lived in almost complete isolation. Thus, during the formative period of the language there was little outside influence. It is known too that half of the Englishmen died within four years and all but one of them within ten years, so it is possible to make some intelligent guesses about the relative influence of various individuals on the language of this small community. Most Pitcairners were moved permanently in 1856 to Norfolk Island (see Ross and Moverley 1964; Harrison 1972; Romaine 1988; and Laycock 1988, for further discussion of the status of Pitcairn-Norfolk English).

In Melanesia contact with Europeans tended to be less than in Polynesia, due in large part to the remoteness of some areas and tribal hostility. The practice of recruiting labour by force and deceit in Melanesia contributed greatly to the spread of an English-based pidgin by dint of the uprooting and transportation of thousands of Melanesians as indentured plantation workers to the Queensland canefields (see Dutton 1980) and to various Pacific Islands. There workers were brought into contact primarily with varieties of Australian English. Although Polynesia was not disturbed by the social upheavals of blackbirding, Hawaii was transformed from a traditional subsistence agriculture into a plantation economy (again, see Sato, this volume).

Contact languages in the Pacific

The contact languages of the Pacific include both indigenous and non-indigenous (i.e., European language based-) pidgins and creoles (see Mühlhäusler 1988). The earliest pidgins in Oceania were Portuguese-based. Most of these are now extinct, except for one used in Timor. A discussion of Spanish-based pidgins and creoles in the Philippines can be found in Whinnom (1956).

Tok Pisin and Hawaii Pidgin/Creole English are the best documented Pacific pidgins and creoles. Less is known about Solomons Islands Pijin (see however, Jourdan 1985) and Bislama, a closely related pidgin English of Vanuatu (see Charpentier 1983; Crowley 1981; and Mühlhäusler 1986).

The best described of the indigenous pidgin languages is Hiri Motu, which is a pidginised version of the Austronesian language Motu, spoken around the Port Moresby area. A greatly reduced variety of Motu was employed on trading expeditions in the Papuan Gulf area. At present, it is one of the officially recognised languages of Papua New Guinea along with Tok Pisin and English. However, it is used by only about 10 per cent of the population (see also Wurm 1971 and Dutton 1983).

Less is known about other indigenous contact languages, which were no doubt widespread before the advent of European languages and the emergent pidgins based on them, particularly in highly multilingual areas like Papua New Guinea. Mead (1938), for example, reported that a simplified form of Iatmul was used as a trade language in the Middle Sepik area. Foley (1986) has identified a trade jargon derived from Yimas in use along the Arafundi River. It is also likely that many present-day pidgin and creole languages have undergone a number of repidginisations and recreolisations. There is, for instance, some evidence that Hawaii Pidgin English was a reflexified pidgin Hawaiian used by Chinese labourers who took over cultivation of taro from native Hawaiians.

Extent of nativisation of English in the Pacific

Most studies of English in the Pacific have concentrated on errors (see for example, Church 1970; Phillip 1986; Smith 1978; Smithies and Holzknecht 1981, on English in Papua New Guinea). As far as English in Papua New Guinea is concerned, Smithies and Holzknecht (1981: 28) concluded that the pattern of errors was still too haphazard and the extent of deviation from standard English too great for it to constitute a distinct variety of English. Earlier, however, Smith (1978: 28) concluded that Papua New Guinea English had developed distinctive patterns of its own.

Following the criteria cited by Platt, Weber and Ho (1984: 2–3) for the recognition of autonomy, Barron (1986) has more recently claimed on the basis of a study of lexis that there is a distinct variety of Papua New Guinean English. One could also argue that Papuan New Guinea English consists of several varieties (see, for example, Yarupawa 1986), thus putting it on a par with other 'new Englishes' such as Singapore and Indian English.

Siegel (this volume) has identified the kinds of grammatical markers which lead him to recognise a distinctive local variety of Fijian English, many of which can be found in other 'new Englishes' as well as in English-based pidgins and creoles (see also Moag and Moag 1979). The dividing line between a 'new English' and an English-based pidgin or creole is perhaps fuzzier here than Platt, Weber and Ho claim on the basis of other cases, even though in Fiji, unlike Papua New Guinea, there appears to be a continuum linking basilectal varieties to a more standard-like English, as in Singapore. Siegel finds that lexical markers seem to have the widest range, which is in apparent contrast to what happens in the Jamaican continuum described by De Camp (1971). The situation in Fiji is also unlike Jamaica in another important respect. DeCamp (1971: 357) reports that relatively few features vary with age, sex, occupation and ethnic group, whereas Siegel found clear sex differentiation. As in Hawaii, Siegel found evidence that the use of some of the salient features of the basilectal end of the continuum were becoming less frequent in the speech of similar individuals recorded in identical situations but eight years later. Sato (this volume) gives examples to show that decreolisation in Hawaii does not affect all linguistic features or speakers in the same way. Prosodic features seem particularly resistant (see also Le Page and Tabouret-Keller 1985 for a discussion of the social forces behind readjustment of speakers' norms, and later in this chapter).

Barron (1986: 9) identified six processes in the lexical nativisation of Papua New Guinea English: lexical borrowing, semantic shift, lexical shift, collocation, hybridisation and abbreviation. A few examples follow. A number of borrowings from Tok Pisin and indigenous languages can be found in the English of Papua New Guinea (see also Siegel, this volume, for similar items in Fiji English from Hindi and Fijian). From pidgin come items such as *singsing*, 'traditional dance and song festival', and *wantok* ('one language'), 'relative or clan member, who speaks the same language'. From indigenous languages there are items like *tultul*, 'chief'.

Cases of semantic shift are found when an existing English item is changed in meaning, for example, the use of the term *cargo* to refer

specifically to European goods. Barron (1986: 12) defines lexical shift as
borrowing items from local languages to refer to items which already have
existing English terms, for example, *balus*, 'airplane'. There are also
orthographic shifts in which items are used with Tok Pisin spellings, for
example, Steamships Department Store's advertisement in the *Post Cour-
ier* (an English language daily) for *nambawan prais* ('number one', 'best
price'). Barron (1986: 14) says that lexical and orthographic shifts are
deliberate sociolinguistic markers of the user's national identity as Papua
New Guinean. Still other examples are found in Mühlhäusler's texts (this
volume). Lexical items such as *fresh*, 'without a boy/girlfriend' have been
extended by urban speakers.

Collocations consist of two English items forming a set whose sense is
one which is peculiar to Papua New Guinea English. One such example I
have heard is 'rascal activity'. This is also used by some speakers of Tok
Pisin. This term is the one used by the media to refer to the crimes
committed by 'rascals' (i.e., criminals). There are also Tok Pisin collocations such as *haus kaikai* ('house food', 'an eating establishment'). An
interesting one I discovered, which is peculiar to the staff at the Papua
New Guinea University of Technology, is *haus kopi/house coffee* ('house
coffee'), a canteen built in the style of a traditional Sepik *haus tambaran*
('spirit house'). This one is unusual in that it is both an English and a Tok
Pisin collocation, depending on its pronunciation. In its English version it
is a case of Tok Pisin syntax influencing English word order.

As an example of hybridisation Barron (1986: 19) cites *wantokism*,
which in this case could be glossed as 'nepotism'. There are also hybrids
consisting of two terms, one of which is English and the other Tok Pisin,
such as *meri blouse* (*meri*, 'woman'). A meri blouse is a distinctly Papua
New Guinean style blouse. Another is *bilum twine* – twine for making a
bilum or traditional string bag. There are also a few indigenous short
forms and abbreviations such as *bro* for 'brother', *POM* for Port Moresby
(from the airline code) and *PMV* for public motor vehicle (see also
Mühlhäusler, this volume, and Smith 1988 for other idiomatic and colloquial expressions).

Papua New Guinea English as yet does not appear to be marked by the
same kind of dense lexical nativisation as Kachru (1982: 335) has described
for Indian English. However, the length of contact has been about three
times as long between English-speakers and Indians. There is, nevertheless, a tendency towards the same kind of lexical creativity which has been
reported for other 'new Englishes'. Smith (1978: 13) cites the use of
hateness instead of *hatred*. Smithies and Holzknecht (1981: 30) report the
use of *transference*. Both studies found a number of non-count nouns
which have become count nouns in Papua New Guinea English such as
damages, *harms*, *informations*, *equipments*. Others which I have found are

stationeries and *properties*. This is paralleled in other new varieties of English.

Attitudes to English in the Pacific

Attitudes to English in the Pacific cannot be discussed without also considering attitudes to other indigenous languages which coexist with it and, in particular, attitudes to various pidgin and creole languages which serve as lingua francas and important symbols of solidarity (see Rickford and Traugott 1985, and Sankoff 1980, on the politics of linguistic inequality). Attitudes to pidgins and creoles are quite often negative, particularly on the part of Europeans. Many reflect their failure to regard pidgin English as a real language: for many, it is nothing more than a bastardised English. Sato's (this volume) extensive documentation of attitudes towards Hawaii Pidgin and Creole English is illustrative of the conflicts faced by those who use these varieties of English.

For the most part, attempts to explain aspects of the structure of pidgin English in the Pacific are confused by the resemblance between English and pidgin words. Pidgin expressions are often seen as clumsy, but amusing and descriptive. Collinson (1929: 21), for instance, comments:

> That word 'stop' is rather a puzzler until you get used to it. It means 'is present' and not 'finish'. Here is an illustration. If you lost your pencil you would probably mutter to yourself, 'now where's that pencil of mine?', but a Solomon Islander would say, 'My gracious, where pencil belong me he stop?'. It sounds rather difficult, but in time this curious phrasing comes naturally.

Europeans commonly make the assumption that pidgin English is just a special form of English. Serious misunderstandings can arise from the assumption that words which look like English ones have the same meaning. One with particularly serious consequences is reported in Nelson (1972: 170–1). In this case a Papua New Guinean stumbled against a white woman coming out of the theatre. When questioned by a man about what had happened, the Papua New Guinean replied: 'Mi putim han long baksait bilong misis' – 'I touched the woman's back with my hand'. The answer, however, cost him half a tooth, his job and three months in prison due to the confusion between the meaning of Tok Pisin *baksait*, '*back*', and English *backside*.

Much more research needs to be done on communicative misunderstandings between Europeans who believe they are speaking Tok Pisin and Tok Pisin-speaking nationals. I witnessed a number of efforts made by Europeans who believe they speak 'good pidgin' (see Mühlhäusler 1981 on Tok Masta; see also Piau and Holzknecht 1985). One of the most notable occurred when a vehicle in which I was travelling came to a sudden halt because a small dog was in the middle of the road. The driver (a woman expatriate, who has lived in Papua New Guinea for around 20 years) was not able to see whether the dog had moved out of the way, so asked a man by the side of the road, 'Em i gone yet'? The correct Tok Pisin would have been: 'Em i go pinis'. I found this particularly odd because the woman regards herself as able to speak pidgin, and surely knows the use of *pinis* as a completive aspect marker. Indeed, a calque based on this construction has entered the English of expatriates in a phrase which is used very frequently, namely *going finish*. There are signs on almost all public notice boards about 'going finish' sales, which expatriates typically hold when they leave the country for good (see also Wolfers 1969 for other expressions). Barron (1986: 15) gives this as an example of a collocation which is peculiar to Papua New Guinea English. It is also, interestingly, another case where Tok Pisin syntax has influenced English.

It is widely believed in popular accounts that Tok Pisin is inadequate for the expression of certain ideas and concepts. Chatterton, a former member of the House of Assembly, commented (NBC, 23 June 1976): 'My eight years in the House of Assembly convinced me that pidgin as it is now is an inadequate medium for conducting the business of a modern nation.' A look at some statistics on the use of Tok Pisin in transactions in the House of Assembly shows a dramatic increase, from 40 per cent in 1964 to 95 per cent in 1975 (Noel 1975: 78). In the first four-year period of its use it was restricted to certain topics and specific purposes. Now any business arising in the House of Assembly can be discussed in pidgin.

In a survey of self estimates of the use of Tok Pisin by students at the Papua New Guinea University of Technology in Lae, Swan and Lewis (1987) found no evidence of any significant decline over the four years and no indication of a move towards the use of English (see also Davani 1984). Some of the younger students appear to be using more Tok Pisin at university than at any other previous time in their educational career since Community School. Swan and Lewis interpret the data as an indication of a very positive attitude towards the language, even in an environment which strongly favors the use of English. In another survey done by Swan (1986) it was found that three quarters of the graduates made considerably more use of Tok Pisin in the course of their professional work than their largely expatriate employers were aware (see Phillip 1986).

Among Papua New Guineans themselves attitudes to pidgin, indigenous languages and English are mixed. Laycock (1981) says that a characteristically Melanesian attitude towards language favours diversity because language differences serve as badges of identity. Grimshaw's (1912: 191–2) remarks about the inferiority of indigenous languages in New Guinea are illustrative of the attitude of Europeans, however, to language diversity:

To be addressed in reasonably good English of the 'pidgin' variety, by hideous savages who made murder a profession, and had never come into contact with civilisation, is an experience perplexing enough to make the observer wonder if he is awake. Yet this is what happens on Rossel Island. English is the *lingua franca* of the place, filling up the gaps – and there are many – in the hideous snapping, barking dialect that passes for speech along the coast, and making communication possible among the tribes of the interior, who vary so much in language that many of them cannot understand one another. How did this come about? I fancy, through the unsatisfactory nature of the Rossel dialects. Any that we heard were scarcely like human speech in sound, and were evidently very poor and restricted in expression. Noises like sneezes, snarls and the preliminary stages of choking – impossible to reproduce on paper – represented the names of villages, people and things.

The imposition of European languages was justified in most of the European-dominated territories of the Pacific both as the solution to perceived communication difficulties and as a means of imparting Western culture. In a village school in the upper Markham Valley of Papua New Guinea I encountered a particularly telling indicator of the present status of English in relation to pidgin and indigenous languages. In one of the classrooms a notice was posted advising pupils about activities and behaviours which were categorised under the heading of 'good', 'bad', and 'worst'. Among them was one relating to language. To speak English was considered good; to speak pidgin was bad, but to speak *tok ples* (i.e., one's local language) was worst. All the schools I visited had signs reminding pupils that English was the language of the classroom. This picture is, of course, in stark contrast to the one painted by Sankoff (1980) for pre-colonial Papua New Guinea, where a state of linguistic egalitarianism prevailed.

It is likely that ambivalence towards the use of and role of English *vis-à-vis* Tok Pisin will continue for some time to come. The former prime minister, Michael Somare, is a case in point. He has on occasion chosen to speak abroad in Tok Pisin rather than English, even though he publicly endorses the use of English as the language of international relations. His attitude towards the role of the two languages can be seen in the following report from *Wantok* newspaper (10 July 1976):

Na praim minista i bin tok olsem: 'Mi ting yumi mas yusim Tok Inglis long skul na long bisnis na long toktok wantaim arapela kantri. Na mi no laikim Tok Pisin long wanem em i gat planti Tok Inglis insait long en. Miting planti yumi long olgeta hap i yusim Tok Inglis pinis, olsem mi laikim em i kamap na nasenel tok ples bilong PNG.' Na taim em i mekim dispela tok, em i yusim Tok Pisin.

The prime minister spoke thus: 'I think we must use English in our schools and for business and discussions with other countries. I don't like

Tok Pisin which is mixed with a lot of English. I feel very strongly that we've used English for all sorts of purposes, and I want it to become the national language of Papua New Guinea.' At the time he made this speech, he was using Tok Pisin.

Here we see a desire expressed for the two languages to remain separate and to be used in different domains. English is viewed as the language to be used in an international context. It is interesting, however, that Somare takes a decidedly negative attitude towards the adoption of English words into Tok Pisin. Although he favours English as the best choice for a national language, it is clear that Tok Pisin has positive affective value for Papua New Guineans (see also Romaine 1986).

In the major urban centres of many island nations of the Pacific, such as Honiara, Port Vila and Port Moresby, where a pidgin language coexists with English, there is great concern that increasing anglicisation is leading to the death of pidgin. Charpentier (1983), for example, says that in Bislama spoken in Vanuatu there is depidginisation without creolisation because the language is still used only as a second language. Among the developments associated with depidginisation is increasing anglicisation, leading to fragmentation of the language into two varieties. In this way a pidgin may in time give rise to a new regional variety of English (see, however, Tryon 1986: 312). This is parallel to what is happening in Tok Pisin, except there the process is occurring at least partially within the context of creolisation (see Romaine 1989b and c). Bickerton (1975) has suggested that a post-creole continuum is developing in Tok Pisin. Mühlhäusler's texts (this volume) show the kind of code-mixing, switching and lexical borrowing which fluent speakers typically engage in.

While it is by no means clear that a full-fledged continuum of the Jamaican type will emerge, it is already the case that varieties which are intermediate between Tok Pisin and English can be found. It is not always possible to distinguish borrowing from code-switching (see Romaine 1989a). As the case of Black English in the United States shows, it is in principle possible for a creole to diverge so considerably that its historical origins become obscured and it becomes very much like other varieties of English which do not have a prior creole history. Some of the more acrolectal varieties of Hawaii Creole English might be thought of as falling into this category (see Sato, this volume).

The situation which I have outlined here for Tok Pisin is of course by no means unique. Similar trends can be found in other parts of the Pacific where a pidgin/creole language exists in close contact with English. Bislama displays morpho-syntactic and lexical variation similar to Tok Pisin. However, in other respects, it is different. Although large portions of its lexicon contain items which predate French influence and are therefore cognate with forms in Tok Pisin and Solomon Islands Pijin, there is nevertheless a French component concentrated in certain lexical fields, for example, food and drink. Lynch (1987) has, however, shown that only about 3 per cent of these French-derived words survive now. Tryon (1988) has also noted that some of the older lexical items in use by older rural informants, like *dampa*, 'damper', and *manowa*, 'warship', which go back to the nineteenth century and are thus shared with Solomons Pijin and Tok Pisin, are now being replaced by English terms. Nevertheless, to the extent that other Pacific pidgins and creoles also draw on English for their lexical innovations, basic historical affinities will not be obscured.

Grammatical changes are, however, another matter. There may be significant divergence in the future, depending on what course these take. For example, with regard to the so-called future marker *bai*, Jourdan (1985) observes that in Solomons Pijin the forms *bambae* and its reduced variants *babae* and *bae* are all currently in use and have been for some time. Older speakers tend to be conservative and use only *bambae* and *babae*. The younger generation tend to use *bae*, but preverbal *bae* is not by any means a frequent variant. In Tok Pisin, however, the general trend is towards the use of preverbal *bai* (see Romaine 1989a and c). Thus, grammaticalisation may be proceeding in different directions in different varieties of Melanesian pidgin/creole.

Another instance where divergence among closely related varieties may increase can be seen in Bislama, where Tryon (1988) reports the coexistence of verb +*i stap* and *i stap* + verb, as in *Em i slip i stap* vs. *em i stap slip* ('He is sleeping'). The latter variant is the usual one in Bislama, but in Tok Pisin, the former pattern is the preferred one. Crowley (1988) has discussed some of the differences in the prepositional systems of Tok Pisin and Bislama.

Different patterns of lexicalisation may also have important grammatical consequences. Watson-Gegeo (1987: 28) has observed differences in Solomon Islands Pijin between rural and urban speakers with regard to verbs which in English would be phrasal, for example, *to find out*, as in *she found out the answer/she found the answer out*. In Tok Pisin the whole phrase is usually reanalysed as an indivisible unit, for example, *painimautim*, but not **painim . . . aut*.

Gaps in research

I have already pointed out a number of gaps in our knowledge of varieties of English in the Pacific, for example, Micronesia. The history of research on pidgin, creole and indigenous languages of the Pacific has been largely dictated by non-scholarly concerns, such as whether a language was seen as useful in missionising efforts. Because Tok Pisin was seen as a valuable medium of communication for government and mission business, there was considerable interest in it. The case of pidgin English in the Loyalties is completely different. Neither the missions or government encouraged its use. There is not a single publication dealing with the language, despite its probable greater importance than Tok Pisin in the development of Pacific Pidgin English (see Mühlhäusler 1986: 183–4).

Our understanding of even the best documented of the pidgin/creole languages, such as Tok Pisin, is fragmentary and information about 'new Englishes' is much more scanty. Handbooks such as Wurm and Mühlhäusler (1985) are urgently needed for other pidgins and creoles. Systematic quantitative work has also been rare in many areas; Hawaii is, however, an exception. My research on children's acquisition of Tok Pisin, some of which is reported in Romaine (1989a, 1989b and 1987c), is quantitative and provides information about differences between varieties of spoken and written Tok Pisin. Given the rapid pace of linguistic development, longitudinal studies are also a pressing need.

Research is underway at the moment on an Atlas of Languages of Intercultural Communication in the Pacific, under the direction of Stephen Wurm at the Australian National University in Canberra. It also involves a research team based at the University of Oxford in the UK which includes myself and Philip Baker. The aim of the project will be to bring together historical and synchronic material, which will allow us to map the present location and distribution of lingua francas in the Pacific area (see Mühlhäusler 1986 for an interview). This will provide much needed information on patterns of contact in the Pacific, and the development and spread of these languages. It will at the same time identify areas which require further investigation.

It is clear that the English language will play an increasingly important role as a means of cross-cultural communication within and outside the Pacific. The future of the pidgin/creole and indigenous languages is perhaps less certain. At the Unit for Pacific languages at the University of the South Pacific in Port Vila, Vanuatu, there is a group of linguists concerned about the future of Pacific languages. It is hoped that they may be able to encourage the Pacific nations to plan their linguistic resources carefully and to coordinate research activities in the various countries.

REFERENCES

Baker, S. J. 1943. French beach-la-mar in New Caledonia. *AS* 18: 12–17.

Barron, C. 1986. *Lexical Nativisation in Papua New Guinean English*. Research Report No. 7. Department of Language and Communication Studies. Papua New Guinea University of Technology, Lae.

Bickerton, D. 1975. Can English and Tok Pisin be kept apart? In McElhanon, K. (ed.) *Tok Pisin i go we?* Special Issue of *Kivung*, pp. 21–28.

Cavalli-Sforza, L. L. and Wang, W. S–Y. 1986. Spatial distance and lexical replacement. *Language* 62: 38–56.

Charpentier, J. M. 1983. Le Pidgin Bichelamar avant et après l'Independence de Vanuatu. *York Papers in Linguistics* 11.

Church, G. 1970. Twenty very common mistakes in secondary school English in T.P.N.G. *English in New Guinea* 3: 20–40.

Collinson, C. W. 1929. *Cannibals and Coconuts*. London: George Philip & Son.

Crowley, T. 1981. *Grama Blong Bislama*. University of The South Pacific. Port Vila: Vanuatu.

1988. Genesis of a preposition system in Bislama. Paper presented at the Fifth International Conference on Austronesian Linguistics, Auckland.

Davani, J. A. B. 1984. Current Trends and Patterns in the Use of English amongst Students at the University of Papua New Guinea. Unpublished BA thesis, University of Papua New Guinea.

De Camp, D. 1971. Toward a generative analysis of a post-creole continuum. In Hymes, D. (ed.), *Pidginization and Creolization of Languages*. Cambridge: Cambridge University Press, pp. 349–70.

Dutton, T. 1980. *Queensland Canefields English of the Late Nineteenth Century*. Pacific Linguistics D-12. Canberra: Australian National University.

1983. Birds of a feather: A pair of rare pidgins from the Gulf of Papua. In Woolford, E. and Washabaugh, W. (eds.), *The Social Context of Creolization*. Ann Arbor: Karoma, pp. 77–105.

Foley, W. 1986. *The Papuan Languages of New Guinea*. Cambridge: Cambridge University Press.

Grimshaw, B. 1912. *Guinea Gold*. London: Mills and Boon.

Harrison, S. 1972. The Language of Norfolk Island. Unpublished BA thesis, Macquarie University, New South Wales.

Hollyman, K. J. 1971. French in the Pacific. In Sebeok (ed.), 1971, pp. 903–37.

Jourdan, C. 1985. Sapos Iumi Mitim Iumi: The Social Context of Creolization in the Solomon Islands. Unpublished PhD thesis, Australian National University.

Kachru, B. 1982. Meaning in deviation: Towards understanding non-native English texts. In Kachru, B. (ed.), *The Other Tongue: English Across Cultures*. Urbana, II: University of Illinois Press, pp. 325–50.

Laycock, D. C. 1971. English and other Germanic languages. In Sebeok (ed.) 1971, pp. 877–902.

1981. Melanesian linguistic diversity: a Melanesian choice? Paper presented at Research School of Pacific Studies Seminar on Melanesia-Beyond Diversity. To appear in Proceedings. Canberra: Australian National University.

1988. The status of Pitcairn-Norfolk: Creole, dialect or cant? In Ammon, U. (ed.), *Status and Function of Languages and Language Varieties*. Berlin: De Gruyter.

Laycock, D. C. and Vorhooeve, C. L. 1971. History of research in Papuan languages. In Sebeok (ed.), 1971, pp. 509–40.

Laycock, D. C. and Winter, W. (eds.) 1987. *A World of Language: Papers presented to Professor S. A. Wurm on his 65th Birthday*. Pacific Linguistics C-100. Canberra: Australian National University.

Le Page, R. B. and Tabouret-Keller, A. 1985. *Acts of Identity. Creole-based*

Approaches to Language and Ethnicity. Cambridge: Cambridge University Press.

Lynch, J. 1987. The French legacy in Bislama. In Laycock and Winter, (eds.) 1987, pp. 411–20.

Mead, M. 1938. The Mountain Arapesh: an importing culture. *American Museum of Natural History Anthropological Papers* 36: 139–349.

Mihalic, F. 1957. *Grammar and Dictionary of Neo-Melanesian Pidgin.* Westmead, NSW: The Mission Press.

1971. *The Jacaranda Dictionary and Grammar of Melanesian Pidgin.* Brisbane: Jacaranda Press.

Moag, R. F. and Moag, L. B. 1979. English in Fiji: some perspectives and the need for language planning. In Richards, J. (ed.), *New Varieties of English: Issues and Approaches.* Occasional Papers No. 8. Singapore: SEAMEO Regional Language Centre, pp. 73–90.

Mühlhäusler, P. 1981. Foreigner Talk: Tok Masta in New Guinea. *International Journal of the Sociology of Language* 28: 93–113.

1982. Etymology and pidgin and creole languages. *Transactions of the Philological Society*: 99– 118.

1984. Tracing the roots of Pidgin German. *Language and Communication* 4: 27–57.

1986. Pidgin and creoles of Australia and the Pacific: current research for an atlas of languages of intercultural communication. *Australian Journal of Linguistics* 6: 181–99.

1987. The politics of small languages in Australia and the Pacific. *Language and Communication* 7: 1–24.

1988. Intercultural communication in the Pacific area in pre-colonial days. Paper presented at the Fifth International Conference on Austronesian Linguistics, Auckland.

Nelson, H. 1972. *Papua New Guinea. Black Unity or Black Chaos?* Harmondsworth: Penguin.

Noel, J. 1975. Legitimacy of Pidgin in the development of Papua New Guinea toward nationhood. In McElhanon, K. (ed.), Tok Pisin i go we? Special Issue of *Kivung* 1: 76–84.

O'Reilly, P. 1953. Le francais parlé en Nouvelle-Caledonie. Apports étrangers et vocables nouveaux, archaïsmes et expressions familières. *Journal de la Société des Océanistes* 9: 203–28.

Phillip, A. 1986. *Communication Skills Needs Survey of the Papua New Guinea Provincial and National Public Service 1985.* Port Moresby: Administrative College of Papua New Guinea.

Piau, J. and Holzknecht, S. 1985. Current attitudes to Tok Pisin. In Wurm and Mühlhäusler (eds.) 1985, pp. 487–93.

Platt, J., Weber, H. and Ho, M. L. 1984. *The New Englishes.* London: Routledge & Kegan Paul.

Rickford, J. R. and Traugott, E. C. 1985. Symbol of powerlessness and degeneracy, or symbol of solidarity and truth? Paradoxical attitudes towards pidgins and creoles. In Greenbaum, S. (ed.), *The English Language Today.* Oxford: Pergamon, pp. 252–61.

Romaine, S. 1986. Sprachmischung und Purismus: Sprich mir nicht von Mischmasch. *Lili* 62: 92–107.

1988. *Pidgin and Creole Languages*. London: Longman.

1989a. English and Tok Pisin in Papua New Guinea. In Watson-Gegeo, K. (ed.), *English in the South Pacific*. Special Issue of *World Englishes*.

1989b. Lexical change and variation in Tok Pisin. In Alatis, J. E. and Walsh, T. (eds.), *Synchronic and Diachronic Approaches to Linguistic Change and Variation*. Washington DC: Georgetown University Press, pp. 268–79.

1989c. Some differences between spoken and written Tok Pisin. *English World-Wide* 9: 243–69.

Ross, A. S. C. and Moverley, A. W. 1964. *The Pitcairnese Language*. London: Deutsch.

Sankoff, G. 1980. Political power and linguistic inequality in Papua New Guinea. In Sankoff, G. (ed.), *The Social Life of Language*. Philadelphia: University of Pennsylvania Press, pp. 5–28.

Sebeok, T. A. (ed.). 1971. *Current Trends in Linguistics. Vol 8: Linguistics in Oceania*. The Hague: Mouton. 2 vols.

Siegel, J. 1986. Pidgin English in Fiji: a sociolinguistic history. *Pacific Studies* 9: 53–107.

1988. Pidgin English in Nauru. Paper presented at the Fifth International Conference on Austronesian Linguistics, Auckland.

Smith, A. M. 1978. *The Papua New Guinea Dialect of English*. ERU Research Report No. 25. Port Moresby: Papua New Guinea.

Smith, G. P. 1988. Idiomatic Tok Pisin and referential adequacy. MS, Department of Language and Communication Studies, Papua New Guinea University of Technology, Lae.

Smithies, M. and S. Holzknecht. 1981. Errors in Papua New Guinea written English at the tertiary level. *RELC Journal* 12: 10–34.

Swan, J. 1986. *Report of an Investigation of Employer Satisfaction with the Professional Communicative Competence of Graduates of Papua New Guinea University of Technology*. Research and Technical Report Series 'R'. No. 52.86. Papua New Guinea University of Technology, Lae.

Swan, J. and Lewis, D. 1987. 'There's a lot of it about': Self-estimates of their use of Tok Pisin by students of the Papua New Guinea University of Technology. In Laycock and Winter (eds.) 1987, pp. 649–3.

Tryon, D. T. 1986. Neologisms in Bislama (Vanuatu). In Fishman, J., Tabouret-Keller, A., Clyne, M., Krishnamurti, Bh. and Abdulaziz, M. (eds.), *The Fergusonian Impact*. Vol. 2. Berlin: Mouton de Gruyter, pp. 305–13.

1988. Regionalisms and the history of Bislama. Paper presented at the Fifth International Conference on Austronesian Linguistics, Auckland.

Volker, C. A. 1982. *An Introduction to Rabaul Creole German*. Unpublished MA thesis, University of Queensland.

Watson-Gegeo, K. 1986. The study of language use in Oceania. *Annual Review of Anthropology* 15: 149–62.

1987. English in the Solomon Islands. *World Englishes* 6: 21–32.

Whinnom, K. 1956. *Spanish Contact Vernaculars in the Philippine Islands*. Hong Kong: University Press.

Wolfers, E. P. 1969. The vocabulary of New Guinea English as used by expatriates. *Kivung* 2: 52–64.

Wurm, S. A. 1971. Pidgins, creoles and lingue franche. In Sebeok (ed.) 1971, pp. 999–1021.

(ed.) 1976. *New Guinea area languages and language study. Vol. 2: Austronesian languages*. Pacific Linguistics C-39. Canberra: Australian National University.

1982. *Papuan Languages of Oceania*. Tübingen: Gunter Narr.

Wurm, S. A. and Mühlhäusler, P. (eds.). 1985. *Handbook of Tok Pisin (New Guinea Pidgin)*. Pacific Linguistics C-70. Canberra: Australian National University.

Yarupawa, S. 1986. Milne Bay Informal Variety of English. Unpublished BA thesis, University of Papua New Guinea.

42

Watching girls pass by in Tok Pisin

PETER MÜHLHÄUSLER

Introduction

Most studies of creolisation have emphasised the massive qualitative changes accompanying the acquisition of a pidgin as a native language by a new generation of children. There are few reasons for doubting the importance of children in the development of some creoles, though the number of such 'ideal' (in a Bickertonian sense) creoles is probably quite restricted. More numerous and, arguably, equally important, are instances where the expansion of a pidgin occurs with a generation of adult speakers who change their primary language as they migrate to the new urban centres of the developing nations. Thus, in the southwest Pacific, in Papua New Guinea (Tok Pisin), the Solomons (Pijin) and Vanuatu (Bislama), this second type of creolisation is becoming increasingly common. Valuable general remarks about the transition from rural pidgin-vernacular bilingualism to urban (creolised) pidgin monolingualism can be found in the writings of Jourdan (1985). Referring to Tok Pisin, the Pidgin English of Papua New Guinea discussed in this paper, Elton Brash made the following observations about the linguistic adaptations accompanying the changeover from a rural to an urban environment (1975: 323):

> Evidence of the operation of ethnogenesis within Papua New Guinea cities can be found in the growing number of original Pidgin expressions covering the shared experience of their black inhabitants. These range from descriptive terms referring to town occupations, the shortage of money, to sport, beer drinking, brawling, sexual adventure, card playing, the police, to whites, and so on, together with more complex terms which recognise the effects of city life on the individual.

At the time of his remarks very little had been written about the urban varieties of Tok Pisin. Moreover, such important work as had been done (particularly that of Sankoff and her collaborators) concentrated on certain aspects of core grammatical development in young children rather than stylistic diversification in adult urban migrants.

In 1976, at the invitation of the University of Papua New Guinea, I undertook a brief period of fieldwork in Urban Port Moresby with the aim of obtaining data covering a maximum of non-traditional domains, functions and registers. Some of my findings were subsequently published in Wurm (1979) and Wurm and Mühlhäusler (1985), though many of my transcriptions still await more detailed analysis.

The present study is concerned with a small number of issues:

a)   sociolinguistic methodology for obtaining 'natural' speech.
b)   data pertaining to the domain of male-female relations among young urban dwellers.
c)   code switching and linguistic innovation.

My emphasis will be on the use that is made of the lexical repertoire of my informants rather than on questions of grammatical expansion.

Some methodological issues

The bulk of texts representing spoken Tok Pisin are either narratives (typically translations of traditional stories (*stori bilong tumbana*)) or dyadic conversations relating to fairly traditional domains of discourse. Moreover, virtually all recordings were made and transcribed by expatriate linguists.

In the wake of the Labovian revolution in sociolinguistics more sophisticated procedures for collecting pidgin and creole data became more widespread, the texts in Dutton's revised *Tok Pisin Course* (1985) containing a number of fine examples. In my own work I adapted a number of conventional sociolinguistic procedures for obtaining Tok Pisin texts, making extensive use of data I had obtained as a participant-observer living in various Tok Pisin speaking communities. Observer participation was not a viable option in the case of my urban fieldwork, however, mainly because integration into a dynamic urban communication network would have taken considerably more time than I had at my disposal. To overcome this problem I cooperated with a student[1] of the university of Papua New Guinea who (a) had a basic training in sociolinguistics (b) was a leading member of a group of male students and (c) was highly motivated to find out more about Urban Tok Pisin. For the duration of about a week, my helper spent every morning recording the conversations he and his mates had whilst playing snooker at one of the open air snooker tables of the university and the afternoon transcribing and discussing his recordings with me. The selection of the snooker table as the setting was motivated by the following considerations:

a) as there is only one player at any one time there is a great deal of opportunity for other players and spectators to talk
b) the participants belong to a close group of friends
c) the participants are involved in conversations as well as watching a game, and there is considerable scope for interruptions and code switches.

An additional bonus was the location of the snooker table in the open air, close to a footpath connecting a number of university buildings. On several occasions, users of the footpath commented on the game and/or its participants and female passers-by were commented on or involved in light-hearted exchanges with the all-male group of snooker players/watchers (this latter aspect forming the principal topic of this paper). The selection of talk about sex is motivated, on the one hand, by the frequency of this topic in my data; on the other hand, it is a particularly interesting domain for studying sociolinguistic change in an urban environment as the traditional sex-roles and associated linguistic activities of the villages are no longer applicable in the towns where new modes of interaction between the sexes emerge and are talked about.

The data

The data considered here fall into two main groups: a) talk about sex and b) direct verbal responses to seeing girls walk past the snooker table. For the limited purpose of this paper the second type of data will be given preferential treatment, as they combine insider conversation with verbal exchanges with outsiders. First I shall present a number of texts together with their translation.

Text 1 Two onlookers discuss how they spent the last weekend. This extract, from a longer speech event, illustrates how their attention is temporarily focused on a girl walking past the snooker table.

A: Mipela painim blekmaket raun i go.
Ol wantok kirap i laik rap long wanpela utility mipela i bin raun longen.
En mi, mi ronewe long T. long lek.

B: Em bilong boi i save wok long ELCOM ya?

A: A, em tasol.

B: Husat pul nem bilongen gen ya?

A: T. M. Ol i laik rap long kar bilongen ya, mi pret na mi ronewe. nogut ol polis i autim mipela.

We were looking for a black market going all over the place.
My mates were beginning to mess about with the utility truck we had been going around in.
This is when I ran away to T. on foot.
Isn't he the bloke who works with the Electricity Commission?
Yes, that's him.
What is his full name again?
T. M. They were beginning to mess about with their car, I was frightened and ran away. I was worried that the police would get us.

B: O pren, dispela meri ya i kam bek   This woman has come back, mate.
gen.
A&B: Sem mo yet (shouting)!   Very attractive!
A&B: Yu save!   You know!

(returning to previous speech event as the girl disappears)

B: Na bihain olsem wanem?   And then, what happened?
A: Mi ron long lek tasol i kam long   I just walked until half past four in the
hap pas po long moning.   morning.

Text 2 Another group of players discuss their exploits at the weekend.
(extract)

A: Mipela i spak, em dispela taim yu   We were drinking, it was when you lost
lusim ki bilong yu ya. Em dispela   your key. That was the time. We
taim tasol. Mipela i spak i go, i go i   drank and drank, the boys beat the
go, ol boi paitim dram na singsing: drum and sang:
Yu ya yu ya, sak meri ya²   You, you, shark woman
Singsing bilong ol Madang ya.   That's a song from Madang
B: Yupela i spak wantaim ol manki   Did you drink with the Sepik boys?
Sepik?
A: Nogat. Mi, mi . . . mi . . . na John   No. I, I . . . I . . . and John S., Louis,
S., Louis, William na husat gen ya?   William and who else? This bloke, S.
Dispela boi ya, S. Dispela boi   This bloke from Morobe. We kept
Morobe ya. Mipela i spak i go i go   drinking. We went to the black
nau. Mipela i go long blekmaket   market and bought more drink and
baim dring gen i kam na dring   bought it back and drank again.
gen.
B: (whistles as a girl passes by and   My God, your skirt is too short.
shouts:) Salawe, he tusot. (the girl
attempts to pull down her skirt)
A: Ais!   You are as sweet as icecream!

(girl laughs)

B: O-a-o (short for kok-kan-kok)   cock-cunt-cock
A: Abus bilong tumbuna kandare!   What a dish for my old uncle (=penis)!
B: Goan yu pinisim stori nau.   Come on, finish your story now.
A: Mipela i spak i go i go nau na mi   We kept on drinking and I saw
lukim samting nogut.   something bad.
B: Samting i gat huk tu?   Something that had a hook?
A: Magnet ya, magnet. Samting i gat   A magnet it was, a magnet. Something
huk ya, i save hukim ol man.   which had a hook, to hook men.
I save go slip nabaut long set ya.   She was in the habit of sleeping around
with this set.
B: Sore!   How shocking!

Text 3 A group of snooker players discusses a recent sports event.

A: Na this people, ting, they really regret they should have put R. in the first half, so he cause a lot of extensive damage.

And these people, I think they really regretted it, they should have put R. in the first half, so he could cause a lot of extensive damage.

B: Dispela Sondoni ya, R. i kam insait ya, i go holim em long nek bilong en, na R. bihain i go pilai?

This R. who entered and held Sondoni by his neck, did he play afterwards?

A: Ating, some fifteen minutes before the game i pinis.

I think some fifteen minutes before the end of the game.

B: (notices a group of highschool girls walk by) O, olsem wanem?

Hey, what's that?

B: (shouts) Baby blue, baby white[3]

Baby blue, baby white!

A: (shouts) Wokabaut bilong yu tasol! He, sis, working with the canteen!

Look how you are walking! Hey sis, working with the canteen?

A: Yufela ting wanem dispela is getting us?

Do you think this one is getting us?

B: So what, mi tokim yupela ya.

So what, as I just told you.

Text 4 The same conversation is again interrupted by a group of girls passing by. This time the reaction of the men around the snooker table is more lively:

A: Na Sondoni takelim em i kirap nau na i rekem Sondoni wantaim bol. Na man ya i kirap na pinalaisim ol.

And Sondoni tackled him and he got up and wrecked Sondoni with the ball. And this man penalised them.

(a group of highschool girls pass by)

Chanting: Mosbi hai ya!

Moresby High School girls!

Voice: Nogat, ol bilong Godons ya.

No, they are from Gordon's.

Voice: He, yagaye, o Clemens!

Heh, gee, Clements.

A: Ol occupied pinis ya.

They are all occupied.

Voice: Ol i kam painim man bilong ol ya.;

They have come to find men.

Voice: Go, go, go wet long toilet ya (general laughter) na pulim em i go insait.

Go and wait in the toilet and pull them in.

Voices: Yagaye!

Jeez, look at that!

Voice: Yu kam we? Em nau ol i Seten tasol i stap.

Where are you from? Now, this is where Satan is.

Voice: Yu, mipela givim long yu.

You, we give it to you.

Voices: Laik ok one, eh, *edeseni oi lao*?[4]

I like the ok one. Hey friend, where are you going? I like the one without a boyfriend. Friend, where are you going? I like a good one just like her, like her.

Laik fresh one. *Tura, edeseni oi lao?*

O laik good one. Olsem, olsem.

Voice: Tambu, can I have the back
  one?

Cousin, can I have the one at the back?

Voices: Ai, yagaye!

Geez!

Voice: Ai, nogat mani ya, yu stupit.

You have no money you stupid.

Voices: Heh!

Hey!

Voice: Laik unused one.

I would like the unused one.

Voice: Nogat mani ya.

You have no money.

Voice: Mai kayo, back one.

My fellow Manus islander, I want the
  back one.

Voices: Laik fresh one.

I like the one with no boyfriend.

(girls laugh)

Girl: I am fresh, na you?

I am unattached, how about you?

Male voice: Na yu yu are fresh.

And you, you are unattached.

Male voice: Oke wan, laik o.k. wan.

OK one, I like the ok one.

(laughter)

Angry voice: Bladi baket!

Bloody dustbin! (someone hurt himself
  on a dustbin)

(laughter)

Voice: Laik fresh one.

I like the unattached one.

Angry voice: What the hell you, shit!
  Fakim, I don't like that.

What the hell you, shit! Fuck it. I don't
  like that.

A: Em bai ol i go long rum. Girlpren
  bilong I. ya.

They will go to their rooms now. Here
  is I.'s girlfriend.

B: I. husat?

I. who?

A: I.S. manki Manus ya.

I.S. the boy from Manus.

Text 5 Conversation as another woman walks past the snooker table:

A: Dispela meri Nu Ailan ya, husat
  ya?

This New Ireland girl. Who is she?

B: R.

R.

C: Em gutpela bilong opim lek ya.

She is good at opening her legs.

B: A opim lek samting nogut ya. Yu
  save, mi misineri pinis na mi ting yu
  misineri yet ya.

A, to open one's legs is bad. You know,
  I am a religious man and I was under
  the impression you were too.

A: Mi wanwe pinis.

I follow the straight and narrow path
  (double meaning).

C: Olaboi!

Good heavens!

B: Wanwe ya, bi yu go painim wanem
  wanwe?

The straight and narrow path indeed,
  what kind of straight and narrow
  path are you after?

A: Em bipo ya, mi wanwe las wik
  tasol, bipo mi tewelman yes, nau
  mipela i misinari.

Well before, I became converted only
  last week, I was a sinner before, now
  we are converted.

The language of the above texts differs in a number of respects from that found in the more conventional texts published by other investigators and thus deserves to be analysed in more detail. However, given the exploratory nature of this paper, its full significance will not be discussed here.

Some linguistic and sociolinguistic aspects of Urban Tok Pisin

Not so long ago, Tok Pisin was known as Tok Boi[5] 'the language of male indigenes in European employment', that is, it was a language spoken predominantly by young males. It was learnt away from the villages on the coastal plantations and in related industries and, consequently, few females had a good command of the language before the Second World War. A number of writers remark on the use of Tok Pisin by returning young men to make sexual innuendos about women back home. As the meaning of these was only partly transparent to the victims of such innuendos an inegalitarian linguistic situation was created. Before the mass influx of Tok Pisin speaking New Guineans into Papuan Port Moresby (where Hiri Motu was the principal pidgin language) from pre-independence days onward, Tok Pisin appears to have been used for making comments about Motuan women in a similar way. Today, there are few young Motuan women who do not understand Tok Pisin and on the campus of the University of Papua New Guinea an understanding of Tok Pisin by female students is virtually universal.

The data on which this study is based could serve as a point of departure for the study of sex-related differences in language use in Tok Pisin and pidgin languages in general. A first impression is one of considerable sexism in male talking to and about females. A pidgin language such as Tok Pisin offers a form of verbal interaction without the restrictions and taboos found in male-female discourse in traditional societies. Further, as the language has grown up as one of a male dominated world and asymmetrical power relations (see Sankoff 1976), it gives men a considerable advantage over women. Note that speech is typically initiated and dominated by males in these texts and that the relationship of males with females is seen in terms of metaphors such as consumption of food, something which is equally common in Western languages. It would be interesting to observe to what extent the male domination of Tok Pisin is attenuated or reduced with increasing creolisation and increasing numbers of female speakers. With very few exceptions (e.g., Troy 1987; Escure, this volume) the question of language and sex in pidgins and creoles remains unexplored territory.

Turning now to more linguistic aspects of these texts, one can observe the following salient features:

i) There is a considerable amount of code switching, both of a genuine type involving Tok Pisin and English and a kind of stereotype tokenism, involving the use of holophrastic sequences from Hiri Motu, such as *edeseni oi lao*? 'where are you going?'

ii) In addition to code switching there is also code mixing. In a number of instances it is not clear whether the speakers use Tok Pisin or English. An example is *laik gut wan*, 'like good one'.

iii) Lexical items are borrowed very freely from English.

Many of these loans would not be intelligible to monolingual or traditional Tok Pisin speakers. Examples in the above texts include both replacement of established items and additions. Examples are:

replacements	additions
utility replacing *haptrak*	*pinalaisim* 'to penalise'
rekem replacing *bagarapim* 'to wreck'	*okjupait* 'occupied'

iv) The fact that we are dealing with a new group of people composed of members of numerous geographic and linguistic backgrounds is emphasised by the use of special forms of address and other markers indexical of speakers' or addressees' place of origin. The following ones were collected during this study:

tobarat	'fellow Tolai'
sunam	'fellow Manus islander'
kas (intu)	'fellow Sepik person'
kayo	'fellow islander (from Bismarck archipelago)
atos	'fellow Siassi Islander'

The formerly widely documented *wantok*, used as a solidarity marker among Tok Pisin speakers, was not in evidence in my recordings.

v) When compared with traditional rural Tok Pisin, certain semantic fields of Urban Tok Pisin, such as talk about sex and drink, are considerably more densely populated in the latter variety. I managed to record a significant number of previously unlisted items and elicited further ones during the transcription with my Papua New Guinean informant. This suggests that much of the lexical growth during urban glossogenesis is catering for stylistic variation in a small range of domains.

vi) The meanings of both Tok Pisin and English lexical items are extended and changed to fit the special requirements of urban Tok Pisin speakers. In the text we note examples such as *fresh* 'without a boyfriend or frigid', *sem* 'attractive' rather than shameful, *ais* (ice) 'sweet' and *magnet* 'magnet or attractive'.

vii) Double entendre and other forms of play language (Tok Pilai) (cf. Brash 1971) are widespread. Such double meaning is either local as in *abus biling tumbana kandare* 'A dish for my old uncle – for my penis', or prolonged over several verbal exchanges, as in conversation no. 5 where the ambiguity of *wanwe* (the straight and narrow path; female genitals; a converted Christian; an erect penis pointing 'one way') is exploited by both interlocutors.

viii) In the texts recorded on the university campus, the frequent use of clipped forms and acronyms was observed, something which is almost entirely absent in rural Tok Pisin. Examples include both items borrowed from English, such as *sis* 'sister' or *Elcom* 'Electricity Commission', and independent creations, such as *ti el* = *trai lak* 'to try one's luck'.

Conclusions

The data presented here illustrate the continued growth of Tok Pisin resulting from its extension to new domains and functions in non-traditional settings. The lexical evidence examined in this paper suggests a number of sources of such expansion, particularly borrowing from English and traditional vernaculars, extension of meaning of existing terms and the formation of acronyms. In the passages quoted, mechanisms such as compounding were less in evidence. However, when considering a larger corpus produced by the same group of speakers the importance of this traditional means of lexical extension could still be seen. It is important to point out that the kind of urban creolisation observed in Tok Pisin, that is, a pidgin language being adopted as the primary language by a group of adults for whom it is not the first language, is characterised by increased stylistic flexibility and lexical choice in a small number of culturally salient domains rather than a jump in referential adequacy. The signalling of group membership, attitudes and other indexical information appears to be more important than having new names for new objects and concepts.

In the domain of discourse singled out for special consideration here, the changes in the language parallel those in relations between the sexes, particularly the transition from conservative rural modes of interaction to new urban ones. It was found that these changes have not led to a greater equality between the sexes but rather perpetuate and accentuate the male domination characteristic of many traditional societies. Data such as the ones examined here would seem to provide an interesting point of departure for the study of sex-related linguistic differences in Tok Pisin and other pidgins and creoles.

NOTES

1. Because of the controversial nature of some of the materials recorded I have agreed not to divulge the identity of this person or that of the other participants.

The transcriptions were made with the knowledge and consent of those recorded.

2. The full song is:

Yu ya, yu ya, sak meri ya,	Hey you, hey you, shark woman (prostitute),
Wan man kam i no nap,	One man comes – that's not enough,
Tu man kam i no nap,	Two men come – it's still not enough,
ol man kam warawara	Lots of men come – now you are getting aroused.

3. Referring to the different colour teeshirts signalling different highschools in Port Moresby.
4. Note the switch to Hiri Motu, the former principal *lingua franca* of the Port Moresby region.
5. In Urban Tok Pisin the meaning of *boi* is 'young man', contrasting with other items such as *manki* 'small boy', *man* 'male of any age, person' and *lapun* 'old person'. Some speakers also use *boi* to refer to young boys.

REFERENCES

Brash, Elton. 1971. Tok Pilai, Tok Piksa na Tok Bokis: Imaginative Dimensions in Melanesian Pidgin. *Kivung* 4 (1): 12–20.
1975. Tok Pisin, *Meanjin* 34 (3): 320–7.
Dutton, Thomas E. 1985. *A New Course in Tok Pisin (New Guinea Pidgin)*. Canberra: Pacific Linguistics D-67.
Jourdan, Christine, 1985. Sapos Iumi Mitim Yumi. Unpublished PhD thesis, Australian National University.
Sankoff, Gillian. 1976. Political Power and Linguistic Inequality in Papua New Guinea. In O'Barr, W. and O'Barr, J. (eds.), *Language and Politics*, The Hague: Mouton.
Troy, Jakeline. 1987. The role of Aboriginal women in the development of contact languages in New South Wales: from the late eighteenth to the early twentieth century. In Pauwels, A. (ed.), *Women and Language in Australian and New Zealand Society*. Sydney: Australian Professional Publications, pp. 155–69.
Wurm, Stephen A. (ed.). 1979. *New Guinea and Neighboring Areas: A Sociolinguistic Laboratory*. The Hague: Mouton.
Wurm, S. A. & Mühlhäusler, P. (eds.). 1985. *Handbook of Tok Pisin*. Canberra, Pacific Linguistics C-70.

43

Sociolinguistic variation and language attitudes in Hawaii

CHARLENE J. SATO

Introduction

Sociolingustic research that acknowledges the importance of viewing language as a human problem attempts to reconcile the facts of linguistic variation with those of social identity and inequality (Hymes 1973). In this paper I present a case study of Hawaii which examines this relationship in a Pacific English creole continuum and, more specifically, calls attention to its dynamic nature.

A history of cultural diversity

Hawaii, with a population of about one million, is the only American state in which no single ethnic group is a numerical majority, and where most of the people are of Asian and Pacific rather than European or African origin (Nordyke 1977). The population of the seven inhabited islands is roughly a quarter Japanese and a quarter Caucasian. Still another quarter is racially mixed (about 16 per cent part-Hawaiian), and the remaining quarter is comprised of a number of groups, including Filipinos, Chinese, Blacks, Koreans, Hawaiians, Samoans, and other Pacific Islanders (Schmitt 1982).

Hawaii's cultural diversity is largely the result of massive labour importation, triggered by the development of sugar plantations by north Americans during the late nineteenth and early twentieth centuries. The islands were transformed from a Hawaiian kingdom with a subsistence agricultural economy into a plantation economy in which sugar became 'king' (Fuchs 1961; Kent 1974, 1983). Political incorporation into the US began with the overthrow of the native Hawaiian monarchy in 1893 and annexation by the US in 1898, and was completed with statehood in 1959. The sugar plantations formed the basis of the islands' economy until the mid-1950s but, since statehood, the economy has been dominated by tourism and, to a lesser extent, the US military and civil service bureaucracies (Beechert 1985; Cooper and Daws 1985; Kent 1983; Takaki 1983).

Hawaiian society was radically restructured by the development of the sugar plantations. Native Hawaiians were politically subjugated and their language and culture were systematically undermined (Day 1987; Huebner 1985; Trask 1984/1985). By the end of the nineteenth century, they accounted for only one-fifth of the total population of about 154,000 (Reinecke 1935/1969); they were outnumbered by the major immigrant groups: the Chinese, Portuguese, Japanese, and Filipinos. All of these groups lived and worked within the constraints of the socioeconomic hierarchy largely controlled by Caucasian plantation owners.

Today, this hierarchy has its counterpart in the ethnic stratification of workers in the tourist industry, which some observers have warily dubbed 'a new kind of sugar' (Finney and Watson 1974, Kent 1974). Native Hawaiians, who earlier relinquished their land to meet the needs of sugar growers, have now grown accustomed to the 'commodification' of their culture for tourism (Kent 1974; Trask 1984/1985). Currently, the bureaucratic-professional middle class is Caucasian and Asian, while the working class is primarily composed of native Hawaiians, Filipinos, and recent immigrant Asians and Pacific Islanders (Kent 1983: 180–1).

The emergence of a creole continuum

The linguistic consequences of plantation labour importation and of Hawaii's economic and political domination by the US have been complex (for fuller accounts, see Bickerton and Odo 1976; Carr 1972; Day 1987; Reinecke 1935/1969; and Sato 1985). On the plantations, which were first worked primarily by native Hawaiians, a pidginised Hawaiian developed by the end of the nineteenth century (Bickerton and Wilson 1987). This later gave way to a pidginised English – Hawaii Pidgin English (HPE) – with the addition of the Chinese, Portuguese and Japanese to the plantation workforce, and as a result of the political ascendancy of English in the islands during the early 1900s. Most scholars agree that HPE was rather unstable and highly variable, both ethnically and geographically (Bickerton 1977; Reinecke 1935/1969). In essence, it consisted of English and Hawaiian vocabulary combined with the phonology and syntax of its speakers' first languages.

Hawaii Creole English (HCE) was initially created by the first Hawaii-born children of the plantation communities and further developed by subsequent generations of 'local' people. It differs from HPE in many interesting ways (see Bickerton 1977, 1981; Sato 1978). One difference is that HCE has an elaborated system for marking tense, aspect, and modality which is minimally evident in HPE. An even more obvious difference is phonological: whereas HPE speakers typically have an accent influenced by their first language, HCE speakers' accent IS that of their first language. Hence, someone of Japanese ancestry speaking HPE can be identified by her Japanese accent, but a Japanese speaker of HCE could not be easily distinguished from a HCE speaker of any other Asian or Pacific Island background.

HCE appears to have been most 'focused', in Le Page's (1980) sense, during the 1920s and 1930s. Thereafter, diversification of Hawaii's economy, accelerated by US military and governmental needs during World War II, led to greater employment opportunities off the plantation. Public education, available since the late 1800s, also increased native creole speakers' exposure to English and, in certain segments of the community, contributed to rapid decreolisation following World War II.

The extremely variable English in Hawaii resulting from the processes of language contact and creation sketched above has been the object of study for over 50 years now. Hawaii is one of the few places in the world where researchers have had access to both pidgin and creole speakers and have thus been able to describe empirically pidginisation and creolisation in a single community. Recently, attention has shifted to decreolisation, the process through which a creole merges over time with its lexically related standard language.

Most studies of Hawaii either explicitly adopt or assume De Camp's (1971) creole continuum model. They take as uncontroversial the view that decreolisation is occurring at the societal level, that is, that there has been an increase over time in the use of more acrolectal, English-like linguistic variants by a larger portion of the community. A number of linguistic features have been described from this perspective, including segmental alternations and other phonological processes (Odo 1975; Bickerton and Odo 1976); the (zero-)copula (Day 1972; Bickerton 1977; Perlman 1973), tense-aspect-modality markers (Bickerton 1974, 1977; Neff 1977; Sato, 1978); existential predications (Perlman 1973); relativisation (Bickerton 1977; Peet 1978); and various noun phrase features (Bickerton 1977; Perlman 1973).

In several studies, decreolisation in HCE is reported to involve implicational patterning among HCE and standard English variants of a linguistic feature. Such patterning was evident in Sato's (1978) analysis of 26 HPE and HCE speakers' marking of *irrealis* (i.e., future, hypothetical or conditional) events and actions with the preverbal auxiliaries: *go*, *gon*, *gona*, and *wil*. The following sentences, glossed as 'I'll leave it/them outside for you', illustrate their use:

a. ai *go liv* om autsaid fo yu
b. ai *gon liv* om autsaid fo yu
c. ai*m gona liv* om autsaid fo yu
d. ai*l liv* om autsaid fo yu

The implicational pattern observed among these forms was that speakers who used *wil* also used *gona*, and those who used *gona* also used *gon*. Interestingly, the use of *gon* did not entail the use of *go*. *Go* proved to be the least frequently used of the four irrealis forms and was favoured by Filipino HPE, not HCE, speakers from Hawaii (arguably the least decreolised island in the state). Those speakers who preferred *gon* as an irrealis marker were either HCE speakers or HPE speakers from the more decreolised islands of Maui and Oahu. From these results, it seems that *go* originated as the basilectal irrealis marker but has been rapidly losing ground to the other forms.

While the cross-sectional studies cited above do reveal clear evidence of decreolisation at the societal level, it is important to realise that decreolisation has not affected all individuals to the same degree. As a result, synchronic variation in the community is extensive, both across speakers and within a single speaker in different communicative contexts (Bickerton 1977; Perlman 1973). A study on code shifting by children (Purcell 1979, 1984) has shown, for example, that the relative frequency of HCE features in their conversational speech covaries with a number of situational factors such as addressee, genre, topic, and psychological factors such as the speaker's emotional state.

Decreolisation does not affect all linguistic features in the same way either. Preliminary findings from longitudinal research on decreolisation (Sato 1986) indicates that linguistic features vary in their 'susceptibility' to decreolisation. Analysis of two samples of conversational speech obtained 13 years apart from a relatively basilectal Filipino HCE speaker revealed decreolisation in two morphosyntactic features but not in a prosodic feature.

With respect to past time reference (shown in table 43.1 below), the speaker shifted from a strong preference for HCE markers (the preverbal auxiliaries *bin* and *haed*, as in *hi bin kawl mi ap*, 'he called me up' and *hi haed chro om aut*, 'he threw them out') in 1973 to a preference for standard English (SE) regular and irregular past markers (as in 'call*ed*' and 'threw').

In referring to indefinite entities in discourse (as in 'She wants *a new bicycle*'), the speaker also shifted from greater use of HCE markers (the zero-article or *wan*, as in *shi laik ø nyu baisikol* or *shi laik wan nyu baisikol*) to greater use of SE *a* (see table 43.2).

A discourse-prosodic feature was also examined: *æh*-tag utterances with rising terminal pitch, such as *no mo jab fo yu æh* ('There isn't a job for you, right?'), which typically function as confirmation checks from speaker to listener. To the SE ear, the *æh*-tag is a striking feature of HCE (akin to Canadian *eh*; see Woods, this volume, note 4), one that would appear to be a prime candidate for decreolisation because of its perceptual salience. However, this proved not to be the case; the speaker did not demonstrate a loss of the *æh*-tag or a change in its accompanying intonational contour from 1973 to 1986.

Table 43.1. *Past time reference: HCE and SE markers*

	%(no.) HCE	%(no.) SE	Total no.
1973	79 (57)	21 (15)	72
1986	54 (51)	46 (43)	94

$1973 \times 1986, \chi^2 = 10.06, df = 1, p < 0.005.$

Table 43.2. *Reference to indefinite entities (existentially asserted or hypothesised): HCE and SE markers*

	%(no.) HCE	%(no.) SE	Total no.
1973	78 (14)	22 (4)	18
1986	44 (17)	56 (22)	39

$1973 \times 1986, \chi^2 = 4.39, df = 1, p < 0.05.$

These results suggest that, in general, prosodic features are more resistant to decreolisation than are morphosyntactic features (see similar findings reported by Escure (1981) for Belizean Creole). Why this should be the case remains problematic. While important insights undoubtedly lie in psycholinguistic accounts of language processing and acquisition, it is also necessary to consider the sociocultural and sociopsychological under-pinnings of language change (Le Page and Tabouret-Keller 1985; Rickford 1983, 1985; Romaine 1982; Sankoff 1980).

Clearly, speakers make linguistic choices based on a number of conscious and not-so-conscious motivations and pressures. Certain speakers have greater loyalty to HCE and/or less inclination to acquire a mainland US variety of English. How such attitudes and preferences are developed by individuals in Hawaii is as yet poorly understood. Equally unclear is how HCE use reflects different dimensions of social identity in Hawaii: ethnicity, class, and what might be termed 'localness'.

Attitudes toward HCE and SE

Studies of language attitudes in Hawaii converge on the general finding reported for other creole communities (see, e.g., Rickford 1985; Wurm 1985) that there is a negative attitude toward the creole variety of English and a positive one toward SE, on the part of teachers and students alike. Further, these studies indicate that HCE is associated with Asians and Pacific Islanders (including Hawaiians), low academic achievement, and low socioeconomic status (see Choy and Dodd 1976; Day 1980; McCreary 1986; Slaughter 1982; Yamamoto and Hargrove 1982). The general conclusion that may be drawn from these studies is that teachers and students alike evaluate HCE negatively relative to SE. While the results might be taken simply as confirmation of community stereotypes concerning varieties of English in Hawaii, these studies warrant careful interpretation. The studies yield important insights; however, there is much more that remains to be described in the dynamic interrelationship of language attitudes, linguistic variation and decreolization.

Rickford (1985) has pointed out that language attitude studies, in general, have tended to elicit the attitudes of middle class or socioeconomically privileged subjects, not the predominantly creole-speaking segments of the communities. As a result, the 'standard' view of language attitudes in creole communities probably underestimates the strength of positive attitudes toward creole varieties. Where the attitudes of working class, creole-speaking subjects have been examined (e.g., in Rickford 1985), clear evidence of the 'solidarity' value of the creole has emerged. Day's (1980) study, for example, found that 'less-advantaged' kindergarteners expressed a clear preference for HCE.

It is also important to note that all of the attitude studies were conducted in Honolulu, that is, in an urban setting where mainland US institutions and values are most pervasive. It remains to be seen what similar studies would yield in rural, working class areas on Oahu and the other Hawaiian islands, areas with a high proportion of native Hawaiians, or areas with a low proportion of Caucasians.

The studies used roughly the same research methods, essentially, elicitation of subjects' attitudes in (quasi-) experimental settings. If only as a corrective to the biasing effect of institutional contexts (Carranza and Ryan 1975), observational data are needed on language socialisation in HCE speakers and the community-at-large that either clarify or belie the stereotypical behaviour revealed by elicitation studies.

Also needed is information on perceptions of *intra*speaker variation as well as interspeaker variation. How would subjects evaluate the social significance of a single speaker's use of HCE and SE in a range of speech events? Not only would such studies be more likely to yield evidence of positive attitudes toward HCE, but they would also enhance the validity of attitude research in general.

A rather dramatic point of departure for observational language attitude studies has been provided by recent educational and legal controversies concerning HCE and SE. During the late summer and fall of 1987, heated and prolonged public discussion erupted over (1) the state Board of

Education's language policy for Hawaii's public schools and (2) the employment discrimination trial of two local weather forecasters (Kahakua *et al.* v. Hallgren). For the first time in Hawaii's history, positive attitudes toward the use and maintenance of HCE were explicitly articulated by different segments of the community and implicitly endorsed by some elements in the local mass media. A full account of these events is presented elsewhere (Sato, in preparation); here, it will suffice to point out some important links between language attitudes and sociolinguistic variation in Hawaii.

HCE in the classroom

Late in the summer of 1987, Hawaii's Board of Education (BOE)[1] formulated a policy on 'Standard English and Oral Communication,' a preliminary version of which mandated that 'Standard English [would] be the mode of oral communication for students and staff in the classroom setting and all other school related settings except when the objectives cover[ed] native Hawaiian or foreign language instruction and practice' (see Sato, 1989, for further discussion). Immediate opposition to the policy was voiced by many:[2] parents, teachers, university faculty, native Hawaiian professionals and community activists, and even some elements of the mass media.

During the final four-hour meeting at which the Board voted on the policy, all but a few speakers testified against it. Several who argued that HCE was a vital aspect of local identity, and that the acquisition of SE should not result in the loss of HCE, drew rousing applause from the audience. Not having anticipated this strong support for HCE and negative reaction to the policy, the BOE eventually adopted a much weaker version which simply 'encouraged' the modelling of SE by DOE staff.[3]

The level of public response to the Board's actions was unprecedented. Letters flooded the newspapers, and radio talk shows and television news programmes carried the controversy every day for a week in September, featuring interviews with BOE members, Department of Education (DOE) administrators, teachers, students, and university researchers. One of the two major newspapers commissioned a special week-long series on HCE which proved informative and generally quite supportive of HCE as a marker of local identity (Brislin 1987; Hartwell 1987; Hollis 1987; Keir 1987; Matsunaga 1987; Reyes 1987a–g). Student newspapers at various high schools around the state debated the policy and the role of HCE in schooling. Never before in Hawaii's history had such widespread, frequently rational, discussion of language politics consumed the community.

Various officials in the DOE made public statements supporting the BOE's policy following its adoption. At the same time, however, it was widely acknowledged that implementation and enforcement of the policy were virtually impossible, given the policy's failure to specify what it meant by the term 'standard English' and how 'violators' of the policy would be identified and sanctioned (Hikida *et al.* 1987; Reyes 1987d, 1987f). It is difficult to imagine how DOE officials might monitor several thousand classrooms on a daily or even weekly basis for HCE use.

Perhaps most importantly, the BOE mistakenly anticipated whole-hearted endorsement by teachers. While some appear to be complying with the policy by punishing students for using HCE in the classroom (Reyes 1987g), many others have indicated their wariness of any policy which would stifle student participation in classes (Hikida *et al.* 1987). Although no quantitative data exist on what proportion of Island teachers oppose the BOE's policy, it is worth noting that the Hawaii State Teachers' Association, the major teachers' union, adopted a resolution at their annual meeting in March, 1988, asking the DOE to develop a comprehensive kindergarten to twelfth-grade language arts curriculum to meet the needs of HCE-dominant children. Shortly thereafter, the State Legislature adopted a (non-binding) resolution requesting that the DOE 'evaluate language arts programs for Hawaiian Creole-speaking students with limited English proficiency' and 'study the feasibility of obtaining federal funds for such programs' (HR No. 371, 1988, p. 2). Given its negative reaction to a similar legislative resolution adopted in 1979 (for discussion, see Sato 1985), the DOE is unlikely to comply with the directives of the present resolution.

A difference of opinion about the Board's policy exists among students as well. Several months after the BOE's action, an informal survey of 986 graduating students at public and private high schools across the state was conducted by a major Honolulu newspaper to gauge student sentiment about the role of HCE in the classroom (Verploegen 1988). Whereas only 26 per cent of the private school students surveyed felt that HCE use should be allowed in school, 54 per cent of the public school students supported this idea (Verplogen 1988: A1). Comments ranged from 'Pidgin English fosters illiteracy; Pidgin is a lazy way to talk; it promotes backward thinking;' and 'Correct English will get you anywhere;' to the polar opposites of 'banning pidgin would violate our freedom of speech; Pidgin is a natural language;' and 'it's our way to make Hawaii different from anywhere else in the United States' (Verploegen 1988: A1, A8).

The survey's results seem to reflect general social class and rural–urban differences, with the working class students attending rural public schools showing much stronger loyalty to HCE than the urban private school students from middle and upper-income families. Moreover, the openly defiant attitude of some of the students indicates increasing political awareness among young HCE speakers today, a distinct shift from the historical pattern of self-denigration in matters of verbal ability (Sato 1985).

HCE on trial

During the same week in September that the BOE language policy was debated, a federal lawsuit filed by three National Weather Service (NWS) employees against the US National Weather Service went to trial in US District Court in Honolulu (Kahakua *et al.* v. Hallgren). The suit was a complex one involving various charges against the NWS. Here, I will be concerned with those brought by two of the plaintiffs regarding discrimination on the basis of race and national origin; specifically, as reflected in their HCE accents.

The plaintiffs were two meteorological technicians, one Japanese-American and the other, part-Hawaiian-American (hereafter, referred to as G and J, respectively), both of whom had worked for the NWS for several years and who applied for two vacancies, one in April, 1985, and the other in October, 1986, in the Public Service Unit of the NWS's Honolulu office. On each occasion, they were asked to submit an audiotaped weather forecast as part of the application process. Both vacancies were ultimately filled by Caucasians with mainland English accents, and it was G's and J's claim that their applications were downgraded because of their HCE accentedness and in spite of their superior qualifications and exemplary employment records with the NWS. The NWS claimed that the Caucasians were selected because, although they were less experienced and had far less training than either G or J, they 'sounded better' than G and J.

Newspaper headlines such as 'Suit says men rejected because of "pidgin" use' (Oshiro 1987a) and 'Complaints about "pidgin" told in job bias trial' (Wiles 1987) strongly suggested that G and J spoke such basilectal HCE that they were unintelligible to mainland English speakers. As an expert witness called to testify during the trial, I countered this view on the basis of a phonetic analysis of taped weather forecasts by G and J such as those they had submitted as part of their applications (Sato 1987). The HCE features observed were the following, given in decreasing order of their frequency in the transcripts:

(1) Full vowels where many mainland varieties of English reduce vowels: /u/ rather than /ə/ in *today*
(2) /d/ where many mainland varieties of English have /ð/ as in *with*
(3) Monophthongs where many mainland varieties of English have diphthongs: /o/ rather than /oʉ/ in *low*
(4) Ø where many mainland varieties of English have a sulcal /r/, as in *afternoon*.

Whereas the first two features were usually present for both G and J, the latter two were infrequent, that is, G and J usually produced the SE variants. These results, together with an analysis of conversational speech from both men, demonstrated that these men were far from basilectal in all of the data examined. This is not to say that they were not in fact capable of using basilectal HCE, of course. The point at issue was that, in carrying out their professional duties, they could and did use standard Hawaii English of the sort spoken by the majority of highly educated, locally born professionals, including the present part-Hawaiian governor and Filipino lieutenant governor of the state and several members of the state Board of Education.

That a simplistic view of 'good' vs. 'bad' English was being conveyed by the local media became clear through a radio interview of G and a TV news programme where G presented a weather forecast as part of a story on the case. Listeners called in during the radio interview to remark with some surprise on how 'well' he in fact spoke. Several university colleagues of mine had similar reactions upon seeing G on the TV news. Local professionals (teachers, doctors, lawyers, news reporters etc.) who speak like G were particularly troubled by the implications for their own careers of the negative evaluation of G's and J's communicative abilities by an agency of the federal government.

The presiding judge (who had been brought in from California for the trial) apparently had no such qualms. Rather than taking a few weeks or longer for deliberation (which is common practice), the judge announced his ruling immediately following closing arguments in the three-and-a-half-day trial. He ruled that the NWS had not discriminated against G and J and even suggested that these men put more effort into improving their speech.

Attitudes and sociolinguistic variation

Neither large-scale survey data nor in-depth interview data are available as yet on community reaction to the educational and legal controversies reported above. However, a certain amount of analysis is possible on the basis of my own participant observation in critical events surrounding both the BOE policy and the court case, including many subsequent discussions with BOE and DOE staff, teachers, students, and various community groups.

First of all, it is undeniable that negative stereotypes of HCE and positive stereotypes of SE are still held by many in the community. This is at least partly due to the World War II experience of the *nisei* (second generation) Japanese in Hawaii, many of whom were deeply affected by the 'Be American' and 'Speak American' (i.e., English) campaigns launched in reaction to anti-Japanese hysteria during the 1940s (Kotani, 1985). As this generation of now middle class Japanese-Americans has largely controlled government and education in post-war Hawaii, it should not be surprising that language policy in the school system should reflect their strongly assimilationist viewpoint (for further discussion, see Huebner 1985).

That many Islanders do not share this viewpoint today *is* surprising. Even as a marker of working class and ethnic (actually, non-Caucasian) identity in the past, HCE was arguably perceived as more of a stigma than an asset (Sato 1985). However, the recent educational and legal controversies seem to have sharpened the community's sense of HCE as a marker of *local* identity. This historic shift was evident in public testimony before the BOE, which frequently referred to HCE as a vital part of local culture needing protection from harmful influences, in much the same way that the islands' natural resources require protection from land speculators and developers.

Open advocacy of this sort on behalf of HCE has never been characteristic of local people, particularly in direct confrontation of the educational and legal establishment of Hawaii. It certainly puts in a new light the generally negative evaluations of HCE and HCE speakers reported by the attitude studies cited earlier. In a time of crisis, it appears that Islanders who might otherwise subscribe to a status-based interpretation of linguistic diversity in Hawaii will be moved to reject it in favour of one which more accurately reflects the social and political reality of their lives. As Milroy (1982) has argued, the existence of contradictory attitudes in socially stratified, multilingual communities is to be expected, given that both status and solidarity ideologies motivate and/or sustain sociolinguistic variation. Creole communities such as Hawaii's are no exception.

Significantly, none of those who argued against the BOE's policy denied the importance of acquiring academic English and, particularly, literacy in SE. However, questions were raised concerning the inherently political definition of standard English (cf. Milroy and Milroy 1985). In the discrimination case, the court's ruling that the weather forecasters' accents were unacceptable made clear that Islanders who speak standard Hawaii English, not only those who speak basilectal or mesolectal HCE, are vulnerable to sanctions in the workplace based on the sociolinguistic preferences of their employers.

As for the question of how attitudes toward different varieties of English in Hawaii are related to variation, it must be concluded that an extremely polarised view of HCE and SE as 'bad' and 'good' English still prevails in spite of the tremendous variability evident in the post-creole continuum. In the debate over the BOE's policy, the central issue was often presented as a choice between HCE and SE, as if one could easily draw linguistic boundaries between these varieties. This mismatch between social perception and observable linguistic behaviour was also illustrated well by inaccurate media accounts of the local plaintiffs' speech in the discrimination case.

It must also be noted, however, that stereotyped perceptions were frequently challenged, not least by the sociolinguists and educational researchers who participated actively in public meetings and served as resources to the educational and legal bodies, the media, and various community groups. As a result of our involvement, much information about pidgin and creole languages and about second language education was repeatedly brought before various public officials and the community at large. Use of the term 'Hawaii Creole English' (rather than, e.g., 'broken English') by public officials and several members of the media was, in itself, a significant change, for it entailed treatment of HCE as a legitimate object of scientific study and, hence, of rational discussion.

Conclusion

The events of fall 1987 mark an important turning point in Hawaiian social history. Public discourse concerning English in Hawaii has been transformed, and public policy can no longer ignore the linguistic systematicity and cultural significance of HCE. This is not to say that social and political conservatism in the community has ceased to operate on questions of language in educational and legal domains. However, it is clear that any future efforts to undermine local language and values will meet with more informed, organised and vocal opposition from various groups in the community.

What effects, if any, the heightened consciousness about language politics will have on sociolinguistic change is the central question to be addressed in future research in Hawaii. Most creolists would probably predict that, in the absence of radical socioeconomic restructuring of Hawaiian society, decreolisation is likely to continue for generations to come. Still, it is simplistic to view convergence with mainland SE as the only, or the most interesting, direction of change in Hawaii. To the extent that speakers choose to accentuate their localness linguistically, there will be some degree of refocusing of HCE (Le Page 1980; Le Page and Tabouret-Keller 1985). Within dense, multiplex social networks (Milroy 1980, 1982) HCE may even increasingly diverge from mainland SE as American Black English appears to have done (Labov 1980).

It will be particularly interesting in future work to examine linguistic variation across different kinds of occupational networks, for example, those which are organised around employment in the tourist industry as opposed to those based in governmental bureaucracies at various levels (city, state, federal). In such comparisons, it may be discovered that class interests motivate greater refocusing of HCE among tourist industry workers as opposed to bureaucrats. By this I mean to suggest that the former may increase their use of particular features of HCE (e.g., prosodic markers), reflecting their alienation from the middle and upper class tourists they serve and resulting in greater divergence of HCE from SE in these networks.

Whatever the outcome of such studies, they will give us a better sense of how English variation in Hawaii reflects different dimensions of social identity (ethnicity, class, localness) as the larger economic and political context changes over time. Such knowledge, in turn, should continue to be used by and on behalf of those seeking remedies for economic, educational, and social inequality in Hawaii.

NOTES

I would like to acknowledge many fruitful discussions with Karen Watson-Gegeo and Michael Long which have influenced my thinking in this paper. Thanks are also due to graduate students Dominique Buckley, Vince Riley and Kent Sakoda for their support during the events of Fall 1987 and their enthusiastic advocacy of language rights in Hawaii.
1. The BOE is an elected body of 13 members which develops educational policy and controls fiscal matters in the state school system. It appoints the Superintendent of the Department of Education (DOE), who implements the Board's policy and administers the public school system. Much of the Board's work is accomplished through sub-committees which draft reports and make recommendations to the full Board. However, meetings at which decisions are taken are open to the public, and members of the community are encouraged to present formal testimony.
2. On a number of occasions, BOE members explicitly stated that the policy was not intended as an attack on HCE. However, in light of Board members' public comments contradicting this claim (see Hikida *et al*. 1987; Reyes 1987) and the logical entailments of the policy statement, many in the community perceived an intent to ban HCE.
3. 18 September 1987 memo from the BOE curriculum committee to the chair of the BOE states: 'Although no field imput was obtained, major arguments against the [English only] policy are not anticipated inasmuch as there appears to be general public recognition of the problem.'

REFERENCES

Beechert, E. D. 1985. *Working in Hawaii*. Honolulu: University of Hawaii Press.
Bickerton, D. 1974. Creolization, linguistic universals, natural semantax and the brain. *Working Papers in Linguistics* (University of Hawaii) 6(3): 124–41.
    1977. Change and variation in Hawaiian English, II: Creole syntax. (Final Report on National Science Foundation Project No. GS-39748).
    1981. *Roots of Language*. Ann Arbor: Karoma Publishers.
Bickerton, D. and Odo, C. 1976. Change and variation in Hawaiian English, I:

General phonology and pidgin syntax. (Final Report on National Science Foundation Project No. GS-39748).

Bickerton, D. and Wilson, W. 1987. Pidgin Hawaiian. In Gilbert, G. (ed.), *Pidgin and Creole Languages: Essays in Memory of John E. Reinecke*. Honolulu: University of Hawaii Press, pp. 61–76.

Brislin, T. 1987. 'Pidgin Laureate' praises both tongues. *The Honolulu Advertiser*, September 27, pp. A6, A7.

Carr, E. B. 1972. *Da Kine Talk*. Honolulu: University of Hawaii Press.

Carranza, M. A. and Ryan, E. B. 1975. Evaluative reactions of bilingual Anglo and Mexican adolescents toward speakers of English and Spanish. *International Journal of the Sociology of Language* 6: 83–104.

Choy, S. and Dodd, D. 1976. Standard-English-speaking and nonstandard Hawaiian-English-speaking children: Comprehension of both dialects and teacher's evaluations. *Journal of Educational Psychology* 68(2): 184–93.

Cooper, G. and Daws, G. 1985. *Land and Power in Hawaii*. Honolulu: Benchmark Books, Inc.

Day, R. R. 1972. Patterns of Variation in Copula and Tense in the Hawaiian Post-Creole Continuum. Unpublished PhD thesis, University of Hawaii.

    1980. The development of linguistic attitudes and preferences. *TESOL Quarterly* 14(1): 27–37.

    1987. Early pidginization in Hawaii. In Gilbert, G. (ed.), *Pidgin and Creole Languages: Essays in Memory of John E. Reinecke*. Honolulu: University of Hawaii Press, pp. 163–176.

De Camp, D. 1971. Toward a generative analysis of a post-creole speech continuum. In Hymes, D. (ed.), *Pidginization and Creolization of Languages*. London: Cambridge University Press, pp. 349–70.

Escure, G. 1981. Decreolization in a creole continuum: Belize. In Highfield, A. and Valdman, A. (eds.), *Historicity and Variation in Creole Studies*. Ann Arbor: Karoma Publishers, pp. 27–39.

Finney, B. and Watson, K. A. (eds.). 1974. *A New Kind of Sugar: Tourism in the Pacific*. Honolulu: The East – West Center.

Fuchs, L. 1961. *Hawaii Pono: A Social History*. New York: Harcourt, Brace & World.

Hartwell, J. 1987. Pidgin was invented by Hawaiians, traders. *The Honolulu Advertiser*, September 27, p. A6.

Hollis, R. 1987. Pidgin called too deeply rooted to die out. *The Honolulu Advertiser*, September 30, pp. A1, A12.

Hikida, A., Chinen, K. Muromoto, W. and Hiura, A. 1987. Pidgin English: the controversy that will not die. *The Hawaii Herald*, vol. 8, no. 9, October 2, pp. 1, 10–11.

Heubner, T. 1985. Language education policy in Hawaii: two case studies and some current issues. *International Journal of the Sociology of Language* 56: 29–49.

Hymes, D. 1973. On the origins and foundations of inequality among speakers. In *Daedalus* 102(3): 59–86.

Kahakua *et al.* v. Hallgren, Civil No. 86–0434, US District Court, Honolulu (1987).

Keir, J. 1987. The great expectations on English in schools. *The Honolulu Advertiser*, September 28, p. A5.

Kent, N. 1974. A new kind of sugar. In Finney, B. and Watson, K. (eds.), *A New Kind of Sugar: Tourism in the Pacific*. Honolulu: The East – West Center, pp. 169–98.

1983. *Hawaii: Islands Under the Influence*. New York: Monthly Review Press.

Kotani, R. 1985. *The Japanese in Hawaii: A Century of Struggle*. Honolulu: The Hawaii Hochi, Inc.

Labov, W. 1980. The social origins of sound change. In Labov, W. (ed.), *Locating Language in Time and Space*. New York: Academic Press, pp. 251–65.

Le Page, R. 1980. 'Projection, focussing, diffusion' or, steps toward a sociolinguistic theory of language, illustrated from the sociolinguistic survey of multilingual communities, Stages I: Cayo District, Belize (formerly British Honduras) and II: St Lucia. *York Papers in Linguistics* 9.

Le Page, R. and Tabouret-Keller, A. 1985. *Acts of Identity*. Cambridge: Cambridge University Press.

McCreary, J. 1986. Attitudes of non-native speakers of English to language variation in Hawai'i. Unpublished MA thesis, University of Hawaii.

Matsunaga, M. 1987. Most officials don't talk li' dat these days. *The Honolulu Advertiser*, September 29, pp. A1, A4.

Milroy, L. 1980. *Language and Social Networks*. Oxford: Basil Blackwell.

1982. Language and group identity. *Journal of Multilingual and Multicultural Development* 3(3): 207–16.

Milroy, J. and Milroy, L. 1985. *Authority in Language*. London: Routledge.

Neff, K. 1977. Theories of the syntax of aspect. Unpublished PhD thesis, University of Hawaii.

Nordyke, E. 1977. *The Peopling of Hawaii*. Honolulu: University of Hawaii Press.

Odo, C. 1975. Phonological processes in the English dialect of Hawai'i. Unpublished PhD thesis, University of Hawaii.

Oshiro, S. 1987a. Suit says men rejected because of 'pidgin' use. *The Honolulu Advertiser*, September 16, p. A3.

1987b. Strong English skills open many job doors. *The Honolulu Advertiser*, September 29, pp. A1, A4.

Peet, W. 1978. Relativization in a creole continuum. Unpublished PhD thesis, University of Hawaii.

Perlman, A. 1973. Grammatical structure and style shift in Hawaiian Pidgin and Creole. Unpublished PhD thesis, University of Chicago.

Purcell, A. 1979. Variation in speech by children in Hawaii. Unpublished PhD thesis, University of Hawaii.

1984. Code-shifting Hawaiian style: Children's accommodation along a decreolizing continuum. *International Journal of the Sociology of Language* 46: 71–86.

Reinecke, J. E. 1935/1969. *Language and Dialect in Hawaii*. Honolulu: University of Hawaii Press.

Reyes, D. 1987a. Panel wants pidgin kept out of schools. *The Honolulu Advertiser*, September 2, pp. A1, A5.

1987b. Panel urges pidgin ban in schools. *The Honolulu Advertiser*, September 16, p. A1.

1987c. Board votes 7–4 to keep pidgin out of classroom. *The Honolulu Advertiser*, September 18, p. A1, A4.

1987d. Pidgin use in schools clarified. *The Honolulu Advertiser*, September 19, pp. A1, A12.

1987e. Pidgin: Teachers – and children – face a dilemma. *The Honolulu Advertiser*, September 27, pp. A1, A6.

1987f. Pidgin: School board, other educators have their say on its place in the schools. *The Honolulu Advertiser*, September 28, p. A5.

1987g. Switch to English may mean talking pidgin. *The Honolulu Advertiser*, September 28, pp. A1, A4.

Rickford, J. 1983. What happens in decreolization. In Andersen, R. (ed.), *Pidginization and Creolization as Language Acquisition*. Rowley MA: Newbury House, pp. 198–319.

1985. Standard and non-standard language attitudes in a creole continuum. In Wolfson, N. and Manes, J. (eds.), *Language of Inequality*. Berlin: Mouton, pp. 145–160.

Rickford, J. and Traugott, E. 1985. Symbol of powerlessness and degeneracy, or symbol of solidarity and truth? Paradoxical attitudes toward pidgins and creoles. In Greenbaum, S. (ed.), *The English Language Today*. Oxford: Pergamon Press, pp. 252–61.

Romaine, S. (ed.). 1982. *Sociolinguistic Variation in Speech Communities*. London: Edward Arnold.

Sankoff, G. 1980. Political power and linguistic inequality in Papua New Guinea. In Sankoff, G. (ed.), *The Social Life of Language*. Philadelphia: University of Pennsylvania Press.

Sato, C. 1978. Variation in Hawaiian Pidgin and Creole English: *go* plus verb constructions. Unpublished MA thesis, University of Hawaii.

1985. Linguistic inequality in Hawaii: The post-creole dilemma. In Wolfson, N. and Manes, J. (eds.), *Language of Inequality*. Berlin: Mouton, pp. 255–72.

1986. Directions of sociolinguistic change in a post-creole continuum: a pilot study. Paper presented at Sociolinguistics Symposium 6, University of Newcastle-Upon-Tyne, England, 16–18 April.

1987. Technical description of plaintiffs' speech. MS.

1989. A nonstandard approach to standard English. *TESOL Quarterly* 23(2): 259–82.

In preparation. Language politics and applied sociolinguistics: Hawaii Creole English on trial.

Schmitt, R. 1982. Hawai'i's social rating. *Social Process in Hawai'i* 29: 151–7.

Slaughter, K. 1982. Attitudes of teachers and student teachers toward varieties of Hawaiian English. *University of Hawaii Working Papers in Linguistics* 14(2): 89–108.

State of Hawaii, House of Representatives, Fourteenth Legislature. 1988. House Resolution 371: Requesting an evaluation of language arts programs for Hawaiian creole (pidgin English)-speaking students with limited English proficiency.

Takaki, R. 1983. *Pau Hana: Plantation Life and Labor in Hawaii*. Honolulu: University of Hawaii Press.

Trask, H.-K. 1984/1985. Hawaiians, American colonization, and the quest for independence. *Social Process in Hawaii* 31: 101–36.

Verploegen, H. 1988. Pidgin in classroom stirs spirited debate by seniors. *The Honolulu Star-Bulletin*, June 1, pp. A1 & A8.

Wiles, G. 1987. Complaints about 'pidgin' told in job bias trial. *The Honolulu Advertiser*, 17 September.

Wurm, S. A. 1985. The status of New Guinea Pidgin (Neo-Melanesian) and attitudes towards it. In Wolfson, N. and Manes, J. (eds.), *Language of Inequality*. Berlin: Mouton, pp. 373–86.

Yamamoto, J. 1982. The perception and stereotyping of speech varieties in Hawaii. *University of Hawaii Working Papers in Linguistics* 14(2): 75–88.

Yamamoto, J. and Hargrove, E. 1982. Teachers' attitudes toward recorded speech samples of elementary school children in Hawaii. *University of Hawaii Working Papers in Linguistics* 4(2): 109–34.

44

Variation in Fiji English

JEFF SIEGEL

Introduction

English is the national language of Fiji, used in government, business, and education. It is also the lingua franca among the many ethnic groups of the country: indigenous Fijians, Fiji Indians, Europeans, Chinese, Rotumans, other Pacific Islanders, and part-Europeans (as people of mixed race are called in Fiji).

A distinctive local variety of English is characterised by certain nonstandard linguistic features. This 'Fiji English', like Singapore English (Platt 1975; 1978), is a linguistic continuum with variation according to the frequency of occurrence of these nonstandard features, here called 'markers'. Speech at the lower end of the continuum contains the highest frequency of these markers, and speech at the upper end contains the lowest frequency. Speakers of Fiji English may differ both according to where on the continuum their speech is located and the range of the continuum over which they have competence.

The linguistic markers themselves differ according to their range in the continuum. Lexical markers seem to have the widest range, with some commonly used items from Fijian and Fiji Hindi (such as *tanoa* 'bowl used for making kava' and *roti* 'Indian flat bread') being found from one end of the continuum to the other. Certain phonological markers range from the lower through the middle of the continuum. These include the absence of certain consonant clusters and the presence of intonation patterns similar to those of Fijian – for example, questions beginning at a higher pitch than in standard English and ending with falling rather than rising intonation.[1] Many of the grammatical markers (described below) are restricted to the lower end of the continuum.

It is this lower part of the Fiji English continuum and its characteristic phonological, grammatical, and lexical markers that have been described in the literature as a distinct variety of English. Kelly (1975), who gives

664

the most detailed description, called this variety 'the dialect'; Geraghty (1977, 1984) called it 'Fiji Pidgin English'; and Moag and Moag (1977) used the term 'Colloquial Fiji English'. In earlier descriptions (Siegel 1986, 1987, 1989) and in this study, I call it Basilectal Fiji English (BFE).

This study

This is an exploratory study which examines the limited data available on Fiji English, rather than follows any particular research design.[2] It has four main aims: (1) to illustrate some of the linguistic variables in Fiji English, (2) to discuss some of the situational and social factors which may account for different degrees of synchronic variation, (3) to identify any diachronic variation, and (4) to suggest areas for further research.

The data for this study come from three different sources. The first source is two hours of tape recorded conversation of third form (9th grade) girls (aged 14 to 16) in a Suva high school. The recordings were made in 1974 by Sister Francis Kelly, a teacher in the school, and provided the basis of her 1975 article. The method she used was to leave a tape recorder with the girls to record their informal conversation during their lunch break at school. In October 1982, I obtained these recordings and the transcripts from Sister Francis. I also asked her to make another 90-minute recording of a similar group of girls, using the same method.[3] This is the second source of data for the present study.

The last source of data is a one-hour recording made for me by Paul Geraghty in December 1983. It is of a group of eight boys (two aged 12, three aged 11, two aged 10, and one aged 4), sitting in a playground and 'telling stories'.

The study uses these recordings to look at variation in the occurrence of 15 linguistic markers (mainly grammatical) associated with Basilectal Fiji English (BFE). Many of these are also features of other nonstandard varieties of English. The linguistic markers examined here are as follows:

a.   *one* as indefinite article (instead of *a*):[4]

(1)   I give you one slap.
         'I'll give you a slap.'

b.   *us two* as first person dual inclusive pronoun (instead of *we*):

(2)   what schoolbus us two go by today?
         'What school bus will we go by today?'

c.   *us gang* as first person plural pronoun elsewhere (instead of *we*):[5]

(3)   Us gang learning about the thing.
         'We're learning about it.'

d. *fella* (/fəla/ or /fɛla/) as third person singular pronoun with [+ human] referents, both male and female (instead of *he* or *she*):

(4)   Fella come, fella go inside.
       'He came and went inside.'
(5)   How Mary climb the tree, fella got hurt?
       'How did Mary climb the tree if she was hurt?'

e. *thing* or *the thing* as third person singular pronoun with [− human] referents (instead of *it*):

(6)   Thing might get stuck.
       'It might get stuck.'
       (Also, see example (3).)

f. absence of copula with nonverbal predicate (adjective, NP, or locative):

(7)   Fella very rude priest, eh?
       'He's a very rude priest, isn't he?'

g. absence of copula as an auxiliary (with *-ing* forms):[6]

(8)   Some gang really studing.
       'Some people are really studying.'

h. verbs unmarked for third person singular:[7]

(9)   She always call me that.
       'She always calls me that.'

i. unmarked simple past tense:

(10)   The police catch him.
       'The police caught him.'

j. past tense marked with *been* (/bɪn/) before the verb:[8]

(11)   He been swear.
       'He swore.'

k. future tense marked by *gonna* (/gɔna/) before the verb:

(12)   You call me and I gonna peep inside the door.
       'You call me and I'll peep inside the door.'

l. direct quotations introduced by *go like this* (/go laɪ ðɪs/) or *went like this* (/wɛn laɪ ðɪs):

(13)   The Chinese man go like this: 'Cheers to the Great Wall of China.'

m. *aks* for 'ask':

(14)   I aks the fella how much for the fish.

Table 44.1. *Percentage frequency of occurrence of 13 linguistic markers of BFE*

Marker		Boys	(N)	Girls	(N)
a.	*one* (indefinite article)	49.1	(30/61)	28.6	(2/7)
b.	*us two*	100.0	(3/3)	–	
c.	*us gang*	18.6	(8/51)	26.3	(15/57)
d.	*fella*	31.6	(30/95)	2.8	(3/107)
e.	*thing*	10.0	(2/20)	37.7	(20/53)
f.	no copula (nonverbal predicates)	23.4	(34/145)	22.7	(16/75)
g.	no copula (as auxiliary)	18.6	(11/59)	36.2	(25/69)
h.	unmarked 3S verb	60.0	(12/20)	53.6	(15/28)
i.	unmarked past	49.0	(78/159)	41.1	(62/151)
j.	*been* past	8.8	(14/159)	0.0	(0/151)
k.	*gonna* future	51.6	(16/31)	24.4	(0/41)
l.	*go/went like this*	53.3	(16/30)	28.1	(9/32)
m.	*aks* ('ask')	88.9	(8/9)	100.0	(6/6)

n. *full* as an intensifier before verbs:

(15)   The fella was full sleeping over there.
        'The guy was sound asleep over there.'

o.   the Fijian focus marker *gā* (/ŋa:/) used:

(16)   You *gā*, you *gā* tell it.
        '*You* tell it.'

Variation in frequency of occurrence

Table 44.1 shows the frequency of occurrence of the first thirteen linguistic markers of BFE in the first 45 minutes of the two most recent recordings. Each figure represents the actual number of times the marker occurred divided by the number of potential occurrences times 100. (The last two markers of intensity and focus are not included here because their potential environments cannot be determined). The numbers of potential occurrences for each marker averaged 60 but ranged from 0 (*we/us two* for the girls) to 159 (marked/unmarked past tense for the boys), as the table shows.

It is obvious that there is a great deal of variation in the frequency of occurrence of the markers, with only two markers, *us two* and *aks*, coming close to occurring consistently in potential environments.

Closer examination of the environments for some markers sheds more light on the patterns of variation. For example, figures show that in BFE there is a more consistent abscence of the copula (as auxiliary) in the present tense, as suggested by Kelly (1975: 23) and as shown in table 44.2 above for

Table 44.2. *Percentage frequency of absence of copula in present and past tense*

Marker	Boys	(N)	Girls	(N)
no copula (nonverbal predicates)				
present	22.0	(27/123)	21.5	(14/65)
past	31.8	(7/22)	20.0	(2/10)
no copula (as auxiliary)				
present	27.3	(9/33)	61.0	(25/41)
past	7.7	(2/26)	0.0	(0/28)

Table 44.3. *Percentage frequency of absence of copula with different persons*

Marker	Boys	(N)	Girls	(N)
no copula (nonverbal predicates)				
1st person	33.3	(3/9)	0.0	(0/2)
2nd person	92.9	(13/14)	69.2	(9/13)
3rd person	11.0	(11/100)	10.0	(5/50)
no copula (as auxiliary)				
1st person	16.7	(1/6)	62.5	(5/8)
2nd person	100.0	(5/5)	88.9	(8/9)
3rd person	13.6	(3/22)	50.0	(12/24)

the current data. Figures also show that absence of copula in the present tense is much more likely with the second person (see table 44.3).

These more precise environments would have to be considered in future studies of variation in Fiji English. For example, the more specific 'absence of copula for second person present' may be a more useful marker.

The marker 'absence of simple past tense marking' also needs to be studied in greater detail. A preliminary examination shows no variation according to person or aspect (punctual – nonpunctual) (see Platt, this volume).[9] However, there appears to be some inherent variability according to phonological factors. As pointed out by Kelly (1975: 22), regular verbs (those normally taking the *t* or *d* past tense marker in standard English) which end in a consonant are more likely to be unmarked in the past tense in BFE.[10]

On the other hand, the past tense forms of certain common irregular verbs, namely *go*, *come* and *say*, are more likely to occur. In other words,

Table 44.4. *Markers with significant differences in frequency of occurrence*

Marker	Z- score (boys/girls)
d. *fella*	$Z = 5.76$
e. *thing*	$Z = 2.93$
g. no copula (as auxiliary)	$Z = 2.29$
j. *been* past marker	$Z = 3.91$
k. *gonna* future marker	$Z = 2.42$
l. *go*/*went like this* quotations	$Z = 2.08$

the marker 'absence of past tense marking' is less likely to occur with these verbs. For example, in the recordings considered here, the frequency of occurrence of the verb *go* unmarked for past tense, rather than *wen* ('went'), is only 23.2 for the boys (as opposed to 49.0 overall, shown in table 44.1 and 17.4 for the girls (as opposed to 41.1).

Differences between groups

The difference between the boys and girls in frequency of occurrence for each of the 13 markers in table 44.1 was evaluated using the Z test of significance. It was found that there is a statistically significant difference at the 0.05 level between the two groups in the frequency of occurrence of six of the markers. These are listed in table 44.4 above with the Z-score comparing the boys to the girls.

These results pose many questions for future researchers to answer. First of all, can these significant differences in the frequency of occurrence of certain markers be correlated with any situational or social difference between the groups? Second, why is the frequency of occurrence for some markers greater in one group and for other markers greater in the other group?

First, the different frequencies of occurrence of the markers may reflect stylistic differences depending on the situational factors of setting and topic. Such contextual variation has been illustrated in the classic studies of Labov (1972b) and Trudgill (1974). Here one would expect a lower occurrence of the markers in more formal situations. The two recordings were made under similar conditions in that the subjects were asked to record their informal speech and left alone to do so. But an important difference is that the girls were in the more formal environment of a school whereas the boys were in a playground. This would perhaps account for the lower frequency of four of the six significant markers among the girls, but it still leaves the question of why the other two markers (e and g) occur more frequently than for the boys.

Another point is that the topics of conversation differed between the two groups. The boys narrated many jokes which, having been memorised, may contain formulaic grammatical structures. This may have lowered the frequency of some markers compared with normal informal conversation. At any rate, both these factors of setting and topic should be more controlled in future research, and recordings should be made of speech in several contexts if stylistic variation is to be examined.

The possible significant social differences between the groups are sex, age, race, socioeconomic group, and education. Sex is, of course, the most obvious difference, and studies made in several different parts of the world show that, with social class and context controlled, boys are more likely to use nonstandard forms than girls (Trudgill 1983: 85–6). But many more recordings of both boys and girls of various age and socioeconomic groups need to be compared before any conclusion can be reached.

Age is also an important difference between the boys and girls, especially in that it correlates with the amount of their formal education in English (discussed below). Race is another important social characteristic (cf. Labov 1972a), especially in Fiji, but it does not seem to be a factor here as both groups had the same racial representation (Fijians and part-Europeans). Socioeconomic differences may also be significant, but no information on the backgrounds of the subjects was obtained (a flaw which should be rectified in future studies).

One of the most significant social differences between the two groups of subjects may be level of education. Jahangiri (1980), for example, has shown that there was an inverse correlation between the level of education and the frequency of occurrence of nonstandard features among speakers of Persian in Tehran. In this study, the girls have an average of two years more education than the boys, and the significantly lower frequency of some of the markers among the girls may reflect this higher level of education. But again there is the discrepancy of the higher frequency of two of the markers, *thing* and 'no copula (as auxiliary)', among the girls. There are also other features, such as absence of copula with nonverbal predicates and unmarked past tense, on which two additional years of education seem to have no significant effect.

There are two schools of thought, however, about how the amount of education may affect BFE. According to the first school, BFE represents a learners' continuum of English. Some markers (such as absence of copula and tense marking) reflect incomplete mastery of the rules of English. Other markers, such as *one* as the indefinite article, and preverbal tense marking with *been* and *gonna*, reflect structures in Fijian, the first language of a large proportion of speakers. So, according to this point of view, with more instruction in standard English these markers of BFE would occur less frequently.

The other point of view is that BFE is actually a distinct colloquial

Table 44.5. *Number of occurrences of two other markers*

Marker	boys	girls
n. *full*	0	7
o. *gā*	1	14

variety learned from contact with other children at school, but outside the classroom. This idea is reflected in one of the common names for BFE: 'Playground English' (Moag 1982: 276). Some of the markers of BFE may originally derive from interference from Fijian and incomplete learning of English, but they have become fossilised (Selinker 1972: 215) or petrified (Platt 1978: 54) as features of this colloquial variety. What the students learn in the classroom increases their range of competence in the Fiji English continuum, and allows them to shift into a more standard variety in appropriate formal contexts. But it does not displace what they have learned from other children outside the classroom as appropriate for informal contexts. So, according to this viewpoint, the amount of education would not affect certain markers of BFE and some would actually increase in frequency with more time spent in school as they are learned from contact with other children.

The data in the two recent recordings seem to show that both points of view are correct, to a certain extent. Certain nonstandard features may occur less frequently in the speech of the girls because of their higher level of education. But other nonstandard features occur more frequently because they may have become more 'standard' features of the colloquial informal variety. These include the two markers mentioned above and, in addition, the two other markers (listed in the first section) which have not been considered so far because they do not have easily predictable environments. Both these markers derive from Fijian – the preverbal intensifier, *full*, reflecting the Fijian preverbal *rui*, and the focus marker, *gā*, coming directly from Fijian. The number of times they occurred is greater for the girls than for the boys (as shown in table 44.5).

Thus, it may be that these four nonstandard features are actually learned in the informal school environment and therefore occur more often in the group with a higher level of education. But, again, more substantial data are necessary to test this hypothesis.

Variation between individuals

Because it was difficult at times to determine exactly who was talking in the recordings used for this study, the speech of all the participants could not be accurately compared, and an analysis of variance could not be

Table 44.6. *Percentage frequency of occurrence of four markers, 1974 and 1982*

Marker		1974	(N)	1982	(N)
e.	*thing* ('thing')	42.2	(22/52)	37.7	(20/53)
f.	no copula (nonverbal predicates)	78.3	(36/46)	22.7	(16/75)
g.	no copula (as auxiliary)	52.4	(22/42)	36.2	(26/69)
i.	unmarked past	45.1	(74/164)	41.4	(62/151)

made. However, it appeared that one of the boys, Jone, differed from the rest in having a lower frequency of occurrence of some markers. In several long narratives where the speaker could be identified, it was found, for example, that the frequency of occurrence for the unmarked past tense was 18.4 for Jone, while it was 68.8 for another boy, Vili. This is important because it shows that Jone's speech may have skewed the totals for the group to show lower frequency of some markers.

Here a study of each individual's attitudes and degree of group member-ship would also be valuable (cf. Milroy 1980; Cheshire 1982) in allowing us to see whether these factors affect the frequency of occurrence of the markers. It seems from the content of the recording that Jone does not have much solidarity with the rest of the group, whose speech is in general less standard. As pointed out by Paul Geraghty (personal communication, 9 March 1984) Jone's 'English-for-school-teacher style sticks out a mile'. There are several instances of his correcting himself and others to a more standard form, and of his making sarcastic comments about others' 'incorrect' English. And many times the other boys tell Jone to keep quiet or they make comments like: 'He want to be fancy.'

Diachronic variation

Kelly (1975) gives statistics on the frequency of occurrence of four markers which make possible a comparison with those of the recording made eight years later of similar subjects in almost identical conditions. The figures are shown in table 44.6.

An application of the Z test shows that there is a significantly lower frequency of occurrence of the marker 'no copula (with nonverbal predi-cates)' in 1982 than in 1974, but no statistically significant difference for the other three markers. Therefore, the frequency of occurrence of some of the linguistic markers which identify BFE may be changing over time while others remain constant. One possible factor which could account for the increase in the use of the copula is more widespread education. But this idea needs to be studied in greater detail, especially since the increase is significant in only one of the two different linguistic environments.

Conclusion

Jahangiri and Hudson (1982: 49) have shown for Persian that 'variation patterns can differ considerably (a) as between linguistic variables, (b) as between social groups, and (c) as between individual speakers.' This study tentatively shows that the same is true for Fiji English, but it is clear that much more data is needed before any definite conclusions can be drawn about correlations between the variation and any situational, social, or individual factors.

NOTES

1. Similar to that of Hawaiian English (Carr 1972: 52–3).
2. Originally I had planned to study Fiji English spoken in various formal and informal contexts. But recordings made in December 1986 were lost when Hurricane Uma destroyed my office in Port Vila in February 1987. Plans to make further recordings in Fiji were cancelled by the military coups which followed in May and September.
3. This time, however, I asked Sister Francis to promise the girls that she would not listen to the recording. Their faith in their teacher is revealed in the content of the recording – containing a good deal of unbridled talk about sex.
4. Also found in Hawaiian English (Carr 1972: 54).
5. *gang* is also used as a plural marker on other personal pronouns:

   > What you gang doing?
   > 'What are you all doing?'
   > We gonna be like those gang.
   > 'We'll be like them.'

6. Lack of copula with nonverbal predicates and as an auxiliary with *-ing* verb forms are considered separately here, following Kelly (1975).
7. This and the following marker are also found in Basilectal Singapore English (Platt 1978: 58–9).
8. This is also a feature of Melanesian Pidgin English and of other English-based pidgins and creoles of Africa and the Caribbean (Clark 1979: 13).
9. Person and aspect also do not appear to affect the occurrence of the *been* past tense marker.
10. The same is true for Singapore English (Platt 1978: 59–60). Also, a greater frequency of *t/d* deletion has been reported for some English dialects of northern England (Chambers and Trudgill 1980: 148) and for Black English Vernacular in America (Labov 1972b: 216).

REFERENCES

Carr, E. B. 1972. *Da kine talk: from Pidgin to Standard English in Hawaii.* Honolulu: University of Hawaii Press.

Chambers, J. and Trudgill, P. 1980. *Dialectology.* Cambridge: Cambridge University Press.

Cheshire, J. 1982. Linguistic variation and social function. In Romaine, S. (ed.) 1982. *Sociolinguistic Variation in Speech Communities.* London: Edward Arnold, pp. 153–66.

Clark, R. 1979. In Search of Beach-la-mar: towards a history of Pacific Pidgin English. *Te Reo* 22: 3–64.

Geraghty. P. 1977. Fiji Pidgin and bilingual educatioin. *Fiji English Teachers Journal* 12: 2–8.

1984. Language policy in Fiji and Rotuma. In Milner, G. B. *et al.* (eds.), *Duivosavosa: Fiji's languages: their use and their future (Bulletin of the Fiji Museum* no.8). Suva: Fiji Museum, pp. 32–84.

Jahangiri, N. 1980. A Sociolinguistic Study of Persian in Tehran. Unpublished PhD thesis, Univerity of London.

Jahangiri, N. and Hudson, R. A. 1982. Patterns of variation in Tehrani Persian. In Romaine, (ed.) 1982. *Sociolinguistic Variation in Speech Communities.* London: Edward Arnold, pp. 49–63.

Kelly, F. 1975. The English spoken colloquially by a group of adolescents in Suva. *Fiji English Teachers Journal* 11: 19–43.

Labov, W. 1972a. *Language in the Inner City.* Philadelphia: Pennsylvania University Press.

1972b. *Sociolinguistic Patterns.* Philadelphia: Pennyslvania University Press.

Milroy, L. 1980. *Language and Social Networks.* Oxford: Basil Blackwell.

Moag, R. F. 1982. The life cycle of non-native Englishes: a case study. In Kachru, B. B. (ed.), *The Other Tongue: English across Cultures.* Urbana: University of Illinois Press, pp. 270–88.

Moag, R. F. and Moag, L. B. 1977. English in Fiji: some perspectives and the need for language planning. *Fiji English Teachers Journal* 13: 2–26.

Platt, J. 1975. The Singapore English speech continuum and its basilect 'Singlish' as a 'creoloid'. *Anthropological Linguistics* 17: 363–74.

1978. The concept of a 'creoloid' – exemplification: basilectal Singapore English. In Todd, L. *et al.* (eds.), *Papers in Linguistics* A–54: 53–65.

Selinker, L. 1972. Interlanguage. *IRAL* 10: 209–31.

Siegel, J. 1986. Pidgin English in Fiji: a sociolinguistic history. *Pacific Studies* 9(3): 53–106.

1987. *Language Contact in a Plantation Environment: A Sociolinguistic History of Fiji.* Cambridge: Cambridge University Press.

1989. English in Fiji. *World Englishes* 8: 47–58.

Trudgill, P. 1974. *The Social Differentiation of English in Norwich.* London: Cambridge University Press.

1983. *Sociolinguistics: An Introduction to Language and Society.* Harmondsworth: Penguin.

Index of topics

675

Index of place-names

	DATE DUE		